6 NOV 77

R Frank

Black Jack

Black Jack

The Life and Times of

John J. Pershing

By FRANK E. VANDIVER

Volume II

Texas A&M University Press

COLLEGE STATION AND LONDON

Copyright © 1977 by Frank E. Vandiver

Library of Congress Cataloging in Publication Data

Vandiver, Frank Everson, 1925–
    Black Jack.

    Bibliography: p.
    Includes index.
    1. Pershing, John Joseph, 1860–1948.
2. Generals—United States—Biography. 3. United
States. Army—Biography. I. Title.
E181.P575   355.3′31′0924 [B]   76-51729
ISBN 0-89096-024-0

Manufactured in the United States of America
FIRST EDITION

Contents

VOLUME II

List of Illustrations

List of Maps

Black Jack

☆ 17 ☆

"¿En Donde Está Villa?"

FRANKIE could not be gone, not the true heart of the family . . . and the girls could not be gone, not all gone save Warren. They could not be gone when they were so needed, so happy with coming to daddy, not when the loneliness parched like the desert wind. Warren? Was he all right? Where was he? How could the terrible loss be lived? Had they suffered; were they awfully burned, or had death come quickly, unsuspected? Questions, questions raced unanswered as the miles dragged to Bakersfield California. There Frank Helm, who had known the family—and there was now no family—boarded the train to share a friend's suffering.

Pershing seemed shrunken, anguish visibly eroding his life. Throwing his arms around Helm's neck, Jack clung in desperation. From Bakersfield to Oakland, Helm held him, increasingly worried about his sanity. Finally he got word ahead to have a doctor meet the train with a sedative. If Warren had been lost, Helm thought that "Pershing would have lost his mind." "I can understand the loss of one member of the family," Jack sobbed, "but not nearly all."

Senator Warren and his wife sped to meet Jack in San Francisco; they, too, anguished. There had been something in Papa's mind that turned it to finite reaches of life, something that led him to think of twice lightning at the time of Frankie's accident. Perhaps, after all, there had been no time left for her at the still tender age of thirty-five —maybe the fates combined to finish a life at full tide and promise.

With typical concern, Papa had wired General Murray to look after arrangements until Jack and the rest of the family could gather. Fred and Bessie, who had just left San Francisco for southern California, heard the dreadful news and turned stunned steps back toward the house they knew so well.

At 8:30 A.M. on August 29, 1915, Jack arrived in San Francisco. General Murray and Maj. Henry H. Whitney had cared for the bodies; Jim Harbord, an honorary pallbearer, offered help. A cold compulsion took Jack straight to the funeral parlor where four caskets stood side by side, one long and three shorter. Of those friends who tried to sustain him Jack asked a time alone. They worried and watched around heavy curtains while the general fell to his knees for a long vigil before each box. Then he came out, wracked but firm in purpose to see the house. Frank Helm protested, to no purpose, and they went together. A haunting question pulled Pershing to the house—did they suffer? Witnesses seemed legion; their stories conflicted in small particulars but comforted in main recollection. The fire probably started in the downstairs fireplace, possibly from a stray coal rolling out on the floor. Frankie and baby Mary Margaret had been in the front upstairs bedroom with Helen and Annie next door; windows were closed because baby had a cold. Warren, tucked in the back bedroom, was separated by the two doors of an intervening bathroom. And the closed doors probably saved his life. Anne Boswell and her children, who were asleep across the hall, had windows open to the roof and escaped unhurt. And all who had toiled against the flames in the weird and foggy light of early morning agreed that the Pershings were suffocated by smoke and were not actually burned to death. That gave an odd comfort to grief.

As Jack looked on the house, on the sagging roof, on the graying char of the walls, the full ending came down. In that finite, shabby tinderbox most of the world stopped. He listened to such words of comfort as friends could voice. To Major Whitney, who fought the fire staunchly in those lost morning hours, Jack listened carefully. Speaking with poignant conviction, the major said that even if the rescuers could have reached Frankie and girls after Anne Boswell screamed warning that they were still inside, too much time had passed. Death had already occurred. As for six-year-old Warren, he had been handed out of his room by a team of men fighting to get to the front of the house. Driven back by smoke, they had failed, and were chagrined.

There had been others in the house—Florentine Pereri, Frankie's Filipino maid, and faithful William Johnson. With the special grief of reluctant survivors, they offered silent sympathy.[1]

[1] There are numerous accounts of the fire. In addition to Donald Smythe, "Pershing's Great Personal Tragedy," *Missouri Historical Review* 60 (Apr., 1966):

Satisfied that everything possible had been done to save his dearest and that they had been spared the worst, the general wasted no time in San Francisco. There would be a short ceremony at an undertaker's chapel, and Jack went to Letterman Hospital for Warren. On the way to the Stewart Hotel—of fond, fond memories now—Jack held Warren on his knee. They rode past the fairgrounds and daddy asked if the boy had seen the fair. "Oh yes, Mama takes us a lot." Pershing broke, his body began to shake terribly, and Frank Helm took Warren in his lap until they reached the hotel.[2]

Mercifully the chapel service ended quickly. The Episcopal rites Jack heard and bore them well. Those friends and acquaintances who came watched for signs of breakdown. The general seemed his stoic self as he came from the chapel with Bessie on his arm. But one observer saw through the iron control—"I shall never forget the look of grief on his face as he came out the door."[3]

Later that Sunday, the twenty-ninth, the surviving family left for Cheyenne. Johnson and Florentine Pereri remained in San Francisco to salvage furniture and such clothes as might be used—the thin line of draggled shoes seen the morning of the fire were wasted and forlorn and best forgotten.[4] But some things could be kept for the heart's sake, some for donation, some were Jack's own.

On the way to Cheyenne the senator's resilience showed. Alone of the mourning group, including Jack and Warren, Lt. James Collins, Bessie and Fred, his own Clara, he did the dark business of preparation. Telegrams came from the train to beleaguered Hiram Sapp in Cheyenne: arrange cars at the station for the party; arrange hearses for the four boxes—dimensions were carefully noted—and alert the local undertaker. One large grave would be needed in the Warren

---

324–28, see *El Paso Herald*, Sept. 8, 1915; *San Francisco Chronicle*, Aug. 30, 1915; E. G. Fitzhamon, "The Only True & Accurate Story of the Dreadful Fire at S. F. Presidio, Where Mrs. Pershing and Three Children Perished" (written Aug. 27, 1915), in Archives of the Presidio, San Francisco, Calif.; Recollections of Mrs. John H. Lindt (who was fifteen at the time of the fire and saw it), in John H. Lindt to Maj. Thomas R. Stone, Riverside, Calif., Sept. 28, 1970 (copy in author's possession); author's interview with Mrs. Myron Steeves, Houston, Texas, 1963 (Mrs. Steeves lived as a child in quarters near the Pershings at the Presidio). See also Maj. Henry H. Whitney to FEW, Aug. 31, 1915, FEW Papers, misc. papers relating to the fire. Some details are offered in *Army and Navy Journal* 53 (Sept. 4, 1915): 10.

[2] Smythe, "Pershing's Tragedy," p. 330.

[3] *Ibid.*, quoting Nellie Tayloe Ross.

[4] Author's interview with Mrs. Myron Steeves, Houston, Texas.

family plot; pallbearers, Papa thought twelve, must be alerted, so must the clergymen who would officiate.[5]

James, May, and Elizabeth Butler met Jack in Cheyenne, and some Warren relatives arrived for the burial on Tuesday afternoon at four. It went swiftly. A stark hole softened by banks of flowers greeted mourners from the Episcopal Church, and added swatches of blossoms surrounded graveside. The children would rest between Frankie and her mother in the Warren family plot.[6] The caskets, so final, came decked with white chrysanthemums. As the solemn words were spoken in the cool Wyoming air, Papa took curious consolation in a glance at Frankie's bier. "One of dear Frances's hands was in plain sight through the glass of the metallic casket, and on it was simply her wedding ring, a gold band; and the hand, so far as could be seen, was in perfect condition." Again, that needed certainty that death came unscorched.[7]

Flowers came from round the world; letters and telegrams, cards, and notes flooded the local post office. Of all the messages of condolence, two were especially interesting. One came to Jack from Francisco Villa;[8] the other, to Papa, came from San Francisco:

My dear Senator Warren,

In your dreadful sorrow may I say to you how my heart goes out to you. I was present at the marriage of your daughter to General Pershing and then you remember she was with us on our Philippines trip. I knew her and admired her sweet and engaging personality. The coming of the beautiful family made every one rejoice and now to have all but one taken, and the Mother. It is such a heart breaking tragedy that you will need all that philosophy you have to endure it. You know you have the deep sympathy of all and especially of those who admire you and have a warm regard for you and of the latter I am proud to feel myself one.

To the poor bereaved husband and father, will you express my profound sympathy. One does not know what to say. Ones words are hushed.

Affectionately yours
Wm H Taft[9]

For a few days Jack and his brother and sisters stayed in Cheyenne. All worried about Warren. He bore the crisis apparently well but had not been strong. Who would care for him? Papa and Clara wanted him, Fred and Bessie opened hearts and arms, but daddy needed him

[5] FEW to Hiram Sapp (telegrams): San Francisco, Aug. 29, 1915; Ogden, Utah, Aug. 30, 1915; Montello, Nev., Aug. 30, 1915 (all in FEW Papers, vol. 74).

[6] FEW to H. Sapp (telegram), Aug. 29, 1915, FEW Papers.

[7] FEW to Mrs. H. E. Santon, Sept. 11, 1915, FEW Papers. For floral arrangements, see Hiram Sapp (?) to Joe Breckons, Sept. 4, 1915, ibid.

[8] Box 314, PP.

[9] FEW Papers, Misc.

most. Finally May agreed to come with Warren and Jack to El Paso and set up housekeeping. Jack had to return to the border, where troubles brewed. On September 10 he left Cheyenne and all of its bursting recollections. Southward he looked toward his brigade and that one sure solace of a soldier—duty.[10]

Death had dimmed briefly Pershing's appreciation of crumbling border conditions. Back in early summer, when he had departed for his last happy vacation with the family, he had reported nervousness among El Pasoans about a possible Villista attack on the city. Disbelieving, Jack nonetheless suggested an additional field battery for show, added that he would return if needed, and guessed that Villa's power waned. Public worry stemmed, he knew, from an early June statement by Wilson on the Mexican situation. Cryptically unaddressed, the statement apparently was designed to explain Mexican conditions to citizens of the United States, but Wilson took pains to have his remarks widely circulated in Mexico, and obviously he spoke for Mexican ears. The United States would support a man or a group of men who could restore order to the distressed southern neighbor. Clearly attempting to unify warring factions, Wilson added a final proviso—if order did not come, the United States would have to help Mexico save itself.

This last stinger ruffled everybody's honor. Such blatant saber rattling earned firm rejection, but the message hung black in border air. As Mexican leaders feared its promise of intervention, so did American officers doing nervous guard duty on the United States–Mexican line. Pershing guessed the final purpose, and hence his promise to return from Cheyenne on call. Now back, he scanned recent history for indications of further trouble.

Trouble clustered more in Washington than in Mexico in early winter. Two decisive defeats in April and June tarnished Villa's gloss; hero-followers fell away by mid-summer, but still he ruled north Mexico and sustained friendship with the gringos. His stout advocate Hugh Scott pushed the Villista cause from the chief of staff's office, but military reality often shapes diplomatic fancy. No matter the hopes of Wilson and his administration, Carranza seemed increasingly strong in Mexico.

Robert Lansing, reserved, dignified, craftier than apparent as secretary of state, had a professional's view of foreign policy. Not always in agreement with Wilson, Lansing nonetheless served loyally to implement some policies likely to fail, to shift others when he could.[11] And

[10] FEW to Mrs. H. E. Stanton, Sept. 11, 1915, FEW Papers, vol. 74.
[11] Arthur Link, *Woodrow Wilson and the Progressive Era, 1910–1917*, p. 27.

the Mexican situation challenged his utmost guile. Subtly but firmly he worked to win South American approval of Carranza's government. Finally, on October 19, 1915, the United States and six Latin American friends recognized Carranza's regime as the de facto government of Mexico.[12]

Naturally Villa's sympathizers recoiled and blustered, and the general himself huddled in growing anti-American anger. But Carranza and his henchmen basked in newfound glory with gringo approval. Old border hands could have predicted the next twist of the plot: Villa would stir up trouble between Carranza and Wilson.

John Pershing anticipated the approaching worst and made his command as ready as training allowed. Winter pulled a cold lull over natural border excitements. Troops marched and countermarched along the west Texas, New Mexico, and Arizona boundaries with Mexico; minor incursions and alarms prevented boredom, but both sides tended to comforts in the biting desert chill.

A blighted life cut Jack off almost entirely from old friends, from El Paso's bustling socializing. May kept Warren and Jack a house and made it as much like home as loneliness permitted. Jack and Papa Warren wrote each other letters of piteous adjustment—the two men tried by an old bond of affection to assuage mutual horror. On September 13, 1915, Papa wrote with special understanding: "If my memory of things is correct, to-day is your fifty-fifth birthday. . . . I am sure you have never passed a birthday anniversary with sadder heart than you are carrying at this moment, and it is only a little to say that all of us are sad for you and with you."[13] Maybe with time, the senator hoped, "we may all feel a little more contented."[14]

In October the trunks came to Jack from the Presidio, filled with dear mementoes, some charred and water stained, some fresh and ready for quick hands to use—and the memories rushed back with tears and hopeless emptiness. "I can feel for you most sincerely," Papa said, and added wisely, "of course you wanted them to come; but knowing how I feel almost every day and sometimes many times a day when I come across some toy or article that the children had or something that was Frankie's when she was a child, I can in a slight degree appreciate how such things must touch you. And the sorrow must be all the more biting when articles, etc., that were theirs at the last moment, appear in a condition which indicates the cause of their sad

12 *Ibid.*, p. 135.
13 FEW to JJP, Sept. 13, 1915, FEW Papers, vol. 74.
14 FEW to JJP, Sept. 18, 1915, FEW Papers, vol. 74.

end."[15] To both shattered men, young Warren remained a shining hope. "I love to hear what you have to say about little-big Warren," grandpa wrote in September, "and wish I might see him every day as his mind unfolds and his body and muscles enlarge. He certainly promises well, and it is a wish of my life that nothing may happen to retard him, but that all may happen to advance him further."[16] One question haunted Jack, Papa, and May: What and when to tell Warren of the deaths? "Have you explained to him the continued absence of his dear mother and sisters?" Papa wrote in November. "What result? My heart bleeds for the poor little fellow when I think what the loss is to him, even though he does not appreciate it so keenly as he would if older."[17]

In the cold of the winter came an added chilling concern—what stones, what color, what writing on them? Papa wanted the family plot divided, with Warren and Pershing families equally honored. But Jack demurred on deciding about stones—some deep conviction of finality held him back.

Fortunately martial matters intruded. Arms and ammunition for Villa were interdicted as the Wilson embargo policy wavered again. Carranza's men sought permission to use North American railroads to reach remote Villa stations, and the crazed schemes of diplomacy roiled around El Paso. Which kept Jack sufficiently busy to dull anguish, and encouraged Papa to a shrewd guess that "you are having your hands full now . . . and are generally busy with correspondence, etc.; and perhaps it is better that way, as I myself find it quite the better thing to be plunging along in work with always something waiting to be done."[18]

May took excellent care of Warren, and, as the winter lengthened, she relaxed the social tether to include him in children's parties at the post. But Jack remained remote. Official entertaining he did when demanded, and May served as hostess. But no longer did his name appear in the gossip columns as a guest or honoree at post get-togethers. He just did not go.[19]

Some old habits remained. Training stayed tough; the Old Man conducted one of his fierce inspections in October and shook the brig-

[15] FEW to JJP, Oct. 26, 1915, FEW Papers, vol. 74.
[16] FEW to JJP, Oct. 26, 1915, FEW Papers, vol. 74.
[17] FEW to JJP, Nov. 22, 1915, FEW Papers, vol. 74.
[18] FEW to JJP, Oct. 13, 1915, FEW Papers, vol. 74.
[19] See, for example, *Army and Navy Journal* 52 (Aug., 1915), and 53 (Sept., Oct., Nov., 1915), passim, for Fort Bliss social notes. See especially *ibid.* (Nov. 27, 1915): 411.

ade in all of its stations.[20] And he talked of war games to sharpen men made lethargic in the cold. Rumor had it, too, that the Liberty Bell would pass through El Paso en route back to Philadelphia from the Panama-Pacific Fair—its visit demanded celebration.

Rumor proved true. The Liberty Bell came in mid-November, and Pershing made it a moment of martial triumph. With the bell on Thursday, November 18, came clouds of dignitaries, including Henry C. Breckinridge, assistant secretary of war, and the 8th Brigade showed all visitors what a first-rate outfit could do. Pershing, his staff, and some eager members of the Chamber of Commerce met Mr. and Mrs. Breckinridge and his sister, Margaret, at the station, then whisked them to the "military tournament" in Washington Park. Breckinridge, with Pershing and aides, inspected the surrounding army camps and was briefed on readiness. Jack knew the visit went well when, at the end of the tournament review, Breckinridge exclaimed: "This is a remarkable group of splendidly equipped and drilled men, and my only regret is that there are not a great many more of them."[21] In the evening Jack gave a dinner at the Paso del Norte Hotel for his superior, while May entertained Mrs. and Miss Breckinridge at a separate supper.[22]

While that same tournament continued after Breckinridge and the bell departed, Jack used one day for pure nostalgia. On Saturday morning, November 20, he invited "the children of El Paso" to the park as his guests. With the cooperation of the troops, a series of events staged earlier were repeated for those bright and shining eyes. "Those events most calculated to please the children were chosen by the General and were thoroughly enjoyed by them," according to a rapt witness. "General Pershing was everywhere with the children, explaining the different phases of the tournament to at least five thousand children from the city. The military bands also played. . . ."[23]

Numbers did not fill a void, and Christmas approached a bleak and empty season for endurance. Mary Butler—Sister Bessie—suddenly appeared in El Paso to spend a season lonely for her, as well—her Daniel was gone now five years, and a chance to be with May, Jack, and little Warren offered comfort while she gave it.[24] Together brother, sisters, and son clustered in one of the staff cars and roared off into

20 *Ibid.* (Oct. 30, 1915): 284.
21 *Ibid.* (Dec. 4, 1915): 443.
22 *Ibid.* (Nov. 27, 1915): 411.
23 *Ibid.* (Dec. 4, 1915): 442.
24 [Edgar J. Pershing,] *The Pershing Family in America*, p. 405.

the New Mexican desert. They spent New Year's in a place of bygone happiness, Fort Stanton, where they showed Warren something of the Old Army posts in Indian fighting trim. Later, when Bessie left, the holidays were over and Jack could claim routine's defense.

News from Europe bothered the general; that, and the dawdling preparations of his country. In France mighty armies slaughtered millions with incredible precision. Training could not come quickly enough should America be hurled into the war. And training alone would be useless. Armament now ranked almost above men in urgency. While the Allies and the Central Powers deployed hundreds of thousands of machine guns, whole armies of cannon, airplanes in awesome panoply, America argued still over which machine gun to adopt, which airplane to purchase, which field gun to issue. Confused delay disturbed a soldier. Compulsory military training—a growing national issue—seemed essential to General Pershing. Writing for the *New York Times* early in 1916, he argued for careful preparation, for universal training on a selective basis. "Universal military training is a necessary prerequisite to effective war time armies," he argued, and added that "the demands of modern war upon the individual are greater than ever before and only the thoroughly trained and tried soldier is able to stand the strain."[25] Senator Warren agreed.[26]

All arguments about preparation seemed suddenly moot to a practiced soldier-diplomat in January, 1916, when Villistas pulled seventeen Americans off a train at Santa Ysabel near Chihuahua and shot sixteen of them. Screams of rage tore congressional calm, even solid peace men wobbled, but Wilson stuck to his purpose. He wanted no Mexican embroilment, especially not at Pancho Villa's whim.

Irked that the Santa Ysabel episode faded from prominence, especially that it did not induce American intervention in Mexico, Villa brooded in mounting anger. His North American friends had deserted him, had turned to Carranza, and the only hope left was that they might be pulled into the Mexican imbroglio and tear down Carranza with everybody else. Santa Ysabel was, after all, in Mexico; what if some outrage were committed on American soil?

Throughout a disturbed February, rumors wafted over El Paso like a Mexican wind. Villa was coming north; he was dead; he was marching on Chihuahua; he was seen, not seen; Obregón had beaten him again. On March 6, 1916, Gen. Gabriel Gavira, Carranza's commander in Juárez, announced to the press that Villa headed for the border to

[25] Quoted in *Army and Navy Journal* 53 (Feb. 5, 1916): 723.
[26] FEW to JJP, Jan. 21, 29, 1916, FEW Papers, vol. 74.

make trouble. This news hardly surprised Pershing. He had heard the same story too often for sudden alarm. On the ninth rumors repeated in the press put Villa near Columbus, New Mexico, and reported that he had killed more Americans and seemed to be bearing down on the border. But reports conflicted, and his location remained uncertain. All rumors went to Col. Herbert Slocum, 13th Cavalry, at Columbus, the apparently threatened point. But Slocum could get no clear idea of what was happening—not until the night of March 8–9. That night Villa struck.[27]

"Immediate and Effective Retaliation"

Rumors and alarms flitted and rang so often that security lapsed to perfunctory pitch in Columbus. True, a kind of eerie certainty colored tales of Villa's coming in the night, but the 13th Cavalry did normal duty—and got badly surprised. Before that lurid night washed in a desert dawn, seventeen Americans, nine of them civilians, lay dead. In the smoulder of Columbus, a cause was ignited that burned wires and hearts across the nation and exploded into the halls of a stunned Congress. Pershing forwarded Colonel Slocum's battle report to the War Department.[28]

War fever surged and cries for vengeance came. A worried president and cabinet pondered action. Newton D. Baker, highly touted pacifist now in his first day as war secretary, emerged from a special cabinet session on the morning of March 10, found the chief of staff, and said he wanted an expedition started into Mexico to catch Villa. Scott modified the objective to the capture or destruction of Villa's band.[29] Then the chief of staff coded detailed instructions to General Funston. The president had authorized an incursion into Mexico "with the sole object of capturing Villa and preventing further raids by his band, and with scrupulous regard to sovereignty of Mexico."[30] Funston would organize a force under Pershing's command—he was picked because of propinquity and experience—which would pursue the Columbus raiders into Mexico. They would withdraw when Carranzistas could replace them or when "Villa's band or bands are known to

[27] See Clarence C. Clendenen, *The United States and Pancho Villa: A Study in Unconventional Diplomacy*, ch. 18 (cited hereinafter as *U.S. and Villa*).

[28] *Ibid.*, p. 249.

[29] Hugh L. Scott, *Some Memories of a Soldier*, pp. 519–20.

[30] See Clendenen, *U.S. and Villa*, p. 251. See also Francisco R. Almada, *La Revolución en el Estado de Chihuahua*, 2: 304, where the message, in longer form, is said to have been addressed to Pershing.

be broken up." Wide authority to press people into service went to Funston, who was especially reminded that President Wilson wanted border commanders alerted to the possibility of "hot pursuit" into Mexico without fanfare. And the instructions closed with special approval of a Funston suggestion:[31] "You are instructed to make all practicable use of the aeroplanes at San Antonio, Texas, for observation." Funston should ask what he needed, report on the force to comprise the expedition, and expedite everything.[32]

Tough little Freddy Funston—he stood 5 feet 4 and hefted about 100 pounds—wanted the field command himself, but he accepted higher dictates and sent friend Jack a good soldier's orders.[33]

Fort Sam Houston, Texas.
March 11, 1916.

General Pershing,
Fort Bliss, Texas.

Secretary of War has designated you to command expedition into Mexico to capture Villa and his bandits. There will be two columns, one to enter from Columbus and one from Hachita, via Culberson's [Ranch]. Hachita column will consist of 7th Cav., Tenth Cavalry (less two troops) and one battery horse artillery. Columbus column will consist of Thirteenth Cavalry (less one troop) a regiment of cavalry from the east, one battery of horse artillery, one company of engineers and First Aero Squadron with eight aeroplanes. Reinforced brigade of Sixth Infantry, Sixteenth Infantry, First Battalion Fourth Field Artillery and auxiliary troops will follow Columbus column[.] Two companies of engineers will be ordered to Fort Bliss awaiting further orders. Necessary signal corps will be ordered from here. Will furnish you War Department instructions later. Have you any recommendations to make?

Bundy. [Adjutant General.][34]

Aware that something drastic must be done about the bumptious Villa, Pershing must nonetheless have wondered at his sudden good fortune in drawing the prime field command available in the army. As Teddy Roosevelt had once commented in excessive candor about the Spanish-American War, the Punitive Expedition was the only war

[31] Frederick Funston, "Annual Report for the Southern Department, 1916" (Oct. 17, 1916), p. 26, in AGO Records, RG 94, National Archives (hereinafter cited as Funston, "Report, 1916").

[32] See Funston, "Report, 1916," pp. 26–27; PM, vol. 2, ch. 22, pp. 10–11. A slight variant is printed in Scott, *Memories*, pp. 520–21.

[33] "Funston and Pershing, the Generals in Charge of the Chase After Villa," *Current Opinion* 60 (May, 1916): 318–19.

[34] This order is copied in JJP, "Report of the Punitive Expedition to June 30, 1916" (Oct. 7, 1916), p. 1, AGO Records, RG 94, National Archives (hereinafter cited as JJP, "PX Report").

America had working at the moment—and Jack would lead the way. Ready always, Jack began the bustle of quitting El Paso. Aides looked after transportation, checked on staff people, inquired about troops going from Fort Bliss, worked on the general's personal kit, gathered up Johnson to drive and cook in the field. Jack himself pondered sudden problems of organization. Time had run out for preparation. Washington and San Antonio wanted speed, wanted a force gone quickly across the border.

Happily Jack operated under a crafty fighter who knew the needs of command. Later on the eleventh, Funston sent another order that gave Pershing unstinted support. "As commander of the expeditionary force," Jack read, "the Department Commander leaves you free to make such assignments of the troops under your command as you think best in order to accomplish the purpose in hand. . . . From the time the troops report to you they will be subject to your orders."[35] Getting the command together might be a good deal harder than Jack expected. Many designated units were strewn around New Mexico and Arizona, even away in Georgia. Orders went from San Antonio directing a gathering of what would officially be known as a "provisional division" at Columbus and Hachita. Pershing decided to go instantly to Columbus, establish headquarters, and receive his men.

Some sadness touched leaving El Paso. For several weeks the sister of Lt. George S. Patton, Jr., 8th Cavalry, had been visiting her brother and his wife. Anne ("Nita") Patton, lovely, with Frankie's set of chin, with warm lips and the kind of eyes that spoke of wise and wonderful affection, caught Jack's tragic look—and she felt instantly the lure of the lost. So wounded he was, his heart so withered, he needed a woman's warmth to kindle the embers of living. They had enjoyed each other's company at various functions; she felt him respond. That tall, gaunt man of fifty-five had a handsomeness made finer by those hurt eyes and he made Nita's heart lurch each time he caught her gaze. Twenty-nine seemed old enough for a girl who wanted to comfort him, especially for a girl who knew the army and her life's purpose. She encouraged the general and they grew closer than friends.[36]

That respite from anguish told Jack he might love again, reminded him of his deep need for women's interest. But now he must go, must again say good-bye to someone he could care for. Warren and May would go to Lincoln and wait—farewells to them were hard.

---

[35] *Ibid.*, p. 2.
[36] See Martin Blumenson, *The Patton Papers, 1885–1940*, pp. 312, 321.

All kinds of distractions marred March 12. Everyone apparently wanted to join the general's entourage, or wrangle an assignment to a field outfit. While Jack and his harassed staff worked through myriad details, streams of petitioners badgered anyone close to Pershing for a chance at Villa. One of the pesterers proved persistent. As it happened, George Patton drew duty as officer of the day on the twelfth. Most of the hours he spent worrying that the 8th Cavalry would not go to Mexico—probably because the commander would fail Pershing's stern physical standards. After lunch that day Patton smoked his pipe on the headquarters verandah and watched frantic packing on all hands. Soon he heard reliable rumor that the 8th Cavalry would not join the expedition. Instantly Patton sought his regimental adjutant and asked for a recommendation as an aide to General Pershing. Next he cornered Maj. John L. Hines, already assigned as adjutant general to the Punitive Expedition, and put the same request. One of Pershing's two official aides, Lt. Martin C. Shallenberger, heard Patton's personal plea.

Later in the day, Pershing called Patton at the officer of the day's office, said he heard the lieutenant wanted to go, got a quick affirmative, and said he would take him if possible. But Patton thought he should follow up and after supper presented himself at Pershing's quarters. He was, he boasted, "good with [newspaper] correspondents," and he would happily go with the general in any kind of job. "Every one wants to go," came the level reply; "why should I favor you?"

"Because I want to go more than any one else."

A cold look from steely eyes, no flicker of a smile, no thawing of official pose, just a short last sentence: "That will do."[37]

At about 8:30 next morning, the thirteenth, Patton's phone rang; he answered and heard a quick question:

"Lieut. Patton, how long will it take you to get ready?" With foresight Patton had packed the night before and replied that he could report instantly.

"I'll be God Damned," Pershing snorted, and added, "you are appointed aide." A catch in the appointment—he would have to give up the job when Little Collins rejoined. But as long as he was with the expedition, he could prove his worth.

By 12:15 he had loaded most of the staff horses and then joined Major Hines in coding reams of telegrams to speed collection of troops

[37] *Ibid.*, pp. 318–20.

in Columbus and Hachita. Pershing and headquarters people would board a westbound train late in the day, and Patton must push arrangements.

In a fiery desert sundown, Patton put wife Beatrice and Nita in a car, picked up the general and Major Hines, and drove to the depot. Brief joy in Nita's welcome eased the ride, and Pershing enjoyed a quiet good-bye at the train—Shallenberger had done a fine job of decoying flocks of newsmen from the general's car, and the small party boarded unseen.

At last time for war came; the train pulled out of El Paso. Slowly the familiar city faded in a dimming orange aurora; out past the mountains beyond the Paso del Norte, the train gained speed on the desert flat. This day Jack rode the El Paso and Southwestern that hugged the border to Columbus. Hungry, he ate a much belated lunch and pored over dispatches until almost 10:00 P.M. About a mile from the suddenly famed settlement, Pershing's party swung from the train, was joined by new staff members, mounted, and rode into Columbus.[38]

By all military standards Columbus was a mess—one to bring horrified recollection of Tampa's awful days in 1898. Troops were arriving from various places, were looking for campsites, for supplies, for orders, for somebody in charge. Until Pershing set up shop, Columbus wallowed in disorder. Trains chuffed into the depot and shunted box cars galore to sidings; trucks roared into town. Cavalry, infantry, and guns bunched in haphazard array. Pershing noted quickly almost hilarious lapses in preparation. Apparently no one thought of quartermaster needs—and that error reproduced Tampa's troubles. There was, in fact, no chief quartermaster available, no one present to designate depots, to classify shipments, to sort the freight from unmarked cars. Puzzling questions escalated into bafflement—what to do, for instance, with the escort wagon bodies arriving by train? They came without wheels, axles, whiffle trees, or traces; finally someone noticed they were marked for use as truck bodies. Motors, frames, tires, pieces of various kinds of trucks arrived for assembly—without directions or tools or people to fit them together. Officers announced themselves detailed for quartermaster duty only to confess total ignorance of forms, materiel, transportation, ration ratios, forage requirements, the barest rudiments of logistics.[39]

Ordnance supplies apparently would be provided by providence— no chief ordnance officer reported. Ammunition, machine guns, rifles,

[38] *Ibid.*, pp. 320, 321.
[39] JJP, "PX Report," p. 34.

pistols, cannon, and shells came with troops; troops could resupply themselves? Acidly Pershing noted that "a continuous flow of ordnance from the Base to the troops . . . seems not to have been anticipated and provided for."[40]

Medical supplies, other than those already with regiments and other formations, arrived in bundles of tenting, instruments, and bottles, and came with distracted doctors. Elements of a field hospital and an ambulance company were identified and gradually assembled. Communications were going to be chancy. No field telegraph wire arrived, so galvanized-iron wire would be tried by willing telegraphers. Pack radio sets issued to cavalry units were handsome things but mystifyingly unreliable. Larger wagon sets promised better, and the big tractor transmitters coming from San Antonio might keep contact with Mexico.[41]

General Pershing's glacial presence brought some order from confusion. Unruffled, he made temporary assignments to staff departments, picked a base commander for Columbus, and made certain a competent chief quartermaster would soon take charge. The expedition would not be stalled by disorder at the start. Orders were left for Maj. John Madden of the Quartermaster Corps: Progress must not be hampered by lack of supply. Take charge, get organized, and send supplies forward to whatever advanced base might be established.

But delay could not be avoided. Too much had been left undone. And Jack could not yet guess the unreadiness at Hachita. He would worry about that as soon as chaos dwindled to confusion in Columbus. But behind his stoic calm he fumed. And he grew alarmed when in the midst of March 13's general disarray came a telegram from Funston, announcing that the expedition must cross the border no later than 6:00 A.M., March 15. That seemed possible, but unlikely. Still, Jack would try. Burdensome, too, was the added injunction that President Wilson put on him—do nothing more than pursue the bandit bands and take all measures to keep de facto government friendship. "The greatest caution will be exercised after crossing the border that fire is not opened on troops pertaining to de facto government of Mexico. As such troops are very likely to be found in country which you will traverse the greatest care and discretion will have to be exercised by all."[42]

Plans had already soured. The Mexican commander of the small

40 *Ibid.,* p. 41.
41 *Ibid.,* pp. 37–43.
42 Funston, "Report, 1916," p. 29.

border garrison at Palomas, six miles south of Columbus, declared resistance to any intruders from the north. Explanations of an agreement between the United States and Mexico concerning mutual border crossings for "hot pursuit" swayed the Mexican officer not at all, and Jack reported a delay until noon on the fifteenth to Funston. Nervous and eager, Funston relayed the disquieting pronouncement of unwelcome to Washington but urged Pershing to move out before diplomatic caution dimmed chances of chasing Villa.

Ready or not, Pershing told the belligerent Carranzista commander, at noon the fifteenth the eastern column of the Punitive Expedition would cross the border at Palomas. Jack bought off the Palomas commander by hiring him as a guide![43] The expedition crossed into Mexico without incident at 12:13 P.M., March 15, 1916. Pershing saw his men safely off, then telegraphed Col. George A. Dodd at Culberson's Ranch in the southeastern corner of New Mexico's small panhandle to wait for him. He rented a car for the fifty-mile run. Dodd had collected his own 7th Cavalry, the 10th, and other units, moved down from Hachita, and was ready to go. Jack intended to go with him.

Whimsical disorder continued that day—Pershing's car broke down! Not until almost midnight did a draggled party of travelers arrive at Culberson's Ranch. Dodd still waited, good soldier that he was, although he had almost dispatched a search party under Lieutenant Patton—whom Pershing had sent earlier with radio equipment —to find his missing leader. After 1:00 A.M. the western column of the Punitive Expedition moved out to cross the border. Troopers Pershing and Dodd rode into Mexico early in the morning.[44]

In lambent moonlight the Chihuahua desert rested far and lovely,

[43] For JJP's hiring of the Palomas commander, see Funston to AG (telegram), Mar. 15, 1916, in 3849 ACP 1886, RG 94, National Archives.

[44] The timing of Pershing's border crossing is difficult. In PM, vol. 2, ch. 23, p. 2, JJP says the Culberson column left "after midnight." He repeats the "about midnight" time in "PX Report," p. 7. Herbert M. Mason, Jr., *The Great Pursuit*, p. 85, says JJP crossed "thirty minutes past midnight on March 16," apparently following Frank Tompkins, *Chasing Villa: The Story Behind the Story of Pershing's Expedition into Mexico*, p. 77. Col. De Rosey C. Cabell, Pershing's chief of staff, reported to Funston's headquarters that Pershing was crossing with the Culberson column at 1:00 A.M. on the sixteenth, but Cabell probably reported the time of departure from Culberson's Ranch. See Papers of Col. Fitzhugh Lee (on Funston's staff), dispatch 32, March 16, 1916, University of Arizona, Tucson. These dispatches from the Punitive Expedition were copied by Captain Lee at the Southern Department's telegraph office. George Patton reported that JJP arrived at Culberson's Ranch at 2:00 A.M. and the crossing occurred at 3:16 A.M. on the sixteenth (Blumenson, *Patton Papers*, p. 321). The text seeks a balance of extreme estimates, hence the equivocation.

and the trail looked easy to the eye. Out in column of twos the Garry-owens rode, their pennons dim and ghostly in the moonglow, some lost bugle sounds of Custer fading in their wake. Behind them came the good black 10th, Jack's old regiment, twos riding with veterans' ease, hunched to rest on the trail. Then came Battery B, 6th Field Artillery, guns broken to mule packs, eager gunners riding limbers and horses.

At the point with Dodd, Jack looked back over the long line of horse soldiers—and all the romance of the cavalry was conjured again in the sight. With them they carried the past and brought the future. To the agony of designer George Patton, the troopers left their sabers behind in Texas and carried rifles, pistols, and the new killing tool of modern war, the machine gun.[45] And Jack knew that soon trucks would crowd the sandy tracks south, that aeroplanes would roar overhead, and that infantry would come for its ancient consolidation. He knew, too, that in the awful mud of the Western Front in France and Flanders swarms of cavalry waited for a break in the trench systems, waited for a chance to maneuver, a chance once more for valor. Would Chihuahua's arid wasteland give the U.S. Cavalry its last full chance for glory?

Dawn camp at Geronimo Rock, an afternoon march to Ojitos, took the column fifty miles into Mexico. By the time the van pulled into Casas Grandes—the rendezvous point—after 7 o'clock in the evening of the seventeenth, Jack knew important things about his mission.

Logistics were going to be a serious problem. Villa and his *ban-didos* skedaddled southward, probably into the fastness of the remote Sierra Madres, that massive range marking the western edges of Chihuahua. If so, he would pull the Punitive Expedition behind him into a hundred-mile-wide corridor of land bounded on the west by the Sierras and on the east by the Mexican National Railway running from Juárez to Chihuahua City and on toward the nation's capital. That corridor might stretch three or four hundred miles south-southeast, but with luck the expedition might keep Villa north of Durango and Sinaloa. If he remained in Chihuahua, even in its mountains, he might be caught or badly punished. Catching him depended on fast moving cavalry columns, which would have to be supplied along a lengthening line of communications. Good roads and good supply men were the keys to success.

Roads looked all right on maps, could be easily seen as firm lines; they seemed to show a workable skein connecting Casas Grandes and

---

[45] See 12th Indorsement in Funston, "Report, 1916," by Col. George Burr, Cavalry Equipment Board, Rock Island Arsenal, Ill., Apr. 2, 1917.

Colonia Dublán—a nearby settlement with likely depot sites—to important towns south and southwest in the mountains. Jack announced Colonia Dublán as his advanced base, ordered infantry supports and supply columns from Columbus, and speculated about the roads. Dry weather gave the trails and traces an illusion of reliability. But they were powder dry and gritty, and the ruts filled quickly with shifting sand. Rains would turn them into slick, unstable quagmires. Engineers must begin a new network of highways, else the Jeffrey Quad trucks, the Whites, Packards, and Locomobiles would sink to their axles in goo.[46]

Jack knew that good roads alone would not guarantee the success of truck-train supply. Skilled drivers were essential and absent. Old-style wagon trains could be used to some extent, but motor trucks were the real answer to distance and mass.

At Colonia Dublán on March 18, Pershing began to plan his full campaign. That evening, after a day of inspections and a fine dinner with a local Mormon bishop, Jack went outside, found a big tree near the Casas Grandes River, took out his notepad and a map of Sonora, Chihuahua, and Coahuila.[47]

Lieutenant Patton watched the Old Man from a distance as his flashlight swept across the map, stopped, moved again, and his pencil scratched out the pursuit. Jack's military problem could be stated simply enough: Somewhere south was Villa and he must be found. How? Down that corridor of dry alkali dirt, its flatness cut by stray arroyos and yucca spears, or off in the sere brown Sierras, Villa's bandits lurked. Pershing's map—not as accurate as he wanted—showed countless towns and settlements where Villa's men might hide, for Pancho ranked a folk hero to the poor of northern Mexico. Vicious, bloodthirsty, the gringos might call him, but he brought fresh winds of revolution to the desert people. These were peons who scoured living from reluctant ground, who starved and burned and stayed alive and had the fierce dignity of survivors. Many of them were Yaquis, fearsome, so proud in battle that they always carried off their dead, and who revered Pancho as a deliverer.[48] Others in that forbidding land were simple souls nurtured in poverty who needed only the small-

[46] See JJP's graphic description of bad roads in PM, vol. 2, ch. 23, p. 2.

[47] A map of these states was issued by the War College Division of the General Staff to Punitive Expedition officers. See papers of Lt. Col. Charles C. Winnia, Rice University Library. For JJP's planning session, see Blumenson, *Patton Papers*, p. 322.

[48] Col. G. A. Dodd to JJP, Guerrero, Chih., Mar. 29, 1916, in JJP, "PX Report," pp. 14–15.

est mite for life—and they loved Panchito for the hope that he was. Most of them tolerated Carranzistas as long as Villa did, and gringos these northern people knew as ranchers, users of the scant good lands, and diggers of gold and silver. Pancho rightly resisted these pale exploiters. And when John Pershing's khaki columns intruded into the old, hard land, its people opened their hearts and their adobe hovels to Villa's desperate men. The gringos would find closed doors, and blank faces long practiced in deceit.

At Dublán, Pershing had scant hope of help in this alien world. Carranza's men, supposedly allies, seemed usually sullen, resentful, and potentially hostile. Wise in the way of unfriendly folk, Jack reckoned that "if this campaign should eventually prove successful it will be without the real assistance of any native this side of [the] line."[49] He planned accordingly. Remarks he made in the *El Paso Morning News* professing hope that the Mexican people would welcome help against brigandage were expected protocol—and should do no harm.[50] Speed seemed the key to the quest, speed and a good deal of luck. If quick columns could find and engage Villa before his bandits blended into the populace, the expedition might do its job and leave Mexico in haste. But if speed failed, Jack would rely on practices from Moroland —would seek friends among the enemy who would identify Villistas. Once exposed, they could be excised like troublesome *dattos*. In hope of a quick roundup—a touch of luck—Jack sent the 7th Cavalry on a thrust toward San Miguel de Babícora. Rumor put Villa and about 500 men in that village only 55 miles due south of the Mormon colony at Casas Grandes.[51]

Before he launched a full campaign against Villa, Jack considered supplies. Carranzista cooperation did not extend to permitting use of the Mexico Northwestern Railroad from Juárez to Dublán, an inhospitality of formidable kind. Knowing he must rely on trucks, Jack had called on an aviator for help.

Back in Columbus, in the chaos of arriving equipment, the commander of the First Aero Squadron, Capt. Benjamin D. Foulois, Aviation Section, Signal Corps, showed himself a man of multiple talents.

[49] JJP to Funston (telegram), probably Mar. 26, 1916, in Funston to AG, Fort Sam Houston, Mar. 26, 1916, 3849 ACP 1886.

[50] *El Paso Morning News*, Mar. 12, 1916.

[51] See Clendenen, *U.S. and Villa*, pp. 256–57; H. M. Mason, *Great Pursuit*, pp. 88–89; Tompkins, *Chasing Villa*, pp. 77–79; JJP, "PX Report," p. 7. JJP in PM, vol. 2, ch. 23, p. 3, gives the time of Erwin's departure as 3:00 A.M. but misdates it on March 19. He correctly gives the date as the night of March 17–18 in "PX Report," p. 7.

Those loose wagon beds that baffled quartermasters baffled Foulois not at all. He and his men were the only "motorized" outfit in the army, the only one with real training in truck usage. The squadron had its eight Jennies—JN-2s—for occasional sky ventures, but it moved mainly by truck, and every man knew motors and the intricacies of mechanical cajoling.[52] Foulois had his men bore two holes on each side of the beds, bend some round iron bars into U bolts, and lash the beds to truck chassis. Impressed always by ingenuity, Jack asked Foulois if he could help find truck drivers. "From the squadron commander right on down . . . to cooks," the captain said, his men "could all drive a truck." He had, he said, "plenty of instructors." Get him some men with a mechanical gleam and he would produce drivers in a week. Pershing hoped fervently in Dublán that the training was going well. But the expedition could not wait—he would gamble that Foulois's energy would prevail and soon produce supplies.

Under his tree on the night of the eighteenth, Jack plotted a thorough search for Villa.

"Fortune might be favoring us."

Put geometrically, the problem was one of triangulation: If Villa was at San Miguel, resting on a broad plateau in the Sierras, he was situated midway on the base of an isosceles triangle of roads and trails. The Garryowens rode along the eastern face, and if Jack could put other columns on route to the west and perhaps south, Villa could be trapped from two sides. Clear and simple on the map, the solution depended on two variables beyond Pershing's control: Villa's doings and the speed of the chase.

Pershing could put more men on the trail. He saw no need to keep the two troops of the black 10th at Dublán. But the 10th had marched since March 10 from Fort Huachuca, Arizona, to Dublán, a total of 252 miles. Although the troopers were eager to get after the enemy, their horses needed rest. Pershing wanted his former comrades to try for Villa's left flank, to sneak into the San Miguel area from the west. That opened a possibility. Main track of the Mexico Northwestern Railroad ran near Dublán south through Cumbres Tunnel parallel to San Miguel Plateau. Although the de facto government denied the use of their trains, no direct orders forbade the use of American rolling stock.

[52] Author's interview with Maj. Gen. Benjamin D. Foulois, USAF (Ret.), Andrews Air Force Base, Maryland, Mar. 8, 1960.

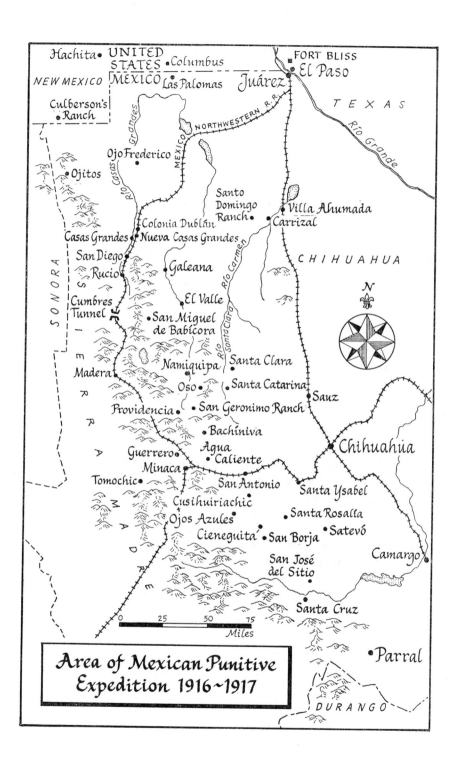

Area of Mexican Punitive
Expedition 1916~1917

To the general manager of the El Paso Southwestern—the U.S. continuation of the Mexican line—Pershing wired for a train. Promptly it came down. As it clanged and puffed into Dublán on the morning of the nineteenth, Pershing thought the chances of catching his quarry loomed bright indeed. But the train was a sham, almost a wreck. Dirty, ramshackle box cars were unfit for use. Hastily men began chopping vent holes in the cars, reflooring many, packing bearings. Late in the afternoon of the nineteenth, troopers and mounts boarded, and the train whooshed toward the mountain grades south. It moved glacially, but it moved, and Jack at last had his plan arail. One troop would detrain at Rucio and head straight for San Miguel de Babícora, the other would go to Las Veras, near Madera, mount up, and ride eastward into the plateau. Now all Jack could do was wait for reports from his columns.[53]

To an old Indian and Moro hunter, the situation had possibilities. "At this early stage of the pursuit," Jack mused, "it seemed that fortune might be favoring us."[54]

On March 20, not long past noon, elements of the Columbus force began arriving. They told tales of sand-bogged trucks, of wandering aeroplanes, of whimsical communications, tales which cast some doubt on fortune's favor.

"Information . . . was very conflicting."

If the trap worked, the expedition succeeded. If the trap failed, the expedition proceeded—and Jack made ready for a longer stay in Mexico. Now that logistical problems were in process of solution, the general began formal organization of his staff. Battle experience at Lake Lanao and Jolo, as well as administrative experimentation at Fort McKinley and Zamboanga, had taught advantages of a small headquarters entourage. Too many staff members tended to impede each other's business, and Jack worked to build a compact, diligent group of trustworthy men. Aides were good—Jimmy Collins, Marty Shallenberger, and George Patton all had the zest of youth. The expedition's adjutant, Maj. John L. Hines, forty-seven, West Point class of '91, an infantry officer until assigned to the Adjutant General's Department in 1901, boasted field experience and sound theoretical training. Since the Inspector General's Department missed a chance to

---

[53] See JJP, "PX Report," pp. 7–8; H. M. Mason, *Great Pursuit*, pp. 92–93; Tompkins, *Chasing Villa*, pp. 78–79; PM, vol. 2, ch. 23, pp. 3–4.
[54] PM, vol. 2, ch. 23, p. 3.

attach one of their own to Pershing's staff, he picked Col. Lucien G. Berry, 4th Field Artillery, as the man to advise on the condition of troops, camps, transportation, and the efficiency of staff and supply systems.[55] Maj. Jim Ryan of the 13th Cavalry drew detached service as intelligence officer. Signal work was handled by Capt. Hanson Black of the flag wavers; Maj. Lytle Brown, Corps of Engineers, had the dubious honor of supervising pioneer troops on the roads and of fixing things in general.

By March, 1916, Pershing's knowledge of the increasing complexities of command, combined with his careful study of the war in Europe, convinced him that the most important member of headquarters was the chief of staff. For that vital post—the chief of staff often functioned as the field commander in the general's absence—Jack had Col. De Rosey C. Cabell, 10th Cavalry. Short, stocky, his full face and chill eyes accentuated by a neat white moustache, Arkansan Cabell was a year Pershing's junior, was a member of the West Point class of '84, and had toured through the 8th, 5th, 6th, 1st, 12th, and 11th Cavalry regiments before settling in Jack's old unit. A 1913 graduate of the Army War College, Cabell was steeped in strategy, tactics, and military organization. Shrewd and tough, horse-soldier Cabell pleased a fellow trooper; he and Jack worked increasingly well together. Jack came to trust Cabell's judgment and to know orders issuing from headquarters would fit his own pattern of campaign. Pershing learned from Cabell an important lesson in delegation of authority with responsibility. Capt. Wilson B. Burtt, 20th Infantry, class of '99, a 1912 graduate of the Army Staff College, served as Cabell's assistant.

Various men passed through the headquarters staff on various assignments, and a few did special, unassigned duties. Probably the most trusted of Jack's official "family" was Capt. William O. Reed, late governor of the District of Sulu. Carried ambiguously on the roll as "on special service with the expedition,"[56] the bulky, forty-six-year-old Reed provided continuity of confidence for Jack, was a man to listen in hard times and to do tasks secret and demanding.

Aides usually feel overworked—Pershing's did. Theirs to arrange headquarters housekeeping, to provide Pershing's transportation when wanted, to pack and unpack documents, to run errands and carry messages. The three young officers contrived a division of labor to lessen individual work and increase efficiency. Collins would do Pershing's personal chores, Shallenberger had charge of all headquarters

[55] JJP, "PX Report," p. 32.
[56] Tompkins, *Chasing Villa*, p. 257.

personnel, and Patton would boss laborers, guides, packers, orderlies, and sometimes assist Major Ryan with intelligence work.[57]

All of them did sometime duty handling the horde of war correspondents that buzzed around Pershing. The general had a smoldering suspicion of newsmen, balked at their nosiness, fended them too brusquely—so the whole staff tried soothing and cajoling in especially difficult moments.

Correspondents led Jack to firm censorship. Difficult enough the campaign would be without important details blared in headlines all over the United States. Major Hines drew the nasty task of censor. Pershing told Hines that he "didn't want anything derogatory to the Expedition, or anything informatory to Villa, to be sent out by the reporters. He was to censor everything most carefully so that nothing detrimental was published in the home newspapers. Major Hines . . . wielded a very heavy blue pencil." And he irritated many minions of the Fourth Estate. In the early weeks of the expedition, Hines let almost nothing through save carefully edited official reports. Even pictures were screened for stray intelligence.[58] Pershing had his reasonable moments and conceded the welcome of correspondents with headquarters—as long as they kept required silence.

Information, reliable information, became a constant necessity. Information depended on communications, which became increasingly undependable as Pershing's columns disappeared into the looming mountains southward. Uncomfortable in the knowledge that separated commands always have difficulties keeping contact, Jack tried to coordinate his three stray outfits. Who should do the coordinating? Hardbitten Col. George Dodd, sixty-three and a fierce old Indian fighter, Pershing thought too old for active service. But the colonel corralled the general at this critical moment with a soldier's boast: "General, I can outride any of them." Here was the man for the toughest task of all.[59] He reviewed the dispositions of the three pursuing forces, learned that the 7th Cavalry camped near Galeana and still waited firm word on Villa's whereabouts. Riding quickly to the 7th, Dodd assumed operations command but left the regiment in Colonel Erwin's hands.

Communications with the two detachments of the 10th were almost impossible. Commanders were unaware of each other's positions and kept such contact as they could with Dublán. Colonel Cabell func-

---

[57] Blumenson, *Patton Papers*, p. 322.

[58] *Ibid.*; Memoir of Gen. John L. Hines, typescript in John L. Hines Papers, U.S. Army Military History Research Collection, Carlisle Barracks, Pa.

[59] PM, vol. 2, ch. 23, p. 7.

tioned as a kind of interlocutor, receiving and sending reports and rumors from one column to another—by courier, by telegraph when feasible, by radio in clear weather. Fuddled by varied reports, Dodd nonetheless trailed southward from Galeana and on the twenty-second met Colonel Salas with some Carranzista remnants of a fight with Villa near Cruces. These forlorn troops held defensive lines near El Valle and were hostile to Villistas and to gringos alike. Salas dickered about American rights to intrude on his country but at last permitted the 7th to trot on toward Cruces. Word from that hamlet on the twenty-third branded it especially anti-American, and Dodd toured round it toward Namiquipa, where several reports placed Villa.

An anguished Pershing read bits and pieces of intelligence flitting between his units, knew that Dodd did his best to coordinate, but realized by March 24 that his trap had hauled up empty. Long rides in grim country and in biting, fearsome weather brought the two 10th Cavalry detachments no contact with Villistas, and the information collected from various sources waxed increasingly confusing. Somewhere between Namiquipa and Santa Clara, Pancho Villa rested, according to rumors given to one of the 10th's detachments; when that news reached headquarters, Pershing directed concentration of the 10th Cavalry.

Confusion confounded headquarters. One column of the 10th received word that Villa lurked near Oso Canyon, and a Carranzista officer promised scouting support for an attack. Everything went awry, and the detachment commander sent a report to Pershing of another empty trap and ended with a rueful comment on his prospective Carranzista ally: "I fear he simply lied to me."[60]

But Dodd persevered. On the twenty-fourth, acting on hints that Villa fled south, the tough colonel put his men on the road early in the morning, turned them southwest through rough hill country and into the teeth of a frigid, driving gale that roared throughout the day. Dodd pushed his men almost beyond endurance in hopes of setting another snare in cooperation with the wandering 10th Cavalry. Night camp settled on the east of the Sierra Madre Orientals, men huddled in blankets, feet to fires, and horses hunched along the picket line in mutual misery. Shortly after 6:00 A.M. on a cold Saturday, March 25, Dodd's men mounted, filed up a high pass toward Babícora. Humped in their saddles against the elements, the troopers managed glimpses now and then of breathtaking scenery, high ridges softened by grace-

[60] JJP, "PX Report," p. 10.

ful pines, oaks, and cedars greened with juniper, and crowned with a lofty, chill sky. In camp near Babícora, the men found ample supplies and ate well.

From there on the twenty-sixth Dodd took his command southeast, learned that elements of the 10th still guarded Oso Canyon, that they had picked up hints that Villa might be heading for the Guerrero Valley. Dodd aimed for Providencia and scoured the trail for signs of bandits. There were none. From Providencia the 7th trotted on toward Bachíniva and on the twenty-eighth captured a Mexican who fearfully reported Villa fighting there a few days past and that just the night before some of Pancho's men had been in a fight at Guerrero. Dodd believed this report—the first that seemed useful in days. Like an old war horse, Dodd got the scent of battle, felt his quarry almost nigh, and made plans to attack. As his column threaded through the cold toward Bachíniva and the trail leading on through the mountains to Guerrero, Dodd heard the strange racket of a plane overhead. One of the Jennies circled his command, found a likely spot, cut power, and sailed in stately glide to land. As the plane skidded to a stop, a bundled figure in leather jacket, helmet, and huge goggles clambered from the cockpit and sought Colonel Dodd. Lt. Herbert Dargue brought dispatches from Pershing—who at last had planes to contact troops beyond telegraph or radio reach. Pershing's orders were most depressing. A detachment of the 11th Cavalry headed for Dodd's territory, the 7th was to rest until relieved by fresh pursuers.

Quickly Dodd scratched a reply, one that marked him Jack's type of commander. Close to the prey, he intended to press on, he said. "I am now satisfied that Villa is not far distant. I shall proceed farther south, and shall continue in such touch as is possible to attain (and attack if possible) with Villa."[61]

Probably Dodd should have waited for fresh men and animals, despite the apparent proximity of the enemy. His own men were worn by scant rations, had been on the march fourteen days out of fifteen, and up on the Babícora Plateau had endured weather cold enough to freeze canteens and ice whiskers. If they had counted, they could have boasted covering four hundred miles since leaving Dublán. But Dodd trusted their toughness. He had to trust, too, guides ignorant of the high country. Hopefully he listened to one guide who had been to Guerrero years before and thought he recognized a trail that led there —although it might be the long way.

[61] See Tompkins, *Chasing Villa*, pp. 80–83.

Faced with a moment of high decision, Dodd elected to take a fair certainty in place of total ignorance and ordered a forced march through the night. That night lingered long in memories of veteran cavalrymen—they struggled with the unknown trail and halted often to check direction; men slept as they could, huddled in coats and blankets, almost numbed beyond suffering. Citizens were conscripted as fresh guides during the march but seemed less informative than others. At about 6:30 A.M., after a harrowing trek of fifty-five miles, the 7th Cavalry drew rein along a precipice and looked down at Guerrero, nestled in a valley far below. There was a way to the town, a hair-raising trail that plunged sickeningly downward. Better guides would have brought the American troops to the valley from the west where the bluffs were less formidable and would have permitted easier surprise. Surprise would surely be lost that morning as horses and pack mules slithered and galloped toward the village. But Dodd made the best of his fate and urged speed. Rumors placed Villa, wounded, somewhere in the hamlet. If any luck held, the campaign could end on the twenty-ninth of March in that little village lost in the palm of the mountains.

Not until after 7:00 A.M. did Dodd's men deploy for attack, but, when they went, they went in two parties and went hard. Soon the colonel realized he had flushed a force of almost five hundred men, but surprise cut their strength. Heavy fighting pushed the Villistas finally out of town, and they broke into small groups as they fled. For almost five hours Dodd's tired troopers pursued. When firing died away and numbers and spoils were counted, the doughty colonel drafted a proud report to John Pershing:

The number known to be killed was 30, and in this connection it must be remembered that four-fifths of the Villistas are Yaquis, who carry off their dead. Undoubtedly a much larger number than this was killed.

We captured Villa's two machine guns, a number of horses, saddles and arms.

Our casualties were four enlisted men wounded, none of them seriously.

The attack was a surprise, but owing to misrepresentation of guide failed to be the total success I anticipated. Had I had a good guide the entire outfit would have been boxed. The attack resulted in the breaking up and scattering of Villa's troops, the greater portion of them being driven in a ten mile running fight into the mountains northeast of the railroad where after brisk skirmishing they separated into small bands, and our horses were too weak to follow them further.[62]

Many Carranzista prisoners were freed, much booty taken, but

[62] JJP, "PX Report," pp. 14–15.

Villa had gone. Once more he had evaded the gringos and his legend grew, although the incredible march of the 7th Cavalry enhanced the regiment's own traditions. Dodd's persistence did another thing of importance—it convinced many in the range of Pershing's horsemen that the Americans were tougher than expected.

That march and fight convinced Jack that he must devise his campaign with increased care. He had guessed the need for close planning as he dispatched Dodd to the front. The sketchy reports, fragmentary dispatches, and eddying rumors finally cracked his patience. Fervently he had hoped that Benny Foulois's planes would solve the puzzle of communicating with distant and disparate columns—but Dublán rested high and the mountains south, higher.

Jack's interest in military aviation stretched back to that remembered day at Tours when he had encountered Wilbur Wright working with French flyers. Orders to use aeroplanes in Mexico came obviously with intent beyond immediate convenience. Secretary Baker and Chief of Staff Scott surely intended campaign testing for the infant air section of the Signal Corps. Foulois's First Aero Squadron gleaned publicity for various experiments at Fort Sill and at San Antonio, but it still lagged far behind British, French, and German air outfits in planes, trained pilots, mechanics, shops, in almost everything. Congressional parsimony seriously hampered aerial development in the United States, and field testing might confirm or deny congressional wisdom.

Experience taught Jack the overall importance of coordinating all the new tools in his division. Planes, field radios, machine guns, trucks were adjuncts to men, horses, cannons—adjuncts to enhance but not replace traditional modes of war. Innovations had always fascinated Pershing—methods used by modern armies, methods used by primitive enemies were noted carefully by a serious student of war. And planes worked their own special fascination on an American soldier. Machines charmed some deep current of tinkerer in all gringos, touched their hands with greasy magic, tuned their ears to a rhythmic noise, shined their eyes with the beauty of iron. When the First Aero Squadron, some of it, had racketed to landings near camp at Dublán, everyone there—Pershing included—looked on aviators as a new kind of knight errant. As Foulois and his men clambered from their planes and walked to report, they had the cockiness long kept to the cavalry. They were the new elite.

But they were an elite with frailties. Two aeroplanes failed to arrive with the rest, and amid concern for pilots Pershing had issued his first orders for aerial reconnaissance. Go, he told Foulois, south toward Cumbres Pass in search of cavalry heading for Babícora.

An uncomfortable impracticality colored this first aviation order from General Pershing. Dublán rested 4,000 feet above sea level; Cumbres Pass climbed to 12,000 feet, and a Jenny's operational ceiling was 10,000! But first mission seemed a poor time to report deficiencies —so Foulois made ready. He had an additional deficiency for personal concern, a hazard to affect performance. By awkward design, the Jenny carried observers in the front cockpit, pilots in the rear. A bad experience at Fort Sill lent special importance to location. As Foulois well recalled, at Sill "one of the pilots took the quartermaster up, he sat in the front seat, came down and made a crash landing and the engine was pushed back into the quartermaster captain's lap. We buried the quartermaster up there. Well, none of those boys wanted to sit in that front seat after that." Who would peer groundward in search of Pershing's horsemen? Foulois resigned himself to the chore. "I did it with the pilot that I had every bit of confidence in. . . . That was Captain [Townsend F.] Dodd."[63]

Off toward the mountains sailed the biplane, growing finite and tiny in the distance, a toy in the hands of Sierra winds. Finally back came the machine with deflated flyers. Little Benny, his broad grin gone, his high forehead creased with disappointment, reported to Pershing. The general heard an almost ludicrous tale of trial and failure calmly enough. Foulois's mission had gone scarcely more than twenty-five miles southward. Underpowered, the plane failed to clear even the foothills of the Sierras at the entrance to Cumbres Pass. Gusty winds played tricks on the plane. "We tried that pass four or five times," the game little captain said, "and every time we'd get into it, we'd get slammed right down almost to the treetops, and we'd pull out and try it again, and couldn't get through." Nature provided a good excuse, but Jack scowled, nonetheless. He would support requests for better planes and in the meantime abandon hope of useful reconnaissance. There was, however, a vital duty which the planes might do—communications. Vagaries of atmosphere, mountain interference, the strange independence of radios reduced effective contact with field units. Telegraphs, maintained against distance and vandalism, worked sporadically. If planes could construct a grid of contact between headquarters and fast-moving columns southward, they would

[63] Author's interview with General Foulois; Memoir, Benjamin D. Foulois, Oral History Collection, Columbia University, pp. 26–28, 76; See also, H. M. Mason, *Great Pursuit*, ch. 6, pp. 103–19.

do inestimable service for the expedition. Foulois and his men did their best.

Jack knew he could not rely on the planes to be measurably more effective than any other avenue of communication. Keeping in touch with roaming troopers remained the toughest task of all commanders of large forces. Jack had encountered the problem slightly on Mindanao and more pressingly on Jolo. Maneuvers with his brigade at McKinley and work with the 8th Brigade along the border during 1914–15 taught the absolute need of being close to troops. A remote headquarters doomed itself to mystifying ignorance. Jack wanted to get closer to his field units, to move along the main road south, perhaps to find Colonel Dodd's persevering men. It was a natural urge, one expected in a fighting general. Was it practical? Or wise? Should the commanding officer expose himself deep in hostile country? If communications might be assured, the risk could be justified. If not, exposure would be simply foolhardy. Weighing the chances of improving contact, Jack decided he must risk jeopardy. Cabell would stay with expedition headquarters at Dublán while the general ranged to the front.

At Dublán, and far ahead as well as far behind on the line of communications, Pershing could count a command of almost 10,000 men—the largest force of his career. The expedition wore heavily on his concern in multiple ways—its men, its circumstances, its mission, its potential. He might kill many, miss his mark, cause war—the chances of serious embarrassment were splendid. Pershing thought cautiously but acted boldly. Boldness could not be pressed without his presence close to the scene. Fortunately his staff were men of like swash.

George Patton organized the small traveling corps. Maj. Jim Ryan (crafty sifter of information), a clerk who doubled as stenographer, a cook named Johnny Booker from the 10th Cavalry, Lanckton the long-suffering, Patton, three drivers, and four guards made up the general's close entourage. Jack would ride in a Dodge tourer rented from a Mormon colonist. A clutch of correspondents wanted to go along. No one save the general seemed ready for desert campaigning. He made his kit of a blanket, shaving bag, razor, and tooth brush, and must have been amused at the impedimenta of the scribbling corps.[64]

[64] For JJP's traveling arrangements, see Blumenson, *Patton Papers*, pp. 324–25; H. M. Mason, *Great Pursuit*, p. 121; Robert Ginsburgh, "Pershing as His Orderlies Know Him," *American Legion Monthly* 5 (Nov., 1928): 13; Frank B. Elser, "General Pershing's Mexican Campaign," *Century Magazine*, Feb., 1920, pp. 438–39.

Floyd Gibbons of Chicago's *Tribune* and Bob Dunn of New York's were temporarily without transport and scampered through Dublán loudly begging a car. Other correspondents, including the *New York Times*'s shrewd Frank Elser, were bandoliered, pistoled, draggled with paper, typewriters, cameras, canteens, tents, and an eye-catching assortment of Fords, Dodges, and Hudsons somehow purloined in El Paso. And they joined Pershing's three small cars to make a motley caravan.

Generous the general had been to the newsmen he usually distrusted. "You can sign for gasoline," Pershing told them, and Patton had happily issued Springfields for defense.[65] Defense could be a problem, since Jack projected a jump to San Geronimo Ranch, 110 miles south of Dublán and probably squarely in Villista country.

"About noon" on March 28, Pershing, straight, thin-lipped, stern, boarded the first car in company with Patton and waited while his civilian driver and others revved engines and contemplated the oozy road ahead. Behind in the second car were four enlisted men and Lanckton, and in the third, Booker with four more guards. With a lurch into the mud, the trip began—it was to linger fresh in memories for hazard, discomfort, and breakneck loitering. Bob Dunn recorded the day's 60-mile trek to El Valle as "over the world's worst ruts, no road whatever, we seldom bettered fifteen miles per hour—through thousand-foot box canyons, over passes with orchids like small pineapple plants on the limbs of oaks. My job was to fill canvas waterbags at the rare water holes and quench our sizzling radiator."[66] Once, during a race around harrowing turns, the caravan burst full panoplied on a solitary peon atop an ancient spring wagon. Wrenching his panicky horse off the trail, the Mexican sat trembling as the gringos thundered by. Pull up, Pershing ordered as he spied the wagon's cargo—lump sugar! As the cars clanked, rumbled, and cooled, men poured around the wagon and bought a good chunk of its freight. Popping a lump in his cheek and sucking slowly, Pershing remounted and waved "forward."

On through climbing land that chilled with sinking sun, the strange invasion continued until, at last, a spreading red glow lit the sky. To one observer the sight reminded of "the concentrated lights of some great summer amusement resort," but it marked instead mesquite fire, distant and wasting.[67] Natural curiosity slowed the writers

[65] H. M. Mason, *Great Pursuit*, p. 121.
[66] Quoted in *ibid*.
[67] Elser, "Mexican Campaign," p. 439.

as they gawked at a fiery spectacle, but Pershing pushed ahead and reached El Valle far ahead of his comrades. When they clattered into the advanced American base, the general could be seen huddled under his blanket in a bed of hay.

That night Dodd's men of the 7th were making their heroic march toward Guerrero, and some extrasensory excitement reached El Valle. At dawn Pershing rose fresh and eager. "I think we've got Villa," he said to henchmen at breakfast. Just as the last coffee washed down hot food, a plane droned in sight and landed. The general read the message from Dodd that told the old soldier's intent to attack. Quick, now, the general urged, and in less than twenty minutes he was speeding southward, guards, correspondents, and others strung behind. News became the desperate need. What had happened? No more planes came, and the caravan plunged southwest through the morning. A quick break for lunch ended with the cars back to their rutted course. Sunset found them still rolling—an heroic day of tire changing and minor rebuilding dim in numbed memory. Finally, at Namiquipa, Pershing heard that Villistas had recently routed Carranzistas there. On he ordered his wearied driver, on toward Bachíniva. Shortly he learned from scouts that Bachíniva was filled with Villistas, and he turned back to San Geronimo Ranch. There, some 270 miles from the U.S. border, he made contact with Dodd.

News ran good—Villa might be caught. The hope burned bright on the thirtieth, as Pershing pulled elements of the 11th and 13th Cavalry regiments into the area around Guerrero. The day burned slowly in shifting fortune and confused reports. Excited by hope, Jack almost ignored discomfort, but he was cold.

San Geronimo Ranch sprawled on flat land 7,500 feet up in the Sierra foothills; a fierce north wind drove sand and snow through coats and uniforms to make misery of walking or riding, to turn horses' backs to windward, heads down "like cattle drifting before a blizzard."[68] Pershing huddled the night in his blanket, campaign hat pulled down against sand and snow. At sun-up he yanked on his boots, ceremoniously shaved—shaving was good for morale—and joined the correspondents in sand-flavored hardtack cooked in bacon grease. It seemed likely that Villa was surrounded. And the general proved uncommonly generous with news. In a talk that sounded like a communique, he even allowed a small boast: "Our troops seem to be pressing him [Villa], but I won't hazard any predictions. Villa is no

68 *Ibid.*, pp. 439–40.

fool. It may be that the campaign has just started." The correspondents, huddled with guards and scouts, scribbled that quotable nugget. Among the listeners was C. E. Tracy, a red-shirted broncbuster in cowboy hat, chaps, and pistols, who squatted on his boots, chewing a straw. When the general quit talking, Tracy drawled, "As I figure it, General, we've got Villa entirely surrounded," a pause, then, "on one side." The whole group collapsed in laughter. Pershing, to everyone's surprise, laughed hardest![69]

Frank Elser noted happily that "General Pershing might have a reputation for being a rigid disciplinarian, he might be a stickler for formality . . . but at any rate it appeared that he had a sense of humor."[70] Elser did not know how long that sense of humor had been quenched, how slow the returning laughter, the smiling eye. Annie would have been eight years old on March 25, and birthdays were poignant agonies now. Warring was a kind of anodyne that pushed grief behind the veil of duty. But always in the lonely dark, anguish seeped anew. Jack knew that he "should never be relieved of the . . . grief at the terrible loss." Time offered no help. "It is just as it was on the dreadful morning when the telephone message gave me the heartbreaking news."[71] Daylight and the puzzle of Villa's whereabouts brought surcease and diversion.

Crisis at Parral

Quick movement, small cars, a penchant for light gear, all reduced accommodations at mobile headquarters. Folks sat on anything handy, and the general usually used an empty supply box for a camp stool. One chilly San Geronimo dusk, air strangely quiet with the wind down, he perched on his rough throne, rested chin in hand, and stared back into some distant past—he did that often and no one dared break his reverie. A faint clank and squawky rumble announced some old Mexican wagon; finally it rocked into sight, a poor thing, tattered, and bulging with people. Silently the riders studied the American camp, the thin man astride the box who obviously bossed the place. A glance at the visitors showed apprehensive politeness; Pershing roused, waved the wagon closer. Holding hats sheepishly, five men approached and with them a woman with three children.

[69] *Ibid.*, p. 438; H. M. Mason, *Great Pursuit*, p. 122, misquotes Elser in a different version of the episode.

[70] Elser, "Mexican Campaign," p. 438.

[71] Quoted in H. M. Mason, *Great Pursuit*, p. 80.

Musicians, they had been playing at a birthday party and wondered if the general would permit . . .? Surely. Fiddler, guitarist, cornetist, plus "a thin little fellow with a huge bass viol," tuned up. Sad love songs floated first in the desert twilight, faster dance music, a momentary hesitation, then the fine tune that told endless ways of Villa's greatness, "La Cucaracha." When the concert ended to loud applause, a sombrero quickly filled with silver.

Musicians were the more peaceful visitors to Pershing's camp. During the days he stayed at San Geronimo, various bands of natives passed by and through the American bivouac. Surely the most interesting visitor came also the most wary. General Luis Herrera, an important military figure in Chihuahua, whose father was *presidente* of Parral (a large city to the southeast in heavily Villista country), approached camp one afternoon with about two hundred men—a force at least ten times larger than Pershing's detachment. Close scouting of Pershing's camp finally convinced Herrera of its hospitality, and he rode in with fifteen or twenty staff officers.

Quickly Pershing rose from his box-stool and strode to meet his guest. Secretly abashed by the bare and mean equipments at hand, impressed by the well-armed Carranzistas atop fine and beautifully saddled horses, Jack offered a warm welcome to the Mexicans. With full protocol, he presented his tiny entourage, greeted Herrera's officers. While formalities continued, Trooper Booker swept a space, hunted every box and gasoline can, and finally ushered all to seats.

Correspondents gawked and cocked eager ears. The Mexican officers were polite and oddly muted. "Standing within ten feet of them, one could scarcely hear them," one newsman noted, and was impressed by the "white teeth" showing in each swarthy face. General Herrera asked quick, incisive questions: Did Pershing know Villa's whereabouts? How many gringo troops were in the field? Where were they going? "About the latter point they wished especially to be enlightened," writer Elser noted. "We did not appreciate it at the time, but that question was later to determine the destinies of the campaign."[72]

Pershing listened for hidden nuances. Dodging Herrera's questions with some of his own, Jack wondered about Carranzista locations, their plans? Herrera finally said Villa was dead—it was a recent

[72] Elser, "Mexican Campaign," pp. 442–43; H. M. Mason, *Great Pursuit*, pp. 122–23.

rumor that Jack doubted. There was a body, Herrera insisted, and Villa's death made continued Norte Americano invasion unnecessary. If a body existed, Pershing would have it seen.

Further sparring yielded no admissions on either side, and finally Herrera mounted and galloped away. Jack watched him, frowning. The Mexican general professed friendship, but Jack felt that "his manner throughout this visit was distinctly surly." [73]

That unsatisfactory encounter enhanced Pershing's skepticism about Carranzista support. Widely announced, assistance rarely materialized. Scant toleration marked most meetings with Carranza's troops. Increasing indications of rising hostility came from far-flung cavalry detachments. On April 5, Maj. Frank Tompkins narrowly avoided trouble with Carranzista General José Cavazos near San Borja. Hot on Villa's trail, Tompkins wanted to gallop on south beyond San Borja, but Cavazos refused permission and looked ready to fight. Wisely Tompkins chose discretion and returned to Cieneguita. But from that day he knew "that the Carranzistas were against us, that we could expect no help from them, and that they would jump us at the first favorable opportunity." [74]

With or without Carranzista aid, Jack felt he might still catch Villa. All reports coming by air, by radio, by horse and auto couriers, put Villa southeast now of the Sierra Madre Oriental range. Apparently wounded, but muchly alive, he seemed headed for the Durango country below Parral. Pershing kept to his plan of parallel columns; they would converge near the Durango line and, with luck, bag Villa and his men. [75]

The three probes Pershing sent southward gave promise of final success. He had Colonel Dodd at Minaca by the end of the first week of April, where his presence was resented but permitted by General Herrera. Maj. Robert Howze, 11th Cavalry, reported himself on April 11 a few days behind Villa on the road south of Santa Cruz. Col. Bill Brown, 10th Cavalry, rode the eastern flank and was at the Media Ranch, near Sapien, not far north of Parral, by April 12. On that day Maj. Frank Tompkins rode into Parral and history.

Columns slowly concentrated in the vicinity of Parral, and San Geronimo seemed remote and far beyond touch with the fluid front.

[73] PM, vol. 2, ch. 23, p. 10. The visit is described in Elser, "Mexican Campaign," pp. 442–43, and in H. M. Mason, *Great Pursuit*, pp. 123–24.
[74] Tompkins, *Chasing Villa*, p. 131.
[75] JJP, "PX Report," p. 17.

Actually communications failed. On April 10, Foulois's gallant remnants tried a grid search of almost 700 square miles of Chihuahua. A vast emptiness sped below the planes, an emptiness of burned, dry hills, adobe villages, scourged ground cut by arroyos, wrapped in blowing dust. Of humans there came scant evidence, only the innocent, upturned faces of the patient desert people. No sign of U.S. Cavalry greeted observers, no sign of Villa's men. The report cut deep, for it brought grim confirmation that Pershing had, for the first time, lost contact with his roving command. Just as he felt victory near, he lost his men, could learn nothing of the trap so near springing! He must get closer to impending operations, must find a new moving headquarters location reachable by all columns and by Cabell from Dublán. On the eleventh, he collected Ryan, Q.M. Capt. Leon Kromer, reliable Bill Reed, Patton, Booker, base people of the First Aero Squadron, and a small guard, bundled them in Dodges and trucks, and took the trail toward Satevó, some eighty miles north of Parral.[76]

Troubles dogged the trip—detours, snipers, lost planes, accidents, and the loss of a Dodge and a side-car motorcycle. Exhausted travelers made camp in a Satevó cornfield.[77] At 4:30 P.M. on the twelfth, a small, provisional squadron of the 11th Cavalry under Col. Henry T. Allen trotted into Satevó. Pershing last had seen Allen on the eighth and sent him wandering southward through rough hill country in general support of Brown and Tompkins. Allen reported tersely; he had followed a spotty trail of a Villista officer that led generally toward the caves near Santa Rosalía, where Villa just might be hiding. From Satevó, Allen's command could march east-southeast into the cave district, but horses were worn almost beyond moving and men were numbed skeletons in the saddle.[78]

Allen and Pershing combined information with Major Ryan, and the emerging picture disturbed them all. The various columns reported varying reception—some communities were friendly, others hostile. Hostility seemed to grow in direct ratio to American penetration southward. How much farther before a coalition of all Mexicans turned on the gringos and made war? Every extra mile toward Durango seemed fraught with danger. But Villa must be somewhere in the grasp of Pershing's converging columns. Speculation proved the weak-

[76] JJP to Funston, Apr. 10, 1916, in 3849 ACP 1886; Blumenson, *Patton Papers*, p. 327.

[77] Elser, "Mexican Campaign," p. 444.

[78] Tompkins, *Chasing Villa*, pp. 124–27.

ness of communications. Although the general recklessly exposed himself with a small guard close to his flying columns, he received no real information throughout early April.[79]

Rumors became their own facts and correspondents traded in them as the only surety. The grim, tall Missouri general, whose form shrank as his wrinkles deepened, offered proportionately less information as his sources evaporated. Censorship clamped tighter, so tight, in fact, that not even Pershing could approve dispatches. He gave Maj. John Hines absolute control over press releases in a memorable encounter. When one of the more enterprising writers snagged the general, thrust a story at him, and badgered a hasty "O.K., J.J.P." on it, he rushed to Hines and said "Please send this off right away." Hines began reading, and the writer broke in irritatedly, "You don't have to read it. Look and you will see there that it has been okayed by General Pershing."

"Well," said the deliberate Hines, "my duties are those of the censor, so I must read it." With maddening thoroughness he read the story, shuffled the pages together, and walked out, saying, "I want to talk to General Pershing about this."

Into the small and squalid headquarters tent came Hines, obviously irked. With full military politeness he explained the need to read several paragraphs. Certainly. When he finished, Hines looked levelly at the commanding general with a question:

"Now, General, is that what you would like to see published in the newspapers back home?"

Badly burned by an early April tirade leaked to the national papers by frustrated flyers,[80] concerned that no internal criticism of any phase of the expedition be permitted, Pershing had listened to Hines's reading with shock. To the question he answered, quickly, "Good God, no."

"Well, look here, it says, 'O.K., J.J.P.' You've already cleared it to be sent."

That smacked of considerable boldness, but Hines's irritation was justified.

Waving a quick hand, Pershing cleared the air.

"Don't pay any attention to what I approve. You're the censor here. Only what you approve is all right to be sent. You censor all these

---

[79] See JJP to Funston, San Geronimo, Apr. 6, 1916, Lee Papers. JJP said he had not been in wireless touch with Dublán for nine days, and that planes were unreliable as couriers.

[80] H. M. Mason, *Great Pursuit*, pp. 115–16.

dispatches the way you see fit and don't pay any attention to what I may write on them. Now you're the final authority on what goes out from this Expedition. It doesn't matter what I say."

On Hines's request, Jack repeated his order to the reporters, who took the news unhappily. But one phase of activities had been solidified.[81]

Around the expedition news leaked from local Mexican sources, from Americans living in Mexico, from Carranzistas with mischief in mind. In recent days expedition news seemed to reach the War Department before Pershing—it happened embarrassingly often and revealed in Washington unwanted inquisitiveness about casualties, plans, rumors, tactics. It also brought a fracture in command. One of the bad moments came in a telegram from Newton Baker to Freddy Funston, who sent a copy on to Pershing:

WAR DEPARTMENT
Washington

April 14, 1916.

We are of course without information as to why commander of American troops entered Parral without consent of Mexican local authorities. The Secretary of War directs that you send general orders to all commanders of troops in Mexico calling their attention to the importance of maintaining the most harmonious relations with all local authorities of the de facto government and urging the utmost consideration for the feelings and sensibilities of such authorities and the people in Mexican towns and villages.

Newton D. Baker
Secretary of War.[82]

In San Antonio, Funston balanced reports carefully and defended his wandering subordinate. To the adjutant general he wired soothing words:

I feel sure commanders of our troops have been discreet in dealing with Mexican authorities this being indicated by apparently cordial relations when they have come in contact. Upon starting expedition Pershing issued stringent orders on subject of relationship with Mexicans generally. I am strongly of opinion that it would be better to await official report before assuming that our troops were in the wrong at Parral. . . . No towns are being occupied or have been occupied by our troops, but they must go through them or they can go practically nowhere as the towns are naturally on the roads. . . . If any stubborn or hostile Mexican commander so wills he can tie up the expedition provided we are dependent on consent of such official before going through a town.[83]

[81] Memoir of John L. Hines, Hines Papers.
[82] In 3849 ACP 1886.
[83] Funston to AG, Apr. 15, 1916, in 3849 ACP 1886.

Such spirited defense brought swift clarification. "The Secretary of War wants it understood," wired the adjutant general, "that our [message] makes no assumption that our troops were in the wrong at Parral. Say so to Pershing. There have been many evidences of fine tact on his part. Also impress upon him the importance of full communications as early and as often as possible to enable Department to give him proper support and prevent other trouble from rumors. Our [message] is not a prohibition upon going through towns when necessary. . . ."[84]

Washington was right about communications. In Satevó, Jack heard nothing, nor did he receive Funston's urgent messages. Still groping for his various elements, he sent out auto couriers and such patrols as he could garner. Almost desperate for contact with Funston and Cabell, he risked sending Foulois to Chihuahua City. Benny, by now almost a veteran at flying into that high town (where he recently had spent some uncomfortable hours in jail), took dispatches to the United States consul, who presumably could use the telegraph line northward. Back he buzzed sometime on April 15,[85] hopped from his plane, and reported to Jack in a lather. Wild rumors flitted the streets in Chihuahua—an American force had been attacked in Parral by de facto troops and badly beaten. People were killed on both sides; Carranza's government fumed officially to Washington and issued its own public version of the "atrocity."[86]

Uncertain who had been involved, if anybody, Jack guessed his nearest unit to have been Brown with the 10th Cavalry. Quickly he sent word to Funston, identified Brown's men as likely victims, announced he had demanded the arrest of guilty Carranzista officers, and asked for help. A big fight with government soldiers pushed peace to the teetering edge; if war came, the Punitive Expedition could manage, but would need its units brought to full strength and could use two more regiments, one cavalry, one infantry.[87]

As full details filtered to Satevó, Jack seethed. Foulois's erroneous rumors explained the absurd dispatches that came at last from Washington but did not relieve their sting. Petty punctilio at so tender a

[84] AG to Funston, Apr. 15, 1916, in 3849 ACP 1886.
[85] The time is uncertain. Elser, in "Mexican Campaign," p. 445, fixes the day Foulois returned as April 14, but JJP in a dispatch to Funston from Satevo, Apr. 15, 1916 (3849 ACP 1886), says he "just received news of unprovoked attack . . . at Parral." Pershing probably sent his message immediately after hearing Foulois's report.
[86] Elser, "Mexican Campaign," p. 445.
[87] JJP to Funston, Apr. 15, 1916, in 3849 ACP 1886.

moment struck Jack as ruinous. War threatened by the minute with the Punitive Expedition deep in hostile land, strung out at the ends of multiple thin supply lines, outnumbered, weary, its animals worn, its men hungry and trail dazed, its communications occasional, its planes nearly wrecks, its trucks mired helter skelter over 300 sand-seared Chihuahua miles. Facing that reality, Jack raged at the flaccid policy pushed by Wilson and Baker.

Funston, at least, understood the tactical emergency and asked Jack to estimate his situation. Carefully the general reconstructed the Parral encounter—by the sixteenth he had a report from Maj. Frank Tompkins—to the credit of the 13th Cavalry. Tompkins had been cordially invited into Parral by military authorities, offered hospitality and permission to buy badly needed food and fodder. About noon on the twelfth he arrived, apparently surprised the local *jefe des armas*, but negotiated for supplies and was finally escorted by a Carranzista general toward a campsite out of town. As his men rode through huge crowds, the people turned ugly, shouted "Viva Villa," and finally someone fired on the gringo rearguard. Tompkins promptly protested to his hosts and tried to extricate his detachment without serious fighting. He failed. At last he began a long, skirmishing retreat that took him to a village some eighteen miles from Parral, where he dug in and waited for help. Tompkins, wounded himself, took several casualties and inflicted more.

Colonel Brown with part of the 10th Cavalry galloped hard and reached Tompkins about 8:00 P.M. His arrival scared off the Mexicans, and the incident ended.[88]

Aftersparks worried Pershing. Parral's wake created an entirely new situation for the expedition. Resentment against U.S. intrusion became a fine tool for Carranza, and he used it. There was also the possibility of German agitation in Chihuahua, of some incitement by the German consul in Parral, which complicated the international picture.[89] For Funston, Jack assessed current Mexican attitudes. "My opinion is," he wired his superior,

general attitude Carranza has been one of obstruction. This also universal opinion Army officers this expedition. . . . Inconceivable that notorious character like Villa could remain in country with people ignorant of his general direction and approximate location. Since Guerrero fight it is practically impossible obtain guides. . . . Small bands Carranza troops under guise Villistas have often fired upon our columns. The further we advance south the less friendly the people have become.

[88] See Tompkins, *Chasing Villa*, pp. 135–44; JJP, "PX Report," pp. 21–23.
[89] JJP to Funston, Namiquipa, Apr. 16, 1916, in 3849 ACP 1886.

Clearly if U.S. troops continued feigned politeness, they would be driven from Mexico. That meant only one thing to Pershing, and he offered a soldier's best suggestion to the tough little fighter in San Antonio:

In order to prosecute our mission with any promise of success it is . . . absolutely necessary for us to assume complete possession for time being of country through which we must operate and established [*sic*] control of the railroads as means of supplying forces *required*. Therefore recommend immediate capture by this command of city and State of Chihuahua also the seizure of all railroads therein as preliminary to further necessary [operations?].[90]

Aggressiveness just might retrieve a dismal situation.

Treachery everywhere infuriated Pershing. For weeks the fiction of friendship with Carranzistas held, to the credit of everyone in the expedition. Correspondents were kept from spilling a bloated spleen by heavy rain and light humor. Early in April, Frank Elser of the *New York Times* had tried to stir up news by questioning the taciturn general who disliked reporters. How would he characterize Mexican reaction to the expedition? That kind of question confirmed old suspicions of reportorial idiocy, and Jack stared quizzically at Elser for a while. Then, smiling mysteriously, he began precise dictation: "After having progressed 350 miles into the interior of Mexico it is very gratifying to be able to state that our relations with the Mexican people, both civil and military, have been exceptionally cordial and friendly. From the military forces of the de facto government we have received hearty cooperation." Elser laughed in amazement at such glib dissimulation and noted a twinkle in placid blue eyes.

But Parral changed Jack's ideas on arranging news. Reporters at Satevó saw a new John Pershing. Barely controlling anger as he learned Tompkins's troubles, Jack blew the lid off censorship. To astounded newsmen he said "nothing, now, should be kept from the public. You can go the limit." He watched as the horde of scribblers composed purple paragraphs about "ambuscades" and "alarms," and reached over one shoulder to add "treachery" to a wild summary of Parral.[91]

Sudden frankness could prove dangerous. Bald attacks on Carranzista "co-operation" could embarrass Wilson's diplomacy and the president's wrath reached long. How much ought a soldier tolerate?

[90] JJP to Funston, Namiquipa, Apr. 17, 1916, in 3849 ACP 1886.
[91] H. M. Mason, *Great Pursuit*, p. 140. For JJP's dictation to Elser, see Elser, "Mexican Campaign," p. 442.

Treachery marked limits of discipline. Wilson's policy of quasiinter-
vention worked hardships unimagined on the Punitive Expedition.
Surely no American field force ever operated under harsher restrictions, or endured worse conditions. Openly critical now, Jack talked
of weakness in high places and grumbled at his shackles. His opinion
spread. Patton, who worshipped at the shrine of a "great soldier full
of energy," reflected his hero's disenchantment. "Wilson ought to take
iron or something to stiffen his back," the young lieutenant wrote his
father, and boasted that the hard-riding Punitive Expedition had improved the American public's view of the army. "We must take it
[Mexico] or leave it," he mused in late April, and guessed that "if we
leave it ruine [sic] total and complete will follow . . . If we take the
country we could settle it and these people would be happier and
better off."[92]

Caution prevailed in Washington; Parral shocked the administration. Extra care would be taken to avoid trouble. Pershing must curb
himself and his men. "No hope of our being allowed to strike the first
blow," Funston wired his frustrated subordinate,[93] and cautioned a
defensive posture pending renegotiation of U.S. rights in Mexico. It
hurt, but made sense. Pershing's forces were four hundred miles from
home, spread wide across southern Chihuahua, and could not live off
the poor land around Parral. Jack sent reluctant instructions to fall
back on San Antonio. There trucks and wagons could provide food
and forage and the town some strategic advantages for larger operations—if they were ordered.

Knowing the importance of quick contact with Funston and perhaps with Baker, vexed by the tenuous communications from Satevó,
aware, too, of his exposed position eighty miles south of San Antonio,
Jack decided to keep headquarters moving. He could wait for his
cavalry to pick him up en route north, or he could risk another of his
wild rides through enemy country with a tiny collection of military
and civilian visitors to sunny Chihuahua. Move, he ordered, and the
harried Patton began sweeping people and equipment into eight dusty,
weary Dodges and several grimy trucks. Bill Reed, a specialist now at
salvaging wrecked autos, piled his peculiar collection of spare parts
into a kind of repair truck while guards checked everyone's arms.
Thirty rifles were counted. Booker rattled his pots, pans, and boxes
aboard one of the trucks, and the general's safari stood ready for
almost anything save travel. About noon on April 15, 1916, Jack

92 Blumenson, *Patton Papers*, pp. 328–29.
93 Funston to JJP, May 1, 1916, in 3849 ACP 1886.

climbed into his car, took his ramrod posture, fixed his eye on some remote vision; and the mechanized column rocked into the ruts. Orders were to run to Namiquipa where Pershing could use the telegraph.[94]

All night headquarters kept the road. Near Santa Ysabel at dark one of the cars broke down, and a wary party deployed to guard repairers. "We feared being shot up," George Patton confessed.[95]

Discipline and care paid off frequently during those hair-raising cruises through the Chihuahua dust. The ride to Namiquipa brought memories of earlier hazards. Pershing did not sleep at all during the night's lurching and had not slept during the previous night's worries about Parral. At sunrise on Sunday, the sixteenth, Namiquipa bounced in sight. After breakfast, Pershing, looking fresh and fit, reported by wire to the War Department, then worked on reorganizing his base. Correspondents who puzzled his plans were doomed to frustration—he explained nothing about the fast ride north, nothing of orders to his men. Frank Elser hazarded a delicate dispatch: "The . . . Expedition . . . had apparently come to a standstill. Whether the halt is to be permanent depends largely on circumstances beyond the control of General Pershing. From a military standpoint he has for the time being come to the end of his lane."[96]

Pershing read it, pensively stroking his chin. Knotting his brow, looking stubborn, he looked at Elser and growled a question.

"Is this your deduction?"

"Yes, sir," Elser nodded.

"Then send it," Pershing said—and Hines was absent, so it went!

At Namiquipa Gen. John J. Pershing took stock of his campaign. Where was Pancho Villa? Or was that now the main problem?

A Good Plan Undone

Almost while Pershing's frightening telegram dated April 17 suggesting control of the whole of Chihuahua clicked from the wire, President Wilson and Secretaries Baker and Lansing opted for cautious talk with Carranza. Hugh Scott, that old hard bargainer, took a late April train for San Antonio, Texas, as soon as word arrived that Secretary Obregón journeyed to the border. Funston reported the delay for

[94] See Elser, "Mexican Campaign," p. 446; Blumenson, *Patton Papers*, p. 327.

[95] Blumenson, *Patton Papers*, p. 327.

[96] Elser, "Mexican Campaign," p. 447. Details of the trip are pieced together from *ibid.*, pp. 446–47; Blumenson, *Patton Papers*, p. 327; H. M. Mason, *Great Pursuit*, pp. 141–42.

discussion to Jack, warned of Scott's descent, and added that "pending his arrival there will undoubtedly be no action taken by [the] War Department on any recommendation you and I have made."[97]

Correspondent Elser's guess had been good. Clearly the expedition bogged in the shadow of war. All must be quiet in Chihuahua while talk progressed; Pershing must harness his men and husband resources. The whole pussyfooting business irked him—he knew Wilson's purposes and thought them wrong. A quick strike to the core of Mexico, a direct excision of Carranzistas and Villistas together Pershing believed possible and the best politico-military policy. But he leashed his men, called the far columns back toward San Antonio, Mexico, and sat uncomfortably lazy. His temper he controlled, but not his opinions. Funston received daily reminders of Carranzista perfidies, of the constant hampers to American troops.

Enforced inactivity brought a chance to refit the expedition; and every man, machine, and animal needed rest, refurbishing, and repair. As he surveyed his first units filtering back to Namiquipa from further south, Jack swallowed anger anew at how much American troops had given for so long to be robbed somehow of final victory. The scrap-clad scarecrows swaying atop bags of bones hardly reminded of the storied U.S. Cavalry—they seemed more like Jeb Stuart's men after a long chase through Yankee country. Supplies were not short. The logistical agencies did herculean work in purchasing everything needed by Jack's men, but distribution failed the challenge of distance from Columbus. The sprawling wasteland consumed machinery with grim impartiality and was dotted now with mute iron skeletons that once were trucks and wagons. Foulois's planes finally were gone, all wrecked or worn away by the cruel, high desert and impenetrable Sierras. Good men were dead, fortunately not many; good men were sick, fortunately not many; lots of good equipment had been lost; and Pershing felt most of these erosions wasteful without positive results. In the hard tradition of George Washington and Robert E. Lee, Jack begged for added trucks, for railroad support from El Paso. But the hardest thing was sticking to orders. Personally busy with inspections and correspondence, Jack devised camp chores with training overtones for the staff and idle troops.[98]

Idleness is military sin, and Jack fought it. Sitting passive would earn Mexican contempt and would not find Villa. Jack improvised an

[97] PM, vol. 2, ch. 23, p. 12.
[98] See Blumenson, *Patton Papers*, pp. 327–39.

active withdrawal from the south, a kind of snooping extraction of his columns—pull back but keep looking.[99]

April burned away in brassy sun and blowing sand. As the driving prairie wind moaned through camp, flaying tents and men and horses with a wicked penance, ennui settled over headquarters and finally plunged Pershing into uncommon self-pity. He was lonely, of course, weakened by work, poor food, alkali water, and endless care. And his situation shook his faith in the wisdom of diplomats. To fellow Missourian Enoch Crowder, now the army's judge advocate general, he wrote some honest musing of a martial stepchild.

I feel just a little bit like a man looking for a needle in a haystack with an armed guard standing over the stack forbidding you to look in the hay. . . . From my own observations, I do not believe these people can ever establish a government among themselves that will stand. Carranza has no more control over local commanders or of states or municipalities than if he lived in London.[100]

Anger at the hostility of professed friendlies crept into most of Jack's personal correspondence and lent his official documents a wry humor.[101]

Throughout late April, Pershing paraded almost daily a list of indignities committed by Carranzistas. Funston read of every rebuff, false promise, feigned act of cooperation suffered by American troops. Finally Jack capped the list with a final arrogance. "Carranza officers," he wired his superior, "have stated openly that they would not allow Americans to capture Villa."[102] Such thwarts demanded response, and Jack devised new tactics. He ordered all of Chihuahua south of Galeana and above Parral divided into districts, each under a regiment commander with permanently assigned troops. Practice sparked the idea. For weeks some of the best work of the expedition had been done by Dodd's hard-riding 7th. They stayed pretty much in one area, learned the ground and the people, traded in local markets, developed special sources of information. Familiarity bred respect; if it worked for Dodd, it should work generally. As soon as units were partly refreshed, they trotted to Pershing's new districts: Namiquipa, Satevó, San Borja, Guerrero.[103]

Dodd, almost on cue, proved the virtue of this scheme. Pushing his

[99] H. M. Mason, *Great Pursuit*, p. 143.
[100] Quoted in *ibid.*, p. 145.
[101] See FEW to JJP, May 10, 1916, FEW Papers, vol. 75.
[102] JJP to Funston (telegram), May 1, 1916, in 3849 ACP 1886.
[103] GO no. 28, HQ Punitive Expedition, Apr. 29, 1916, in JJP, "PX Report," pp. 24–26.

men in the best 7th tradition, he struck a big camp of Villa's *bandidos* at Tomochic on April 22, routed nearly two hundred men, killed at least thirty of them, and pursued survivors into the mountains. Delighted, Pershing reported success to Funston, who reacted nervously. Contact, even positive, might jiggle the forthcoming talks near the border. "Situation very tense regarded as dangerous," Funston wired Jack, but allowed as much latitude as his own trammels permitted. "Use your best judgment as to disposition of troops and inform me what you do. Take all possible precautions against troops from Sonora and against the movement we are informed is in progress from south. . . . Suggest desirability of shortening your lines."[104]

Nervousness came from several causes. Funston was in El Paso with Scott, preparing for talks with Obregón, and had heard of Mexican concentrations building against Pershing's men from the west and south. When actual palaver started at Juárez on April 30, Scott alone seemed ready for the battle of repetition. Obregón pressed the question of Pershing's withdrawal; Scott, the question of cooperation and use of railroads by the Punitive Expedition. For two hours futile exchange continued. Not accustomed to long pow-wows with Indians, not initiated to nuance as communication, Funston fidgeted as time passed. Good soldier that he was, he wanted to get to agreement quickly. Laborious ratiocinations tired the little general. Threats to Pershing from Sonora and elsewhere seemed vital to Funston. He listened to the infinite trivia Obregón and Scott rehashed until he could stand it no longer. Slamming his fist on the table, leaping to his full diminutive height, he—according to Scott—"allowed his real sentiments to be expressed so brusquely that he lost his influence. . . ."[105] Mexican newsmen saw the eruption through a window and wrote lurid exaggerations of the moment. That afternoon Scott reported Obregón's refusal to "discuss anything but withdrawal."[106]

With almost unctuous duplicity, Newton Baker counseled dissimulation. "We of course cannot foresee result of further conference with General Obregon but suggest that if deadlock seems imminent you adjourn further instructions from Department so as gain time to pull together outlying part(s) of General Pershing's force. Every precaution should be taken against sudden general attack."[107] At the same time, Baker authorized negotiation of Pershing's situation. In a

[104] Funston to JJP, May 1, 1916, in 3849 ACP 1886.
[105] Scott, *Memories*, p. 525.
[106] Clendenen, *U.S. and Villa*, p. 272.
[107] AG to Scott (telegram), 11:59 P.M., Apr. 30, 1916, Lee Papers.

"convenient number of days," the expedition might be pulled back "to a place nearer the border . . . from which place should further trouble appear we can act promptly and effectively in cooperation with the forces of the de facto Government or independently if the need be urgent." Complete withdrawal could be promised on the capacity of the Mexican authorities to control the border.[108]

Perils for Pershing clouded the conference. Rumors of hostile troop concentrations were confirmed when Funston received, on May 1, a copy of orders going to a Carranzista general from the First Chief of the Mexican government: "Dispose your troops so that they shall be in a position [to] cut off American expeditionary forces now in Chihuahua. The action must be sudden and will take place after the Scott-Obregon conference. It will make no difference what else may be decided upon in conference; unless there is absolute withdrawal of American troops the above plans will be carried out. The Sonora troops will be assisted by the troops in Chihuahua."[109]

A sudden surge of truculence around the expedition convinced Jack of real threats. Robert Howze with his detachment of the 11th Cavalry barely avoided a bad fight near San José del Sitio, and a general ostracism cut troopers off from local markets. All of which, duly reported, excited Funston's belligerence and may have firmed the administration's feelings. At any rate, on May 1, Secretary Baker stated the boundaries of possibility: "This Government can not withdraw troops from Mexico until it is satisfied that danger to our people on the border is removed. . . . On no account give excuse for attack. If attacked, take all necessary steps to make answer decisive and speedy."[110]

In El Paso, Washington, probably in Mexico City, fears ran for war. Less anxiety troubled Pershing's headquarters. News of growing success with the district scheme lured a weary general again closer to his front. At San Antonio, headquarters deployed for reports, and, on the evening of May 4, Pershing learned that three leading Villistas, Julio Acosta, Cruz Dominguez, and Antonio Angel, were near Cusihuiriachic with about 120 men. Cusi, a mining community, was protected by a small Carranzista unit. Townsfolk asked for American protection; also, a Major López of Carranza's army reported a severe defeat at Ojos Azules and politely asked for men to protect Cusi. Who

[108] AG to Scott (telegram), 7:50 P.M., Apr. 30, 1916, Lee Papers.

[109] Quoted in H. M. Mason, *Great Pursuit*, pp. 152–53. Also in Clendenen, *U.S. and Villa*, p. 273 (a variant version).

[110] Baker to Scott (telegram), May 1, 1916, Lee Papers.

could go? Howze was ready. Take six troops and the Machine Gun Platoon of the 11th Cavalry, Pershing told his good major, ride for Cusi, and attack the raiders if possible. About midnight of the 4th, Howze reached Cusi. From partially intoxicated Carranzistas—who were not especially friendly—he learned that the brigands were still enjoying victory at Ojos Azules.

Carefully picking guides—Howze was a veteran now at deceit— he put his men in column for a night march. A little after daybreak on the fifth—after a thirty-six mile nocturnal ride—Howze's men surprised the Villistas at Ojos Azules.

Howze had ordered an attack at sight. When the advance, including a number of Apache scouts, saw the rancho *cuartel*, they spread out in skirmish order and started in. The Indians, long customed to brush fights, dismounted, fell on their bellies, and returned desultory rifle fire. Long strands of barbed wire guarding one approach to the rancho slowed and skewed Howze's battle, and quickly he saw that nothing went right for a real, true, set-piece cavalry charge. Somewhere back in the dust trailed the Machine Gun Platoon. Various mounted units straggled forward without formation and joined in the tumult and shooting. Battle was on, but Howze would not be robbed of a final glory. Where was his bugler? The trooper rode up, got the word, raised the short brass bugle, wet the mouthpiece, took a breath, and suddenly over the popping clatter floated the chilling call— "Charge!" By fours, forward, and all columns spilled onto the flat field in front of Ojos, drew pistols; "gallop," came the order, and men hunched a little, horses began their stately run. In no more than twenty minutes Troops A, C, D, E, F, and G had cleared the *cuartel*, broken resistance into small, splintering pockets of desperate horsemen, and driven well beyond the rancho into small, spare hills to the southeast. For almost an hour and a half running skirmishes flared in the hills. Small bands were caught, killed, or scattered. Venging American troopers pursued until some horses dropped. Not until Howze knew all organized enemy units were dissolved did he call a halt.

There were several fascinating sidelights to the fight. Five Carranzista prisoners doomed to death were rescued. And although sixty-one Villistas died in an action wild with bullets, not a single U.S. trooper had even been wounded, although several carried bullet holes in clothes and equipment. "Consider this a brilliant piece of work," an elated Pershing wired Freddy Funston.[111]

111 JJP to Funston, San Antonio, Mex., May 5, 1916, in 3849 ACP 1886. For the battle, see JJP, "PX Report," pp. 26–27; H. M. Mason, *Great Pursuit*, pp. 159–

Funston may have been elated, too, but the news of Ojos Azules came at a tender moment. In a conference at El Paso on May 2—a twelve-hour marathon—Scott and Obregón hammered out an agreement that satisfied Wilson, Scott, possibly Obregón, and apparently averted immediate war. According to the protocol, which Carranza must ratify, Mexican troops would increase efforts to repress Villa and guard the U.S.-Mexican border; in return for these vague promises, the United States would "gradually withdraw the forces of the punitive expedition from Mexico, commencing the withdrawal immediately." Only continued chaos and troubles near the border could deter full extraction of Pershing's force.[112]

Agreements with Carranza always seemed doomed. On May 5 a bandit raid against Glenn Springs and Boquillas, Texas, in the Big Bend wastes, showed the impotence of Carranzistas, but the First Chief laid blame on American outlaws and told Obregón to talk again with Scott, this time to get a firm date for Pershing's removal from Mexico. And anyone, Carranza said, who chased after the recent raiders would be treated as invaders. Scott and Funston weighed the situation and asked Washington for 150,000 men to guard the border. "It is recommended," the two generals said, "that militia of Texas, New Mexico and Arizona be called out at once." In another wearying round of talks, Obregón and Scott achieved no solution. When they parted amicably but finally on May 11, war seemed the only option for either government.[113]

Tension, mounting and almost tangible over Headquarters, Southern Department, drove Funston to a reluctant order. Pull back to Colonia Dublán, he wired Pershing on May 9; deteriorating relations might require quick concentration.

Aware that the president had called out elements of the National Guard as requested, that Scott and Funston—normally glacially calm —were concerned, Jack issued general orders for retreat. Some units began backing up by afternoon on the ninth of May. Exposed the expedition surely was, pieces of it isolated, but Jack suspected "that

---

68; Clendenen, *U.S. and Villa*, p. 275; Tompkins, *Chasing Villa*, pp. 191–94; H. A. Toulmin, Jr., *With Pershing in Mexico*, pp. 81–88; S. M. Williams, "The Cavalry Fight at Ojos Azules," *U.S. Cavalry Journal* 37 (Jan., 1917): 405–8.

[112] See "Memorandum of Conference Between General Alvaro Obregón, Secretary of War of the Republic of Mexico, Major General Hugh L. Scott, Chief of Staff, U.S.A., and Major General Frederick Funston, U.S.A. . . . ," El Paso, Texas, May 2, 1916, copy in Lee Papers. See also Link, *Progressive Era*, pp. 139–40; H. M. Mason, *Great Pursuit*, pp. 154–56; Scott, *Memories*, pp. 525–28.

[113] H. M. Mason, *Great Pursuit*, pp. 174–75; Link, *Progressive Era*, p. 140.

north of the border there was much anxiety for the safety of the expedition that was not entirely warranted." Although rumors told of arms being given to civilians, of clustering troops on all flanks, Pershing thought their leadership would be poor, their loyalty doubtful, their effectiveness nil.[114] But orders would be obeyed.

As trucks, wagons, horses, autos began rolling out of camp at San Antonio, and footsoldiers began that slow, swinging gait northward in the sand, Col. John Beacom, the 6th Infantry's Old Man, waited by the flagpole for the sad honor of lowering Old Glory. Dust blew already through deserted streets, stray tumbleweed bounced through a ghost community. As the colonel drew to attention and watched the flag come down, he looked quickly to find a sad companion standing rigidly beside him—John Pershing. A soldier looked proud when the flag went up or down, and Jack's lined face was rock-like. His far-looking eyes were reddened—not from the blowing sand—and he confessed to Beacom as they left the lonely post a heavy and uncertain heart. "I shall never cease believing," he said, "that but for this turn of affairs the arch-bandit would have been captured." Going backward always galled, and doing it under threats put severe strain on discipline. "To turn our backs upon the further possibilities was as great a disappointment to the command as it was to me," Pershing admitted.[115]

The need for going seemed increasingly less. Politicians made their bargains, but soldiers faced realities. Back in the Alamo City's fevered clime, Funston must be sweltering under suspicions and beguilings to fog the hardest brain. Tough, his professionalism charged with a small man's pugnacity, Funston believed in boldness. His new caution must be uncomfortable, probably insecure; Pershing, even as he headed north, wired his superior a careful assessment of the situation. Not as serious as painted, threats against the expedition evaporated with shows of force; retreat simply encouraged the weak. Was Dublán a nonnegotiable destination? Better coverage of possible Villa country could be kept from Namiquipa, and from there a concentration of all forces would be quick and easy. Withdrawal to Dublán not only blunted all hope of catching Villa, but also undid everything so far done.

Risking high wrath, Funston approved Namiquipa as Pershing's advanced base and headquarters. Questioned by a touchy War Department, Funston gave Pershing's smooth rationalization. "If he [Pershing] were to retire to Dublán it would give Mexicans impression

[114] PM, vol. 2, ch. 23, p. 15; JJP to Funston, May 11, 1916, in 3849 ACP 1886.
[115] PM, vol. 2, ch. 23, pp. 15–16.

that he was afraid of their concentration and would unquestionably greatly encourage them."[116]

To Namiquipa came the scattered elements of a moribund expedition. Pershing kept up patrols, worked on refitting and logistics, and hoped to be unleashed by some diplomatic legerdemain. Throughout May he collected intelligence, surveyed the surrounding ground, estimated Carranzista intentions, probed carefully southward for whiffs of Villa, and scribbled incautious letters against politicos. Some rumors of his sentiments reached Washington, apparently, and tweaked a presidential ear. Scott, queried as to Pershing's loyalty by Secretary Baker, asked for time to investigate. Quickly he wrote Jack that "enemies were working against him" in the capital and requested words of explanation. "A frank manly letter" came from the beleaguered general, which Scott passed on to the president, and the issue closed.[117] But it rankled and seemed symptomatic of a static sort of unrest.

Jack knew those rumors floating in Washington carried too much truth for comfort. He did think Wilson's policies vacillating and probably wrong; he did think excessive courtesy toward Carranza's government bred contempt, and he said so in more letters than were prudent. Papa Warren, whose sympathies ran rarely for Democrats, agreed with Jack's assessment of Wilsonian oscillation, but old army friends who read of unrest in Mexico often passed on juicy tidbits of gossip from an unhappy general.[118] Off in a forlorn waste, fettered by uncertainty and official confusion, Jack's morale slipped; he could not, for the moment, appreciate pressures on the White House.

But some reflection renewed perspective on the view from Pennsylvania Avenue. A long look showed that Jack's good plan of district management was undone for large reasons of the future. Too effective, the plan piqued general Mexican resentment and nudged war closer— and war had to be avoided. Daily dispatches from Europe told terrible Allied news. Casualties piled across the Western Front in a kind of reckless race against humanity. Into the consuming cauldron at Verdun, France and Germany still fed men and munitions without stint in a daily sacrifice that had begun in February and seemed destined to last to the end of the world. Both sides dreamed of a "breakthrough" in the trench system that snaked across 400 miles of

---

[116] Funston to AG (telegram), 8:30 P.M., June 12, 1916, in 3849 ACP 1886.
[117] Scott, *Memories*, p. 532.
[118] For an example of Jack's complaints, see FEW to JJP May 10, 1916, FEW Papers, vol. 75.

France, but the dream warped into a bleeding nightmare that eroded hope and courage. From the mire that was the Western Front came hints of one final, gargantuan British drive to wrest the Somme valley and break on into good cavalry ground. If it succeeded, the Allies might win; if it failed, they might lose. And if they lost, they would call with blood kinship to America for men. A Mexican tangle might prevent an American decision in a war for destiny, decency, and democracy. All of which forced Pershing to play reluctant possum.

"Responsibility here has fallen on my shoulders very heavily."

George Patton learned from his heroes, many of them dimly lustrous in martial history, one of them close by in camp. From one touchy encounter with Pershing and three carloads of men against hordes of Mexican horsemen, he learned the truth of Caesar's alleged dictum that "fortune favors the bold." Desperately did he hope to re-prove the point, took every opportunity for scouting, and at last found and killed one of Villa's generals, Julio Cárdenas. *Times*man Frank Elser wrote a lurid account of "one of the prettiest fights of the campaign," and attributed new mobile tactics to Patton of the cavalry—he had ridden to battle in an automobile! Pleased with his young apprentice's daring, Pershing dubbed Patton his "bandit" and let him keep his victim's silvered saddle.[119] Newsmen caught some yearning touch of glory in the thin, reedy-voiced lieutenant who strove to look like John Pershing; his exploit hit the wires and spread wide around the country.

Patton's feat won more attention than one of greater import a few days later, when a detachment of enlisted men was attacked by Villistas, lost one killed, two wounded, and managed to kill two in return —one being Candelario Cervantes, Villa's ablest subordinate.[120]

Gradually Villa's good men fell. Attrition told Pershing that pressure counted. With his men scattered as far as Providencia and San Geronimo, he kept a semblance of pursuit. Patrols were part of general security necessary to the expedition's new defensive. Security loomed an increasing concern as reports of Mexican concentrations building in Chihuahua multiplied. If rumors were right, Pershing might be flanked east and west. Denied the luxury of attack to improve the odds, Jack decided the time had come to talk to Carranza's commander in

---

[119] Blumenson, *Patton Papers*, pp. 327–28, 330–39; JJP, "PX Report," p. 28.
[120] Blumenson, *Patton Papers*, p. 339; JJP, "PX Report," p. 28; H. M. Mason, *Great Pursuit*, pp. 184–93.

Juárez. If some kind of cooperation could be established between generals, the expedition might continue in relative ease. Would Gen. Gabriel Gavira come to Dublán? He would, and on May 31 Jack and two staff members climbed into a car for an eighty-mile run over the worn road north.

On June 1 Gavira's private railroad car was spotted between Carranzista and American camps, and Pershing climbed aboard. At first it seemed nothing but trouble would come from the meeting— Gavira wanted to occupy every town on Pershing's line of communications from Dublán to Namiquipa. Fixing the Mexican officer with cold eyes, Jack sat firm, jaw fixed, and reckoned that large movements of de facto troops along the railroad and his left flank would be considered by his government as hostile acts. After two hours of conversation with the unswerving American general, Gavira wilted. By the end of the afternoon session, Jack had gained almost every point. "Final conclusion . . . as follows," Jack wired Funston,

Carranza troops occupy four stations on Central Railroad north of Sauz with garrisons 50 men each, also four stations Carmen Valley from Santa Rosalia north 50 men each. Total number on my left flank north of Sauz not to exceed at any time more than 400 men. Same number now occupying garrisons along Northwestern Railroad not to be increased. . . . In return it was agreed on my part that I should advise General Gavira of our retirement if made from any town along my line of communication so that his forces could occupy it. Also that I should investigate and settle any complaints against American troops made by local presidentes in towns within our lines not occupied by Carranza troops.

It had been a good day's work and Pershing said so: "Regard conference as very satisfactory inasmuch as we are committed to nothing we should not otherwise do, and no restrictions are placed upon our movement. . . . General Gavira is committed to limited number of troops on our flanks."[121]

Whether the agreement would hold depended on Gavira's suasion among other Carranzistas and on the tense relations between governments. Diplomatically the situation crumbled. A virtual ultimatum to Wilson in mid-May was long ignored, and the First Chief decided to shift pressure from Washington to Namiquipa. On June 16 a telegram arrived from Gen. Jacinto B. Treviño in Chihuahua City that nearly declared war.

I have orders from my Government to prevent, by the use of arms, new invasions of my country by American forces and also to prevent the American

[121] JJP to Funston, June 1, 1916, in 3849 ACP 1886.

forces that are in this state from moving to the south, east or west of the places they now occupy. I communicate this to you for your knowledge for the reason that your forces will be attacked by the Mexican forces if these instructions are not heeded. Courteously, J. B. Treviño, the General in Chief.

Long practice in diplomacy shaped a quick answer, one soldier to another.

> Field Headquarters, American Expedition
> Casas Grandes, Mexico, June 16, 1916.

General J. B. Treviño,
  Chihuahua, Mexico.

I am in receipt of your telegram advising me that your government has directed you to prevent any movement to the east, south or west of the American forces now in Mexico. And that should such movement take place the American forces will be attacked by Mexican forces. In reply you are informed that my government has placed no restrictions upon the movements of American forces. I shall therefore use my own judgment as to when and in what direction I shall move my forces in pursuit of bandits or in seeking information regarding bandits. If under these circumstances the Mexican forces attack any of my columns the responsibility for the consequences will lie with the Mexican government.

> Respectfully yours,
> John J. Pershing, General,
> Commanding American forces.[122]

The answer went before Pershing reported to anyone higher up. He wanted to establish his position, to act without involving the administration, and to frighten Treviño with speed. Other Carranzista commanders who reported hostile orders received the same cold assertion of American independence. Pershing refused to be bluffed and told Funston that he would "continue reconnaissance necessary to keep in touch movement of Carranza forces."[123] Orders from Pershing to his field units offered some comfort to nervous folk in the War Department. "Make every effort to avoid collision, but if attacked, inflict as much damage as possible. . . ."[124] Scrupulous attention to politesse would govern every encounter with Carranza's followers— if they allowed time for politeness. Reckless Pershing was not; firm he was.

Washington was confused. Negotiations suspended, no one quite knew the status of U.S.-Mexican relations. Wilson, Lansing, and Baker,

---

[122] Texts in JJP, "PX Report," pp. 29–30. Also in JJP to Funston, June 16, 1916, in 3849 ACP 1886.

[123] JJP to Funston, June 16, 1916, in 3849 ACP 1886.

[124] JJP, Field Notebook, Punitive Expedition, Box 2, PP.

though, came to the end of ravelling patience. On June 20, after due recasting, a brutally blunt reply went to Carranza's May ultimatum. Rejecting all allegations of wrong by the United States, refusing to withdraw the Punitive Expedition, the American government announced that any resort to war by Mexico would bring its own reward.[125] Growing militia strength along the border backed the State Department's uncommon bluntness. Baker ordered most of the Regulars to the border to aid the gathering National Guard and hoped—a bit wistfully—that enthusiasm would recruit numbers above 200,000. War plans were based on 150,000, and Funston received orders to prepare three possible columns for invasion; one from El Paso under George Bell was to consolidate with Pershing's command.

Washington's purposes were complicated—war without fighting seemed the hope—and the orders ran long. Long orders always confuse, and Funston soon wallowed in conflicting discretions. He could, said Baker, occupy international bridges and Mexican border towns in case of attack or to protect Americans. If Pershing got into serious trouble, Bell could advance from El Paso along the railroad and join forces. At the same time, Funston was strictly forbidden to put any troops across the border without permission. Perplexed, he asked for clarification and read again dual authority—he must act without boiling the war kettle.

Virtually spitted by responsibility and vague power, Funston fumed and spilled some of his temper on Pershing. Communications became stiff, and the little man in San Antonio required unusually full summaries of the expedition's doings.

Drab routine plagued the line from Dublán through El Valle to Namiquipa. Regular patrols were increased as local intelligence dwindled. Whispers of Mexican hordes gathering to throw the gringos out chilled all natives. Friends turned away, people on the spy payroll quit spying, everyone wanted to get right with the revolution. Understanding human frailty, Pershing avoided pressure and relied on reconnaissance for information. But internal reliance demanded extra vigilance—and extra vigilance meant increased chances of hostile contact.

Boredom worked against vigilance. Days grew longer and hotter, desert winds seethed constantly, and camp seemed like a sand-blast furnace. Troopers sweltered in field khakis or anything else, horses wilted in the awful aridity, and out in the burning hills shimmered

[125] Clendenen, *U.S. and Villa*, p. 278.

Villa's mirage. Men doomed to camp service hunted duck, antelope, anything for diversion, and worked on their personal gear; officers badgered noncoms and filled out the army's ancient forms. Pershing did his stint of paper work and rebelled. Couldn't the supply services simplify their infernal machinery? Mindful of Cuban lessons and already responsible for innovations in base camp administration in Columbus, Pershing pestered his logistical staff until, at last, traditional requisitions were scrapped in favor of simple signature issues and memorandum receipts for depot needs. Intermediate depots were essential, and Pershing found good men to run them. The Punitive Expedition relearned many supply lessons of the Civil War. Big field forces cannot be supplied according to regulations designed to sustain posts, camps, and small stations.[126]

Persistent rumors from the east nudged Jack's concern for the railroad line from Juárez to Chihuahua City. Word was that 10,000 Carranzistas clustered near Villa Ahumada, 75 miles east on Dublán's left flank. All of northern Mexico tensed for explosion. Doubting the rumors of hostile hordes, Jack nonetheless took a good soldier's precautions. Pulling headquarters back to Nueva Casas Grandes for better communications, he shortened his patrol perimeter and urged special caution on his commanders. If only Foulois had one plane.

Scouting was the cavalry's business, and troopers must discover the situation near Ahumada. Pershing had a soft spot for the 10th Cavalry, knew the hard mettle of its troopers, and expected full duty always. Happily some of the 10th rested handy, and the general asked Col. Ellwood Evans, the regimental commander, to send to his tent "the most diplomatic officer" available for service. Capt. Charles T. Boyd, leading Troop C, got the call and went to headquarters in the evening of June 17. He had known Pershing for years, had crossed his path in the Philippines, and respected him highly. Respect was mutual, and Jack greeted the grizzled captain with pleasure. Boyd's experience gave him perspective on the mission Pershing outlined. What was going on at Ahumada? How many Mexican troops gathered near there? This information, urgently needed, might be gleaned at Santo Domingo Ranch, short of Ahumada—which would be less hazardous. In a relaxed conversation, Pershing made a serious point. "This is a reconnaissance only, and you will not be expected to fight. In fact, I want you to avoid a fight if possible. Do not allow yourself to be surprised by superior numbers. But if wantonly attacked, use your own judgment

---

[126] See JJP, "PX Report," pp. 34–36, 41–42.

as to what you shall do, having due regard for the safety of your command." Treviño, the Mexican general, had warned against just this kind of nosiness, Jack explained, and specially cautioned Boyd against daring Carranzista garrisons. A clash probably would start a war—the situation looked about as tense as it could get. And if fighting erupted, Boyd's troop would be too remote for help from Dublán. Boyd asked questions, took notes, seemed eager. And when Boyd left Jack "felt confident that [he] fully understood the importance and delicacy of his mission."

Boyd's ambition worked behind his smiles, and it showed on close reading of his eyes. Long years of solid work had brought a spectacular opportunity—Pershing's precious information could be the key to fame. Good soldier Boyd, class of '96, was a "distinguished graduate" of the army's School of the Line, and his active career sparkled with considerable combat service. Normally careful, precise, Boyd brimmed with excitement over his assignment; in camp after leaving Pershing's tent, he talked too much of his mission and its potential. But he made proper preparations for getting Troop C ready.[127]

With Boyd under orders to beat the trail eastward, Pershing doubled the chance of picking up intelligence by sending another troop east from Ojo Frederico. The job went to Capt. Lewis S. Morey, commanding the 10th's Troop K. Lean, thin-lipped, scholarly looking Morey, class of 1900, was one of the bright boys of the service; at forty he was a "distinguished graduate" of the Infantry and Cavalry School and also of the Army Staff College.[128] Convinced his routine snooping missions were in competent hands, Pershing took a brief respite from official worries.

Weatherbeaten like his men, burdened beyond the ken of his colleagues, Jack had stuck to his job without stint, but relief must come even to compulsion. When Bishop Call of the Mormon colony invited Jack to visit Aztec ruins on June 19, he gathered up some gleeful staff members and journeyed to the Casas Grandes valley. Surprisingly enough, Mexicans everywhere on the route welcomed the party and were especially courteous. Jack did ceremonial sightseeing, not only at the ruins but also at the San Diego Ranch. Delighted by numbers of school children who pressed to see him, Jack thought of Warren's com-

---

[127] For the Boyd-JJP meeting, see Clendenen, *U.S. and Villa*, p. 279. For JJP's belief that Boyd understood his orders, see PM, vol. 2, ch. 23, p. 19. For some of the odd circumstances of the meeting, see H. B. Wharfield, "The Affair at Carrizal," *Montana, The Magazine of Western History* 18 (Oct., 1968): 28.

[128] See *Army Register, 1918*, p. 215.

ing birthday—he would be seven on the twenty-fourth—and showed
unsuspected gentleness.[129]

That day he wrote nostalgically to Frank Helm, who had shared
the death trip to San Francisco. Family thoughts crept through his
martial barrier, and he admitted that "responsibility here has fallen on
my shoulders very heavily. I have very little time to think of anything
except the conduct of the expedition." And he added, sadly, "in many
respects this has been fortunate for me."[130]

"Peculiar conditions surrounding expedition not fully appreciated"

"Why in the name of God do I hear nothing from you the whole
country has known for ten hours through Mexican sources that a considerable force from your command was apparently defeated yesterday
with heavy loss at Carrizal." The frenzied words were Funston's; they
came in a wire on June 22 and reflected agitation in high places. They
were awkward, embarrassing, and infuriating, especially since the
little general added caustic criticism as a query: "Under existing order
to you why were they there so far from your line being at such distance that I assume that now nearly twenty four hours after affair news
has not reached you who was responsible for what on its face seems to
have been a terrible blunder."[131]

Hysterical accusations from his superior Pershing did not need at
the moment; he laboriously pieced together snatches of information
about disaster at Carrizal. As first he learned of losses there, Jack assumed war had come, asked authority for a dash toward the Mexican
Central, thence on to Chihuahua; he expected Bell to help. But quickly
he cooled with facts.

Dejected stragglers drifted into Casas Grandes, and gradually a
mosaic of blunders was constructed from their stories. One of the survivors brought a letter written by the wounded Lew Morey that summarized early parts of the action. By the afternoon of June 23, Pershing had wired a lengthy appreciation of the Carrizal action to Fun-

129 Press dispatch to multiple papers, Dublán, July 16, 1916, in "Punitive Expedition to Mexico, Selected Documents, Records of U.S. Army Overseas Operations and Commands, 1898–1942," RG 395, National Archives.

130 JJP to Frank Helm, June 19, 1916, Box 92, PP.

131 Funston to JJP, June 22, 1916, in Punitive Expedition, Selected Documents, RG 395, National Archives (hereinafter cited as PX, Selected Docs.).

ston which admitted that two troops of the 10th Cavalry—Morey met Boyd at Santo Domingo Ranch on the night of the twentieth and since their missions were similar had offered to join forces—had attempted to pass through Carrizal and were denied permission in several lengthy conferences with Carranzista officers, and that Boyd finally determined to fight through toward Ahumada. During the conferences, Mexican troops deployed toward Boyd's flanks, set up a machine gun, and clearly outnumbered the Americans. Stubbornly Boyd dismounted his men and advanced in separating groups, echeloned to the right. Boyd led the advance of his troop, charged the machine gun, and was killed; his second-in-command, 1st Lt. Henry R. Adair, fell at about the same time. Morey, trying to rally Troop K, flanked on the right, was hit in the shoulder and sought refuge in a nearby building while remnants of both troops left the field. Fighting had been close and heavy, with successes going first to the 10th. Even the loss of all officers did not demoralize good troops, but, outnumbered and outflanked, they gradually lost cohesion and fled. Twelve men were dead, ten wounded, and twenty-four were prisoners.[132]

What had happened? How could Boyd so mistake his mission? He seemed, that night in Jack's tent, sure and willing and careful. Added details confirmed Boyd's curious audacity. When, at last, Morey returned, he recounted the history of his march, his link-up with Boyd, and the conference at Santo Domingo Ranch. Talk ran long that night, he said, with the officers haggling over their orders and listening to the ranch foreman, an American named W. P. McCabe, who thought further advance absurd. About 400 Carranza cavalry were in Carrizal, he reported, and agreed with Mormon scout Lem Spillsbury that if getting to Ahumada was essential, Boyd should by-pass Carrizal. Morey recapitulated his own orders, which cautioned against aggressiveness, and he urged that the column miss Carrizal. If the two troops went there, he said, they would start a fight. Boyd bowed his neck and said he would go to Ahumada through Carrizal. Everyone at Casas Grandes wondered what madness seized a seasoned soldier. He had engineered the only full-blown disaster experienced by the expedition, and the knowledge that good men had died in a pointless skirmish brooded in the air over headquarters. Gloom spread far and quieted the camp.

---

[132] JJP to Funston, June 26, 1916, in PX, Selected Docs.; H. M. Mason, *Great Pursuit*, p. 211; Heath Twichell, Jr., *Allen: The Biography of an Army Officer, 1859–1930*, p. 190.

What would the Old Man do? Would the president at last cut him loose for Chihuahua City?[133]

Privately Jack worked on the mystery of Carrizal. He knew he would be accused of sending Boyd with deliberate orders to start a war. Some of the captain's boasting on the night of the seventeenth might tend to confirm the charge. Silly as it seemed, out of character and out of orders, Jack knew the suspicion would lurk. What had happened out there in the Chihuahua wastes? Puzzled, Jack tried to reconstruct Boyd's thoughts. "Before he started," Jack remembered, "I told him personally, among other things, that Trevino had sent a threatening letter, that the Mexican situation was very tense and that a clash with Mexican troops would probably bring on war and must be avoided. . . . No one could have been more surprised than I was to learn that he had become seriously involved."[134] To Col. Henry T. Allen, who took command of the 11th Cavalry, the general wrote in frank puzzlement: "I am very much cut up over the calamity caused by the error of judgment on poor Boyd's part, and which cost such a heavy toll. It is entirely inexplicable to me in view of the fact that I personally gave him instructions, and especially cautioned him against exactly what happened."[135] In preparing his official report of the action, Pershing did his best to put most of the blame on the Mexicans and avoided any guesses as to Boyd's motives. "Error in judgment" was Pershing's final assessment.

Pershing had no illusions of unleashing his forces. Quickly he sent troops to aid the sixty survivors wandering toward camp. "It is highly important . . . that a fight be avoided," he wrote one detachment commander. "Our War Department is not ready for the war to begin."[136]

Funston's and the War Department's confusion confirmed the unfortunate possibility that the "peculiar conditions surrounding [the] expedition not fully appreciated." Most information was untrustworthy; and although he doubted alarming rumors, Jack sent patrols to invesigate. "No aggressive act ever ordered," he announced, "and none ever committed unless Boyd's action be considered as such." A single failure should not condemn a proved system—and Jack intended to continue patrolling.[137]

133 For the mood at Casas Grandes, see Frank Elser's dispatch to the *New York Times*, Dublán, June 23, 1916, PX, Selected Docs.
134 PM, vol. 2, ch. 23, pp. 18–19. See also Wharfield, "Affair at Carrizal," pp. 33–39, for suspicions of JJP's duplicity.
135 JJP to Allen, June 23, 1916, Box 9, PP; Twichell, *Allen*, pp. 190–91.
136 JJP to Maj. J. M. Jenkins, 11th Cav., June 24, 1916, in PX, Selected Docs.
137 JJP to Funston, June 26, 1916, Lee Papers.

Cool assessment of the fight at Carrizal encouraged Pershing. His men fought well while any chance of success permitted; even in defeat they killed thirty (including a general) and wounded forty with deliberate, accurate rifle fire.[138]

Funston judged that another American defeat would lure the Mexicans to war. Stay put, he told Jack, and attempt invisibility. Obediently Jack began consolidating his position, drawing patrols closer to Dublán, and covering exposed points with field batteries.

But the emergency passed. Apparently all Mexicans but Carranza wanted war. Perhaps even he wanted it but assessed its outcome too well. Grudgingly he agreed to return the Carrizal prisoners but clouded the gesture with atrocity allegations against the Punitive Expedition. Pershing quickly disposed of the charges as false Carranzista rumors. On July 4 the Mexican government suggested negotiation. Quickly the United States agreed, and the summer passed in selection of delegates to a conference scheduled for New London, Connecticut, in September.[139]

An Adobe Xanadu

A relentless sun scorched Chihuahua, winds swept hard across an empty land, and tents burned and bounced and blew away. Flies buzzed in incredible defiance of the wind, crawling things infested every bedroll, and snakes were sporting enemies. Boredom stalked the expedition. Inactivity saps energy and makes good men lazy. Empty hours stretched beyond the alchemy of cards and talk, sometimes even drink. At headquarters, Jack's time filled with the army's constant avalanche of paper, but he knew the dangers of idleness. Patton and other staff officers went to work planning rigid training schedules.

With almost 11,000 men filling campsites at Dublán and El Valle, Jack recognized opportunity as surely as obligation. Large field forces were rare in modern American annals. A provisional division blended every arm of the service and all new, modern tools of war. Mexican campaigning had not taught real lessons in combined arms or modern war—the cavalry still held sway in this old Indian land. In Europe infantry and artillery were lords of the mud. In a few weeks, surely, rains would march spitefully across Chihuahua, turn the roads and

---

[138] For casualties, see H. M. Mason, *Great Pursuit*, p. 211; Twichell, *Allen*, p. 190.

[139] Clendenen, *U.S. and Villa*, pp. 281–88; H. M. Mason, *Great Pursuit*, pp. 215–18.

trails and camps to bogs remindful of the Western Front, and give soggy realism to full maneuvers. Jack planned special courses in musketry and practice with varied types of machine guns. Infantry tactics in open order were taught by experienced men. Officers received classroom instruction—shades of Fort McKinley! Staff people worked feverishly on daily maneuver problems, maps, and intelligence evaluation.

Unobstrusively Jack worked diversion into necessity. Shelter would become critical in the rainy season—luck alone had held it off—and in the desert winter. During moments free from combat simulation, troops began building adobe huts. First efforts were hilariously bad—some leaned crazily, others sagged in the middle like tired camels, a few simply collapsed. How did the Mexicans make those infernal bricks? A few hints from natives, and a little experience wrought dramatic architectural art. Builders vied for best designs, and finally one caught on, to become a rough standard for both base camps. Company buildings ran along regulation lines and were built in neat, sanitary "streets." When the rains came toward the last of summer, they washed through the camps, swamped the truck parks, maneuver fields, and baseball diamonds, drummed incessantly on the barracks, but did no real damage. The Punitive Expedition had snuggled in for as long as Wilson wanted.

By late July supplies began rolling in on the Mexican Northwestern Railroad from El Paso; quartermasters could vary the dreary field ration with meat and vegetables, a few gustatory luxuries.[140] Obviously a kind of truce prevailed in Chihuahua, and with it came not only better food but also more people. As Pershing increased camp sophistication, created large repair and assembly shops, and improved depot procedures, additional troops and civilians were essential. About 2,000 of the 2nd Massachusetts Infantry and 1st New Mexico Infantry, plus a 13th Cavalry troop and assorted supply soldiers worked with more than a thousand civilians to expand and organize at Dublán one of the best base camps ever constructed for the U.S. Army.[141]

At headquarters Pershing watched proudly as his camp became a post of substance. Old army practice gave the outlines of his creation, but his own experience in field necessity gave Dublán its big ordnance repair shops, its bustling railhead, its aeroplane engineering works.

[140] "General Pershing's Report of the Punitive Expedition, July 1916–February 1917," p. 19, in AG Records, RG 94, National Archives.

[141] See H. M. Mason, Great Pursuit, p. 221. It is possible that the National Guard troops remained at Columbus. See JJP, "PX Report," 1916–1917, p. 25.

Efficiency pleased Jack always, and he took special pride each morning when reveille spilled sleepy men into the streets, as they meandered to the latrines, to breakfast mess, and to work. He listened as first a kind of low whispering clangor began and grew to the din of a thousand forges—the city's workday started early.[142]

Work at headquarters started earlier; Jack kept his staff small and efficient and overworked. Daily administration he dispatched quickly, looked around his camps for problems, handled them swiftly, and taught valuable lessons in management to each young man who walked those daily rounds. But the Old Man, too, needed diversion. Often he joined Patton and other venturesome staff and line officers on hunting safaris in the hills around Dublán. Antelope, various fowl, and snakes were frequent targets. Those trips were often endurance sessions for unsuspecting officers. Example: On the way back to camp from a mid-August antelope hunt, the hunters' car stuck in the mud. Pershing hopped out, motioned George Patton and a guide to follow, and began walking. "We did four miles in 50 minutes, the General setting the pace," Patton moaned, "hardest walking ever did. . . . stiff for several days."[143]

Late in August, after six hard months in the field and with all well in camp, Jack decided he could risk a short leave. Would Patton like to join in a jaunt to Columbus? He most certainly would—wife Beatrice awaited him there! Had Nita come from California? Was she, too, waiting? She was! With clerks, some reporters, photographers, and George, Pershing decamped on August 31.

Longer than usual the run to Columbus, this one tingled with expectant anxiety. Would she be there? Finally Columbus loomed in view the next afternoon. Usually it came to sight a straggling break in a drab landscape, but that Saturday it shone brightly to a wistful soldier. Nita was there—she and Beatrice clasped the thin and toughened troopers with fervor, and hope again was good.

Talk channeled to personal matters. For that large-eyed girl with the sweet mouth, Jack reviewed some of the campaign, surely boasted a bit, but complained, too, of the neglect, the misunderstanding, the grinding frustration. He had obeyed orders, orders he hardly approved, had done all expected of a good soldier. After each fight Washington flared with concern; after Carrizal even friend Funston erupted in suspicion of military incompetence. Obedience deserved better. In July

[142] H. M. Mason, *Great Pursuit*, p. 221; JJP, "PX Report," 1916–1917, pp. 14–28.

[143] Blumenson, *Patton Papers*, p. 348.

Jack had hoped for promotion. Papa Warren kept abreast of Washington matters and guessed Jack would win a second star in the summer elevations. Field service seemed to make it a certainty—but he had lost out to Albert Mills and it hurt. What, after all, must a soldier do to please a mercurial War Department? Yes, he was sure his chances were better because of field service; Senator Warren, who sedulously cultivated General Scott and other dignitaries, reported the chief of staff pleased with the expedition.[144]

Nita cared, offered the hints of an army sister with a political and financial father—Jack ought to push himself harder! Warren could not help directly. Republicans hardly counted in Washington now, and the administration rejected political pressure. If General Scott liked what Jack had done, why not report informally on the hidden difficulties of Mexico?

For most of a happy week Nita and Jack rode, dined, and talked together. With George and Beatrice—proper chaperones—they visited the new aerodrome at Columbus, toured the suddenly fascinating New Mexican wasteland. And too soon the idyll ended. Soldiers said farewells and headed for Dublán. Longer now the miles dragged, for Nita's presence fresh in mind charmed Jack to long discussion. Praises, questions, speculation almost palled on brother George.

A lovely lady's flattering attention waked again Jack's special magnetism. A surprised staff found him witty, humorous, laughing, a warm companion. What caused the change? Patton knew but kept quiet. Daily he heard Jack's recitation of Nita's fascinations and reckoned friendship close to love. "He's all the time talking about Miss Anne," George wrote Beatrice, and added with some envy, "Nita may rank us yet."[145]

Nita sparked Jack's ambition, convinced him of a good future. It was September, a mystic personal month, one that boded big changes. What could kindle a career wasting in Chihuahua? Nita's idea of pushing friendship with Scott seemed worth trying. A dinner given for Scott by the Warrens offered personal entree for a semiofficial report. It would have to be carefully written.

Just how carefully came clear in news headlines on September 19. Albert Mills died the day before, and Pershing seemed the obvious replacement. Now the time for subtle suasion or direct attack? Jack tried both tactics.

---

144 FEW to JJP, July 15, 1916, FEW Papers, vol. 76.
145 Blumenson, *Patton Papers*, pp. 349–50.

On September 22 he composed a blunt telegram to the adjutant general:

> Colonia Dublan, Mexico,
> September 22, 1916.
>
> Adjutant General Army, Washington, Through Military Channels.
>
> I hereby present formal application for promotion to vacancy in grade of Major General. Attention of Honorable Secretary of War invited to ten years record as General Officer. During this time commanded and organized brigade post fort McKinley; was in command department Mindanao and governor Moro province jointly for over four years; Pacified Moros and other wild tribes; also planned and recommended civil government and transferred province to civil control. Commanded reinforced brigade on border two years and have commanded punitive expedition since March. Refer to every General officer under whom have served as to Qualifications. Have had more foreign service than any other General Officer. Request full consideration of my record of accomplishment. Also of my present rank as senior Brigadier General of the Army.
>
> Pershing.

Funston kept the wire a day and on the 24th forwarded it with this endorsement: "I consider that General Pershing being senior Brigadier General and his very excellent services through his last ten years in that grade make his promotion to next higher grade a matter of almost foregone conclusion. His very excellent service in command of punitive expedition would seem to be sufficient in itself without any further recommendation from me."[146] If the endorsement read a bit thin, Funston meant no harm. Long since had his pique at Pershing dissolved in admiration; his comments were honest.

Jack followed his Washington wire with a chatty letter to Scott on September 23 confessing no real military need to keep the expedition in Mexico. Diplomatically he suspected his men served a threatening purpose. Criticisms of operations had been few, he said, and those stemmed from unappreciated realities. Villa remained loose, true, but vigorous pursuit in face of popular hostility and deliberate misdirection had broken his power. "It may be that Villa will be able to 'come back,'" Jack mused, "but I do not believe it probable that he will ever become an important person in Mexico or have any permanent standing." Villa's capture would not, Jack said, solve the Mexican problem —too long had anarchy weakened nationalism, too long had banditry defied government. A pitiful sort of affection sprang up around the expedition as peons for the first time learned the blessings of money,

---

[146] See Funston to AG, Sept. 24, 1916, in 3849 ACP 1886.

justice, honor, safety. Many neighbors hoped that the expedition would remain until Mexico achieved a government.

Soldier Scott would appreciate how much the expedition did for America's prestige. Never had respect for gringos run so high. Discipline was the main reason for success. All arms were superb in the field. "You have no doubt been especially pleased with the work of the cavalry," Jack said, and added that the horse soldiers in Mexico had done the hardest duty in the history of the U.S. Cavalry. Infantry and artillery, less useful on the far desert tracks, sustained the best service traditions. "Long marches with full packs have surpassed anything that I know of since the civil war."

Logistics became the prime concern of command, and Jack boasted splendid development of truck supply. Important, indeed, he emphasized, for "if another war breaks out we will be far more nearly prepared, as far as transportation is concerned, than we would otherwise be." Roads, those often bottomless puzzles to men, animals, and machines, had at last been solved by diligent engineers who perfected a serviceable all-weather artery from Columbus to Dublán.

Deficiences there were. Foulois's first Jennies proved too slow and fragile for war conditions, but Jack had praise for the men who dared those crates against winds, rains, and mountains: "They have demonstrated that American aviators can do wonders. They have also shown our people and congress our hopeless deficiency in aeroplanes and aviators." New planes, fortunately, were coming—Curtiss R-2s with big, 160-h.p. engines.[147]

As he ended his letter, Jack pushed a little. "Regardless of whether this expedition has a right to be in Mexico, the army has completely obeyed its orders and under the existing circumstances, has, in every respect, played its part well."[148] He closed with thanks for Scott's kind words reported by Senator Warren.

Nothing more could he do for his cause but wait. The whole expedition waited—rumors flitted quickly through the tight communities at Dublán and El Valle. Officers and men expected their general's reward. George Patton put the feeling clearly: "I guess Gen P will be a major General. I hope so. He ought to be."[149] He could miss again, of course, especially if Leonard Wood or some other envious malcontent

[147] See H. M. Mason, *Great Pursuit*, p. 221.
[148] JJP to Scott, in the Field, Mexico, Sept. 23, 1916, Scott Papers.
[149] Blumenson, *Patton Papers*, p. 350.

muddied procedures in Washington. Senator Warren was cautiously optimistic and hoped for Baker's wisdom.[150]

Baker pondered the case and on September 23 wrote Wilson a long, judicious appraisal of the promotion question. "I feel that the Army and perhaps the country will expect this reward to go to General J. J. Pershing," he said, adding that command of the Punitive Expedition had been "the most difficult sort of work . . . in that he had been stationed in another country where the possibility of bringing on conflict by indiscretion was very great and where he himself has been obliged to wait rather than fight." How had Pershing borne the tether? "I am impressed," said the secretary, "with his general steadiness and good service to the extent that there have been evidences of impatience and failure to comprehend the duty intrusted to him. I doubt whether they are more striking than would be the case of any soldier who looked at the situation purely from a military point of view." A political point intruded, since Pershing was Warren's son-in-law. "I have not, however, been able to discover the slightest evidence of political activity on his part, nor have any requests or recommendations come to me from any source in his behalf." Baker recommended the promotion.[151] Wilson appointed Pershing to be major general on September 25, 1916.[152] Congratulations from Enoch Crowder and Papa Warren anticipated word from the White House, which reached Dublán late on the twenty-fifth, and Jack asked the staff to a lemonade reception in the evening.[153]

It was a recess commission and needed confirmation, but Jack knew he had no troubles. A second star gave a kind of jauntiness to his tall frame, seemed, somehow to hint a smile in the weathered lines of his face. It made no difference in his work.

Winter demanded careful gleaning of forage, food, and fuel. Depots were slowly filled with anticipated wants—a fact to impress old army hands who appreciated a careful man's concern for troops and animals.[154] Diversion in winter came hard. After some maneuvering, Jack secured projectors and screens for nightly movies at both Dublán

[150] FEW to JJP, Sept. 10, 27, 1916, FEW Papers, vol. 76.

[151] Baker to Wilson (Confidential), Sept. 23, 1916, in 3849 ACP 1886.

[152] *Army Register, 1918*, p. 5.

[153] JJP to Crowder, Sept. 27, 1916, Box 56, PP; FEW to JJP (telegram), Sept. 25, 1916, FEW Papers, vol. 76, which reads: "Congratulations. It makes us all happy." For the reception, see Blumenson, *Patton Papers*, p. 351.

[154] Lt. Col. Thomas Stone, USA, interview with Brig. Gen. Isaac Spalding, USA (Ret.), Jan. 6, 1971, transcript in author's possession.

and El Valle. Football replaced baseball as the popular sport, though some polo persisted.

A delicate matter took unusual time—women. Sexual problems arose in direct ratio to dwindling action. The permanent camps were besieged by Mexican prostitutes who showed no racial or rank bias; they met anyone with money in the bushes and in convenient shacks. Sick call produced alarming numbers of men with venereal disease; regulations, orders were useless. When Bishop Call complained that flagrant excesses near the Mormon colony frightened ladies, Pershing asked his advice. The bishop suggested a "restricted district" be located at the southern limits of Camp Dublán and even found a reliable Mexican manager. Pershing agreed, assigned one of his doctors as health inspector, fixed the fee at two dollars, and watched the disease rate shrink quickly. It was a bold, chancy solution, but it worked without undue outcry in the States.[155] "Everyone was satisfied," Jack boasted, "as the towns have been kept absolutely clear of that sort of thing." Success confirmed the method. "The establishment was necessary and has proved the best way to handle a difficult problem," Jack noted.

Other diversion suddenly seemed likely. In mid-September Chihuahua chilled to Villa redivivus. Just as the Joint High Commission struggled to maintain peace, war flamed again in northern Mexico. From some lost haunt Villa came, bandoliered and blustering, with five hundred followers to snatch land and people and munitions, to kill and to burn and to drive Venustiano Carranza from power. Chihuahua City fell to a quick attack, yielded men and munitions, and was left stunned and bleeding as Villa rode victorious. What of Carranza's vaunted border protection, his "control" in the north? Hastily he denied Villa's resurrection, blamed small bands of dissidents, and announced peace would be kept. Bluster is the best diplomatic substitute for strength, and Carranza's position hardened again to the finite point of Pershing's withdrawal. Such buffoonery adjourned the New London talks. Villa rode against Portrero, spread troops across the State of Chihuahua, and achieved heroic anarchy.[156]

Clearly the expedition would not soon leave the war zone. Pershing's force was Wilson's needed fulcrum in the Mexican political turmoil. Excitement banished boredom at Dublán, El Valle, and the

---

[155] JJP to Scott, Jan. 21, 1917, Scott Papers; H. M. Mason, *Great Pursuit*, p. 219.

[156] H. M. Mason, *Great Pursuit*, pp. 223–25; Clendenen, *U.S. and Villa*, pp. 288–90.

new zones of reconnaissance. Villa's rampage rolled on, picked up Carranzista defectors with every success, and spread terror through the entire state.

To Jack decisive intervention seemed imperative, else anarchy would decay to savagery. On November 2 he suggested an old desire— "it would probably not be difficult now to seize Chihuahua City, as there would be little opposition on the part of the de facto troops, while the populace would doubtless welcome us." Ensconced in the capital, Pershing's force would be closer to Villa's vicinity. Funston liked the notion of a final military finish to the pestiferous Villa, but the War Department vetoed aggression.[157]

Parral, Torreón, Camargo all fell to Panchito's villains; wild scenes of mayhem were reported, but the rebel armies grew with every sacking. Careful eyes were kept on the south by Pershing's cavalry, but Villa maintained healthy distance from the gringos—only against the de factos did he charge. And on November 23—Thanksgiving Day for U.S. troops—Villa shattered all pretense of Carranzista power. In the morning about nine, thundering columns streamed again into Chihuahua City; all day the battle raged, all the next, and the next, bitter fighting flared in the streets and continued until the city fell on Monday. Victory brought a new viciousness to Villa, which he aimed at the large Chinese population that ran restaurants and laundries. Mercilessly his men stalked the Orientals and shot them where they stood—more than a hundred died, some escaped, but the lesson was told afar that the slant-eyes were taboo.

For a terrible week Villa looted and raped the city. When a big Carranzista force came against him in early December, he evacuated a ruined capital.

At Dublán, Villa's success now threatened directly. Part of his supposed 6,000-man force occupied Carrizal, dominated the Santa Clara Valley, and could soon squeeze communications back to the Columbus road. Never accustomed to receiving attack, Pershing again urged initiative. "A swift blow . . . should be made at once against this pretender. . . . In the light of Villa's operations . . . further inactivity of this command does not seem desirable."[158] Funston agreed that Villa threatened to take all of northern Mexico and urged Pershing's proposal. Wilson could have agreed now that he had won the election, almost did, but still hoped for something positive out of the somnolent Joint Commission; Pershing was kept tethered.

[157] H. M. Mason, *Great Pursuit*, p. 225; Tompkins, *Chasing Villa*, p. 217.
[158] Tompkins, *Chasing Villa*, p. 218.

It proved a bad winter. High-plains weather beat down the morale of men toughened to almost anything else; snow and sand came in fatal alliance, worked into clothes, food, forage, medicine, into eyes and mouths, and haunted imaginations. Expectation became a buffer against the chill—everyone looked toward Christmas, hopefully the final Christmas in Mexico. Staff and line officers cooperated in gathering supplies for a huge celebration. Spits were built for a mammoth barbecue. The superior black cooks of the 10th Cavalry promised to prepare food for the entire complement. Scavenging produced the ingredients of eggnog, and gaiety increased. Vast surges of packages, cards, mail of all kinds choked the small postal service, and Pershing choked in rage at a misprint on his personal Christmas greetings. He cherished each Christmas card he received and took pride in those he sent. When he saw the spinning wheel and the fireplace, the cozy scene looked pleasing, but the "Brigadier General" ruined everything. Replacements were rushed by air but arrived on December 21; Jack kept the aviator handy while he addressed the urgent ones and sent them to Columbus for quicker posting. It was a bad beginning to festivities—but it proved to be no bad omen.

Working with Mabel Boardman of the Red Cross, Jack had arranged a gift for everyone in camp, and gifts came in great bundles that prompted cheers and wild guesses about content.[159]

A cold, clear Christmas morning brought cooks out early to begin a barbecue historic. But soon a rising wind whirled dust through the streets, temperature dropped, and snow mixed in the sand; the wind kept rising to a vicious, moaning force that scoured and froze the waiting carcasses beyond use, blew tents and roofs away, beat walls down. The chill and cut of the storm forced men to huddle wherever shelter offered. Jack called it "a combination Montana blizzard and Sahara dust storm."[160] When it finally gusted down late in the day it had pretty well ruined the barbecue, but turkeys were washed and roasted and eggnog flowed freely. Pershing promised Christmas on the twenty-sixth. That last celebration on Tuesday was touched with twin nostalgias—longing for home and for lost comrades. Everyone felt the expedition would soon go home and they were glad, but shared dangers made men close, and they would miss each other.

There was a great 70-foot tree made of seven trees, and there were

[159] PM, vol. 2, ch. 23, p. 21.
[160] *Ibid.*, p. 22.

10,000 boxes wrapped and waiting near it. Around the tree and the presents circled all the cars and trucks in camp. Another hearty meal was washed down in bounteous spirits, and thousands of happy men clustered toward the tree as darkness fell. Suddenly the lights of all the cars and trucks flicked on, the tree decorations glistened. The laughter and the shouting hushed as a huge Star of Bethlehem was outlined on the ground. The men lined up around it, a band somewhere began soft carol chords, and the army's voice rose in old, familiar song. Some prayers were offered. A loud fanfare of trumpets quieted the soldiers, and Santa Claus crashed the circle with his great sack of presents. Fireworks banished briefly the cold Chihuahua dark. They marked the high point of a celebration Jack thought "the greatest . . . that ever has been pulled off by any similar body of American Troops on Foreign soil."[161]

"The key to happiness is a clear conscience."

Shabbiness could not be tolerated in camp; cold could not long excuse sloth. Pershing pushed renewed training schedules for winter practice and set a gruelling personal pace to shame the youngest on the staff. Patton might be the quickest study of those close to headquarters. Intelligent, devoted to soldiering, he hated idleness and worked easily. A quaint devotion to the saber—apparently because great captains of the past praised it—could be toned with experience, since his mind stayed open. Jack enjoyed his enthusiasm, his quiet adoration, his almost comical tries at emulation.[162]

A burning professionalism touched a kindred current in Pershing; he read Patton's frequent papers on tactics with interest and criticized them carefully. Patton's effervescent nature brightened headquarters considerably, and his eagerness lightened the work of inspections. Inspections were the key to soldiering, and Jack taught Patton the virtues of close troop knowledge by example. "Under the personal supervision of the General every unit went through a complete course in range and combat firing, marches, maneuvers, entrenching, and combating exercises," Patton noted in awe. "When I speak of supervision I do not mean that nebulous staff control so frequently connected with the work. By constant study General Pershing knew to the minutest detail each of the subjects in which he demanded practice, and by his

[161] JJP to Mayor Tom Lea of El Paso, Dec. 30, 1916, Box 115, PP; PM, vol. 2, ch. 23, p. 22; H. M. Mason, *Great Pursuit*, p. 230.
[162] See Blumenson, *Patton Papers*, pp. 360–62, 364, 368, 370.

physical presence and personal example and explanation, insured himself that they were correctly carried out."[163]

Familiarity with his own troops gave Pershing insight into general army knowledge. His own appreciation of tactics and administration could be seen in his quick correction of maneuver errors, his swift perception of poor tactical problems, and his smooth-running headquarters. "Gen. P. is certainly a fine leader and tireless worker," Patton proclaimed in December, 1916, and he noted that "it is [his] personal care which gets the results and only this *personal* care will."[164]

Winter passed with efficiency increasing among all units of the expedition; clothing and equipment arrived in goodly amounts, and appearance improved; men took better care of themselves and animals, as befitted trained veterans.

Pershing assumed the expedition could not remain much longer in Mexico. It would be nice to have a break in January, to run up to Columbus again with George and steal a few days with Nita. She crowded martial thoughts too often from the mind. All the Pattons crowded his conscience; he liked Beatrice and George immensely, their children, too, whose little Christmas notes started old and tearful recollections.[165] Could Nita come to Columbus in mid-January? There might be a chance then for a few days away. She wanted to, but Funston suddenly decided to visit Dublán and all gave way to his whim, for his coming sparked rumors of home.

Old friends were ever welcome at headquarters, and Funston ranked a cherished ally. When the dapper little general arrived, he reviewed the Dublán contingent, then whisked Jack off to El Valle. He cast shrewd eyes on men, equipment, housing, horses, mules, and planes and talked with all kinds of people. While he rushed through Pershing's camps he talked frankly to the new major general. At last the order had been given—the Punitive Expedition would leave Mexico. Pershing should decide if his men would be extracted by foot or rail and give some idea of when he wanted to start. Should the Mormons be given warning? Did they want to come out with the expedition? When should the public be told that he was coming home? Unofficial as yet, Funston's questions were easily answered by a man who had thought of every mile northward for months. At the end of

163 *Ibid.*, p. 362.
164 *Ibid.*, pp. 366, 370.
165 *Ibid.*, p. 369.

four days Funston sped back to Columbus; Pershing waved him off with the happy thought of meeting soon.[166]

On January 19, 1917, almost on Funston's heels—the order came: Withdraw at an early date. Pershing, primed, confirmed that he would march everyone out; marching would give time for orderly extraction of surplus supplies and equipment. He would move not later than January 28 and asked no announcements before that day. Alerted already, the Mormons had divided on leaving Dublán; some would anticipate the expedition, others would take their chances with Villistas or Carranzistas. El Valle and other southern stations would be evacuated first, and surplus property would start prior to January 28. All elements of the expedition would assemble at Palomas, Chihuahua, on February 4 and march together into the United States.

Evacuation began on January 27–28, 1917. The big camps became ghost towns surprisingly fast, and demolition crews began turning them back to the desert. Roofs were pulled off, then a truck backed against adobe walls and whole buildings broke into dust.[167] Tall and solitary, his campaign hat at correct angle, Jack watched his base city vanish to the winds. That set face told no feelings; the eyes looked for little blunders. Then he turned, found Patton, and rode to the squalid refugee camp near Dublán. Men, women, Mexicans, astounding numbers of the newly persecuted Chinese, Mormons, old, young, hardy, lame, rich, and poor clustered against fate. They would go north to whatever destiny Uncle Sam allowed, and Patton agonized at the human woe he saw. "It was the most pathetic sight. . . . " Pershing encouraged as much as facts allowed; he urged the Chinese to come, the Mormons, too, who stood small chance against Villa. A camp, he said, would await them in Columbus with shelter and food and safety until some future could be found. A thin column of war's dispossessed joined his men going north.[168]

Rigged out well in the best regulation issue, Pershing's men stood at attention at Palomas. It was Sunday, February 5, and it was their last day in Mexico. Horses were brushed shiny, guns burnished in the sunlight, pennons snapped in a gentle breeze. The general looked spruced as ever as he led them out to cross the border toward Colum-

---

[166] JJP to Scott, Jan. 21, 1917, Scott Papers.

[167] Blumenson, *Patton Papers*, p. 375.

[168] *Ibid.*, pp. 374–75; JJP, "PX Report," 1916–1917, p. 14; JJP to Scott, Jan. 21, 1917, Scott Papers; Edward Briscoe, "Pershing's Chinese Refugees in Texas," *Southwestern Historical Quarterly* 62 (Apr., 1959): 467–88.

bus. He stood to watch as headquarters personnel rode first, then the 8th Brigade, the 1st Provisional Infantry, the 2nd Engineers. The horse soldiers followed smartly, in order of regiments, 5th, 7th, 10th, 11th, 13th, with newly minted Brig. Gen. Eben Swift riding herd on every horseman. Next rolled the 4th and 8th Battalions, Field Artillery, trailed by the Signal Battalion, ambulance companies, field trains, and wagon companies.

Pershing noted that the last of his men crossed at 3:00 P.M. "We had not captured Villa, to be sure, as we hoped to do," he thought, "but when active pursuit stopped we had broken up and scattered his band, which was our original mission."[169] "The key to happiness is a clear conscience," Jack had written to a cousin years before. That was an apt motto as the Punitive Expedition faded into the echoes from the Western Front.

[169] PM, vol. 2, ch. 23, p. 22.

☆ 18 ☆

"Lafayette, We Are Here"

As the last khaki clads crossed into the United States that happy February morning, they trailed dust like the curtain on an era. Their thinned and toughened general watched the cavalry ride out, watched the guns rumbling back, saw the smart lines of infantry swinging gaily home, and knew that for them the task had yet to come. Down against Pancho Villa the U.S. Army practiced old war in the shadow of newer ways. Across the Atlantic whole armies smashed against cannon and wire and weird engines in a new cacophony of slaughter. Were all lessons learned in Mexico lost lines of history?

To a long-time student of war the answer clearly would be "no." Tactical lessons might be useless in a war devoid of elegance and enmeshed in mass, but war's verities remained to recognize. Experience reminded Maj. Gen. John Pershing of command's necessities. In Mexico he began learning the heavier burdens of large commands, the complex personality problems, and the endless logistical attention vital to success.

Handed a command at the start, Pershing pursued Villa with many units under men unknown to him. The regular officers he trusted, but found some of them wanting. Older colonels, many, showed a sloth and uncertainty irritating to a general who expected energy in everyone. He shed them without rancor but without regret. And he promoted men who showed spirit and sense. In the Mexican months Pershing came to realize an important fact—modern war was for youngsters. Endurance and quick reactions were essential in commanders, perhaps even more essential than experience. Officers who led effectively usually trained their men with care, and Pershing long had known the value of training. Now, more than ever, training loomed important. The dismal record of militia along the border told a tale of ineffective leadership that boded trouble for the whole army. Pershing knew, as he watched his campaign-wise men returning to the States, that they were the best the country boasted.

He read words of praise from Fred Funston with a professional pride but without surprise—he had done well.[1] A carefully picked and pruned staff ran the Punitive Expedition with minimum fuss and maximum achievement. Logistics had been a constant bugaboo—lines of communication stretching across burned wastes and vicious hills tested men, animals, and machines. And while food and forage oftimes shrank, a system at last came. For the whole of the permanent camp at Colonia Dublán, supplies were varied and sufficient.

That same staff did as well as possible in managing tactics. Diffusion of force Pershing hated but accepted as the price of circumstance, and diffusion imposed special requirements on a small staff. Careful organization, deftness in alternatives, and special loyalty to the general and the mission were imperatives. Men like Collins, Reed, and Patton who ran close to Pershing became a well-knit "family"; men like Cabell, Hines, and Ryan made headquarters work. Field leaders like Tompkins, George Dodd, Swift, and Howze responded swiftly to Pershing's wishes, when they could learn them through defective communications, and proved the importance of informed tactical subordinates. Initiative these men had, showed it wisely, but depended on overall leadership for strategy. Valiantly they and their men displayed the virtues of American training, the strength of American soldiery.

Valiantly, too, such derring-doers as Foulois and Townsend Dodd proved the possibilities of an air service with proper airplanes, proved that communications might be vastly enhanced and that reconnaissance no longer belonged to the cavalry. But equipment failure dogged them, niggardly appropriations doomed them to planes antique in the infancy of flying. They knew the growing sophistication of a war abroad. Not even the R-2s gave parity with Allied and German planes, and American flyers could only yearn as they read news of aerial progress.[2]

Radios, machine guns, trucks, and cars—all these newfangled adjuncts to war Pershing had tested. In the harsh Mexican environment the tests had been tough, and lessons learned sometimes depressing. Trucks and cars broke down often in the rarified heat, on the dismal

[1] See Funston to JJP, Feb. 6, 1917, Fitzhugh Lee Papers, and Funston to Scott, Feb. 7, 1917, Scott Papers, in which Funston said: "I think Pershing deserves a tremendous amount of credit for the way he's handled things. Today, I wrote him an official letter telling him so. He seems to be in fine physical condition, and his mind is keen as could be."

[2] Benjamin Foulois, *From the Wright Brothers to the Astronauts*, pp. 133–34.

roads; radios were effective sometimes, depending on distance, intervening mountains, and vagaries of atmosphere. Machine guns worked well; tactics adapted more to close unit action had been proved by the Mexicans at Carrizal and by the Americans at Tomochic and Ojos Azules. Pershing gave hopeful reports of his newer tools—their potential he recognized, their present development he deplored. Equipment for cavalry, artillery, and infantry was fine, sturdy, and plentiful. Too little attention and money had been spent on war's modernities, and Pershing urged quick improvement.

With the perspective of a hard campaign, Pershing reckoned his growing competence and marked the changes he had learned. He would have a chance, he thought, to apply them in Europe.

War in France and Flanders went poorly for the Allies, and Jack had watched its decline carefully in the press. All he could do, all any good American soldier could do, was prepare himself as fully as possible for the awful challenge of rescue. Under that threat, Pershing distributed his command throughout Funston's department and journeyed to take charge of the El Paso District. The old town would be familiar, and in his old area Jack could indulge his whims for training, could strive to make soldiers of militiamen, and could shore up the loose bulwark of the border.[3]

Friends of the Punitive Expedition staff he sent away regretfully, but kept Collins and a close eye on favorites who filtered through the army. Good units he marked, so bad ones, and knew the war men available to the nation. El Paso enthusiastically welcomed its new hero.[4]

On Monday, February 19, 1917, Frederick Funston fell dead in San Antonio's Menger Hotel. Word came to El Paso and brought stinging sadness and the guilty thrill of chance. Protocol demanded that Pershing as next in seniority assume departmental command pending word from the War Department. Pershing followed regulations and announced himself in charge on the twentieth.[5] Memories flooded the act of assumption. Funston could not be gone, not a friend so constant, a soldier so stalwart, a man so firmly at the peak of his profession. Phrases flickered from that letter he had written Jack scarce a fortnight before, phrases that fitted fighting Freddy so well—"great good judgment and tact," "discipline . . . at the highest notch," and one that spoke a proper epitaph, "the fine standard of loyalty and

[3] JJP left Columbus for El Paso at noon, Feb. 7, 1917 (see document 2524419, Feb. 7, 1917, in RG 94, National Archives).

[4] Martin Blumenson, *The Patton Papers, 1885–1940*, p. 379.

[5] See doc. 2538668, Feb. 20, 1917, RG 94, National Archives.

efficiency . . . fully maintained."[6] Good soldier Funston would have urged the army's continuity and denied that any man was indispensable —but he nearly was. What would the army do without him in its nearing hour of trial?

To the sudden widow, he surely was indispensable, and her plight caught Jack's heart. He and other army friends asked for help, and San Antonio poured sympathy and money to the stunned and helpless lady.[7]

General Orders Number 30, February 21, 1917, gave Pershing formal command of the Southern Department. His assignment came in wake of frantic puzzlement in Washington. When Maj. Douglas MacArthur presented himself at Secretary Baker's home on the evening of February 19, he interrupted the secretary, the president, and the chief of staff at dinner. At attention, he read the news of Funston's death. "Had the Voice of Doom spoken," MacArthur said, "the result could not have been different. The silence seemed almost like that of death." Somberly the president asked Baker who would command in Europe. Turning to the young MacArthur, Baker asked: "Whom do you think the Army would choose, Major?" The major had two nominees, personal ones since he denied he could speak for the army: Pershing or Col. Peyton March. Good choices, Baker acknowledged.[8]

Experience and reliability were the key measures of Pershing. He had done a hard job according to Wilson's rules; his years ran rich with varied responsibilities and department command would be easy. As for larger stages, Baker would think. Rumor mongers reported Pershing as disloyal to Wilsonian Mexican policy, offered affidavits to prove bitter comments from a frustrated warrior. Was Pershing trustworthy?

Fortunately Baker put the question to Hugh Scott, and that doughty friend promptly pooh-poohed the tales and told Jack, "I suggest to you that you have many enemies and it would be a good thing if you were

[6] Funston to JJP, Feb. 6, 1917, in 3849 ACP 1886, RG 94, National Archives.

[7] JJP to J. Franklin Bell, Mar. 18, 1917, Box 23, PP.

[8] See statement by Gen. Douglas MacArthur, Aug. 22, 1960, issued to the press (copy furnished by Gen. Courtney Whitney), in which MacArthur recalls recommending Pershing only. See also Harvey A. DeWeerd, *President Wilson Fights His War: World War I and the American Intervention*, p. 204 n., quoting a letter from Baker to Frederick Palmer, Mar. 10, 1931, in which the former war secretary recalls that MacArthur recommended both Pershing and March. Donald Smythe in *Guerilla Warrior: The Early Life of General John J. Pershing*, p. 280, accepts MacArthur's version. There is no doubt that the news of Funston's death reached President Wilson at Baker's home on the evening of the nineteenth (see Hugh L. Scott to JJP, Feb. 20, 1917, Scott Papers).

extremely careful about such matters."[9] That caution told a grateful general the high possibilities Scott considered. In the midst of learning his new domain, Jack took time for defense. To Scott he sent lavish thanks for the warning, for scoffing at the charges, and enlarged a bit on constancy.

> I am in a position to assure you that these reports were entirely without foundation. . . . I have been just as guarded in my remarks as I could be. No one in my position could, I think, have a larger view of the situation in general than I have had. I have realized from the start that the President has been confronted with very serious conditions as to our foreign relations and I have fully realized that his acts have been prompted by the very highest of motives. Being in this attitude of mind, I have not only not criticised him, but I have stated the above views time and again to others. The very first attribute of a soldier is loyalty. It is a part of my creed to which I have always clung tenaciously. . . . My attitude is, and has been, one of entire friendliness to the President, fortified by my own strict sense of loyalty. I hope you will do me the favor of placing this clearly before the Secretary and I assure you that you and the Secretary and the President can count on me to the last extremity, both as to word and deed, for loyalty and fidelity, in any task that may be given me to perform.[10]

With luck, Scott would soon see that the hierarchy read that; meantime the Southern Department would bustle. First Pershing faced the amorphous militia.

Clotted haphazardly in border stations, alarmingly zealous militia units had paraded, drilled, fussed, and fumed for a part in Pershing's expedition. By all accounts they would have been dubious allies in Mexico. Many militia officers boasted heavy seniority and nodding knowledge of modern warfare. No regulars wanted to recall the awful muddle of mobilization as thousands of willing martial misfits came in variegated array to the border. They huddled in confusion to baffle even the surest system—equipment they lost, guns they treated like baseball bats, uniforms they designed with casual abandon. But behind their infuriating indiscipline Pershing saw the core of a great army. In the camps sprawling through his department he glimpsed democracy rampant, and it touched the farmer deep within him. He coped with easy confidence. These good men would go home—for a time—and their going must be worked efficiently. He put inspectors at every departure point to oversee accommodations, unscramble snarls, and instruct in basic logistics.

In March he trekked his department and planned careful reorgani-

[9] Scott to JJP, Feb. 24, 1917, Scott Papers.
[10] JJP to Scott, Mar. 3, 1917, Scott Papers.

zation of the regular outfits remaining in his hands.[11] Large-unit training must be continued, practice in open maneuver increased. And the border must be guarded against a resurgent Pancho Villa.

Moments of congratulation relieved routine. Friends in and out of the army basked in Jack Pershing's new elevation. Theodore Roosevelt, gadfly of war, pronounced himself "tickled to hear of his boy's success," and a cascade of letters brought welcome pledges of support.[12] Old friends forgot him not, especially the loyal Patton clan. Nita's pride spilled from various letters, and brother George in El Paso hoped for reunion with his hero.[13] While still at Fort Bliss, Jack had looked expectantly for a visit from Nita's father, but the sudden shift to San Antonio doomed the meeting. Neither Patton nor an eager soldier abandoned hope; finally Jack agreed to come to Los Angeles sometime in March. For a delightful week—the last week of the month— Jack relaxed with dear friends. Nita monopolized him, but no one objected. California's cold memories faded in a new warmth of affection.

Seven quick days and Jack went back to the army; he arranged a stopover at El Paso with George and Beatrice to tell the Patton-Pershing news. He took his young friends to dinner and talked of family and of Nita. And in a serious interlude he spoke of ominous things in Europe. Recent events told a fearsome story. Steady erosion of neutrality put the United States on the brink of war with Germany. In February the Imperial German Government announced resumption of unrestricted submarine warfare and sanctioned the astounding "Zimmerman telegram," which proposed a German-Mexican-Japanese alliance, with Mexico to get large slices of Texas at war's end. Wilson, woebegone peacemaker, tried "armed neutrality" but had finally broken relations with Germany. Rumors inflamed America's mind. German saboteurs were suspected everywhere; legions of spies purloined such secrets as an unguarded country kept. Pershing knew personally of German agitation in Mexico aimed at re-igniting the border.[14] In that sober conversation with the young Pattons, Pershing could recall

---

[11] See doc. 2548248, Mar. 10, 1917, announcing inspection of Brownsville District; doc. 2548921, Mar. 14, Laredo District; doc. 2553282, Mar. 19, announcing general inspection (all in RG 94, National Archives).

[12] Lt. Col. Henry T. Allen to JJP, Camp Travis, San Antonio, Tex., Mar. 1, 1917, Box 9, PP.

[13] Blumenson, *Patton Papers*, pp. 379–83.

[14] See JJP to H. L. Scott, Apr. 7, 1917, Scott Papers, in which JJP wrote: "As to the operations of Germans in Mexico, there is little doubt that they are active and I think it certain that those in Mexico intend to give all the trouble possible."

vividly the sinking, a scant two weeks before, of three American ships, the *City of Memphis*, the *Illinois*, and the *Vigilancia*. So blatant a challenge demanded answer, and a battle-toughened general, who now knew the president a harder man than he seemed, felt the answer would come soon.

Again in San Antonio, Jack watched peace disintegrate. An anguished chief executive called the National Guard to the colors on March 25, authorized joint naval talks with Great Britain, and finally summoned Congress to meet on April 2, 1917. The nation waited in a sudden hush to hear Woodrow Wilson speak. Pershing thrilled at the president's words:

> With a profound sense of the solemn and even tragical character of the step I am taking and of the grave responsibilities which it involves . . . I advise that the Congress declare the recent course of the Imperial German Government to be in fact nothing less than war against the Government and people of the United States; that it formally accept the status of belligerent which has thus been thrust upon it; and that it take immediate steps not only to put the country in a more thorough state of defense but also to exert all its power and employ all its resources to bring the Government of the German Empire to terms and end the war. . . . It is a fearful thing to lead this great peaceful people into war. . . . But the right is more precious than peace, and we shall fight for the things which we have always carried nearest our hearts—for democracy, for the right of those who submit to authority to have a voice in their own governments, for the rights and liberties of small nations, for a universal dominion of right by such a concert of free peoples as shall bring peace and safety to all nations and make the world itself at last free. To such a task we can dedicate our lives and our fortunes . . . with the pride of those who know that the day has come when America is privileged to spend her blood and her might for the principles that gave her birth and happiness and the peace which she has treasured. God helping her, she can do no other.[15]

In the wake of that honest summons the world saw a new champion of liberty, saw once more the promise of America; small nations especially thundered approval. Allied response, quick, warm, prophesied victory. In San Antonio, Texas, John Pershing read in those words of war the whole meaning of his life.

For four days a great republic exhumed its conscience to search the future. In Congress men of concern opposed war, and one of them, Nebraskan George Norris, thought not of the dead thousands already but of the blighted generations to come. The war resolution under debate, he said, had hidden import. "Upon the passage of this resolu-

---

[15] *Congressional Record*, 65th Cong., 1 sess., 1917, 55, pt. 1:102–4.

tion we will have joined Europe in the great catastrophe and taken America into entanglements that will not end with this war, but will live and bring their evil influences upon many generations yet unborn."[16] Fighting Bob La Follette, keeper of reform's keys, joined in urging delay. But a nation so long thwarted by neutrality, so long watcher while Britain, France, Italy, and their thinner allies stood off titanic hordes, leaped at war with relief. No voice could stem the urge to blood.

For four days caution flickered and on April 6 it died. At noon that day President Wilson signed the war resolution and his own proclamation of hostilities. During those dragging days of debate Jack Pershing devoured each scrap of word from Washington. Wilson acted rightly and the challenge had been met. No man had put America's place so clearly for the world, so summoned the heritage of a nation ever on liberty's side. Caught on the crest of enthusiasm, the general, on April 10, wrote his commander-in-chief:

Dear Mr. President:

As an officer of the army, may I not extend to you, as Commander-in-Chief of the armies, my sincere congratulations upon your soul-stirring patriotic address to Congress on April 2d. Your strong stand for the right will be an inspiration to humanity everywhere, but especially to the citizens of the Republic. It arouses in the breast of every soldier feelings of the deepest admiration for their leader.

I am exultant that my life has been spent as a soldier, in camp and field, that I may now the more worthily and more intelligently serve my country and you.

With great respect,
Your obedient servant,
JOHN J. PERSHING
Major General, U.S. Army

His Excellency
   The President of the United States
      Washington, D.C.

On the same day, still in ardor, Jack wrote Secretary Baker, his unseen immediate superior, in much the same sentiment. He made a special point of subtle volunteering: "In view of what this nation has undertaken to do, it is a matter of extreme satisfaction to me at this time to feel that my life has been spent as a soldier, much of it in campaign, so that I am now prepared for the duties of this hour. . . . I wish thus formally, to pledge to you, in this personal manner, my

[16] *Ibid.*, pp. 212–14.

most loyal support in whatever capacity I may be called upon to serve."[17]

Enemies, and he had them, would have read these missives as raving cant, the kind of currying done by a toady. But Jack burned with patriotism and yearned to serve. A blend of desire and persuasion came naturally.[18] No simpleton, Baker read his letter with pleasure, passed it to the president, and told Pershing he had done so. Wilson read his own letter with his own leashed zest. "Thank you for your kind letter," he replied on April 16, and admitted that "it is an inspiration to me to receive such messages, and I appreciate deeply the sentiments to which you give expression."[19]

A new urgency tinged Pershing's work in San Antonio. All stations in his department were urged to special security. German machinations in Mexico were watched; arms smuggling dwindled to a trickle under Pershing's personal bane. Spit and polish worked overtime in the Southwest as men, guns, and animals were burnished into models. At last Jack ventured to call his doings to higher notice. Hugh Scott read a few days after war came of a bustling border command. "I have finished a complete tour of inspection," Jack told the chief of staff. "Some changes have been necessary on account of the withdrawal of the militia, and we are still occupying many small stations. . . . As to internal affairs . . . I am having a complete list of public utilities in strategical places made and shall send militia troops when available as far as expedient to do so."[20]

Increasingly Pershing wandered from the large and lovely gray stone house at Fort Sam Houston reserved for department commanders. Big and rambling, it almost matched the Zamboanga "barn" in elegance, but it stood only a stone bedroom, a place sometimes convenient. Shallenberger, Collins, Sgt. Lanckton, Johnson, the whole official clan kept the house spruced and polished, but they had no magic to make it home. Frankie would have loved it, would, too, have thrilled as war rolled slowly over the land and touched old virtues in Americans. But she was gone, and war came, and her general savored duty for them both.

[17] JJP to Baker, Apr. 10, 1917, Baker Folder, PP.

[18] See Edward M. Coffman, *The War to End All Wars: The American Military Experience in World War I*, p. 46, citing Robert Bullard's comment that JJP "was always a good courtier."

[19] In Letter Book 40 (Apr. 11–May 14, 1917), p. 74, Woodrow Wilson Papers, Library of Congress.

[20] JJP to Scott, Apr. 7, 1917, Scott Papers.

In April friend J. Franklin Bell, former Philippine superior, wrote a surprising guess that Jack would lead the American forces going abroad. So sure was the canny major general that he asked assignment to Jack's command.[21] And on May 3 came a cryptic telegram from Papa Warren: "Wire me today whether and how much you speak, read, and write French."[22] Jack's struggles with French at West Point flooded fresh to mind, but he quickly sent a response: "Spent several months in France nineteen eight studying language. Spoke quite fluently; could read and write very well at that time. Can easily re-acquire satisfactory working knowledge."[23] His chance was coming.

The American Expeditionary Forces

A spasm of relief flexed the country. Americans doffed their false role of spectators. Never in the memory of most had there been a moment quite like it. Rebirth, some said, virtue's just reward others intoned, and some saw destiny achieved. For John Pershing only the crusade mattered. Never had he felt so close to his nation, never so ready, so useful.

Certainty and excitement he had admitted to his superiors, and to Papa Warren he confessed an enthusiasm to assuage sad memories from the past. "The world is certainly going through a trial," he wrote the senator. The challenge none could miss—"Democracy pitted against Autocracy." Never had history known such a moment, Jack thought, and he was glad. "I should rather live in the world now than at any previous time, and I am exultant. . . ." Caught in passion, Jack saw new dimensions to the president. "I think Woodrow Wilson is going down to posterity as the greatest man of this time," he announced to his Republican father-in-law.[24]

There must be months of preparation, a hard waiting time for valor, but the weeks would fill with soldier's duties and pass finally into battle. Fortunately for Jack, calls came from the full reach of his department for guidance in the war: commanders for orders about local security, mayors for hints on urban girding, governors for ways to mobilize. Some of these calls puzzled Jack, who hoped the War De-

21 JJP, *My Experiences in the World War*, 1:3.
22 FEW to JJP (telegram), May 3, 1917, FEW Papers, vol. 79; JJP, *Experiences*, 1:1.
23 JJP, *Experiences*, 1:1.
24 JJP to FEW, Apr. 8, 1917, FEW Papers, vol. 79.

partment would quickly decide on mobilization plans—the draft was his loud preference[25]—and begin the giant job of making an army. As department commander in the Southwest, Jack saw the need to guide the reckless zest of his fellow patriots. Without direction fervor can be dangerous. So he accepted many invitations to speak and became familiar with civic, fraternal, patriotic, and social organizations. The podium at last lost its horrors, and he charmed a growing following. Some of his speeches were quick, frothy, and short; others, careful, directive, and fairly long. He had a program in the midst of confusion, and people listened. Curtail social activities, he urged, conserve human and material resources for the war. He ordered military families in his area to practice his plan and urged civilians to follow. "I do not mean that people should go about with long faces, and renounce the pleasures of social intercourse," he explained, but added that "the public as well as the Army must come to full realization of the fact that the United States is at war with a world power. War is a most serious business and this war will entail the greatest of sacrifices. . . . Excessive social activity and the keeping of late hours will sap vitality and make citizens less able to give the full measure of service."[26] He carried the scheme of mass cooperation to frequent platforms and fully endorsed reasonable plans for civilian effort. Ladies were encouraged to expand their capacities in nursing, stenography, tailoring, and Pershing urged Texas ladies to prepare to fill jobs vacated by men gone abroad.[27]

Some of his speeches won wide press coverage, and the better ones hit wire services. Papa Warren read these avidly, passed a few along to the War Department. A little insurance on the loyalty front would not be wasted.[28]

Primary attention Jack gave to military affairs. Training increased under his cold eye, and he chafed at congressional tardiness in accepting conscription. Wilson's firm demand for a draft won Jack's added praise; history and experience had taught the vices of untrammeled volunteering. Senator Warren agreed and worked to sustain

[25] See FEW to JJP, Apr. 18, 20, 1917, FEW Papers, vol. 79; JJP, *Experiences,* 1:13.

[26] *Army and Navy Journal* 54 (May 5, 1917): 1151–52.

[27] *Ibid.*, p. 1152.

[28] FEW to JJP, Apr. 18, 1917, FEW Papers, vol. 79. See also JJP to San Antonio, Tex., Rotary Club, Apr. 16, 1917, thanking for expression of appreciation for a talk he made to that group (Box 47, PP).

administration aims in a congress willing to declare war but unwilling to wage it.

All the agonies Hugh Scott and the tiny General Staff faced concerning conscription Jack did not know; he did note opposition. Firm in his lessons of muddled Civil War mobilization, he urged frequently full drafting of able-bodied men. To War College staffers, to old hands in the field, conscription alone would do the job. But Jack's friend Enoch Crowder summed antidraft sentiments for Secretary Baker in February: "A military draft," he said, "is not in harmony with the spirit of our people. . . . Our people prefer the volunteering method."[29] Since the pesident had already accepted the draft in his proposal to Congress, the argument ended at high levels. An old specter of the New York draft riots during the Civil War chilled a few hearts, but Baker and Crowder, Scott and Bliss, plus their small cadre of cohorts had composed a bill resting all draft administration in local boards—which, they hoped, would draw the sting of an impersonal military police force pressing men into the ranks. Whatever the reaction, the draft was set.

Enormously pleased with Scott's plans, Jack noted resistance with disgust. Politicians who saw votes in harangues for local control of the war focused on the draft as a harbinger of regimentation. The draft, these opportunists hinted, would combine with all the "boards" Wilson spawned to rob Americans of their rights. If conscriptors roamed the nation in tandem with watchmen from the Munitions Standards Board, the General Munitions Board, and if all other clap-trap regulatory agencies went unchecked, the United States might easily resemble its imperial enemy. Even in Texas, that normally militant domain, politicians mounted hustings in opposition to Wilson's war.

Political wrangling had a sound peacetime role, but John Pershing considered open disapproval of war plans a kind of treason. When he learned that some of the Texas congressional delegation might oppose conscription, he wrestled with a soldier's conscience. Open political intervention could cost a soldier dearly, could brand him insubordinate, a conniver, a power seeker. Always careful in his political maneuvers, Jack pondered how to influence the Texas delegation without breaking cover. No masked route offered, and in the emergency he made direct contact with Governor James Ferguson. The governor hesitated himself and wondered about the proper ways of levy. Jack talked earnestly

29 Coffman, *War*, p. 25.

and persuasively, and finally the governor agreed to use his influence with the Texas congressional corps in support of the draft.[30]

Arguments had come easily to the serious general who leaned into his conversation with a passion to catch the governor's spirit. "We must avoid creating the impression that we are sending a political army to Europe—the day of political armies is past." That might have caused a gubernatorial wince, but it made sense. Other Pershing points were equally telling. Restrain national enthusiasm for American colors on ✓ the Western Front until men were properly trained for the new war. Only the Punitive Expedition veterans boasted needed professionalism, and probably many of them would be kept home to train others. "The only way we can hope to succeed is by dogged determination and perseverance. . . . no half-way measures are going to solve this problem. I am with the President in this matter, heart and soul. . . . The President feels the importance of this situation and every honest American should stand right behind him and help to the utmost."[31]

Help washed in huge waves over the War Department, eddied in goodwilled confusion around Newton Baker's office, and engulfed the Allied commissioners who came quickly to steer American strength aright. Late in April, while Congress wrangled about conscription and the nation poised for some great step somewhere, Arthur James Balfour led a British mission to Washington. Not to be elbowed out of Yankee aid, the French quickly shipped experts led by former premier René Viviani, but dominated by "Papa" Joffre, renowned to Americans as France's bulwark on the Marne in 1914. These Allied leaders told woeful tales of military erosion in Europe. Jaunty Gen. Robert Georges Nivelle's 1917 offensive—he said it would crack the main German defenses along the Chemin des Dames ridge—had failed in a welter of blood and bodies. Over one hundred seventy thousand French casualties dotted the shell-swept Aisne Valley, and France's ardor dampened everywhere. As Nivelle's battle ground to its grisly end, Field Marshal Sir Douglas Haig, commanding the British Armies in France, gazed again beyond the squalid ruins of Ypres to an old enchantment—the draggled village of Passchendaele five miles beyond British wire and eons beyond hope. He would drive there as the British shouldered the Western Front burden, would drive the Hun from the war before the American amateurs mucked up the front. Haig might

---

[30] See JJP, *Experiences*, 1:13. See also M. S. Stump to JJP (cable), July 24, 1918, concerning impeachment proceedings against Governor Ferguson (Box 73, PP).

[31] JJP, *Experiences*, 1:13–14.

plan his mud march, might postulate victory in 1917, but old realist Joffre knew everything depended on the Americans. "We want men, men, men," he said to American officers and civilian war leaders in talks frank and shocking.

Joffre, Balfour, and the British military advisor Maj. Gen. G. T. M. ("Tom") Bridges could agree on one imperative: American troops must soon be seen in France. Joffre urged Wilson to send a division, and Bridges strained Allied relations by suggesting that Americans be recruited into British ranks! Impolitic Bridges seemed, but his idea had been broached earlier by Herbert Hoover, who cited the comparatively easy expansion of the U.S. Army made possible by infiltration into veteran British units. But the plan charmed no army men and chilled Baker. President Wilson accepted the notion of a quick American division abroad. That decision[32] saddled Baker with a familiar problem—finding a commander. Maj. Douglas MacArthur's suggestion of Pershing and March was not forgotten. Baker welcomed suggestions but made an independent study of available officers.

Four major generals competed for the most important command in America's gift: Leonard Wood, Thomas H. Barry, J. Franklin Bell, and John Pershing. Barry and Bell were apparently disqualified by poor health. Wood laid siege to a great segment of American sentiment. Just as Teddy Roosevelt charmed thousands with his offer to muster and lead a division of volunteers to France—the Rough Riders reincarnated—so Wood's touted career rang familiar from San Juan to Manila to Mindanao to the chief of staff's office. Known and admired on both sides of Congress, welcome ever with the mighty, Wood exercised the power of intrigue better than any soldier in the country. He guessed the country expected his elevation to high command, and he probably guessed right. Baker knew him by irritation and by repute. Out of Washington now, apparently isolated as commander of Governor's Island, Wood turned that New York rock into a power base for insinuating his views along Wall Street and in Gotham's political and social swims. He corresponded freely with hordes of congressional friends. Out of Washington he seemed more irksome than in it. Baker tried further ostracism by shunting Wood to Charleston in command of the Southeastern Department—a maneuver resented by the Wood clique in New York and everywhere else. But Baker held politely firm.[33]

[32] See Coffman, *War*, pp. 8–10; DeWeerd, *Wilson Fights His War*, p. 202; Frederick Palmer, *Newton D. Baker: America at War*, 1:112–13.

[33] Palmer, *Baker*, 1:163–65; FEW to JJP, Apr. 18, 1917, FEW Papers, vol. 79.

To critics of the general's banishment, Baker made blunt explanation: "I think General Wood has been very indiscreet and . . . I think the appearance of political activity which he had allowed to grow up about many of his actions has been unfortunate for his splendid reputation as a soldier. . . ."[34]

Baker reviewed his own knowledge of Pershing. Senator Warren's report that Jack's knowledge of French stemmed from study on the ground Baker counted a distinct plus. But Pershing's iron subordination in Mexico counted for more than anything else. Rumors of Pershing's criticisms had been pretty well negated by the general's own declarations, and Baker would risk some disagreement in exchange for obedience. Pershing seemed the best man. Hugh Scott, that tough old rawhide soldier Baker so admired, agreed, and the president got word of Baker's choice. On May 2, 1917, Scott sent a telegram to Pershing in San Antonio. The message began in clear: "For your eye alone." In code the chief of staff sent the order Jack had dreamed of getting. "Under plans under consideration is one which will require among other troops, four infantry regiments and one artillery regiment from your department for service in France. If plans are carried out, you will be in command of the entire force. Wire me at once the designation of the regiments selected by you and their present stations. . . ."[35]

So Papa Warren's question about French had a point! Better yet, the secretary obviously had made a decision before knowing about Jack's linguistic skills. He wanted the general, not the diplomat. Carefully Jack kept his counsel and pondered Scott's purposes. Apparently a division must be pulled together, given necessary logistical troops; once the division was mobilized, Pershing would lead it abroad.

For a day at least Jack consulted no one else about his orders. Punitive Expedition units he knew well, and conjured a list in his mind before talking to classmate Col. Malvern Hill Barnum, departmental chief of staff. Who should go? Barnum, excited and impressed, suggested almost the same units Pershing had picked—the 16th, 18th, 26th, and 28th Infantry Regiments, the 6th Field Artillery. More batteries would be needed for a division, plus added support troops, but the nucleus was obvious. Final selection must wait for full definition of an American division. No such element existed in the army, had not

[34] Palmer, *Baker,* 1:164.
[35] Quoted in JJP, *Experiences,* 1:2; Order to report to Chief of Staff, May 7, 1917, doc. 2591581, RG 94, National Archives.

for years, and efforts to create one before the Mexican venture brought low comedy to the border.[36]

With troops picked, Jack next considered staff. Who could run a modern division under war conditions? That question had teased his thoughts as he dissolved the Punitive staff, and he kept an eye on old comrades with competence. Some members of that old group could be tapped, others forgotten. Myriad concerns burdened Pershing in his preparation for Washington. Lanckton and Johnson and the household staff must pack a minimum kit, arrange storage of the rest. In the midst of excitement loomed urgent personal questions if Jack went to Europe. What of Warren? Should he remain with Jack's sister, May, or should he go to Cheyenne and Papa's ranches? Ranch life would be good for the boy, would throw him with men for a change.[37] Suddenly fatherly responsibility bore heavily. Suppose death waited in France? How would Warren fare? That specter Jack attacked with a long business communication to Senator Warren. Would he permit Jack to invest in the family companies for Warren's and his own benefit? The senator jumped at the chance and secured Warren's financial future in a grandfather's confession of love.[38]

San Antonio clutched a soldier's heart. Fort Sam Houston, with its sprawling parade, its elegant general's quarters, called back images of the Old Army, of that small professional corps that hunched together in remote posts and made the West safe for civilization. There was a family quality to that army, a sense of belonging that seemed somehow fading in an age of mass and machines. For the last days in that Old Army, Jack took comfort in his guests. The Patton family— minus George and Beatrice—journeyed from California and expected a decent stay with the general. Nita's hopes for quiet days and happy nights, for perhaps a decision with Jack about their lives, went glimmering with Scott's order. But Jack suggested the Pattons join him for the Washington trip. They wanted to go East anyway to see George, who waited restlessly for some call to glory. Pershing wanted George on his staff—he ranked high on that list of Mexican reliables—and possibly the whole clan could congregate during lulls in emergency.[39]

On that happy trip Jack kept secret his intentions. Rumors circulated with irritating publicity about his possible marriage. To Papa Warren

---

[36] JJP, *Experiences*, 1:17.
[37] JJP to Anne Boswell, May 26, 1917, Box 32, PP.
[38] See FEW to JJP, Apr. 19, 1917, FEW Papers, vol. 79.
[39] Blumenson, *Patton Papers*, p. 386.

went his assurances of constancy, and to several dithering suitors went amused confessions of bachelorhood.[40]

A saddened party—Nita probably ranked the saddest—climbed from their Pullman on the evening of May 9 in Washington's lofty, echoing station. Jack took hasty leave—he must see Senator Warren, who wanted to brief his son-in-law before the War Department devoured him.[41]

What could a proud father-in-law have said that night? He knew, from his sudden associations with the administration, that Jack stood well with Wilson. If Jack needed things, men, arrangements, old maneuverer Warren could have suggested methods, suasions to apply. He could, too, have talked of people, of their predilections, of congressional problems with the nascent war, of legislation clogged in committees appalled by mass and money. He might have told the amazement of his friend Senator Thomas C. Martin, chairman of the Finance Committee, at the first emergency appropriations call for three billion dollars. "Three billions! What do you want it for?" he had gasped during a hearing.[42] And the response in detail by a staff officer had stunned Martin's whole committee. Papa Warren certainly explored congressional sentiments with Jack and prophesied few troubles should he win command of much more than one American division.[43]

On Thursday morning, May 10, Jack presented himself at the rambling State, War and Navy Building, entered its maze of halls to seek Gen. Hugh Scott's lair. Labyrinths stretched everywhere in a kind of hectic challenge to visitors; the building slumped old now, its mansarded roof spotted with Washington's permanent reminder of fowl population. Across the street the White House gleamed in clean contrast to the gunnish gray of the building Pershing penetrated. In a hive of hallways dulled in nameless official coloration and remote on a lofty floor, Pershing found the War Department, the jumble of

[40] FEW to JJP, Mar. 14, 1917, FEW Papers, vol. 78; JJP to Mrs. Alice M. Kelley, May 2, 7, 1917, Box 110, PP. In reply to Mrs. Kelley's plea to keep a friendship even if the marriage rumor were true, Pershing denied the story and added that "none of us know what we are to do, [but] please remember that I shall always hold our friendship in very high esteem, and in the future as in the past I shall regard it a very great privilege to hear from you when you find the time."

[41] FEW to JJP (telegram), May 7, 1917, FEW Papers, vol. 79: "When you arrive in Washington please arrange see me few minutes before talking with others."

[42] Palmer, *Baker*, 1:120.

[43] See letters from FEW to JJP, Mar.–May, 1917, FEW Papers, vols. 79–80.

offices assigned to Newton Baker. Quickly Jack located the chief of staff's office—next to the secretary's—entered, and felt instantly the warmth of an old friend's affection. Scott's politeness, his old-fashioned sense of the fitness of things, demanded a slight linger on formalities, the trip from San Antonio, health of the senator, the son, the general. Then to business. Much of what he said in confidence Jack knew, but the words echoed in that cluttered office with an electric excitement. Pershing would go to France; he would command the first U.S. division to show the Stars and Stripes abroad. There were problems. Almost in chagrin Scott confessed an absolute dearth of plans for European involvement. The War College, charged with war schemes, had stopped—on Wilson's request—its gaming of the war on the Western Front. As Scott tolled inadequacies, Jack almost quailed. "Figuratively speaking," he noted, "when the . . . Chief of Staff went to look in the secret files where the plans to meet the situation that confronted us should have been found, the pigeon-hole was empty."[44]

Pressed, Jack would have admitted astonishment at so little preparation in face of the war signs of the past months. "The War Department," he confessed, "seemed to be suffering from a kind of inertia, for which perhaps it was not altogether responsible."[45] Some comfort came from military history, the sort of comfort born of philosophical desperation. Never in the long roll of American wars had the nation girded ahead and entered prepared. Always there had been a period of holding while the country heaved itself into a great effort. Now, though, there had been three years of European holding and a Mexican expedition that stripped mythology from military weakness; the comfort of precedents wore thin.

That day, May 10, Scott could boast of two plans finally grinding through bureaucracy—one, from the War College, covered five closely typed pages and proposed an expedition to France; the second, with Wilson's approval freshly scrawled, was Baker's own suggestion for a flexible response to war. Both postulated a small division—some 12,000 men—sent to France. Planning duplication, with the president unaware of it, seemed typical of Washington's ways at the time.[46]

With the idea of a division firmly in mind, Pershing went next door to the secretary's office. Long correspondence conjured an image of his unseen superior, and it shattered at first sight. Baker bobbed from behind his big desk, stood short, "diminutive," and shrank lower as he

[44] JJP, *Experiences*, 1:78.
[45] *Ibid.*, p. 16.
[46] See Coffman, *War*, p. 47.

doubled himself in his chair. But as Baker talked of the Punitive Expedition, border conditions, and the state of the Southern Department, Jack's old impression of force and foresight grew. The secretary's mobile face, his clear, large eyes magnified by round glasses, his strong mouth and chin showed a blunt man of decision. Pershing, Baker said, had been selected for the foreign command purely on his record. His deeds in hectic circumstances south of the border proved the general a self-contained, reliable soldier. Pleased hugely at the compliments, Jack spoke his appreciation of the appointment, noted its large responsibilities, and hoped the secretary would "have no reason to regret his action."[47]

Baker spoke directly about the division and about Pershing's selected troops. What did he plan? How could the War Department help? Swift-running events had offered little time to assess needs; Jack wanted to determine the organization of a division and its auxiliaries. He would keep the secretary informed as he went.

First, of course, he had to name a divisional staff. In the free moments on the train from San Antonio, moments stolen from Nita and her family, he had thought further of staff members, made notes. In San Antonio he had enjoyed the able assistance of Malvern Barnum as his chief of staff. Should he come to Washington? Who else? Like all soldiers building their administrations, Jack called the long roll of his friends. "Cronyism" many critics branded this penchant for allies, but what better way to pick reliable men? From the '86ers still on duty Jack could choose the best easily; from those who served with him through the years he could also name the ablest. Several lists he made and culled them carefully. His general staff men would do the business of the division; his personal staff would run his headquarters and tend his personal wants. Jimmy Collins, Marty Shallenberger, Lanckton, Johnson, and possibly George Patton would make up the personal group.

From his temporary office across the hall from Scott—number 223 —Jack began checking assignments of men he wanted. Some he had anticipated in early May when first he designated troops for Scott, and these he had asked the adjutant general to "hold" from other duties (Patton learned of his hero's interest when he was "held" by the War Department).[48] Personal staffers were easy; the general staff would be vital, and its chief the most important appointment Jack would make. For almost two days he pondered his picks and the over-

[47] JJP, *Experiences*, 1:17.
[48] Blumenson, *Patton Papers*, pp. 385–86.

all question of organization. In the midst of administrative planning, he received an utterly unexpected summons to Baker's office. Not two days before he had sat in front of the big desk and shared Baker's schemes for a division. Now the little secretary peered fixedly at his general and told him everything had changed. The president had decided, Baker said, to go beyond one division, to commit a large force to the war. John J. Pershing would be commander-in-chief of American forces abroad.[49] How large an army did the administration plan? Baker spoke of "several divisions," of added support and specialized troops, and confessed that numbers were uncertain because of unfinished War Department plans and of haphazard shipping.

For a long moment the burden bowed Pershing's back as his imagination called out the legions of men, the mountains of munitions, the utter effort of a people needed to sustain him and his troops. He would lead phantom phalanxes in a war already beyond the bounds of history. Then Jack straightened, looked his superior in the eye, and talked of the challenge and the opportunity. A keen-eyed war secretary did not miss the moment when the general took his own measure and found it sufficient for his tasks. "There was no doubt in my mind then, or at any other time," Pershing said, "of my ability to do my part, provided the Government would furnish men, equipment and supplies."[50] There was no doubt in Baker's mind, either; he had seen Pershing grow. The general and selected staff officers would go abroad ahead of divisions—observation on the battlefield seemed essential to planning.

Added tasks meant added risks. Obviously the United States intended to commit at least an army to France, certainly a force larger than any put in recent fields. Staff officers would have to learn new dimensions of administration as they groped forward in the war. War College education, branch training, even instruction at the revamped General Service and Staff College at Fort Leavenworth, could not prepare American officers for the stress of Western Front operations. Those myriad Allied missions that prattled daily about the nature of the trench battling made the intricacies of staff work painfully clear. Logistics and the uses of great war engines replaced tactics in martial importance. Those grim ditches writhing from Switzerland to the English Channel showed that firepower and engineering had once again prevailed over mobility and that massive armies were now great, boundless consumers. They demanded management more than com-

[49] JJP, *Experiences*, 1:18.
[50] *Ibid.*

mand. As the American Army swelled to parity with its Allied "Associates," its bureaucracy would also spawn managers. The kind of men Pershing sought were trained in old methods but open minded and innovative, the sort who conceded ignorance as the foundation of progress. The chief of staff would make or break the American effort abroad. Who? De Rosey Cabell, whose service in Mexico Pershing approved, was too old. That brought a twinge, since he was a year younger than Pershing. But staff officers must have more vigor than the general, must be unset in their ways. Barnum? Why not? Still, his deep loyalty to Funston left some chill in his life, a frost that old friendship might melt with time. But time pressed beyond delicacies. What paragon existed to fit all of Jack's criteria?

Around noon on May 15, Maj. James Harbord received word that General Pershing would like to see him at the War Department—quickly. Caught eating lunch, Harbord pondered the summons. A guilty sense of impoliteness tinged the call with fear. Pershing had come to town a week or so earlier, and old friendship dictated that Harbord pay a visit. But rumor put Pershing in line for the chief of staff's job when Scott retired—he had four months to go[51]—and Harbord feared a call would be unseemly. Now he wondered. At the War Department he found Pershing's office and an aide, who pointed him to Scott's office. Awed by the rarified air he sniffed, Harbord found his friend. Pershing, looking older and browner and tougher than he did that awful day in San Francisco two years before, shook hands heartily, smiled familiar greetings, and quickly got to his point: He wanted Harbord to be chief of staff of American forces in France. Did he speak French? Unfortunately, no.

"Well, you could learn it, couldn't you?"

With something of Jack's own confidence, Harbord guessed he could—after all he had learned Spanish tolerably!

"Well, that might make a difference, for one of us ought to know French, and I do not speak it except very poorly."

No worry, though, Pershing would take Harbord in some capacity—in the meantime he could help with general organization.[52] Beckoning Harbord to join him across the hall, Pershing put him to work immediately on questions of staff and headquarters personnel. Logistical staff slots had to be filled quickly, and recommendations from supply-bureau chiefs were usually accepted. In cases of doubt, "understudies"

[51] James G. Harbord, *The American Army in France, 1917–1919*, p. 60.
[52] James G. Harbord, *Serving With Pershing*, pp. 8–9; Harbord, *American Army*, pp. 60–61.

were inserted to shore against trouble.[53] As the list of men grew, Pershing wondered about Baker's feelings. The secretary had originally talked of sending "one or two trustworthy aides" with his general; a muster of more than fifty might frighten him. But Harbord kept reminding his chief of the huge foreign staffs and asserted that Americans must learn all the functions of an army and the only way to do it was to put counterparts on the scene with British and French staffs.

In those hectic days of enrolling able men Pershing watched Harbord. No youth at fifty-one, the balding trooper with much Philippine service had Pershing's one indispensable quality—drive. Early mornings he arrived and wrestled with lists, telegrams, letters, suggestions, and recommendations all day, did the special chores the general threw at him, and stayed till long after dark. Pershing stayed with him, save for those increasing times when social and official duties called.

A few days after setting up shop, Pershing announced himself away to New York—Harbord would run the office. In solemn splendor Harbord summoned an official car—the first one he had ever used—for a trip to the War College, where he collected his books. He could not hazard a guess when he would see the place again. The office kept at its work, and when the tough chieftain returned he called in his subordinate. Two names he had as possible chiefs of staff; what did Harbord think? Embarrassed, he shuffled a bit and said his position made it hard to reply.

"Well, Harbord" came the stern voice, "if you are going over on my staff we must be damned frank with each other."

That message being clear enough, Harbord spoke his mind.

"Well, I think I could do the job better than either of those men."[54]

Silence greeted the boast, but Pershing showed no displeasure. On May 18 orders assigned Pershing to expeditionary command, and with public notice came public swarm. Everyone—well, almost everyone—wanted to go with Pershing. Prominent military men, including Gen. J. Franklin Bell and Enoch Crowder, prominent public officials, diplomats, people of all stations and conditions of collapse, asked for place. Requests came by letter, by wire, and often in person. Frequently these pleas were embarrassing to a general sensitive of prestige. Worst troubles came from special friends like Bell, and some troubles were

---

[53] James G. Harbord, *Personalities and Personal Relationships in the American Expeditionary Forces*, pp. 4–5.

[54] Harbord, *Serving With Pershing*, pp. 9–10.

surprises. One morning, for instance, Pershing opened the door to Room 223, stepped into the hall and into Lloyd C. Griscom, old Tokyo ally. Griscom looked into those keen blue eyes, saw the crinkle of a slow smile, and grasped his friend's hand in warm recollection. Flustered, the former ambassador could only blurt his feelings half facetiously.

"I wish you'd take me to France with you."

Shaking his head, Jack answered:

"Sorry. I'd like to, and I certainly would if you were a trained officer."

An understanding handshake lingered briefly, the two said "good lucks," and Griscom headed for the adjutant general's office, where he hoped his age and health would permit service.[55]

One old friend proved bullish as ever and a real problem. For weeks the country had rooted for Teddy and his proposed volunteer division. Jack had opposed it from the first and rejoiced in Baker's firm resistance. "I do not approve of Teddy holding up Congress," Pershing wrote a friend on May 18, adding that "he is a very warm friend of mine and I am a great admirer of him. . . . It is a pity that he has not been able to take a broader view of the situation . . . but I presume that a man's ambition eventually will warp his view of things."[56] Quickly Jack must have cringed in shame, for on the twentieth Roosevelt wrote him in bluff admiration.

MY DEAR GENERAL PERSHING

I very heartily congratulate you, and especially the people of the United States, upon your selection to lead the expeditionary force to the front. When I was endeavoring to persuade the Secretary of War to permit me to raise a division or two of volunteers I stated that if you or some man like you were to command the expeditionary force I could raise the divisions without trouble.

I write you now to request that my two sons, Theodore Roosevelt, Jr., aged 27, and Archibald B. Roosevelt, aged 23, both of Harvard, be allowed to enlist as privates under you. . . . The former is a Major and the latter a Captain in the Officers' Reserve Corps. . . .

Very sincerely yours,
THEODORE ROOSEVELT

P. S. If I were physically fit, instead of old and heavy and stiff, I should myself ask to go under you in any capacity down to and including a sergeant; but at my age, and condition, I suppose that I could not do work you would

[55] Lloyd C. Griscom, *Diplomatically Speaking*, p. 369.
[56] JJP to Guy S. Preston, May 18, 1917, Box 164, PP.

consider worth while in the fighting line (my only line) in a lower grade than brigade commander.[57]

The request for Roosevelt's boys could hardly be ignored by a soldier so much the creation of a former Rough Rider turned president.

Now that Pershing's headquarters functioned, the War Department sloughed its lethargy and a great urge for speed swept the halls of the old gray building. Americans must get to the war immediately; Pershing's deliberations must not be too deliberate—he must collect his men and be gone. Days flew in seemingly endless conferences. Baker stinted his general no information on the woeful unpreparedness of the army. Small arms were ludicrously absent and manufacturing facilities unready. Purchases of the Enfield seemed the best solution, since British orders in American plants had already achieved assembly-line production of that rugged rifle. Money had been appropriated for machine guns, but only 1,500 were available and these fell into four types. No decision had yet been made on which field gun to adopt as standard. French guns would be used until the Ordnance Department made a bureaucratic move. Artillery ammunition, despite production for the Allies, could not sustain front-line action for more than nine hours.

Reports of only thirty-five qualified army pilots, of only fifty-five training planes airworthy, failed to surprise the former commander of the Punitive Expedition. Benny Foulois and his heroic few won Pershing's sympathetic admiration and his constant support. He agreed fully with the proposed 300 squadrons in France and urged special efforts to provide planes, men, and parts. Air support from the United States was a special Allied hope. The French expected 4,500 American planes for the 1918 campaign! Congress provided $640,000,000 for planes in July, but money alone would not create an air armada.

Baker, in his usual direct way, accepted the idea of at least 500,000 American troops as a first objective and had begun building training camps around the country to produce the officers for so large a force. With the National Guard mobilized and the draft at last accepted and almost working, Baker also proposed cantonments for rendezvous and training of all branches of service. These feverish programs, these hectic revelations impressed Pershing and made him resolute. "The deeper we went into the situation," he noted, "the more overwhelming the work ahead of us seemed to be. As the degree of its accomplishment within a reasonable time would be the measure of our aid to the

[57] Copy in JJP, *Experiences*, 1:23.

Allies, extreme haste in our preparation was urgent. We were called upon to make up in a few months for the neglect of years. . . ."[58]

At last Pershing's own work matured. A tentative list of thirty-one officers took shape (Harbord was chief of staff); a tentative date for sailing alerted headquarters, but suspected submarine operations delayed departure. While he waited, Jack kept to the speaking circuit, talked to a Red Cross national conference, and put his increasing aides to work on plans to mobilize and transport the first American division.[59] And as the time drew down, Baker suggested a visit with Wilson. Jack had hoped to see the president for some time, to get a reading on his views on the war and on command relationships. The date was set at last—May 24, in the afternoon.

Baker and Pershing went together to the White House, and the meeting began with an exchange between President Wilson and Baker about shipping. Then the president turned to his general and said with his cool cordiality,

"General, we are giving you some very difficult tasks these days."

"Perhaps so, Mr. President, but that is what we are trained to expect."

Talk turned to the Punitive Expedition, and Pershing basked in an unexpected compliment. The president emphasized that command came to the general because "of our experience in having you in similar positions." Probing questions about Pershing's acquaintance with France showed Wilson's knowledge of the general's record. Although the thin-faced chief executive seemed uncomfortable in military matters, he had considerable interest in the way the war was going. Joffre had, he thought, been unnecessarily negative in his views of tactics. "Delaying actions" were not the way to win. Pershing listened intently as the president made a forceful point—we must begin where the Allies have left off; we must do new things, must profit by their mistakes and go beyond their achievements. All this made good sense; the president surely would comment on Allied pressures for amalgama-✓ tion. But he avoided that issue.

Instead he turned to cordialities. Would Pershing please extend greetings to the king of Great Britain and the president of France? Certainly. Then back to a serious vein.

There would be problems, the president reflected, especially with sea transport. The War Department would do its best to support the American Expeditionary Forces.

[58] *Ibid.*, p. 28. For a summary of problems, see *ibid.*, pp. 26–28.
[59] *Ibid.*, pp. 35–36.

Finally the visitors rose to leave. Pershing had a statement.

"Mr. President, I appreciate the honor you have conferred upon me by the assignment you have given me and realize the responsibilities it entails, but you can count upon the best that is in me."

Those assessing eyes looked through the nose glasses and the president's manner grew formal.

"General, you were chosen entirely upon your record and I have every confidence that you will succeed." Then he made an important promise: "You shall have my full support."[60]

On May 27, Jack, with Harbord in tow, made a farewell call on the secretary of war. Too many things crowded for discussion, and the two kept to small and special things. Both knew the problems beyond the Atlantic, knew prediction pointless, and exchanged good hopes. Pershing had a nagging worry.

"If I cable requesting that the two Roosevelt boys be sent to France, will you grant the request?"

"Certainly."

An old debt neared discharge.[61]

The secretary had something for the general, a letter of instruction, an order covering his authority.

"Here are your orders, General. The President has just approved them."[62]

Pershing and Harbord had thought such an order needed and drafted one which Tasker Bliss, the acting chief of staff, had signed on the twenty-sixth. But Pershing happily accepted Baker's letter. It read almost a model order, reflected a deeply rooted historical worry of Baker's, and spoke to many of Pershing's concerns.

WAR DEPARTMENT
Washington

May 26, 1917

SECRET

From: The Secretary of War.
To: Major General J. J. Pershing, U.S. Army.
SUBJECT: Command, Authority and Duties in Europe.

The President directs me to communicate to you the following:

1. The President designates you to command all the land forces of the

---

[60] The meeting is covered in *ibid.*, p. 37. Details are given in JJP, AEF Diary, "Notes from Conference with the President," Box 2, PP. See also F. E. Vandiver, "Commander-in-Chief–Commander Relationships: Wilson and Pershing," *Rice University Studies* 57 (Winter, 1971): 69–76.

[61] Palmer, *Baker*, 1:205.

[62] *Ibid.*, p. 170.

United States operating in Continental Europe and in the United Kingdom of Great Britain and Ireland, including any part of the Marine Corps which may be detached for service there with the Army. From your command are excepted the Military Attachés and others of the Army who may be on duty directly with our several embassies.

2. You will proceed with your staff to Europe. Upon arrival in Great Britain, France or any other of the countries at war with the Imperial German Government, you will at once place yourself in communication with the American Embassy and through its agency with the authorities of any country to which the forces of the United States may be sent.

3. You are invested with the authority and duties devolved by the laws, regulations, orders and customs of the United States upon the commander of an army in the field in time of war and with the authority and duties in like manner devolved upon department commanders in peace and war, including the special authorities and duties assigned to the commander of the Philippine Department in so far as the same are applicable to the particular circumstances of your command.

4. You will establish, after consultation with the French War Office, all necessary bases, lines of communication, depots, etc., and make all the incidental arrangements essential to active participation at the front.

5. In military operations against the Imperial German Government, you are directed to coöperate with the forces of the other countries employed against that enemy; but in so doing the underlying idea must be kept in view that the forces of the United States are a separate and distinct component of the combined forces, the identity of which must be preserved. This fundamental rule is subject to such minor exceptions in particular circumstances as your judgment may approve. The decision as to when your command, or any of its parts, is ready for action is confided to you, and you will exercise full discretion in determining the manner of coöperation. But, until the forces of the United States are in your judgment sufficiently strong to warrant operations as an independent command, it is understood that you will coöperate as a component of whatever army you may be assigned to by the French Government.

6. You will keep the Department fully advised of all that concerns your command, and will communicate your recommendations freely and directly to the Department. And in general you are vested with all necessary authority to carry on the war vigorously in harmony with the spirit of these instructions and towards a victorious conclusion.

NEWTON D. BAKER.[63]

In that order Pershing received authority to do virtually anything with the American Expeditionary Forces he thought would contribute to victory. His various powers made him almost a czar over American troops abroad. The comments about cooperation and keeping the U.S. Army a "separate and distinct component of the combined forces" answered Pershing's lingering question about amalgamation into Allied

[63] JJP, *Experiences*, 1:38–39.

units. He could play that game as the thought best. Baker's letter, carrying Wilson's personal approval, gave Pershing more responsibility and more power than any American general had carried before. And the order, in tandem with the one Pershing and Harbord had written for Bliss's signature, seemed to cover all specific and general contingencies.

In their deliberations, Pershing and Harbord had thought of several points covered in Baker's instructions: liaison with Allied governments and forces; cooperation with the French armies; location of bases; lines of communication; camps of instruction for receipt, care, and training of troops; full discretion in using American troops when ready; keeping the War Department fully, freely informed; overall authority needed "as will best contribute to the fulfillment of your mission in France."[64] But Baker's sweeping collection of powers, the elegant arrangement of duties and responsibilities to concentrate all necessary authority in Pershing's hands, went beyond anything military men would have dared suggest. The special provision for American identity could not have been written save on the president's approval. Although Jack had agreed fully with Baker's personal ideas on using American forces, on authority and command, he appreciated written orders, a charter of authority, to use in any arguments abroad.[65] It was time to go.

Headquarters, American Expeditionary Forces, would sail from New York on the White Star Line's *Baltic*, May 28. Officers and men and civilian assistants must be collected, processed, boarded. Final details must be smoothed by the staff—and the staff at last was set. On the twenty-sixth Pershing issued General Orders Number 1, AEF, which named his personal and general staff, and all "attached" officers. A quick glance confirmed Jack's predilections for old reliables.

Little Collins remained on the personal roster along with 1st Lt. Martin Shallenberger and Capt. Nelson Margetts. Harbord read his official appointment as chief of staff, assisted by two members of the

[64] *Ibid.*, pp. 39–40.

[65] A curious historiographical debate swirls around the authorship of JJP's two instruction letters. No doubt clouds the origin of Bliss's letter, since Harbord explains its composition in his *American Army*, p. 64. But JJP's confession of puzzlement over receiving two letters (*Experiences*, 1:40) has probably caused the interest in authorship. Various sources (Palmer, *Baker*, 1:172–73; Harbord, *American Army*, p. 64; DeWeerd, *Wilson Fights His War*, p. 205; Coffman, *War*, p. 49), show that Brig. Gen. Francis J. Kernan, an assistant to the chief of staff, wrote Baker's letter at the secretary's request. Palmer, in *Baker*, 1:173, is doubtless correct in saying that JJP's memory failed him about the two letters.

General Staff Corps—the only General Staff Corps men Pershing had been permitted to name!—Maj. John McAuley Palmer and Maj. Dennis E. Nolan. Supply slots were filled by professionals. Among representatives of the Inspector General's Department, for instance, was Maj. Fox Conner, who had enjoyed temporary attachment to the French army several years earlier.[66] On some of his early lists, Jack had included George Deshon for the Medical Corps, but he could not be had. The aviation officer needed no introduction to his old chief—Maj. Townsend F. Dodd, late of Colonia Dublán. And there were several other Villa chasers or San Antonio officers among the "attached": Capt. Hugh A. Drum, late of the Southern Department; Capt. William O. Reed, late of Mexico, out of Sulu; 1st Lt. George S. Patton; Maj. John L. Hines, of the Adjutant General's Department and of Mexico. There were certain special appointments to the "attached" group—Capt. David Hunter Scott, son of the chief of staff; 1st Lt. Richard B. Paddock, nephew;[67] Maj. Robert Bacon, former ambassador to France and secretary of state, one of the few personal applicants to get Pershing's appointment, whose long friendship with Jack rated less important than Bacon's familiarity with the Allies.[68]

Old reliables already showed value. Patton, who came gleefully to Washington, assumed the dingy duty of assembling and instructing headquarters orderlies and took charge of the entire enlisted contingent. In that job he performed one secret and vital service—the day of the orders and hectic bustlings, May 26, he discovered that Collins and Nelson Margetts both had forgotten to get Sergeant Lanckton travel orders. "I was much upset for fear the general would find it out." He put the problem to a friend in the adjutant general's office and got the orders without fanfare.[69]

A general sort of dithering cluttered the last days. Everybody wanted to entertain General Pershing, to see him, to put in some kind of word or request. A few intrusions had to be welcomed. French Ambassador and Madame Jean Jules Jusserand gave a luncheon at the embassy "memorable for its cordiality and charm."[70] Madame, an American, took special pride in her country's entry into war. Arthur Balfour entertained the American general and talked of practical Allied matters. And the secretary of state with his charming lady displayed

[66] Coffman, *War*, p. 12.
[67] See GO no. 1, AEF, May 26, 1917, in Harbord, *American Army*, pp. 68–70.
[68] JJP, *Experiences*, 1:23.
[69] Blumenson, *Patton Papers*, p. 389.
[70] JJP, *Experiences*, 1:36.

several Allied missions for Pershing's acquaintance.[71] All of these diversions, welcome as they must be, tested the ingenuity of the headquarters staff. Progress toward departure continued smoothly.

At 11 o'clock in the morning of Sunday, May 27, the headquarters contingent boarded a Baltimore and Ohio train for New York. A spectacular casualness marked the gathering at Washington's depot—men came in mufti, took elaborate pains to look inconspicuous, all conscious of Pershing's passion for secrecy. But once on the train, the appearance of several medical officers in new khaki and new enthusiasm made Harbord wonder just how secret the whole thing might be.[72]

For the Patton clan the trip to New York had sad overtones. This train ride might be the last time they would all cluster together, and a kind of sweet melancholy tinged their conversation. At 4:00 P.M. the train chuffed into New York, and George departed to usher his enlisted men to quarters. Later he would join the family at the Walcott Hotel. Nita fussed and worried about Jack. Rumors fluttered publicly now about their marriage "after the war," even some of Pershing's staff expected engagement before sailing.[73] They would have last moments together in a decent isolation. That night they pledged their love and kissed each other's tears away.[74]

Rain shrouded New York that Monday, May 28; it pelted and sluiced the streets and made them shiny and slick. A gray day seemed appropriate to Nita and Beatrice, to Mama and Papa Patton—but the day glistened for Georgie in the special hue of glory. By six in the morning George had taken leave of tearful ladies; his father went with him to the Governor's Island ferry. There George took care of arrivals, directed baggage, and checked tickets for men and officers. Secrecy by now had become a joke: numerous boxes on the White Star docks were marked "S.S. *Baltic*, General Pershing's Headquarters."[75]

At 10:30 Pershing and Collins arrived, collected all staff members present, and went to Department Headquarters at Governor's Island. There Gen. J. Franklin Bell greeted his old friend warmly and presented his officers. Onlookers clustered at the island, including several army wives who wanted to bid good-bye to husbands, some to sons.

[71] *Ibid.*, pp. 36–37.

[72] Harbord, *American Army*, p. 71.

[73] Author's interview with Brig. Gen. James L. Collins, Carlisle Barracks, Pa., Apr., 1974.

[74] Blumenson, *Patton Papers*, pp. 389–90; Anne ("Nita") Patton to "My dearest Love," Oct. 14, [1917,] Box 3, Additional Material, PP.

[75] Harbord, *American Army*, p. 71.

Mrs. Hugh Scott came to bid her David farewell.[76] At noon[77] Pershing's party moved to the pier where the government tug *Thomas Patten* waited to take them out to the *Baltic* in Gravesend Bay. Pershing motored to the pier in Bell's car. That short ride brought acute agony to Jack, since his old ally reminded him of an earlier letter asking for assignment. Pershing "was forced to remain noncommital to this very dear friend," whose health prevented foreign duty.[78]

As the whole group huddled in the *Patten* and it turned outward for Gravesend, the guns at Governor's Island fired a major general's salute—and shredded the last secrecy from departure.

An anticlimatic return for mail interrupted the drenched pomp of departure, but the *Patten* finally took station in the bay. Leaden waters heaved, and the lowering sky sank spirits in queasy concern. Late in the afternoon the *Baltic* hove in sight. She lurked in a gray background, her former grace as passenger favorite lost in ugly warpaint. It was now around four and nearly twilight; in that gloaming the *Patten* steered to the *Baltic's* weather side, found the swells too high and put round to the lee. Up the gangway and into the warm and lighted saloons, then Pershing's party dispersed to assigned quarters.[79]

Baltic's passenger list spread beyond the Pershing party, although the bulk of 188 Americans took precedence among 600.[80] A few civilians headed back to England—a theatrical company, an opera star, and Mrs. Frederick Palmer, who accompanied her correspondent husband and would plunge into Red Cross work in Britain. Several British officers journeyed home. Pershing determined to put the crossing to good use.

There were several competent interpreters aboard, including Winthrop Astor Chanler, Major Bacon, and Col. Benjamin Alvord, former French instructor at West Point. Classes were organized several times a day and much agonized mouthing reflected a Yankee incapacity with Gallic *r*'s. Pershing attended regularly.[81] When his officers were not floundering with the language that still plagued him, Pershing con-

---

[76] *Ibid.*

[77] The timing is Patton's. See Blumenson, *Patton Papers*, p. 390. Harbord, in *American Army*, p. 71, agrees.

[78] JJP, *Experiences*, 1:41.

[79] The time of boarding is given as "about four p.m." by Hugh Drum in "Diary of General Hugh Drum, USA: 17 May 1917–15 May 1918," copy furnished by Prof. Alan R. Millet, Ohio State University. Patton puts the time at three o'clock (Blumenson, *Patton Papers*, p. 390), but Harbord, in *American Army*, p. 72, says "we boarded the *Baltic* as twilight fell."

[80] James G. Harbord, *Leaves from a War Diary*, p. 10.

[81] Blumenson, *Patton Papers*, p. 391.

signed them to study groups; pondering lines of communication, base ports on the French coast, depot sites, staging areas in England, and tonnage requirements for an American force of expanding size, initiated the small staff to the huge task they faced. Harbord, who fitted into the chief of staff's role with growing ease, summed the problem of his colleagues aptly: "Officers whose lives have been spent in trying to avoid spending fifteen cents of Government money now confront the necessity of expending fifteen millions of dollars,—and on their intellectual and professional expansion depends their avoidance of the scrap heap."[82]

At the highest level of planning Pershing, often with his old private secretary from Mexico, George Adamson, with Harbord, Palmer, Nolan, Alvord, and Hines, listened to British experiences and saw quickly that current schemes were too small. Slowly the old Indian fighter, whose field command had not yet reached beyond a provisional division, came to a vital decision: 1,000,000 American troops must reach Europe rapidly![83] Jolted by this figure, staffers shifted mental gears; they dug deep in old lessons for poor precedents and produced programs they hoped had tangents with reality. Pershing called for an outline of a greatly increased staff to match Allied models and approved it in a few days.[84] The general created boards to investigate artillery wants and supplies, engineering problems at base ports, and railroad lines to the French interior. Maj. John H. Parker, he of the Gatling guns at San Juan Hill, would join with others to report on machine-gun types, equipment, and transport.[85]

Activity banished boredom and almost banished terror—but not quite. As the Baltic slipped northward toward Halifax, the British rendezvous point for North Atlantic runs, the U-boat specter billowed. Would the Baltic enjoy the comfort of a convoy? The Admiralty kept its usual silence, and Captain Finch, that huge-girthed, florid-faced, merry man, laughed at nervous questions of safety.[86] No one—unless it was Pershing—knew whether the ship closed on Halifax or whether it sailed on some lost ocean encased in a mysterious fog that choked and blinded and echoed the endless, haunting horn. And then suddenly the Baltic broke into clear ocean and blue sky. Lovely cruising weather brought mixed relief—such good weather beckoned torpedoes.

[82] Harbord, Diary, p. 12.
[83] JJP, Experiences, 1:43.
[84] See Drum, "Diary," May 28–June 5, 1917.
[85] Harbord, American Army, p. 75.
[86] For Finch see Harbord, Diary, p. 5, and JJP, Experiences, 1:43.

Veterans of any danger long to preach to neophytes, and the *Baltic* had its share of gleeful doomsters. On the way to the States, according to stateroom gossip, two "fish" narrowly missed the ship; only her quick rudder saved her! Jim Harbord hoped the rudder remained nimble, especially since the *Baltic* steamed toward England unescorted. Daily boat drills were mandatory.[87] Strict blackout of every porthole matched prohibition of smoking on deck at night. And the moon glowed on the cold sea as only a shadow marked the *Baltic's* course.

Gradually routine accommodated fear. Evening festivities diverted the morbid. One gala night the traditional entertainment to benefit British seamen's families attracted the services of the resident theatrical troupe, the opera star, General Pershing himself, plus Freddy Palmer and his fellow correspondent Charles H. Grasty of the *New York Times*. Allied anthems rang the rafters; maudlin songs and speeches touched a surging patriotism to bring tears abounding.[88]

A close eye on the staff showed that choices largely had been good. Varied talents were available and conversations with friends opened areas of future organization. Palmer, that old Manchurian hand who had reported every kind of war in a tumultuous career, talked seriously of public-relations problems in Europe. Someone with a knowledge of news and newsmen ought to handle that delicate area. It was a point to remember. The special isolation of the dining salon at a private table made secret interviews or calm reflection possible.[89] And in those closed moments Pershing read his roll of staff, line, and civilians. It ran like a kind of new *Who's Who*. Down with the enlisted men, for instance, was a speed-demon racing driver with the hands of a mechanical genius, Sgt. 1st Class Edward V. Rickenbacker. Among the Johns Hopkins Medical Unit—those newly fitted doctors from Harbord's train ride— was Dr. Hugh H. Young, likely the best authority anywhere on urology and "social diseases." He must lecture on venereal problems since they plagued the Allied armies. George Patton watched the welfare of the enlisted men and reported that many of them spoke French and one had taught it at the City College of New York. Language classes flourished below decks. And Patton kept the men drilling, for morale's sake.[90]

When even the timid ventured boldly to bed without life jackets, the *Baltic* began zig-zagging. On June 5 the captain told Pershing

[87] JJP, *Experiences*, 1:43; Harbord, *Diary*, p. 10.
[88] See Harbord, *Diary*, pp. 14–16.
[89] See *ibid.*, p. 7, for JJP's table arrangements.
[90] Blumenson, *Patton Papers*, p. 391.

that the danger zone lay ahead. Tension quickly stalked the ship. Uniforms disappeared; rumors said that U-boat crews were less likely to shell civilians in lifeboats. Old hands advised that the coats stay handy —people had perished from exposure in the cold Atlantic—and the great icebergs passing ominously to port told the chill of the deep. Boat drills were fully attended. Men listened with one ear to lectures on disease, logistics, ammunition, and organization; with the other, for the five short whistle blasts that would call all hands to the boats.[91]

That first full night in the danger zone passed in special anxiety, since the Admiralty messaged that two American destroyers, *Tucker* and *Rowan*, would meet the Baltic about dawn on June 6. If she lasted the night all would be well—even if a U-boat sank her then, the destroyers would pick up survivors. At dawn, wracked passengers clustered the rails for a sight to touch red American blood. Abeam to port and starboard and well out rode the trim four-stackers. Among the lookers stood John Pershing. Those good gray ships with their snapping Stars and Stripes brought that rare and marvelous smile. The sight, he knew, "gave all on board somewhat of a thrill and fully restored confidence."[92] A third destroyer joined early on June 7 and led a procession into the Irish Sea. By eight o'clock that night the danger had passed; the run to Liverpool was a cruise. *Baltic* had run the gauntlet to bring a new partner to the war. All of the seventh, as the tranquil water broke in frothy bow waves and glistened in the friendly sun, a new tension built on shipboard. Everyone caught the feeling of a special kind of beginning. Out from her sea-girt shores America ventured to a foreign conflict for the first time since the Spanish-American War. She reached now across the Atlantic to take the Allies' hand at a dark and desperate time. On the *Baltic* solemn thoughts of the long debt to France tinged many a talk; some said that Rochambeau would soon be repaid. But the thrill was more than that of an unpaid obligation, more than a joining of armies—it was as if America stirred from some long sleep to meet its destiny. Once awake it would never again shirk its role. Those few with John Pershing knew they were the spearhead of a world made different by America's righteous wrath.

Baltic dropped anchor in the Mersey for the night of the seventh. Slowly next morning—it was a bright Friday—the *Baltic* eased to a Liverpool dock. About 9:30 the AEF vanguard landed on foreign soil and met a welcome beyond belief.[93]

[91] Harbord, *Diary*, p. 11.
[92] JJP, *Experiences*, 1:43.
[93] See Harbord, *American Army*, p. 76.

"We're coming over"

For Pershing it had already been a day of recall. As the ship steamed dead slow up the Mersey and the forests of cranes stalked the skyline, old memories flooded back of that long ago visit in 1899—then he had been on the verge of the world, just going to the Philippines. And even then he had noted the great capacity of Liverpool's port. Now shipping filled the river, ships tied at every dock in a swarm of commerce to sustain the greatest war in history—yet the Hun blockade was feared. Now he was coming back and would bring behind him another surfeit of tonnage to strain those cranes and piers.[94]

Events followed tradition. A party of visitors climbed aboard, led by a smiling old friend, Bill Lassiter, now a colonel and U.S. military attaché in London—his happy face brought a tiny vignette of the wedding that blustery day in Washington when Bill had stood with the ushers. Smartly present, too, was venerable Lt. Gen. William Pitcairn Campbell—a Maj. Pitcairn it was who commanded "Disperse, ye rebels," at Lexington on a fateful day in 1775—and with him a local admiral as well as the lord mayor and lady mayoress of Liverpool. Joyful handshakes and pleasantries exchanged, the visitors asked Pershing and his ranking staff to come ashore. Campbell led the party, and when, at last, John Pershing trod the soil, Campbell turned and gave a formal handshake in welcome to Great Britain. A cluster of newsmen buzzed around the party as it moved toward a guard of honor awaiting inspection. The troops stood rigid, left shoulder arms, and showed the polish of a crack unit. In front their mascot, a well-groomed goat, identified them as clearly as the small black patch on the back of their uniforms—Royal Welsh Fusiliers, 3rd Battalion. That regiment charged at Bunker Hill and marched with Yanks to Peking in the great China Relief campaign. For the British the symbolism of an old enemy coming to help demanded honors from the past. Compliment understood —down the ranks the smiling American marched, nodded approval. A stripe on one of the men's arm caught his eye: "Where were you wounded?" "At Givenchy and Laventie, sir" came the proud reply. "You are a man," said the white-haired American with the steely eyes. Floyd Gibbons, American correspondent in the pestering hive, beamed in pride at his countryman; "sincere, all-meaning," he thought. And as the general and his escorts turned back to the ship midst strains of the "Star Spangled Banner"—the sound on British soil brought a chill to

---

[94] See JJP's reminiscent passage in *Experiences*, 1:44.

listening Yankee ears—a quiet approval touched old soldiers. To the notes of "God Save the King," the party climbed the gangplank.[95]

Back on the *Baltic* Pershing and friends awaited dispatch of baggage, and the correspondents crowded for pictures and comments. These pestiferous people always impeded business, but war forced concessions. Harbord, by now something of an expert on his boss, noted that Pershing "has the political instinct well developed, and realizes the necessity of playing up to the British public a little. . . . "[96] A look at the eager newshawks—about fifty of them—sparked a thought: "This was not the time to do much talking." But the war-weary Allies needed a voice of help coming.

Several questions were fended while ideas jelled. Finally the words sounded right:

Speaking for myself personally, the officers of my staff, and the members of my command, we are very glad indeed to be the standard bearers of our country in this great war for civilization. To land on British soil and to receive the welcome accorded us seems very significant and is deeply appreciated. We expect in course of time to be playing our part, and we hope it will be a very large part, on the Western Front.[97]

No Yankee bluster here, no conceit about tipping the balance of war, just an earnest man's earnest hope to help. It seemed to register well. A movie camera ground away; the cameraman longed for a group picture of staff department heads with their general. It offered an opportunity to get the formalities done quickly. Together they came, all smiling, then the microphone and sincere words of praise in that Missouri voice, words for Captain Finch who "brought us through the submarines"—avid nods of approval from the posers, and the interview happily ended.[98]

About noon good-byes were finished—the baggage hopelessly strewn in shreds, vans, in vagrant porters' hands—and the American Expeditionary Forces, documents firmly clasped in Harbord's dispatch case,[99] entered a waiting train of sumptuosity. The royal coach and other special cars had been sent for Pershing and his men. The king's carriage offered wide glimpses of the green and tranquil country. As

---

[95] There are two accounts of JJP's exchange with the Fusilier and the dialogue is at variance. The text represents a blend of the sources. See Editors of the *Army Times, The Yanks Are Coming: The Story of General John J. Pershing*, pp. 60–61, and *London Times*, June 9, 1917.

[96] Harbord, *Diary*, p. 22.

[97] Text in JJP, *Experiences*, 1:45–46.

[98] See Harbord, *Diary*, p. 22; *London Times*, June 9, 1917.

[99] Harbord, *Diary*, p. 22.

the rails clicked a somnolent measure, tidy patches of rich tilled ground marched by. Frugal British farmers filled the smallest plots in firm alliance with the men in France.

Into the general's car during the run to London came several members of the U.S. Mission in France; with them came Capt. Count Charles de Marenches, tested, wounded veteran who brought Henri Pétain's greetings and assignment as aide to Pershing.[100] Close to six o'clock the royal train rumbled into London's Euston Station. In that high-vaulted echo chamber bustling with traveling troops and civilians, a group of greeters waited to open London's doors.

Among the welcomers stood Adm. William Sims, and his American blues looked good amid the black frock coats and the stark khaki of U.S. Ambassador Walter Hines Page, H. M. Secretary of State for War Lord Derby, Lt. Gen. Sir Francis Lloyd, and Brig. Gen. Lord Guy Brooke. But one figure caught Pershing's eye—a fine old soldier with the typical British trim and the quiet pomp of a field marshal's garb. Lord John French, heavy with South African honors, late chief of the Imperial General Staff, had come for a personal greeting. Pleased and a little stunned, the Americans shook hands effusively and were sorted into groups, each herded by an appropriate British officer.[101] Lord Brooke quietly announced himself as the general's aide for his British visit and urged him gently toward a waiting car. But before they cleared the platform for the run to the Hotel Savoy, Harbord whispered a suggestion. Quickly the engineer and fireman, grimy, beaming with pleasure, were escorted for a handshake. That touch of expected American democracy seemed worth recording, and the whole thing was repeated before cameras. At last, then, the general and his staff rode away. George Patton, helped by Dick Paddock and a captain of the Honorable Artillery Company, herded the enlisted contingent to transport for the Tower. There, in that firm bastion of empire where the blackbirds proved permanence and where the Beefeaters walked their stately measure, there the Yanks formed column and, led by the artillery band, swung smartly through gates crowned that special day by the Stars and Stripes.[102] Frowning battlements were crowded by men of the 1st Battalion, Honorable Artillery Company, and as their fresh allies marched in they cheered long and lustily. "It seemed like a dream," thought Hugh Drum.

[100] JJP, *Experiences*, 1:46; Harbord, *American Army*, p. 76.
[101] See JJP, *Experiences*, 1:46; Harbord, *Diary*, p. 23; Harbord, *American Army*, pp. 76–77; *London Times*, June 9, 1917.
[102] Drum, "Diary," June 8, 1917.

Harbord and the other staff department heads found the Savoy dreamlike. As guests of the British government, they wallowed in comfort unusual to field soldiers. Right away Harbord liked Lord Brooke, whose worshipping aide told of his fighting prowess on the Western Front. Brooke had a gentleman's courtesy; he and Lady Brooke kept Pershing's room "piled with flowers."[103] For the first evening he had arranged an "informal" dinner and introduced to Pershing the permanent secretary of the War Office along with Gen. Sir Nevil Macready, the adjutant general, and several other officers of influence and distinction. But Brooke must have noted the general's aversion to large gatherings. It had been a long and eventful day, and work must begin in the morning.

After breakfast on June 9, Lord Brooke, Bill Lassiter, and Maj. Maitland Kersey called for General Pershing and his senior staff. Official and calm, Brooke arranged cars for a ride to Buckingham Palace. The king had invited the American Expeditionary Forces for an audience—and excitement crackled among the younger officers whose touch with the mighty had been scant. Expectation almost ruined the sightseeing, but the charm of the Strand, of Pall Mall, of the stately towers of Saint James Palace sharpened the feeling of living history.

In Buckingham's imposing halls everyone waited—and Harbord fidgeted. "I am rapidly getting to be a professional waiter since I joined this staff," he mused and then watched as the general was ushered alone into the king's apartments. Twenty endless minutes later the remaining party entered. George V stood waiting for presentations, took bows from the door, bows with each handshake, and then the officers fanned out beside their general.

Pershing watched his staff with pride. They might be new at high diplomacy but they showed no fright or awe. Simple good manners marked them, and the king approved. Jack surveyed the king with interest. During their short private session Wilson's greetings had been given; his majesty spoke admiringly of the president and a little wistfully of his war powers. Short and dapper in the uniform of a field marshal, the king gazed with keen eyes from an angular and aristocratic face. A clipped white moustache conceded to popular style and added subtly to the king's charm. Affable and interested in his guest, he seemed somehow nervous and excited. Glad words spoken—the king admitted special pleasure in the Anglo-Saxon alliance forged by war—sober ones followed. Britain's enormous losses he mentioned, the

103 Harbord, *Diary*, p. 24.

treasure wasted in campaigns that sank always into bottomless mud. His strong, manly voice dripped venom when he talked of Germans. Submarine warfare struck him as sinful, but its deadly qualities he admitted. America, he hoped, would send "a large number of destroyers." What of the American army? How fast would it build; how fast would it arrive? Were those happy rumors true of 50,000 American planes? They might turn the tide. Something dramatic must happen, for the Allied future looked foreboding.

Truth alone mattered—the army would build slowly and arrive as soon as possible; planes were hardly even on drawing boards, much less in production. America's whole heart was with the cause—nothing would be stinted. Satisfied apparently, the king talked of the recent mining success at Messines Ridge with knowledge and zest. The little man was no figurehead.

To the staff the king made a short, apt comment about Anglo-American unity in common cause. "Together we are fighting for the greatest cause for which peoples could fight. The Anglo-Saxon race must save civilization."[104]

By contrast the next call on the American ambassador offered stiff and repelling officiousness. Walter Hines Page boasted high repute as a literary gadfly and a Democratic nobleman. Through the war his popularity rose in England in direct ratio to his lamenting America's neutrality. He welcomed the first American soldiers with tasteless relief. "Now I am able to hold up my head and look people squarely in the eye."[105] That kind of comment showed why his popularity sank at home. And, truthfully, Page, with his receding hairline, big nose, small round glasses, and scraggly moustache looked more like a Bolshevik agitator than a clean-cut American diplomat. Still, Pershing knew him for a shrewd and useful hand in London and showed proper respect for a presidential crony.

Impulsive, Page fancied his own machinations and resented alternatives. With the zeal of the dilettante he cultivated the brittle British haute monde and danced attendance on the William Waldorf Astors. Viscount and Lady Astor gathered at Clivedon a curious, self-approving salon. Page boasted entree to that circle and wanted Pershing as proof of his pose. The Astors could receive on Sunday afternoon, June 9, and Page confirmed the date despite knowledge that Pershing had accepted a luncheon invitation from Gen. Sir Arthur and Lady Paget. Pershing must alter his plans. Aware only that Page considered the Astors im-

---

[104] See JJP, *Experiences*, 1:47–48; Harbord, *Diary*, pp. 25–26.
[105] JJP, *Experiences*, 1:48.

portant friends of America, Pershing accepted Lord Brooke's suggestion of lunch at Lady Paget's—she had invited Arthur Balfour, Field
Marshal French, Gen. Sir John Cowans, quartermaster general of the
British army and an authentic expert on mass supply problems—and
then a run to Clivedon for dinner.

Pershing gathered nine of his close staff Sunday morning and went
to Westminster Abbey. That soaring building wrought again it mysterious magic. As the Americans entered, they saw Pitt's statue, with
outstretched arm, on their left and filed to seats in the choir. In the dim
but oddly clear light of the venerable building loomed all the spirit of
the empire—tombs of the great were everywhere, inspiring words
graven in stone told the faith of the past in the certainty of the future.
On one marble figure group were piled high the banners of all Guards
Regiments at war, and the blended colors seemed soft and safe in
candleshine.

That morning the archbiship of Canterbury took the service, and
the portents thrilled the congregation who saw those khaki, stiff-backed
figures muted near the pulpit. Sacrifice great and searching had been
called from the British people, the archbishop intoned, and the end
was not yet. A glance toward the Americans and the sermon rose with
certainty that strengths combined in a virtuous cause must prevail.
Shadows etched figures somehow vital still, and voices rose in sweet
songs of old religion and renewed belief. Familiar to Jack from an
earlier visit, the Abbey seemed today more a place of promise than
preservation. He groped for his feeling and found it: "This joint meeting there with the British, high and low, amidst the old things, the
traditions, the history, seemed to symbolize the unity of aims and purposes of our two peoples, through which, fighting shoulder to shoulder,
we should one day achieve the victory."[106]

Return to social pettiness brought a cultural shock. Page had decided Pershing would ride with him and his wife to Clivedon for lunch,
would later motor to the Pagets for tea. He had announced his plans
to Lady Paget, who, ever courteous, had regretfully excused her other
guests and made ready for her later afternoon visitors. Harbord and
two other staff officers journeyed to the Pagets' lovely place in the
suburbs to try soothing the general and his lady. They encountered
such bountiful kindness that Harbord felt especially ashamed.

Out through the lovely English countryside Pershing breathed
easily at last. The full import of Page's gaucheness missed him, happily,

---

[106] *Ibid.*, pp. 49–50; Harbord, *Diary*, p. 28; Harbord, *American Army*, p. 77.

and he waxed enthusiastic about sights and sounds and plans for the future as the car rolled steadily toward Clivedon. The Astors wrapped their guests in welcome, presented their four children to Pershing—who looked long at a familiar number of youngsters—and then ushered everyone inside. Nancy Astor (everyone called her that) showed her Virginia background in casualness and competence. Twenty people for lunch caused no problems; she blended them well, stirred with easy conversation, and watched the friendships rise. After lunch, a decent digesting time, a walk around the grounds, and then they visited a Canadian hospital where she urged her trim American general inside. Patients she knew by name, was warmly welcomed, and somehow conjured beauty from things broken. Would John speak? He did, to a group of convalescents on the rich green lawn, and the Canadians liked those American tones, the bluff and honest manner of a soldier more concerned with deeds than words.

At last the Pages agreed to drive Pershing to the Pagets—for a brief hello and then on to London. By now darkness gathered and teatime passed to dinnertime. Page finally admitted he had invited them to dinner at the Pagets'. After eight in the evening his car rolled to the Paget's door, and the amiable general and lady made the newcomers welcome without rancor. Page announced they were about to leave, but the much beleaguered Harbord urged his chief aside and "told him he simply had to stay." Obviously his host and hostess had ruined their day for him, had waited on his tardiness without complaint, and seemed eager to know him. Pershing wanted to stay and told Page. Instantly the ambassador agreed to drive the general to London later.

Dinner seemed strained to Harbord, now hopelessly caught in the Paget's charm. Page kept looking at his watch, mumbled short responses, and seemed altogether distracted. With the growing guile of an old social hand, Harbord "managed to interest Ambassador Page about himself and got the General a few minutes' talk with Sir Arthur Paget." It was a profitable snatch of conversation—Paget promised to stage for the Americans a full divisional trench attack at the practice fields on Tuesday![107]

Society intruded on business as obligations burgeoned, and Pershing accommodated fate by working longer hours. An old bent to be tardy worked havoc with his schedule, and he used his disarming smile overtime, wore his American enthusiasm thin, and kept the friends just met. Increasingly consumed by a social whirl, Pershing appreciated

[107] Harbord, *Diary*, pp. 30–31; JJP, *Experiences*, 1:50.

fully the importance of proper staff appointments. While he served as a kind of exhibit, proof that the Americans were coming, his men worked with English staff officers to firm mobilization, supply, and transportation arrangements. Rather alarming stories in British papers, especially the *Times*, painted the commander-in-chief of the American Expeditionary Forces a tough, frightening man. One reporter wrote that "it is not hard to see that it is not a difficult matter for him to claim absolute obedience. Any man with that thin-lipped mouth, square jaw, and firm chin must be obeyed when he is in authority."[108] But old practice with diplomacy softened that chill exterior, and as he bustled through London his smile flashed as often as his foreboding scowl. Lord Brooke found him easy to manage, if certain penchants were observed. Large gatherings were painful, small ones pleasant.

On Monday, the eleventh, Brooke produced the general along with the Pages in time for lunch at Buckingham Palace, then retired to host a staff luncheon himself at the Savoy. The king, queen, and Princess Mary presided over a "plain" lunch and talked easily of the war, of their happiness at America's help. Afterwards the king, Pershing, and Page stood together by a window and looked out at the garden now turned potato patch. George V reminisced a little about times before the war, recalled the last visit of the kaiser to London, and grew angry at the thought. Pointing to the great Victoria memorial in front of the palace, he said, "The Kaiser has even tried to destroy the statue of his own grandmother."[109]

Air raids that killed indiscriminately irked a sovereign still idealistic, and a lesson might be learned from that reaction. "There is no doubt that these attacks served to strengthen British determination to fight to the last man."[110]

Obviously time in England dwindled; everyone looked eagerly toward France. But certain ceremonials remained, and some loose contacts for the staff. Monday afternoon offered a visit to Gen. Sir William Robertson—the famed "Wully"—Chief of the Imperial General Staff. Up from the ranks, a tough, heavy-set man with stolid Scottish forebears and a laconic bluntness to shock his high-born colleagues, Robertson showed common sense in his gaze. He seemed, by reputation, a

---

108 *London Times*, June 9, 1917.

109 JJP, *Experiences*, 1:51. According to Eds. of *Army Times, Yanks Are Coming*, p. 62, "Pershing, with his 'grim sense of humor,' thought this remark [by the king] very droll." No source is given for the observation and the serious way in which Pershing recorded the incident seems to point to an opposite interpretation.

110 JJP, *Experiences*, 1:51.

disciple of Haig's, and certainly he thought the Western Front the focus of the war.

Tea served—both men looked incongruous sipping it—Robertson listened to Pershing's account of American plans, of raising the regular and National Guard units to war strength and raising draft divisions for training. Stressing the need for time, which Robertson ought to understand, Pershing urged the need for shipping. Robertson, never enthused, suggested funneling Americans into existing British units. Anglo-Saxons, you know, common language, no barrier in getting into it.

That argument would obviously linger, and Pershing plotted a careful reply. The U.S. Navy now cooperated fully with the Royal fleet; it seemed only fair that the U.S. Army align with the French. Operations in France based on French ports and communications should go better in close association. That curious American penchant for the French— something left from the Revolution, apparently—many British officers noted. Robertson paid it small service. Clearly tonnage should go to the Americans if they fleshed wasted British corps. Insertion into French lines put them in French hands—let the French transport them. Britain's food crisis required every available bottom. Pershing felt the dwindle in attention and left the meeting uneasy.[111]

Tours through London blended history with the present in curious and disturbing ways. A kaleidoscope of uniforms paraded the Circus, Haymarket, Whitehall—British troops, Canadian, Anzacs (Australia–New Zealand Army Corps), French, a scatter of other nationals. But London life crept its ancient pace. Officers visited their old clubs— Lord Brooke's entree was staggering—and bought uniforms on Saville Row. (In one of these bastions of taste Pershing met Gen. Edmund Allenby, whose British Third Army fought fiercely in the Ypres area.) Streets beguiled a tourist, piqued old memories and longings. Whitehall led down from Trafalgar Square to Parliament and late on Monday afternoon, the Robertson meeting rankling still, Jack went back to those stately buildings that had so awed him eighteen years ago.

This time he would not gawk and wander with the sightseers— Winston Churchill, minister of munitions, waited to give him tea. Quickly Churchill's intensity, his boldness and American zest, forged admiration. Out on the terrace of Parliament—that long balcony siding the Thames—Churchill took his guest, presented him to members, and

---

[111] *Ibid.*, pp. 51–52.

then plunged eagerly into questions of America's war. The man's knowledge of trans-Atlantic affairs showed his dual background; his exactness on munitions showed his professionalism. Controversy swirled around him, of course; his Gallipoli venture ranked as the bloodiest sideshow of the war. And before the war his political maneuvers had earned him a wild reputation. His role in the strange "Curragh Incident" in Ireland remained as obscure as his explanations.[112] He sparked energy like a human dynamo and worked prodigiously in a kind of personal waging of the war. Ambitious, many said of him, ambitious to the point of conspiracy—it may have been true. He had Lloyd George's restless drive, and those two swelling egoes might collide. But Churchill made a fascinating host. Spilling ideas in undistilled spate, he listened sometimes to America's problems. Artillery he generously offered to supply and ammunition—which caused Pershing to shift the conversation: "we had . . . practically decided to adopt the French types of artillery."[113] But the minister and the American general parted friends.

By now the social whirl had become work. Harbord shared much of the chore with Pershing, but no shifting of symbolism was possible. Monday evening demanded more hours with the Pages. They staged that night a formal dinner for the general and his staff chiefs. In glittering pomp it set records—at least in the untutored eyes of Pershing's men. Harbord, who kept pinching himself to recall that "but a month before I was a Major of Cavalry and student at the Army War College,"[114] thought the galaxy of stars at those two tables formed a constellation "rarely equaled in the English-speaking world, or perhaps in any other part of the world. . . . "[115] Stiff in his high-necked tunic with its fresh silver lieutenant colonel's leaf,[116] Harbord sat down at the ambassador's table and surveyed power all around him—the prime minister, Arthur Balfour, Pershing with his own immaculate khaki tunic sticking high in his neck, French Ambassador Paul Cambon, Minister of War Lord Derby, Lord Robert Cecil, Adm. Sir John Jellicoe of Jutland fame, Admiral Sims, Gen. Sir William Robertson, Q.M. Gen. Cowans, Gen. Jan Christiaan Smuts, late of the Boer forces. Once aware of his confreres, Harbord saw the second table in true perspective:

[112] See James Fergusson, *The Curragh Incident*, ch. 16.

[113] JJP, *Experiences*, 1:52.

[114] Harbord, *American Army*, p. 78.

[115] Harbord, *Diary*, p. 35.

[116] Promoted as May 15, 1917. See *Army Register, 1918*, p. 195.

"Many prominent men but not quite up to the level of the dignitaries among whom General Pershing and I were located."[117]

If only the ambassador had followed hints—a small dinner would have been welcome now. "I much preferred not to have a formal dinner, as we had come on a serious mission. . . . " But Page's beaming face and his obvious glee at the glittering turn-out smoothed feelings. And the guests were impressive. That they should take time from daily crises just to come to dinner fanned a smoldering suspicion to flame— the Allies were worried, worn, and weak. They needed the United States. More than that, though, they saw beyond the war to some greater world of decency, a future born when America shook off isolation and accepted power. Conversation sparkled and only rarely became serious.

Later the other staff members came to a reception at the embassy and shared the growing popularity of their general.

Tuesday brought war closer. Paget, true to his word, demonstrated trench-warfare tactics at his training camp in Essex. Bayonet techniques, gas usage, the eerie "creeping barrage" laid down by Stokes mortars, all fascinated Americans. A cold Missouri eye surveyed the scene, noted the school for tactical instructors, the high importance given to training, and approved. A small notebook recorded tactical lessons. But "much to my surprise they gave little thought to the possibilities of open warefare in the near future, if at all."[118] A march past by the 17th Yorkshires completed Paget's show, and Pershing bade quick good-byes to join Lord and Lady Derby for lunch. Already friends, the secretary of state for war and Pershing developed a lasting admiration during that luncheon, and it seemed likely to smooth any troubles ahead.[119]

Reluctant adieus and then the most important call. Short and impulsive, Prime Minister Lloyd George had a Welshman's humor and twinkling eye. Hair quite white now in the war, moustache short and also white, he had a rounding high-foreheaded face and long nose, and when he smiled, he looked a little like an actor prominent in America, Charlie Chaplin. Two canny gentlemen took quick measure and wasted no time on frippery. When will the American army be trained, how big will it be, and when will it come? Mobilization begun, the draft would

[117] Harbord, *Diary*, p. 37.
[118] JJP, *Experiences*, 1:52–53; Harbord, *Diary*, pp. 35–38; JJP, AEF Diary— Notebook on AEF, Box 2, PP.
[119] JJP, *Experiences*, 1:53.

bring in thousands soon, and some men—possibly a division—might arrive in a month. Anything at all that the British government could do, all assistance would be a pleasure. Ships were the critical need. They were everyone's critical need—nations rather had to fend for their own tonnage. And with that the interview sputtered, with the same sense of truncation that followed the Robertson meeting. At the prime minister's state dinner that night—another wearisome duration—more might be accomplished, but Jack doubted real help on the shipping problem.

At Lancaster House the dinner had happy informality, speeches were limited to toasting the king and the president, and the prime minister seemed in fine fettle. Lord Curzon's tardiness sparked Lloyd George's guess that his new and young American wife was the cause. French officials, he cautioned Pershing, were also late. The warning amused a professional late-arriver. And in the course of the festivities Jack confirmed a growing idea—these dinners might be tedious, but they created working goodwill for the future. He noticed how well his senior officers fitted into various groups—how Harbord held Curzon's attention with recollections of relying on British colonial precedent in the Philippines.

Before six in the morning of the thirteenth, headquarters struggled with breakfast and baggage and lingers from the evening, but finally gathered at nearby Charing Cross station and boarded a special train for Folkestone. Lord Brooke still attended and made the run to the coast typically comfortable. At the port, fond farewells said, headquarters boarded a channel boat under a blanket of secrecy and steamed toward France. Flanking destroyers showed British concern for U-boats in that "English Lake." An uncommonly smooth crossing rested everyone for the 10:00 A.M. landing at Boulogne.

"Vive l'Amerique"

During that quiet time on the channel, a harried and socially tried general could assess things learned. Clearly most information on French bases and ports had to come from there, so a board of officers, including Hugh Drum, had been sent ahead. Recommendations had gone to the War Department concerning additional officers for logistical work —all British experience showed logistics the key to modern battles. Jack had learned, too, about the press in wartime. Badgered, begged, and browbeaten, Pershing had gradually unbent before cameras and inquisitive newshawks. Shreds of that former private person cringed at such exposure, but this war ran to a large degree on morale and that fed on quotation, illustrations, communiques, and arranged hope. The correspondents who had come with the AEF proved that some fourth estaters were discreet. And Frederick Palmer emphasized the need for news control from headquarters. The War Department had been cabled from London to look into proper numbers of correspondents as adjuncts to coming troops.[120]

Paget's demonstrations, though, had been the best lessons so far. Trench tactics, although practiced by the Punitive Expedition's men during the Colonia Dublán lull, were harder and more compact than Jack had expected. Special instruction could be started at home, but intensive training must be given in France. All kinds of questions crowded, plus one confusion dumped in Europe by Secretary Baker— or someone in the War Department. Apparently almost coincidentally with departure of Headquarters, AEF (HAEF), a "mission" under Col. Chauncey B. Baker—happily an '86er—also headed for France. Charged with recommending organization and general policy, Baker's officers might well develop an entire war plan to be foisted on the AEF. Cooperation seemed essential, and Jack proposed a chat with his old friend.

Problems, worries, flooding questions all faded as Boulogne approached. Two transports loaded with British and colonial troops on the way home slid out of the harbor; seaplanes and dirigibles plied the clear sky, and plainly seen on the dock stood another guard of honor. Even from a distance they looked different from the British, roundish in their coats folded oddly back at the bottom, their helmets ridged along the top and their varied moustaches blatant. Territorials, they were, a strong contingent at attention. As the channel boat touched the dock, a French army band struck up the "Star Spangled Banner," Pershing and his men drew to attention, saluted, and listened. On the band went, through a chorus, another, until Harbord guessed they had been standing at attention "for several days." To Harbord, Pershing muttered at the endless rendition but kept his iron-backed salute. No sooner did the American anthem end than the band, now warmed to work, slid into the "Marseillaise" for multiple variations. At

[120] Headquarters American Expeditionary Forces War Diary, June 8, 11, 12, 1917, typescript vols. in Records of the AEF, RG 120, National Archives (hereinafter cited as HAEF Diary).

last, "our hands having broken off at the wrist," the music stopped and a clutch of officers clambered aboard. Each saluted General Pershing, spoke briefly, and stepped aside for his colleagues.[121]

Carefully Pershing noted his greeters—M. René Besnard, undersecretary of war; Brigadier General Peltier, heading the French Mission with the AEF; two generals representing General Pétain and Marshal Joffre; a French admiral; Gen. J. B. Dumas, commanding the Region du Nord. Colonel Daru, governor of Boulogne, did the proper honors of local welcome. Pershing noted that the adjutant general of the British Expeditionary Forces (BEF) stood diffidently in the crowd and that a youngish French colonel looked eagerly for notice. As he shook hands with Lt. Col. Count Jacques Adalbert de Chambrun, he learned this straight, friendly officer would be his aide and liaison with the French. It was a grand gesture, for de Chambrun descended from Lafayette. Married to Nicholas Longworth's sister, the young colonel had unusual command of English and shared American citizenship.

Some kind of delay kept the party milling around the docks. Harbord and the general, warned by Paget, cast wary eyes for kissing and crying among their hosts—but a curiously unemotional tone prevailed. Harbord seemed disappointed; Pershing was not. Finally a guide led the Americans on a tour of the sixteenth-century fort built to protect Boulogne harbor. Dutifully impressed, the Americans at last were ushered to a waiting train.

At about eleven the ride to Paris began. Pershing, confessing pent-up fatigue, went to bed in his compartment, but his officers eagerly watched the growing signs of war. Stray detachments trudged the roads; rest camps flitted by the carriage windows; villages crowded with Allied soldiers; guns, trucks, wagons toiled somewhere; and a subtle excitement charged the train.

Back in Boulogne the general had spoken briefly to reporters and hit again the theme of participation, of America being at war to stick. He promised America could be counted on for whatever victory demanded. Those drab towns, the slouching troops, the nervous enthusiasm of the welcoming party underscored rumors of a morale crisis. Nivelle's disaster shook France brutally, and a fresh voice talking of victory, not merely of survival, revivified the war. Arrangements for the Paris arrival showed importance given to morale. The Boulogne delay had official sanction—Pershing's train should arrive at the Gare du Nord as Paris offices emptied and the people could see the Amer-

---

[121] Harbord, *Diary*, pp. 40–41; HAEF Diary, June 13, 1917.

icans. For months now visiting dignitaries had arrived secretly in Paris; they were simply not worth noting. But the Americans were different.[122]

At about 6:30 the cars rattled over switches in the yards, and slowed to a stop in the great chasm of a station. A small party stood to meet the visitors. Joffre, good old blunt hero now stuck on a dusty shelf, had been trotted out for the occasion—Pershing was known to like him. With the marshal were the American ambassador, William G. Sharp; M. Paul Painlevé, the French minister of war; M. René Viviani, former premier and head of the Joffre Mission to America; Gen. Ferdinand Foch, now French chief of staff. All were suddenly lost in the crush of throngs eddying into the station.

Floyd Gibbons, eager newshound who preceded Pershing to Paris, tried to see the general but abandoned hope and simply basked in the sight of the age. "The sooty girders of the Gare du Nord shook with cheers when the special train pulled in [he wrote] . . . flashlights boomed and the Garde Republicain blared forth the strains of the 'Star-Spangled Banner,' bringing all the military to a halt and a long standing salute. It was followed by the 'Marseillaise.' "[123]

People crowded into a kind of mass, burst through station gates, and swayed to their own cheering. As the official group fought its way to waiting automobiles, the crowd became a wall. Some embarrassing delay occurred when Joffre found himself bumped down the line of cars to a remoteness reserved for the useless. Pershing and Painlevé rode in the first car and were soon swallowed in a sea of people. Stunned, Pershing waved and waved. People crowded the car, reached to touch; little American flags waved from windows, rooftops, tops of marooned cars. Children climbed trees and lightposts to wave paper, handkerchiefs, to cheer. Often the car doors burst open and tearful ladies fell in screaming "Vive l'Amerique" and throwing flowers everywhere. Almost buried in blossoms, Pershing beamed, waved, and fought a sense of shock. Men, many of them beribboned of earlier wars, some freshly maimed and gaunt, others old and weary and fading in hope, wept openly, their tear-stained faces wreathed in happiness—"Vive l'Amerique! Viva la France!"

That tall American, so straight, so strong, so clearly a fighter, waved and smiled, but a close look would have showed a sadness in his eyes.

---

[122] JJP, *Experiences*, 1:57–58; Harbord, *Diary*, pp. 42–43; Harbord, *American Army*, p. 79; HAEF Diary, June 13, 1917; "General Pershing in France," *Army and Navy Journal* 54 (June 16, 1917): 1374; *London Times*, June 14, 1917; Blumenson, *Patton Papers*, p. 395.

[123] Quoted in Eds. of *Army Times*, *Yanks Are Coming*, p. 62.

"It was most touching and in a sense most pathetic," he thought, and it burdened a good conscience with worry. These surging, shouting people have not cheered nor laughed nor really hoped for long, long months. And now they think Americans are coming in great legions with guns and planes and endless treasure. He could announce that the first division would leave for France tomorrow—but the news was secret and the help so small. Better far to smile and wave and look so rightly like a soldier, for this moment belonged to Frenchmen and to a spirit that had not died.

Through surging humanity the auto crept in a kind of Roman triumph. The other cars of Pershing's caravan? Lost in the multitudes. Harbord found his own car alone, sat numbed with de Chambrun, who kept saying, "Salute, Colonel, salute. It is for you." Pelted by flowers and deafened by acclaim, the chief of staff suddenly had the ghastly thought that the pulsing crowd took him for General Pershing! "It took all the joy out of life until finally after our motor was smelling with heat from running so long on 'the low,' we reached the Hôtel de Crillon in time to see him trying to force his way through the mass from curb to hotel door."

Once clear of the broad boulevards and into the Place de la Concorde, Pershing almost gave up hope of reaching the Crillon. That stately mansarded place, redolent of Paris's many palaces, often entertained celebrities—but Pershing's status ranked him somewhere between President Poincaré and Louis XIV. The sedate lobby throbbed with excitement; reluctantly Parisians permitted Pershing to reach his room. But the tumult increased in the great sweeping Place de la Concorde; the police stood helpless, caught in this frenzied release from fear. "Pershing! Pershing! Pershing! Viva l'Amerique!" rang again and again.

In his room Jack found banks of flowers, flags, messages, and heard that happy roar. Bareheaded, his khaki uniform showing well, he went to his portico to wave, laugh, bow, say things lost in the crowd. People interrupted—stray Americans who bluffed their way in, "missions" who wanted to report, a bevy of reporters determined to record words from him that day. In the crowded suite he tried French, and he stumbled and stuttered and recalled those days of terror at West Point. In English he thanked France for her welcome and said he and his men came to fight, not talk. Superb, the words of a true American. An ally who would fight! He could have said anything that evening and been eloquent.

Ambassador and Mrs. Sharp snatched the general and his senior staff to a dinner that night. The embassy glittered with French military and naval folk, high government officials, and important Americans who happened to be handy. Sharp spoke his feelings and sounded a bit like Page. "You cannot realize the satisfaction I feel that we are in the war and that you are here to prepare for our participation. It is a great day for America and for France. The civilian now gives way to the soldier. I hope you have not arrived too late."

That last phrase hung leaden in the air and touched most of the late conversation between the general and Harbord. In the quiet post-mortem session at the Crillon, the two compared notes. So high the hopes of France, so electric was the national spirit that Pershing feared a bad reaction when great legions from the States did not arrive. Aware clearly of the burden and the problem, he urged a certain sobriety on his staff, a "down to business" manner, and careful planning for the early contingents of the first division.

Sobriety was not in the Paris air. A soldier eager to work languished still in ceremonials. On Thursday, June 14, zestful hosts planned a visit to Les Invalides in the morning. That baroque building of sun-brown stone seems somehow to sum so much that war has done, to hold within its marbled walls much more than Napoleon's tomb. Draped with banners of bygone legions, the walls are guarded by a stone phalanx of great captains, and some subtle genius lingers in the air. The stone warriors gaze toward the graceful sepulchre in silent admiration. Visitors gaze, too, in silent awe. Some few may sign the Golden Book, a muster roll of glory, and John Pershing joined those ranks. Down to the sepulchre's floor he went to stand by the tomb. The guide, a veteran beribboned, carefully took Napoleon's sword from its display case, reverently handed it to the American soldier so obviously touched by the scene. Pershing took it and it felt delicate, as though it might break and with it all touches of victory. Gently, after a moment's hesitation, Pershing bowed and kissed the sword. That gesture was told by the press, by recollection, by some mysterious emotional telegraph all across the nation, and a link of two generals forged.

Next a visit to President Raymond Poincaré gave an opportunity to convey President Wilson's greetings. Formal, more reserved than most, Poincaré said that "the French people are very happy that America is in the war. Your coming is a great satisfaction to us." Details of American preparations he sought, news of troop arrival. Pershing's news ran less optimistic than perhaps the day before. Luncheon in the Presidential Palace almost boggled the minds of Pershing's staff. Sixty guests sat at one long table. Sèvres porcelain paraded endlessly, as did superb wines. "Nowhere," Jack thought, "are such things done so well as in Paris at the Palace of the President."[124]

Madame Poincaré's charm engulfed the American general. Speaking flawless English, she described the sufferings of her country, the endless travail, and the losses, defeats, disappointments. So long a roll of doom deflated her guest; could morale be restored, he asked? "Your presence has already heartened," she suggested, and the evidence everywhere seemed proof.

More proof came for Pershing in the afternoon when he went with Ambassador Sharp to visit the Chamber of Deputies. They entered the diplomatic gallery unobtrusively, but heads turned quickly—Pershing was there! In a wave the deputies stood and cheered; visitors in the gallery forgot protocol as they joined in thunderous applause. Smiling yet serious, the American general bowed. M. Viviani spoke in high emotion of his own reception in the United States, of the meaning of America's help; a new wave of tearful clapping, cheering erupted.

Something closer to business consumed part of the afternoon. At Le Bourget "aviation field," Pershing saw a great bustle of planes landing, taking off, many standing ready for instant use against German raiders. Modern antiaircraft guns ringed the field and intrigued the Americans, unused to such sophisticated operations. For the general there were demonstrations of formation flying by pursuit planes, of air fighting tactics, and such precision that Pershing nursed a "painful thought that our aviation had a long way to go. . . ."[125] Captain Patton, ogling the mock battles in frank amazement, realized that "I have never before known what flying was. It is impossible to imagine the perfection which these people have attained. . . ."[126]

Grimmer realities of war were confided at a meeting later in the day with the minister of marine. Submarine losses, he told Pershing, had created a real food crisis. France, he said, depended on some 1,200,000 tons of British shipping; as that tonnage sank, so the food reserve. Pershing knew a little of the other side of the argument. British officials had told him the French refused to ration food as stringently as necessary. It seemed a national laxness with them.[127] Although France's munitions industry had grown with war, some necessary raw

---

[124] See JJP, *Experiences*, 1:57–61; Harbord, *Diary*, pp. 43–44; Harbord, *American Army*, pp. 79–83.
[125] JJP, *Experiences*, 1:61–62.
[126] Blumenson, *Patton Papers*, p. 396.
[127] JJP, *Experiences*, 1:62.

materials must come by sea. If losses continued, all kinds of failures promised.

Suitably sobered, the general attended in the evening a dinner given by War Minister Painlevé. The War Ministry lost its drabness for the occasion. A special dining hall had been created by hanging Gobelin tapestries around the walls, filling corners with American and French flags, opening tall doors to the garden where a small ensemble played. About thirty people came, bureau heads in the ministry, some General Staff types, a few cabinet members—really a working gathering. Pershing appreciated his first real contact with those his staff must know.[128]

Business picked up as American troops sailed closer to France. Staff discussions, led by the base and communications group that preceded headquarters, selected Saint Nazaire as the first landing site. Would the general approve? He considered it. A tentative site for GHQ had been found, over on the left bank, 31, rue Constantine, a place isolated from city bustle and near the Invalides. That seemed all right. Organization plans continued, with help coming from some of those myriad "missions" already trudging France. Careful planning of billets and supply centers around Saint Nazaire must continue, and the general wanted attention paid to a proper place in the front line for American troops. Staff could study that and report.

He must report to the man leading the armies of France. By the time the visit was confirmed for Saturday, the sixteenth, Pershing had enjoyed another public triumph. Friday morning a call on Marshal Joffre had stirred cameramen to a joint photo boasting Allied unity, lunch with the marshal at the Military Club had been interrupted by frequent calls to the balcony, and Joffre wallowed in attention. That afternoon a Senate appearance had destroyed the dignity of that chamber. Prolonged cheering, an endless ovation, brought the general to his feet for multiple bows. Harbord muttered to him that if Parisians had the say, he could be elected king of France![129] In the afternoon they went to Picpus Cemetery and Lafayette's tomb, where Pershing laid a wreath and heard an affecting speech by the Marquis de Chambrun. But he and everyone on the staff looked forward to Saturday's trip. Pétain seemed the man of the hour, a steady, somewhat stolid soldier who had picked up morale and was holding the lines after Nivelle's carnage.

French headquarters at Compiègne lacked the flair of Paris. A

---

[128] *Ibid.*
[129] *Ibid.*; Harbord, *American Army*, p. 83; Harbord, *Diary*, p. 46.

businesslike atmosphere impressed the Americans. Pétain, fairly tall and large, wore the light-colored, big-pocketed French officer's tunic and a high, pot-like cap swirled in gold braid. A prominent nose and brushy moustache accented his wide, quiet, and probing eyes. Essentially a silent man, he had a keen sense of humor, and Pershing liked him immediately. They enjoyed lunch; the staffs traded introductions and chatted while the commanding officers discussed the war. America, Pershing said, could hardly do much until the following spring. Pétain brooded and understood, but when saying his good-byes, he made a plaintive comment: "I hope it is not too late."[130]

In care of Gen. Franchet d'Espérey—the British called him Desperate Frenchy—the American group went to the area of Saint Quentin, where d'Espérey's army group held the line. Two miles ahead sprawled the "front," and, although activity was said to be light, shells dropped in nervous rhythm. After that first sniff of war, Pershing took his troops back to the Crillon.[131]

One final entertainment bedazzled Paris that night. A special performance of the Opéra Comique dedicated to Pershing flushed thousands of celebrants into the streets. Every seat was sold, aisles jammed, and people cheered endlessly while Pershing and his familiars entered the presidential box. Everyone in that huge theater rose to cheer while on stage a marine tableau of flags featured Old Glory and the Tricolor. As the "Star Spangled Banner" was sung beautifully by the girl carrying the American flag, Harbord wept. The girl with the Tricolor started the "Marseillaise," and tremulous voices joined in rising chorus. For at least fifteen minutes the demonstration continued. And the meaning of all the days in England and France suddenly struck Harbord—"We are all living history. . . . our coming is hailed as the coming of the Lord."[132]

Moved beyond words, Jack reminded himself that the joy was for his country and for freedom—with perhaps just a little for him.[133]

A lot of the joy was for him. As Charles H. Grasty wrote Col. E. M. House—a particular Wilsonian agent—"General Pershing has been an unqualified success in Europe. So far as fitness to deal with these people socially and diplomatically is concerned, he is America at its very best. . . . France has thrown its arms around him. . . . So great has been

130 Harbord, *Diary*, p. 47.
131 *Ibid.*, pp. 47–48; JJP, *Experiences*, 1:63–64.
132 Harbord, *Diary*, p. 48.
133 JJP, *Experiences*, 1:59.

his instant success. He reminds one of Robert E. Lee in his mien."[134] Harbord, by now a total convert, gave a close observer's appraisal: "General Pershing certainly looks his part since he came here. He is a fine figure of a man; carries himself well, holds himself on every occasion with proper dignity; is easy in manner, knows how to enter a crowded room, and is fast developing into a world figure."[135] That kind of word reached Baker's ear and he passed it on: "On every hand," he told Wilson, "I hear . . . stories of good nature, tact and good sense on General Pershing's part."[136] Tact, manners, and diplomacy continued through the run of lunches, dinners, and outings, but Pershing's true interests lay southward at Saint Nazaire. There on June 28 elements of the U.S. 1st Division arrived, Maj. Gen. William J. Sibert commanding. As men of division headquarters, of the 16th Infantry, two battalions of the 28th Infantry, and one battalion of the 5th Marines landed, they saw standing on the dock a tall man in khaki staring intently at them. So straight he stood, so narrowly he surveyed the ranks that old Mexican veterans pegged him immediately—JJP. They knew, some of those men, that the Punitive Expedition troops were now often called "Pershing's darlings," a sobriquet their general did not deny but which perhaps counted a mixed blessing. He did stare hard![137]

Sibert, a Panama Canal engineer, Jack knew less well than the two infantry brigade commanders, Robert L. Bullard and Omar Bundy. Old days at the Point plus years of tangential service bound them together. The tall Bullard who strode from the gangplank with confidence knew his superior extremely well. Back at Marahui he had expected a great future for Jack, but hardly as a fighter. Now he would lead all Americans in the worst war ever.

There were socials and problems and meetings every day; statistics burgeoned, and paper cascaded across all the desks in the small quarters on rue Constantine. Irritations compounded as the War Department apparently ignored HAEF's recommendations for almost everything. But troops were coming, staging areas were preparing, and America's aid became obvious. By July 4 France expected a great celebration for Independence Day. Even England proposed to fly Old Glory from the Houses of Parliament in honor of her new ally.

That sunny Wednesday, Paris glimpsed its first American battalion

[134] Grasty to House, June 16, 1917, Woodrow Wilson Papers, Series 2, Library of Congress.
[135] Harbord, *Diary*, p. 85.
[136] Baker to Wilson, July 24, 1917, Box 4, Baker Papers, Library of Congress.
[137] Eds. of *Army Times, Yanks Are Coming*, p. 64; JJP, *Experiences*, 1:87–88.

as men of the 16th Infantry marched out to Les Invalides. There a formal presentation of colors by the President to the troops and of guidons to their general solemnized a rekindled alliance. As the battalion—Pershing thought its marching sloppy by old standards—marched to Picpus Cemetery, crowds thronged the way, bewreathed those startled fighters, and festooned rifles and bayonets until they looked to Pershing like "a moving flower garden."

At the cemetery Fourth of July oratory praised French heroism, pledged American admiration and eagerness to aid. French speakers heaped affection on the Americans. To old friend C. E. Stanton, now a colonel and chief disbursing officer of the AEF, Pershing deputed the task of response. Stanton, gifted orator, had written short remarks. As the solemn and impressive ceremonies, punctuated by American troops at rigid attention, by proper martial music, drew to an end, M. Painlevé turned to Pershing to ask: "Aren't you going to speak?"

"No, Colonel Stanton is speaking for me."

"But you must speak."

Urged, too, by Ambassador Sharp, the general added short words to the sum of enthusiasm. And then Stanton made formal comment for the United States. "What we have of blood and treasure are yours," he said, and then earnestly: "In the presence of the illustrious dead, we pledge our hearts and our honor in carrying this war to a successful conclusion." In the silence light filtered through trees and a wind touched leaves. Men stood bareheaded and then the last line came. "Lafayette, we are here!"[138]

[138] See C. E. Stanton to Kate Louise Roberts, July 12, 1927, Box 189, PP; JJP, *Experiences*, 1:93.

"The Standards for the American Army Will Be Those of West Point"

BY mid-1917 war had changed. All illusions of 1914, most hopes for a "breakthrough" had washed away in the blood and ooze of Flanders, Artois, Picardy, Lorraine, and Champagne. A close look at France behind the war, at the drawn and sober faces of a naturally gay people, showed pitiless human erosion. A look at the *poilus*, at their slumping pose and dragging gait, showed martial decay. All the dash, the *audace* of earlier days lay behind somewhere with comrades on the Marne, the Somme, at Verdun, on the bitter slopes of Chemin des Dames. In that earlier, different war had been hope for the world, for the saving of decency, the triumph of goodness. Not even the evil of Wilhelm II could long restrain human progress. But progress halted— not, perhaps, at the kaiser's hands, but because of some ineluctable process released by war. As thousands upon grisly thousands fell along the 400 miles of trenches soiling France from Switzerland to the English Channel, a kind of unstoppable consumption sucked men to butchery. Different surely from all trenches before, these ranged through high land and low, split towns and families, and were marvels of engineering waste. Sublimely sophisticated, the trenches existed in a time of their own, a world apart, a reality of carnage. Between the lines stretched a ghost-ridden, barren, blasted universe called "No Man's Land." And all things said of the trenches were untrue. For no voice could tell, no eye could see the truths of soul learned in those ditches of the damned. In that alien world men burrowed, scurried, slithered, snatched existence in a mutant incarnation. Sometimes, under an awful howling sound, they groveled "over the top" in a grotesque mime of a charge, bent against a chattering, leaden wind. Some tumbled like winter leaves, others fell bleeding in a gaseous pock of dirt, some few gained the enemy's wire or a shard of his trenchline. Survivors learned to live with daze and to charge again at dawn. And in the horror came faith—faith in challenge and companions and death. There was in all that mud-slimed squalor awesome, piteous heroism. Men daily did deeds beyond belief, dared carnage and waste and uncertain profit for reasons of the heart. For three years the trenches ground lives in the mincing machine of the Western Front until, at last, there seemed no other kind of life.

Fatalism tinged all ranks of *poilus* and Tommies, depressed civilians in France and England, turned their desperate eyes to America. There seemed no solution save attrition to a trench stalemate—and America could sustain the Allies beyond the pool of German blood.

A different kind of winning had charmed every leader of the war. Both sides began with splendid plans that were ruined by the sudden triumph of machines. Firepower negated numbers and compelled defensive tactics. As the trenches lengthened and mobility ended, old martial theories faded in frustration. Count Schlieffen's bold scheme for turning the Allied left went awry through misjudged opportunism; French valor *à l'outrance* crumbled against machine guns and wire and cannon. Early leaders faded with their hopes; replacements followed to their own oblivion the illusion of a breakthrough. Moltke, Falkenhayn, Joffre, Foch, Sir John French, all were sacrificed to attrition.

Pershing knew the fate of generals who fail. He had the recent example of Robert Georges Nivelle to vivify martial mortality. Douglas Haig alone kept his stolid perch atop the British Armies in France. Apparently unemotional, aloof, Haig burned with an ambition unquenched by the blood of thousands. Fighting always in suspicion of the French, smugly taking up the burden when Nivelle failed, Haig sought a grand gesture of victory.

If his dream was absurd, his preparations were earnest, and his record beckoned study. From the depths of the First Marne he had rescued the BEF, had survived the Somme debacle, and had won constant support from a government bankrupt of alternatives. Lloyd George came to power with an eye cocked eastward, with an urge toward Egypt or Salonika. But Haig's argument, always echoed by Wully Robertson, reminded Lloyd George of Gallipoli, of the dismal excursion to Kut el Amara, of the liabilities abounding in Italy. The war, Haig intoned, must be won in the West. Dwindling manpower and fewer ships combined to limit British logistical possibilities beyond France. So the dapper field marshal who looked so like his king kept his armies and his plans for a push toward Passchendaele in the summer of 1917. Haig's example had a lesson: Determination makes converts.

John Pershing had determination and he, too, had plans. Converts might be few, but Baker and the president were the only ones who mattered. A pacifist secretary of war and peacemaker president held surprisingly firm vision of America's martial destiny. An American army fighting on its own front, led by its own officers, would wage its own crusade for freedom in a way the world would know. That single view of America's portion fixed Pershing's plans during the *Baltic* voyage. And as his young, inexperienced staff wrestled with sudden and stupendous dimensions of modern war, Pershing had worked during the trip, and in the weeks since, to grasp dimensions of his challenge.

His task transcended Grant's or Lee's or any other predecessor's, and his command might be larger than all of theirs combined. His responsibilities were beyond anyone's guess, his powers to be made. Critics, and they growled in a growing chorus at home, suggested an obvious weakness—limited imagination. Veteran of small wars, citizen of the U.S. Army's little world, Pershing had insufficient vision for the World War. Such jealous carps ignored a special background in diplomacy dating back to service on General Miles's staff in Washington and running through the governorship of Moro Province. Such carps, too, ignored a grasp of organization that matched diplomatic exposure. Experience John Pershing had; the only question was whether it was usable in the World War.

Expansion proved really a matter of observation. Although physical ravages extended not far behind the zone of the armies, the frenzied welcome for Americans, the worn people, and the grinding drabness of everything marked a war that reached the core of nations. From Pétain's woeful hope of timing, from visits to British General Headquarters, looks at the Allied lines, the daily increase in violence and consumption came clear. Talks with Marshal Joffre, shelved though he seemed, won shrewd estimates of Allied weaknesses and needs. The officially forgotten hero of the Marne kept a closer touch with the war than politicians knew and confided in his newfound American friend. Field Marshal Sir Douglas Haig acknowledged the real French need for men and confessed that good recruits would not be scorned in

Flanders. Staff discussions focused on new sinews of war—railroads, ships, docks, highways, trucks, gasoline, and airplanes.[1] Old scales of American fighting were scrapped. Quickly Pershing came to a new estimate of America's role in the war. A cable to the War Department on July 6, 1917, sent shock waves all the way up Capitol Hill and showed how quickly Pershing had adjusted to an unprecedented challenge: "Plans should contemplate sending over at least 1,000,000 men by next May."[2] Jack explained to Baker:

It is evident that a force of about 1,000,000 is the smallest unit which in modern war will be a complete, well-balanced, and independent fighting organization. However, it must be equally clear that the adoption of this size force as a basis of study should not be construed as representing the maximum force which should be sent to or which will be needed in France. It is taken as the force which may be expected to reach France in time for an offensive in 1918, and as a unit and basis of organization. Plans for the future should be based, especially in reference to the manufacture of artillery, aviation, and other material, on three times this force—i.e., at least 3,000,000 men."[3]

"What a road we have before us."

If Congress could scarcely imagine a war large enough to need a million men, Baker seemed unruffled. Committed to winning peace at any kind of rates, Wilson followed Baker's calm. But Tasker Bliss, acting chief of staff, and his henchmen in the War College reacted in alarm. They were bankrupt of suggestions; they had no real war plans beyond a gesture division. And when Pershing supported his bombshell with a detailed scheme for raising his legions, a scheme with Col. Chauncey Baker's approval, all opposition collapsed. Under the unportentous title of General Organization Project, Pershing's program arrived full buttressed with charts, schedules of mobilization, shipping, and equipment, and it detailed the structure of divisions to the last sanitary train. Divisions, corps, and armies were created on paper, their lines of communication described, the command chain for operations and logistics arranged. The General Organization Project prescribed a complete system for making a huge American Army fight in France. Under its provisions the AEF would finally boast five corps, each of 187,000 men, each corps to have six divisions,

[1] Martin Blumenson, *The Patton Papers, 1885–1940*, p. 408.
[2] JJP, *Final Report of General John J. Pershing, Commander-in-Chief, American Expeditionary Forces*, p. 8 (hereinafter cited as JJP, *FR*).
[3] *Ibid.*

of which two would be replacement and training divisions. Armies would control two or more corps in the field.[4]

In the whelm of surprise and euphoria generated by a truly professional scheme for making the AEF, only scattered doubts were raised. Shipping loomed the most serious obstacle to Pershing's hopes. By pressing all kinds of tubs into the sea, by combing yards and neutral fleets, by browbeating the Allies, there simply would not be enough ships to get a million men in France by mid-1918. A fraction over 600,000 men might make it by the next June, Pershing was told, but he stuck to his demands and increased them to include special troops on the lines of communication.

With the problems of providing men handed to Washington, Pershing eyed places to use them when they came. Staff studies underway since early June focused on proper placing of American troops. Maj. Hugh Drum, with Col. Daniel McCarthy and Capt. H. B. Moore of the Quartermaster Corps, Col. Harry Taylor of the Engineers, and Lt. Col. Merritte W. Ireland, Medical Corps, made careful reconnaissance of French railroad and shipping facilities and surveyed existing lines of communication for Allied forces on the Western Front. Pershing wanted this team to recommend the best French ports for AEF use; more than that, he wanted some idea of where the American army might best be supplied while fighting. None of the *Baltic* veterans underestimated the problem of location. Drum, forty-seven, a line infantryman with service dating from the Spanish-American War, caught a vision of the future while laboring on initial plans aboard the *Baltic,* and everything seen since he arrived in France enlarged his horizons. "What a road we have before us," he mused in his diary on June 10. When he and his teammates plunged into the port and supply imbroglio, confusion escalated to alarm. Railroads were the key to modern war. Rail routes in central France supported French armies defending Paris and the Allied right; those in the north served the Channel ports and the BEF. Although the British suggested that America might double up on the northern lines to fight on that front, Pershing gave no serious consideration to areas already strained by freight and troop trains. He agreed with his staff investigators that southern French ports tied to the interior by rail lines largely untrammeled by war traffic were the places for AEF depots. "The only ports on the west coast of France that would accommodate vessels of more

---

[4] U.S., Army War College, Historical Section, *Order of Battle of the United States Land Forces in the World War, American Expeditionary Forces, General Headquarters, Armies, Army Corps, Services of Supply, and Separate Forces,* p. 20.

than moderate draft," he noted, "and that were otherwise free, were St. Nazaire, Bassens and La Pallice, while Nantes, Bordeaux and Pauillac were capable of taking light draft shipping."[5] Saint Nazaire, already suggested by staff studies, Pershing approved as a main entrepôt; the other west coast ports he accepted as he glanced at a rail map of France. Double tracks connected Saint Nazaire with Tours and ran on to Bourges, where they crossed another set coming up from Bordeaux. From the Bourges hub, main arteries served Nevers, Dijon, Neufchâteau, and Chaumont-en-Bassigny (Haute-Marne). From that nexus in northeastern France, feeder lines fanned toward Lorraine. Marseilles, on the Mediterranean, was also connected by trunk lines to Dijon and Neufchâteau and could serve as an additional American port of necessity.

Obviously logistics would dictate strategy and tactics. With communications aimed northeastward leading to the Chaumont-Neufchâteau sector, Pershing thought the likely spot for insertion of his khaki-clad Doughboys would be somewhere east of Verdun in the wooded hill country of Lorraine. Calling in Hugh Drum, John McAuley Palmer (a new lieutenant colonel of the General Staff), Fox Conner of the Inspector General's Department (also sporting shiny silver leaves), Maj. Frank Parker of the cavalry, and Maj. Sanford H. Wadhams of the Medical Corps, Pershing charged them with recommending the exact place to fight the enemy![6]

Men picked for this mission were unusually gifted. Palmer, ten years younger than Pershing, enrolled at the Military Academy in 1888. Entering infantry service in 1892, Palmer did honors work at the Army School of the Line, served a year on the General Staff (1911 to 1912), and had rejoined the brain-trusters in January, 1916. Known for his quick mind and easy manner, Palmer had deceptive shrewdness and a keen eye for military ground—he would make a good team leader. Fox Conner, artilleryman, USMA class of '98, was a Staff College graduate, had served on the General Staff from 1907 to 1911, and had done a tour at the Army War College. At forty-two, the robust Conner with the laughing eyes and ready smile had both the experience and temperament for operations planning. Wadhams was forty-three, had served the Army Medical Corps since 1900, and would give some appreciation of sanitation to soldiers mainly interested in the

[5] JJP, *Experiences*, 1:81–82.
[6] Diary of General Hugh Drum, U.S.A., 17 May 1917–15 May 1918," entry for June 21, 1917.

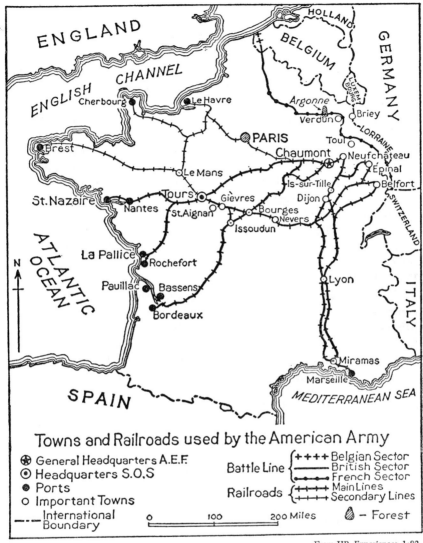

Towns and Railroads used by the American Army

⊕ General Headquarters A.E.F.
◉ Headquarters S.O.S
● Ports
○ Important Towns
—·—· International Boundary

Battle Line { ++++ Belgian Sector
      —— British Sector
      •—•—• French Sector

Railroads { +++ Main Lines
      +++ Secondary Lines

0   100   200 Miles

◍ – Forest

From JJP, *Experiences*, 1:82.

tactical possibilities of ground.[7] With them the Americans would take Col. Jacques de Chambrun, whose knowledge of English and wise assessment of his countrymen seemed invaluable.

Palmer's team knew from Pershing some of the boundaries to choice that were set by logistics and French schemes. They must work within

[7] For background on the operations team, see *Army Register, 1918*, pp. 572, 337, 36 respectively, and Drum Diary, June 21, 1917.

those limits for freedom of action. Some limitations became clear in the early stages of the inspection trip. When the inspectors reached Bar-le-Duc, halfway between Paris and Strasbourg on June 21, they found a bustling semi-industrial town torn between present war and past glories. This former capital of the Duchy of Bar seemed a good base; from it roads fanned in various ways, one ran a scant few miles southeast to Gondrecourt. French authorities intended to put America's early units into training camps at Gondrecourt, which nestled in a relatively quiet sector of the Zone of the Armies. Close by the Meuse and not far from the bulge of the Saint Mihiel Salient, which had threatened the northeastern French flank for three years, Gondrecourt sat surrounded by hills and good infantry ground. "Here we found the 47th French Div[ision]" Drum noted, and here, too, the inspectors found little extra living space. "Our men will have to billet in French houses," they observed, and Drum guessed that would please every Doughboy![8]

Neufchâteau itself—"In this vicinity the French plan our large concentration & schools"—boasted adequate space for 50,000 trainees. At Mirecourt, thirty kilometers east of Neufchâteau, the Americans met a hero of France. Gen. Edouard de Castelnau, one of the high priests of attack in the days of dreaming before 1914, survived the Verdun cauldron and now commanded an army group. "A fine old soldier of the French type," he greeted his American guests with continental courtesy and impressed them with his enthusiasm. Germans he loathed with the knowledge of a thrice-bereaved father of sons. America's entry de Castelnau assessed as essential. Simply the presence of U.S. troops on the Western Front would encourage the Allies, depress the enemy— and he made a gallant offer: "If necessary, I will use all my Army to make your first fight a success."[9]

A night's car ride through the Vosges brought Palmer's party to Besançon. On June 23 the surveyors viewed an artillery-school site offered by the French. Near the picturesque village of Valdahon, the camp area loomed large and convenient for at least an artillery brigade, and it could be used. Retracing steps toward Paris, the American officers visited Epinal and Nancy, and through the courtesy of the French VIII Army's commander, got a view of the front lines near Metz.

War's technology could be seen full blown. Aerial photography bulked large in French operations planning. Antiaircraft artillery worked hard through that summer afternoon, and some air skirmishing

---

[8] Drum Diary, June 21, 1917.
[9] *Ibid.*, June 22, 1917.

fixed all eyes skyward. Against a vast blue backdrop smudged with blobs of smoke and streaked with tracer lines, French and German planes circled and dipped in oddly graceful warring. At last one broke contact to glide earthward and crash in crumpling slow motion. From the gathering wreckage two aviators ran, and, when they were clear, German cannon blew the wreck to pieces. Hugh Drum saw it as a new dimension of experience and labeled it all "a most interesting & instructive afternoon."[10]

Monday morning, June 25, General Pershing greeted his inspectors; they looked a little worn and complained of no wagon-lits on French railroads. Some toughness would come in time, and the general pressed on for data. He listened carefully as they assessed the French offers and described the training areas proposed. Talk shifted to strategic concerns. How decisive would American fighting be in Lorraine—the area dictated for U.S. participation by logistics and by French wheedling? Answers were impressive. An American force inserted into the line east of Verdun, with opportunity stretching as far as the Vosges, would have the largest latitude of attack. West of Verdun French and British operations continued and were essentially defensive. Pershing said always that his men would attack—and in Lorraine attack seemed likely to bring rich rewards.

German positions in Lorraine, apparently strong, were economically and logistically exposed. Coal fields of the Saar and the Longwy-Briey iron region were not far behind the front, as well as an essential rail line connecting Mulhouse and Colmar with Metz and all points west. An American push into Lorraine might snatch the coal and iron reserves of the Central Powers and cut the main rail artery sustaining German armies on the Western Front. Those losses would force a hasty retreat from northern France. Maps showed other American advantages in Lorraine. Rough and lofty land in the Vosges guarded the right flank of any advancing force. Driving east-northeast across the Meuse, Americans would soon push the enemy from the ridges surrounding Verdun and out on to the broad Woëvre Plan, which offered scant cover for defense.

Two salients intruded on the Lorraine situation. A shoulder of the Allied line hung on the Verdun salient punched into German positions; that shoulder slumped on the right into the Saint Mihiel Salient, which for three years had dented the Allied flank.

Saint Mihiel's weakness glared on the map; that salient seemed a

[10] *Ibid.*, June 24, 1917.

comprehensive objective for a neophyte army—and once past the salient, Americans could drive for Metz, Saarbrücken, and the innards of Germany. If Doughboys took responsibility for the Lorraine sector, French armies could cluster in the center, could even aid the British.

Pershing agreed on Lorraine, accepted even the French proposals for training and staging areas. Arriving infantry would train around Gondrecourt and Neufchâteau; artillerymen would go to Valdahon to work with veteran French gunners.[11] Some attention must be paid the British, who viewed American alliance with the French as a kind of Revolutionary aberration. But with main details of training sites and ultimate employment settled, Pershing left the routing and assignment of troops to unit commanders and his staff and turned his own attention to tougher matters of diplomacy.

Diplomacy became one of myriad pressures. Pressures increased constantly, confounding Pershing's hectic work schedule. He "set the pace in his attention to everything needful," Harbord conceded wearily,[12] and watched amazed as his fifty-six-year-old boss kept herculean hours filled with conferences, briefings, visits, and trips. Staff teams did a lot of work for the general, but he reviewed carefully each report, knew intimate details of all, and could recite almost instantly important provisions of significant documents. Nothing escaped his interest. Operational planning obviously concerned the commanding general; logistics became an alternate interest; personnel assignments he watched with professional eye. No technical subject defied his ken; esoteric topics simply piqued his attention. Specialists were often confounded by "JJP's" close awareness of their activities.

Scrutiny often discomfits, and some staff officers complained that the Old Man kibitzed too much. There were problems. For the most part the officers who came on the *Baltic* and who had slowly clustered since headquarters opened in Paris were a good lot, youngish, eager, teachable. But they were inexperienced and awkward in their jobs, unpracticed in the ways of big armies. Consequently Pershing held fairly tight rein, tighter than he wanted. And because every responsibility rested squarely on his big shoulders, he delegated with caution. In the early going, prudence dictated that he edit all documents from headquarters; he wrote many, including all general orders.[13]

---

[11] See *ibid.*, June 25, 1917; JJP, *Experiences*, 1:81–86.

[12] James G. Harbord, *Serving With Pershing*, p. 13.

[13] JJP, Memo for the AG, AEF, Apr. 11, 1918, AEF, GHQ, Office of the CIC, File 16118, RG 120, National Archives; James G. Harbord, *Leaves From a War Diary*, p. 124.

Frankie would have seen the symptoms, worked the magic cure of caring—those hours of close detail, the dragging meetings, the constant compulsion to politeness drained the patience of a robust man. He longed for Nita, for a woman's soothing, for a remembered understanding. The fullness of his need he confessed to no one, not even Georgie Patton. Now in the lofty confines of full command, human weakness must be denied, male anxieties ignored in an aura of aloof assurance. At the pinnacle of military power Jack anguished alone. His kind of loneliness a few others shared—high commanders on the Western Front. Earlier in the war leaders had failed and fallen, their perches taken by followers soon their equals in isolation and responsibility. Colleagues in command all knew the precarious footholds of power. Joffre, ever quick to relieve incompetents and himself at last a victim of attrition, warned Foch of fame's brevity and guessed Pershing's tenure might be long but troubled and ultimately severed.[14]

What solace could a high commander take? Nivelle had apparently feasted on visions of glory, and, when they faded, his life quenched. Falkenhayn yielded high command but kept an army and a part in the war—war was his life. Sir John French, misfit from littler wars, crept home to the comforts of promotion to figurehead. In his months of rejection after the Somme, Foch buried himself in work and plans and accepted the role of chief of staff in 1917 with professional assurance. Pétain, called to command the Armies of the North and Northwest and to minimize the wreckage of Verdun's shocks, received word of his assignment while enjoying the charms of a *fille de joie* in Paris—women were his pleasure.[15] But these were veterans of long anguish. What might a novice commander be allowed as diversion from decision?

Some old Calvinism joined with a nice grasp of the fitness of things to shape John Pershing's personal and official lives in France. He would meet friends, special ones, when he could, would try for such normal society as responsibility allowed, but would strive for an image of ruthless worker, try to be an example for the whole AEF.

He could at least be comfortable. The rue Constantine accommodations were tight, the location really inconvenient. Something larger, more accessible, would be welcome. One of the most accomplished and unobstrusive members of the staff, Maj. Robert Bacon, gentleman, diplomat, friend to almost everyone, reported with typical diffidence an offer of quarters that seemed suitable. Ogden Mills, a rich American whose French connections were large and affectionate, had offered

[14] B. H. Liddell Hart, *Reputations Ten Years After*, p. 167.
[15] See Alistair Horne, *The Price of Glory: Verdun, 1916*, pp. 136–37.

his palatial residence at 73, rue de Varenne, for Pershing's use during the war. Once the residence of Napoleon's Marshal Lannes and one of the magnificent townhouses of Europe, the mansion was set in a garden to charm Louis XIV. Would the general accept the palace as residence, office, and site of American business?[16]

Ostentation seemed a problem. Too many people thought Americans too affluent; how could America's general preach a hard war from a soft berth? Good question, but easily smothered. America's position as powerful ally demanded some show of wealth, some pomp to match aims. And Pershing's schedule would squelch rumors of oriental languor! "After a certain amount of deliberation"[17] Jack accepted the house with pleasure—and vastly pleased Robert Bacon, as well as Ogden Mills.[18]

Lovely and welcoming, the Mills's house charmed visitors with reckless abandon. Americans of all ilks who were in Paris without purpose suddenly decided to aid the war and flocked the manse for guidance. Pershing's known opposition to mere spongers deterred a few of the volunteers, but they finally bulked to problem size. Work out a policy, Pershing told his staff, and soon regulations commanded U.S. citizens from Allied armies, voluntary organizations such as the Red Cross, and simple tourists yearning to stay.[19]

Other visitors fragmented the commanding general's time. French and British officials must be met and soothed; Allied businessmen with legitimate interests for the U.S. Army—such men as Herman Harjes, long-time Paris resident and member of the Morgan, Harjes financial firm—had to be welcomed. And personal friends who called for old time's sake, or on Papa Warren's introduction, what of them? There were a few acquaintances scattered in France who had known Jack over the years; most were diffident about imposing, a few wrote notes of distant welcome, one put welcome with charming abnegation: "When I was a little girl, I was in your class in geometry and you gave me some fencing lessons. You have always been an object of extreme admiration and pride for our family. Brother Jim and his wife . . . are never through talking about you. They were both of them under your instruction. You may remember. I want to add my welcome to France. . . . " Signed by Dorothy Canfield Fisher, the note brought a whole

[16] See James G. Harbord, *Personalities and Personal Relationships in the American Expeditionary Forces*, p. 6.
[17] Richard O'Connor, *BJP*, p. 167.
[18] James Brown Scott, *Robert Bacon: Life and Letters*, p. 283.
[19] HAEF Diary, June 30, 1917.

block of life back in view—the genial, bespectacled chancellor of Nebraska's university and his affectionate family; Dorothy, the precocious girl who sat in math with the now widely known novelist Willa Cather. No door of Mills's palace would be closed to Dorothy. Come, Pershing wrote her at her duty station with the French War Blind, come to Paris, come to a meal. She did, to breakfast at the Crillon in late June, and talked of home and friends and of the hope of the world fixed on the former lieutenant of Nebraska's cadets. That touch of the past somehow seemed to knit a life together, to connect all the agonies, heartbreaks, all losses and honors to the purpose of the present. Jack had faced bullies and challengers before and won; Dorothy basked in the coming of the right man for victory. She was charming, reassuring—and touched that old gallantry. Business had crowded women—even Nita —from consciousness for weeks; Parisian ladies in super abundance had intimidated rather than beckoned, but Dorothy touched the flirt in Jack and brought a twinkle to cold blue eyes.[20]

If anyone noticed a special verve lighting Pershing's eye, it would have been George Patton. He and Pershing talked of Nita through a late night's chat in June. Relaxed and easy with an old confidant, Pershing expanded in conversation to touch on U-boats, American mobilization, and finally on the chances of Nita's coming over. He suspected, ruefully, she ought not come; it would hardly do to have the commanding general's lady arrive just when he was urging no passports for dependents.[21] But he wanted her to come desperately, and George was amused and touched by his chief's emotion: "It certainly is the most intense case I have ever seen."[22] It proved a rare lapse into personal longing.

At HAEF staff members learned Pershing's symptoms of fatigue— the deep gruffness, the baleful eye, the swift complaint. But they learned, too, the ways to run an army. During the weeks since they all left Washington, the general had tinkered with staff organization. Compared to the entourage clustering at other Allied headquarters, Pershing brought a corporal's guard to France. His small coterie of planners had worked overtime to devise the General Organization Project with Baker's commission; that chore done, the staff had shifted to local concerns, to matters of frontage, logistics, training, to difficulties of coalition warfare.

[20] Dorothy Canfield Fisher to JJP, June 15, 1917, Box 29, PP; JJP, *Experiences*, 1:74.
[21] JJP, *Experiences*, 1:105; Blumenson, *Patton Papers*, p. 401.
[22] Blumenson, *Patton Papers*, p. 402.

Coalitions were new to Americans whose only real experience with allies ran back to the Revolution—and history upheld an old American initiative. Increasing concerns forced Pershing to revise staff structures. Originally American practice indicated that the General Staff activities might be divided among three components—Administration, Intelligence, and Operations. But even limited experience, combined with Allied advice, indicated an organization geared to five broad functions —G-1: Administrative Policy; G-2: Intelligence; G-3: Operations; G-4: Training; G-5: Coordination.[23] All these sections plus the technical staffs for logistics functioned directly under the commanding general through the chief of staff, and Jack arranged trustworthy chiefs for each section. Harbord, who rose in competence with each crisis, remained as chief of staff. As his secretary of the General Staff, Harbord appointed friend Frank McCoy, a regular cavalry major who would meet any emergency with cool determination. Jim Logan, thirty-seven, boasting a silver leaf, headed the Administrative Section; his years in the Quartermaster Corps fitted him for army administration, but he had the saving imagination to ignore pernicious regulations. Lt. Col. Dennis E. Nolan, forty-five, class of '96, long-time infantryman shifted to the General Staff Corps in 1915, ran the Intelligence Section with growing guile. Nervous John Palmer, forty-eight, class of '92, nearing his eagles, rode herd on a brilliant corps of Operations planners, including deputy Fox Conner. Training activities, G-4, came under the close control of Lt. Col. Paul B. Malone, forty-five, class of '94, graduate of the Army School of the Line and the Staff College, who shaped up recruits with an infantryman's zest. Lt. Col. William D. Connor, forty-three, class of '97, ran the Coordination Section with an engineer's precision.[24]

Each department head commanded staffs of varying size and competence, and the overall expectations were extremely professional. The same high performance could be expected of the technical bureau heads, the men who served as AEF adjutant general, inspector general, judge advocate, chief quartermaster, chief surgeon, chief engineer officer, chief ordnance officer, chief signal officer, chief of air service, provost marshal general. Most of these men were known to Pershing

[23] Army War College, *Order of Battle of the United States Land Forces*, p. 5 n.; Historical Division, Department of the Army, *United States Army in the World War, 1917–1919*, 16:14 (hereinafter cited as *USWW*).

[24] For the staff department heads, see *Army Register, 1918*; James G. Harbord, *The American Army in France, 1917–1919*, p. 97.

or Harbord, sometimes to both, and came with high marks from those old autocrats of Washington, the bureau chiefs.

No bureaucrat by service or temperament, Pershing nonetheless knew the need for careful martial management. His own experience, combined with Allied advice, showed how far war had strayed from history. Old glories of personal leadership vanished in the snarl of men, material, and mass—small chance came now for high commanders to command anything save experts and statistics. Precedents long solid in most armies crumbled in the new realities of France. The Haigs and Pétains and Pershings filled new and perilous executive positions that seemed often somehow tangential to the fighting—they were elevated above the battlefield to an oddly savage arena of logistics, diplomacy, and mutual persuasion. Their new roles sometimes chafed, sometimes conflicted with soldier's intuition, and often nudged them too closely to politics, but they were a new breed of leaders who made daily precedent.

A good deal of his new job Pershing grasped clearly; its full dimensions he would learn. While learning, he would rely on methods that had worked for him before.

In Mexico his small staff had functioned in familial ease, the members attuned to the chief's personality. Pershing ran a tight organization, but listened for all shades of view. Finally he made his decision and the staff implemented it—but full consultation brought unity and understanding. In France Pershing relied increasingly on consultation. In a way this reliance reflected the Western Front "conference syndrome" that found all high commanders proliferating committees in a kind of desperate diffusion of decisions. But unlike many commanders who nursed the dread of disaster, Pershing used committees to shape his thought, not supplant it. And as AEF business burgeoned and committees multiplied, he learned to listen through Harbord's ear. From the chief of staff's daily meetings with his assistants, Pershing kept posted on the general state of the AEF.

High morale showed the health of headquarters, the confidence in success, the self-esteem of a staff that grew in competence with each challenge. Harbord, a fairly tough judge of subordinates, rated his henchmen "a most efficient body of highly qualified officers." Morale and enthusiasm might reflect ignorance, however, and Pershing would not know fully the virtues of his staff until the test of battle.[25] Until

[25] See Harbord, *American Army*, pp. 95–98.

that test he would watch how well his chosen few learned from Allied counterparts the mysteries of organization, supply, and training.

Pawn between Allies

Competition encouraged British and French courting of American affections. Pershing's argument that oceanic comradeship with the British made shore friendship with the French essential seemed logical to Americans and Frenchmen—it soothed few feathers of Albion. Quickly Americans noted the crippling rift weakening the Allied cause in France. Napoleon had disdained coalitions, and the thinly veiled contempt abrading Franco-British relations seemed to confirm the Corsican's wisdom once again. A close glimpse revealed that contempt rankled mainly at high levels. *Poilus* and Tommies fought Germans and left backyard squabbling to generals. Combat brought tolerance to fighters and a cynical acceptance of silliness at the top.

Lofty idiocy had its inconvenient side; sometimes it cost the lives of soldiers and sometimes it aggravated difficulties of survival. In the summer of 1917 it threatened to fragment American strength and fritter Yankee determination. Specifically idiocy that summer caught Americans between two eager swains untrammeled by restraint. Whichever won America's support on the Western Front would boast success in bloated battalions. France had a head start. Plans lingering from early days of Joffre's mission to America proposed places and programs for Doughboy use in the Lorraine sector. Assiduous cultivation, careful flattery, and shameless resort to sentiment welded an old affection of common cause. Outside stood the British, long storied foemen and strange in Allied garb. It was a dangerous distortion of history, but strangely strong. And it took obvious forms. For instance, Pershing had been warned early by American military liaison men in London that he ought to visit French officials in strength before he turned to Haig and British armies. After all, the visit to London, the adulations of king and country, offered sop enough to English spirit. France needed attention, proof of some kind of worth, puffing of the ego in a time of deflation. It made sense and it made trouble.[26]

But an old call of blood combined with profound interest in British

[26] See Lt. Col. James A. Logan to JJP, Paris, June 3, 1917, in AEF, GHQ, Off. CIC Correspondence, File 21510, RG 120, National Archives: "I believe it would be better for you not to call on Sir Douglas Haig before you see the French authorities. . . . I am afraid that if you do not do this, you may perhaps 'hurt' the French sensibilities."

operations urged a visit to the northern front. Amidst a mass of paper work at rue Constantine, Pershing had easily postponed departing the capital after the Saint Nazaire excursion. As organization of headquarters and the staff departments continued, he decided he must learn more of Haig's procedures. British system many American observers lavishly praised, and part of it might be borrowed.

Before the trek to Saint Omer and Headquarters of the British Armies in France, one more Parisian ceremony claimed American presence—Bastille Day. The special attention lavished on July Fourth activities compelled similar attention to France's great holiday. In Paris, though, Bastille Day took on oddly American trappings—more people cheered and applauded John Pershing than the French officials who tended the tokens of remembrance. Embarrassed but game, Jack did plucky duty as President Poincaré's guest through a morning of sentiment. Special reviews and presentations of the croix de guerre and Crosses of the Legion of Honor rewarded new heroes on that old occasion. Jack watched the parade of martial colors by 11,000 veterans with a practiced, appreciative eye—it was, he said, "an inspiring sight."[27]

For impressionable Jim Harbord the day ran far beyond inspiring —it almost matched the glory of his chieftain. At the Trocadero in the afternoon, Harbord basked warmly in Pershing's prominence. Watching the Franco-American celebration in that famed theater, he recorded that when Pershing, the American ambassador, the military governor of Paris, and the prince of Monaco filed into their box the audience— 3,000 strong—erupted in frenzied glee. On stage the aged Camille Saint-Saëns, fabled composer, played his own music and was encored gustily. The inevitable tableau of Tricolor and Old Glory stood the audience for national anthems.

That day the 26th U.S. Infantry left Saint Nazaire for Gondrecourt.[28]

Music and flags and shouted troths rang falsely to Pershing. He wanted to attack the problems of coalition, to define bounds of American participation, and to discover how much independence had been bartered from him by events—and previous secret agreements. In endless gatherings of Allied leaders, gatherings often aimed as much at mutual comfort as on serious war planning, a few real crises were faced. Russia's shocking instability boded the imminent collapse of a great ally; creeping decay among Italian troops beckoned help to the south. Although diversions from the Western Front might please an anti-

[27] JJP, *Experiences*, 1:105.
[28] See *ibid.*; Harbord, *American Army*, pp. 108–9; HAEF Diary, July 14, 1917.

trench man like Lloyd George, the new prospects of frittered strength were hardly encouraging, especially with the chances growing that Germany could soon concentrate many eastern divisions in France. Old Allied hands read the import of the future; they were, consequently, pardonably urgent in wanting American help put directly on the threatened front. And the loom of danger forgave, partially, the rising call for filtering American troops into tried Allied units. That really was the quickest way to use these big, healthy, optimistic men so eager for the fray. Yet how urgent was the need? How honestly did British and French fear the chances of holding lines? To an old Moro negotiator customed to nuance, the arguments from both sounded more jealous than scared. There was, for instance, a matter of spacing. French discussions had pushed American eyes toward Lorraine, had induced the visitation to Gondrecourt and Valdahon, and staff consultations supported the location. But British fancies ran otherwise. Aware of the peculiar American affinity for helping France, British government and army leaders schemed ways to purloin at least some of Pershing's divisions.

Some of Haig's staff—the marshal kept a decent distance from such conniving—suggested that American forces might be inserted between the French and British on the Western Front. Two obvious advantages sprang from this possibility: the British right would be anchored by troops likely to learn proper fighting ways, and the fading French would be separated from the British by younger, more eager hands. It was a typical plan of military snobs and was boasted by staff nabobs who enjoyed some contempt for Americans, much for the French.

French intelligence flourished in British clubs; the plan for a Yankee buffer zone leaked quickly and brought swift countermaneuver. Pershing's plans for Lorraine were encouraged, his desires concerning port and railroad facilities were soothed with promises, and he heard subtle litanies on the perfidies of Albion.[29]

An inherent embarrassment clouded America's position in the war —the role of Associated Power. Short of full ally, she could join the crusade and cavil at its sacrifices. Woodrow Wilson's careful avoidance of tainted partnership apparently stemmed from some lurking Calvinist morality that put America above the horrors of war. Pershing and his shadow legions denied the total of Wilson's wishes, but his ill-

[29] See General Vignal to the French Minister of War, Washington, July 8, 1917, in Records of the Quai d'Orsay, Etats-Unis, Armée Américaine, 1:163–64; Maj. Gen. "Tavish" Davidson to Lt. Col. C. M. Wagstaff, British GHQ, Dec. 13, 1917, in Papers of Douglas Haig, National Library of Scotland, Edinburgh.

concealed contempt for mass war irked all his "associates" aligned against the Hun. The anomaly of Pershing's job robbed him of his fullest powers, made him and his army more easily bait for Allied hooks, and almost achieved Wilson's worst fear that the AEF might become a makeweight in French and British politics.

Pershing, whose political perspicacity many missed to their detriment, recognized how easily he and his men might be squandered as pawns to Allied expediency. Close reading of war news since 1914 would alert any American to Lloyd George's obligation to win at almost any constitutional cost[30] and showed the thin stability of the coalition. Britain's mandate to its new tribune ran clear, but the prime minister juggled relations with Wully Robertson and Douglas Haig. First their supporter, he turned at bay after their assured victory at the Somme dissolved in British blood. Now that canny Welshman looked for surrogates for British bodies—and Americans might just do. In France, Prime Minister Ribot writhed in the despair of Nivelle's failed drive on the Aisne; his government rested, really, on stemming mutiny in the ranks. America thrust swiftly into Lorraine battles would delay the Germans, revive the nation, and renew a sense of *gloire*. On either side Americans might be pawns to survival.

Pershing rejected a pawn's role for himself, his country, and his army. Against that demeaning chance he cast his full authority and his unexpected determination. First lessons in Missouri patience he gave at Saint Omer in Flanders.

Pershing's visit to Headquarters, British Armies in France, followed in wake of careful preparations. George Patton, still clinging to the periphery of an aideship, still making himself as useful as possible, stood handy when the general began serious planning of the trip to Sir Douglas Haig's establishment. To Patton and to one of Bill Lassiter's brightest attachés, George Quekemeyer, Harbord gave a quick and hectic assignment—find the best route to the British. At 4:30 on Saturday afternoon, July 7, the two young officers piled into an auto and struck north.

Out of Paris the country splayed beautifully into rolling hills and streams and blends of green and brown. The happy scapes of Picardy lured the Americans onward toward Artois as gloom settled over slopes of land long anguished by men and blood and iron. Roads declined to tracks churned by guns and animals and the endless coils of infantry.

[30] A. J. P. Taylor, "Politics in the First World War," *Proceedings of the British Academy* 45 (1959): 86–95.

Slitted headlights lost battles with the night and speed slackened in uncertainty. But young men shared hopes and ambitions, not worries.

Patton and Quekemeyer liked each other. A year and a half separated their ages; they had overlapped at West Point, with "Quek" receiving his commission in 1906, Patton in 1909. Patton's California aggressiveness blunted against Quekemeyer's Mississippi manners.

Around 10:00 P.M. they rolled into British headquarters brimming with sightseers' comments—columns of British, Canadian, and Australian troops had shared roads with them in twilight and the friendly dark—and they eagerly boasted the better looks of the British. Although they came late, they forged their own welcome with a fresh and open naïveté so different from war-jaded Britons at headquarters. Both were strong and manly men. Patton's piercing glance caught both facts and others' eyes; Quekemeyer's tall frame, his dark, handsome face etched with a Pershing-type moustache—he looked much like his new chieftain—and his quick courtesy attracted notice and almost masked his measuring mind. Hungry, they rummaged for food and companionship, and they soon found themselves fascinated by the urbane and witty Gen. John Charteris, who headed Haig's Intelligence. Taking especially to Quekemeyer's southern mein, the general chatted through a hasty dinner, checked roads with the visitors, suggested that if his new Mississippi friend were to return as liaison, they might mess together. Then again into the roiling black the young Americans went, for a six-hour plunge to Paris.[31]

Equipped with a map carefully marked by his scouts, steeped in their lore of the north country, estimates of British capacities, and first impressions of some of Haig's staff, Pershing left for Saint Omer on July 24. It was a Saturday, clear and balmy, and Harbord, Col. Ben Alvord, Patton, and Quekemeyer climbed with Pershing into two cars (Pershing's bearing Patton's hasty blazon "U.S. No. 1"). The general told Lanckton to unleash the drivers, and they lurched toward the war.[32]

Up through Saint Denis the road led and triggered Harbord's latent romance. His unexpected historical knowledge sparkled as he recalled old kings of France, the Hundred Years War, and fierce moments of the Revolution. "Our journey lay through rolling hills and valleys," Harbord remarked, "through a land smiling with summer crops." Like ave-

[31] See Blumenson, *Patton Papers*, p. 404, and George Quekemeyer to his mother, Paris, July 10, 1917, Quekemeyer Papers, Yazoo City, Miss.

[32] See Harbord, *American Army*, p. 112; Blumenson, *Patton Papers*, p. 407; Quekemeyer to his mother, Paris, July 18, 1917, Quekemeyer Papers.

nues the roads ran, bordered each with straight lines of trees, and the vista was tunneled and green. But to Harbord the view was ghostly with Napoleon's legions, the trees there "to facilitate the parallel marching of his columns. . . ."

An arboreal reverie broke finally as the big autos encountered French troops on the road and passed some rest camps for *poilus*. The white label on the car snapped sentries to salute, brought waves of interest through much of Picardy. In Artois, where the war was harder, French troops looked worn but responded on sight. Finally into the British sector as Flanders approached, the Americans noted wear but not special tear. British discipline showed in the smartness of salutes, the quick formations and stiff officer punctilio. Through Beauvais Pershing's expedition ran, on to Abbeville and the Somme, then near the Channel coast to Montreuil—not far from the popular old British tourist port of Le Touquet. Two stops en route slowed arrival to a decent time.

Almost at noon the Americans pulled up at one of Montreuil's gates and were met by a stiff and proper aide who brandished a "program" for the visit. First there was an inspection of the Guard of Honor, composed of elements of the Ancient and Honorable Artillery Company of London, resting at Montreuil after a month in the line; next, luncheon, then a visit to the staff organizations at this huge second-echelon headquarters.

Among the first hosts to appear came Lieutenant General Fowke, adjutant general of the British Armies in France and old crony of Pershing's from Manchuria days, who had been among the Boulogne greeters. Jovially he bade the Americans welcome, escorted them to a courtyard where the "very smart-looking" guard of honor presented arms, then showed them around the military secretary's offices and whisked them two miles to his quarters for lunch. Pershing and Harbord flanked Fowke, the talk ran easily and sometimes reminiscently, the food steamed tempting odors, and the Americans ate with the gusto of the road.[33]

After lunch Fowke threw his departmental offices open to inspection, handed the inquisitive Americans on to the quartermaster general. Myriad "sections" sprawled through the old French military school serving as staff headquarters. Quartermaster operations included almost everything. Harbord, who felt diminutive in rank and stature

[33] Harbord, *American Army*, p. 112. The initial visit to Montreuil is covered in *ibid.*, pp. 111–13; Harbord, *Diary*, pp. 104–5; JJP, *Experiences*, 1:111–12; Quekemeyer to his mother, Paris, July 18, 1917, Quekemeyer Papers.

compared with all the brigadiers heading sections—he noted how "topping" and brawny the British stood compared, even, with General Pershing—gawked at the puzzles of transport and supply. "There is, for example," he noted, "one section devoted entirely to getting forward ammunition. A brigadier general is chief of a labor section, handling laborers of eleven races; Chinese, Indians, even nations of the Fiji Islands are included. In one section graphics are applied to the ammunition supply: a vertical line representing the rounds fired by every gun, enabling a curve to be constructed showing consumption of artillery [ammunition] by periods."[34]

Pershing's calculating eye consumed the various offices. He noted approvingly the quick interest of his officers, heard their intelligent questions, and compared American and British organizations. There were tangents, familiar echoes. It was hardly surprising, since "our military system had been practically copied from the British a century and a half earlier," but this war and intervening ones wrought expansions and improvements. Jack took consolation in the things he recognized.[35]

His officers swarmed the staff departments; especially they concentrated on the maze of British records that kept so many armies so handy to general headquarters. Here there were really new techniques to learn. But Jack shuffled in anticipation of getting on to Saint Omer. Harbord could admire with the British quartermaster general Montreuil's ramparts, could muse about the Hundred Years War and Henry V's archers possibly stalking the walls, but Haig waited, and so did Jack.

Impatient Pershing was, but aware of the good impression his intelligent officers made, aware of the surprised pleasure the British took in American knowledge of Europe's history. He fussed just enough to shake the expedition loose.[36]

An hour's ride through lowering dusk, through ordered roads of lorries and lines of men, showed a rear zone well organized and compact. German prisoners could be glimpsed tilling fields en route. At last came a column different in dress and manner, dark men who looked with Latin frankness at the khaki cars of Americans. Portuguese, the hosting British aide announced, adding that an individual soldier would be called a "Portugoose." With that sally, the party chuckled until at last Saint Omer hove in view. On through the town the cars were sent,

[34] Harbord, *Diary*, pp. 105–6.
[35] JJP, *Experiences*, 1:112.
[36] Harbord, *Diary*, p. 106.

on to a superb grove of great trees and to a gem of a chateau nestled among them—Blendecques, Douglas Haig's residence. Smaller than Ogden Mills's mansion, it had a curious ordered elegance that touched callers with respect. Out in front of the entrance stood a group, and, as the cars rolled to a stop, a smallish man, dapper in the perfectly fitted uniform of an officer, strode forward with a measured, friendly smile. His long face made almost somber by a clipped moustache and deep-set eyes, his frame taut in nervous courtesy, the man seemed somehow eager and remote. Tabs on his tunic collar and pips on his shoulders marked him a field marshal. This graying, tended dandy was Sir Douglas Haig.

He greeted Pershing as a friend, almost an equal, shook hands with Harbord and smiled, gave the other staff over to his own retinue, and escorted the American commander to rooms for the night. Would the travelers care to freshen up? They would, of course, dress for dinner. There was an English week-end quality to the meeting, a sylvan tranquility marred only by the low and constant rumble of the front.

Dinner had that peculiar comradely formality of a British college common room, with the field marshal at the head of the table, much as the senior fellow, his senior staff members circling in junior descent, his guests seated with regard to rank. Pershing and Harbord flanked him; Alvord, Patton, and the others scattered amid British generals. Conversation flowed easily as the wine, but Harbord still pinched in a lieutenant colonel's discomfort—"to an officer of the American Army where rank has never . . . been commensurate with command . . . there seemed a great many Generals"[37]—and he was surprised at Haig's cordiality to so junior a man. Haig kept his guests engaged and entertained with talk of French problems, of Nivelle's offensive and the total lack of security before it was launched, of the grinding battles in Flanders that had kept some pressure from the French, battles that had wasted more Britons than Frenchmen that summer—175,000 men—and had inched the line forward a bit.[38] Preparations bustled for resumption of attack.

While the marshal chatted, his staff filled their newfound allies with stories of past British glories, of the problems involved in preparing an attack on the Western Front; the details astounded men still really unaware of the monstrous maw of war. Trenchlines lay in reluctant permanence, sometimes wracked by some reflexive spasm; dirt and death, a dailiness well known. But behind those nervous, static boundaries of

[37] Harbord, *American Army*, p. 112.
[38] JJP, *Experiences*, 1:113.

the war the "rear areas" seethed with activity unguessed by men holding the firing steps. There, behind the fighters, war now was geared and waged. Sustaining eighty miles of trenchline required a mighty British effort of procurement, transport, management, and distribution. At Montreuil the maze of records wrote the story of organization, of a system bloated beyond all chance of martial movement, a system aimed at bringing men and material to the trenches, at feeding and clothing and arming them, at bandaging and encouraging and burying them, at replacing blasted, lost, and worn equipment, at simply holding long ditches against Germans and rain and heat and cold, at pressing outward Britain's banners with all the trove of home. And if the British effort seemed gargantuan, the French seemed greater still, for they held more than 300 miles of line. Somewhere in that belt of conflict the Americans must go. Had they the foggiest of the job ahead?

As they listened they got some slight notion, and the awesome complexity defied belief. But that small dawning of reality encouraged Haig and his men. Pershing seemed a man with beguiling eagerness to learn. More, he had a "quiet gentlemanly bearing—so unusual for an American"—that enabled him to listen.[39] The American general might have picked better assistants; Harbord and Alvord seemed "men of less quality" than their chief, ignorant of modern war. One alone among them caught Haig's special eye—George Patton, "The A.D.C. is a fire-eater! and longs for the fray."[40]

That old country gentility comforted another English morning as the American visitors straggled to breakfast on Saturday. Each man walked a great long table, helped himself to bacon, eggs, fish, and a brigade of British breads, then found a linened place gleaming with proper service. Slowly came a khaki crowd; conversation buzzed about the war, the churlish weather, the food. A quick hush, a shuffle to stand, and Haig arrived to choose his breakfast. That courtly moment lingered briefly in the soft haze of morning, and then the war returned.[41]

Pershing's schedule looked hectic. Impressed with the importance of organization at each command level, he wanted first to see how Haig's headquarters functioned; he would enjoy a guided tour under Maj. Gen. R. H. K. Butler, assistant chief of staff. When the progress through all offices ended, Butler gave Pershing and his staff a detailed briefing on general staff procedures. In the afternoon the British suggested a visit to a field army staff and escorted Pershing's party to Gen.

[39] Diary of Field Marshal Sir Douglas Haig, July 20, 1917, Haig Papers.
[40] *Ibid.*
[41] See Harbord, *Dairy,* p. 109.

Sir Herbert Plumer's II Army headquarters at Cassel. With Plumer absent in England, the army was temporarily commanded by the senior corps commander, but the army's chief of staff, Maj. Gen. Charles Harrington, answered every question and arranged a working luncheon.

A close inspection showed the army staff organized as at Saint Omer but on a smaller scale. Operations and intelligence were busy, but logistics ran the show. As afternoon gathered and a bluish haze hung over a bleak world, the Americans drove to a tiny clutch of Belgium for a visit with the corps commander, Lieutenant General Morland, and a glimpse of corps staffwork. Cordial and typically helpful, Morland put Harbord and Alvord with his own staff chiefs. To Pershing, the veteran commander talked of corps functions and coordination of subordinate divisions. In the midst of instruction came the inevitable five o'clock interlude with tea. The sudden appearance of Gen. Tom Bridges, who trekked over from his 19th Division, brought happy memories of early war days in Washington—and proved the full success of British staff planning.[42]

Dinner at eight back at Saint Omer sparkled with excitement. Haig's innate courtesy expanded to cordiality. His private stock of Haig and Haig—he owned part of the distillery—flowed freely with congenial talk. Putting his newfound fighting friend Patton on his right, Haig waxed warmly for sabers and for cavalry and won an adoring ally. To Pershing the field marshal confided the reason for enthusiasm—the British cabinet had finally discovered the inevitable and agreed to his plan for a great Flanders drive toward Passchendaele. The lulling bombardment, now a forgotten background to conversation, was early preparation for the battle Haig had known he would fight.[43]

There were problems to the drive—problems stemming from a fractured alliance. "What a nuisance these French are," Haig commented, as he scolded their timidity. Apparently France's generals shared her politicians' hope for peace without further price. Rumors of Austria's disaffection charmed Paris and combined with absurd dreams of Bavarian and Saxon secession to banish thoughts of attack. Haunts following Nivelle shattered France's fragile élan.

On Sunday morning, July 22, Pershing saw a new dimension to

[42] For the day, see *ibid.*, pp. 109–10; JJP, *Experiences*, 1:114–15; Harbord, *American Army*, p. 115; Blumenson, *Patton Papers*, p. 408 (where the timing is confusing).

[43] Haig Diary, July 21, 23, 1917, Haig Papers. For Haig's private stock, see Memoir of John P. Frey, p. 5, Oral History Collection, Columbia University.

attack preparations. Gen. Hugh Trenchard, commanding the Royal Flying Corps, took the Americans in charge that morning—off they went for a visit to a working airdrome, base repair shops, and all the paraphenalia of modern sky fighting. Patton's eyes bulged at the spit and bustle everywhere, the bulboid "sausages," hanging almost obscenely in the air around the Royal Flying Corps's base of operations. Harbord's eyes bulged at the forty-five-year-old major general running the RFC. Bristling with un-British zest, Trenchard pushed himself and all his men to a kind of frenzied compulsion. Staffers whispered to the visitors parts of Trenchard's growing legend—in the early days of the war, for instance, when nobody in London guessed anything about the nature of fighting, he had waded into heavy machinery plants and ordered aircraft engines by the thousands. Authority? His own seemed enough—at least his certainty carried through.[44] His enthusiasm infused the RFC; his men followed blindly his gaze to the future. And he ran a loose but superb organization.

Pershing's eyes swept the giant repair shops, approved the quick "attention" he got in each building, watched as Trenchard's pleasantries returned everyone happily to work. Mechanics, carpenters, new specialists flocked wrecked planes, studied captured enemy machines for new ideas, and salvaged far more than they scrapped. Impressive? Certainly. And depressing. How pitiful Foulois's little Mexican squadron seemed in comparison, almost antique and comical. Those shrewd Missouri eyes betrayed none of the dismay Pershing felt. Well he knew how the Allies looked to America for clouds of planes, expected miracles from Yankee factories; well he knew, too, that there were no clouds, not even a thin mist of modern combat ships to come. As the RFC's efficiency glistened in both men and equipment, Pershing's humiliation grew.[45]

Shops and organization touched Jack's special soul, but his heart went with the young men with wings. Boys they seemed, but their exploits—recounted always by others—ran timeless and heroic. One drew the chance to show General Pershing what his ship could do. It looked capable of anything, "climbing nearly vertically, looping loops in either direction, spinning 'nose-dives' as though falling from hundreds of feet," and showed Jack how far aeronautics outran American technology.

[44] Harbord, *Diary*, p. 110.

[45] See JJP, *Experiences*, 1:159. A school just established at Fort Sill, Okla., would train forty pilots a month (see E. L. Spiers to War Office, July 25, 1917, in AEF WO 106/468/E.L.S. 116, pt. 3, no. 91, Public Records Office, London.

Spirit, though, smartened the whole corps. "Incomparable," Pershing thought the morale of the young men he met. "Every man seemed to be disappointed when a flight of planes departed for the front without him." Trenchard's own longing ran through his courteous briefings.

Could one of the young men tell about air fighting? Instantly a lad, no more than nineteen, marched forward, snapped to attention, saluted with British spring. It was one of those uncomfortable meetings between commanders and commanded, an encounter between generations and dangers that fractured understanding. But Pershing struggled manfully to learn. "The General asked about his methods of fighting and he didn't seem to have much to say; asked how many he had brought down of Hun planes,—for his reputation in that line was really why they turned him out to talk,—he said 'I really don't know, Sir, fifteen or sixteen.'" Youth burgeoned everywhere. Pershing liked the freshness, but a disgruntled Harbord felt aged.[46]

George Patton, happily tagging with British staff friends, gawked at the balloons awhile, then marveled at the "parishoots" used by the intrepid men who swung in those stationery gondolas that so attracted German fighters. Alvord wondered about organization and listened as boys talked like old generals long in command. Lunch with Trenchard brought musings about youth and mortality and the future of air warfare. The RFC's leader knew the future secure, felt that a new dimension in military surprise lurked aloft.[47]

Exhilarated at war free from trenches, Pershing's party returned in the afternoon to British GHQ for a lengthy session with General Charteris on the Intelligence Service. If the Americans hoped to see real cloaks and daggers around they were disappointed. Instead the cool general who had remade British Military Intelligence introduced endless charts, showed how "nearly every thing is reduced to diagrams." Spies there were, of course, but Military Intelligence concerned itself with front- and rear-area security, with tracking at least 300,000 "suspects" in France and another 6,000 in German-occupied Belgium.[48] As the Operations Section splintered into subsections, so did Intelligence. Complicated at first, Charteris's organization soon came crystal clear. Things he knew of the war and the people waging it on both sides were astounding. It seemed almost impossible that so much might be gleaned from air observation, scanning mail, careful interrogation of

[46] Harbord, *Diary*, pp. 111–12; JJP, *Experiences*, 1:115.
[47] Blumenson, *Patton Papers*, p. 408.
[48] *Ibid.*

prisoners, reading captured documents and enemy newspapers, filtering rumors through neutral sources, and hearing public pronouncements.

Pershing's interest centered on information first hinted at in England, now learned in detail. Much of what he heard represented the most secret knowledge sifted by the British and constituted a rich gift to friends. Some items were ritual: France teetered toward ruin. That fetish charmed all British commanders, apparently, and would not now have impressed Pershing, save for added details. "On a cold mathematical comparison of figures," the British learned, "the position on the Western Front as a whole, and of the French Army in particular, is not such as to give us confidence in any immediate decisive result." Then some sobering statistics: "Our General Staff estimate the combined *combatant* strength of all the Allies on the Western Front at 2,545,500 men (French 1,310,000; British 1,061,300; Belgian 131,000; Portuguese 25,200; Russian 18,000), as compared with 2,149,000 Germans. In field guns the Allies have a great prepondrance, namely, 9,126 to 4,556 German. But in heavy artillery, which has proved of such vital importance in the present war, the Germans still have a superiority, possessing 7,520 weapons of 4.5 inch calibre and above against 6,614 Allied weapons of corresponding calibre." The small numerical superiority, almost half of which could be figured as "a non-homogeneous force," was offset by the heavy gun shortage.

Reserves were the frightening factor.

The rate of wastage of human life in the present War has far exceeded all previous experience and estimates, and . . . no serious offensive operation can be undertaken without a definite provision beforehand to replace casualties on a very large scale. It is just this process that has now become so difficult for France. We estimate that, including both [the] 1918 and 1919 classes, France has in sight a reserve of 510,000 men. At present . . . these reserves are not liquid. . . . The German position, with an estimated million men in her depôts, including the 1918 and 1919 classes, is not enviable, but, having regard to the fact that they are able to stand on the defensive in their elaborate fortifications, and to the lack of fighting on the Russian front, it is better than the French. . . . This reacts on the success of our operations, since we can no longer count on France to draw the German reserves away from the front on which we are attacking, and our task is by so much the more difficult. . . . It was with little surprise . . . that we learned recently that there had been serious, though not widely spread disturbances in certain French regiments, which had come under the influence of pacifist propaganda. . . .[49]

49 See M. P. A. Hankey to the Prime Minister ("Secret"), June 16, 1917, F/23/1/12, Lloyd George Papers, Beaverbrook Library, London. This document

Sufficiently impressed with British pluck versus French *dépérisse-ment*, a solemn company of Americans rode back through Sunday's clear sunlight for dinner with the field marshal.

Gen. Wully Robertson, Chief of the Imperial General Staff, joined the table that night, caught Pershing's full attention, and rambled about manpower. Rumblings from England—Pershing had noted some of them through War Department cables—indicated a struggle between Western Fronters like Haig, Robertson, Secretary of State for War Lord Derby, and the prime minister, who wailed over casualties and pointed with horror to the costs of 1917. Robertson that evening talked straight about numbers. British capacity to replenish losses waned. Still, there had been results, said that tough former enlisted man. Heavy losses on the enemy, some advances into his lines, that sort of thing. "It was obvious," a bemused Pershing noted, "that the serious aspect of the general situation had not noticeably dampened their [the British] aggressive spirit." Apparently they ignored their own concern for reserves.[50] It was a national trait, this rising above distress, and never did it show more brilliantly—or uncomfortably—than that night.

After dinner the guests lingered in the garden. Pershing and Haig walked together in deep converse; their staffs and orderlies drew close in growing acquaintance. A different roar filtered through the British bombardment, then a higher screaming sound, a booming explosion, and dirt, grass, dignity erupted near Blendecques. Sergeant Lanckton, who had been chatting with Haig's orderly, dove for the palace "without a thought about my General." He and Haig's men finally grew ashamed as later bombs fell farther away. "We looked out on the lawn and there stood both Generals Haig and Pershing, seeming unconcerned, talking along as if nothing were happening." Carefully Lanckton snuck back to his duties, pierced by one long glimpse from an all-seeing blue eye. But Pershing said not a word until Monday morning. How, he asked at breakfast, had Lanckton enjoyed the air raid? A few stumbling attempts at a confession Pershing waved aside with a veteran's advice: "Lanckton, bullets have a way of chasing

---

represents Hankey's collection of data for the prime minister's use in persuading Americans of the urgent situation in France. Certainly it was not used at the Charteris briefing, but the same kinds of information were doubtless confided. See, for instance, Harbord's comment (*Diary*, p. 113): "That afternoon we spent with the General Staff at G.H.Q., and were fed up on sacred valuable information destined never to be read by the profane eyes who will possibly scan this journal."

[50] JJP, *Experiences*, 1:113–14.

after those who run." Frank Lanckton tucked that wisdom away for future consolation.[51]

Monday found the Americans heading for British V Army Head-quarters and a day largely in the hospitality of Gen. Sir Hubert de la Poer Gough. Gough's career looked even quicker than Haig's—a meteoric rise to brigadier general had almost ended in the curious Curragh affair in Ireland, but he had emerged bucklered with respect and came into the war the youngest man of his rank in the army. The V Army seemed to flourish as his command. His front looked well or-ganized, the long lorry trains crawling forward were carefully handled, the men slogging toward some forlorn trench were happy enough. In this shell-beaten stretch of the persistent Ypres Salient, mud had subsided into pernicious dust, the sun beat down on khaki with almost colonial spite. Closer to the front than usual, the Americans came to great gouges in the ground, craters from stray long-gun shells that searched British supply lines often.

Lunch with Gough proved companionable and paraded for Yankee view an oddly typical British general in his full glory. Gough, now looking fiftyish, still sported that round, boyish face with its arrogant moustache that kept a hint of lancer dash in his gaze. He was an en-tertainer born and practiced, a man of the moment. While he and his guests ate lunch, an Irish pipe band played outside, the skirling sounds of "The Campbells are Coming" and "The Harp that Once Through Tara's Halls" setting feet atap. No one enjoyed the music more than Jack Pershing. He listened, head moving in time, body arched to dance. For one moment the young lieutenant broke through the years and touched a soldier's blood. "The effect was such," he said, "that I think any of us, with small encouragement, would have tried a jig or a clog dance."[52]

There were war scenes in the afternoon, a camouflage school mys-terious and Merlin-like in product, a great sprawling engineer work-shop that revived maimed machines of Mars. Late in the afternoon Pershing's expedition headed back for Paris.

Pershing had taken leave of Haig in the morning; they had come to some touch with each other, a reach across lands and traditions to fledgling appreciation. When his guests pulled away that dusty Mon-day, Haig made a sober note in his diary: "General Pershing and party left this morning for Fifth Army H. Qrs. They were all very much

[51] Robert Ginsburgh, "Pershing as His Orderlies Know Him," *American Legion Monthly* 5 (Nov., 1928): 55.
[52] JJP, *Experiences*, 1:115–16; Harbord, *Diary*, p. 114.

pleased with their visit, and have begun to realise the great task which lies before them in order to prepare their Army to engage the enemy in battle."[53] That was true enough and yet distorted—for John Pershing had begun to learn the pressures on a pawn.

What other lessons came from the visit? One impression hovered over the conferences: "I had long since held that real teamwork between the . . . [Allies] was almost totally absent."[54] Haig's own resolute drive spoke well for British purpose. If Britain could sustain his massacre tactics, Haig might someday succeed in outbleeding the enemy. But such grinding seemed an awesome waste, an inhuman way to thin humanity. Positive things did linger from the trek to Flanders, of course, things of organization, of staff acquaintances likely to wear well in future, and a deeper knowledge of the massive march of modern war. Old Field Service Regulations of the United States, already outmoded in Mexico, had to be modified to fit Western Front realities. Units were too small on paper, staffs too naïve in outline, tactics too open for the finite trenchlines. Much had been seen and learned from the British, some of it worth borrowing.

As the khaki-colored car marked U.S. No. 1 sped toward Paris, some puzzles charmed the miles. Why so much attention to French perfidies, such conviction of sudden Gallic collapse, combined with inflexible urges forward to unalloyed British triumph? Was this a hint that Americans should hitch their destiny to Albion, link on the British right, and be ready to stem a French retreat when the Germans advanced? How much of this worry reflected natural British xenophobia, how much the distilled terror of experience? Haig talked of his manpower needs, asked openly for American help, suggested cooperation in staff and line training, rehashed arguments about language compatibility and the thickness of Anglo-Saxon blood. But if his staff talked straight, the French stood in most dire need of quick help.

Nothing done back at Blendecques could be taken to token subordination. Sandwiched by Wully Robertson and Haig, exposed to British gallantry and style, Pershing resisted any temptation to blurt promises or hints. Courteous, affable, admiring, always studious, the quiet American departed uncommitted. His careful neutrality made some impression. Suspicions already rife in London of America's favors bestowed on British ships and French soldiers appeared confirmed. Lloyd George told the War Cabinet that "as a counterpoise to ap-

---

[53] Haig Diary, Monday, July 23, 1917, Haig Papers.
[54] JJP, *Experiences*, 1:113.

pease the French, the United States would probably, at least for the present, coöperate with them in military matters."[55]

Paris that July steamed in heat and hostility; the air hung a fetid blanket of animus soaked in fear. Rounds of socials dragged Allied leaders to brittle cordialities. Diplomats, officers, dilettantes gathered in poisonous concourse to spy, gossip, and purvey delicious hints of doom. Through this hectic miasma came finally some distant clang of reason. At last even the British and the French recognized they needed each other, at least until America could inherit the burden of Albion's triumph. Cooperation must come; there would be a conference to that purpose in Paris late in July.

That welcome word Pershing passed to Washington along with requests from various French officials for American participation. Obvious benefits beckoned Yankee presence in the Paris consultations, but Wilson had reservations about admitting hostility to Austria, Bulgaria, or Turkey, and had vigorous objections to any peace dealings. Some lingering stiff-necked honor recalled the picky president of Mexican days, but Wilson had an innate sense of the fittest way for America.

At breakfast with Lloyd George on Thursday, July 26, Pershing told Wilson's reasons and added his own sense that only military matters ought to concern America for the present.[56]

If American ways perplexed the Welsh war horse, they also seemed opportune—America's portion of influence might pass to Britain. With that chance in mind, the prime minister cooperated heartily in arranging separate talks for political and military representatives.

Nothing heard from other Allied leaders rang especially optimistic. Much muttering about Russian demoralization suggested the horrid possibility of a German victory in the East. Faces turned to Pershing, and voices asked for hope. Carefully he told of his cable asking for one million men by the middle of 1918 but dampened rising spirits with sober questions about ships.

[55] Minutes of the British War Cabinet, July 16, 1917, Cab. 23/3, Public Records Office, London.

[56] According to JJP (*Experiences*, 1:116–17), both Ribot and old friend Jules Cambon sought his participation in the Paris talks. He consulted Ambassador Sharp and both arrived at Wilson's view before they heard from the president. See Ray Stannard Baker, *Woodrow Wilson: Life and Letters*, 8:177: "The President [is] unwilling to be represented by conference of all powers engaged in the war, as we are not at war with Austria, Bulgaria or Turkey. Attendance . . . also might give the impression to this country that this Government was discussing not only the conduct of the campaign, but the ultimate purposes having to do with peace terms."

Washington rightly wondered if tonnages could carry a million Americans and feed the British. "By using all shipping which is now in sight for the purpose,"—Pershing was quoting from a fresh War Department message—"the plan proposes to transport to France by June 15, 1918, 21 divisions, comprising about 420,000 men, together with auxiliary troops and replacement troops, line of communication troops, and others, amounting to 214,975 men, making a total of 634,975 men." Into the sighing despond Pershing's clipped midwestern words told harsher dimensions of the truth—"even this schedule could be carried out," he said, "only by a very large increase in tonnage." Timing worked. Pressures and worries broke through conversatism, and some colleagues suggested that more shipping might be available than predicted; perhaps some could be released for American troops. Pershing had guessed as much,[57] but even wild guesses could not conjure ships enough for a million troops. He would push as best he could.

Conferences thrive on consensus, which vitiates initiative. Pershing hardly flinched to hear Wully Robertson, Henri Pétain, and Luigi Cadorna reach an obvious conclusion: "After canvassing the whole situation, the conference expressed the unanimous opinion that a defensive role should be adopted on all secondary fronts. The British and French representatives hoped that the surplus troops resulting from this course might be available to strengthen their armies in France, and General Cadorna, of course, thought the Italian armies should have their share." Clearly the war was waiting for Pershing's legions. Coolly Jack assessed the meeting for Baker and the president, summed the caution shrewdly as a gamble to hold the Western Front "until American forces in sufficient numbers arrive to gain ascendency."[58]

Behind his colleagues' nervous hedging Pershing saw the terrible chances of ruin. Secret information confirmed his fears that submarine warfare consumed ships too fast for replacement and unless sinkings slowed, "the war would be lost before we could fire a shot."[59] A natural Yankee bent for pooling of resources met hesitant agreement. An Inter-Allied Shipping Commission seemed worth trying. Increased security measures were ordered to minimize chances of troopship schedules reaching German ears.[60]

[57] JJP, *Experiences*, 1:117–18.
[58] *Ibid.*, p. 119.
[59] *Ibid.*, p. 120.
[60] See *ibid.*, pp. 119, 121–22; JJP to AGWAR (cable), Paris, July 28, 1917, par. 2 (confidential), reporting various ways the enemy learned of American shipping schedules. In GHQ, AEF Cables to War Department, Pershing Papers, RG 200, National Archives Gift Collection (cited hereinafter as HAEF Cables).

For Pershing the main task remained making ready for the men he hoped might someday reach France. British precedents were splendid, but Pershing wanted to share more of France's front-line lore, to combine everything learned into a final program for American organization. More than that, he wanted to encourage his allies while profiting from their agonies. Valuable information came from the American mission to Pétain's headquarters, but personal contact of the sort developed at Blendecques might produce special and long-term insights. And a visit to Pétain might soothe any jealousies festering from the British expedition. What of a Pétain visit to American troops in training? That kind of camaraderie opens friendships and could establish lasting liaison. Would a visit to Gondrecourt and a parade of Sibert's men win the heart of France's silent soldier? First Jack wanted to see if the 1st Division could survive a veteran's cold judgment.

At about three on Tuesday afternoon, July 31, 1917, Pershing, the wearying Harbord, and an eager George Patton joined a small coterie of orderlies and drivers, climbed into a Hotchkiss and a Packard, and sped out of Paris via the Bastille column. Harbord's historical nerve twanged as Napoleon's country whizzed past the window—Champaubert, Montmirail, Fère-Champenoise, country that reached a deep romance in Harbord's expanding soul, a country that reminded of the mighty falling. "It was the man Napoleon," he mused as the river ran, "the lion brought to bay." Patton's memory ran back too toward 1814, but his eye swept the Marne battlefields with fresh concern. "Many graves along [the] road," he noted, and recent signs of war.[61]

In that land of sorrow the skies lowered and the rains came late in the afternoon; the wind-lashed water smashed windshields and marched on towns like some ghosting army. With the storm came an odd depression, a brooding of the air that softened the will to travel, and at Saint Dizier Pershing called a halt. The general and Harbord dashed through the downpour into the Hôtel Soleil d'Or—a name not matched by building or by clime. Patton and Chambrun found shelter in a residence.[62]

By now the general's companions guessed the Old Man had a dual reason for the trip—he wanted to see Sibert's camps well enough, but he kept an eye toward a spot for Headquarters, AEF. Out of Paris he wanted to move his shop, out where society would beckon less, where

61 JJP, *Experiences*, 1:126–27; Harbord, *Diary*, p. 115; Blumenson, *Patton Papers*, p. 410.
62 Blumenson, *Patton Papers*, p. 410; Harbord, *Diary*, p. 116.

obligations would decline, and where soldiers could be soldiers. But the cruel Marne valley seemed repelling.

Wednesday's weather raised spirits and spread charm over "pretty valleys and picturesque hills"[63] as the American cars meandered toward Gondrecourt and its tiny neighboring hamlets, places suddenly clustering Americans far from home.

Up in that Lorraine land, Americans were homesick but rustically cheerful, busily making friends of the families who sheltered them in billets. Billets were not part of the American military tradition, were, in fact, one of the reasons for the Revolution, but they had peculiar interest, some of them. Farmers' daughters, often beauties, beckoned lonely Doughboys, despite fatherly frowns. Friendships formed sometimes expanded into family ties. But for many lost soldiers, French billets were grimy barnyards, manure-crusted holes famed for mud and wet haylofts. As winter approached comforts loomed scant, since fires were forbidden in the flammable barns. For romantic American soldiers who felt beyond the slime and cold, French billets formed a reason for the war. In those small villages of Lorraine, thinned now of men and pruned of luxuries, in those meandering streets and clotted houses, behind those whitewashed wattled walls, tough families struggled for freedom and for France. In dim centuries past their peasant ancestors in Lorraine joined the Maid of Orleans in her crusade. Born in Domrémy, near Neufchâteau, Joan of Arc cast a lasting spell of honor on her countrymen that touched still the strong faces of the northeast.

At Naix and Meneaucourt, Pershing stopped to visit U.S. Marine billets, dug into those of the 28th Infantry at Saint Amand and Tréveray (Col. Beaumont Beauregard Buck had his men reasonably well fixed), then pushed on to Saint Joire for lunch with an old friend. Each stop had impressed the staff with Pershing's eye for detail. Undaunted by repetition, Pershing strode through hayloft after hayloft and drove Harbord to note that "we inspected them with considerable detail, those billets."[64]

At Saint Joire, Col. George Duncan, now commanding the 26th Infantry, squired Jack around with the special propriety of a classmate. On the roads toward Duncan's headquarters, Americans drilled, marched, worked on entrenching with some shreds of competence. Duncan's men were fairly sharp, and George watched proudly while Jack swept battalion areas with calculating eyes. Good, good, but not

[63] Harbord, *Diary*, p. 116.
[64] *Ibid.*, p. 117.

perfect—here and there the general caught a detail, offered a suggestion, and sustained George's respect. "His alert eye took in every detail of what we were doing," and his criticisms were "helpful."[65]

Lunch with Duncan brought old thoughts of West Point, straying classmates, and serious rumination on the war. Duncan, a month younger than Pershing, had the kind of drive expected of an 86er and was about to win his first star. Jack judged him a likely division commander when organization progressed, knew his experience with the General Staff and his stint at the War College ranked him among the select few real "professionals" in France. To a comrade Jack confessed some chagrin at the relaxed training apparent in the American zone. Why? The French 47th Division of Chasseurs Alpins, the famed "Blue Devils," were serving as teachers, and each of them knew the hard facts of war. "The French troops made a fine appearance," noted a rueful Pershing. In the afternoon at Abainville, Pershing watched training of Col. Bill Allaire's 16th Infantry, and at Houdelaincourt he saw Col. Ulysses Grant McAlexander's 18th Infantry put on a respectable show. But in general, his impressions were still poor. To the young officers along, Pershing pointed out defects, noted sloppiness in dress and performance, and prompted a patronizing comment by George Patton: "Men did not look smart, officers were lazy, troops lacked equipment and training, were listless."[66]

A late afternoon meeting with news correspondents at Neufchâteau banished all traces of depression. Frederick Palmer, now a major in charge of managing the picky press folk, wanted a happy colloquy. Impressions were good. "All troops [were] well turned out," even the billets were "reasonably comfortable." But the press must cooperate. Too much had leaked already of American positions in France, and these leaks had probably cost lives on the Atlantic. Questions might be answered, but the answers would be off the record. Piously Pershing voiced "regret we cannot permit them to tell what we are doing."[67]

Irksome the newsmen were, but their questions and interests showed America's exploding awareness of war's necessities, the brooding concern at home for every Doughboy in France. Curiosity at home had its virtues, would probably ensure a constantly expanding war effort; mishandled, though, curiosity could ensure confusion in France. Palmer's delicate job might prove decisive.

[65] George B. Duncan, "Reminiscences of the World War," p. 27 (typescript in University of Kentucky Library, Lexington).

[66] Blumenson, Patton Papers, p. 410; JJP, Experiences, 1:126.

[67] JJP, Experiences, 1:126.

A tight schedule extricated Pershing from the scribblers. At Mirecourt, south of Nancy, the Americans met Gen. Edouard de Castelnau, commanding the Eastern group of French armies, the group likely to use the first American troops at the front. A sprightly old man—Pershing guessed him about seventy—de Castelnau had been in the war since the beginning; his honors were legion, his reputation formidable. Welcoming his new allies, he spoke of the war, listened to Pershing's plans for rustic headquarters, and offered assistance. At least consoled, the Americans rode on to Vittel for a night's rest.

Rest might be rare—rumor put the pack of correspondents on Pershing's heels. But if they caught up with the expedition, Vittel seemed just the place for entertainment. A "watering place" since 1854, the small town—scarcely 3,000 people—nestled on the slopes of the Monts Faucilles; it boasted elegant hotels and world renown. Its bottles of "Vittel water" graced tables to the reaches of civilization, and its people were cosmopolites. Younger eyes sparkled at the sight; some of the staff thought the place an ideal headquarters site. But distractions were too clear; "social attractions objectionable," Pershing thought, and the hunt continued.

Early on August 2—departure time was set to avoid the rumored correspondents—the American site searchers rode to Joinville and on to Chaumont. There Pershing looked carefully for adequate facilities, for transportation possibilities, and for size sufficient to sustain a growing American community. The special interest in Chaumont stemmed from a report submitted by a board of officers charged with finding a new headquarters. This board, boasting among its members Robert Bacon, had selected Chaumont. Keeping the secret, Pershing did his own searching of the surroundings. Now he found Chaumont eminently suitable. A city of some 20,000 people, it connected with upper Lorraine by good roads and rail lines, with Paris by the Marne and by rail, with southern French ports by several tracks. This was the place.

Most local citizens were enchanted with Pershing, with his entourage, with his plans. The mayor of Chaumont, M. Lévy-Alphandéry, extolled the marvels of the selection, pledged the effusions of his people; the local French commander offered glum prophecies of trouble. The large, obviously comfortable regimental barracks would be lost to the French army, hence the coolness of martial welcome. Pershing accepted the invitation and the warning—the AEF would move as soon as possible.[68]

[68] See *ibid.*, pp. 126–28; Harbord, *Diary*, pp. 116–18; Harbord, *American Army*, pp. 129–32; J. B. Scott, *Robert Bacon*, pp. 286, 290.

Relieved, tired, Pershing's party headed for Paris—and arrived too late for the general to keep a dinner date with the American ambassador. That typical tardiness nonetheless put the general out of sorts.[69]

Unanswered still was the question of whether the 1st Division could survive a Pétain inspection. The men working under the Blue Devils just did not look like soldiers, were sloppy, ungainly, mostly awkward squads in baggy uniforms. But off in their Lorraine training grounds the Americans had a mysterious martial quality that showed in their untoughed youth, their eagerness for war, their terribly fresh courage. Perhaps France's first soldier could see what those brave, raw boys might become.

Pétain solved the problem. Coming to dinner on Monday evening, August 6, he was loquacious and more optimistic than usual. To Pershing he excitedly revealed plans for a French advance in the Verdun area—the first attack since the Nivelle mutinies. Preparations were stupendous, security absolute. This test of France's armies must succeed! Would Pershing come to the battle? His presence would be an important morale and propaganda factor. Certainly. Would General Pétain visit the U.S. 1st Division before the French attack? A visit on the eve of important operations would cement comradeship, would inspire the Americans to hurry into battle. Gladly Pétain accepted.[70]

On August 18 Pershing collected John McAuley Palmer and Capt. Carl Boyd, a new aide (Patton sulked), and headed for Pétain's headquarters. The coming meeting was even more important than expected, since in the interim new questions of Franco-American cooperation had confounded Jack. Aware of problems in staff discussion, always hopeful of direct personal contact, Pershing had gathered M. René Viviani, M. Painlevé, and M. Clavielle to lunch on the fourteenth; over good food, talk flowed freely and difficulties surfaced. French officialdom's goodwill continued untainted—down the bureaucratic chain friction clogged liaison despite orders from the top. Politicians apparently had limited powers against the French civil service; Pétain's awesome stature could grease the ways of friendship, and he must be nudged to action.[71]

Pétain's stiff formality unbent during dinner on the eighteenth; he discussed plans for visiting American positions near Gondrecourt and

---

[69] Harbord, *Diary*, p. 119.
[70] JJP, *Experiences*, 1:130.
[71] *Ibid.*, p. 132.

announced that everyone would spend the night en route—on his private railroad train. The brusque French commander, much in charge of things, showed the impressive program for attack that had occupied his staff for long weeks. Organization and enthusiasm were apparent everywhere; French staff people were quick to show the special effectiveness of their system to the inquisitive visitors. Pressure for emulation mounted.

Sunday morning, the nineteenth, Pétain's train chuffed to a siding near Gondrecourt, and a party of American and French officers climbed aboard. First stop for the day proved to be a plateau near Houdelaincourt where the Blue Devils were paraded for inspection. Stiff-backed, cold-eyed, Pétain marched the lines, noted the faded smartness of the uniforms, the battle honors everywhere. Then he strode front and center to present decorations. Pétain and his cohorts did ceremonials well. Spread on the plain were soldiers in the Alpine blue, at attention and hushed. In that silence the men who had earned the thanks of France marched before their comrades, who knew the truths of courage. Each man walked forward to Pétain and the light wind whispered across the field of honor, uniforms flapped slightly, flags moved, and the general embraced his heroes, gave ribbons of the Legion, of the Military Cross, kissed the cheeks of the brave. And then music floated over the plain, the strains of "Sambre et Meuse," and the 47th Chasseurs Alpins swung into column and passed in review. Pershing saluted as the lines moved along, straight, rapid, precise; and he marveled at the élan of old veterans. If the Americans ever matched these men, they would be soldiers.

Morale Pétain understood, and Pershing watched, impressed, as France's first soldier built spirit with his charm. After the review Pétain asked the 47th's commander to assemble his officers for a conference. Pétain complimented them on the looks of the division, praised its record, urged them to encourage their men to further efforts, for the war would get harder. Your men, he said, have served in every great battle of France in this conflict; your losses have been heavy, your sacrifices match your country's, and you must do more. A glance around the assembly showed Pershing the eagerness in the young faces—faces of youth grown old—as Pétain's words touched French hearts. Because of sacrifice, because of incredible feats of bravery, Pétain said, the division had been given the honor of training the American 1st Division. Those allies, trained well, would surely someday distinguish their teachers.

For a tiny moment that summer morning in Lorraine, the past touched the present to acknowledge the courage of men—and the pageantry seemed altogether proper to a soldier recalling West Point.[72]

Now Pershing took over. With officers of the 1st Division and his French guests, he descended on various units. First honors fell to Bill Allaire and his 16th Infantry; some of his men huddled in rough new barracks of an uncommonly flimsy type that offered special interest to visitors. "These buildings were constructed of thin boards not tightly joined and it is apparent that they must be strongly reinforced by tar paper or some other material before they can be made suitable for winter occupancy." But a cheery welcome met inspectors in these "Chambourcy" billets and helped soothe Pershing's dismay. Lunch raised spirits higher, and an optimistic crew began the afternoon viewing various training activities. "A portion of the men were engaged in physical drill," Palmer noticed, "others were in a system of trenches that had been prepared for their instruction; another detachment was observed in practice at bomb throwing and another was engaged in practice with the Chauchat rifle."[73]

What did their instructors think of these untested Yanks? They were especially good at grenade throwing—baseball's influence?—and they were accurate with the Chauchat automatic rifle, but not fast. One instructor had a good story of a grenade student who listened to instructions about setting the fuse and slowly counting to seven before throwing the bomb. He just could not wait; time after time he threw the grenade too soon, and it rolled around long enough to be thrown back before exploding. Several times the instructor fumed his displeasure and finally the Doughboy said, "Captain, I just can't hold these grenades any longer because I can feel them swelling in my hand." Laughing, Pershing and Pétain moved on to billets of the 47th French Division, then into the camps of Colonel Buck's 28th Infantry, and finished with a look at the marine regiment's area.

A lot of work preceded the visit; troops looked good, spruced and military, their billets clean, comfortable, and the "command made a most creditable appearance."

Pleased, not a little proud, Pershing joined his French colleague in a journey to the front. At Souilly, French II Army headquarters, Per-

---

[72] See *ibid.*, pp. 136–37; John McAuley Palmer, "Report of Official Journey—August 18–21, 1917," ("Confidential"), p. 1 (typescript in AEF, GHQ, G-3, Folder 1108-A, "Comments on Visits to Fronts"), RG 120, National Archives.

[73] Palmer, "Report of Official Journey," p. 2.

shing met Gen. Marie Emile Fayolle, heading the Armies of the Center, and General Marie Louis Adolphe Guillaumat of the II Army. At a briefing conducted by II Army staff, Pershing learned the plans for the next day's battle. Fayolle impressed Pershing as extremely able, though frail. Pétain took his guests to a French hospital in the afternoon, where he gave the croix de guerre to a nurse who had been wounded by shell-fire. Pétain presented Pershing, and the young lady's eyes sparkled. "I am glad you are here, General, to see how a French woman can suffer for her country." A sham, thought Pershing as she glowed at the decoration—"I am sure that for the moment she had entirely forgotten her pain."[74]

Once more entrained in the evening, Pétain's party traveled westward to give Pershing a look at one of the main regulating stations on the French front. At Saint Dizier on the Marne, all Americans were enthralled at a logistical triumph unimagined in any staff school. "Regulating stations" were a product of mass. As armies choked front lines, supplies clotted behind them, packed rear areas into snarls of camions, wagons, trains, caissons, and slogging infantry. Moving rations, water, ammunition, medical stores, artillery, all tools of human survival forward into combat zones demanded special management techniques. Traffic control was an obvious problem, but control of the flow of supplies became an equal burden. Uncontrolled shipments from the rear produced either plenty or paucity; regulating stations were designed to send proper amounts of all supplies to proper places for issue to the front-line units. They were not warehouse points—supplies moved through these stations rapidly. Daily shipments went up over a skein of roads and small-gauge tracks connecting with the front. "The system seemed simple," Pershing observed, "but to make it work successfully thorough organization and expert management were necessary."[75]

In the ordered chaos of that great station, Painlevé and M. Albert Thomas, French minister of munitions, joined the sightseers and marveled at the extent of attack preparations. All of II Army's logistical support sped through Saint Dizier, and, although the army would launch a big battle on the morrow, no confusion or congestion could be seen. Experience had taught the French the importance of good order. "It was stated that during the Verdun operations 2,000 carloads of supplies were forwarded each day for a period of 100 days.

[74] *Ibid.*; JJP, *Experiences*, 1:137–38.
[75] JJP, *Experiences*, 1:139; Palmer, 'Report of Official Journey," pp. 4–5.

During this period 100,000 rounds per day of 75 MM. ammunition were forwarded. . . ."[76]

After lunch Pétain took his party to an observation point behind the XVI French Corps, which would carry the attack. And here Jack had an unexpected treat—the XVI Corps's commander proved to be Maj. Gen. Charles Corvisart, old colleague in Manchuria. Greeting friend Pershing heartily, Corvisart took him to high ground for a panoramic view of the battle. Little had been left to chance. For four days French guns rained shells on German positions at Le Mort Homme and Hill 304—landmarks poignant in memories of the Verdun horrors in 1916. Spread before Pershing and all visitors was a vast wasteland of trenches, straggling wire, and mud crazed with oozing geysers that erupted as the French barrage rolled on. Into that roiling gray morass at last charged the *poilus*. They came hunched and huddled; trying hard to avoid bunching against bullets, they ran on in groups, leaping for shell holes, looking oddly restless and unstoppable from high distance. Corvisart had no real doubts of success—a limited attack for well-defined objectives put in behind an iron storm unknown since the hardest days at Douaumont could scarcely fail. As the day dwindled, thousands of dazed prisoners came into Corvisart's lines—their condition ample evidence of effective bombardment. Objectives taken, Corvisart ended the attack.

Pershing watched, fascinated, and noted especially the quick need of both sides to huddle in their lines. Attack formations withered under modern firepower; men were clearly out of their element in the open. But Corvisart consoled his American friend with assurances that entrenchments did not quench fighting spirit. As the battle became an obvious victory, he and Jack talked of older times, of youth. What, Jack wondered, had happened to Maj. Enrico Caviglia, the opera buff who waked them each morning singing? Corvisart had kept up with most of his Manchurian colleagues and reported Lieutenant General Caviglia now commanding an Italian army. Ian Hamilton, a British general when they were junior officers, had suffered the burden of Gallipoli. Fowke, now a lieutenant general, Pershing had met as adjutant general of the BEF. Max Hoffman served as German chief of staff on the eastern front and was clearly destined for high command. Von Etzel, the chilly senior German, so aloof in the observer's mess, what of him? Smiling, Corvisart pointed to the battlefield and said, "I have just beaten him today. He is commanding a division opposite me."

[76] Palmer, "Report of Official Journey," p. 4.

That little community of soldiers who followed Kuroki's fortunes had won more than their share of honor, were responsible for much of this war. Professional pride tinged those reminiscent moments and was shared even with the enemy. Good soldiers like their kind.[77]

Gleeful with Verdun victory, Pétain and the high politicos with Pershing at his viewing point guessed French morale repaired—at least improved enough to continue the war. Pershing shared their elation; his own concern for French staying power he had confided to Baker several weeks before and suggested the possibility that America might have to assume the main burden of the Western Front in 1918. Time had seemed critical; it would be almost impossible to complete training much before 1918's summer. But now time pressed more easily; the French could hold the front until the AEF arrived in force.

For Pershing the French visit went far better than hoped. Not only did the U.S. 1st Division impress Pétain, not only did the renewed friendship with Corvisart open extra doors of cooperation, but the staffs exchanged invaluable information. More importantly, relations with Pétain reached cordiality. The cool French leader waxed enthusiastic in personal talks. Eloquently he spoke of the fierce fighting of 1916 when the fate of France hung on the thin thread of the Voie Sacrée from Bar-le-Duc to Verdun, praised the men who bore the challenge. And gradually he relaxed and commented sardonically on France's political leaders. With that confidence, Jack knew he had made a friend. So had Pétain. "I found it most agreeable as well as instructive to be with Pétain in this intimate way and have an opportunity to hear something of his experience."[78]

On their return to Paris, Harbord was reassured that the Old Man had not been bamboozled by Pétain and the "smooth Minister of War, M. Painlevé." Clearly Pershing had known from the start the intention to persuade an amalgamation of Americans into existing French units; he had listened, sifted, profited, been agreeable but unfazed, and returned to push plans for divisional and staff training based on Allied precedents but geared to American needs. The trip, obviously, had been good. The Chaumont shift would be better. Out of the dense political miasma of the French capital, the staff might escape intrigue and try working.[79]

Staff sections moved on Saturday, September 1, 1917; Pershing quit Paris on the fifth, and headquarters opened in Chaumont on the

[77] JJP, *Experiences*, 1:139–40, Palmer, "Report of Official Journey," p. 5.
[78] JJP, *Experiences*, 1:141.
[79] *Ibid.*, pp. 142–43; Harbord, *Diary*, pp. 133–35.

sixth. Warmly welcomed by the citizenry, the Americans settled in swiftly and Pershing relaxed in "surroundings [that] give relief from [the] depression of Paris."[80]

Outline of an Army

Shadows had been forming for weeks. Through hectic Paris meetings with French officials, with itinerant American boards and visitors, with Allied generals in their sectors, Jack glimpsed fleeting images of the army he wanted in France. The full picture came slowly. The men would be smart—amateurs could still look like soldiers. Only smartness impressed veterans—the cool contempt of French officers embarrassed a West Pointer. Poor first impressions would be corrected.[81] "The conspicuous position in a foreign land which our officers and men occupy makes every slouchy officer and man a reflection on the whole American army."[82] Better uniforms were ordered, cut more to size and warmer for French winter. Men would stick to clothing regulations. Staff officers were authorized white shirts with collars and cuffs. Quartermaster clothing-repair shops were established to mend tatters. For easy identification, officers were strapped in the neat (Sergeant Lanckton hated to shine it!) Sam Browne belt.[83]

Overall conduct might decide delicate matters of cooperation. The AEF ought to be famous for manners and morals. After considerable thought, Pershing, in August, put the delicate matter of image to his men. "For the first time in history the American Army finds itself in European territory. The good name of the United States and the maintenance of cordial relations require perfect deportment of each member of this command." European experience notwithstanding, Pershing felt that a guest army had special obligations, knew that American history boasted many instances of responsible military conduct among civilians, and knew his men capable of gentlemanliness. More than that, he knew them capable of conduct becoming the finest

[80] JJP, *Experiences*, 1:163.
[81] *Ibid.*, p. 130.
[82] GO no. 23, AEF, Paris, Aug. 20, 1917, in *USWW*, 16:56–57.
[83] JJP to AGWAR, May 23, 1918 (Cable 1172-S), JJP Papers, Cables Sent (Open), Box 6, RG 200, National Archives (hereinafter cited as Open Cables Sent): "I am decidedly in favor of retention of Sam Browne belt as an article of uniform for officers serving in Europe. Without it there is difficulty, particularly for troops of our Allied nations, in recognizing our officers. The American uniform without the belt does not lend itself readily to easily distinguishable insignia for our officers. I am satisfied the wearing of the Sam Browne belt adds to esprit and to discipline." See also Ginsburgh, "Pershing as His Orderlies Know Him," p. 53.

of their kind. In those early Chaumont days as he formed his visionary legions, Jack decided to set an aiming point for his men, a gauge to measure by. "The standards for the American Army," he announced, "will be those of West Point. The rigid attention, upright bearing, attention to detail, uncomplaining obedience to instructions required of the cadet will be required of every officer and soldier of our armies in France." Charlie Rhodes would have groaned along with a bitter cadet company who remembered 1897. Could a whole army aspire to corps precision? John Pershing had no doubts.[84] So part of the picture came clear. Doughboys would be martial in their khaki, would stand tall, know courtesy, have pride in themselves because they belonged to the AEF.

Other parts of the picture came into focus. Headquarters took shape quickly. At first glance the Caserne de Damremont in Chaumont would be too sumptuous for hard work, but, despite its palatial exterior, the old regimental barracks proved ideal for the staff and supporting units. With three large buildings fronting a bare parade, the Caserne boasted adequate space for offices, billets, garages, stables, and kitchens. Communications were ample via telegraph and wireless with Paris, Lorraine, London, or Washington. In the largest building, the one facing the great gates, Pershing established his office. Vast acres of floor space proved ample for all staff elements, for burgeoning files, for clerks, orderlies, and visitors.

Visitors found General Pershing with some difficulty. His lair defended by aides and secretaries, he worked in a smallish room behind a modest desk, his chair padded but straight, his conveniences restricted to a book table, a huge wall map of the Western Front, a big clock over the door, one easy chair hidden in a corner, and *Webster's Unabridged Dictionary*. A few straight-backed chairs repelled lengthy visits, and the general tone ran Spartan.

September came a lovely month to the upper Marne country, where rustic splendor was disturbed only by the far rumble of the war. Morning horseback rides were pleasures snatched sinfully, assuaged by talks with fellow sinners about the business of the day. Time became a talisman of danger that dimmed the splendor of the fall. Each day spent with plans and preparations seemed somehow mortgaged at the front. Reports came steadily of fighting in Flanders, of the endless combats at Verdun, of the steady pace of death. Pressure must not bring panic. Routine must be fixed and kept. From his small desk at

[84] JJP, *Experiences*, 1:15, 129; JJP, *FR*, p. 15.

Damremont, Pershing fought a war of organization—a fighter's hardest war.

General organization of headquarters came first and involved various compromises. British and French influences competed within staff conferences; some officers wanted to move faster with training than others thought possible. Harbord let everyone talk out his prejudices, sifted results, and pushed for consensus. His own inexperience balked originality and sometimes encouraged lack of coordination.[85] Early plans for the building skeleton of the AEF Pershing read with a quick eye to interests and capacities shown by his men. Harbord's adroit handling of people, his ways of suasion, outweighed his weaknesses. What coordination might be needed could be furnished by adding a section to the table of organization—a point Pershing pressed.

Schools he pressed, too, harder than almost anything else. Traces of the old schoolmaster could be glimpsed in his passion for instruction, a schoolmaster frightened of ignorance. Mindanao and Mexico proved that soldiers could be taught far beyond the reaches of experience. Training might not make recruits into veterans—it could make them into soldiers. Never had the need been so urgent for skilled military instruction. The staff must devise a system for teaching harsh ways of killing to boys of good will. Who might produce the best scheme of initiation? A careful watch on performance suggested Hugh Drum. Already far advanced with a program to organize logistics for the AEF, he had energy, Leavenworth trappings, and originality. Pershing picked him to educate an army.

Drum would not really instruct troops—his task was harder. He would devise the plans for schools of the line, of division, of officers. The assignment carried full powers—he could do the thing his way. No staff officer worthy of the brass needed a general watching over his shoulder, but, if he failed to do the job in reasonable haste, Pershing would shift the business to a better man. Everybody knew the Old Man worked that way, that you could trust him to leave you to it, that you could report and give strong opinions, that he would listen if the facts ran true, would halt the flow when rhetoric intruded. So Drum began. And he justified faith. Not long after settling in Chaumont, Pershing received the plans.

There had been haggling. John Henry Parker, he of the Gatlings,

[85] Drum Diary, Aug. 9–31, 1917.

wanted to create an army line school immediately by borrowing instructors from General Sibert's thin 1st Division. Did speed justify the shift of men? At first thought, Pershing rejected the idea; he had pretty firmly decided not to disturb the nascent organizations of units already in France. But no rule was irrevocable. There might be a way to follow Parker's push for haste and still aid Sibert. Detailing divisional staff officers for temporary duty at headquarters would familiarize them with high command procedures while they worked on special assignment.[86] Orders to try borrowing irked Sibert, his staff, and hurt Drum, who felt Parker was intruding on his scheme. But so persuasive were Drum's plans that they forced acceptance. The energetic new lieutenant colonel had conducted a comprehensive survey of British and French schools and marshaled evidence to show that officers ought to grow into army schools, level by level.

Impressed, Pershing decided to put some of his best men into Drum's system; Drum would indoctrinate the new "faculty." Once a small group learned the Allied system, they would come under the AEF's training section and begin the classes. Pershing picked that early group of teachers with care—listened to Drum, to Harbord, considered old friends, and then pulled Robert Bullard out of his brigade, along with his adjutant, Maj. Harold Fiske, joined them with Col. James McAndrew, fresh from his infantry regiment, and gave them to Drum's tender care. He shipped them promptly to Allied schools for enlightenment. An odd lot, they seemed likely to work well with training commander Paul Malone, who gave them simple instructions: "Go and establish the schools."[87] At Gondrecourt the first divisional school opened with a complement of teachers, cooks, laborers, orderlies, and students totalling less than one hundred, but the staff had zeal and expected to keep pace with army expansion by broadening work to the corps level.[88]

As that pioneer effort began in Sibert's camps, Pershing watched to see how well he had picked men and how carefully they had listened to him. Through long sessions with Drum and Malone, with the later arrivals, one theme had been hammered hard—American schools should teach American methods. Drum listened and parroted; Pershing wanted the whole curriculum at Gondrecourt pointed toward

[86] *Ibid.*, July 16–19, 1917; JJP to Sibert, Aug. 9, 1917, Box 184, PP.

[87] Drum Diary, July 16–19, 1917; Malone's quote is in R. L. Bullard, *Personalities and Reminiscences of the War*, p. 63.

[88] *Ibid.*, July 20–27, 1917; JJP, *Experiences*, 1:164.

"the importance of teaching throughout our forces a sound fighting doctrine of our own. . . ."[89] Schools based on that principle would succeed.

Announcing the school's program to the War Department on September 8, Pershing confidently included the schedule of development: division schools begun; corps "centers of instruction to train commanders of all arms and units" to start probably in mid-October; army schools "to train instructors for corps schools and preserve accepted doctrine of combat" to begin in mid-November. A General Staff College at Langres—for selected officers—would follow, along with base and technical schools. Everything depended on proper personnel.

Nothing would succeed unless qualified officers were selected to continue instruction. Earlier requests for staff assignments remained unattended in Washington. Could the War Department hasten help?[90] Headquarters would keep a close eye on Gondrecourt, would aid and cajole as necessary.[91]

Until American instruction matured, French and British officers would train the 1st Division in rudimentary trench warfare. Pershing realized the necessity but deplored it. Warworn and wasted, the Allies thought defensively and overemphasized trench tactics. Time and more Americans would change the doctrinal climate.[92]

Concern spread far beyond training. Everything at headquarters focused on getting into the war, which meant constant concern with effective strength. Magically deceitful statistics appeared at Chaumont to comfort or convulse, and Pershing read them with a realist's suspicion. By September he counted 1,616 officers and 35,042 men in the AEF and heard wildly varying guesses about how many men could arrive each month, how many would be in France by mid-1918. Staffers worked on the estimate of 600,000 in a year[93] for planning and requisitioning services and supplies. That kind of growth confounded all human problems. Social control of those thousands demanded new techniques of management, of military policing, and of physical preservation. Again, Allied precedents were invaluable. To British and French counselors went officers saddled with herding and preserving people. Col. Hanson Ely became the AEF's first provost marshal

[89] Drum Diary, July 20–27, 1917; JJP, FR, p. 13.
[90] JJP to AGWAR, Sept. 8, 1917 (Cable 147-S), in Open Cables Sent.
[91] JJP, FR, pp. 12–14.
[92] Bullard, *Personalities*, p. 61; JJP, FR, p. 14.
[93] Drum Diary, July 28–Aug. 2, 1917.

and prepared a modest corps to greet thousands of countrymen with rules, regulations, and restrictions. Among the most important, if delicate, duties that came to Ely's unabashed eye was management of prostitutes in French ports. That duty impinged heavily on Medical Corps sentiment—and heavily, too, on General Pershing's serious concern.

Experiments in Mexico with the segregated brothel near his main camp Pershing now recalled unhappily—isolation and regular medical inspections had helped reduce venereal disease but had done nothing to reduce venery. In France, Pershing wanted to improve the morals of his men, to build an army virtuous. The hope seemed absurd to Allied generals who had contended unsuccessfully against venereal absenteeism for three years. Pershing wondered. During the *Baltic* voyage he had spotted among the medical contingent Dr. Hugh Young, of the Johns Hopkins University's Brady Urological Institute, and discussed with him army sanitation at length. Young, a remarkably able surgeon with an earthy sense of his profession, found a kindred soul in Pershing—their humors matched as well as their jokes. Young's shipboard lectures painted the horrors of venereal disease in awesome hue and won Pershing's instant attention. What could be done to prevent a diseased army in France?

Realist Young cherished few illusions about chastity in bulk. He shared the Australian surgeon general's view that "there are chaste men, but all of them are impotent."[94] Young thought chastity a needless sacrifice to Mars. A crusade for cleanliness might curtail the wages of sin. By the time headquarters settled at Chaumont, Young's visits to Allied hospitals made him an expert on *morbus gallicus* in military history.[95]

Things he reported impressed Pershing forcefully of the degenerative effects venereal disease could have on an army. British experience alone would frighten the most outrageous optimist—Young described the forty-six-day treatment given in the BEF, the 23,000 beds assigned to VD cases. His statistics were terrifying: almost 70,500,000 soldier days per year wasted treating a social ill![96]

Young's expert grasp of the subject could not be lost to the AEF. Despite frowns from some regular medical officers, Young must be used. How? Give him the recognized status of a medical consultant,

[94] Hugh H. Young, *A Surgeon's Autobiography*, pp. 270–73.
[95] *Ibid.*, pp. 272–87.
[96] *Ibid.*, pp. 276–77.

but give him special authority. Would he accept the job of director of urology, AEF? He would, did, and made a whirlwind inspection of facilities. British methods against syphilis Young rejected in favor of French use of novarsenobenzol, a kind of neosalvarsan. French success in handling gonorrhea locally inspired Young's scheme of issuing prophylactic kits to front-line units. Properly used, the kits would cure easy cases and significantly reduce the hospital load.

In the midst of organizing his plan for the AEF, a plan he hoped would win Pershing's support, Young received an urgent call to Saint Nazaire. Statistics on VD rates in the AEF rose alarmingly in November; the new cases concentrated in the port city. Go at once, Young was told by Pershing, find out what had happened. Hasty inspection revealed the problem. Faced with clogged port facilities, transports lingering over-long in the harbor awaiting discharge, crowded reception depots, American medical officers in Saint Nazaire granted frequent shore leave and resorted to the French system of regulated prostitution combined with prophylaxis. Normal precautions lapsed in drunken crowds and fabricated recollections of leave; most men returning to their ships simply did not remember if they had been treated. Heroic measures alone could prevent an epidemic. Rushing back to headquarters, Young worked on a comprehensive report of conditions and recommendations. Just as the ink set, he heard the general wanted to see him; about to leave for a Paris meeting of Allied leaders, Pershing installed the major in his car and started off. At first he read Young's report with impatience, then with anger.

"Major," he stormed, "this is one of the most disgraceful things that has happened to the American Army. Drastic measures must be taken immediately. I have agreed to meet the chiefs of the Allied armies in Paris, but this is more important, and I shall take the earliest train to Saint-Nazaire and put into effect your recommendations."

Complacent officers in that hapless French town suddenly saw their commander-in-chief as never glimpsed before. Raging into offices, barracks, headquarters of medical, line, and military police units, he ripped men of all ranks with withering contempt. Dereliction of duty rang the easiest of his charges; criminal neglect, conduct unbecoming Americans, abysmal ignorance of two earlier orders against VD, ignorance of the army regulations—these were among the snarled charges. Stern, glacial, he confronted port officers with their outrageous sloth—troops would be debarked and shipped through the city with dispatch or reputations would end faster. Young's words blazoned on his conscience, Pershing ordered the houses of prostitution put off limits to Doughboys; saloons, likewise. All troops would receive prophylactic treatments in cases of the slightest doubt.

Pershing's hot words fumigated Saint Nazaire. Young, amused and amazed, reported that "a veritable transformation occurred. Never again did such disgraceful happenings occur in Saint-Nazaire, or any other seaport." But the general's anger lingered; from it stemmed General Order No. 77, December 18, 1917, written under Young's eye and regarded by him as "the most drastic and far-reaching health order ever issued to an army." Pershing directed that "all Commanding officers . . . give personal attention to matters pertaining to the prevention of veneral disease. . . . No laxity or half-hearted efforts in this regard will be tolerated. . . . The number of effectives in a command is an index to its efficiency and this depends upon the efficiency of the Commanding Officer." The order then spelled out drastic regulations governing conditions in ports of embarkation, enjoined cooperation with French officials in putting brothels and bars "off limits" to Americans, and required all arriving ship commanders to report the venereal condition of their complements. Urologists supplied from General Headquarters would work with local surgeons in following regulations for VD prevention and treatment; relentless vigilance was expected. Daily reports of VD cases would be forwarded from all units to General Headquarters for Pershing's personal information. And there came in this general order a special incentive for compilation of VD statistics: "These reports will be filed at . . . Headquarters with the personal records of organization commanders, and will be used as a basis in determining the commander's efficiency and the suitability of his continuing in command." Since intoxication inevitably contributed to sexual excess, the general order inveighed against imbibing and sought a kind of army prohibition.

All provisos, tough and resented though they might be, were carefully planned by Pershing and Young; they would, if followed, do more to sustain the health of the army than anything in American military history. Young guessed Pershing's experience in Mexico and his problems in the Philippines the efficient causes of his concern. There were other causes, not the least of them a kind of paternalism. He wanted the AEF to remain clean, wanted his men to return home in moral and physical strength. It seemed a large hope, but hope ran with the American cause in Europe—if the war might make the world safer for Democracy, Democracy should defend the purity of its knights.[97]

Nothing seemed more important to Pershing than the welfare of his men, and once that came clearly to subordinates, the climate expanded. Young, whose gadfly activities for urology amused and shocked some of his associates, had no firmer friend than the general. After General Order No. 77, he encountered almost obsequious assistance. Let him chortle: "Previously, when I called upon the general of a division and asked about the venereal rate, I was usually told that he was very busy and to see Lieutenant So-and-so. After General Order 77, whenever I inquired at the headquarters of even the most high-ranking officers, they immediately replied: 'There's no subject in which I am more interested. Please let me know in what way we can co-operate more effectively.'" Pershing's penchants were pervasive.

Young's surprised pleasure at the weight of Pershing's support many other AEF officers shared. Support Jack dispensed freely along with careful assessment of the men who got it. Increasingly he asked the same question of each man put in charge of some phase of America's European venture: Does he get the job done? If so, he got all the backing necessary; if not, he found himself in Cannes as a reluctant sightseer. Cannes rapidly became a place of dead dreams, a place of oblivion to match France's baleful Limoges. There officers went to "await orders" for transfer.[98]

Did Hugh Young have the stuff of success in him? Jack did like him, enjoyed his easy humor, his calm professionalism—but nothing really mattered save success. Could Young make good the promise of his plans? Spirit he conveyed, and Jack watched approvingly as Young cut miles of red tape to snatch prophylactic kits and urological supplies from depots and dispensaries unwilling to cooperate. Finally there were no more doubts—Young had the artist's gift of improvisation. When medical stores failed him, he turned quickly to the Red Cross for temporary assistance; he had the needed sense of urgency.

Cooperation with the Red Cross came easily. That honorable

[97] See *ibid.*, pp. 307–12, 328–33; Harbord, *American Army*, pp. 143–47. The text of GO no. 77 varies between *USWW*, 16:144–46, and Young, *Autobiography*, pp. 310–12. The differences are not substantive, and the text follows Young's version. See, for details about port conditions, Yves-Henri Nouailhat, *Les Américains à Nantes et Saint-Nazaire, 1917–1919*, pt. 1, ch. 1, and pt. 2, chs. 1–3.

[98] Later the "Classification Depot" was shifted to Blois ("Blooey" in Dough-boy parlance), which became the last stop on failure's road (see Harbord, *American Army*, p. 376).

organization increasingly became a fixed auxiliary of the AEF. Its leaders in France received honorary commissions from Pershing to speed work with the army, opened their stockpiles to AEF necessity, and showed success in supply coordination.[99]

Logistics hung a heavy darkness over headquarters. From early moments of accepting the European command, Pershing brooded over supplies. Ancient War Department methods of sustaining the relatively small United States Army in peacetime had collapsed under the mild strain of the Punitive Expedition. Militia mobilization along the Texas-Mexican border simply overwhelmed supply officers untrained in anything save company support. Those fateful months between February and April, 1917, months when all lessons from Mexico should have been studied by the War Department, went wasted. True, the War College devoted attention to logistic plans for the single division expected to go abroad; training in staff work and in higher planning at the War College gave graduates at least the rudiments of broad supply bases for large campaigns—and Pershing sought graduates diligently. But they had run thin as the AEF siphoned away most of the real talent in the army. Now the demands increased daily—reports of troop transport arrivals came in happy profusion[100]—and skilled staff manpower dwindled.

Shortage of specialists made careful evaluation of available officers vital. The kind of work done by Hugh Drum and others on the General Organization Project showed the kind of talent handy; the cluster of young men at General Headquarters represented a kind of brain pool collected to help organize everything. That sort of ability accepted only the deftest leadership. Slowly Pershing found a way to extract the best efforts from the best men. Young's experience seemed fairly typical—Pershing found the man he liked, pointed to problems bearing on his competence, turned him loose with full support.

[99] For Red Cross activities, see JJP, *Experiences*, 1:35, 71–74, 108; HAEF Diary, July 31, 1917; JJP to AGWAR, July 28, 1917 (Cable 66-S), in Open Cables Sent: "After further consultation with Red Cross officials am of the opinion that some sort of militarization of Red Cross within certain limits probably desirable. Red Cross officials strongly of opinion that no appointments to such assimilated rank under executive order should be made above the grade of Major and then for actual service performed and only upon recommendation of head of Red Cross in Europe approved by these hdqrs." See also Young, *Autobiography*, p. 293.

[100] See HAEF Diary, June 25; July 23, 24, 25, 26, 27, 29; Aug. 1, 3, 8, 15, 19, 20, 21, 22, 26, 31; Sept. 10, 11, 22, 23, 25, 30, 1917, for examples of troop and supply traffic.

That same broad approach to delegation of mounting responsibility shaped plans for a new scheme to supply the AEF. So complex a problem, one that impinged on domestic supply, on shipping, and on Allied cooperation required organization as intricate as the AEF itself. And no sooner had the staff completed the General Organization Project than Pershing put them to work on a similar program for supplies. Weeks of study produced a comprehensive report that Pershing accepted and put into General Orders No. 20, August 13, 1917. The logistical support for his troops would be handled by "The Line of Communications," a command extending from the sea to railheads behind the front line and embracing all units and establishments outside the Zone of the Armies. The LOC were divided into the three traditional broad divisions—Base, Intermediate, and Advanced Sections—and had such hectic concerns as all categories of supplies, policing of all rear areas, timber cutting, and transportation management.[101]

no existing doctrine

Who would command this vital link from home to the war? Pershing looked hard for his man. He must be tough, willing to take authority, bear responsibility almost as great as Pershing's, think broadly enough to expand his endeavors apace with the AEF. One henchman from Mexico loomed as possibly qualified—he had done well in troop command as a colonel—Richard M. Blatchford. A brigadier, soon for two stars in the National Army, Blatchford was Pershing's senior by a year but seemed hearty and vigorous. Good soldier always, Blatchford took the job. Pershing discussed its dimensions carefully—everything would depend on how effective the supply system became. Blatchford's organization could truly make or break the AEF. He would have all necessary authority; his headquarters in Paris could issue all orders to build an organization, could purloin such men as were essential, could make rules for life behind the lines. Blatchford would have the power to plan the sustenance of one, two, or three million men, would have the support and all resources available—the work was up to him. With that old trait of seeing ahead, Pershing pointed out special concerns. As the men began to flood in from America, as divisions and corps took shape, as an army emerged, Blatchford must not only supply them but also guard against possible transportation failures by stockpiling reserves. Conservative always when thinking of troop safety, the com-

---

[101] GO no. 20, Aug. 13, 1917, in *USWW*, 16:52–53; Harbord, *American Army*, pp. 120–21. JJP gave final approval to the LOC Project on Sept. 10, 1917 (see HAEF Diary for that date).

mander-in-chief talked of forty-five days' reserves in the base sections, thirty days' stored in intermediate depots, and fifteen days' handy in advanced stations.[102]

Blatchford would be left to his designs—as long as supplies were plentiful and efficiently handled. But Pershing's eye strayed often to Blatchford's activities, and he kept in close touch.

Both Pershing's own staff and Blatchford stressed some problems simply beyond the scope of any logistical command. Rail lines were the AEF's arteries and should have been fully controlled by American officers, but France could not concede control of even a portion of its own veins and capillaries. Coordination of all Allied rail needs in France ought to come from the French. Britain had, by hard bickering, gained some control over the lines serving Flanders and the northern coast, but total control eluded even Haig. French trainmen still confused British operations with irritating regularity. And France, of course, held the trumps in the railroad stakes—rolling stock, trackage, repair shops, people. In one area a deficiency made her vulnerable to pressure—and Pershing pressed. America could supply locomotives to French gauges—how many were needed? With desperate greed, French rail authorities asked for boundless numbers but settled on three hundred.[103] Using such special inducements, Pershing enhanced his chances of coordinating rail services in the south of France.

Coordination was really the polite consideration. Maintenance and repairs of French railroads languished in a kind of Gallic disarray; many roadbeds simply could not stand heavy military loads and must be relaid. Workmen for train and repair crews were scarce and many must come from America. Presuming French approval came for AEF control of its own rail support, how best control? Pershing guessed the best plan was Britain's. The finest railroad men in England had been put in charge of Haig's rail lines and worked wonders. A hasty suggestion to Washington: "I am convinced that operation of railroads must be under [a] man with large experience in managing commercial railroads at home. . . . Handling our railroad lines so important that ablest man in country should be carefully selected."[104]

When William W. Atterbury, general manager and operating vice president of the Pennsylvania Railroad, reported to Chaumont in September, Jack had found his man. Businesslike, willing to learn the

[102] JJP, *FR*, pp. 10–11; JJP, *Experiences*, 1:109.
[103] HAEF Diary, Aug. 3, 1917.
[104] JJP to AGWAR, July 29, 1917, in Open Cables Sent.

baffling ways of the army, Atterbury showed impressive knowledge of AEF rail conditions. "His personality, his force, his grasp of the difficulties of the task and his willingness to undertake it appealed to me at once. So, without hesitation . . . I told him that he would be placed in charge of railroad transportation." Atterbury, for a time clinging to his civilian status, worked under the impressive guise of director general of transportation. Familiar with power, he grasped it quickly and forced subordinates to his plans. It would be easy to support a doer.[105] Only a tiny cloud shaded Atterbury's attributes—obedience. And appointment of a director proved no grand panacea. Supplies continued a plague on all consciences at headquarters. Approval of the Line of Communications Project and of another announcing priority of shipments apparently brought order to logistics—or would if Washington overcame natural bureaucratic inertia and hastened implementation of Pershing's programs. Patient but irritated, increasingly importunate, Pershing tried to hurry help.[106] But troubles continued. Blatchford and Atterbury dug into their assignments—problems spilled beyond their control. What had been left undone? What was left to manage?

Finally Pershing realized that the ultimate management had been ignored—control of purchasing. Disorganized procurement encouraged unit avarice, and supply officers vied fiercely for French resources in all possible markets. Old phantasms of Tampa and Columbus, N.M., haunted Pershing. How to curb confusion?

Since preparations in the States suffered from endless dawdling, vital supplies for the AEF obviously must come from France. Someone must take charge of all French purchasing, give order and discipline to the procurement of all kinds of materiel—simply take charge of sustaining the AEF in a businesslike way. Awash in high business competence, the United States surely could provide some tycoon equal to the challenge of France? Who?

In the last days of August, in those hectic days before quitting Paris, came news that Charlie Dawes had worked his way to France. Snagging an appointment as lieutenant colonel in the 17th Engineers, Dawes had virtually transformed a potentially staid railway engineer regiment into an outfit with panache and verve, boosted by a newly equipped (by Dawes) and raucous band and inspired with a front-line urge. Unspoiled, undaunted by military circumstance, Dawes expected swift

---

105 JJP, *Experiences*, 1:156; Harbord, *American Army*, pp. 142–43.
106 For JJP's patience amid Washington's sloth, see Harbord, *Diary*, p. 124. His attempts to urge speed are illustrated in JJP to AGWAR, Oct. 8, 20, 1917, in Open Cables Sent.

contact with Jack, swift approval of extensive plans for rebuilding the port of Saint Nazaire, instant fame for the best regiment yet created. He did get swift summons to Pershing.

At headquarters Dawes greeted his old friend in the morning of August 29, found him surrounded by people and problems, apparently handling all with his usual poise. No inhibitions of rank or status balked old friends as they brought lives to date, remembered good times, wondered about people, things, recollected the sad times they shared. But Jack needed to know of the docking problems in Saint Nazaire, to hear of plans to solve logistical snarls. As that dapper figure—Charlie always had a way with tailors—leaned into his enthusiasm, Jack listened in rising relief. Behind that high forehead the mind worked with baffling speed, those piercing eyes emphasized the sense the thin lips were telling—brilliance and energy Charlie scattered everywhere.

Amused and impressed with Charlie's grasp of logistical foibles, Jack waited for an ebb in the flow, broke in to say that Saint Nazaire's crises were known and being attended. More important were other, realer crises.

Charlie watched his friend as he hunched in earnest converse. Grayer he looked, possibly a little more lined in the face, but he had uncommon strength and excitement in him, a feeling of power altogether attractive. Pershing enjoyed his job. As he talked of purchasing problems, Dawes recognized an old persuasion at work—Pershing still knew how to get men to do what needed doing.

Old American practice caused the trouble. As Jack spoke, gestured with his fluent hands, Dawes realized that the Old Army had lived in the trough of luxury. No one ever had worried about coordinating orders for anything—the United States had so much of everything that horribly unbusinesslike democracy prevailed in procurement. All bureaus bought what they wanted without worrying about centralized control. Now, though, with Allied agents falling over each other for every factory, every rail line, airplane, port, for every spare stevedore and skilled mechanic, democracy had reached its ultimate fruition—chaos.

Things had been tried. He had, Pershing said, created a board of officers to study methods of regulation. He ought to have guessed the outcome, did, really, but still fumed when he read a strong recommendation for laissez faire. Ruefully he explained: "In a rather extended discussion, the board came to the conclusion that a centralized agency to control purchases would be illegal and unanimously recommended the continuance of existing methods." That conclusion was unacceptable. Tearing up the report, he turned to Charlie for the kind of business sense so clearly needed. Work in the engineers would be useful, the chance for service good, but Charlie could do so much more for his country, especially for his friend, if he accepted the role of general purchasing agent for the AEF. Under him a board of representatives from all supply branches of the AEF would serve, together with delegates from the Red Cross and the Young Men's Christian Association; as needs expanded, Dawes would regulate everything purchased by the Americans in France and would coordinate supply relations with the Allies, especially the French.[107]

Jack had picked his man shrewdly. For the next several days, days crowded with obligations and farewells before the Chaumont venture, he and Dawes conferred frequently about the general purchasing scheme. Dawes needed no prompting to see the opportunity Jack offered and confided in his journal:

He gives me practically unlimited discretion and authority to go ahead and devise a system of coördination of purchases . . . to arrange the liaison connections between the French and English army boards and our own; to use any method which may seem wise to me to secure supplies for the army in Europe which to that extent will relieve our American transports in their enormous burden. . . . He gives me such authority as I may deem wise to execute in regard to all methods of purchase and general supervision of them. In other words, he makes me an important element in this war.[108]

Just how important he was, Charlie soon saw as Pershing paraded him before a host of French high officials, introduced him as the virtual czar of procurement. It was heady business, this swift elevation to peaks of power, but Pershing eased the way with his custom and good manners. The two took time together, time to set lines right, to confide, and to soothe. Not all moments were happy, not all giddy at the heights of the world. One of these good days of reacquaintance found Jack and Charlie in a car heading for lunch at the Ogden Mills mansion. As Paris's boulevards flicked past the windows in a delicate August sunlight, a curious quiet settled. It was, Dawes knew, "an instance of telepathy which was too much for either of us. Neither of us was saying anything, but I was thinking of my lost boy and of John's loss and looking out of the window, and he was doing the same thing on the

107 See JJP, *Experiences*, 1:148–49; Harbord, *American Army*, pp. 124–26; and especially Charles G. Dawes, *A Journal of the Great War*, 1:19–22 (hereinafter cited as Dawes, *Journal*).
108 Dawes, *Journal*, 1:21.

other side of the automobile. We both turned at the same time and each was in tears."

A long look, then John said, "Even this war can't get it out of my mind."

Power, success, prominence beyond the dreams of a Missouri farm boy seemed often pointless without sharing. Those hard moments came less often now as time and challenge sapped recall. New happinesses came less guiltily, and laughter sparkled frequently at headquarters. Staff members noted gladly that Dawes brought new pleasantries, that his humor touched old mirth in the general and kindled the man lost in the image. At one luncheon with Harbord, Alvord, and Little Collins, Dawes swept his hand around the plush dining hall at the Mills mansion and quipped:

"John, when I contrast these barren surroundings with the luxuriousness of our early life in Lincoln, Nebraska, it does seem that a good man has no real chance in the world."

A moment's sadness, a melancholy look, then Jack answered, "Don't it beat hell!"[109]

Humor sometimes riles the jealous. Dawes's humor combined with his sudden exaltation triggered hopes for his failure in a few of the staff and many in the old supply bureaus. But Dawes used power like a silken snare, and soon even skeptics were fans. Harbord, who knew his boss relied on men who had proved themselves one way or another, thought Dawes's experience admirable for the tasks set, his personality splendid for the difficulties of connivance. "From what I have seen of his friend," Harbord mused, "I share the Chief's feeling" of confidence in Dawes.[110]

With a characteristic zest, Dawes leaped into a billowing coal crisis, found sources of purchase in England, arranged railroad carriage from the French coast to American depots, and bludgeoned the War Department into extra tonnage for channel crossings. That done in a few weeks convinced Jack his purchasing troubles were over. Dawes probably would need no backing beyond announcement of his appointment —he commanded cooperation as he demanded success.

One quality Dawes had in generous measure, one to endear him to a lonely, isolated general often the target of ignorance and envy. Charles Dawes was loyal. "Dear fellow and loyal friend," he said of Jack, "I hope I do not fail him." And, too, Charlie understood his new

[109] *Ibid.*, p. 23.
[110] Harbord, *Diary*, p. 141.

boss. "General Pershing demands results. Unless one can show them, he must step aside. When one does show them, the General does not stint his appreciation either in word or act."[111]

With Charlie at work, Jack turned to worries about consolidation of artillery ammunition resources for American field guns, and he soon chastised Washington for compounding confusion by permitting some bureaus in the War Department direct contact with their officers in France. Impatience ran through an early September message to the chief of staff:

With reference . . . my [cable] regarding failure Ordnance Department to keep these hdqrs. advised on important matters, following is case in point: The personnel for the divisional ammunition train motor section first division has arrived in France; vehicles to be furnished by the Ordnance Department but none have yet been received. Information requested concerning shipment of these vehicles and the kind of vehicles to be furnished whether motor caisson or escort wagon.[112]

When discordant work at home could be discovered and announced, Pershing knew his own logistical situation improved.

Everything really depended on people, on cajoling aid and sympathy, on urging, watching, praising, complaining until order and system replaced confusion.[113] The supply organization's officials were men Pershing liked and thought cooperative. Relations with the Allies were edgy, as usual, for an increasing variety of reasons. Relations with the War Department continued exemplary, in the main. Secretary Baker's communications were inquisitive of ways to help, his response to suggestions from Chaumont always cordial. And as long as Hugh Scott remained chief of staff, special friendship charmed support for every Pershing wish. Tardy responses from bureaus to many Pershing desires eluded control from above—the high brass simply could not move minions lost in the mass. Would a younger, stronger chief of staff be able to achieve quicker support? The question had moment, since Scott was about to retire.

That doughty old Indian battler had gone to Russia with Elihu Root, had helped report on Eastern conditions, and had returned to Washington with a short time left in office. His concern for Pershing's personal and official welfare prompted a letter as he picked up the reins again: "I have inquired around the War Department and find that

111 Dawes, *Journal*, 1:22, 27.
112 JJP to AGWAR, paragraph for chief of staff, Sept. 8, 1917, in Open Cables Sent.
113 See JJP, *Experiences*, 1:157.

everything seems to be going well with you. I thought that I would write you a note to assure you of my cooperation and to ask you to let me know how things are going with you." Traces of Jack's impatience surely sparked an important offer: "Any criticisms on the ways things are being supplied to you, or changes you want made will receive very careful attention here. I am anxious for your personal official success and will welcome your views on methods of attaining it."[114] Who really could replace so constant a friend?

Baker worried about a replacement for wider reasons and shared his musings with Pershing. Scott's departure would open the chief of staff's slot for Tasker Bliss, long the second man, whose stint in the wings entitled him to promotion. Bliss, too, teetered on the edge of retirement. Baker thought of a younger man who could handle the growing sphere of war, manage with diligence and current knowledge. What did Pershing think?[115]

Bliss could handle the War Department, at least for a while, although criticisms of his own bumbling disarray mounted. Even George Goethals, now freighted with Panama laurels and lofty in the councils of his country, carped at Bliss's labyrinthine administration.[116] Pershing could scarcely quarrel with Bliss's succession; that grand old soldier had always held out a strong hand. But friends could be problems—age and long measurement in the army regulations cut patterns in men hard to alter. Bliss's penchant for correctness was commendable but he took it to such long lengths. Hours he would devote to things worth minutes; cables and messages he received seemed somehow devoured in a lost cache of secrets. If a younger man familiar with business management could take charge of the War Department, Pershing's problems would instantly dwindle.

Baker suggested Peyton March, vice Bliss. March had been an attaché in Japan, almost contemporaneously with Jack, and had fullest knowledge of the army building in France. His command of an artillery brigade at Valdahon earned plaudits from every witness and had impressed Pershing mightily during a September visit. In fact, the energy, personal devotion to details, and discipline March had infused into his men convinced Pershing he would be the right man to command the AEF's artillery. As a newly minted major general, March had plunged into larger problems with accustomed order and kept an eye cocked

[114] Scott to JJP, Aug. 11, 1917, Box 29, Scott Papers.

[115] Baker to JJP, Sept. 10, 1917, in JJP, *Experiences,* 1:225–26.

[116] Edward M. Coffman, *The Hilt of the Sword: The Career of Peyton C. March*, p. 43 (hereinafter cited as *March*).

toward the First Artillery Brigade. Pershing appreciated a good officer, hated to lose him, and urged engineer Maj. Gen. John Biddle as chief of staff—he would do splendidly in Washington. If the alternate were selected, Jack had saved himself a fine artillery chief. If Baker decided, finally, on March, Jack knew he would be efficient, would clean out the War Department's Augean mess, and surely would not lose most of the AEF's cables![117]

Baker's questions showed continued confidence and reminded of old obligations. Scott would be recalled to active service, Baker said, to command a training camp in the States. That would assuage the wound of departing duty in a war. So much that man had done for the army, especially for John Pershing, that his departure demanded a moment from the AEF. A cable on September 24 carried to Scott honest affection and professional admiration: "Please accept sincerest wishes from this command for your future long life of happiness and well-earned rest. Congratulations on the valuable and honorable service you have rendered your country. You have our love and admiration.[118] That cable seemed a kind of punctuation to an older, milder life. Traces of it lingered in the Blisses, the Bells, and the Woods, but it faded rapidly in new men hardened in a graceless world.

Indications of Baker's support were comforting, especially in the intricate maze of Inter-Allied relations. Despite Pershing's careful cultivation of Haig and Pétain, Robertson and Lloyd George, French and British thoughts still ran urgently toward amalgamation of American units into their own. A disaster in Italy and the long-expected collapse of Russia added urgency to Allied hopes. On October 24, 1917, a sudden, smashing attack by combined German and Austrian forces along the old Isonzo front developed into an overwhelming Italian defeat at Caporetto. Riddled by Bolshevik propaganda, poorly led, wretchedly prepared either for winter or the enemy, thousands of Italian soldiers surrendered while their armies fled toward the Piave. On that broad barrier in November the Italian front stablized, but the southern ally had taken more than 300,000 casualties, lost thousands of guns, incredible amounts of supplies, and avoided total ruin only by enemy exhaustion. If the southern front opened again, if Central Powers forces occupied Rome and overran all of Italy, the whole strategic picture on the Western Front and in the Mediterranean would shift. Whatever inconvenience resulted, the French, British, and surely the Americans must save Italy.

[117] *Ibid.*, pp. 44–48.
[118] JJP to Scott, Sept. 24, 1917, Box 29, Scott Papers.

A close look at Caporetto raised some military eyebrows. Gen. Oskar von Hutier plied the Isonzo front with his specially trained troops and his tactics of surprise, infiltration, isolation of strong points —and was as successful as he had been at Riga in September.

In the east the Russian bear, stirred too long from hibernation, turned on his tormentors. Revolt swept the Russian forces; revolution shattered the monarchy. From the ashes of the czar's empire came red flags, "soviets," and a strident call for peace. Negotiations began at the end of the year. Russia's failure would free thousands of German troops for the Western Front. In the darkening winter, gloom spread across France, tinged all Allied thoughts with defeat, and made American determination for a private army absurd. Pétain raised the old issue in person late in the year. He wanted, he said, to arrange "for the collaboration as rapidly as possible of your forces. . . ." because of the gathering crises. Trapped and not wholly unsympathetic to Pétain's position, Pershing argued firmly for continuing the collection of his own army. Careful instruction seemed essential, indeed Pétain had urged deliberate preparation—hasty commitment of Americans to battle would simply add to Allied hazards. There were other considerations—national and linguistic barriers, predilections of the American public, political pressures on President Wilson, for instance—that forced American policy. All these things Pétain grasped; his shrewd sense of realities made him especially sensitive to democratic military problems. But emergencies change circumstances. "A menace by the enemy of an imminent large scale general offensive on the French front," he urged, "obliges us to utilize all resources, not omitting the support of the American forces. Without prejudice to the duration of the war it is then believed that we can not wait for these troops to be organized and instructed as would have been desired had we disposed in all tranquility [*sic*] of considerable time."

Specifically Pétain wanted to speed the preparation of the 26th Division by breaking it up among four French divisions for two months' intensive trench training. Then the units could be regrouped for brief instruction and inserted in the line alongside the U.S. 1st Division, which would have completed its slow indoctrination by February, 1918. Later American arrivals should be filtered in regimental strength to French divisions. Infantry, with some artillery and engineer adjuncts, would stick with French divisions for first front service and would stay with their "parent" units until "hardened." "Thus," Pétain boasted, "the different arms of the American Army would be trained in close liaison with one another in the school of a French division." American officers would work with their Gallic counterparts in learning ways to run modern war. There were charms to the idea, and Pétain summed them craftily. "The American units thus trained will then be grouped in American divisions whose successive entry beside one another on the front would form progressively an American sector of increasing importance, unless most pressing need necessitate making other dispositions. . . . I request you urgently, in the common interest, to adopt this solution without delay."[119]

None of the arguments here were new; they reflected much of the old "Nivelle Plan" bruited before Pershing and his staff sailed on the *Baltic*. Counterarguments still applied—but a new dimension appeared in Allied supplication. Ever jealous of each other's place with the Americans, they connived for preeminence, for aid. Shameless with inducements, each paraded advantages: the French, supplies, especially artillery and ammunition; the British, shipping and that old call of kinship. Now, late in 1917, as Haig's grinding drive in Flanders produced "wastage" beyond even his estimates, a real manpower pinch sharpened British reaction to Russia's demise and Caporetto. Lloyd George, casting still for alternatives to Haig's abattoir, glimpsed the power of dwindling numbers—the power to persuade. Britain, he knew, faced cutting divisions from twelve to nine battalions, with matching cutbacks in support units. Germany soon would boast troop superiority on the Western Front, especially if Allied forces had to sustain Italy. America's help must come now or it might be wasted. Britain would be able, with careful planning, to release additional ships for Yanks destined for service with the British! That bait supreme might charm increased alliance between the English-speaking armies, an alliance likely not only to steady the war but also to pressure Haig. Lloyd George had tried to counterbalance Haig's prestige by supporting Nivelle, and the Frenchman's failure left the prime minister weaker against his generals. If America's role expanded, if she took increasingly important places in councils and battles as her numbers swelled, Haig's position would dwindle. Lloyd George might somehow control the war. It seemed a high gamble with Britain's sacrifices, but political necessities dimmed future portents.[120]

---

[119] Henri Pétain to JJP, Dec. 28, 1917, in "Important Documents Concerning American Troops for Employment with French and British," bound vol. D-4, AEF, GHQ, G-3, Folder 651, Employment of Troops Correspondence, Jan.–July 1918, RG 120, National Archives.

[120] For background considerations affecting Lloyd George's attitude toward American participation, see Joseph E. De Francisco, "Amalgamation: A Critical

Britain's canny war leader sought American participation in a series of Allied conferences scheduled for late in 1917—conferences likely to map military and logistical strategy for 1918. In September he wrote Col. Edward M. House, Wilson's brilliant unofficial advisor, that "I think it is essential to the cause of the Allies that a representative of the United States of the first rank should come over here officially as soon as possible."[121] This smooth invitation showed some misapprehension of America's government and a serious misreading of America's president. Wilson had seen little through the first war months to increase his faith in the Allies. That strain of morality running deep in him lent suspicion to diplomacy. And war was diplomacy gone bad. Baker had his confidence and ran the war with as little fuss as necessary. Pershing had done well through the hard beginnings of America's crusade and had Baker's support—so he had Wilson's, too. Which meant that he had as much power as necessary to direct American affairs in Europe. This kind of authority cast on a general seemed senseless to Lloyd George. Rich in his troubles with Haig and other martinets, the prime minister saw power in terms of politics only as practiced by politicians. That Pershing might wear both helmet and bowler strained British imagination.

Not that Wilson remained utterly aloof from war's intrusions. Capitol Hill intruded its own twisted version of the war increasingly through a long, hot, and oddly fruitless summer. Restive at staggering costs, nervous about the draft, irked by docile Doughboys languishing on French farms, lawmakers grumbled about investigating the conduct of the war. The ancient precedent of the Civil War chilled all War Department heads and achieved Wilson's notice. Aware of some cabinet sentiment favoring increased interaction with the Allies, the president brooded on ways of achieving it without yielding the war's morality to blood-stained hands in France and England.

Baker, for his part, played a deft game of keeping out of the way. As he and Pershing grew close through frequent confidential communications, the secretary of war appreciated his general's hope for closer Allied ties. Pershing's difficulties were magnified by exclusion from Inter-Allied discussions; his absences were easily mistaken or inflated into slights; he missed many chances for coordination. To an increasingly frustrated general who asked for a sustaining visit from

Issue in British-American Command Relations, 1917–1918," Master's thesis, Rice University, 1973, pp. 66–69.

[121] Lloyd George to House, Sept. 4, 1917, in Charles Seymour, *The Intimate Papers of Colonel House*, 3:174 (hereinafter cited as *House Papers*).

his chief, Baker wrote a long survey of his own situation and included a paragraph that reminded Pershing of his duty and confirmed his absolute authority:

I am especially concerned that our troops should not be engaged in actual fighting in France until they are there in such numbers and have made such thorough preparation that their first appearance will be encouraging both to their own morale and to the spirit of our people here. I think it goes without saying that the Germans will make a very special effort to strike swiftly and strongly against any part of the line which we undertake to defend, in order to be able to report to their people encouragingly about our participation and also with the object of discouraging our soldiers and our people as much as possible. I have no doubt this has all been present to your mind and I refer to it only because I want you to know that we will exercise all the patience necessary on this side and will not ask you to put your troops into action until in your own judgment both the time is opportune and the preparations thoroughly adequate.[122]

After that it seemed unnecessary to add that "your course from the moment you landed in England has given both the President and me the greatest satisfaction and pleasure." But it was nice to read. And the authority did make relations easier. Without that assurance, Pershing might have resented news that Colonel House with a sizable mission would come over and take part in the conference Lloyd George had been pushing for in late fall. Especially might Jack have worried to learn that Gen. Tasker Bliss, chief of staff, would be among House's party. But Baker had removed concern.

There was another proof of success and prop to power. Negotiations had been bandied in the Senate concerning promotion of a long slate of generals. Among these, Jack's name appeared for elevation to the exalted glitter of four stars—the rank of full general. Papa had worked his smoothing deftly, and in early October the confirmation came in the form of a bill creating the rank to fit both the commander of the AEF and the chief of staff of the army.[123] A happy Bliss cabled Pershing's promotion, and, in the evening of October 7, kind Robert Bacon, commanding Chaumont post, put a bottle of champagne on Jack's table—just one for ten men, but it brought grand toasts and smiling recollection of another lonesome bottle some three weeks before and of toasts to a fifty-seventh birthday.[124]

Amid pleasure and reams of congratulations there was quiet satis-

122 Baker to JJP, Sept. 10, 1917, in JJP, *Experiences*, 1:224.

123 FEW to JJP, Oct. 4, 5, 9, 1917, FEW Papers, vol. 80.

124 See JJP, *Experiences*, 1:170, 193; Blumenson, *Patton Papers*, p. 428; J. B. Scott, *Robert Bacon*, pp. 292, 305, where the champagne is mentioned for both occasions; Harbord, *American Army*, p. 152.

faction and some longing to share the pinnacle of military prowess. There was, too, some thought about a personal future. Although the four stars were temporary, the command conferred a lifetime's prominence. After the war, whenever that ended, high reputation would carry burdens and responsibilities. They would be heavy borne alone; what of Nita? George had been quiet about her as he wrestled with his cars and correspondents. Bemused by a possible shift to the new Tank Corps, Patton seemed present but not fit for duty. Finally Jack came to a decision. Would George ask Beatrice to invite Nita for a visit? Nita seemed now "very much alive to the responsibilities she will one day assume," and felt too tied to her mother. George sent the message with a brotherly suggestion: "You might coach her on maternity?"[125]

With time for personal plottings, Pershing knew he had his army shaped in outline, had the men in charge he thought could run it, had the Allies impressed—Ambassador Jusserand wrote Clemenceau in October that "it is for us of extreme importance . . . that he judge us favorably and write to Wilson in that light"[126]—and he had the rank to match his hero, Ulysses S. Grant!

All of which gratified but did not satisfy Jack. An outline of an army, efficient as it was, only teased a soldier—he wanted the AEF to fight.

[125] Blumenson, *Patton Papers*, pp. 434–35.
[126] Jusserand to Clemenceau, Oct. 19, 1917, in Records of the Quai d'Orsay, Etats-Unis, Armée Américaine, 2: 130.

☆ 20 ☆

Agitated Allies

*"If you want to know where the generals were . . .
Back in gay Paree!"*
—I'll Tell You Where They Were," Doughboy Song

"How many times have you sat for your portrait?" The sudden question from normally taciturn Henri Pétain startled Pershing. It dropped into an afternoon's war talk and sparked a quick answer—"several times"—and a private muse on fame. Ambitious always, questing to crown service with acclaim, John Pershing now stood squarely in the eye of the world. His old aloofness, so much the mood of grief, had hardened with a sharpened sense of martial security—but he yielded to the thronging adulation of France, surprised his staff with good press manners, and tolerated autograph hunters, gawkers after the great, photographers, and "several" portraitists with becoming modesty. He knew his role better than anyone guessed. America looked to him as democracy's captain, expected him to be firm, fatherly, honorable, fearsome in battle, magnanimous in victory. For a time, at least, he was the most important symbol his country had; and symbols have no privacy.

"Several times already" he had sat for eager artists to catch such signs of triumph as they might. A good subject and disciplined model, he looked on most portraits with neutrality; one he liked and discussed with Pétain.

"The last one, which I thought very good, was done by a distinguished artist by the name of Jonas for *l'Illustration*."

"Don't let them publish it! Don't do it!" Pétain exclaimed. "Every officer whose portrait by Jonas has appeared in that journal has been relieved from his command."[1]

---

[1] JJP, *Experiences*, 1:141.

Pétain had a long list of ruined leaders to spur his own concern with precedent. And he knew his American friend sat a precarious and lonely perch. Superstitions usually rated a hearty Missouri laugh— but not against Pétain's desperate seriousness. Pershing listened and stopped publication. Why risk an added omen? Commanders in France had enough real problems to plague survival without tempting fate.

War leaders were expendable, much more so than their men. Pershing knew the reward for martial fools, knew, too, how fickle democracies can be with fame. Americans watched paladins with suspicion. Uncomfortable with contemporary heroes, Americans endowed them with mythic strengths and virtues to make them bearable —and heaped gleeful scorn on those who proved too human.

Failure could come for various reasons, but Pershing knew the surest cause to be poor subordinates. If he picked his henchmen badly, he would suffer most. This challenge came as nothing new. He had wrestled with finding the right men for a wide range of jobs at Fort McKinley, in Moroland, and especially along the border and in Mexico. But earlier problems were small by comparison to those dogging him at Chaumont. With the regular army expanding, with the sudden surge of enlistments in the National Army, with the call-up of the National Guard, American military leadership became scarce. There were simply not enough trained officers to work the camps building across the country, to control the units preparing to sail, to organize others still recruiting. As in the Civil War, experience would be the main teacher. Costly as this lack of system was, it seemed the only way to provide a commissioned cadre for the army. What of higher commanders, of men to lead battalions, regiments, brigades, divisions, even corps and armies?

High commanders were critically scarce. When the United States entered the war there were comparatively few generals on the rolls. Some were of recent minting, some had seen service with Pershing in Mexico, but most were administrators of a small and untried army. And Pershing knew from his Mexican experience that most generals were too old or too soft for field duty. Border testing showed, too, that most field-grade officers barely grasped the intricacies of small-unit management; coordination of larger forces baffled most Old Army staff-bureau officers and simply stupified national guardsmen. New levies of civilians were malleable but incapable of any kind of leadership without training. So the AEF must make do with such higher commanders as looked competent.

Unfamiliarity dogged the whole organization process. In the
doldrum years since the Spanish-American conflict, the army had
fussed with the problem of mobilizing a division—and the failures
were too sad to be funny. Along the Texas-Mexican border, divisions
had straggled into rag-tag existence, but their overwhelming unreadiness embarrassed the country. What was a division? American attitudes
toward the new unit varied from the Allies and from the Germans.
Attrition along the Western Front showed the need for a flexible force
of sufficient size to hit hard, but not too big for movement. American
planners in the War College urged a large, 28,000-man division as the
best response to the dual problems of plentiful men and scarce officers.
American divisions, as they slowly clustered in France, were amazing-
ly large to Allied eyes; they were also filled with great, strapping,
fine men, prime subjects for the front. Such superb raw material ought
not suffer under tyro leaders, commissioned or noncommissioned. That
argument heard so often by Pershing piqued his nationalism. American officers were as good as their men, or would be with proper
training.

Proper training would have to come, of course, from Allied
teachers. But during the schooling time, Pershing insisted that American officers control their own units. And as the 1st Division toiled
grimly in the icy mud of Lorraine, Pershing watched divisional officers with cold assessment. Especially did he watch the generals.
Generals were the real key to AEF development—all enlisted rumors
to the contrary considered. Generals would set the tone of the divisions and brigades, would finally forge the corps and armies to win
the war. And the earliest generals to join the AEF were surely the
most to be pitied. Pershing's concern for Gen. William Sibert's command of the 1st Division mirrored his concern for every general permitted to serve in France.

Devoutly Jack hoped Sibert's cause untypical. The man seemed
progressively incapable. An easy sort of lethargy charmed his camps,
and the frequent visitors Pershing took to Gondrecourt came away too
often pointedly polite. Pershing fumed at the condescension. With
each awkward display, Sibert's life got harder. Constant public
scrutiny seemed supremely unfair to Sibert's harassed officers. His
staff resented the role of foil to Pershing's ego. The 1st Division had
come to learn the fighting business; to display neophytes as America's
finest seemed cruelly harsh. Big Red One would rank with the best
in time, but it should be left alone during adolescence.

Propinquity proved part of the problem. Gondrecourt lay a convenient motoring distance from Chaumont, and Pershing had special pride in the 1st Division; many of its regiments had toiled with him on Villa's trail. Naturally he wanted to show off Americans to distinguished visitors—and he expected his Mexican veterans to shine. When the division paraded at Gondrecourt in muddy puttees and baggy pants and stood awash in slime, the vision curdled the soul of an old tac from West Point. And when military nonprofessionalism muddied the talk of division officers, Pershing cringed. Poor appearances he blamed on poor officers; training and tactical confusion he blamed on generals.

Sibert's career added to Jack's worries. An engineering background had earned Sibert renown for Panama Canal work, but this training hardly charmed line officers. Affable, a man of considerable scientific attainment, Sibert enjoyed good army repute. Long acquaintance with Pershing had seemed a guarantee of support from the top—but Sibert's years away from troops bothered the commander-in-chief. Once suspect, Sibert's every act seemed to confirm Pershing's prejudice. Sibert simply could not "stand the gaff";[2] he "let his division run down"[3] and relied too much on his staff. Worse yet, he showed no real energy, seemed lackadaisical in pushing open warfare training, and preferred camaraderie to discipline.[4] Harbord, sharing Pershing's growing dissatisfaction, concluded that Sibert was "a positive danger as the second senior officer in France."[5]

In September, when Pershing took President Poincaré to watch a review, everything had gone wrong. An aggregation of French brass joined the inspection, and the AEF's commander winced on his first view of parade arrangements. Whoever had selected the site lacked any sense of ground—the assembling area looked like an uneven plateau sliced from a muddy hillside. The men stood at parade weary in the muck and were woebegone and sullen as the galaxy of stars marched along each line. The president of France, always courteous, smiled, talked to various men, and roundly complimented the inept marching of troops just barely aware of the evolutions of the line. Graciously Poincaré asked to meet the division's officers, "made them a very happy speech," which won him three loud cheers.

If Poincaré seemed pleased, Pershing was not. "From the purely military point of view," he judged, "the impression gained by the

2 Edward M. Coffman, *The War to End All Wars*, p. 142.
3 James G. Harbord, *Leaves From a War Diary*, p. 201.
4 Coffman, *War*, p. 142.
5 Harbord, *Diary*, p. 202.

President . . . could not have been particularly favorable. . . ."[6] Fixing on Sibert, Pershing vented his chagrin. What was happening with the division? Why was progress so slow? Surely the French trainers were not coddlers—spit and polish might not be possible in a Lorraine winter, but some start on precision might be expected. Aware of the pressures, Sibert kept a tactful, if mistaken, silence, and Pershing stalked away in a sulk.[7]

Sibert's embarrassment pinched hardest on Capt. George Marshall, the brilliant Virginia Military Institute man who served as acting divisional chief of staff. Marshall, saddled with arrangements for the parade on short notice, coordinated the arrival of units far sprawled over the training area, picked the review site in fading daylight, and failed to see the abounding ooze.[8]

Marshall shared the staff's possessive affection for Sibert. This affection, partly defensive, came from a deep respect for the general's manliness and cheerful subordination. He bore suspicion like a gentleman. And he treated his staff like colleagues, took advice readily, never showed the hauteur of uncertainty. Pershing's spiteful vendetta —for that it seemed to Sibert's friends—sparked no responding feud. Sibert's honor earned devotion.

In Chaumont, Sibert's stoicism smacked of sin. If there were reasons for such bad shows, why did he not say so? Did he really know the dismal look of his awkward squads? If Sibert's silence came from kindness, could he really command on the Western Front? That, of course, was the acid question. Kindness had small room in a trench, where survival went to the strong.

Strength haunted the Allied world. Russia's situation worsened daily, and distressed French leaders pressed harder for Americans in the line. How long did Pershing intend to train those fine, big soldiers? The French Blue Devils would take them into line any time. Did the general not think that front-line experience would aid morale? Certainly it would aid Allied morale! Pressures for participation Pershing felt keenly, though he ignored them well. But certain principles of trench warfare could not be ignored. For each unit in the line, another should be in reserve. Rotation every three or four days kept men fresher and allowed replenishment of equipment and provisions, and

[6] JJP, *Experiences*, 1:163–64.
[7] Forrest C. Pogue, *George C. Marshall: Education of a General, 1880–1939*, pp. 151–52.
[8] *Ibid.* See also George C. Marshall, *Memoirs of My Services in the World War, 1917–1918*, pp. 21–22.

the reserve unit could replace any sudden casualty losses. Replacement potential must be achieved, and no American division would try the front until two could go. So, four divisions ought to be ready for combat before any full commitment occurred. Meanwhile Pershing could not deny the practical sense of sharing trench duty with French divisions. The 1st Division could have a touch of the line.

Before it went forward, however, it ought to be shaped up considerably. On October 3 Pershing and a small group climbed into a khaki staff car and took the hour's ride to Gondrecourt. At "Washington Center" training site things looked some better. With a little warning of Pershing's impending descent, French and American officers arranged a trench attack demonstration. Skirmish fire, booming grenades, men scurrying from hole to hillock to trench were everywhere. Clutches of troops rose from cover, rushed forward, dropped from sight; some jumped up to hurl grenades, others sprayed the "enemy" lines with covering machine-gun fire. A regular battle flourished in view. One of the men leading the attack, Maj. Theodore Roosevelt, Jr., came to report on his own scheme for assault. Even the French approved!

Finally the shooting stopped; Pershing and the divisional staff gathered for a critique of the exercise. Turning to Sibert, Pershing asked his views. Unfortunately Sibert had seen the maneuvers for the first time himself; his comments were halting, confused, and obviously inexpert. A junior staff officer entered the fray and muddled matters worse than his general. A sweep of the group showed fear and uncertainty—not a man seemed to know what had happened or why! What was everybody doing up here? Obviously training had been low on the list of activities! Directives from GHQ about open warfare formations apparently had gone unread. As for Sibert—what kind of leader would permit such unprofessionalism? Did discipline ever occur to the general? Was Sibert ever close enough to training for discomfort? Furiously Pershing raked the whole staff with scorn, then turned to the chief of staff—just assigned two days before—and asked if he had the faintest notion of the day's lessons? He had not, clearly, since he stammered, looked desperately for help. As a critique the session had gruesome likeness to a mass court martial.

Obviously nothing could be learned here. A wave of dismissal to the hapless chief of staff, a whirl toward the door, while the wretched tableau stood mute, then an irritated, insistent voice stopped Pershing's exit. A tall captain, that VMI man Marshall, talked rapidly, with growing anger, of Pershing's gross unfairness. Shrugging his shoulders, the general turned back toward the door, only to feel Marshall's hand grab his arm.

"General Pershing, there's something to be said here and I think I should say it because I've been here longest."

A cold, appraising glance, then,

"What have you got to say?"

In a passionate torrent Marshall explained that he had served as acting chief of staff and that Pershing should have asked him most of the questions put to Sibert and the crushed new chief of staff. Sibert's absence had been on legitimate business; the division did work hard, harder than anyone guessed, but it was difficult to look good on hasty display—soldiers ought to be allowed to get on with soldiering was the gist of the verbal assault.

Everyone else present shrank in horror; Marshall had clearly committed professional suicide. The general stood and looked at the captain and finally, with remarkable calmness, said,

"You must appreciate the troubles we have."

Marshall, aware now that he had "gotten into it up to my neck," plowed ahead.

"Yes, general, but we have them every day and they have to be solved before night."

Pershing looked hard at Marshall, then left. The captain had a wealth of facts at his lips, spoke with convinced boldness, and knew what was happening. He might be a soldier, even a fighter.

Behind him Pershing left stunned silence for some time. Sibert finally sympathized with his loyal captain and regretted he had sacrificed himself for a fading cause. Most of the junior officers guessed George would "be fired right off." So what, Marshall answered—the worst fate possible would be the best, a shot at field duty![9]

Surprisingly enough, no retribution came. On Pershing's next visit—dreaded in anticipation—he took Marshall aside and asked the real condition of the division. Pershing's curious detachment to criticism impressed Marshall increasingly. Finally he grasped one of Pershing's special qualities: "You could talk to him as if you were discussing somebody in the next country. He never [held] it against you for an instant. I never saw another commander I could do that with. . . . It was one of his great strengths that he could listen to things."[10]

As the 1st Division's moment of war approached, Pershing came

9 Pogue, *George C. Marshall*, pp. 152–53.
10 Quoted in *ibid.*, p. 153.

oftener to Gondrecourt, toured all the neighboring training towns, watched the men practice improved martial arts—and he worried about their welfare. Some snarl in Washington denied the AEF winter clothes in proper quantities; shipments of shoes and blankets, of socks and underclothing, lagged. Local procurement, the kind that Dawes could push, went fairly well. British and French depots yielded a good deal of important gear, especially steel helmets. Rifles and small arms came with officers and men; ammunition lingered to vex a fighter's ire. Field kitchens were scarce, transportation incomplete, and divisional artillery still practiced down in Valdahon. But the French would fill the needs in gun support and kitchens—Big Red One would go into line on the twenty-first of October as part of a veteran French division.

In those exciting weeks Marshall noted Pershing's capacity for detail. While his heart rested with the men about to taste battle, the commander-in-chief kept a close eye on general organization, did his social duties by bringing a continuous stream of guests to Gondrecourt, and pondered the toughest of his problems—high command.

Short association with Pershing showed his teacher training. Important things were repeated, stressed in various ways until they seemed extensions of his thought. The staff at Chaumont could recite the lessons on qualifications for command, and Marshall could have embellished them easily. And the Old Man was right, of course, in stressing youth and vigor, mental agility and character. Early in October he hosted the first visitation of generals from home. They came as a result of Secretary Baker's well-meant scheme to familiarize all potential division commanders in the States with front-line conditions. To the harried staff, especially to unobtrusively efficient Robert Bacon who was charged with housing all VIP's, they seemed an ill-sorted Baker's dozen—really fourteen—who swept in with chiefs of staff and aides for a tour of the war.[11] While Bacon bedded them, Little Collins, Shallenberger, and Patton wrestled with protocol and transportation. Harbord and the staff department heads briefed them all on their vacation plans in France.

Elaborate itineraries greeted this first star-bearing contingent. They would alternate visits to British and French line units, would watch divisional operations, corps activities, army coordination, and would study Allied staff work and the intricacies of running the rear areas of modern war. While they studied they were studied—by Allied

---

[11] James Brown Scott, *Robert Bacon: Life and Letters*, p. 310.

officers, American liaison people, guides, and hosts everywhere. Each general prepared a report of his observations with suggestions for American improvement. A month's indoctrination brought them all back to Chaumont.[12] Pershing's staff watched with interest the grilling the generals got while they listened to the Old Man.

Pershing, who had had some doubts about wholesale junkets of generals from the first, doubted the system more deeply as he greeted his war-exposed guests. November came chill and gray to Lorraine, wet and grimy like the war, and the visitors huddled against the gloom and John Pershing. Several of them knew him, all knew his reputation—which left a few insecure about their futures, since they now knew the pressures of the Western Front. He marched in to greet them at a convocation—tall, as straight as ever, face etched a little deeper, hair lighter but still sandy, moustache trimmed, eyes alive and searching. His four stars glittered atop an immaculate tunic modest in ribbons, his Sam Browne belt a tribute to Frank Lanckton's polish; his flared breeches were razor-pressed and his boots were mirrors to the room. As his good Missouri voice welcomed them, the generals listened intently, touched by a subtle force that straightened them perceptibly and sharpened their gaze.

Rumor made Pershing a tough, unbending martinet at GHQ, a dapper dandy of a gentleman in Paris salons. He might be all that and more. Certainly here with American generals he had warmth, ease, and persuasion in his word and gesture, wisdom in his mind.

As he talked of Allied training methods contrasted with American realities, he studied his guests. Who listened and got the point? It would be hard to tell. The men had an odd similarity that blunted personalities: they all looked alike, with their moustaches, heavy girths, and jowls, and they seemed somehow settled into age. Undaunted, if dispirited, Pershing praised the British and French systems, noted especially British discipline, French physical training, but pointed to America's special mission in France. Doughboys would tip the balance toward victory; they would carry the brunt of attack. Allied methods were splendid for trench training but lacked emphasis on open-warfare tactics—these would be the heart of the American system. Nods, smiles from many, murmurs of approval showed a few brains alive in the room. You are here, Pershing continued, to study the organization of the biggest army America has ever created— charts and statistics and suboffices and battalions of staff officers were

---

[12] See Hunter Liggett, *Commanding an American Army: Recollections of the World War,* pp. 14–18.

the hallmarks of a military program designed to move America's full power against the Germans. Close study of GHQ would give each general an idea of the things he must teach his troops from the earliest training days.

Not everything could be learned in a short visit—although one general recalled that "no other two weeks of study . . . ever so greatly profited me"[13]—and a good deal had to be left for reading. Pershing spoke fully his view on command, words the staff could quote: "We must not stand for any laxity or lack of energy or competency to train and handle our troops. The situation is grave and important. I shall take summary actions" against incompetent commanders.[14] Neither the challenge nor the threat were missed.

As he looked at his discomfited guests, Pershing began to appreciate Baker's idea. Not all of them, perhaps few of them, were fit for line service, but their tour of the front would lend invaluable perspective to any training or logistical assignments they got at home. If they took up time and eroded patience, the result seemed worthwhile.

Some intensely personal inconveniences came from the visitation plan. Friends were the harshest liabilities, enemies the meanest. What could Jack say to reliable J. Franklin Bell, crony so often in parlous times, but friend now aged sixty-two and saddled with diabetes? What to Thomas Barry, just ahead of Jack in the promotion scramble, old hand in army politics, competent but also sixty-two and more an administrator than commander? To tell these good men they could not stand the strain would break their hearts. But the truth would be told, and another heart would bend.

Dear old Bell tried hard to come—he had a fighter's spirit. Balked by Pershing's dictum against older generals—a rule broken by the rarest exceptions—Bell secured a physical examination to show his diabetes controlled and his constitution stout. Faced with that medical report, Jack had to explain things. It was one of the hardest letters he ever wrote, and it was gentle and firm and full of affection.

No officer in the army with whom I have served has inspired in me a more sincere affection nor a higher opinion of personal character and worth than you. It hardly seems necessary for me to say these things, but I am anxious that you should fully appreciate the fact that my recommendation in your case was based solely upon my conception of what is required of an officer in command of a division, and of your ability to fulfill to your own satisfaction and mine the duties imposed. . . . No one has a higher regard

---

[13] Robert L. Bullard, *Personalities and Reminiscences of the War*, p. 74.

[14] JJP to Chief of Staff, GHQ, Oct. 2, 1917, in AEF, GHQ, CIC Correspondence, File No. 3358, RG 120, National Archives.

for you personally and for this reason no one has had a more difficult decision to make in such a case than I have been called upon to make. My personal advice to you, if I were not in command, would be exactly to the same effect. I must hold to this opinion. . . .[15]

Bell's case brought anguish; Leonard Wood's, anger. For Wood came to France arrogant and with influence highly placed. For months he had sulked, and he had avoided oblivion by political machinations, by offering unbidden advice, and by conniving for some kind of command. Using his reputation in society, his knowledge of high members of Congress, his potential as embarrassment to President Wilson, Wood badgered his way to the war. His way proved longer, loftier, and more potent than the route of his fellow major generals.

Although he would go to France as one of Baker's trainee division commanders, Wood wangled a shift in direction through London. Well-known there before the war, he came as a kind of symbol of an older Anglo-American comradeship in imperialism. Once the crony of the revered Lord Roberts, accepted by such higher-ups as Sir John French, and famed to late comers like Lloyd George, Wood prowled like a lion through Albion's salons. Tuned to his audience always, Wood waxed eloquent on America's awful unreadiness, on War Department chaos that had triggered a congressional investigation. President Wilson's weaknesses were acidly reviewed by the fluent general so veteran in American councils; Pershing's innocence of large affairs livened many a dinner. These things were true, obviously; they fitted British prejudice. And Wood must be speaking with a kind of authority, else why did he tour so loftily?

Reports of his procession preceded him to Paris, where again he mingled with the great. He attracted notice like some migrant plague, far more than all the other American generals together. Parisian gaiety, the natural exaggeration of French natures, touched Wood's deep sense of drama—he talked longer, wilder than ever of America's martial lapses. Nothing would come, he guessed, from so feeble a logistical system—and the sudden stoppage of railroad shipments in the eastern United States (the trains were snowbound) confirmed his wisdom.[16] Bounding from dinner to party to tea to conference with superb Gallic zest, Wood stole the whole American show in France. Pershing, the burgeoning AEF, the Red Cross, the great ports in the south, all trailed Wood's sparkling self. His sturdy figure and round countenance, his bristling hair and moustache, all added to the

[15] JJP to J. Franklin Bell, June 25, 1918, Box 23, PP.
[16] Frederick D. Palmer, *Newton D. Baker*, 2:233–34.

valor of his oddly halting gait—tough soldier was he, wounded surely in his country's cause. His wizardly role fitted well as Wood bestrode Paris and dispensed war opinions with the ease of ignorance. And to those Allied friends who wondered why America's "ablest soldier" hugged the fringes of conflict, he turned a modest silence or muttered possibilities of "politics."[17]

Pressed finally into the usual itinerary of a neophyte division commander, Wood's luck held—he was wounded while watching a Stokes mortar exercise at the French front, his chief of staff lost an eye, his aide had an arm disabled, and several French officers were killed. To Wood's hospital room trooped correspondents in platoons. Somehow the story emerged that he had been wounded in action—he made whispered protest—and a wave of admiration washed across America.

Touched by violence he came at last to Chaumont. Pershing had followed Wood's pilgrimage with distaste. Whatever Baker's own preferences, decency had demanded that Wood be shipped abroad. If some were shocked by Wood's raucous indiscretions, Jack had expected worse. Especially he expected a haughty visitation at Wood's convenience. But when the touring expert at last favored Chaumont's halls, he met higher hauteur.

Wood saw his old subordinate at Chaumont in early spring, a budding time of power for the AEF, a time of testing for John Pershing. Complaints of things American swelled the news by now; that vaunted Yankee urge to speed rang a hollow joke in France. And when Leonard Wood presumed to patronize the commander-in-chief, he ran against the grain.

From all signs along the front, Wood said, American troops were poorly treated—doubtless the fault of an archaic, red-taped War Department. He would tell Baker, tell Congress, tell all who lent their ears, how shabbily the nation supported good John Pershing, and would urge redoubled efforts. It seemed the least one general could do for another, especially for a former junior now saddled with such mountainous problems. A detailed report to Harbord showed weaknesses in the AEF organization for which Wood offered remedies.[18]

In an earlier world the meeting might have gone Wood's way; in Manila, perhaps, when Pershing struggled for repute. Now a full general simply squashed the stubborn two-starred man who talked too much. You will say nothing, Pershing bluntly commanded. What the

[17] *Ibid.*, p. 234.
[18] Wood to Chief of Staff, Feb. 24, 1918, Box 215, PP.

AEF needed Pershing would provide.[19] And the meeting, short, brittle, and glacially correct, apparently ended on Pershing's terms.[20] Wood remembered conveniently, and when he got home, he touched his training division briefly, then accepted a senatorial command to talk. In front of Papa Warren he kept quiet about Jack's deficiencies, spoke temperately of Allied problems and confidently of victory.[21] Clearly he thought he would soon return at the head of his troops; he and his public were shocked when some odd fate snatched him almost from the gangplank to stateside duty. Baker took the blame for animus, but the secretary knew that Pershing would have shipped Wood home unceremoniously. And Baker bluntly explained the reasons to Wood: "the indirect and insubordinate disposition on your part . . . which made it difficult to combine you with an organization of which you are not the head with any expectation of harmonious cooperation."[22]

For Pershing the issue closed when he rejected a Baker question about using Wood in Italy.[23] Staff chiefs at Chaumont relaxed when the Wood specter faded, many of them now more convinced than their chief of the conniving doctor's unprofessionalism. Several of them noted that other visiting generals listened closely to lectures on AEF policies, but Wood "was inclined 'to tell us instead of being told.'"[24]

Agreement with the Chaumont assessment came from the field, especially from officers who watched Wood's dilettantish flit along the front. George Duncan, now a brigade commander, noted Wood's departure with grim glee. "In my opinion," Duncan said, "General

---

[19] JJP to Wood, Mar. 5, 1918, Box 215, PP.

[20] Palmer, *Baker*, 2:234.

[21] FEW to JJP, Mar. 27, 1918, FEW Papers, vol. 82.

[22] Baker to Wood (copy), June 5, 1918, Box 19, PP; also in Palmer, *Baker*, 2:243–44.

[23] Baker to JJP (Private Cable), June 1, 1918, and JJP to Baker ("Personal and Confidential"), June 10, 1918, both in Box 19, PP. Pershing's reasons for rejecting Wood's Italian service were consistent: "Regardless of his physical unfitness, if sent to France or Italy it would introduce a disturbing factor in an already difficult situation as he would certainly endeavor to undermine the structure that only loyal co-operation could build or maintain. . . . Having his own political ambition always in mind, he would, without question, endeavor to lay the foundation for his own political future. No matter what he promised, he would never be subordinate to discipline under his former junior. His entire army career has fully demonstrated that loyalty is not a trait in his character. Both his reputation and character inspire only mistrust, even among those who know him best. He is unscrupulous, and I should have no confidence in him in the conduct of operations nor under any other circumstances. He would carry out orders only if it suited his purpose. He is superficial in military knowledge and training, and inclined solely to the spectacular" (see *ibid.*, and also Palmer, *Baker*, 2:240–41).

[24] Palmer, *Baker*, 2:234–35.

Pershing was perfectly right in not wanting an officer who had so much hostility toward him and was notoriously undisciplined in his attitude to constituted authority when decisions ran contra to Wood's opinion."[25]

Vexing questions of friends and foes might rile tranquillity occasionally, but careful selection of high officers, of competent staff assistants, produced visible results. Jousting with the War Department often as to proper staff assignments, haggling with local commanders who wanted to keep their best, gave Jack deep knowledge of the AEF's hierarchy.[26]

Nagging doubts of command competence plagued Pershing most when they focused on possible casualties. Now that the AEF began to share something of the war, Jack suffered the anguish of a parent trying to let a splendid child mature. The 1st Division carried so much of Pershing's own pride, so much of America's hope, sustained the dual roles of fighting machine and Allied symbol so completely, that its appearance against the Boche must be successful. Obviously the division had been prepared as well as the crack Chasseurs and the French 18th Division could achieve—but Papa Pershing fussed at the division's exposure.[27] He watched Sibert coldly and thought seriously of putting Robert Bullard in his place.[28]

In the regiments, in the battalions and brigades, a kind of thrilling release had come with the order to take positions at the front. What mattered that small dribbles of the division would go in at one time, would serve only ten days and yield to other units? Finally everyone would get a crack at the fire-step—and the regulars with their recruit buddies chafed to put Gondrecourt's drills behind them and kill Germans.

Were they really ready? Had they learned enough in simple charading to counter veteran cunning? Did they know the ways to get forward, the strange rituals of trench "relief?" French officers assured Pershing his men lacked only battle experience to be equals in the line.

Those good men started off well enough, with the kind of order and zest West Pointers approved. On October 14, 1917, the word came

[25] George B. Duncan, "Reminiscences of the World War," p. 67 (typescript in University of Kentucky Library).

[26] See JJP to AGWAR (cable), Mar. 18, 1918, in Open Cables Sent; JJP to AGWAR for Chief of Staff (cables), Sept. 7, 1917, and March to JJP, Mar. 21, 1918, in CIC Reports, GHQ, AEF, Box 2, Folder 15, RG 120, National Archives.

[27] Coffman, *War*, p. 138.

[28] Bullard, *Personalities*, p. 93.

that the division was moving up. Orders came "in great detail"—staff officers fussed with every regiment; detachments went from the lead battalions to scout the ground and test the atmosphere of the real war.[29]

What lay ahead? Where were the French putting the Doughboys? Everyone knew the general rumors—they were going up as part of the veteran French 18th Division, commanded by Gen. Paul Emile Joseph Bordeaux, and that division would hold a stretch of trenches in the Sommerviller sector, not far from Nancy. *Poilus* spoke of the area as "quiet," a kind of resting line where routine amenities regulated hostilities. German and French guns exchanged daily bombardments aimed at empty fields. French trenches ran along lovely rolling hills in Lorraine and looked across at German lines equally comfortable, rustic, and happy. Not always had that stretch of front been quiet. Doughty Gen. Edouard de Castelnau blunted the German fall drive in 1914 in the Nancy area, and after that a stalemate settled along the opposing armies all the way to the Swiss border. But quiet sectors had their excitements, or could be stirred up with proper zeal—and there would be plenty of chances to shoot Germans!

At the start only the first battalions of the four regiments marched out on Saturday, the twentieth, leaving behind the envious remnants who would follow as the chances came. Into the rain-lashed, swallowing dark the fresh boys walked in joy—the whole division looked as spicked and spanned as long-sodden summer khakis allowed.[30] Old Papa Joffre had reviewed them on the fourteenth, the day they became part of the French 18th Division, had spoken glowingly to the officers, and had thought the Yanks a match for any Hun around. And he was right—every man in the division would prove him right.

All of the twentieth and twenty-first passed in marching, waiting, listening to the dull, constant clangor of conflict. With commendable self-discipline the Old Man stayed away from his boys. Pershing, in fact, did plan a visit to the front on the twenty-first or twenty-second, but as sightseer during a big French drive in the Chemin des Dames, against the Malmaison and Condé forts. Six days of bombardment preceded the proposed push, and the French hoped to do something decisive. Pershing could watch close up and in uncommon glamour as

[29] See FO no. 1, Oct. 11, 1917; FO no. 2, Oct. 14, 1917; Operations Table, Oct. 14, 1917, copied in Society of the First Division, *History of the First Division During the World War, 1917–1919*, pp. 391–95 (hereinafter cited as *First Div.*).

[30] Pershing fumed at a Quartermaster Department that hoarded winter garb for troops in the States (see Pogue, *George C. Marshall*, p. 154).

On August 26, 1914, Pershing met with Villa (*center*) and Obregón (*left*) in El Paso, Texas. Pershing later led American troops into Mexico in pursuit of Villa. *Smithers Collection, Humanities Research Center, University of Texas at Austin.*

Pershing (*center*) poses with war correspondents from the major U.S. newspapers in Columbus, New Mexico. *Smithers Collection, Humanities Research Center, University of Texas at Austin.*

Pershing and his staff ford the Río Casas Grandes on their return to Columbus, January, 1917. The officer on the left is Lt. George S. Patton. *National Archives.*

Loading the supply wagons at Dublán. *National Archives.*

Jeffrey quad truck used in the Punitive Expedition. *National Archives.*

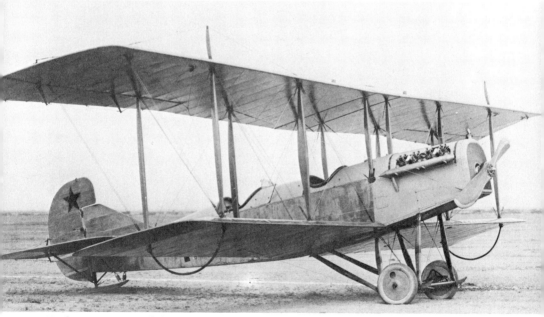

Biplanes were used for reconnaissance but encountered great difficulties in the mountainous Mexican terrain. *National Archives.*

Pershing at Casas Grandes ruins. *Rita Paddock*.

Landing in France, June 13, 1917. The first American troops reached St. Nazaire two weeks later. *World's Work.*

All Paris turned out to welcome the commander of the AEF. *World's Work.*

Pershing's first headquarters—31, rue Constantine, Paris. *U.S. Signal Corps.*

The Mills home at 73, rue de Varenne, Pershing's Paris residence. *U.S. Signal Corps.*

Field headquarters at St. Nazaire. *U.S. War Dept. Gen. Staff.*

Aerial view of Chaumont, AEF headquarters in France. *U.S. Signal Corps.*

Pershing and Marshal Pétain inspect a supply station in the Verdun region. *René de Chambrun.*

American advance northwest of Verdun. Such traffic jams aroused Allied criticism of American discipline. *National Archives.*

Pershing and Maj. Gen. C. P. Summerall inspect the 1st Division at Vertuzey, France, September, 1918. *Lt. Col. Thomas R. Stone.*

American tanks going into action in the Argonne forest, September, 1918. *National Archives.*

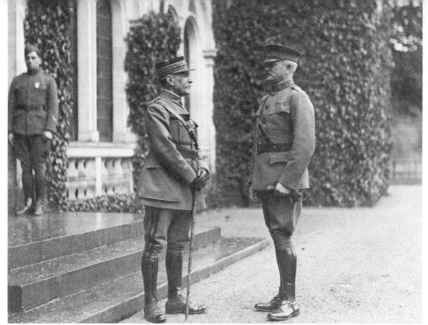

Pershing and Foch at Chaumont. *U.S. Signal Corps.*

Brig. Gen. Douglas MacArthur receives the Distinguished Service Cross from Pershing. *U.S. Signal Corps.*

Pershing reviewing the 32nd Division in Germany, 1919. *Lt. Col. Thomas R. Stone.*

The commander-in-chief at Genicart Embarkation Camp, June, 1919. *Left to right*: Captain Ryan, Gen. Charles D. Rhodes, Charles Dawes, and Pershing. *USMA Library.*

Pershing and Wilson at Chaumont, after the armistice. The Hôtel de Ville is in the background. *U.S. Signal Corps.*

Gen. Peyton March, chief of staff, and Pershing on the reviewing stand in Washington, D.C. The nation's capital welcomed Pershing home on September 8, 1919. *Marlene Muffie MacNeal.*

Pershing leads the crack 1st Division down Pennsylvania Avenue. *Marlene Muffie MacNeal.*

Pershing and George C. Marshall at Marfa, Texas, January, 1920. Marshall had been an operations officer with the U.S. First Army in France. *Smithers Collection, Humanities Research Center, University of Texas at Austin.*

Pershing at Ft. Sam Houston, Texas, 1923, with soldiers and nurses from America's wars. Represented are the Mexican War, the Civil War, the Spanish-American War, and World War I. The cadet (*front*) was in civilian military training. *Smithers Collection, Humanities Research Center, University of Texas at Austin.*

The Allied commanders-in-chief review the American Legion parade in Paris, 1927. Pershing is second from the left. *Goldbeck Collection, Humanities Research Center, University of Texas at Austin.*

Pershing, Foch, and other dignitaries at Château-Thierry in France, 1927. *Goldbeck Collection, Humanities Research Center, University of Texas at Austin.*

Pershing and Pétain review the Corps at West Point, October, 1931. *USMA Library.*

Pershing and the Prince of Wales in Washington, D.C., mid-1930s. *Marlene Muffie MacNeal.*

Pershing on his seventy-first birthday, Lincoln, Nebraska, 1931. *USMA Library.*

a guest of Gen. Franchet d'Esperey, heading Groupe du Nord. It would be a big, loud, smashing battle any fighter would revel in watching, but Jack's heart would be in Sommerviller in that quiet sector where America's first test was coming.[31]

Night approaches were the order of Western Front activity, and the trickiness of relieving units coming out of the line defied explanation on blackboards. Up toward the front on the evening of the twenty-first, American companies found a growing clutter, ground barer than common, the scattered detritus of hasty men; French companies coming out were edgy though welcoming, worn and glad to give up even their "quiet" shelters to younger, fresher troops. Carefully the American staffs had prescribed the battalion trains for support. Ammunition and supply dumps were established already, along with hospital and ambulance stations.

Plans called for American and tutelary French companies to alternate in the fire lines. Confusion plagued the glories of the first moment at the front—companies blundered around in search of parents, staff officers quarreled with line brass, and the Doughboys gawked at No Man's Land. Not that much could be seen in the black night. Sometimes there came a ghostly glow as a star shell burst, swung slowly groundward, and winked out in the rain—in those weird moments an eager eye might glimpse the roils of barbed wire guarding the parapet, a forbidding metaled wall that seemed, suddenly, the boundary of freedom. Beyond that prickly barrier lay a black world, and beyond it the redly winking reaches of enemy country.

Good teachers that they were, the French let the Americans hold strongpoints, resistance centers, and observation posts on their own. French officers were there to help, French units handy for emergencies. And, wonder of wonders, some American guns from Valdahon had rumbled into supporting positions behind the front and would grid their fire with French batteries for security. Given the inexperience of the Yanks, the horrid dark, and the muddled traffic in the communicating ditches, the whole relief operation went well. To the sere comforts of the Western Front, Yanks settled gingerly, in awe.

Perhaps the Germans knew they were coming, the first of Big Red One—rumors said the Huns knew everything all the time—or perhaps

---

[31] See JJP, *Experiences,* 1:202–3; Laurence Stallings, *The Doughboys: The Story of the AEF, 1917–1918,* pp. 36–38 (hereinafter cited as Stallings, *AEF*); Pogue, *George C. Marshall,* pp. 154–55; Sir Rex Benson, "Diary of the World War," Oct. 22, 23 (Monday and Tuesday), 1917, in possession of heirs of Sir Rex Benson, London.

some primal urge to action midst the flood nudged a company raiding party out of the kaiser's lines. Whatever the impetus, a sudden clamor at a strongpoint, a rattle of small arms, the quick loud stutter of machine guns, the sharp cough of a Stokes mortar broke the fragile hopes of night. As suddenly came silence, and the raiders shaded into that land the living did not hold. It was a small but important first combat—for it showed that solders could survive.[32]

Other firsts came quickly. Just after six on a cloudy, blustery Friday, October 23, Sgt. Alex L. Arch of C Battery, 6th U.S. Field Artillery, pulled lanyard on the first gun shot against the enemy. In the close dark of November 2, other Americans relieved the 1st Battalion. As the cocky veterans wound out of the line, they listened in amusement to the 2nd Battalion talking of courage. What would shelling be like? Would they get a better chance at the Hun? How many raids would they run? This relief followed old ritual. Battalion commanders stayed behind to supervise posting of defensive positions: 18th Infantry on the right, facing Parroy, with the 16th, 26th, and 28th strung out left. Artillery officers worked on liaison. Comrades passed the word on good billets. And at last the drifting mist swallowed both American columns.[33]

Luck took the 2nd Battalion, 16th Infantry, to a stretch of line hugging the rim of a bald hill near Bathelémont, and the hill jutted out toward the Rhine-Marne Canal. A happy darkness cloaked exposure. Only stray rifle fire cut the stillness as men found their places and settled to duty. By 9:30 P.M. the battalion reported relief accomplished.[34] That first war night lingered with its shadows and fears, and the wind seemed to bunch the mist by the wire as a fragile marker of life. Some men slept, weary beyond worry; most rested, stood the fire step, and wondered how it would be when they went for the Hun. Midnight came its goblined time, then the early hours of November 3, the long hours until dawn. But dawn came in wild, white, blinding flashes at 3:00 A.M., came roaring out of blackness to blister minds and ears. Ground heaved and rolled, billows of mud and dirt erupted everywhere. The German quick barrage searched trenchlines and gun positions with

---

[32] Evidence for a German raid during the first American night in the trenches is in "Historical Sketch of the First Division, American Expeditionary Force," in G-3 Reports, 1st Division, AEF, GHQ, G-3, Folder 12, RG 120, National Archives. Other sources ignore a first-night raid, so it must be regarded as a possibility, not a certainty.

[33] See *First Div.*, pp. 27–30; Coffman, *War*, p. 138–39.

[34] *First Div.*, p. 30; Coffman, *War*, p. 139.

horrid wisdom. Alarm rockets bloomed along the American front; flares joined in a lurid aurora of war. Suddenly the pounding stopped; German gunners shifted range into a precise box barrage. Raid! Raid! screamed men caught in the raining walls of steel—a platoon of the 16th left now to fight unaided. In moments waiting for the enemy men did the few things possible to be ready—checked arms, ammunition, bayonets, pistols, mortars. Out along the wire came the shattering boom of Bangalore torpedoes as the Germans blew approaches to the trench. Next came grenades that rolled on the duckboards and exploded, then the Germans themselves who rushed with veteran cunning, hacked with trench knives, fired Lugers point blank, bayonetted where room allowed, took a sergeant and ten men prisoner, and vanished into the suddenly ominous darkness.[35]

In the shocked silence men began to explore the seared area. A German deserter wandered aimlessly—his unit was Bavarian—gaps showed prisoners taken, and three men lay dead. These three seemed sadly smaller than real men, crumpled in the grotesquery of sudden death, but they had the purest dignity of sacrifice.

Tender hands took the bodies of Cpl. James B. Gresham, Pvt. Thomas F. Enright, and Pvt. Merle D. Hay to a peaceful place behind the lines to wait for burial.

Battles always spawn investigations, and in the early morning came General Bordeaux to the troubled sector in company with Capt. George Marshall. Together they toured the battalion position, questioned survivors and observers. Marshall listened in growing anger as Bordeaux's questions probed how stiffly the Americans had resisted. In the dressing station where they talked with the lightly wounded, Marshall braced the French commander hotly. Why were the Americans not permitted to put out defensive patrols beyond their wire? Why was counterbattery fire scattered, even disapproved by French advisors? General Pershing would be much interested in the answers! Bordeaux's neck reddened, he retreated into Gallic dignity, and the sudden hostiles parted.

Those first three Americans dead in France were to be buried in the battered village of Bathelémont. American officers and men arrived for honor, and they saw, then, the gallantry of their French comrades. Bordeaux, in the finest of apologies, sent a French infantry battalion, a dismounted cavalry troop, and other units as a guard of honor.

---

[35] Details from *First Div.*, pp. 30–31.

Americans and French formed a hollow square around the open graves, and out from his men walked the French commander to speak of his dead.

The death of this humble Corporal and these Privates appeals to us with unwonted grandeur. We will, therefore, ask that the mortal remains of these young men be left here, be left to us forever. We will inscribe on their tombs: "Here lie the first soldiers of the famous United States Republic to fall on the soil of France, for justice and liberty." The passer-by will stop and uncover his head. The travelers of France, of the Allied countries, of America, the men of heart, who will come to visit our battlefields of Lorraine, will go out of the way to come here, to bring to their graves the tribute of their respect and of their gratefulness. Corporal Gresham, Private Enright, Private Hay, in the name of France, I thank you. God receive your souls. Farewell![36]

The rest of that first tour went without real incident for all the other battalions, and when the division effort ended on November 20, total casualties were one officer and eighty-two men.[37]

General Sibert congratulated his men warmly, thanked them for fortitude, and warned of the toughest period of training ahead—the so-called third phase, when the division would be pulled together for combined operations. After that last hard stint, the whole division would be ready. Now that other AEF divisions were moving into more advanced training, Big Red One would get a sustained chance for renown. There were by early November 87,000 Yanks in France and thousands coming each month.[38]

No special words of praise came from the Old Man in Chaumont— it was hard to do things he thought beyond the call of manhood. And he had learned a good deal about new dimensions of courage in this war of daily dying.

"I have the most burning desire to . . . go over the top, but I can't."

Pétain's stolidity had considerable virtue. If he seemed sometimes un-Gallic in his tranquillity, that quality proved the precise medicine for a war-draggled France. Allied weaknesses plagued Pétain's work

---

[36] The speech is a combination of versions in *First Div.*, p. 31, and Pogue, *George C. Marshall*, p. 156. See also Marshall, *Memoirs*, pp. 47–50.

[37] *First Div.*, p. 32.

[38] AEF—Statement of Strength, in PRO, AEF, W.O. 106/465, Public Records Office, London; JJP, *Experiences*, 1:213. These sources differ. The British estimate is 77,606. See James G. Harbord, *The American Army in France, 1917–1919*, p. 165.

of army reconstruction, and he sought ways to shore a fragile strength. In the gray chill of 1917's fierce winter, the scales of Mars seemed slowly dipping on the side of the Central Powers. Pétain and his generals, using the newly annealed loyalties of some divisions, tried to win the short favor of fate with courage.

Restoration of morale depended much on renewed success, which sparked Pétain's interest in small, finely tuned operations designed to nibble at the German line. Each nibbling rejuvenated lost French élan, and in October the French commander planned an attack near Nivelle's old ground in the Chemin des Dames. Desperate importance shimmered around this offensive—victory on a losing field would truly revive *audace*. To his American colleague at Chaumont, Pétain sent an invitation—come as a spectator to see how attacks now were done on the Western Front.[39]

Techniques could always be improved; Pershing gladly accepted the summons. On October 22, the day after Big Red One entered the line, Pershing gathered Harbord, de Chambrun, aide Carl Boyd, and Maj.[40] Jim Logan, piled with them into the familiar khaki staff cars, and roared toward Headquarters, Army Group North, at Vic-sur-Aisne. There Gen. Franchet d'Esperey, doughty fighter of high repute, held his strike in abeyance until weather permitted air surveillance of the battlefield. That delay touched off talk on the trip—Harbord noted that planes foisted new requirements on tactics. Aerial observation came as nothing new to war; balloons had figured in frequent campaigns. But now careful guidance from planes sighted guns and charging men.[41] Pershing seemed eager to reach d'Esperey—one fighter's interest in another, certainly, but also an innate fascination for battle drove him on. Soon out of Paris fog shrouded the way; the cars crawled as daylight faded, and not until after eight did the Americans straggle into French headquarters.[42]

Staff schedules projected a dinner hosted by d'Esperey, followed by a briefing on tomorrow's attack, then a run to Compiègne for a rendezvous with Frank Parker (liaison with the French), a visit with Pétain, a night's rest, then a look at the battle.[43] Fortunately d'Esperey, who bristled crotchets constantly, seemed in a good mood, not irked by waiting supper. He presented his staff cordially, especially Maj. Rex

[39] JJP to Enoch Crowder, June 28, 1918, Box 56, PP.
[40] Rex Benson called him "colonel" ("Diary," Oct. 22, 1917).
[41] Harbord, *Diary*, p. 175.
[42] *Ibid.*; JJP, *Experiences*, 1:200–1.
[43] Harbord, *Diary*, p. 175; JJP, *Experiences*, 1:202–3.

Benson, British liaison officer, who seemed a kind of unofficial host to the Americans. Benson knew his chief closely, knew how Franchet d'Esperey disliked English-speaking folk, and moved gallantly to prevent any *dérangement.*

This English major had poise, Pershing quickly concluded. Not too tall but imposing in a squirish kind of way, Benson spoke beautiful French and Oxford English, had a large, open, friendly face, clear, light, candid eyes, and a subtle humor to match his wit.[44] Skillfully he filled lapses in table talk, but the chances happily came rarely.

Dapper in his light uniform, dark little General d'Esperey bubbled with excitement and waved Pershing into his confidence. With that special gusto that comes often to Frenchmen, d'Esperey charmed with his verve, his manner, and his courtesy. Benson later sketched some of d'Esperey's history for Pershing and cohorts. They had met the driving little general before but in rather closed circumstances and knew him mainly by glowing report. Reports, Benson confirmed. Franchet, as Benson affectionately called him, came up the hard ladder of French colonial service—those years in the blistering sun accounted for his Riffish brown complexion, his scowly squint, and that frequent far gaze to the eye. When Adna Chaffee and the U.S. relief column smashed through to Peking during the Boxer uprising, Franchet had been there, and by 1914 he commanded a corps. Of all the higher French commanders in that hectic year, he and de Castelnau alone remained![45] Ability, tenacity, much of the vaunted offensive spirit were d'Esperey's hallmarks.

These qualities glowed in the after-dinner briefing Pershing heard. Benson interpreted when Franchet's words blurred into Gallic enthusiasm, and the attack plan emerged clear, concise, and inexorable. For six days French guns thundered against the seven-and-a-half-mile stretch of front to be overrun; for six days a steady pounding churned and pummeled the Chemin des Dames ridge in a searing surely beyond endurance. Tomorrow, d'Esperey boasted, eight fine divisions of the VIth Army would go "over the top." Objective? A stronger defensive position for winter, but especially a stronger French morale!

As Pershing swept Franchet's map with keen eye, Benson measured him. "He is a big man but somewhat bewildered at present by the intricacies of modern warfare!" As Franchet's explanation continued in detail Benson's impression deepened. Pershing "knew exactly what he

---

[44] The description stems from a meeting between the late Sir Rex Benson and the author in London, 1964.

[45] Harbord, *Diary,* p. 177; Harbord, *American Army,* p. 157.

wanted . . . and put his finger on the spot each time." No doubt about his being a fighter—"looks as if nothing could frighten him."[46]

A short night at Compiègne ended with Pershing leading his coterie to breakfast and on toward the front by seven in the morning of October 23. Hurry! Dawdling might cost a good view of the battle, surely would if French plans matured. Franchet reported an intercepted German radio message the previous afternoon that gave accurate prophecy of the French drive, even down to the starting time, 5:30 A.M. With that piece of intelligence, the schedule shifted to a silent start earlier than planned. By the time the German protective barrage started, the attackers would be well ahead of it and into No Man's Land. If the Germans were surprised, they would lose their first line almost at the moment they opened fire.

By eight on a cloudy morning, Pershing had reached the throbbing scene of battle. Major Benson touched his cap in gleeful greeting. By 6:00 A.M. Fort Malmaison, a big, tough one, had fallen to the French 4th Zouaves! Prisoners, many of them dazed by the long preparatory bombardment, streamed by the thousands toward the French rear. Victory had happened already. Benson mused to his distinguished guest on the odd German reaction. "It is difficult to understand why [the German] stood his ground when all was ready for a retirement. He must have realised that an attack like this one preceded by 6 days [of] bombardment and with a limited objective was bound to succeed. It has succeeded every time this year: Messines, Ypres, Verdun." Why, wondered the American general? "He is evidently in a period of indecision as to how to hold the line against these attacks," Benson surmised. "At first he put few men into the front line: a month ago he decided that the front line must be strongly held. This idea has failed lamentably: what will he do next?"[47]

Franchet roamed the field "in excellent humor," insisted on badgering every batch of Boche prisoners, noted they mostly fell into the 1918 class—though he guessed some of 1919 were faking age—and met Pershing at the Condé fort for a victor's lunch.

After a fine field meal, Franchet beckoned Benson, suggested a tour "pour distraire le Général Pershing!" Benson blanched—Franchet would escort his guests up to Laffaux, near the hottest front line. If Benson had qualms, Pershing showed bursting excitement. At Laffaux the safe road ended, and everyone dismounted. Forward Franchet took his party into the churned recency of battle. The Soissons-

[46] Benson, "Diary," Monday, Oct. 22, 1917.
[47] *Ibid.*, Oct. 23, 1917.

Maubeuge road cut across No Man's Land and led into German territory. Out along the road Pershing and Franchet talked of the battle, looked at the dead, apparently oblivious to the random shells, the roaring artillery, the rattling machine guns. By 2:00 P.M. Pershing and Franchet were close to the Malmaison at Vaurain's Farm, in the old German second line. There, to Benson's great relief, the advance ended.[48]

A hearty farewell, a quick trip to Compiègne for congratulations to a much-relaxed Pétain, a visit to a Compiègne hospital where Phillipe Bunau-Varnilla, of Panama fame, rested after losing a leg in the last Verdun attack, then back to Paris.

A few days earlier Pershing had cabled Secretary Baker that "the Germans on the Western Front have been reenforced by four divisions from the Russian front, giving them a present total of 150 divisions. Persistent reports . . . of an (early) offensive by Germany and Austria against Italy. . . . Manifest that Germany is making determined effort to use present economic difficulties of Switzerland to excite Swiss people against Allies. . . . " The divisional problem was worse than it looked, since peace with Russia would release 74 German divisions for the west. The Allies counted 169 divisions, including 2 American, 6 Belgian and one Portuguese.[49]

Numbers lent scant comfort to d'Esperey's little attack.

Back in Paris Pershing worked hard at the old headquarters in the rue Constantine, heard Charlie Dawes's summary of supply success,[50] took a look at the problems of the Line of Communications with General Atterbury, caught up on the recent battle history of the 1st Division, and planned a whirlwind inspection of ports and rail lines to begin on October 24. A young portrait painter confused the schedule —a Russian girl, lively, lovely, and talented. Micheline Resco had no reputation for ruining careers. She did have a gift for friendship.

[48] JJP, *Experiences*, 1:202–4.

[49] *Ibid.*, p. 198; JJP to Secwar (Confidential), Nov. 15, 1917, Box 19, PP.

[50] Dawes had worked endlessly to produce his first quotas of coal, and had succeeded through hard bargaining for miners, laborers, specialists, from France, England, and even the United States. His bargaining also aided the transportation people. Mules in bounty Dawes found in Spain and Portugal; "several hundred" locomotives he finagled from the Belgian government. Charlie basked in notable accomplishment. "You arrived in France June 13, 1917," he recalled for Jack in December. "Let me congratulate you upon the figures . . . showing that your wonderful army organization has brought within less than six months from this date a total of one and three quarter million tons of material on this side of the ocean." It was for Jack to say how much Charlie had contributed! (Dawes to JJP, Dec. 10, 1917, in AEF, SOS, GPA, HQ Official Correspondence, Box 3, Folder 55, RG 120, National Archives; Harbord, *American Army*, pp. 159–60.)

Female companionship Pershing needed often—that old strain of romance ran strong in the blood. And the staff knew and was glad for ladies' company—they made things easier around GHQ. Staffers nodded sagely at the added secretarial staff at Chaumont, smiled appreciatively at such comely visitors as Dorothy Fisher. Ladies of all kinds clustered at headquarters, many of them on official, more on semiofficial business. Red Cross volunteers, members of the Ambulance Service, representatives of Wellesley's Ambulance Unit memorializing Frankie sometimes appeared without warning—a deep, almost Southern courtesy never turned these charming guests away without some word or gesture from the CIC. Moments of great emergency might interfere, but apologies were handsome. Ladies of station Pershing handled easily. Often they proved remarkably helpful. Daisy Harriman (wife of J. Borden), a kind of grande dame in the airy realm of Washington's politico-society, came to France to work with the Red Cross; she also worked for Jack. Rumors, gossip, planted intelligence, all touched her subtle social antennae, and her reports were often surer than G-2s![51]

But in Paris in October, 1917, no one had expected the sudden delay in one of the Old Man's vaunted inspection trips. Irked, but apparently not hotly so, Pershing explained that he had lent Mlle. Resco his campaign hat and belt for close picture details and she still had them. At five o'clock on October 24 he sent his chauffeur in retrieval. Pershing, whose full day had been filled with problems, wanted to quit Paris. When his chauffeur had not returned by six, Pershing began to fuss; the train was at seven. His baggage had been dumped at Colonel Boyd's place, thirty minutes from the Mills's House; de Chambrun was to meet the American party at the Gare Quai d'Orsay. Officers were sneaking away for the station, and, as his comrades dwindled, Pershing's patience frayed. At 6:30, still uncapped and unbelted, Pershing told Harbord to round up the baggage and head for the train. If the chauffeur arrived in time, he would bring Pershing direct to the station. If everything failed, the general's special railroad car must be shunted to a siding and departure delayed.

Harbord's trip to the station aged him. He piled into a car with a French chauffeur who took a gingerly view of Parisian traffic. "Allez plus vite," Harbord yelled, startling the driver, who jammed his foot on the accelerator and promptly stalled the engine. "Three or four good minutes" crept away, then the driver plunged into the busiest of

[51] Richard O'Connor, *BJP*, pp. 312–13.

Paris's avenues—not quite sure how to reach his goal. Arriving finally at Boyd's, Harbord gathered up baggage and with three aides urged heroic driving on their timid chauffeur. They arrived at the station to find Count de Chambrun *"very much excité."* In less than an hour, he fussed, the train would depart—where were the General and Colonel Boyd? "Pershing twenty blocks away" flitted through Harbord's humorous head.

Please delay departure, Harbord implored the conductor. Pershing's car sat well in the body of the train; it could not be extracted until reaching the Gare d'Austerlitz—and if the car laden with all the party's baggage disappeared into the French railroad system, consequences numbed the mind. Huffily noncommittal, the *chef de train* stalked away, surely with one Gallic eye cocked at his sempiternal watch.

Out to the curb Harbord ordered such troops as he had; find the Old Man, hurry him to the track! Eight minutes after departure time, Pershing and Boyd arrived. Pershing took Boyd's hat and belt, told him to collect the missing items and follow next day. A late report indicated the chauffeur had never gone to Mlle. Resco's. She was guiltless! At seven in the morning of October 25, Pershing and Harbord breakfasted in Saint Nazaire, and the general shopped for a hat to fit him—Boyd's pinched. Happily Jack noted his head size larger than that of his staff—and Harbord choked back a career-ending comment.[52] At last a quartermaster hat with gold cord borrowed from Harbord looked acceptable; the two officers collected their traveling companions and climbed into staff cars about 9:00 A.M. for a run up to artillery training camps at Coëtquidan and Meucon.

Journeys through Brittany charm the eye. Straight, maybe a bit self-conscious in the make-shift headgear, Pershing relaxed as the scenery worked its balm. Windmills with their quaint and famous towers crowned almost every hill, and, as the autos followed the twisting roads, orchards touched the world with red and yellow apples. Startles of red brushed the landscape from stray holly bushes; the scattered farmhouses with their special Brittany slopes fetched eyes and hearts with their beauty. Harbord, his romantic pulse running deep, felt the pull of the past. "The country was hilly and picturesque," he noted, and with an eye to talismans, added that "almost every crossroads bears a huge stone cross, generally with a life-size figure of the Saviour on the Cross, for Brittany has always been a stronghold for the cross and crown; firm for monarchy and religion; the old

52 Harbord, *Diary*, pp. 181–84.

royal line and the old faith, very loyal to the king and country and *très Catholique*." Down in this ageless place war's scars were scarce, the red-cheeked peasantry cheery and smiling.[53]

Watching from his fleeting window, Pershing caught the uncommon sense of place—"the quiet countryside," he felt, "the quaint houses with their thatched roofs, the people in old-time costumes, all suggested happiness and contentment regardless of the war."[54] Finally at Coëtquidan the war returned.

At this French artillery post clustered cramped camps of gunners and guns. Bill Lassiter commanded the Yanks and worked to train the U.S. 26th Division's artillery in cooperation with a tutelary French regiment—but that day the commander was absent. Lassiter's deputy, Col. Morris E. Locke of the regulars, did the tour honors. All other officers were New England Guard types who showed an appealing new eagerness. They would, finally, support Clarence Edward's forming division and wanted to be ready quickly. Troubles? Some, especially with French barracks construction and general mismanagement —a kind of *mañana*ish indolence hindered work—but the New Englanders would push.

Again on the road, Pershing accepted hints about the route to Meucon. A little diversion would lead through the Landes de la Lanvaux, a curious, scrubby lowland near Brittany's most famous chateau, the residence of the ducs de Rohan. Stern and formidable that medieval work looked on approach; closer, the lines softened. Colonel de Chambrun asked for the castle's lady, the duchesse de Rohan. The young duchess, whose husband had recently died in battle, had met Pershing during the past summer in Paris and had invited him to visit her castle. She greeted him and his companions warmly and took them on a pilgrimage through her lofting home and her ancient family's past. The castle's interior glowed with likenesses of former dukes, including the great constable of France, Olivier de Clisson. Tapestries graceful beyond description and varied *drapeaux* celebrating old glories touched the stone halls with a haunting life. Out on the battlements Pershing looked almost straight down into the Oust River valley, saw the little town of Josselin with its eleventh-century Notre-Dame-du-Roncier and the panorama of a Brittany close to past and present.[55]

On that parapet the tall American general stood protectively close to the mourning girl—surely no more than twenty-six or twenty-seven

[53] The description follows *ibid.*, pp. 184–85.
[54] JJP, *Experiences*, 1:208.
[55] *Ibid.*; Harbord, *Diary*, pp. 187–89.

—who kept her two children, her household, her family glories to-gether in a kind of huge mausoleum. A golden Brittany sun settled, burnished the town, the castle's walls, the viewers on a balcony who seemed caught by history. And then the charming duchess and her polite children shook the general's hand, the hands of his friends, said *au revoir*, and watched as allies of France rode again to the war.

For long minutes that castle loomed over the valley, and their eyes turned back to hold it in memory until, at last, the words on the great, streaming banner at the gate faded into the heart—"Roi ne suis; prince ne daigne; Rohan je suis."[56] That style of independence a Missouri soldier understood.

At Meucon a nascent camp took only a quick glance—no Americans were there yet—and the road led back toward Saint Nazaire. Happily bemused, the American caravan meandered through a somehow mellower Breton landscape until, after dark, hunger beckoned them to a restaurant in a village by the Vilaine River, a village carrying its castle's name, La Roche-Bernard. Inside, the cafe shed the present and became a small, medieval inn. One long, rough table served travelers, a dozen of them now, bunched toward one end. Already tuned to the past, the Americans clustered at the other end, caught the eye of the gnarled old mistress, and asked for such as the menu offered. At first uncertain of these strange soldiers, she squinted at them, her eyes sparkled as she recognized *le grande général* Pershing.

For those friends of France she would provide more than the menu, some of the specialties of Brittany—boiled chestnuts, wine made from the third pressing of the grapes, other delicacies reserved for heroes. Touched and gracious, Pershing sampled everything with a gourmet's appreciation, thanked in fine American style, and left a charmed, flustered hostess with stories for the years.[57]

Saint Nazaire's dirty streets, its clutter and strangely modern bustle wrenched Jack back to the war. His railroad car standing alone and cold in the yards hardly fitted the triumph of a new crusader, but it had a Spartan dourness becoming to a soldier.

Next morning, October 26, local officers appeared as guides. Colonels Samuel D. Rockenbach and Louis Bash knew the docks, shops, and warehouses well and would display them for the most exacting eyes in the AEF. Harbord and Nolan, plus two French officers, de Chambrun and Captain the Marquis de Ferronays (amusingly jealous

---

[56] "King I am not; Prince I do not choose to be; Rohan I am" (Harbord, *Diary,* p. 188). Harbord translates the middle phrase as "Prince I would not be."
[57] *Ibid.,* p. 189.

of each other's influence with Pershing)[58] started for the port. A certain gloom dimmed that Friday—a gloom of war, not weather. Rumors of disaster at Caporetto came in waves of worry. If the smashing Austro-German drive continued long beyond the Isonzo and flanked the mountain fortresses, Italy could soon join Russia on the defeated list. Quick Allied aid for Italy taxed all facilities, and Pershing noted the lackluster attention given to American problems. Troop and supply trains chuffed southeastward toward Italy in a race for time. But Allied needs displayed only part of Saint Nazaire's problems. The harbor really cramped shipping, was old, walled, needed a lock system for depth. No rational traffic management appeared at work, and had there been, facilities still would have hampered mass usage of the port. In the small approach available a great unfinished ship, the *Paris*, bulked in her yards and blocked part of the harbor entrance. Pershing noted the number of ships, all varieties, snarled in mysterious French admittance procedures. Too many ships crowded the Loire estuary; numbers of them should have been shunted to other ports.

What of shore facilities? Piers, happily, had been poured in cement, and were strong, but rail utilities were short of turntables and switch engines. Cranes and tractors were virtually invisible; few of America's standard port tools were to be found. Workers? Labor, naturally, came at fierce premium, stevedores even higher. Efforts to bring trained stevedores from the States had met with limited success—limited in the sense that untrained men and managers came to fuddle an already serious mess.[59]

Just beyond Saint Nazaire's limits, toward Nantes, American engineers labored on avenues of warehouses. This storage settlement at Montoir would offer adequate rail and shelter facilities. But French workers and managers dawdled to Pershing's rising irritation. No well-run army permitted stores to accumulate in the open, yet great piles marked "AEF" stood exposed to the elements.

All through the morning Pershing's eyes flashed over the scenes of cramped chaos. Organization must come; schedules must be met; cover for men and materiel must be built. By afternoon a decision formed: "If any further evidence had been needed, the situation thus created proved conclusively that we must develop and control our port accommodations and our own means of land transportation to the fullest extent possible."[60]

[58] *Ibid.*, p. 190.
[59] JJP, *Experiences*, 1:208–209; Harbord, *American Army*, p. 162.
[60] JJP, *Experiences*, 1:209.

A night's run in the private car brought Pershing and his fellow inspectors to Bordeaux. All hoped to find conditions good or promising. Bordeaux, a city of some 300,000 people, a bustling wine and industrial center, offered resources unknown in Saint Nazaire. Well up the Gironde, the port's ancient docks ran along the river; for American purposes they were small and already strained with French traffic. Here, though, planning impressed Pershing. Gen. R. M. Blatchford, harried head of the Line of Communications, his deputy, and other officers familiar with Bordeaux boasted of arrangements to use space at Bassens, downriver and in a wide turning area. Everything would be built by the Americans, docks, storage facilities, rail connections; much material had already arrived, and Col. Hugh Cooper, builder of the Keokuk Dam, had firm charge of activities.

In his rapid way, Pershing probed everything, measured the needs, the space available, the new artillery camp at Souge where Americans would soon train; especially did he measure the men he met. Vastness of details overwhelmed Blatchford; clearly he missed the scope of his job. Brig. Gen. Mason M. Patrick, the deputy, looked a man of sense with vision for miracles. He might be the proper commander of the LOC. Certainly he would do for the moment. Blatchford would go home. And Pershing got amusing measure of his two French liaison officers. Since de Chambrun rode with him that day, Pershing accorded the honor of finding a good lunch to de Ferronays, who had a Frenchman's concern for his palate. To Le Chapon Fin (the Fine Capon) he took his American charges. "It was surely a delicious but horribly fattening affair," Harbord thought, but confessed special interest in the restaurant. Both de Chambrun and de Ferronays whispered of Le Chapon Fin's reputation, not only for food but also assignations! Here ladies and gentlemen met paramours in delicate tête-à-tête. Pershing cast unabashed glances around for the assignees, but the place remained uncorrupted save by American soldiers. The French guides assured everyone that the place picked up in the evening. Very well, Pershing announced, they would come for supper. They did. Again the restaurant "seemed as proper as a prayer meeting."[61] Without other spices, the food failed a third charm. Pershing decided on further foraging for the next day.

Sunday proved a day of unrest. Unwilling to leave too much free time open, Pershing's hosts scheduled a run out to a French camp housing some Imperial Russian troops—sort of semiprisoners. Bordeaux

[61] Harbord, *Diary*, p. 190. For details of the day's inspection, see *ibid.*, pp. 189–90; Harbord, *American Army*, pp. 161–64.

on a lazy Sunday beguiled visitors. Jack succumbed quickly. "The city has real charm, with its broad proportions, public gardens, quaint old houses along the quays, its modern cathedral and old churches built a thousand years ago."[62] Accustomed to world commerce because of its vineyards, Bordeaux assumed war's bustle and did its business.

Forty miles from Bordeaux at Le Courneau, Pershing got his first glimpse of Imperial Russia's troops. Czar Nicholas's deposition left this brigade orphaned on the Western Front—it had been his token of help to his friends. Quickly a kind of anarchy seeped through this once crack outfit. Red flags appeared in the companies, "soldier committees" emerged in command, some tough officers were murdered, and others were permitted only tactical functions. Le Courneau showed woeful human erosion. Virtually a swamp it was, made worse by ennui. Men uncertain of the future and officers adjusted to martial democracy created conditions beyond belief. Relieved from the French front because of possible political infection, the Russians slogged to the rear mumbling about rights and privileges, a few about fighting. Why were these Russian casuals permitted such latitude? They were, it developed, still armed! Gallic realism denied them the war but allowed them the honor of their weapons. Pershing and Harbord were astounded, even more when they learned the French were feeding and paying them.

French suggestions that Le Courneau might be an AEF site were absurd. Stalking to the gate, Pershing met two Russian colonels who introduced themselves as a chief of staff and a regimental commander. Beribboned by the czar, one by the French, these officers sought to ingratiate themselves. Their general, they announced, had gone to Paris to negotiate a return to the front. A cold look, then a soldier's question: Did the chief of staff think his unit had the discipline for war? Yes, certainly, came a confident answer. Harbord backed away when he saw the Missouri eyes cloud, the face turn granite. In voice chillingly calm, Jack scourged the colonel on officers and men who would allow themselves a camp so slovenly, on discipline sunk to anarchy, on a state of morale and readiness worse than the vilest militia. Defensively the colonel whined that the conditions were inherited from the French, but he had lost his audience.

As Pershing assessed allies who coddled chaos, others who "were drunk with liberty,"[63] still more who ran from the Isonzo, some who talked of attrition as the road to victory, as he weighed enemies

---

[62] JJP, *Experiences*, 1:209–10.
[63] Harbord, *Diary*, p. 192.

gathering strength from victories in the east, who fought with dogged tenacity and proud skill, who wasted men and material to purpose, he saw the path of America looming long and full of trouble.

Aware more than ever of mounting pessimism—even in himself—Pershing left the Russians behind and pressed his inspection to Arcachon for lunch. At a winning little cafe, Russian officers were seen enjoying the blessings of Bolshevism—good food, good clothes, attention—but the sight failed to quench American appetites whetted by fetching odors from the kitchen.

Attention went not only to the Russians—as Pershing and his men started to leave, the proprietor obsequiously asked the general to sign the guest book. As he did a good-looking girl approached, said her mother was English, and asked, too, for the American general's autograph. Taking her little book, Pershing wrote with a flourish: "To my fair Ally!!!!" Rewarded by a huge smile, Pershing left, trailing freshly impressed staff members. Harbord, accustomed to Pershing's graces, caught the moment in a word: "Smooth!!!"[64]

Back to Bordeaux and the train Pershing went for a run to the big hospital building at Châteauroux. From there he whirled through Issodun and the aviation school, the planned supply dump at Montierchaume, the great, sprawling depot almost completed at Gièvres, and on to the infant ordnance installation at Méhun—all on October 29. Each place got the full treatment; cold eyes swept the men, the place, the equipment and material. Efficiency won a plus in the record; inefficiency, a questionmark toward Cannes.

Finally nearly satisfied, Pershing turned completely to the joys of traveling. An avid sightseer, he delighted Harbord with historical interest and architectural appreciation. At Bourges he tested everyone's knowledge of medieval history.

Moonlight washed a hushed world as the American staff cars rolled into that old town; cool, pale light touched the cathedral and caught Pershing's eye and heart. "The view of this wonderful example of 12th Century architecture . . . was one of the most impressive sights I have ever seen."[65] A dinner stop gave moments to savor the cathedral by candleshine, to walk those old streets and feel the strengths of history. A night drive for thirty miles to Nevers caught up with Pershing's train, and a long, fascinating day ended in his freezing private car.[66]

[64] *Ibid.*, p. 193; Harbord, *American Army*, pp. 164–65.
[65] JJP, *Experiences*, 1:212.
[66] *Ibid.*; Harbord, *Diary*, p. 193; *id.*, *American Army*, p. 165.

A night's run to Paris gave silent hours for reflection. In France's heartland, American preparations lagged, with some exceptions. Port facilities must be increased, rail lines expanded and coordinated in rational ways, depots hastened, camps opened. Blatchford's excision might hasten achievement, but other incentives were needed. What seemed the most serious problem? To Pershing the confusion of multiple agencies clearly hampered cooperation. A remedy occurred to him, on consideration: "I sent to each base section a competent general officer with an organized staff to coordinate and systematize the management of affairs, and in a brief time considerable improvement was noticeable in methods of handling troop arrivals and cargo and in the increased progress of construction."[67] More than that, the CIC redrew the territorial limits of base sections and other logistical commands, combined various activities, and clarified the three-phase system of supply—procurement, care and storage, transportation. Bureau chiefs were responsible for procurement; the commanding general, LOC, for care, storage, and depot distribution; and the director general of transportation, for movement and unloading. All of this fitted the AEF's general pattern of condensing responsibility behind authority.[68] And the system worked where good men were in charge; Pershing could count the instances.

Brief delay in Paris brought good news. Large shipments of lumber, pilings, and crossties were en route from home. Work ought to go a good deal faster now. Other news concerned men and numbers and a new division. As transports did manage to unload at Saint Nazaire and other ports, Pershing counted enough men to form the 2nd Division. Putting Maj. Gen. Omar Bundy in command, Jack expected fast results. Experience with the 1st Division had solved many training problems, and succeeding units ought to form easily. It was good, indeed, to have another division, at least on paper, and another headquarters. For as he trekked back to Chaumont, Pershing thought the Allies faced their hardest test. He would have liked to command one of those divisions, to have a crack at the Hun. American troops, raw and unskilled yet, were nonetheless the hardiest men on the Western Front—any man lucky enough to lead them in battle could be proud. He had a curious avuncular pride, a satisfaction muted by removal. But he knew the AEF to be shaping well enough. If the enemy gave time.

[67] JJP, *Experiences*, 1:212.
[68] Army War College, *Order of Battle of the United States Land Forces*, p. 41.

Conflict in Coordination: The Supreme War Council

Pershing's role at the pinnacle of the AEF irked lesser folk of ambition who fixed on him all the venom of frustration. In those fashionable Paris salons where gathered migrant Americans and Frenchmen touched with ennui, rumors carved reputations with surgical precision. Tongues withered great men nightly, and heroes eroded according to gossip. Pershing's Americanness served him up nicely for dissection. Amiable, some said, but ignorant, crusty yet with the dust of Indian wars; cold, others said, his aloofness cloaking uncertainty. And others pointed gleefully to frontier ingenuousness to prove his incapacity for world affairs. He talked rarely, but sometimes wrongly. Where was it that he had voiced fears for victory? Sometime in November to some unnamed gossip Pershing unburdened his conscience, spoke of French exhaustion, of British fatigue, of the apparently endless German reserves pouring westward from Russia. If he spoke his heart, he could not hope for privacy. An eager ear listened, a quick hand wrote, and a volatile document circulated among the socialists in the French Chamber of Deputies. Loyal Allies branded it a rank bit of German propaganda, but the words rang true to many: "The end of the war can only come by America's making a very great effort in the first line. But America needs four or five years to complete her military preparations. The consequence of this will be a six years' war." [69] Picked up, allegedly, by the *North German Gazette*, these sentiments surely offered comfort to the enemy.

That unfortunate bit of indiscretion spiced other tales about John Pershing. A few friends bristled to hear of his provincialism, of his unappreciative view of the Allies. Willard Straight, old Manchurian comrade, who wangled his way to France in charge of the War Risk Insurance program, circulated in the airiest Parisian circles and brooded about some things he heard. "As to General Pershing," he wrote associates on the *New Republic* in 1918's early days, "there are varying reports. There is much criticism—most of it unjust I should say—some of it due, in that I don't believe he has had the imagination to visualize this situation and to prepare to deal with it in all its ramifications. . . " [70]

[69] Anonymous document, "Subject: General Pershing's Pessimism," quoting Worthington Dawson, Nov., 1917, who reported information given him by a member of Marshal Joffre's staff, in General Correspondence of the Information Division (G-2-A), AEF, GHQ, Folder 34, Memoranda, RG 120, National Archives.

[70] Straight to [?], Jan. 2, 1918, in Willard Straight Papers, Collection of Re-

In the hectic days of Leonard Wood's peregrinations, when he dazzled such visiting American highbrows as Daisy Harriman, Straight found himself swept into the whirl of Ethel Harriman's wedding. The crowd, more like a waspish swarm of New Yorkers than a Paris cabal, buzzed about each other, about friends in France for the war, about Wood's rights to preference, and about the Missouri upstart, John Pershing. His masque of modesty suggested disorganization, indecision, the lapses of inexperience. "There are all manner of mean and petty intrigues going on here about Pershing," Straight complained, and fixed much blame on Wood, who "has been talking and his pink tea friends have been gossiping and criticizing the C. in C. and saying that nothing has been done." He centralized too much, Straight supposed, perhaps groped toward delegation of authority. But the carpers disgusted a friend who knew Pershing from old. "He is learning, and he's infinitely better I am convinced than anyone in the army." To his beloved Dorothy, Willard gave stern advice: "If you hear any kicks about Pershing, get after them. He's the best man that could be in this place." And a few weeks later he strengthened his admonition.

I have heard much for and against [Pershing] . . . My best impression is this: He is not a great man. There are few *great* men. He didn't see the thing as big perhaps as he should have done when he came. Neither did anyone else. He might have moved faster. So might the President. He has made mistakes. So has W. W. and even the Allies! He's the best man available in the army for his job. He's bigger and better than anyone else. . . . and above all, he's open minded. He learns. He has learned much and is now at the point where he'll learn more rapidly. . . . Of the Major Generals of the Army there's no one . . . who could touch him. *State that too*, for there will be plenty of knocking.[71]

All kinds of Allied schemes wafted in the winds of rumor. Italy's Caporetto tragedy had kindled at last some real smoke of cooperation. Lloyd George, fretting mightily over the Allied world, cocked a questing eye toward the Americans. Would Pershing come to Paris for a hasty conversation? Discourtesy toward the British prime minister seemed hardly prudent; a conversation would be welcome. So, on Saturday, November 3, 1917, Jack returned to Paris and the Hôtel de Crillon. Out before that stately building the Place de la Concorde seemed empty, far less welcoming than in those heady June days of celebration. A hectic trip ended in the soft clutches of the Crillon's

gional History and University Archives, John M. Olin Library, Cornell University, Ithaca, N.Y.

[71] See Straight to Dorothy Straight, Jan. 30, Feb. 10, 1918, Straight Papers.

practiced staff, efficient, delicate even in the wrenches of war. Pershing registered with his aide and turned toward the elevator. A few steps brought him to a familiar figure, also walking toward the elevator—Field Marshal Sir Douglas Haig. Warm greetings, exchanged introductions (Haig squired Lord Esher of the War Office), then Haig begged a moment.

Privately the generals speculated on the frenetic deeds of politicians—deeds suddenly ominous for determined meddling. Pershing confessed that he thought Lloyd George's desire to see him had some murky purpose, likely, but not certain, to be revealed at tomorrow's breakfast. For ten serious minutes Haig talked of the problems concerning command on the Western Front. Pétain had broached a scheme, Haig said, of dividing the front between the British and French that the prime minister seemed to accept. And Lloyd George's descent on Paris looked like a side gamble on his way to Italy.

Reportedly, British, French, and Italian leaders were gathering in Italy to spawn some kind of cooperation. Haig could accept the obvious need for cooperation; the need for a supreme command on the Western Front he disdained as absurd. Pershing listened, nodding sometimes in his quick, jerky way, and sympathized with a colleague politically harassed. Haig went off to bed content with his chat. "It was a great piece of good luck and I was able to have ten minutes talk with P[ershing] before he went to L. G."[72]

Sunday breakfast was revealing enough. That odd dullness of winter Paris days depressed spirits, and Lloyd George's energy hardly brightened Pershing's prospects. The prime minister burst into his program upon greeting. The Allies were in trouble; the need for unity required no further proof than Caporetto. Carefully his American guest agreed that unity had never been in evidence in France, as far as he could tell. Unhappily the prime minister conceded that disunity offered the clearest present danger in the war. Central Powers forces might attack either the British or French separately, might reap another Caporetto. What did Pershing think of creating a supreme war council? Thinking first of war councils in the field, Pershing deplored them, said they usually advised caution, and added that Lloyd George's "proposition did not appeal to me."[73] Hastily the prime minister expanded, and Pershing changed his tack.

Despite his evident agreement with Haig the night before, Jack nursed suspicion of a war run by hallway conversations and character

[72] Douglas Haig, Diary, Saturday, Nov. 3, 1917, Haig Papers.
[73] JJP, *Experiences*, 1:214.

sniping. The best way to handle the present crisis, surely, would be to create a supreme commander for the Western Front? Surprised, Lloyd George agreed, but guessed the Allies unable to unite on a commander. A council could serve the useful purpose of bringing Allied political plans together and into perspective. True, but military operations—the general spoke emphatically—must be left to soldiers.

A gathering of Allied leaders was planned for Rapallo, Italy, Lloyd George announced; there a supreme council would be proposed in what might be the most important decision of the war. Surely America should be present at such a momentous moment; Pershing must come. Since the meeting would be political, not military, Pershing said, "I consider it inadvisable . . . to participate without some intimation from my Government to do so." And, of course, time prevented Washington's approval.[74]

Parting amiably from his host, Pershing mused on the whims of the mighty. Clearly the prime minister sought ways to control "the activities of the British Army." Long months of continuous attacking had sapped British blood in the west, and public opinion floundered for alternatives to perpetual sacrifice.

Luncheon with Haig confirmed Jack's suspicions. The field marshal chafed under rumors that Sir Henry Wilson would be British representative on the council. Probably that pompous soldier would be used as a foil against Haig. Lloyd George would do anything to weaken the armies in the west. Haig opposed the war-council scheme and found it impossible to name an acceptable supreme commander. Unity and cohesion seemed as distant as ever.

Depressed, Pershing called by invitation Monday afternoon on M. Painlevé, who broke the news of Rapallo triumphantly, extended an invitation, and heard the same refusal.

Pitifulness tinged the squabbling in Paris, the noble posturing about the Supreme Allied War Council and about collaboration against disaster, and silliness tinged Haig's personal pique about his prerogatives. In that winter of the cause twin disasters chipped Allied foundations. Italy alone would have been enough, but on November 8, the day after hopeful ministers postured at Rapallo, Kerensky's government fell and Nikolai Lenin took Russia's reins. No longer could the hopeful wish; Russia was now out of the war. Rumania tottered toward collapse; her leaders called for food, supplies, and help.

Politicos shared problems. In the overwash of Italy's catastrophe,

[74] The quotation is slightly altered into the present tense. See JJP, *Experiences,* 1:214.

Painlevé's government fell. At last to the head of France came "Le Tigre," Georges Clemenceau, who had stalked the dark corners of high counsel with epithets and admonitions through defeats and vacillations until he seemed a kind of national alter ego. Short, apparently stooped with age, his face revetted by a huge, drooping moustache, Clemenceau had eyes that burned with surprising fervor. He came, he said, to redeem old promises of glory, to cleanse France of corruption and creeping despair; patriots would know his favor, slaggards his contempt. Pershing enjoyed his energy and appreciated his program.

Clemenceau could easily have denounced the conciliar idea—sponsorship had been one of Painlevé's burdens and had troubled Lloyd George in Parliament[75]—but the fiery new prime minister approved cooperation and worked to unravel red tape in martial administration. Passionately sensitive to the war's malign trends, convinced that France's blood ran low, Clemenceau sought ways to save his country by passing part of its torch to stronger Allies. He nurtured some suspicion of British effort; tucked away in their Flanders pocket, they hugged a short trenchline and slogged forward with glacial intensity. Surely they could take over more line—a feeling bound to irk Lloyd George, who sought more French take-over. On the Americans, though, the Tiger focused his fiercest hopes. They must come faster, be used more directly, contribute while still the war survived. John Pershing he knew from varied associations, guessed him deliberate and unmovable. With the odd directness the French sometimes show, Clemenceau decided to circumvent Pershing through Washington. His efforts infinitely confounded Pershing's relations with France and with the Supreme Allied War Council.

From Rapallo had come a council outline. Focused on the Western Front, the council would "watch over the general conduct of the war," but military leaders would "remain responsible to their respective Governments"; "the general war plans drawn up by competent Military Authorities are submitted to the Supreme War Council, which, under the high authority of the Governments, insures their concordance, and submits, if need be, any necessary changes." One permanent military representative would sit for each government, would "act as a technical adviser," and would "watch day by day the situation of the forces, and of the means of all kinds of which the Allied Armies and the enemy Armies dispose." Ferdinand Foch would be France's military representative; Sir Henry Wilson, Britain's; Luigi Cadorna, Italy's.

[75] Charles Seymour, *House Papers*, 3:219–22.

America's had yet to come, but Lloyd George had wrung from Woodrow Wilson an agreement to participate—an important concession at a tender political moment in England.

As he walked Paris's wide avenues with their monuments of past glories, Jack Pershing pondered his own uncertain future. For on November 7, Col. Edward M. House, President Wilson's powerful crony, landed in England with a sizable "House Party." Whisked into British circles with gusto, House, that scant-chinned, fine-eyed little gentleman, came apparently for information and for consultation. He would in time visit France, perhaps soon, as America's first council delegate. General Tasker Bliss would serve as military representative. Did House's mission mean that important folk at home had doubts about the AEF and its leader? Did his coming mean that Pershing, like Haig and Pétain, was to be prodded by politicos, despite Baker's assurances?[76]

There would be a full-panoplied gathering of Allied leaders in Paris —concession supreme by the British!—on November 29, and House would attend the Inter-Allied Conference. Stagecrafted carefully, this initial consultation would resolve into the Supreme War Council for real work. Every warring Ally would have a place at the first meeting; the major ones only would sit on the council. The House party arrived in Paris on November 22, properly British in sympathy but open to French flattery, and in a social daze.[77] The attention of the French is overwhelming, their hospitality staggering, their influence subtle and persuasive. In Paris the pitch came almost in mirror image to London —American troops are needed in French ranks. There Americans can be better trained, closer to their prospective sectors, by men more skilled in modern war. House heard this reprise with amusement and with his usual sympathy. And much to Pershing's pleasure, the little colonel sought his views on vying Allied propositions.[78]

[76] For Britain's flirtation with House, see *House Papers*, 3:210–49, 306–7; JJP, *Experiences*, 1:215–16.

[77] In fact the French snickered privately that the British had missed their best chance. Paul Cambon gloated, mildly, that although the British welcomed the Americans "warmly," they disappointed by the paucity of information offered. The "British were badly organized and conferences always disintegrated into mere conversation. British only presented general solutions. Everyone recognized confusion which can't be stopped. Americans are intelligent, well-instructed, but new in statesmanship. They look for example and advice, which weren't forthcoming from British. Americans now count on us" (Paul Cambon to Stéphane Pichon, Nov. 20, 1917, in Quai d'Orsay, Opérations Stratégiques, Dossier Général, 7:75–77.

[78] For Clemenceau's artistry in candor, see "Memorandum of Conversation of Colonel House and General Bliss with M. Clemenceau and General Pétain," Nov. 25, 1917, quoted in *House Papers*, 3:257–59.

Promptly House must have seen how the French counted on Pershing. The general ranked higher in consideration than even he knew. Daily associations with French purchasing, transportation, and operations leaders involved the AEF's commander in myriad relationships across France, but especially in Paris did he touch most important officials. As some Frenchmen complained that he did not delegate enough authority to underlings, so he complained that they delegated too much. Offices and suboffices proliferated in the Parisian hierarchy; those layers buffered decision. And Pershing approved greatly the centralization of American relations announced by the French in early November. He would keep his own liaison with Pétain; a French liaison officer would remain at GHQ, and in Paris "a central office for purchasing and an office to deal with AEF affairs" was created. Reasons, had he known them, would have brought that wintry smile. So important did he rank in French thinking that his prejudices shaped French policy. "If we don't satisfy JJP," Clemenceau guessed, "we will not be able to change his view of us and we will be open to new criticisms of our organization. We must remember that Tardieu told us in October that Wilson trusts JJP implicitly and listens to him, so try to keep him happy."[79]

While trying to jolly Pershing, the French added to the pressure for deployment of American manpower through thinning Allied ranks. Almost every meeting with Allied leaders touched on the issue of cooperation, even of amalgamation. House, who felt the pressure keenly, also felt the resolution of the issue beyond his powers. So he talked with his general. The pleas from harried friends made some sense— without more blood the front would wither. House heard the pleas in mounting alarm. From London's heated requests to Paris's impassioned demands came impressions of a cause nearly dead. What did Pershing think?

Pershing calmly explained his conviction that the president meant what he said in his original orders. An American army would be built; it would be commanded by its own officers and would fight independently. There might come a crisis demanding release of American troops to Allied units, but there would surely be problems in getting them back. He worried about men sent to French units for training— they might never return.[80]

[79] "Notes on organization of relations with General Pershing," unsigned appreciation, dated Nov. 2, 1917, in Clemenceau Collection (Fonds Clemenceau 61), French Military Archives, Vincennes.
[80] *House Papers*, 3:269.

In frenzied conference halls America's troops might also disappear. Almost everyone dreaded the Inter-Allied gathering as it loomed at November's end. By now, with rumors and whispers and fears rife, it seemed probable that such a monstrosity might degenerate into bickering and petty enmities beyond redemption—Germany might win while watching the Paris talks! House wanted Pershing present.

A call to Paris conflicted with reorganization efforts at Chaumont. Maj. Gen. F. J. Kernan replaced the temporary Mason Patrick in command of the LOC; Patrick took charge of construction. Brig. Gen. Benjamin Foulois became chief of the Air Service; Red Cross officials were worked more closely into army administration. Since the staff could handle details of these changes, reluctantly Jack thought he could leave for the conference nobody seemed to want.

A comfortable night at the rue de Varennes mansion, a day spent in proper calling, and then, on November 29, Jack took Harbord to the Crillon for a meeting with the House party. Pershing fitted well into the gathering of civil "experts," many of whom he knew. Harbord took thinly veiled umbrage at the entire gathering. "I met the great little man," he remarked of House, "the man who can be silent in several languages, the close friend of Woodrow Wilson, the man who carried the Texas delegation from Bryan to Wilson at Baltimore, the creator of Governor Hogg, Culberson and others in Texas." First appearances were poor. "He is one of the few men with practically no chin, whom I have ever met, who were considered forceful." But Harbord did confess the colonel's eyes were impressive and that he acted pleasant enough.

Collecting his corps around him, House made a short talk that struck Harbord as "baldly cynical." Nothing would be done at the Inter-Allied meeting, House said. "It will be our business to be pleasant and sympathetic with the small nations. Listen to what they say. Do not promise them anything. Do not tell them anything about tonnage. Be pleasant. It is our day to smile. Just circulate among the little fellows and listen to their stories. Be kind and agreeable." Harbord found it hard to swallow—"If that isn't giving a stone when they ask for bread, then I dunno."[81]

At the Quai d'Orsay everyone took assigned seats, gawked around the large conference room, whispered about arrivals, about rumors, smiled, smiled, smiled.

Clemenceau had the first words, cut them short, and set an agenda

---

[81] Harbord, *Diary*, pp. 196–97.

of appointing committees; chairmen rose to name their members. After an hour of droning charade, Pershing, who sat next to Tasker Bliss and two American admirals, tired of it all and left, trailing Harbord. House had been right—nothing was done.

For Pershing the meeting's importance came in a private meeting with Generals Foch, Robertson, Bliss, and Vance McCormick, chairman of America's important War Trade Board. If the Allies were bent at last to coordinate activities, the time had come to make formal arrangements about American troops. Foch and Robertson eagerly agreed, Bliss, too, and McCormick listened with interest. Carefully Pershing told of the General Organization Project's schedule, refreshed his confreres on shipping problems and production lags that had already skewed the timing. But he set a new target for troop arrivals: twenty-four American divisions comprising four army corps, some 650,000 men, would be in France by July 1, 1918. Allied shipping must adjust to the new program. All parties accepted the scheme. Foch and Robertson were elated. Pershing had offered more than they expected —but he had reasons. "I thought," he confessed privately, "that the larger the program that could be agreed upon as necessary and possible the more likely we should be to obtain tonnage concessions from our own and British authorities." [82]

On a note of Allied depression—British successes at Cambrai in late November, made spectacular by the use of tanks, had crumbled under heavy German counterattacks—the second War Council session met on December 2 in the odd sumptuosity of Versailles's Trianon Palace Hotel. House and Bliss attended, heard anew the reliance on American manpower and the importance of winning in the west, and lamented the academic tone of proceedings. "While a good many subjects were brought before the Conference, not one, I think, was brought to a conclusion," House noted. One of his impressions surely irritated Pershing: "Clemenceau, Pétain, and Bliss did more in our conference of last week than was done at the Supreme War Council, for we at least determined how many American soldiers should come to France, when they should come, and how to get them here." [83]

Pershing had pushed for the agreement and had reported it to Baker on December 2. Russia's defection and the erosion of Allied

---

[82] JJP, *Experiences*, 1:249. For the general tenor of the special meeting, see Harbord, *American Army*, p. 180. Clemenceau clutched the agreement to heart and sought House's confirmation when the colonel returned home (see *House Papers*, 3:308–9).

[83] *House Papers*, 3:273.

positions in the east generally would give a "60 per cent advantage [to the Central Powers in a few months] and make it difficult to hold them. The Allies have had about 30 percent advantage all summer." That alarming prospect made American participation urgent. "Have impressed the present emergency upon General Bliss and other members of the conference. Generals Robertson, Foch, and Bliss agree with me that this is the minimum [24 divisions] that should be aimed at. This figure is given as the lowest we should think of, and is no higher because the limit of available transportation would not seem to warrant it."[84]

Relieved from the tedium of conference-going, Pershing invited the House party, Ambassador and Mrs. Sharp, and Lord Northcliffe, of the British Air Board, to America's training area. Whatever their impressions, Pershing himself relaxed near the army. And the train trip to Gondrecourt and Chaumont gave Pershing an unsuspected ally.

Lord Northcliffe talked enthusiastically about an American army and about the British helping more fully with transportation, but he echoed an old theme—"he argued in favor of the proposal that Mr. Lloyd George had recently made to Mr. House that we should incorporate in their units any infantry that we might not be able to organize immediately into complete divisions of our own." Candor met candor.

"It is all very well to make such an appeal to us but it is impossible to ignore our national viewpoint," Pershing answered.

Warming to a favorite theme, the general talked forcefully. "The people themselves would not approve, even though the President should lean that way. I am strongly opposed to it. We cannot permit our men to serve under another flag except in an extreme emergency and then only temporarily. . . . No people with a grain of national pride would consent to furnish men to build up the army of another nation."

Precedents from the Revolution bolstered Pershing's point—not even the colonials were amalgamated into British units in America!

Northcliffe listened with growing interest and, after thinking awhile of the arguments, agreed that Pershing was "perfectly right."[85] It was a notable and timely victory, for House pressed Jack with questions about Lloyd George's scheme. Fervently Pershing rejected this revival of Balfour's early plan. It would, he argued, retard if not prevent the establishment of an American Army. House seemed to agree, but lingered on problems. Pétain, he mused, complained about American

[84] JJP to Baker (cable), Dec. 2, 1917, in JJP, *Experiences*, 1:249–50.
[85] *Ibid.*, pp. 254–55.

training methods, and added that other French officials grumbled about American competition for supplies driving prices up. But House was pleased at Pétain's pronouncement that America's first offensive would hit the Saint Mihiel Salient!

How far did House agree with French criticisms? Did he think there should be more amalgamation? Did he chafe at deliberate preparation? Was there, after all, some high discontent with John Pershing? As usual Jack asked. A full, frank discussion brought reassurance and a budding friendship between the general and the emissary. No, House could find no fault; he knew of no Wilsonian suspicions. As for amalgamation, it would likely continue a rankling problem, but House "was convinced that the President and the Secretary of War would leave the whole question of the disposition of our troops to [Jack's] judgment."[86] There was one blemish on the new friendship's surface— House had sent Lloyd George's proposal for amalgamation to President Wilson! Pershing's independence hung on the answer.

On a cold Christmas day the cable came:

December 24, 1917

Pershing, Amexforce,

Both English and French are pressing upon the President their desires to have your forces amalgamated with theirs by regiments and companies, and both express the belief in impending heavy drive by Germans somewhere along the lines of the Western Front. We do not desire loss of identity of our forces but regard that as secondary to the meeting of any critical situation by the most helpful use possible of the troops at your command. The difficulty of course is to determine where the drive or drives of the enemy will take place; and in advance of some knowledge on that question, any redistribution of your forces would be difficult. The President, however, desires you to have full authority to use the forces at your command as you deem wise in consultation with the French and British Commanders-in-Chief. It is suggested for your consideration that possibly places might be selected for your forces nearer the junction of the British and French lines which would enable you to throw strength in whichever direction seemed most necessary. This suggestion is not, however, pressed beyond whatever merit it has in your judgment, the President's sole purpose being to acquaint you with the representations made here and to authorize you to act with entire freedom to accomplish the main purposes in mind. It is hoped that complete unity and coördination of action can be secured in this matter by any conferences you may have with French and British commanders and line of action that may be agreed upon.

BAKER[87]

---

[86] *Ibid.*, p. 257.
[87] See JJP, *Experiences*, 1:271–72; Wilson Papers, Series 2, Box 160.

Lloyd George's attempted flanking movement had failed. Wilson and Baker considered the highest implications of the amalgamation controversy, decided it must be kept a military issue, and left the whole matter to their general. True, they had some guidelines for him, wanted cooperation in crisis and efforts at Allied consultation, but clearly would support any decision Pershing made. Two things about the cable must have warmed that chill December day, must have made a heady Christmas present for a general far called from his country. First in importance ran the clear restatement of "entire freedom" to act, but almost as vital was the crafty equivocation—surely in Baker's language —about difficulties in "any redistribution of your forces" until solid information on enemy movements came. Make your decision, Jack read, without feeling any compulsion to shift men anywhere.

As Jack's "official family" gathered for Christmas dinner, a special kind of joy touched the table. The general's slight, triumphant smile played around the corners of his thin mouth, his eyes twinkled, and the stories grew louder—the Lion and the Tiger must come to that old Missouri Mule!

Since diplomacy broached the issue to the president, Wilson's reply was copied to British and French embassies. Reaction ran hard. Neither Lloyd George nor Clemenceau could understand a general disposing so much power—but they now knew the lines of approach. With a certain Spartan acceptance the British War Cabinet took its medicine. The prime minister read his colleagues a paraphrase of Baker's cable "giving General Pershing a free hand regarding the decision . . . concerning the amalgamation of American forces. . . . " Clearly one course lay open: the cabinet requested Lord Milner, the secretary of state for war, to visit Pershing in Paris and "urge him to accede to the representations . . . by the British Government and the General Staff."[88]

Disbelief wracked French politicians. They read Baker's message for any shreds of hope—and some crumbs of concession might be twisted from scrutiny. Loss of American identity had been considered "secondary" to meeting a crisis in the west. If the crisis were painted luridly in Washington, would further orders go to Pershing?[89] Chances were slim, and French hopes turned to Pétain's direct negotiations with the intransigent American.

Secure in his authority, Pershing risked a game of suasion. "In all

[88] Minutes of the War Cabinet 304, Dec. 21, 1917, PRO, CAB 23/4.
[89] That hope was expressed in Jusserand to Pichon (cable), Dec. 30, 1917, in Quai d'Orsay, Opérations Stratégiques, Dossier Général, 7:178.

these discussions, the British were bargaining for men to fill their ranks and were trying to get shipping to carry over our armies."[90] The Allies worked against terror, and terror Jack counted on with a kind of Moro craftiness. At what point would terror produce tonnage? Jack guessed ships would be found in emergency to carry his gaudy, big divisions and such other men as he agreed to give the Allies. It was a gamble, of course, one that might lose the future, but if it worked, the rewards were an American kind of victory. Pershing coolly played his baiting game. Opponents were legion, numbering among them Haig, Pétain, and most Western politicians. And they played their roughest rounds at Versailles midst the jabber of the War Council.

Through tedious negotiations with Haig and Pétain about training of units and officers, about numbers and equipment available, about men to be loaned and returned, Pershing watched askance the continued skirmishing on the diplomatic front. Agreements might be reached with military colleagues only to have them rejected or twisted beyond achievement by higher authorities or by diplomats. And sometimes the fine understanding between Washington and Chaumont wore thin. On at least one occasion Tasker Bliss, wafted by exposure toward ambition, disagreed with friend Jack's hard-nosed policy of American cohesion. He could not, Bliss pronounced, support Pershing's views against one of Gen. Sir William Robertson's juggled schemes for building up British divisions with Americans. Bliss's switch to the British, irritating though not surprising, Pershing met firmly. He worked for tonnage, not amalgamation in any form. Stubbornly Bliss suggested both men submit their views to Washington.

This kind of obstruction deserved contempt. No, came the cold Missouri reply—not now or at any time would Pershing "put anything up to Washington that I could possibly decide myself." And on troop use his decision would stand. Bliss glowered in sulky disagreement.

"Well, Bliss, do you know what would happen if we should do that? We would both be relieved from further duty in France and that is exactly what we should deserve."

Struck, Bliss listened carefully to Pershing's oft-told reasons for AEF integrity. National sentiment ran against service under another flag, and if amalgamation prevailed it might cripple President Wilson's administration. Germany doubtless would make propaganda capital in the United States about America's subordinate role in the war. Jack thought the worst result would be the delay in creating an American

[90] See Coffman, *War*, p. 169.

Army, a delay confounded by problems of fragmented Allied training experiences and all the bickering of enforced competition. Finally, if security of the war ranked a real concern, troops could be brought for emergencies more efficiently by direct dispatch than by amalgamation.

As Bliss listened he caught some of Jack's clear vision, caught, too, his iron devotion to the AEF. Nodding, he said, "I think you are right and I shall back you up in the position you have taken."[91]

Confrontation had been inevitable between Jack and Bliss, and much depended on its outcome. Pershing forced his point, bent Bliss to his will, and victory by persuasion freed Pershing of worry about the War Council. Usually a forum of discord, it would echo now to Pershing's own passion for American goals.

That council's original aim of unity had been only partly realized in its early meetings. Bliss and Pershing talked of unified command among piercing Allied plaints. If, somehow, political coordination could bring command cohesion, the council might hasten success. It must be sustained and coaxed toward the idea of a Supreme Command for the Western Front.

An American Army

Troops came slowly but in comforting numbers. By the end of December, the AEF counted 9,804 officers and 165,080 men—a gain of 2,108 officers and 46,826 men in one month. Monthly arrivals would vary according to available transport and submarine efficiency—but the tide began. Divisional organization became increasingly important, which emphasized again staff training and experience. A 2nd Division, formed from bits and pieces of units arriving in France, including a brigade of regulars and one of marines, had been organized in France. Omar Bundy, a year junior to Pershing in age, three years senior from the Military Academy, appeared energetic in command of the 2nd.[92]

---

[91] See JJP, *Experiences*, 1:304–5, for the quotations. The paraphrase of JJP's argument is extracted from Coffman, *War*, pp. 170–71.

[92] *Army Register, 1918*, p. 10; JJP, *Experiences*, 1:208, 264; Index and Case Files Relating to Reclassification and Reassignment of Officers. Papers of General John J. Pershing, 1916–1924, 1931–1939, Box 8, RG 316, National Archives. Bundy had many characteristics JJP considered essential in general officers: character, willpower, decisiveness, judgment of men, clarity of thought, endurance, military bearing (see LeRoy Eltinge, "Plan for Keeping Lists of Officers for Staff Duty and Higher Command," attached to JJP to Chief of Staff, HAEF, Oct. 2, 1917, in AEF, GHQ, Office of CIC Correspondence, File 3358, RG 120, National Archives).

But Bundy would be only as good as his staff, and staff officers were in critical scarcity, especially since Washington continued its strange policy of sending and recalling potential staff specialists.[93]

Pieces of a National Guard division—the 26th ("Yankee")—arrived in September along with Maj. Gen. Clarence Edwards as commander. Edwards, old friend from the Insular Bureau, boasted long repute for command potential, although not all of his former superiors trusted him.[94] His chances for success seemed good; his men, New Englanders all, ranked high in zest and drive and plunged eagerly into training near Neufchâteau. If officers did their duty, the National Guardsmen would show the regulars how well civilians could soldier.

Another Guard division, the 42nd ("Rainbow"), appeared, parts of it, in November, and Pershing assigned classmate Charles Menoher as commander. Friend Menoher, artillerist who had taken over the gunnery schools when March had been tapped for stateside duty, had the toughness and professionalism needed in France. Two years Jack's junior, he showed the stamina and competence to weld men from twenty-six states and the District of Columbia into a tough, hard-hitting outfit.[95]

In December some of the westerners from the "Sunset" Division, the 41st, arrived to meet their commander, Maj. Gen. Hunter Liggett. Liggett, class of '79, had age and heft against him, and Pershing questioned his capacity. But he had trained his men well in the States, was in Europe when they began arriving, and took them to La Courtaine for continued practice.[96] His energy and diligence Pershing appreciated, and Liggett's determined physical conditioning reshaped Pershing's impression—and also Liggett!

Myriad support units clustered at Saint Nazaire and other AEF ports: engineers for work on construction of docks, buildings, railroads, all pioneering needs of the army; service troops for work with

[93] See JJP to Chief of Staff, HAEF, Oct. 2, 1917, File 3358, RG 120, National Archives. JJP to AGWAR (cable 144-S), HAEF, Sept. 7, 1917; AGWAR to JJP (cable 956-R), Mar. 21, 1918; JJP to AGWAR (cable 793-S), Mar. 27, 1918 (all in AEF, GHQ, CIC Reports, Box 2, Folder 15, RG 120, National Archives).

[94] See Efficiency Report by Maj. Gen. William H. Carter, 1914, summarized in document entitled "In the Matter of the Investigation of Major General Clarence Edwards, N.A." (Personal file of General J. J. Pershing), May 7, 1919, in Reclassification and Reassignment of General Officers—Maj. Gen. C. R. Edwards, RG 200, National Archives Gift Collection.

[95] For the composition of the division, see Stallings, AEF, p. 375.

[96] Liggett, Commanding an American Army, p. 19; JJP to AGWAR (cable 280-S), Nov. 10, 1917, JJP Papers, Cables, Box 3, RG 200/316, National Archives; Harbord, Diary, pp. 200-1.

the LOC in organizing and running supply depots of all sorts; medical companies for assignment to hospitals dotting the map of southern France. With men came, not often enough, equipment and materiel.

In the vast sprawl of his command Pershing glimpsed first signs of organization amid mass. Good will burgeoned everywhere—every man pined to do his best. That kind of zest needed direction and considerable tethering. Eagerness can breed recklessness, but eagerness thwarted can be dangerous.

A dangerous threnody of pessimism did creep into units near the front—a pessimism caught from weary Allies and worsened by routine, by rumors of swift German victory, and by the squalor of the tortured war zone. Clearly in the hectic, baffling months of training, divisional commanders must act firmly against war weariness and despair—Germany's subtlest weapons. Where centered the softness, the decay that could spread so swiftly?

Answers hardly encouraged a touchy commanding general. Gloomy rumors crept the camps of the 26th Division, of various brigades, and even wafted from the stalwarts of "Pershing's Pets," Big Red One. Those rumors Pershing considered evidence of some kind of command failure; they had to be met directly. Sibert and Clarence Edwards, and some brigade leaders, received a precise warning from the CIC:

Americans recently visiting our training areas and coming in contact with officers in high command have received a note of deep pessimism, including apprehension of undue hardships to be undergone, of the disadvantages of billeting as compared to field conditions that have prevailed in our own country, of the great numbers of our enemy, and a belief in the impregnability of his lines, mingled with some comment on the peculiarities of our Allies, and generally have come away with an impression that the war is already well along toward defeat for our arms. It is especially to be regretted that such an impression has been derived mainly from general officers, who, if prompted by considerations of soldierly duty, of leadership, of patriotism, fortitude and ambition, should maintain quite an opposite attitude.

While realizing that optimism cannot be created by order, it should be unnecessary to point out that such a state of mind on the part of officers in responsible positions is at once reflected among their troops. . . .

The officer who cannot read hope in the conditions that confront us; who is not inspired and uplifted by the knowledge that under the leadership of our chief executive, the heart of our nation is in this war; who shrinks from hardship; who does not exert his own personal influence to encourage his men; and who fails in the lofty attitude which should characterize the General that expects to succeed, should yield his position to others with more of our national courage. The consciousness of such an attitude should in honor dictate an application for relief. Whenever the visible effects of it on the command of such an officer reach me in future, it will constitute grounds for his removal without application.[97]

This stinging assault from the chief prompted some ill will: Sibert demanded a court of inquiry; Edwards explained that he had struggled against "a widespread feeling that the war is near its end . . . before our forces can become engaged with the enemy," and confessed fairly free admissions of discomforts to visitors "in order better to emphasize the fine spirit in which my men have accepted them." Brig. Gen. Peter Traub "emphatically and seriously" objected to being classed a faint heart—he had come, he said, to fight, to die if fate willed, for his country's triumph, and suggested that anyone who reflected on his optimism ranked as an enemy agent!

But the point struck home. Pershing would relieve the careless. A special vigor bustled American units in wake of the Old Man's warning. More might have to be done. Morale demanded careful nursing. French *poilus*, brave as many were, showed the wear of trench existence, had fought so long for so little that their own weariness could infect the men they taught. In a delicate situation of mind, little things counted. Especially chilly eyes surveyed Lanckton's work on Pershing's uniforms, leather, and brass; the commanding general must show his own confidence in every American camp. Visits increased; the Old Man's attention fixed on appearance, on soldierly bearing, on military courtesy. And if word spread that the CIC had a martinet's fondness for picky details, fine. Morale rose in anger and anger could best focus, in the doldrums of training, on the highest man around.

Compliments went to men of spirit. Frequently during that hard first winter, Pershing watched his men dredging through mud and mazes of entanglements as they learned the burrowed life of the front. He brought, still, myriad visitors, an increasing number as American skill developed; he showed vigorous approval to units with professional aplomb. Men could tell his pleasure in the smile, the sharp nod, the handshake, the personal questions.

But progress came so slowly. How much time would the enemy permit the Americans? Information mounted regarding enemy divisions moving to the west and concentrations of guns, transport, and supplies as the Germans disengaged from Russia. Experience comforted a bit; the rains that seemed always part of winter trench life, the squidgy

[97] JJP to Sibert, Edwards, B. B. Buck, Peter E. Traub, Dec. 13, 1917; Sibert to JJP, Dec. 15, 1917, copies in AEF, GHQ, Office of CIC Correspondence, File 21510, RG 120, National Archives. "In the Matter of the Investigation of Major General Clarence Edwards," May 7, 1919.

land of northern Franch, the piercing cold that numbed minds, hands, and hearts—all those old enemies of war—curtailed operations to raiding and sniping and surviving. Winter, then, seemed the safe time for building. Spring would bring clearing skies, breezes to brace men and dry ground, and with the greening of the battlefield would come the Germans. February? March? Would those veteran enemy hordes wait until April?

Those questions plagued every Allied commander in France and sparked the arguments about amalgamation that smoldered yet in Versailles, in Paris, in London, in Haig's and Pétain's councils.

There was luxury in waiting, in building an army of size and strength, an army filled with big, healthy men bursting with a valor mindful of 1914. And that luxury neither Haig nor Pétain could enjoy. For them winter dragged its toll of comfortless attrition.

Since the last spring in France, Haig's legions had fought a battle forward through Flanders, a battle that raged from April into October, a grinding, consuming, killing battle for some lost stretch of trench-lines and forlorn, draggled Passchendaele village. Throwing his men forward, first to aid Nivelle, later to sustain an offensive that would drain German reserves, finally to get out of low swamps into high ground, Haig had seemed reckless. His Tommies were magnificent; ditch by ditch, they kept going over the top into storms of fire, into iron grottoes of death, until at last they reached the muddy sprawl that once had been Passchendaele—five miles they had eked from the Hun at costs beyond American belief. But Haig spent a discontented winter for he had relinquished the offensive, and the Germans would dictate the next year's war.

British divisions shrank against the increasingly intricate German defenses; the usual twelve battalions were cut to nine, support troops were combed for front-line duty, pleas went in solemn cadence to London for still more men for the front. Crippled and thinned, the British army stood formidable yet in its lines beyond Ypres. And as winter wore away Haig shifted his tactical stance. He gathered strength toward the north of his line and built up defenses to hold the scant sixty miles of ground from Ypres to the sea, ground dotted with dumps and hospitals and regulating stations that sustained the BEF. He weakened the southern stretch of his line that linked with French divisions—for there, he guessed, the French would rush reserves to help in case of need.

Reserves became the great question of the winter.

The Supreme War Council urged formation of an Allied general reserve pool. Haig and Pétain both argued against withdrawing divisions to form the reserve; instead they promised cooperation in crisis. And they used the argument for reserves against John Pershing. He had the freest divisions in France, could afford to spend them in threatened places, ought to commit himself to a kind of fireman's role when the Germans came.

Pétain urged closer use of Americans in French units. His divisions had withered in the limited attacks of fall and in the steady erosion of the front. France had peaked in mobilization; her ranks would wane through 1918. Pershing could pump new blood into the martial veins of France, could flesh out the frail divisions that stood bulwark against barbarism.

Those catechisms rang in every talk with Allied leaders, stalked the halls of diplomacy, and affected America's position in Europe. French and British officials all claimed time for talk, and Pershing found that most of his hours fled in daily parlays about trivia. Apparently even the most efficient staff—and his improved daily—could not satisfy every detail, fend every pleader, turn away all wrath. No staff, of course, could handle queries from loftiest Allied chieftains.

Those old days of diplomacy in Washington, Tokyo, Manila, Moroland, even in Chihuahua, taught the essence of successful negotiation—inscrutable patience. Patience and courtesy were essential in coalition relations. Even more important was a firm grasp of objective—and Jack knew exactly his objective. The American army would build its own future without hindrance; emergencies might slow, but would not stop, development. His clear conception of objective made him a tough man to persuade.

Through the winter he heard from everywhere—especially from House and Bliss—of the almost frenzied Allied pressure for American amalgamation. He watched for signs from Washington and kept council of his own concerns. He welcomed friendly discussion of his problems, hoped to sway French political leaders to fuller cooperation, and accepted every invitation for talks with Clemenceau and his ministers. To a lesser extent he met British officials—they were not concerned with the daily sustenance of the AEF. Suspicious, Pershing approached elaborate conferences with raised guard, tight lip, and a close hand on his men.

Wully Robertson, bluff Chief of the Imperial General Staff, proposed a Paris meeting in January, 1918, to discuss the tentative arrangements made between Haig and Pershing for the transport and training of American divisions and staffs. If Robertson had questions, they needed answering. And urgent questions hung between the French and Americans about training and troop usage. They might be tackled at the same time, might, perhaps, impinge on the Robertson discussion.

Collecting aide Carl Boyd, fairly good in French, Pershing headed for Paris on Tuesday evening, January 8.

Next morning Robertson came and brought with him Sir Joseph Maclay, British shipping controller. Quickly to business, Robertson pitched his questions toward technical matters of the Haig-Pershing discussions. What ports were to be used? What logistical support facilities would sustain the American troops, once in France? Useful improvement of schedules seemed Robertson's aim. Open answers were quickly given—Southampton had been discussed since it had deep water, exceptional facilities to ensure quick turn-around. Robertson balked a bit; Southampton, already crowded, might be overstrained by men and baggage.

Clearly the Chief of the Imperial General Staff (CIGS) had some plan to offer. He had, he said, mentioned the problem to French shipping officials the night before; they had suggested using Cherbourg, perhaps Brest or Lorient. Those ports offered rail facilities to the American sector, lessened convoy problems, and lightened the drain on British resources in France. Robertson's talks with French officials seemed a bit presumptive, but if better arrangements could be made, fine. Obviously technical experts should be consulted about port and rail facilities.

An afternoon session convened in the office of the French minister of public works with General Atterbury and General Nash, British chief of rail transportation, in attendance. Quickly Brest dropped from consideration because of small docks; Cherbourg seemed a likely harbor and could be lent the Americans.

Housekeeping business done, Robertson had different questions. What about the troops brought over in British bottoms? Haig's plan, Pershing explained, proposed the training of perhaps six U.S. divisions with British units, the preparation of command and staff officers with their troops, then the transfer of ready divisions to the AEF. Quirky Robertson listened in evident distaste, and when Pershing finished the British general suggested an alternative. Bringing whole divisions would be uneconomical, would consume valuable space for such oddments as forage, engineer equipment, medical stores—men were the desperate necessity. What of Lloyd George's proposal to President Wilson, the plan to incorporate battalions into British divisions?

Direct shipment of men would be quick, would meet an urgent need, and would maintain BEF strength.

Sir Joseph Maclay agreed that men were easier to carry than supplies. Robertson, serious, his heavy brows working, added that "it was quite possible to get over infantry men by battalions about 5 times as quickly as battalions could be brought over in divisions." When agitated, the cockney accent thickened in Robertson's speech and he hunched into his words vigorously—he did now, and Pershing pondered.

Parrying with remarks about a similar discussion slated for later in the day with French authorities, Jack considered the propositions. Plural, for there were two propositions dangled by the English— Haig's straightforward "train and return" plan and Robertson's "bring and keep" scheme. By far the most interesting suggestion concerned shipping. How far were the British prepared to go in providing transports? A little sounding produced cautious guesses by the CIGS that space for 100,000 to 150,000 men might be found—numbers that would sustain normal twelve-battalion divisions.

What about leaving British divisions at nine battalions and filling the line with American divisions? That proposal brought a firm restatement of the speed argument. Would Pershing please consider the battalion scheme? Yes, but a question about shipping. To Maclay: Could ships be promised for the battalions? If so, how? Carefully the polite Englishman answered that fresh men were worth grave risks. England would be prepared to divert ships from food cargoes temporarily, would venture short rations if America would match English boldness with troops.

Another question Maclay anticipated: Britain "could not however well take the risk for the transport of complete divisions as not enough men would be brought in this manner to justify the great risks involved." Robertson echoed Maclay's sentiments, reiterated his plea. Then, leaning forward, he talked solemnly of portents. "Unless something of this kind is done"—the general spoke in hard, measured tones—"there is the possibility of the British becoming so exhausted . . . in the severe fighting which is undoubtedly coming, that the Entente would have a very heavy task in . . . order to win the war."[98]

[98] The quotations, altered into present tense, are from "Account of a Meeting between General Pershing, Sir W. Robertson, and Sir T. [sic] Maclay, Shipping Controller, on 9th January 1918," in "Important Conferences, Memoranda, Etc., Affecting Employment of the A.E.F.," AEF, GHQ, G-3, Folder 655, RG 120, National Archives.

Scattered comments on Western Front strengths, on German ability to snatch spectacular successes from each war year, ended a long meeting. Everyone agreed to convene the next day.

Bemused by the sudden offer of supposedly nonexistent ships, Pershing and Boyd journeyed to Clemenceau's office. It would likely be an unpleasant meeting. Meeting the Tiger always proved a challenge, and this particular session promised challenge sharpened by hostility. For a week relations between the AEF's chieftain and France's had stretched in anger. Clemenceau, in a typical eruption, had cabled his Washington representative to see Baker and protest troubles between Pershing and Pétain. They did not agree on training American regiments with French divisions before consolidation for line service. Baker, who refused both to agree to the plan or to order Pershing to agree, referred the matter to his general.

Too often in recent months had Allied politicos tried the Washington "run around." Apparently undismayed by repeated referrals to Pershing, they kept up their irksome harassment—the kind of sniping likely to erode confidence at home. Clemenceau, since he seemed the worst offender, must learn the toughness of Yankee diplomacy. On January 5, 1918, Pershing wrote him a note:

May I not suggest to you, Mr. President [President du Conseil], the inexpediency of communicating such matters to Washington by cable? These questions must all be settled here, eventually, on their merits, through friendly conferences between General Pétain and myself, and cables of this sort are very likely, I fear, to convey the impression of serious disagreement between us when such is not the case.[99]

Clemenceau, surely seething at such insubordinate words from a soldier, bit nails in reply:

I hasten, without losing a moment, to reply to your letter. . . . I found myself under the necessity of cabling to the Ambassador of France at Washington because the two contradictory responses which I had received from General Pétain and from yourself . . . obliged me, in the interest of the common cause, to seek an arbitration between the two Commanders-in-Chief.

I need not conceal the fact that I placed full confidence in this regard in the American Government. However, it was not to the American Government that I addressed myself. I cabled to the Ambassador of France, as was my right and duty, in order to give him directions for the conversations which might take place either with the Secretary of War or with the President. . . .

So I am giving you here the explanation which I owe you and I shall

[99] JJP, *Experiences*, 1:275.

exercise all the patience of which I am capable in awaiting the good news that the American Commander and the French Commander have finally agreed on a question which may be vital to the outcome of the war. . . .[100]

Frigidly, then, two stubborn men met. Contrasts they were in manner, method, and mein: Pershing, austere, blunter than usual, grave and exquisitely polite; Clemenceau, eyes ferreting, rumpled figure rolled into his aggressive talking stance, fenced with politesse like Tallyrand. Clemenceau had heard the generals with different ears, surely; he wanted only cooperation. Old misunderstandings Pershing recalled and knew that Clemenceau and Pétain really wanted to steal American divisions for the French army. Training principles were the difference; the prime minister had often heard the American position on the need of practice in "minor tactics," the practice of open warfare. Pétain, the prime minister must know, favored only trench training. Both methods were necessary in American preparations. He must, Pershing said, insist on his own program. But harmony would take precedence over other considerations.

Gruffly France's Tiger had to growl approval of harmony and listen as the formal American urged wider understanding among the Allies. Pershing put his sense of urgency into a plea for coordinated effort. Cordial agreement would be essential in planning to meet the pending German drive—extensive operations demanded comprehensive preparation. American forces had not arrived in expected numbers, a sad truth openly confessed. Only four divisions, in various training phases, were on the Continent; ten should have arrived. Supplies lagged, rail transportation languished for locomotives (which the Belgians would now supply), and port facilities pinched badly. Forty-five divisions in the States awaited ways to reach the war.

Ports were the burden of the meeting. Could the prime minister aid in cutting through the petty punctilio entrapping operations at the ports? Previous promises—by the former government—to hand over control of Saint Nazaire traffic went unkept. Bureaucratic entanglements snarled activity at every hand. Faced with a solvable problem, a favor he could do, Clemenceau reiterated good will, agreed to help. Also, he said, he accepted the need for coordination on the Western Front. Pershing, though, must do his share.

Ever willing to match offers, Pershing could easily repeat his constant promise of aid in any real emergency. He would see Pétain

---

[100] Quoted in *ibid.*

on the morrow and restore relations. Restored amiability with the Tiger proved the best result of the meeting.[101]

Paris nights, even winter nights, have strange qualities of soul— the ancient pavements, the reminders of old glories, touch memories and longings and hearts. Going that January night toward the Mills mansion, Pershing felt the special poignance of responsibility. Was Robertson right? Were American soldiers essential to Britain's continuance in the war? He had talked to Clemenceau of emergency— was it now at hand? Was this the time to yield a bit, to slow further the building of the AEF and sustain a failing cause? Perhaps there would be an answer in the next day's talk with Robertson.

That talk rang the same staid changes on British needs, pushed harder now by an old soldier nearly pleading to a comrade. No answer here, merely repetition, and Pershing made a lonesome decision. He would help the British. Not wholly persuaded of necessity, he was persuaded of advantage. Added tonnage must not be lost, and America did have men in bounty yearning for the front. And there seemed strong sentiment at home for open aid to the Allies. The decision went to Baker in an oddly uncertain cable:

This whole question seems to me to be one of necessity. . . . While it would not be advisable in any way to alter our own program for bringing our divisions yet the offer of the British to provide sea transportation for such extra men as we may be able to furnish for temporary service with their Army would not interfere with that. . . . I would therefore recommend that this request . . . be given serious consideration from the point of view of our national attitude regarding service in another Army; that it be regarded as a temporary measure to meet a probable emergency; that as soon as possible the remaining troops of divisions thus temporarily broken up be brought over and the divisions reorganized; . . . that the infantry be taken from these divisions that would not otherwise be transported until after June.[102]

On close reading, Pershing's message looked like a request for approval.

By the time he received approval, he had talked constructively with Pétain. The French commander, who resisted Pershing's early suggestions about training separate American brigades because of

---

[101] For the meeting and its background, see JJP, *Experiences*, 1:283, 296–97; Harbord, *Diary*, pp. 215–16; Harbord, *American Army*, pp. 188–90.

[102] JJP to Chief of Staff (cable 487-S), Jan. 14, 1918, in "Important Letters and Memoranda on Employment of the AEF," AEF, GHQ, G-3, Folder 675, RG 120, National Archives.

command confusion, had happily accepted a modification: the 42nd Division would be rushed through four weeks of American open-warfare training, then its regiments would join French units for trench instruction. That plan, Pétain commented, would permit proper induction of staffs and general officers into the intricacies of front-line management. The 26th Division? Far along in preparation, it would be ready for front duty in early February, and Pershing approved its assignment to General de Maud'huy's army somewhere near Soissons. Elements of the 42nd might also enter the line in February, while the 2nd shaped rapidly and would soon be active.

Oddly Pershing found Pétain willing to accept Robertson's program of American infiltration of British units; he did muse, wistfully, that it could happen to his own divisions. But that acceptance, ready and willing, marked a shift in French thinking. Why?

While he wondered at possible Allied collusion against him, Pershing offered Pétain four Negro regiments of the 93rd Division. They were coming at the special insistence of the War Department, had caused some friction with color-conscious British authorities, and Pershing hoped they would be acceptable. Pétain had no color blindness—his own colonials were splendid troops—but wondered about quality. Pershing knew two of the regiments from border duty, approved them, confessed no acquaintance with the others. Officers were mixed. Pétain took them happily.[103]

In two days Pershing had restored the French front by hard bargaining and shrewd concession. But the new Anglo-French attitude toward using Americans rankled. Had the Robertson agreement been sound?

Conferencing demanded special sensitivity and usually revealed the pettiness in coalitions. British and French negotiators talked usually of the "common cause" but worked for national interests. Uncommon cause between them stemmed obviously from some secret scheme for profit. Nothing done in war ought to disillusion an old soldier; Jack knew that, but the coils of deceit tangling every talk seemed sadly shabby. Open and honest he went to these meetings, and suffered deception; now that the rules were clear, he would go guilefully to future gatherings.

Suspicions of the Robertson plan were confirmed by Bliss's persistent support of it and by a special visit to Marshal Joffre in January.

[103] See "Resume of Conversation between G[eneral] P[ershing] and P[é]t[ain]," January 11, 1918," in "Important Conferences, Memoranda, Etc. Affecting Employment of the A.E.F.," AEF, GHQ, G-3, Folder 655, RG 120, National Archives.

The old soldier, always friendly to Pershing and Harbord, greeted them warmly and confessed that he brooded much about the coming campaign. Estimates of enemy strength, he said, were overdrawn—the Germans would have superior, but not overwhelming, numbers to throw into the spring battles. Agitation about possible defeat Joffre thought silly; the Allies were in better posture than ever. And if American strength increased rapidly, victory loomed certain. Proudly Pershing boasted of his forming divisions, of their impending line service, but avoided pledging schedules.

Joffre pulled his visitors close for confidential words. He spoke, he said, as a friend of Pershing's when he cautioned against British amalgamation plans.

There would be an adverse effect on the [American] division [he confided]. American battalions would find themselves commanded by a British general with a British staff. They would resent orders received under such circumstances which they would accept without question under an American commander. In case of a reverse there would be the tendency to assess the blame to the command. . . . The British have never found it advisable to incorporate in the same divisions Canadians, Australians, New Zealanders, Indians, Portuguese, or even Scottish with English. . . . There must also be considered the effect on the American people. . . .[104]

Here was honesty from a crony! Joffre's conversation Pershing found "profitable" for many reasons, not the least being the perspective it gave to two January meetings between Allied generals. Pershing had forced the first meeting with Haig and Pétain—not that he needed more conferences, but he thought the public ought to know that Western generals did speak to each other, did plan coalition war. He knew, so did the other Allied generals, that hectic business had kept them apart, that working friendship prevailed, but a conference could move further toward cooperation.

Compiègne on Saturday, January 19, sparkled in a winter sun, breezes were mild, and only the uniforms at Grand Quartier Général (GQG) reminded of war. With Boyd, Pershing arrived late in the afternoon. Haig and Pétain with their aides were already together in the "Château du Marechal"; clearly they had been talking earlier. Both leaned to the idea of adding Americans to British battalions, and their mutual agreement again ignited smoldering suspicion. Almost smug in understanding, they turned on Pershing as the outsider. Did

---

[104] "Memorandum of Conversation Between Marshal Joffre and General Pershing, January 26, 1918" ("Secret"), in "Important Conferences, Memoranda, Etc."; JJP, *Experiences*, 1:305–6.

he realize, the glacial Haig inquired, how important it was to get American troops into line quickly?

Patiently Jack turned impertinence to discussion and reminded his colleagues of the determined formation of an American army. With painful self-control Pétain settled his large bulk for preachments, fixed his sunken eyes on Pershing, and spoke quietly. There can be no American army without properly trained divisional and artillery commanders, he argued, and added that their training would prevent effective American help on the front until next winter. That doubtless would be too late.

Haig's coolly superior gaze swept both Pétain and Pershing as they talked; he enjoyed the dialogue, agreed with Pétain, and finally joined with advice: put American battalions and brigades into the line quickly under their own officers. Both could train together.

A "most friendly" dinner found colleagues avoiding argument, talking easily of old friends and shared adventure. Still, Pershing felt estranged from the camaraderie of GQG. Obviously Pétain had closed ranks with Haig, which had one happy result in announced plans for coordinated defense. But they treated the Americans like rookies, almost like parasites on Allied stores.

Pershing disliked being rebuffed; he disliked even more any slights to his country. Musing on the course of selfishness, he returned to Chaumont.[105]

France's chief of staff, General Foch, joined with Robertson in assembling the generals on January 24, again at Compiègne. Up from Paris came Pershing with Carl Boyd; they arrived not long before the appointed time of 10:00 A.M. Haig, tediously prompt, had come early and had taken breakfast with Pétain at the château; it was anybody's guess as to whether they bandied any secret agreements.

For a few minutes the conferees enjoyed the crisp sunshine and the handsome grounds of GQG, then clustered in a large, lofty room charmed with huge windows. A round table took stage center, where the delegates furtively found marked places and checked others. Pershing noted his spot on Pétain's right; Haig took his big armchair directly opposite the French commander; Foch and his aide faced Robertson and two henchmen. All looked to Pétain for host's duties. He began by deferring to Robertson, who had, it seemed, summoned them all hence.

[105] For the conference, see Haig Diary, Jan. 19, 1918.

Interesting tensions gripped the room. Haig, settled comfortably next to his own chief of staff, showed his usual glacial ease, while Robertson, heavy with portents, flicked nervous glances round the table. Nominal host Pétain, sided by two other French generals, sat stoically polite, waiting. Almost consumed by his chair, short, dapper Foch, flanked by an aide, sparked energy and interest. But Jack caught some strange current between the two French leaders, some *dérangement*.

Bluntly Robertson opened—he and Foch wanted the meeting, he said, to find out what defensive plans were prepared. Responsible to their governments, to the War Council, the staff chiefs needed the information. What, too, was the state of American forces? Could a general reserve be formed? Could reinforcements be pulled from Italy?

Pétain spoke next. He and Haig had decided on a defensive posture in the spring; offensives were prohibited by thin ranks. France counted ninety-seven infantry divisions, each with four battalions of four companies, but with divisional rifle strength cut somewhere between five and six thousand. Two dismounted cavalry divisions were supported by six mounted. A third of his army he kept in reserve. Probably, Pétain said without conviction, the divisions can be kept to strength until April; after that, even without battle losses, some divisions must be broken up to sustain others. "Without any action," he said calmly, "the French army would have to be reduced 20 divisions before the end of the year." As for defensive measures, he and Haig agreed to sustain each other in emergencies with available reserves.

Quietly Haig supported his colleague. A third of his divisions, he said, were in reserve also, with his forward troops holding three lines of resistance. Like Pétain, he had fixed on certain possible fields for small counterstrokes.

Foch broke in animatedly. Offensives, he said, were the key to victory. Lessons of 1916 should not be forgotten—the only thing that had halted the Verdun onslaught was the Allied Somme attack. "The way to stop an offensive," Foch's eye flashed to echoes of *attaque à l'outrance*, "in this 4th year of the war is by a counter-offensive with all the force of arms at our disposal." Verdun left lasting wounds, he reminded, wounds of body and spirit in France; another great German drive might make those old wounds fatal.

Carefully Pershing surveyed the table. Haig looked vastly unimpressed—he was, in fact, thinking that Foch's outburst was "admirable in theory, but not practicable."[106] Robertson simply brooded, but Pétain seemed irked. It was Pétain who argued.

In 1916 at Verdun, he said, the Germans boasted only 125 divisions and attacked at one place; now they counted 170, 180, perhaps would soon have 200 divisions and could sustain two or three simultaneous drives. With fervor uncommon, Pétain queried his colleagues: "When they attack at one point, should we then launch a counterattack?" No, because other points would be exposed. Defensive-offensives on limited fronts were the only possibilities.

Squabbling erupted, Foch stressing the need for a carefully planned general attack, Haig willing to charge if he had men, Pétain agreeing with troop needs. Robertson, sticking to the point, asked if victory would come from defensives. Pointedly Haig preached the facts of attrition—the defensive was forced on the Allies. Robertson asked, hopefully, if "it was General Foch's theory to introduce more offensives into the tactics?" No, he advocated "one grand offensive action." Pétain objected strongly. Where should the one great stroke go? Robertson wondered, and Foch casually admitted that he "had not studied this plan." Pétain suggested several potential German objectives on the French and British fronts: Alsace; between the Aisne and Reims to include the Chemin des Dames; between Arras and Saint Quentin, but probably not in Flanders. Haig stiffly said that not much ground could be given up in his area. Reims or Nancy could not be lost, Pétain argued, since they covered the rich Douai coal fields. Robertson liked Foch's big attack scheme but thought it impossible.

Pershing listened to the debate, broke in at last with a question: Would Foch elaborate his plan? Foch confessed he had none, had not been asked to bring any, but if the Germans drove like they did two years before, the Allies would be scrambling from one front to another for reserves in defense—planned counterstrokes, much bigger than Pétain proposed, were needed. Pétain said they were impossible without American aid. Haig broke in belligerently: "Give us back the troops from Salonika and we will commence offensives." Foch snapped that "we are not speaking of offensives but of counter-offensives."

Tiredly Pétain mused that all possible measures had been taken.

---

[106] *Ibid.*, Jan. 24, 1918; Carl Boyd, "Report of Meeting at Compiègne, January 24, 1918, between Generals Pershing, Pétain, Sir Douglas Haig, Sir William Robertson, Foch, Davidson and Lawrence," in "Important Conferences, Memoranda, Etc.," Folder 655, RG 120, National Archives.

Foch wanted another Somme offensive prepared; Pétain urged the Arras–Saint Quentin area for a limited counterstroke. Then he and Robertson chimed together that American troops were vital. Pétain, looking at Pershing, commented on the four divisions currently in training and said that by May an army corps might be in line but would be inexperienced. Training, he added dryly, "was not going on exactly according to the scheme he would like to see adopted." A brief allusion to possible amalgamation with the French gave Jack an opening. Would anyone care to hear a statement on the American situation? Yes, indeed.

Aware now that wrangling and seeping bitterness soured the meeting, Pershing made a firm declaration of problems. Since everybody seemed to want to get the worst on the record, he followed suit. Transportation hampered all phases of American operations in France —shipping and railroad shortages were obvious, port bottlenecks were worsening, and promised French assistance did not come. But progress had been made.

He might as well say here, and Jack spoke with clipped, brusque Missouri tones, "that any real offensive in which the Americans take part should be executed by them as an American army." Firmly he announced disapproval of loaning men to anyone, save in dire emergencies. Language clearly barred French amalgamation; British commanders knew his willingness to help in time of trouble.

A general outburst of surprise about transportation problems ran the table. Could something be done to help the port stoppages? The question from Robertson, Pershing fended with praise for Pétain's efforts, feeble as they proved, but Foch broke in heatedly: "None of these questions has been referred to me." Pétain snorted: "One should not wait until such things are brought to his attention but should look around and find them." He would send officers immediately to assist Pershing.

Responding to general questions, Pershing announced hopes of having twelve to thirteen divisions in Europe, certainly en route, by July, but training would be needed once on the Continent.

Dispirit congealed discussion. Could troops be brought back from Italy? Robertson wondered in a kind of final hope for decision. Foch regretted the impossibility; British and French divisions were propping up the south. And so the meeting ended without action and with scant hope.

For Pershing the lessons were large. Critics of Western generals were right—they had no plans for victory! Depressed, not surprised,

Jack came to a firm certainty of the future as that conference concluded: America would inherit the war, if not in 1918, surely in 1919. His course had become clear in all future dealings with his martial colleagues; nothing would deter formation of the ultimate American force.[107]

Looking back for personal implications, Pershing recalled not only the obvious contempt Pétain had for Foch but also Pètain's petulance toward everything American. The French general's gratuitous comments on training disagreements served as only one example; a kind of irritated shortness colored most remarks to Pershing, and Pétain almost dismissed the United States as a parasite. Haig had been his usual lofty self, polite and only a shade condescending, and had emphasized the need for specialized instructors in troop training, but a growing friendliness could be felt. Pershing chatted privately with Haig before leaving for Paris. Wearily Pershing confessed he found "the French very trying," and struck long-suffering sympathy. Haig commiserated and pressed his own independence of French schemes.[108]

Scant respites came in the campaign to keep an American army. In Paris on Friday, January 25, Pershing encountered Bliss, who bubbled with excitement over Britain's troop plight. Together they joined Wully Robertson, also jaded from Compiègne, and launched again into the intricacies of shipping, battalions, and amalgamation. The discussion began with Robertson's usual blunt declaration of crisis; Bliss nodded vehemently. Disaster stalked the Western Front; Germans were lurking behind each tree in the Bois de Boulogne! Bliss nodded vehemently. But their private argument—the one that had established Pershing's supremacy in France—set common American policy and again frustrated Robertson's cannibalism.

Four days later, at a War Council gathering in Versailles, Lloyd George, Robertson, Sir Henry Wilson, Lord Milner, Col. Maurice Hankey, and, finally, Haig clustered around Bliss and Pershing.[109] Again came the demands, raucous now with the prime minister's Welsh righteousness. Clearly everyone counted on Bliss to bend the iron Missourian. Lloyd George fixed on Bliss a steely eye, canted in a

---

107 Pershing's account of the conference, in *Experiences*, 1:300–3, follows Carl Boyd's minutes of the meeting, given in "Report of Meeting at Compiègne, January 24, 1918" in "Important Conferences, Memoranda, Etc.," Folder 655, RG 120, National Archives. Haig copied a seating chart of the conference, which is followed in the text. His written account differs from the chart. See Haig Diary, Jan. 24, 1918, for important additional details.

108 Haig Diary, Jan. 24, 1918.

109 *Ibid.*, Jan. 29, 1918, says Col. Maurice Hankey was also present.

mime of cordiality: What did he think? Pershing watched his colleague closely; here was the testing moment.

Without heitation, Bliss answered: "Pershing will speak for us and whatever he says with regard to the disposition of the American forces will have my approval."[110]

Crestfallen, the Englishmen turned to their old nemesis. Amused at them, pleased at Bliss's appreciation of the obvious, Pershing rejected earlier arrangements and talked of a compromise proposal. Robertson protested that Pershing had already agreed to putting 150 battalions into the British lines. This new recalcitrance amounted to reneging. Haig, who joined the discussion at its loudest moment, listened quietly, wondering what had upset his new Yank friend.

Forcefully Pershing talked, his clipped Missouri tones almost menacing. At home, he said, people were attacking the administration for "no results to show for the money which America has been spending. No troops in the field, no aeroplanes, no guns, no nothing yet in fact!!"[111] News of amalgamation would confirm worst suspicions of a governmental giveaway. All notions that permanent amalgamation had ever been contemplated were wrong. It never would be.

Haig quietly joined the conversation with a soothing reassurance that if he got 150 American battalions he would train them for return to Pershing. Originally that plan seemed good; now Pershing offered a compromise proposal with cordial finality. Glumly the Englishmen adjourned to study a scheme requiring them to transport 6 divisions during the affluence of shipping. Infantry and auxilliary troops would train with Haig, artillery with the Americans on French guns. When "sufficiently trained," the units would "be united under their own officers for service."[112]

Bliss and Pershing wondered at acceptance chances; the scheme would produce additional men for Pershing, drain British training and logistical resources, confuse command arrangements. Six divisions counted some 72 battalions, hence would be far less than Robertson expected. But for a time the plan would put fresh flesh in British units. Was the price too high? No matter, it served as sufficient salve to such veterans of collusion.[113] Pershing would be generous in real crises, selfish otherwise.

At Versailles next day, a cool one, almost frosty, bright and promis-

[110] JJP, *Experiences*, 1:308.
[111] Haig Diary, Jan. 29, 1918.
[112] JJP, *Experiences*, 1:309–10.
[113] See Coffman, *War*, p. 171.

ing, Lloyd George opened proceedings. You are right, he said to John Pershing, in your opposition to amalgamation. Astounded, Pershing listened in growing glee as the prime minister accepted the 6-division plan.[114]

A fuddled secretary of war must be told of Pershing's change of mind and of his final triumph. In mid-January Jack had cabled tentative approval of Robertson's 150-battalion request, and Baker agreed. On Wednesday, the thirtieth, Jack cabled a carefully arranged explanation:

> Your conclusion that the proposition to send infantry battalions for service with British divisions was recommended by me was erroneous. Have had the matter under consideration for some time and am convinced that the plan would be grave mistake. Stated my views fully to Sir William Robertson which resulted in delay until arrival of British Prime Minister yesterday.[115]

Repeating the full agreement signed with Lloyd George, Pershing concluded with a small boast: "If carried out this arrangement will provide six additional divisions to be brought over by British shipping." If the secretary read carefully he would see his general's skill in "conferencing."

It would take something beyond tough talk and skilled suasion to achieve the thing Jack thought vital to the war—coordinated command. The ramblings of the War Council served some purposes, good and bad. But those ramblings indicated continued resistance to a Supreme Commander for the Western Front. In the dragging meetings during January and February, political and military representatives argued over minute shreds of big problems. Clearly the political members had one eye to objective: a general reserve for spring. Generals squabbled over how men could be pulled into it, who would command. Lloyd George clearly resented the uncooperative attitude of Robertson in most of the War Council sessions and focused his resentment of Haig also on the field marshal's henchman. Neither British general seemed willing to discuss coordination or alternatives to attrition. Pershing worried about the corroded relations between London and Montreuil, worried, too, that Foch did most of France's business in Versailles without a nod to Compiègne. Clemenceau quietly shoved Foch forward at every chance, said nothing of Pétain—the Tiger understood the need for a supreme commander and had his candidate.

[114] JJP, *Experiences*, 1:308–10.
[115] JJP to AGWAR, Jan. 30, 1918 (cable 555-S), in AEF, GHQ, G-3, "Important Letters and Memoranda on Employment of the AEF," Folder 675, RG 120, National Archives; JJP, *Experiences*, 1:309–10.

Anyone would do, within limits. Pershing could take orders from Haig, Pétain, or Foch gladly if cohesion resulted. He and Bliss pushed the idea in each War Council session.

On February 2, 1918, a bright, warm Saturday, sparkling after a frosty night, the War Council made the first move to win the war. Lloyd George, ever trying for changed command, talked with Clemenceau before anyone else arrived for that day's session, arranged his plans, and at 11:00 A.M. rose to suggest an executive war board, with Foch as chairman, charged with organizing a general reserve. Pershing knew the implications; so did the unhappy Haig, who said that "to some extent it makes Foch a 'Generalissimo.'" Who gives orders? Haig wanted to know, and watched in wry amusement as the political members fell into embarrassed haranguing. Finally Lloyd George said that "orders would be issued by the members of the body nominated by the Supreme Council."[116]

Happy, Pershing listened to Haig's questions about taking over more French line. Attempts to refer the question to the War Council and its War Board were frustrated by Haig and Pétain, and Pershing realized coordination had yet to come.[117]

Much of the problem hung on political aims at variance with military objectives. The politico-martial mix at Versailles ought to smooth rough edges but seemed, really, to expose a kind of general incompetence. War had worn the Allies, warped their political views, jaded their generals. Was this the time for special American initiative?

Distance and constant siege strained Pershing's position in France. Troubles with Bliss, though apparently ended, reminded of martial mortality, and the two American generals suffered acute buffeting in War Council sessions attended by British and French heads of state. Voices for rational command were drowned in a babble of ambitions. But suppose . . .

"May I . . . Mr. Secretary, suggest to you the advisability of making a visit to France. Beside being profitable to see the procedure from this point of view, it would give a new inspiration to the Allies and would especially encourage our own forces."[118] Jack wrote in mid-January, and his invitation contained a good deal of personal longing. Troubles with Allied leaders sparked only part of his interest in Baker's coming; problems with the War Department, with logistical arrangements, problems, even, of self-confidence needed Baker's eye. Rein-

---

[116] Haig Diary, Feb. 2, 1918.
[117] JJP, *Experiences*, 1:311–13.
[118] *Ibid.*, p. 297.

forcement of Pershing's position by the secretary in high councils would strengthen the fight against amalgamation, enhance the quest for effective command.

On February 22, the president told Baker he could visit France. He would go as an observer and as John Pershing's friend.

☆ 21 ☆

Generals, Doughboys, and a Few Marines

HE watched them like a father—with pride and a little fear. They were better now, battle wise and tougher, fine-looking soldiers, those 1st Division men. "Pershing's Pets" had stuck as their nickname, but they bore it now with confidence. A stint in the line with their good French teachers put swagger in their walk and touched up their natural cockiness. And because the Old Man always watched, they did their work with special zeal. Reports from Gondrecourt were good, and Jack thought the selection of Robert Bullard to division command sound. A man to measure his chieftain's penchant for success, Bullard wrote orders for speed, professionalism, and discipline; his men liked him, worked for him. They were going up again in mid-January, half of the 1st Division,[1] to a slice of line near Ansauville. American morale was good, the men were eager and edgy, showed no real ill effects of a long, harsh winter spent in uncommon privation. This time they went up as trained troops and would relieve the veteran 1st Moroccan Division of a 7.5-kilometer stretch of trenchline north of Toul, from Seicheprey to Bouconville. An American division would at last hold an entire section of front. Pershing waited with parental anxiety for first word back.

The 1st Division's new responsibilities were vital. The men must prove to the Allies that Americans were capable of sharing the war. Word came to Chaumont slowly but told of solid professionalism. Careful staff work produced prudent marching schedules that brought all units to the frontal zone on time; transports and supplies kept close to the troops.

In the War Room at GHQ Jack conjured the ground his men de-

---

[1] Robert L. Bullard, *Personalities and Reminiscences of the War*, p. 128.

fended. Hugging a kind of last wrinkle of rough land, the line looked toward Mont Sec, standing some 400 feet above the flattening terrain leading into the vast Woëvre Plain. Deceptively named, the Woëvre spawned villages, forests, ravines, all kinds of cover for enemy forces, and it lay behind formidable German defenses. Trenchlines in depth, festooned with wire, crusted with pill boxes, all under an umbrella of well-sighted guns, barred progress northeastward. On the American side everything seemed, somehow, Lilliputian and feeble. French troops dug trenches where they were stopped, and chance had denied the high ground. Big Red One took over a low-lying stretch of front protected by shallow, water-sogged ditches largely dominated by enemy artillery. Behind the front about a mile ran a key ridgeline that carried the Saint Dizier–Metz highway through Beaumont—here hinged the main American defense.

According to agreement, the French 69th Division, as neighbors in the front, controlled Bullard's command. A veteran, careful general led the 69th, and he charmed his new subordinates—both with his Americanized name, Monroe, and his courteous concern for everyone. He would yield to Bullard as soon as the Americans were comfortable in the line.

Comforts were scarce, and Pershing worried about his men. Training had gone as far as possible; practice now remained. But training had involved problems with the French. Pétain's odd insistence on teaching only trench tactics conflicted with Jack's insistence on open-warfare methods. Compromises crumbled in fresh eruptions of French pique; finally tough orders requiring adherence to American regulations went to all units. The French grumbled and were hurt.[2]

---

[2] For problems in training, see *ibid.*, pp. 101–4, where a general critique is offered. For specific Franco-American disagreement concerning open warfare training, see Pétain, "Memorandum on Instruction of American Infantry Units Attached to Large French Units" (GQG, Armées du Nord et des Nord-Est, Staff, 3rd Bureau, No. 736 [Secret], May 1, 1918, p. 8, in AEF, GHQ, CIC Reports, Folder 265, "Secret Instructions to French Commanders re—Training American Units" [Appendix 41 to G-5 Report], RG 120, National Archives), in which Pétain says: "Americans dream of Operating [*sic*] in open country, after having broken through the front. This results in too much attention being devoted to this form of operations. . . . " See also Col. H. B. Fiske to Chfstf AEF, France, July 4, 1918 (Secret), AEF, GHQ, G-3 Folder 695-B, "French Memoranda on Training of American Troops," RG 120, National Archives, in which the ACS for Training comments on the Pétain memorandum as follows: "The offensive spirit of the French and British Armies has largely disappeared as a result of their severe losses. . . . In many respects, the tactics and technique of our Allies are not suited to American characteristics or the American mission in this war. The French do not like the rifle, do not know how to use it, and their infantry is consequently too entirely dependent upon a powerful artillery support. Their infantry lacks aggressiveness and disci-

Wounded feelings impinged not at all on general admiration for American élan. Those stalwart men in khaki showed so much of almost forgotten verve, oozed confidence and certainty, and challenged the Germans by their presence. They went forward toward the eternal trenches over icy roads, through snowy drifts, burdened with the tools of death—rifles, bayonets, gas masks, bandoliers—and with the housewifery of bachelor life—blankets, rations, tent halves, shoes, underwear, mess kits, digging tools—but light in heart and conscience.[3]

Bullard's own aggressiveness showed in orders for harassment of the enemy lines, for intrusion into No Man's Land, for continuous activity.[4] But late in February a clammy cloud of gas seeped from the Boche trenches into Remières Wood and registration fire searched American battery positions. Clearly the enemy's plans ran parallel to Bullard's. At 5:30 A.M., March 1, a storm of shell raked the woods held by the 18th Infantry and rained generally along the American sector with special concentrations flailing artillery batteries.

Swift adherence to training took most Americans to reserve positions; those caught under the barrage fought fiercely, aided by artillery and steady machine-gun fire. When the searing ended with the Germans repulsed, 20 Americans lay dead, 12 had been captured, a number wounded. Estimates put the enemy force at 220, and of these 17 were killed, 4 captured, and 62 wounded. Behind them the Germans left considerable equipment and the jubilation of battle-ready Americans. A congratulatory order from General Passaga, commander of the French corps sheltering the 1st Division, read extremely well at Chaumont.[5]

French enthusiasm at American pluck ran embarrassingly fulsome. The Tiger of France himself descended on the division, in company with the French I Army commander, redoubtable Gen. Marie Eugène Debeney, with Passaga and others. "At a little ceremony near Beaumont," Passaga and his superiors handed out decorations with almost reckless abandon; strutting members of the 18th Infantry and some artillerists sported the croix de guerre!

---

pline. The British infantry lacks initiative and resource. . . . I strongly recommend that the earliest practicable opportunity be taken to secure our emancipation from Allied supervision." JJP endorsed: "This is entirely my own view."

[3] For conditions on the advance, see George B. Duncan, "Reminiscences of the World War," p. 52 (typescript in University of Kentucky Library).

[4] *First Div.*, p. 48.

[5] The order, dated Mar. 2, 1918 and signed by General Passaga, is printed in *ibid.*, pp. 57–58. For other details of the German raid, see Duncan, "Reminiscences", pp. 72–73.

There would, of course, be retaliation. Word was that the American blow would fall early on March 4, 1918. Pershing went to see it.

In the restless dark, time stretched, and men shuffled, did busy things, and wondered. At 1:00 A.M. an eerie, cracking, crowning sound tore through tension; the sharp staccato of 75s and the heavier, angrier booming of 155s mixed in a cacophony with machine guns. Everyone hung on word from the raiders in the 16th and 18th Infantry —men who would soon "go over the top" to repay that previous call. In the thunder of preparatory shelling, minutes passed without any visible movements in the American coils of wire. Finally came cancellation orders in a kind of silly anticlimax. The bangalore torpedoes slated for use against German wire proved too long for turns in communicating trenches—they could not be carried to the front!

Pink-faced and abashed, divisional leaders confessed the absurdity to a stony John Pershing. Amusement may have twinkled an eye, but haughty displeasure reeked along the lines. Happily no distinguished visitors shared this Yank faux pas. Rescheduled for later in the month, the raid would be part of a series aimed at building morale. Morale ran high, though; shamed amusement rather than horror showed the quality of confidence. Pershing had no real worries about Big Red One.

Other divisions, too, impressed the commander-in-chief. Omar Bundy's 2nd Division with its regulars and marines would soon enter a quiet sector south of Verdun. Clarence Edward's 26th Division had done a stint along the Aisne and was readying for work in the Woëvre area. The 42nd ("Rainbow") Division, in classmate Charlie Menoher's hands, had served near Lunéville but now headed for the line near Baccarat. And the "Gemütlichkeit Boys" of the 32nd, those eager Michigan and Wisconsin guardsmen under Gen. Bill Haan, were training furiously near Prauthoy for an early shot at the Hun. By the end of February, Pershing counted 16,547 officers and 235,342 men in the AEF.[6]

In January, anticipating the early front-line service of three big divisions, Pershing had asked Hunter Liggett to organize the I Corps. Old worries about Liggett's corpulence vanished as his alert good sense and his vast military knowledge were seen. Field experience on the border and at Fort McKinley in Manila, training at Leavenworth and the War College—where he finally was president—gave Liggett

---

[6] See JJP, *Experiences*, 1:338; James G. Harbord, *The American Army in France, 1917–1919*, pp. 225–26.

horizons almost as great as Pershing's. Clearly the new I Corps commander was the right man to be second to the CIC.[7]

Affable and friendly, Liggett had, too, the hard sense that soldiers admire, a strategist's mind, and a leader's poise. He took the job without qualm.[8] At Neufchâteau he began shaping his headquarters. Pershing gave him Malin Craig as chief of staff. Administrative responsibility for active American divisions quickly went to Liggett, and he supervised logistical, training, and housekeeping matters. When all American divisions were ready for the line, they would gather under Liggett's tactical command in the Woëvre area. And that moment would mark the beginning of America's full partnership in war.

Pershing wanted to show Newton Baker a solid stretch of line in U.S. control when the war secretary arrived in March. He nearly did.

"And next, Mr. Secretary"

Baker's coming brought uncommon opportunity. Few bureaucrats attract soldiers, but years of association with government at all levels had taught Pershing the qualities of diplomats, cabinet folk, and that great flood of civil servants who increasingly ran the nation. Perceptive soldiers could see, even during the small crises of the Spanish-American War, that a burgeoning civil list intruded new layers of civilian control over the military. Anyone who prated about growing martial manipulation simply had not seen bureaucracy as practiced in Washington. Newton Baker, though, came cautious to his job, came with a local politico's penchant for small power spent well. So he came refreshingly like Elihu Root—disdainful of precedent. And he had full faith in John Pershing. Relations waxed so cordial that Jack considered Baker's trip almost a personal visitation.

From Brest, where he landed on March 10, Baker moved on Paris in a strained cloud of anonymity. He wanted to hold official visits to a minimum and keep everything at a low key.[9] Pershing would do his best, despite a desire to boast his friend.

Tall, neat in his long khaki coat, Pershing waited in Paris for Baker's train on March 10. He greeted the dapper little man warmly. Baker had a beaver's fervid eagerness and spouted questions instantly. He liked what he saw of his military friend. Pershing's color seemed

---

[7] For Liggett's career, see Liggett, *Commanding an American Army*, ch. 1.
[8] See his laconic announcement of assuming command in *ibid.*, p. 21.
[9] Frederick Palmer, *Newton D. Baker: America at War*, 2:89.

better than Baker had ever known it; he had a robust good grace to him that showed him easy in his work. And he had as much eagerness as the war secretary. A Monday morning offered full opportunity to start learning the war. First, a trip to the Hôtel de Crillon to check Baker in, then a round of needful calls. To Ambassador Sharp, Pershing took Baker and his small traveling party. Next they went to the Tiger's lair, where Clemenceau spun his usual noisome web only to find the ebullient American minister deft, polite, and bafflingly voluble.[10]

Then Pershing escorted his chief on a ceremonial pilgrimage to Marshal Joffre's quarters. (Did Baker, on the way, confide the president's fear that Pershing relied too much on the shelved Hero of the Marne?)[11] Unlike as possible, Baker and Joffre seemed typical contrasts in a sprawling coalition.

Warned by Baker of a short visit, Pershing planned packed days of inspection across the AEF's domain. First, he said, the secretary should view the intricacies of the Services of Supply—SOS, as the old LOC had been renamed. Once he trailed the arteries of the American army from the sea to the front, Baker could judge how the awesome masses of men, materiel, and money were building toward a million-man, perhaps even a three-million-man, force. Then he would go to the front, see the wasteland served by Doughboys far from home, would learn the rigors of trench life, the layers of command.

On the thirteenth, after an efficient train trip southward, Pershing showed Baker and his party the huge projects at Bordeaux and Bassens. Local officers, French and American, basked in approval. Even General Pershing beamed at progress visible everywhere. Baker's excitement rose at the Saint Sulpice warehousing area, just outside Bordeaux. Here "a network of railway sidings led to row after row of new storehouses being filled with property that required cover, while other classes were being accumulated in the open storage space." A base-hospital visit led to a gourmet lunch at Bordeaux's Chapeau Rouge. Afternoon inspections included the artillery instruction camp at Souge—Baker almost fell into a 155mm gun![12]—another vast base hospital at Beau Desert, and finally an eerily empty remount depot.[13]

[10] JJP, *Experiences*, 1:342–43.
[11] See Ray Stannard Baker, *Woodrow Wilson*, 8:333.
[12] See photograph in Frank Freidel, *Over There: The Story of America's First Great Oversea Crusade*, p. 120; see also JJP, *Experiences*, 1:343. Harbord, *American Army*, p. 231, gives a list of JJP's fellow travelers.
[13] JJP, *Experiences*, 1:343.

Skipping lesser ports, Pershing pushed his visitors on to Saint Nazaire on the morning of the fourteenth. Here a terrified *sous-prefect* read his couplet of welcome in quivering voice, and then the proud section commander became a boastful guide through the maze of docks, announced a new record of ship unloadings that day—thirteen —and confessed lack of materials had slowed expansion. Baker listened carefully to needs and causes of delay. Pershing, enthusiastic in his knowledge, waved at the growing engine assembly plant, the car assembly plant, pointed glumly to the fine, but almost empty, motor parks near La Rochelle.

After a hasty luncheon, Pershing put Baker aboard a flatcar equipped with seats and showed him the buildings in Saint Nazaire's suburbs at Montoir. The sightseers rolled "over miles of sidetracks through the immense storage yard covering acres. We passed rows of warehouses, finished and unfinished, being filled with perishable supplies, while out in the open were quantities of various classes of material for which cover was not necessary."[14] At the Savanay hospital, filled already, Baker talked cheerfully to patients.

On the fifteenth the travelers toured Saumur, site of the famed French cavalry school. Part of the austere buildings now housed American artillery officers, who were suffering firm training by French gunners. A demonstration of battery technique on the drillfield "left in our minds a good impression of efficiency."[15]

Services of Supply Headquarters at Tours occupied Baker for a brief time—he dashed through offices, spoke cordially but hastily to officers, and eagerly rushed on to an immense salvage plant. Here Baker listened carefully as the commandant reported on reclamation of uniforms after every American trench stay, reclamation of footgear, camp and garrison equipage, arms, helmets, everything likely to be repairable. Money and tonnage were saved impressively, and Baker spread congratulations. A midday run to Gièvres, east of Tours, brought an unexpected vista—here was the biggest AEF depot in France, a hive sprawling over 12 square miles, boasting 165 warehouses, 20,000 workers, 4 million square feet of storage space, and 143 miles of track. Those statistics Pershing paraded for Baker, then translated them to usage: Out there, he said, was "storage for 2,000,000 gallons of gasoline, refrigerator capacity for 6,500 tons of fresh meat, and warehouse space for clothing and food for 30 days' supply of 2,000,000

[14] *Ibid.*, p. 344.
[15] *Ibid.*, pp. 344–45.

men, not to mention the thousands of tons of medical, signal, engineering, and ordnance supplies, excepting ammunition."[16] Pershing impressed everyone with details and with vision during a two-hour tour.

Wearied from watching, stuffed with figures and projections, Baker heard Jack talk in the evening of places time ruled from their schedule —the great ordnance works at Méhun, the burgeoning ammunition depot at Jonchery, hospitals (so many on every rail line), air-service centers, flying fields, small posts straying along the SOS. Next day, said the proud soldier, Baker would visit the Air School at Issoudun.

There, in the care of Brig. Gen. Benjamin Foulois, the commander-in-chief and the secretary saw the fledgling American air service fly. There were embarrassing overtones to the Issoudun day. America sported no military aircraft at the start of the war, had struggled mightily with plane production, and suffered nagging shortages. Generous with all kinds of equipment, the French had had to provide American pilots with aircraft, guns, munitions. Mechanics came from America along with increasing amounts of raw material needed in airframe production, and engineers in the United States had produced an important new aircraft engine—the Liberty. But the planes at Issoudun were as French as the instructors. Baker must have felt that unease common to Americans in France, the interloper sensation.

Clearly Benny Foulois had no doubts of belonging. Little and wiry, his long face twisted with a flyer's squint, Foulois knew Pershing of old. Friends and appreciative colleagues from Mexico, they worked well together. Pershing had wanted Foulois on the *Baltic* team but had to leave him home to organize a skeleton air service. Finally in France, Foulois had at last taken the job of AEF chief of aviation.[17] One of that reckless breed of early birdmen who had virtually taught himself to fly—he corresponded with the Wright brothers after each crack-up —Foulois had uncanny practicality in logistics. The small miracle he worked in Columbus when he supervised the assembly of wagon beds on truck chassis showed his ingenuity, but he had, too, the skilled manager's aplomb. Tuned to the sky, he nonetheless knew the business of supply—to him fell the burden of procurement.

His veteran eye swept the machines maneuvering for Baker; types and characteristics he explained to the secretary, described the acrobatics and their purposes in combat flying. Pershing, too, watched closely and spoke quietly of advances in American air skills. Earlier

[16] *Ibid.*, pp. 345–46.
[17] *Ibid.*, p. 317.

comparisons with French and British flyers had been frightening, now the smoothly cavorting ships showed Yank aviators ready for the Boche.[18]

Shy as Baker tried to be, his company with Pershing and Foulois attracted notice; men recognized him, clustered, some wanting words, others pictures. The school's commander, Lt. Col. W. G. Kilner, wanted an official memento of the secretarial visit—would Pershing, Baker, and Foulois stand close together, please? Pershing glanced at Benny, suddenly snapped, "Foulois, take that pipe out of your mouth!" And a solemn trio stared at the lens, Foulois's pipe safely smoldering in his hand.[19]

Now the route turned northward toward the front and parts of the SOS most fascinating to Jack. They were coming, he told Baker, to Nevers, a rail center converted into a gigantic automobile factory and a locomotive repair shop. Here Pershing showed the newest in hospital trains, several of them painted in dull green and initialed USA— these were an innovation of the World War, railroad ambulances equipped not only to transport wounded to hospitals but also as advanced dressing stations. Sleek and modern, they stretched along their tracks like reptiles stalking blood. On up the line toward Neufchâteau, Pershing announced, Baker would see the regulating station at Is-sur-Tille.

Regulating stations clearly intrigued Pershing. New, he said, they were spawn of modern war's confusion behind the lines, a kind of logistical valve that controlled the flow of supplies from advanced depots to front-line units. Technical and dull as they sounded at first, Baker warmed to them in Pershing's words. Not merely solutions of age-old problems of distribution, these stations of war were marvels of human ingenuity. "All the details were explained to the Secretary, who took pains to understand the mechanism of the system." Details were inescapable![20]

By car through Dijon—that ancient pastel town—the vistors rode to Langres and the AEF's great schools of combat and theory. Here Pershing basked in the enthusiasm of officers crowding the secretary with data on teaching, on lessons, on the newness of fighting ways. General staff officers talked of running divisions and corps and armies; branch trainees spoke eloquently of new tactics and weapons, of lead-

---

[18] JJP's opinion is given in *ibid.*, pp. 346–47.

[19] Author's interview with Maj. Gen. Benjamin Foulois, Washington, D.C., Mar. 9, 1960.

[20] JJP, *Experiences*, 1:347.

ᴏᴦᴏʜɪᴘ ᴀɴᴅ ᴄᴏᴍᴍᴀɴᴅ. Fine men, Pershing thought, and noted Baker's pleasure at the zest and excitement everywhere.

So the trip through the SOS ended—by car through the rolling Lorraine country in the varied ambience of a cool March evening.

Pershing learned perhaps more than he taught during the SOS visitation. Baker spoke of problems at home, of simmering congressional unhappiness at War Department bungles, unhappiness that had brought on investigations and would probably bring more. Jack knew something of these troubles from Papa Warren and spoke soothingly of friends in the Senate. There had been errors, awful errors of omission and commission, but Baker was sure General March would reduce chaos quickly. Pershing hoped so, confessed his own lingering irritation at requisitions ignored, promotions mishandled, supplies confused.[21] Baker had read Pershing's frequent cables of complaint and promised better when the system improved. Pershing knew the secretary had never denied or delayed a sound AEF request and thanked him for the support. Something of bureaucratic pressures Pershing glimpsed in Baker's conversation about War Department failures. Bureau heads, men in those ancient enclaves of privilege, wallowed in old rules and ignored the new needs of war. Baker would break their power by centralizing administration through the chief of staff.

A strong War Department would not impinge on Pershing. In France, Pershing had authority supreme, which Baker would sustain to the fullest. Reassured in his opinion of his chief, Pershing packed him off on a front-line inspection with some misgiving. Escorts were chosen carefully, the visit planned in detail. Should the Germans learn of Baker's presence in the line, they might put on a big raid to capture him, might, at least, flail the line with shell. A quiet sector would be best, perhaps one, Baker hoped, held by fellow Ohioans. His guides would be the best—Harbord and Frederick Palmer. Palmer, a long-time Baker fan, relished company with the witty celebrity, and Harbord took his assignment with skeptical stoicism.

Harbord schemed for secrecy uncommon even in the AEF. Baker would make a planned visit to Langres for a tactical demonstration on March 18, full girded with official party, hangers-on and aides. No sooner the demonstration ended than Baker, Harbord, and Fred Palmer would sneak east toward Baccarat and the Rainbow Division's stretch of front. And he had a splendid time, though he missed Ohio's best.

[21] For a summary of these problems, see Edward M. Coffman, *The War to End All Wars*, ch. 6, especially pp. 159–86.

Iowans saw him and heard his special kind of eloquence about being on the frontier of freedom. He flew along an exposed road in a staff car with de Chambrun, chased by three 105mm shells. Back at Tréveray for a review, Baker joined a relieved John Pershing—secretaries like Baker were all too rare—and boasted of being under fire. A smile for enthusiasm, a glare at the guides, then the general heard the fine impression Baker had of the AEF.[22] He heard, too, the fine impression Doughboys had of the spunky little secretary who wanted to hear complaints so he might improve things.[23]

What next for the secretary? Almost anything else would be anticlimax, but Pershing proposed a visit to General Pétain's headquarters at Compiègne; the French leader would be flattered by the call, and Baker enthusiastically agreed. They would lunch on Thursday, the twenty-first, with Pétain, then Palmer would escort Baker over British ground at the Somme.

Gaily Pershing ushered Baker into a staff car with Palmer on Thursday morning, and they rolled westward toward Compiègne. Baker chattered about the AEF, how fine the men looked, their high spirits, the growing mass of American presence in France; as he talked he looked at the serenity of the country behind the lines. Morning brought a newness to life in this old land that seemed to awaken hope. Not far now to Compiègne as noon approached, and the riders heard something that rose above the rumble of the car, a roar that lifted a strange and beating wave. Greeted cordially by Pétain, Pershing and Baker joined him for a pleasant lunch. Conversation, relentlessly casual, waned under the umbrella of noise. Pétain's French sang-froid never cracked, but after *déjeuner* his guests listened to him discuss the war. He and Haig had agreed on cooperation in crisis. And now the crisis came—that heavy, echoing bombardment signaled a long-pending climax, the great German attack.[24]

"*Tout ce que nous avons est à vous*"

In March, 1918, Gen. Sir Hubert Gough's V Army held a section of Artois and Picardy covering Amiens, a section squarely in front of the German attack. Code-named "Michael," the drive had been carefully

[22] See Palmer, *Baker*, 2:100–103; James G. Harbord, *Leaves From a War Diary*, pp. 241–51.
[23] Colonel de Chambrun and Captain de Marenches, *The American Army in the European Conflict*, p. 130.
[24] Palmer, *Baker*, 2:103–4; JJP, *Experiences*, 1:352.

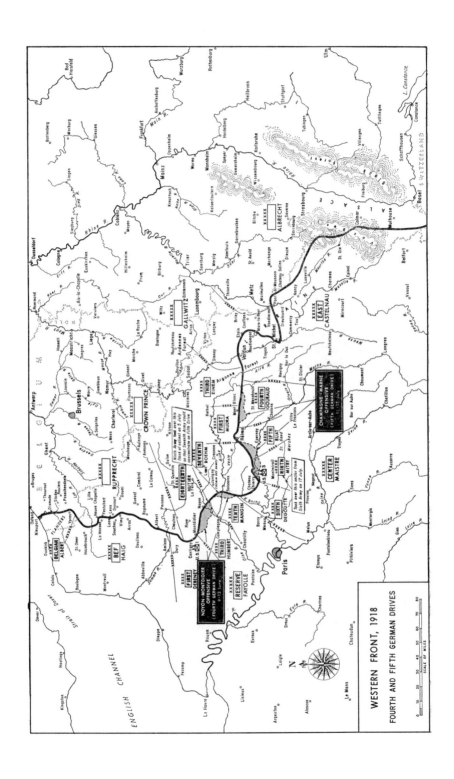

WESTERN FRONT, 1918
FOURTH AND FIFTH GERMAN DRIVES

planned by Gen. Erich Ludendorff. His objective was to break the French and British fronts at the point of juncture between the Oise and the Scarpe, to roll the British armies back to the channel, to drive the French scattering toward Paris, and to complete the unfinished Schlieffen scheme. Roads were choked for weeks from Germany to the Western Front, arteries pulsing men, food, munitions, guns, men, men in great gray waves, men who had served in the east, either in Russia or with the Austrians at Caporetto, men who came now flushed with the prospect of winning the war this spring. Many of these men were trained already in the now famous Hutier tactics, in the "maneuver of rupture" that apparently restored mobility to the battlefield by probing with shock units, by passing strong points and hitting fast to the enemy's rear. Once out of the trenches, Oskar von Hutier's minions knew exactly what to do.

Ludendorff's guns, 6,473 of them, came in a kind of iron avalanche that teetered along forty miles of British line, ready to spill death toward Paris. Gunners were trained by canny Col. Georg Bruchmüller, who counseled secret targeting, massed cannon, and a rolling barrage. Those guns opened fire at dawn on March 21 in a barrage beyond comprehension, a great gout of noise and eruption that scourged the lines of the British V Army, roiled the trenches, turned men to numbed automatons stumbling backward across a demonic No Man's Land. Out of the trenches, Gough's men were lost, unable to resist. In a fog- and dust-muddled respite, survivors reeled to find lost comrades and were razed suddenly by a barrage of 3,500 mortars. Five minutes quick fire, silence, then three full German armies streamed out of the boiling mists—Storm Troops led 32 divisions, backed by 39 more. Gough's 15 divisions—three of them cavalry—vanished before his eyes.[25]

Into the backwash of this stupendous attack, the determined Baker and Palmer drove, hoping to find Haig's headquarters. The secretary wanted especially to see the field marshal. Palmer recalled other scenes of heartbreak in the Somme, lines of broken men and vehicles, wildly galloping animals, units marching to and fro in a kind of martial coagulation. After a hasty visit to BEF Headquarters, Baker headed for England, and he hoped for news of Germans thwarted once again.

Pershing heard the bombardment, filtered by echo across distant hills, gauged it through the day, and knew the German light guns were advancing, that the British must be yielding ground. Quickly,

[25] German strength is taken from H. Essame, *The Battle for Europe, 1918*, pp. 39–40; Barrie Pitt, *1918: The Last Act*, pp. 75–77; JJP, *Experiences*, 1:35–54.

after hearing Pétain's briefing on the situation—which included nothing on the day's experiences—Pershing and Carl Boyd headed for Paris. That war-seasoned city's life bustled with trained tension. The far rumble could be felt almost more than heard, but Parisians seemed oddly gayer, as if released by knowing where the blow had fallen. In high councils the talk was muted and hesitant, all thrown against a great unanswered question. Reserves were marshalled from far points of France; there were none really collected for the enemy attack, despite the vaunted agreement between Haig and Pétain. Trains shrilled through Paris carrying whole men forward, shattered men back.

On Friday, the twenty-second, Pershing drove out to Versailles for a talk with Bliss. What news? Confused reports tumbled back from the riddled front. Backward the British came, a dangerous rupture had opened along the 40-mile attack zone, and the Germans seemed close to a major success. Rumors were bad; officials talked of moving the government to Bordeaux; perhaps AEF offices should be alerted. Possibly, but experience dictated patience. Clearly the French and British were surprised, although why they should have been escaped Pershing. American intelligence, green though the operatives were at the game, spotted the junction of Allied armies in the Somme as a logical point of attack. Surely older, presumably wiser, heads had guessed the same. And yet reserves were scarce, confusion abounding. More than that, the Allies were tactically stunned. It gave small comfort to think that American emphasis on open warfare seemed justified by the smashing German success. What counted now was reaction time. How many men could be pulled to the breach in how many days? What was the German schedule? Was this the main thrust?

Back in Chaumont on the twenty-third, Pershing could note the lowering weather, the foggy conditions reported in the battle zone—proper cover for Ludendorff's gray legions. Excited reports came to Pershing that day of a miraculous gun fired on Friday against Paris, a great German engine with a range of something like 75 miles! New tactics, gorged resources, secret weapons—suddenly that darkening March day Odin's great omens ran for Germany. Patience wore thin as the day dragged on—somewhere in the British cauldron several companies of the U.S. 6th Engineers must be fighting for their lives.[26]

Everyone expected better news. Western Front attacks followed

[26] JJP, *Experiences*, 1:355.

a kind of ritual—big gains the first day, smaller the second, then a nibbling fadeout for several more days. This time, though, news grew worse with each dawn. From La Fère to Arras, the German hordes rolled on; Gough committed his last reserves on the twenty-second; two French divisions joined the British retreat on the twenty-third; on the twenty-fourth, four more French divisions arrived. Watching carefully, Pershing noticed that during the first three days of the battle only one British division joined Gough. Something was seriously wrong at British headquarters, obviously, or Haig had miscalculated grossly. By March 26 the Germans had thrust 37 miles through the British front and threatened Amiens. If that rail center fell, the Allied lines would crack.[27]

Everything pointed to a growing disaster. Pétain, with uncommon eloquence, summoned his Gallic cohorts to renewed heroism: "Soldiers of the Marne, of the Yser and of Verdun, I call upon you. The fate of France hangs in the balance."[28] Casualties piled higher daily; the British reported no less than 150,000 lost. A subtle tocsin sounded in Paris, and the faithful began to leave. Ludendorff's gamble just might work. Here was the moment Pershing dreaded, the one he fended for months—the crisis of the AEF.

To Compiègne Pershing drove Monday afternoon, March 25, for a hasty meeting with Pétain. Roads were wet and clotted now with the jetsam of despair. People shuffled away from the front, people long accustomed to threatened war; they moved in that ageless daze of refugees without purpose, without hope. In a curious passive resistance they clogged roads for armies always. It was almost 10:00 P.M. when Pershing's car sloshed into Compiègne. He found Pétain and his chief of staff nervously waiting—they were packed and ready to move GQG to Chantilly.

Pershing and Pétain pored over a map showing the latest reported Allied positions. Enemy forces drove a sagging wedge sharply south of Amiens, threatened Montdidier and Noyon, scarcely fifty miles north of Paris, and showed no signs of stopping.

In this emergency no considerations of forming an American corps counted. What divisions did Pétain want? He could have any he thought useful, remembering, of course, they would be recalled. Oddly unenthusiastic, Pétain wondered about the fighting quality of

[27] *Ibid.*
[28] *Ibid.*, p. 356.

Pershing's divisions. Some of them, he guessed, might go into battle—but this seemed hardly the moment to consign a portion of front to the American army. If things worsened, he might have to drain his own men from quiet sectors and replace them with Doughboys.

Clearly Pétain's concern lay with Paris; as the threat mounted, his concern concentrated. Secretly he had decided to cover the capital if the Germans drove on toward Amiens—and if he did that, the British army would be stranded in Flanders. Haig worried about that possibility a good deal, suggested it to London, and began to consider his own safety. By the time Pershing talked to Pétain, the Germans had almost achieved a psychological split in the Allied front. Unaware of fragmenting unity, Pershing made his divisions ready for orders anywhere.

From London he got something of a jolt. Baker, several days in Lloyd George's persuasion, cabled British anxiety on the twenty-fifth. The prime minister suggested to Baker that American divisions instantly replace French line units in quiet sectors, that all U.S. engineers be stripped from the SOS and sent to construct secondary British defenses, and finally, that only infantry of the six divisions to be transported in British bottoms be shipped for the present! Obviously the iron Welshman had not abandoned hope of amalgamation, was using crisis diplomacy. But Baker seemed alert to the portents, for he delayed answering until he saw Pershing. The needs were great. Rawlinson at Versailles and Italy's new representative to the Supreme War Council, General Giardino, echoed calls for Pershing's men. With those fresh pleas in mind, Jack rode to Paris's Gare du Nord on Tuesday evening, the twenty-sixth, to meet the secretary of war.

Scenes at the station reinforced Allied cries of agony. Crowding the platforms were throngs of refugees, people with their small packs of belongings going somewhere—some to relatives in the south, others just going from the Boche. In that hectic maelstrom Pershing glimpsed the first disintegration of French morale. Helplessly Jack watched and his anger mounted. "War in its effects upon the armies themselves is frightful," he thought, "but the terror and the suffering that it causes women and children are incomparably worse." [29]

Desperation caused mistakes. The Supreme War Council made one on March 28 in the form of Joint Note 18. This note suggested that all previous American troop-shipment arrangements lapse and that only infantry and machine-gun units be sent until further notice.

---

[29] *Ibid.*, p. 359.

Lloyd George's wishes seemed dominant. Pershing got Baker and Bliss together in Paris on Thursday to thresh out American policy.

Obviously irritated, Pershing pointed out that the proposed arrangement would put the use and disposition of American troops entirely in the hands of the War Council and would probably "destroy all possibility of . . . forming an American army." It was, obviously, the worst possible plan. How did Bliss bring himself to sign it?

Soothing his generals quickly, Baker agreed with Pershing. Loss of control could not be permitted. What did Pershing suggest? Retention of control, surely, but concession in crisis. Rescheduling of shipments toward infantry and machine-gun units for the duration "of the present critical situation and continued only so long as that situation necessarily demands it." Finally Baker cabled the Joint Note to the president with a careful recommendation of approval, with final disposition of American troops left entirely up to Pershing. And Pershing would keep in mind "the determination of this Government to have its various military forces collected, as speedily as their training and the military situation will permit, into an independent American army, acting in concert with the armies of Great Britain and France. . . . "[30]

Bliss had other important news that indicated desperation could sometimes achieve miracles. On March 26 at Doullens, behind the British front, Clemenceau, Lord Milner (the British secretary of state for war), Haig, Henry Wilson, and Foch met in emergency session. Sparked by mutual distrust, the conference focused on joint command problems. Much wrangling produced a consensus: Foch, as senior military member of the War Council's Executive War Board, was "charged with coordinating the action of the Allied armies on the Western Front." Foch accepted.

Such a step ought not have been taken without an American present, but Pershing agreed to the arrangement happily. Joint command was overdue. American cooperation ought to be expressed quickly; while Baker rode to Chaumont, Pershing, Boyd, and Capt. Charles de Marenches headed for Foch's headquarters at Clermont-sur-Oise.

Again the trip followed a trail of woe. Roads bulged with troop-carrying camions, with supply wagons, with guns, with all kinds of equipment. Traffic crawled. Once in the town, which housed headquarters of the French III Army, Pershing could find no one who knew Foch's whereabouts. Confusion and chaos reigned. Captain de Maren-

[30] *Ibid.*, pp. 360–62.

ches, peerless aide, found a friend who put a guide in the car. Around the town they went, "through a lane of tall poplars to a small, typically French farmhouse well off the road, and hidden among the trees."[31]

People milled in the house; General Foch was busy. Pershing, Boyd, and de Marenches waited outside in a moment's quiet. Clear sunshine showed a happy countryside; the farm's shrubbery bloomed in spring colors and a lovely cherry tree blossomed on the lawn. Finally the visitors were beckoned inside. There they met the Tiger of France, Foch, Pétain, and aides. All eyes focused on a map-covered table. Foch motioned Pershing for a look. There was the battle line. The French were now counterattacking at Montdidier—if they failed, the line would sag again. The British, Foch said, had already used 30 divisions, the French 17, against a total of 78 German divisions. Apparently remnants of the British V Army had stiffened with help; the line just might hold for awhile.

A glance around, a long look at Foch, conveyed Pershing's purpose, and the others politely went into the yard. To Foch, Pershing spoke in hurried, passionate French. Foch listened in rising excitement; when Pershing stopped, the French general grabbed him by the arm, rushed him outside, and asked him to repeat what he had said. All listened with interest, especially Clemenceau, as the stubborn American spoke unhalting French:

I have come to tell you that the American people would consider it a great honor for our troops to be engaged in the present battle. I ask you for this in their name and my own.

At this moment there are no other questions but of fighting.

Infantry, artillery, aviation, all that we have are yours; use them as you wish. More will come, in numbers equal to requirements.

I have come especially to tell you that the American people will be proud to take part in the greatest battle of history.[32]

General joy greeted Pershing's pronouncement, although Pétain grumped that the use of American troops had already been discussed. Foch left details to the two commanders; Pershing announced faith in all five AEF divisions in France. Pétain considered the 1st Division probably useful.

No one else grumped about the gesture at Clermont. Papers carried Pershing's offer across France next day, and praise came from

---

[31] *Ibid.*, pp. 363–64.

[32] *Ibid.*, pp. 364–65. The important lines were : "Infanterie, artillerie, aviation, tout ce que nous avons est à vous. Disposez-en comme il vous plaira." See also de Chambrun and de Marenches, *American Army in the European Conflict*, p. 134.

everywhere—even from the British! Secretary Baker lauded Jack in a message to the president. Reaction from the AEF ran well.

All could not be considered well with the Allies. Jack doubted the solidity of the Doullens arrangement. Knowing that Haig succumbed only to considering Foch a liaison officer between himself and Pétain, Pershing guessed that a command crisis might come soon. Gladly, then, he accepted an invitation from Clemenceau to a War Council meeting scheduled at Beauvais on April 3—the agenda fixed on the command problem.

Forty-five miles north of Paris, Beauvais had an ancient charm punctuated by its gloriously Gothic, thirteenth-century cathedral. Surprisingly Pershing's car arrived early, and he suggested a tour to companion Boyd. The two walked the winding streets in clear sunshine,[33] visited the cathedral, then sauntered to the Hôtel de Ville for the meeting. Everyone else was late, and for an hour the Americans waited. At last Clemenceau and Lloyd George came. Haig and Henry Wilson arrived; so did Bliss, Foch, Pétain, and Gen. Maxime Weygand, Foch's chief of staff. Col. Maurice Hankey served as recorder.

Clemenceau opened with a succinct statement of purpose:

We have come together to settle a very simple question regarding the functions of General Foch. I think we are all in agreement as to the coördination of Allied action, but there is some difference in the understanding of General Foch's powers as conferred upon him at the Doullens conference of March 26th. General Foch will explain his difficulties.

Pointedly Foch reminded his colleagues that the powers granted at Doullens were for coordination during the battle then raging. Now that the battle ebbed there was nothing to coordinate. But there were things to prepare against resumption of the German drive, plans to be made for stabilizing the lines, for the transfer of reserves—and realignment of divisions—and he had no authority to command armies under Haig and Pétain.

Haig sat stoically and knew the conference really aimed at him. Watching Lloyd George, Haig assumed the prime minister's hand had stirred the cauldron on supreme command. And the fiery Welshman did speak to the point. "We have had more than three years of this war," he piped, "and we have not had unity of action during that time." Sweeping the table with his piercing gaze, he plunged on: "During the last year we have had two kinds of strategy, one by Haig and another by Pétain, both different, and nothing has been gained.

[33] Haig, Diary, April 3, 1918.

The only thing that was accomplished was by General Nivelle when he was in supreme command."

At that odd distortion Haig leaned forward, waved a hand to speak, and drew a hard reprimand from his chief—no interruptions! "The Germans," Lloyd George announced, "have done exactly what General Nivelle tried to do." Then he recalled the War Council's efforts to create a general reserve and pointedly said that it was a nullity "through the action of those concerned." The British people would not stand more dismal defeats; they would fix blame; they want "some sort of unity of command." Foch needs more authority, Lloyd George added, but stopped short of moving action. Instead he asked Bliss's and Pershing's views. Bliss, a masterful conference man, gave a lengthy kind of legalistic reinterpretation of Foch's existing powers—he wanted simply to clarify where matters stood.

Pershing wanted action. He knew Baker did. Making notes during the discussion, he now read from them: "The principle of unity of command is undoubtedly the correct one for the Allies to follow," he said, and made the point of the gathering when he added that "I do not believe that it is possible to have unity of action without a supreme commander. . . . There has never been real unity of action." Reasons he understood. "Each commander-in-chief is interested in his own army, and cannot get the other commander's point of view or grasp the problem as a whole." Now speaking firmly and with emphasis, he went on: "I am in favor of a supreme commander and believe that the success of the Allied cause depends upon it. I think the necessary action should be taken by this council at once. I am in favor of conferring the supreme command upon General Foch."

Lloyd George agreed fully and nodded to Pershing "this is well put." Next he called on Haig.

Haig liked none of the conversation and recognized now some kind of collusion against him. Besides, most of what had been said was rubbish. "We have had practically complete unity of action," he said with reined anger. "I have always coöperated with the French, whom I regard as in control of the strategical questions of the war." Recalling his earlier subordination to Nivelle, and observing that he and Pétain got on well, Haig bowed to the inevitable. "I agree with General Pershing's general idea that there should be unity of command but I think we have had it."[34] No one seemed to listen except Pétain, who shared suspicions of subordination. Lloyd George asked

[34] See Haig's views in his Diary, April 3, 1918.

that a draft resolution be read. It was and it irked Pershing mightily. No mention did he hear of the American army.

Once before the Allies had cast up a leader without consulting the Americans—this time they blundered into an invitation, and they would pay a price. "I think this resolution should include the American Army," he said in those flat Missouri tones that carried. "The arrangement is to be in force, as I understand it, from now on, and the American Army will soon be ready to function as such and should be included as an entity like the British and French armies."

Pétain, somewhat testily, observed that there was no American army yet and added that its units were training or "are amalgamated with the British and French." His choice of terms, perhaps deliberate, drove Pershing further.

"There may not be an American army in force functioning now but there soon will be and I want this resolution to apply to it when it becames a fact. The American government is represented here at this conference and in the war, and any action as to the supreme command that includes the British and French armies should also include the American army." Soothing agreement met his speech, and a final draft of the resolution was ordered. It announced that Foch was "charged by the British, French and American Governments with the coördination of the action of the Allied Armies on the Western Front; to this end there is conferred on him all the powers necessary for its effective realization. To the same end, the British, French and American Governments confide in General Foch the strategic direction of military operations."

There was a hitch in the totality of power revealed in the final paragraph: "The Commanders-in-Chief of the British, French and American Armies will exercise to the fullest extent the tactical direction of their armies. Each Commander-in-Chief will have the right to appeal to his Government, if in his opinion his Army is placed in danger by the instructions received from General Foch." Only Pershing could have hoped for support from his superiors in response to such an appeal.[35]

A mass scribbling of names created the Supreme Commander of the Allied Armies in France—it was, Pershing thought, a momentous achievement.

[35] The minutes of the conference are contained in "Memorandum of the Conference of the Allied Representatives at Beauvais, April 3, 1918" (Confidential), in AEF, GHQ, G-3, Folder 1338-A, RG 120, National Archives. Pershing used this summary in his own version, JJP, *Experiences*, 1:373–77.

Foch wondered what the Germans planned next. Would they continue against the British? It was the logical strategy in view of success. They might, also logically, attempt diversionary attacks to drain Allied divisions away from the Somme, then hit Haig again. Whatever Ludendorff intended, he must be anticipated or subverted. And merely waiting for his pleasure made no military sense—the Allies must regain initiative somewhere. An attack while Ludendorff regrouped might dislocate his planning. Men were the key to attack.

Pershing had a sinking feeling that the Beauvais conference coupled with his own passionate offer of help to Foch and the persistent misconstruction of Joint Note 18 would cost him anxious moments about his men. Right he was. On the day that Baker left for home, April 3, two British generals called to discuss integrating the 60,000 men per month they were shipping over and the remaining 60,000 to be brought by U.S. ships. Obviously they thought the full 120,000 would serve as replacements in Allied units. The whole weary fight resumed, with Baker taking a tough stand on an independent American army.[36] Pershing bade him farewell with real sorrow. Paris seemed lonelier and more hostile than ever when the generous little man waved good-bye. He was a model war secretary who "gave . . . from the start that strong and sympathetic support which means so much to a military commander in the field."[37]

Pétain at last asked for the 1st Division; he would put it in an active sector.[38] Orders went to Bullard, who was ill, and the division made ready for the Somme. On April 9, Ludendorff struck once more at the British, this time between Ypres and Lens. The ground was tight, close to the channel, pocked and ploughed from old fighting, and the British fought desperately.

There would be a final maneuver practiced by the 1st Division, a test of open-warfare tactics. Pershing journeyed to Chaumont-en-Vexin to watch. It was Monday, April 15, weather chilly and dull, and Pershing joined Bullard (he had recovered quickly) and General Micheler (with whose French V Army the division would serve), to see the big American soldiers show off proudly. Pershing watched longingly. If only he could command those men! They were splendid. Micheler and Pershing visited all brigades, regiments, and battalions,

[36] JJP, *Experiences*, 1:382–84.
[37] *Ibid.*, p. 384.
[38] See Pershing's Diary, March 29, 1918, extract in "Copies of Important Letters bearing upon Employment of American Troops and various subjects," AEF, GHQ, G-3, Folder 657, RG 120, National Archives; JJP, *Experiences*, 1:391.

asked piercing questions, commented helpfully. When he left for Paris, Pershing announced he would return in the morning to address division officers before they went to battle.[39]

Spring mornings in Picardy are sometimes gems of sunlight, roses, and happiness. Men of the 1st Division had hurriedly grown fond of their billet area near Gisors; some found time to sightsee and to shop in the well-stocked stores of a thriving town. People were friendly, despite the near anger of the front, and plied strong French cigarettes freely. When word came that the division would probably leave for the front by April 18, men gathered in camps to make ready. Veteran French officers counseled them, but front-line experience taught most of the chores of "going up." They were as ready as they could get. In the morning of April 16, the Old Man came out from Paris. At Officers' Call, he stood in a circle of khaki-coated men. Bullard, wracked by neuritis, huddled in a huge wolfskin coat.[40]

Pershing glanced around the circle at "these splendid looking men," caught the courage coming from 900 patriots, and spoke from the heart. Harbord, who listened, noted his chief had a simple, direct manner that appealed to his audience. Straight and immaculate in his great-coat, uncomfortable as usual in front of an audience, Pershing began with an apology—he had not been able before to speak to the men, "but I did not want you to enter into real participation in this war without my having said a word to you as a body." He went on, with frequent lapses, with "eh, eh, ehs" every few words. But the message came through.[41] "I believe that you are well prepared to take your place along with the seasoned troops of our Allies." War, though, "is the real school where the art of war is learned," the general said, punc- tuating now with a gloved hand. Tactical principles that had been learned were absolute and should always be in mind. But "when confronted with a new situation, do not try to recall examples given in any particular book on the subject; do not try to remember what your instructor has said . . .; do not try to carry in your minds patterns of particular exercises or battles, thinking they will fit new cases, because no two sets of circumstances are alike. . . ." Main reliance, Pershing said, pointing a monitory finger at the men, "must be upon your own determination, upon the aggressiveness of your men, upon their stamina, upon their character and upon their will to win." Be

[39] Harbord, *Diary*, p. 265; Bullard, *Personalities*, pp. 178–82.
[40] Bullard, *Personalities*, p. 178; photograph in JJP, *Experiences*, vol. 1, facing p. 392.
[41] Bullard, *Personalities*, p. 181.

concerned for your men, he said, and they will reciprocate with duty well done.

I am not given to speechmaking [he remembered, but added that] I have every confidence in the 1st Division. You are about to enter this great battle of the greatest war in history, and in that battle you will represent the mightiest nation engaged. . . . We come from a nation that for one hundred and fifty years has stood before the world as the champion of the sacred principles of human liberty. We now return to Europe, the home of our ancestors, to help defend those same principles upon European soil. Could there be a more stimulating sentiment as you go from here to your commands, and from there to the battlefield?

Our people to-day are hanging expectant upon your deeds. . . . You are going forward, and your conduct will be an example for succeeding units of our army. I hope the standard you set will be high.

He stopped, then said positively,

I know it will be high. You are taking with you the sincerest good wishes and the highest hopes of the President and all of our people at home. I assure you in their behalf and in my own, of our strong belief in your success and of our confidence in your courage and in your loyalty, with a feeling of certainty in our hearts that you are going to make a record of which your country will be proud.[42]

Finished, he looked around, nodded at greetings, and left those special men he so admired.[43] Leaving them came hard for a soldier mired in administration. If he could gather enough of them, could at last create an army, he could take command at the front.

That afternoon, resolutely turned away from Big Red One, Pershing visited Foch at Sarcus. The supreme commander looked tired, drawn, but extended a cordial welcome. What, asked Jack, were the prospects for uniting American divisions in a section of their own? Baker, during his visit, urged swiftest possible cohesion of the Yanks; the president shared that desire. With the 1st Division engaged, America would expect an army soon on the front. Could the I Corps organize near the 1st Division? Foch understood Pershing's eagerness, but could promise no early release of divisions. The Lys offensive continued, and the British were much pressed. True, but the 26th and the 43rd U.S. Divisions could be taken from their somnolent sectors anytime, collected with the 2nd, 3rd, and 32nd in a force equivalent

---

[42] Text is given in JJP, *Experiences*, 1:393–95. A variant is in AEF, GHQ, Office of the CIC, Correspondence, File no. 16526-A-29, RG 120, National Archives; George C. Marshall, *Memoirs of My Services in the World War, 1917–1918*, pp. 78–79.

[43] Bullard, *Personalities*, pp. 181–82.

to twelve French divisions. Surely it was better to use these fresh units in battle and rest tired French troops? Foch appeared in full agreement, and Pershing gathered orders soon would come creating an American sector.

By April 11, the British had grown desperate. Haig, with muffled eloquence, addressed his weary stalwarts: "With our backs to the wall, and believing in the justice of our cause, each one of us must fight on to the end."[44] The stain of German conquest seeped across the Flanders map almost to Ypres at last, almost to Kemmel Hill, to the rail town of Hazebrouck. Hazebrouck stood the key to Haig's front; if it went, his lateral communications went also, and Calais would be his beachhead. French reinforcements were sent as rapidly as possible, and American divisions crept in behind them. By the end of April, Pershing counted almost 430,000 men in the AEF.

For more than a month the 1st Division held a stretch of front opposite Cantigny, near Montdidier. That month Pershing spent fighting French and British demands for more infantry and machine gunners and consequent delays in building an American army. Conferences again drained his energies, but he had learned well enough. Wrangles with Lord Milner and with the War Council at Abbeville in early May produced violent arguments—Pershing at one point announced flatly that "I . . . will not be coerced" and sounded as though he would permit the Allies to retreat to the sea before giving up his men—but at last produced a kind of understanding about troops, transport, and command.[45] More men would come for the Allies, but they would have to bring more for Pershing's army and his SOS on a schedule that he could terminate.

In all those hectic fights with friends, Pershing's eye kept straying to the near fields of Picardy, to the increasing stretches of line held by his men. Larger rosters gave him more strength at the negotiating tables—and beckoned an old soldier forward. In May the day seemed close when Americans would feel the fullest brunt of battle. In the giant bulge of the Noyon Salient, activity continued; guns pounded each other daily, and heavy raids contained the front—but German aggressiveness had to be controlled. Ludendorff's drive in the Lys sector stalled at the end of April, and Foch thought wistfully of putting in a counterattack on prepared ground. One place needing help was the southern part of the salient near Cantigny. There Big Red One held the line confidently, and if the Americans could do a limited attack successfully, Allied morale would improve. Besides, the Yanks abominated their trenchlines. From high ground, German gunners sniped incessantly at the Doughboys and took a steady toll. An attack to improve position made good military sense.

The 1st Division should be able to take Cantigny. There must be the fullest preparation, every attention given to staff coordination—this would be a showcase maneuver for Allied and German eyes, and to encourage the folks back home. There were doubters of the plan, but none in the 1st Division.

Cast again under General Debeney and his French I Army, Bullard's men knew they were hardly orphans. Debeney they liked of old, and the special telephone line to Chaumont linked them to Pershing almost constantly. If Liggett knew of Pershing's direct touch with one of his corps cadres, he made no fuss. And Bullard accepted parental concern with understanding.[46] Hard it was to cut the main active force of the AEF adrift, to leave it in other hands. Pershing did not command, but he hovered.

Big Red One found itself too busy for petty concerns of punctilio. Preceding French divisions had left an unfinished defense line; Doughboys fumed and dug their own communication trenches, finished front-line configuration at night, and worked on defensive lines, often under angry harassing fire. Veterans they thought they were, but Picardy had frills of war unknown in "quiet" sectors. German artillery mumbled constantly; nights filled with eerie varicolored lights that bloomed with sleep-rending frequency, and quiet shattered often in a murderous rage of machine guns. Raids were frequent and fierce, those small combats that tested human endurance.

Close to the front, too close for safety, divisional combat headquarters rested in the ruined village of Mesnil–Saint Firmin. Deep dugouts in the chalky ground offered damp protection from enemy shells hunting the ammunition dump and railroad station a mile behind the town. Frequent gas attacks kept everyone in a Martian kind of headgear. Above ground the scenery had a crazed and crumpled look. Lathe and plaster buildings tumbled into streets, and the town sprawled in sad collapse. A few citizens clung somehow to their wasted homes, eked shelter underground, and kept that strange cheer of survivors.

Bullard carefully circulated his brigades, working to prevent trench

[46] Bullard, *Personalities*, p. 144.

fatigue. Gradually artillery came in to help the division. French commanders increased ammunition allowances when impressed with American gunners. More 75s arrived along with corps support, and Bullard noted proudly that his guns often drove German batteries to cover.[47]

Those hectic weeks of holding seared memories. Gas held special horrors for the Doughboys; stories told in training camps at home fostered dread of suffocation, blistering, slow death. And the constant air raids frayed nerves. German planes bombed Mesnil–Saint Firmin, Villers-Tournelle, and Boyes nightly. Bombs were small fragmentation, anti-personnel types, and rarely did much harm, but gliding enemy aircraft aloft brought fearsome frustration.[48] Out of all the raging came an odd routine. Daily fire schedules set battery work, American guns rained thousands of shells on German trenches, billets, roads, kitchens, and villages, and the screeching din settled into background noise. A wasteland met the eye by daylight; in darkness the area teemed with working parties. Kitchens and water carts toiled the roads; on bad nights German planes caught them on the chalky ribbons and flailed them with bombs and machine-gun bullets. Raids and patrols continued. Casualties mounted in surprising numbers[49] —during one night's work alone, 800 were gassed at Villers-Tournelle.[50] Attrition ran to almost 60 men a day.[51]

Pershing went up to the Cantigny sector whenever he could, checked often for word of progress. Commanders were growing in competence; Bullard had already proved a prudent, determined general who handled men well, whose administrative qualities expanded with responsibility. Losses were distressing, but losses were part of war. If Americans at home complained, they should not have made war. And American losses were so miniscule they were hardly bruited by the Allies. What counted was growing competence, develop-

[47] *First Div.*, p. 71; Bullard, *Personalities*, p. 192.

[48] See Bullard, *Personalities*, pp. 189–90, where he says: "Airplanes were terrible mainly because they were a new and unfamiliar arm. . . . Inexperienced soldiers in the trenches and soldiers and civilians in cities and villages visited by the enemy's planes, far to the rear, became sometimes almost hysterical in the feeling of helplessness and defenselessness that comes over a man at seeing or hearing the enemy circling deliberately above him and earnestly seeking to take his life."

[49] *First Div.*, p. 76.

[50] Bullard, *Personalities*, p. 193.

[51] *Ibid.*, p. 194. See, for specific details, "Special Report, 1st Division, 25 April to 7 July 1918. Operations West of Montdidier (Including taking of Cantigny, May 18–30)," in AEF, GHQ, G-3 Reports, 1st Division (Box 3245), RG 120, National Archives.

ment of toughness and staying power. Big Red One showed those qualities. Debeney heard from corps commander Vandenberg on May 12 that the 1st rated as an assault division—his highest compliment. A limited attack would be easy.[52] Foch's eagerness to push the Germans somewhere brought the chance Bullard had sought for weeks. Sitting in the bubbling cauldron exchanging daily attrition lists made soldiers tired. Up on the high ground around Cantigny, the German 82nd Reserve Division held lofty sway. To drive them off their perch would delight Bullard's men and leave the Germans in a weak position.

On May 15, Debeney told Bullard to take Cantigny. Pulling his staff together—among them came George Marshall, now a lieutenant colonel, as assistant chief of staff for operations, and Charles Summerall, now a brigadier general and chief of divisional artillery—Bullard laid out the assignment. Quickly the choice of assault troops fell on the 28th Infantry, of B. B. Buck's 2nd Brigade, largely because it was commanded by one of the toughest colonels in the division, Hanson E. Ely. As a staff officer Ely had complained long to Bullard of being ignored for stars and finally got a regiment for his vehemence. Men who knew him counted him almost whang-leather mean. Laurence Stallings saw him with a kind of awed reverence: "He was six-feet-two, with 220 pounds of bone and gristle. . . . If Ely asked his mess attendant for a cup of coffee, the request had the tone of a battalion fire chief ordering a hoseman back into a burning building. When he was silent, which was not too often, he continually worked the leathery muscle at the corner of his jaw, as if banking the fires that smoldered in his rasping vocal chords."[53] A West Pointer, Ely had scraped most of the polish off through the years since graduation in 1891.

In whatever he did at Cantigny, Ely would be supported by the rest of Buck's brigade and any other units needed. Preparations were elaborate, detailed, almost overdone. Date and time were fixed for the jump-off: May 28, 6:45 A.M. Four days before the attack, elements of the 28th Infantry were filtered out of line (replaced by the 18th Infantry) and retired to ground specially suited for rehearsal. Aerial photographs were used to reconstruct German trenchlines; supporting outfits—kitchens, ambulances, hospitals—drilled in field service, and airplanes practiced liaison work. Through the night of May 27, the men filed back into line, and by 5:00 A.M. the three assault battalions were in position, machine-gun companies attached.

[52] Laurence Stallings, *AEF*, p. 58.
[53] *Ibid.*

Artillery had thundered throughout the night; at 4:45 volume increased as gunners probed German battery positions; at 5:45 all 250 guns available to Bullard blasted a fierce preparation barrage. For an hour enemy ground trembled under this iron rage, smoke roiled from German trenches and from communication areas, weird flashes lit the dawning sky, and the attackers watched—and hoped the fire killed. At 6:40 the American barrage rolled forward; up, out of the front trenches came the Doughboys, three long lines of them. The first line closed to 50 yards of the barrage to minimize German reaction time; the others followed into the auroral field of war. Enemy reaction seemed slight, German artillery subdued by American drum fire, machine gunners huddled for cover. The three battalions moved on their objectives steadily, almost in parade formation; terrain promised difficulties but they proved minor, and by 7:20 Cantigny and environs were in American hands. The advance, helped by twelve French tanks, cost few men; consolidation, many. But the line had gone forward at least 1,600 yards.[54]

German gunners got the range on new American positions, machine gunners readied for sweeping fires along Yank lines, and men died throughout the morning. Counterattacks came as expected, feeble at first, then fiercer as German officers fumed at the failure of their men.[55] When it was over, Ely had suffered 823 casualties, but the American total ran to 1,067.

At Bullard's command post, Pershing, who had come up from Paris, read the reports of success. He and Bullard noted the lines of prisoners coming back—a sure sign of victory—and listened to awakening enemy anger. Until all objectives were reported secure, the two kept vigil, both of them oddly detached, unexcited. But the moment sparked remarks about the Allies.

"Do they patronize you?" Pershing asked Bullard, with a keen glance. "Do they assume superior airs with you?"

---

[54] Bullard to JJP, May 28, 1918 (telegram), 5:00 P.M., in "G-3 Reports, Journals of Operations—1st Division," Box 3074, Folder 117-A, RG 120, in National Archives.

[55] Stallings, *AEF*, pp. 72, 74; Bullard, *Personalities*, p. 197; Coffman, *War*, p. 158. Statistics for the fight vary greatly. Cantigny is recounted in myriad sources. The text follows JJP, *Experiences*, 2:59–60; Bullard, *Personalities*, pp. 192–201; Stallings, *AEF*, pp. 56–74; Bullard to Commanding General, Tenth French Army Corps, May 29, 1918, "Preliminary Report on Operations against Cantigny," and Maj. Gen. E. F. McGlachlin, Jr., "Report on Cantigny Operation, May 28–30, inclusive, 1918," Dec. 18, 1918, both in AEF, GHQ, "G-3 Reports—1st Division," Box 3245, RG 120, National Archives; Marshall, *Memoirs*, ch. 7.

"No, sir, they do not. I have been with them too long and know them too well."

"By God!" Pershing fumed, "they have been trying it with me, and I don't intend to stand a bit of it!"

Bullard noted: "He meant it."[56]

Satisfied with this first American attack, quietly assured, Pershing headed for the British front. He wanted to see American divisions working with Haig—and he wanted information on Ludendorff's latest gamble, a great drive against the French in the Chemin des Dames region, just at the point suspected by American intelligence. As with so many of Ludendorff's ventures that spring, he calculated better than the Allies. First reports of success exceeded possibilities, and the numbness of disbelief assuaged shock for a time. But as Pershing toured the quiescent British zone, he caught the same bafflement and uncertainty that plagued the French when Haig's men reeled backward in March. Pessimism seeped from the ground; where would all the attacks end? Surely the British and French were beyond real resistance. Why had Pershing taken so long; where were the stalwarts from America who had come to save the world? A few men husbanded carefully were not the answer to emergency. A kind of courteous disdain colored Allied relations now—the open patronizing Pershing resented he found again as he traveled from Cantigny. Good small effort his men had put up; they could not, of course, hold their ground. They had gone to stay, said the man from Missouri. But worry clogged certainty, and late in the afternoon of the twenty-eighth, Pershing wrote Bullard an injudicious note: Cantigny must be held at all costs! Bullard read the words in disbelief: "After his quiet, unquestioning assumption while with me, that we were there and would stay there, this letter astonished me beyond measure." Probably the Allies had been at him, Bullard thought. And if they were, he had boasted and would not be wrong.[57]

He had boasted and was irked by the need. Part of the trouble he had discussed with Bullard—too many Allied colleagues now treated the AEF as a kind of silly figment of Wilson's and Pershing's egos. Cantigny might change some of that, might show that Yanks were better than guessed. The French soon lavished praise on their pupils.[58]

[56] Bullard, *Personalities*, p. 198.

[57] *Ibid.*

[58] Corps commander Vandenberg began the paeans with a report to Debeney: "The action was conducted in an orderly manner. The spirit of the American troops was magnificent. . . . In resume—excellent operation from every point of view." Debeney happily forwarded praise to higher headquarters: "Operation well

As approbation grew to effusive admiration, Pershing became increasingly resentful of any criticism.[59]

Haig had touches of hauteur, always. But necessity seemed the mother of understanding. Divisions training in the British zone praised their instructors, and the commanders were pleased with treatment accorded. Pershing inspected the 35th Division and the 82nd, and found things proceeding well. Col. Robert Bacon, that "admirable liaison officer," escorted the commander-in-chief through familiar camps, reported on blossoming relations with English colleagues, and handed Pershing over to his other hero, Haig.

At breakfast with Haig at Montreuil on Thursday, May 30, Pershing heard alarming reports of German progress. A trifle scornfully Haig confessed wonder at the full extent of French surprise—but, as Pershing concealed a smile, Haig admitted his own record gave small room for boasting. The French, though, were in trouble deeper than the British. At 1:00 A.M. on the twenty-seventh, Bruchmüller deviltry came again—4,000 guns brought daylight on the Chemin des Dames in a masterpiece of bombardment. Bruchmüller had plotted every target perfectly—no trench, command post, headquarters, dugout, battery, or depot was missed as a great slice of France churned over. Into the boiling gap Ludendorff poured 14 assault divisions just at dawn, and, by 6:00 A.M., 2 British and 2 French divisions were almost obliterated; Germans raced across intact Aisne bridges—no one had bothered to tend them since no attack was coming. Three French reserve divisions rushed into the breach were chewed up in the German rush, a two-mile gap yawned in the Allied line, and by evening Germans held a long stretch of dominant ground on the Vesle.

Ludendorff's men had thrust a 25-mile-wide salient 12 miles into the soft belly of France, had consumed 8 Allied divisions, had taken hordes of dazed prisoners, immense booty, and poised for a complete breakthrough toward Paris. Ludendorff shared his enemy's surprise— he had launched the Chemin des Dames thrust as a feint to drain reserves from the British front where he still intended the *coup de grâce*. But his battle gained momentum, set its own pace, and beckoned his men toward victory. By the twenty-eighth, Soissons

---

prepared and rigorously executed, which will serve to give the Americans, and others, a realization of the offensive valor of our Allies." Endorsements to Bullard's report, May 29, 1918, in AEF, GHQ, "G-3 Reports—1st Division," Box 3245, RG 120, National Archives.

[59] See, for instance, JJP's cold demand for respect in a confrontation with André Tardieu, in *Experiences*, 2:65–66.

teetered almost in the hands of 20 German divisions, and French generals sacrificed fresh troops in fruitless frontal assaults that evaporated in the backwash of defeat. All main objectives were gained in little more than 36 hours—and Ludendorff faced a command decision: Should he stick to his plan, halt the attack, shift to Flanders on his inner lines, and hit the British while they rushed to help their fading friends? Or should he follow the promise before him toward the Marne? Once on that river, he could sweep westward and engulf Paris, wreck the French, and isolate the BEF. He could win the war, possibly in a few days. Surprise had won much more than expected— it must be pushed hard. The road to the Marne lay open, guarded only by the ghosts of 1914.

On went the Germans. Late on May 30, they reached the Marne east of Château-Thierry and snared a bridgehead 40 miles from Paris. Ludendorff's situation was complicated by resistance at Reims and French resilience west of Soissons—he decided to flatten the salient pointed between the two great bulges his men drove into the Allied lines. To do that he called reserves from the Flanders venture.

Pershing and Haig talked on the morning of May 31 while Ludendorff was shifting to follow opportunity. Haig's reports were nearly catastrophic: enemy advance, 30 miles; prisoners taken, 60,000; machine guns taken, 2,000; ammunition, gasoline, airdomes—a trove beyond counting.[60] Feeble stories of a masterly French withdrawal Pershing and Haig ignored; disaster loomed stark and instant. British reserves would go as available, but distance might make them useless. Meanwhile, the British would plug on in Flanders.

Pétain, who kept his head midst panic everywhere, had asked Pershing for help, and on the thirtieth two American divisions, the 2nd and 3rd, were ordered to the front. Bundy's 2nd Division, which had done front-line service and was scheduled to replace the 1st at Cantigny, changed direction and moved by truck toward Meaux. Joseph Dickman's 3rd Division, green, still in training, was closer than any other full-strength unit. Dickman had coolness, his men were eager, and Pershing banked on a good showing.

Pershing left Haig and journeyed to Sarcus and Allied Supreme Headquarters. Gloom hung over Foch's entourage. Normally gay French officers sat strangely muted and stared at a horrid future. Pershing tried encouragement. Two divisions were en route to Pétain— nods, general silence. As the dismal group broke up, Pershing had a

---

[60] The summary of Ludendorff's attack is taken from H. Essame's admirable *Battle for Europe*, pp. 60–62, and JJP, *Experiences*, 2:61–62.

session alone with Foch. There were more American outfits usable; what about counterattacking against the flank of Ludendorff's new salient? Confidentially Foch admitted he had that in mind. Anything Pershing had was offered; Foch knew it, was grateful. Then the supreme commander talked of bringing more infantry and machine gunners from the States. There must be a delay in forming complete American units. Pershing argued, firmly now, and pointed out the logistical snarls growing out of skewed organization. His depots, his SOS, had to sustain Americans, most of them, and he was not getting supply troops. Unless artillery, engineer, and other support regiments arrived, American effectiveness would dwindle. Foch seemed puzzled still and "could not see the advantage of having complete American combat units."[61]

Lectures had been too often repeated, and time was short—but Pershing now had even stronger reasons for keeping his own men. As they came from America in growing numbers, they were greener, even less trained than before. Some kind of rotation mania seized the War Department, and trained units were broken up, filled with greenhorns, and shipped. Those boys, thrust into hard training, often into battle, under foreign officers, would wither, sulk, perhaps fail. They would also starve, for the Allies ate smaller, different rations.[62]

Unhappily Pershing rode back to Paris. Foch's pessimism, his lackluster talk of attack, clouded everything. Pétain apparently worked desperately to build a force in front of the Germans; clearly he had not given up. And in Paris Pershing learned, too, that Clemenceau's belligerence grew.[63] It showed at Versailles sessions of the SWC on June 1 and 2, 1918. Things got off to a prickly start when Pershing denied the right of the council to discuss the character or disposition of troops coming from America. The Abbeville agreement needed updating, continuation; this was the reason for raising these questions. Consultations in crisis were acceptable, and he suggested an informal discussion outside the council. At a late afternoon military gathering, Foch tolled the plight of the Allies and called for shipment of infantry and machine-gun units from the States during June and July, at least 250,000 each month. That raised a serious problem, Pershing said, since America had about reached the limit of trained

[61] JJP, *Experiences*, 2:65.

[62] Haig, Diary, May 31, 1918: "I spoke to Q.M.G. about feeding Americans more as they have been in the habit of feeding, that is, they must be given more bulky food, Hominy, rice, vegetables, etc." See also, Essame, *Battle for Europe*, p. 54.

[63] Essame, *Battle for Europe*, p. 63.

men. General consternation greeted that pronouncement. Clemenceau suggested the virtues of training in France; Pershing restated the logistical argument and hit hard on the conditions of French railroads as likely to throttle all American effort unless repairmen were found.

Foch, much distracted, apparently paid no attention to these reasons. Instead, he waved his hands wildly, shook his head and repeated "the battle, the battle, nothing else counts."[64] Which had been Pershing's point, made differently. Even agreement from Graeme Thomson, British transport expert, made no impression on Foch, who ventured wandering criticism of training methods in the States. All of which convinced an increasingly angry American general that Foch had no idea of "our requirements for the services of supply and transportation, and for artillery, engineers, and other auxiliary arms."[65] Truth was told—a relaxed draft at home had cut the pool of trained men, but numbers were increasing.

Back in the council without agreement, Pershing found Lloyd George eager to submit the whole question of troops again to Wilson. Patiently Baker's and the president's views on military matters being settled by the commander-in-chief of the AEF were repeated. Since nothing was being done, Pershing suggested adjourning until the next day.

When everyone arrived on Sunday, June 2, the room bulged with newcomers, and tension throbbed the air. Pershing guessed the whole attack would come again. It did. Lloyd George opened with the idea of recommending larger shipments of troops to President Wilson; Pershing intoned the scarcity of trained troops; Clemenceau suggested training in France; Foch demanded troops, trained or not; then the discussion digressed to questions about causes of troop shortage in America. Foch interrupted in singleminded zest—troops must come, as many in July as in June. Was Pershing prepared to risk defeat? Absolutely!

Lloyd George suggested sufficient tonnage might be available to bring over Pershing's extra troops in addition to the infantry and machine gunners so desperately needed. He proposed that 170,000 of the "priority" men be sent in June and July, leaving space for 160,000 support troops during that period.

[64] JJP, *Experiences*, 2:71.
[65] *Ibid.*, p. 72.

No one seemed to care about the scant training the Americans would have. Besides, Pershing said bleakly, the Allies were asking for both fighting and technical troops for their own ranks, while ignoring the AEF's housekeeping needs. He did not ignore these needs; better far, he said, to ship technical troops in July and return to shipping fighting men in August—by then they would have some training. Clemenceau suggested that the Germans might not wait. Our men, snapped Pershing, would be too green to help you.

Lloyd George then suggested that American troops training with the British might be sent into battle when their British commanders pronounced them fit. Astounded at such direct effrontery, Pershing exploded. Prerogatives could not be given up, nor responsibilities. What could justify "anyone bringing up in a meeting like this such a proposition, especially without having said anything . . . about it beforehand?" And the Americans, Pershing said pointedly, knew better than anyone else their state of training.

Foch finally made a direct appeal: The United States should raise 100 combat divisions "to be sent over at the rate of 300,000 men per month." America would do what was necessary, nothing less—Foch could rest assured. Pershing would even support the need of 100 divisions—more than three million men!

Clemenceau wondered how many divisions the British could maintain in France, and that question triggered long, absurd arguments about statistics. How, wondered the English prime minister, did the Allies always have dwindling numbers and the Germans always keep up ranks from a smaller manpower pool? Foch made an incautious answer: they manage better. Finally Pershing, Foch, and Milner were asked to suggest a program. In their discussion Weygand broke the deadlock by suggesting that the American troops might as well stay home for an extra month's training. Foch instantly saw the point—he had missed it all day—and Baker received a proposal to ship 170,000 combat troops in June, 25,400 men for French railway service, and to use remaining available tonnage for Pershing's support troops. July quotas would be 140,000 combat troops, the remainder Pershing's selections. If some of the men lacked training, the Allies lacked time.

Finally, in effusive bonhomie, the prime ministers cabled President Wilson thanks for his promptness in sending American troops abroad. Pershing read their message with a cynical eye. "While they declared that there was great danger of the war being lost unless the numerical inferiority of the Allies could soon be remedied by the addition of

American replacements, their statement did not convey the extreme apprehension that prevailed."[66]

Fortunately these arguments never seemed to carry over into personal relations; the arguments those two June days Pershing recognized as distorted by fright. Each man wondered as he talked what was happening on the Marne. Pershing worried especially. Not only had he committed Bundy's and Dickman's divisions, but he had also released five divisions training with Haig to Foch's disposal. Foch had called for them, which irritated Haig and increased Pershing's concern for the battle. Shortly most of the combat units of the AEF would be somewhere in the line.

"Little Marine Went Over the Top, Parley voo"

Ludendorff's *Marneschlacht* had already made considerable changes at HAEF. Always preaching the need to bring in fresh minds from the troops, to send staff officers up to the shooting, Pershing had been trapped into freeing Harbord. That redoubtable chief of staff, asking for troop duty months before, had wrested a quasi-agreement; in May when real fighting started, he asked to go. Shrewdly, he had found a spot. Recent medical discharges opened command slots, and one he truly coveted—the Marine Brigade of Bundy's 2nd Division. Harbord had taste. No better command could he have; no better man could have it, obviously. On May 5 reluctant orders took a good friend to the war and brought "Daddy" Jim McAndrew to the chief of staff's troubles. Pershing knew the nickname, though it never was whispered around HAEF—at least not in McAndrew's hearing. The fatherly McAndrew had commanded the Staff College at Langres, was known as an intellectual soldier, unusually well informed about all phases of war. Harbord thought him excellent, and Pershing hoped the same.

Harbord had a future, if he just survived combat marine experience. He had joined his brigade in the line near Verdun, went with it westward toward Cantigny and on that frenzied road to Meaux and the bulging Marne Salient. While Pershing had been talking in the windy halls of Versailles, Harbord and the marines and Bundy's other men climbed out of trucks, into utter chaos. An amalgam of terrified creatures—human and animal—choked the main road from Metz to

---

[66] *Ibid.*, p. 79. For the conference, see *ibid.*, pp. 70–79; "Notes—Discussion on Subject of Transportation of American Troops, at Versailles, June 2, 1918," in "Important Conferences, Memoranda, Etc., Affecting Employment of the A.E.F.," AEF, GHQ, G-3, Folder 655, Box 3110, RG 120, National Archives.

Paris in a long tide of woe. French troops fought with their countrymen for inches of highway in a mounting certainty of doom. From the east and from the northeast over the ranging hills of oft-wartorn Marne country came a defeated band of Frenchmen. No one seemed to know where the marines were going, or what to do with Bundy's 26,000 men.

Harbord had gotten ahead of his men in search of orders, tried to carry out a confused conflict of instructions, and finally, on the night of May 31–June 1, pulled the marines into night bivouac along the road. General Jean Degoutte, commanding what was left of a French corps, tried to form a line astride the highway roughly on the southwestern point of the German advance. Germans had spilled across the Marne at Château-Thierry a scant few miles eastward, and obviously they were trying to break their salient on toward Paris. Degoutte's line, if established, would be the last bulwark before the capital.

Distracted, in anguish, still a warrior, Degoutte knew there was a little time to get the marines and the rest of the 2nd Division into position. They would form near Lucy-le-Bocage, try to hold some high ground north of the Marne, and let broken French units filter through them to the rear. By dark on June 1, all of Bundy's regiments were roughly in position west of Château-Thierry. Most of them were tired —Harbord noted that his orders were to "hold the line at all hazards," and he passed the word to the brigade. Slowly his men fanned out north of the highway, connecting on their left and right with Bundy's army infantry. A parting thought from the French command—dig trenches several hundred yards back of the line "just in case"—met stony rejection. Orders to hold were taken literally, and if defensive lines were started men would recognize rhetoric. "We will dig no trenches to fall back to," Harbord replied; "the Marines will hold where they stand."[67]

Refugees, retreating troops, the ominous rumble of cannon were the only reminders of war that June day. Sometimes sharp popping rifle fire came, distantly filtered by Marne valley hills, sometimes the urgent rattle of machine guns from Château-Thierry. There rumor put elements of the U.S. 3rd Division in hot contest for the Marne bridges. But in front of Harbord's Leathernecks stretched greening wheat fields nodding with red poppies, a few small forests, red-roofed

[67] The quotations are from Harbord, *American Army*, p. 283. For other details of deployment, see *ibid.*, pp. 270–82, and Harbord, *Diary*, pp. 287–92.

French farmhouses. His men, as they lined themselves for battle and dug into the ancient loam, seemed defilers of serenity.

On June 4 Degoutte turned seven and a half miles of front line over to Bundy's division, again with the order to hold at all costs. Those eager Americans had worked wonders with retreating Frenchmen. As broken units streamed through the tough, big men facing eagerly toward the Germans, shame rekindled honor. Degoutte regained optimism sufficient to order an advance to clear some woodland and improve positions. Across from him German General von Contra, vexed with problems of supply and changing front, forced to stall his attack for regrouping, also ordered limited improvement of position.

For the Americans everything looked hopeful. Excellent staff work shuttled support units forward; an ammunition dump miraculously appeared at Lizy-sur-Ourcq replete with a million and a half artillery shells; a railhead opened at Meaux; engineers began digging comforting cover; and rolling kitchens substituted hot food for "corned Willy." There had been contact since June 2, when a German attack on the left of Bundy's line failed. Probes and shelling filled the days since, but no test in anger came until 5:00 A.M. on June 6. Harbord, ever valiant in carrying out orders, tried to clear some woods in front of his marines and push his line up toward Torcy's higher terrain. First Battalion, 5th Marines, under Maj. Julius Turrill, struck in dawn's dim light up toward the distant town. Light resistance brushed aside, Turrill soon announced capture of good ground and began to dig in.

During the day Harbord scanned his position. On his right loomed Bouresches village, about half a mile beyond his front. Its houses and barns and its road intersection might be invaluable—it should be taken. From the center of his line at Lucy-le-Bocage, Harbord looked at the small Bois de Belleau, a copse some 1,000 yards wide and 3,000 deep, perhaps a square mile of trees in spring green. Once a hunting preserve for the Château of Belleau half a mile north of the wood, the *bois* seemed a fairly innocent obstacle. French reports indicated it was defended by a German trenchline in the northeast corner. If the marines could get through the woods, they might push the Germans off the Château-Thierry road and clear a rail line—they would also hold good, commanding ground. At 5:00 P.M. Harbord scheduled an advance by three companies of the Third Battalion, 5th Marines, under Maj. Benjamin S. Berry, the Third Battalion, 6th Marines, under Maj. Berton W. Sibley (aided by part of the Second Battalion, 6th Marines). Berry's men would drive into the western edge of the woods while Sibley's reinforced battalion would assault Bouresches and move into the woods from the south. Preparations were casual—no artillery would ruin surprise on that lazy June afternoon. By jump-off time, gathering twilight should provide some cover. Promptly at five the marines moved forward.

Reconnaissance had been lulled by appearances, and the men walked almost nonchalantly out into the wheat fields. Poppies beckoned a few pickers, some officers smoked pipes on an afternoon stroll. One Medal of Honor noncom with veteran shrewdness yelled "Come on, you sons of bitches. Do you want to live forever?" Long lines of khaki filed out through the fields west of Belleau Wood, neat, good lines that rolled on almost like human scythes through the grain; then the machine guns hidden in the woodland opened in ranging bursts, settled into killing cadence, and the men went down in those neat lines and lay still in a reddening stain. Anger filled the survivors; they leaned into the race now, broke up into bunches, ran for the guns, for some cover of trees. Some men reached the wood line, smashed against an unseen tangle of wire and heavy German trenches, broke and recoiled to the edge of the road, and hung on for contact with Sibley's men.

Out against the village through open fields, lines bent a little to hit the wood flush, Sibley's men also strolled into the slaughter of crossfire, of nests spurting bullets that mowed men down in windrows. Clutches of men, formation gone, raced for the village, for the woods, for those terrible, killing guns. Sharp mortar fire broke the formations further, but finally hand-to-hand struggles pushed the enemy from Bouresches and back into the southern feather of the woods. Sibley's men held the town, refused to yield their thin strip of woods. By dark the attack ended with limited success. It had been the costliest day in Marine Corps history: 1,087 casualties.[68]

And that merely began the battle. Floyd Gibbons, noted correspondent, wounded in the day's fighting and temporarily lost somewhere on the field, had filed an unfinished story that morning. The Paris censor cleared it out of sadness, and the marines were suddenly world-famed fighters in Belleau Wood. Other units resented the news blackout, which the marines fortuitously escaped, but all through June's boiling days the marines slugged it out with rotating German divisions. Why? That straggled strand of trees had no military value, served neither side's strategies, was in fact tactically useless. But day

[68] See Harbord, *American Army*, pp. 289–90; Harbord, *Diary*, p. 295; JJP, *Experiences*, 2:63–64, 90; Coffman, *War*, pp. 214–17; Essame, *Battle for Europe*, p. 65.

after day dribbles of men went up through Gob Gully, the one covered avenue into the woods; hundreds came out bleeding, battered, shocked into numbness by the close machine gunning, the bombing, grenading, gassing, the cold-steel combat that turned days into hell and nights into some mad purgatory. Only once were the marines and elements of the 2nd Engineers relieved, only once because Fox Conner, in one of his rare lapses, decided things were not really bad in the woods, and the relief came at Harbord's insistence. But it was temporary help from June 18 to 24 by the 7th Infantry from the untested 3rd Division. In the outcome the 7th, too, failed to advance, was chopped up in the bitter close attacking, and yielded the "dark, sullen mystery of Belleau Wood" again to the marines.

Tanks could have done it; violent gassing could have done it; massed big guns could have obliterated that forlorn forest. But men with rifles, grenades, bayonets, pistols, and some obscure determination were the instruments of fate. Some strange understanding touched friend and foe alike; Belleau Wood meant more than any other spot in the war in June, 1918. The German commander put it succinctly: "It is not a question of the possession or nonpossession of this or that village or woods, insignificant in itself; it is a question whether the Anglo-American claim that the American Army is equal or even the superior of the German Army is to be made good." That was the question, all right. And when Maj. Maurice Shearer, Third Battalion, 6th Marines, reported on the morning of June 26, "This Wood now exclusively U.S. Marine Corps," the question had been answered. "A storm troop" the Germans branded the 2nd Division, and added a prophecy: "The moral effect of our own gunfire cannot seriously impede the advance of the American infantry."[69] Rarely had answers cost such agony, so much blood. In those raging twenty days of fighting, the Marines lost 5,200 casualties, more than half brigade strength. There were lapses, for the men had been green when they entered the test at Belleau; Harbord underappreciated his artillery—officers, many of them, were confused, reckless, addled; men broke, a few of them, under the endless pressure—but of those men who daily tried Harbord said, perhaps, the fittest thing: "I cannot write of their splendid gallantry without tears coming to my eyes. There has never been anything better in the world. What can one say of men who die for others, who freely give up life for country and comrades? What can be said that is adequate?"[70]

69 Coffman, War, pp. 221–22; Harbord, American Army, p. 297.
70 Harbord, Diary, p. 295.

For their part the French changed the name of the place of such gallantry—now it became Bois de la Brigade de Marine. One man got the Medal of Honor for the stand there, countless others wore various decorations; bravery had been commonplace. For Harbord the finest accolade came from John Pershing. The Old Man handed out promotions sparingly, and a second star was approval of the best kind—Harbord was a fighter! And Pershing unbent when next they met. The management of the Marine Brigade sustained every hope, every standard, conformed to the best West Point tradition. "The General," Harbord basked, "has great native charm when he chooses to exercise it, and a message that one's brigade has done well would have to be very untactfully communicated to be unwelcome."[71]

Others had done almost as well—even Harbord would admit it.

"Division of responsibility . . . would be fatal."

Dickman's men were the first Americans to engage the Germans streaming toward the Marne. While the whole French front near Soissons wilted during the confused afternoon of May 31, the 7th Machine Gun Battalion, a motorized unit of the U.S. 3rd Division, moved into position at Château-Thierry. The Americans found Germans crowding the part of town north of the Marne and working desperately to get across highway and railroad bridges. One Yank company of eight guns contested the secondary bridges, another with nine guns defended the railroad bridge. All though June 1, the Germans swarmed at the crossings, all day the American guns cut them down. By evening, bridges still inviolate, Dickman's infantry filed into line south of the river, and the Marne line held.

Foch had built up reserves, including some British divisions, and the new strength in front of the Marne Salient stalled Ludendorff's drive. No small credit for halting the Germans went to the U.S. 2nd and 3rd Divisions. Their tough resistance, their eagerness in battle infused tired French legions with an old élan, bolstered Allied spirits everywhere. Ludendorff correctly felt that he must press on for victory quickly ere too many of those good American troops overwhelmed the Western Front.

Plans had not worked out well for him. The spring series of attacks had cost 600,000 casualties already. The glittering prospects of the Marne drive faded, logistical snarls developed in the newly won

[71] *Ibid.*, pp. 310–11.

salient, and Ludendorff grappled with strategical problems. Realizing that a tactical battle had so far produced little, he returned to his old plan of drawing in Allied reserves by threatening Paris; then, when the French had panicked sufficiently, he would unleash the Crown Prince's Army Group upon the British in Flanders. Von Hutier and Bruchmüller prepared a narrow attack along the Matz valley—objectives were obscure but a straightening of the lines out to Compiègne-Montdidier would free lateral communication lines, thwart French logistics, threaten Paris and, most importantly, eliminate the threat of a counterattack against the flabby western face of the Marne Salient.

Throwing twenty-one divisions forward on June 9, Ludendorff ran into new French defenses. Bruchmüller's guns had bombarded empty trenches, trained legions charged largely undefended positions, and, when they took the French first line, they were ravaged by a horrendous bombardment. Defeats had taught the French something; defense in depth combined with aggressive counterattacks led by the redoubtable Gen. Charles Mangin stalled the Germans from the start. After a costly advance of some nine miles, Ludendorff called off the attack.[72]

Now Ludendorff became a victim of statistics. Germany would not stand so many casualties for nothing—victory must be snatched while still initiative remained. And initiative teetered in balance. Foch's careful pinching of reserves posed a serious threat to the Marne pocket, and rapid arrival of Americans might soon achieve Allied strength superiority on the front. Optimism faded in German ranks. Excited with prospects of victory in March, the German armies had fought valiantly and now rested checked, uncertain, and riddled by influenza. Peace talk at home sapped morale, too, and the last chance must be taken.

Ludendorff probably guessed that German depression matched rising enemy morale. If so, he was right. The dramatic shift of fortune at the Marne, in the Matz fighting, the continuous flood of American troops into the battle line, inspired Foch's old fascination for *attaque à l'outrance!* Even Pétain, phlegmatic and suspicious of flamboyant optimists, shaped plans for attack. Haig, normally the optimist among Philistines, nursed worries about the Crown Prince's Army Group facing Ypres and the Flanders area. Convinced Ludendorff still cherished plans to push the BEF into the channel, Haig resisted giving

[72] W. H. Nelson and F. E. Vandiver, *Fields of Glory: An Illustrated Narrative of American Land Warfare*, p. 202; Essame, *Battle for Europe*, pp. 65–78.

too much help to the French. But Foch's request for divisions could not really be refused.

Alone among Allied leaders, Pershing thought strategically in the wake of Ludendorff's failures. The Marne Salient offered a huge prize for the plucking. The chance ought not be missed. To Clemenceau and Foch on June 23 Pershing broached his idea. Did Foch recall the discussion at Sarcus on May 30, the suggestion of a counterattack on the developing Marne pocket? He did, had in fact ordered a study made of the possibilities. Pershing, surprised at Foch's languid response, spoke forcefully of "the strategical effect of a successful blow just south of Soissons and the material results it would have, to say nothing of its stimulating effect on Allied morale." He had at least six, possibly eight, divisions that could be used in a counterthrust—forces equal to some sixteen British or French divisions. Clemenceau showed interest and Pershing expanded. "It will be evident to any one who will glance at the map that once the line there was pierced the German rear would be threatened and their position within the salient would be untenable." The Germans, he argued, had given the Allies the best chance of the war![73]

Foch's sphinxlike manner cloaked an ambition boundless and a devious intellect. Pershing's strategic ideas were sound, but they were not Foch's. It would scarcely be right for someone other than the supreme Allied commander to think strategically. Pershing's main function, obviously, lay in the provision of manpower. At the conference, held at Pershing's residence outside Chaumont, Clemenceau talked again of troops, and Foch wondered openly about America fulfilling the 100-division scheme. Pershing, glad of second thoughts, doubted that facilities would produce so much. André Tardieu, who shared the discussion, agreed and suggested a reduction of demands. Clemenceau and Foch quickly disagreed—100 divisions were essential for victory in 1919.

A curious, shifting sentiment charged the meeting, although it was marked by uncommon courtesy. Training and supply facilities in the States, Pershing suggested, would be strained furiously to produce 3,200,000 men—the equivalent of 80 divisions and support troops—in 1919. But the smaller figure seemed a reasonable target. Response from the War Department to Pershing's June 21 request for 66 divisions had yet to come; he guessed it would be cautious alarm. But recent events did prove the absolute need for men. Were the Allies

[73] JJP, *Experiences*, 2:120.

putting in everyone they had? Assurances were loud that the barrels were swept clean until the 1919 class could be processed in September.

German replacement problems happily multiplied, according to Allied intelligence. Although troops still came from the eastern areas, Germany's reserve pool had shrunk to 340,000; there would be more, of course, with the 1919 class.

Reluctantly persuaded, Pershing agreed to support an 80-division target for April and 100 for July, 1919. But he wrung an important concession from his colleagues—six whole divisions a month would be shipped from the States and they would be under American command. The idea came easier in wake of American prowess on the battlefield. The Tiger himself had conceded the wisdom of building up an American army as the best way of strengthening the cause.[74]

All the varieties of suggestions from HAEF produced confusion in Washington. Pershing had worried about that after the June 1 meeting of the War Council. A "succession of demands," he mused, "must have created consternation at home."[75] For a man isolated in France trying to build a huge organization against the combined efforts of ennui, inertia, the enemy, and the Allies, the logic of shifting proposals came clear. At home, though, the logic might be construed as indecision. Always tuned to snipes from the rear and to the need for solidarity in relations with Baker, Pershing hated these examples of uncertainty among the Allies. And with good reason. The impression did mount in Washington that Pershing had too many things on his mind. Rumors wafting from carpers in France that the SOS lacked cohesion, might even collapse under an avalanche of maladministration, increased concern. Combined with combat problems Pershing faced, the rumors posed questions that Baker and the president discussed seriously.

That strange moves were afoot in Washington Pershing guessed through the early part of 1918. Despite efforts to keep friendly with Peyton March, petty incidents mounted to show that the new chief of staff pursued a course independent of the AEF. Not that the AEF should receive all attention, of course, but parity with home forces at least seemed fair. March had infused new zest into War Department procedures, and his reorganization of staff functions produced more and quicker supplies for the AEF.[76] But increasingly March—who became a full general in late May—sent peremptory messages to HAEF, couched in terms of direct command. And some kind of perversity

74 *Ibid.*, pp. 120–24.
75 *Ibid.*, p. 83.
76 Edward M. Coffman, *March*, p. 76.

prodded March into direct confrontation on the issue of promotions. AEF officers who fought well and deserved elevation were duly recommended; March promoted others, usually men on stateside duty, and sometimes men in France were advanced without Pershing's nomination. March argued the broad needs of the army in justification. Fighters deserved recognition, and Pershing fired cables galore defending his views on promotion. The secretary of war, normally sympathetic, read reams from Pershing on the subject but seemed unwilling or unable to act. The problem festered.[77]

March's truculence might be a reflection of cooling affections in Washington. Little hints of it worried Harbord, who, while still AEF chief of staff, called each one to Pershing's notice. The promotion matter especially fanned Harbord's suspicions. Then came a long missive from Baker, dated July 6, 1918, touching on myriad problems. Tucked deep in the letter was a wrenching paragraph:

The President and I have had several conferences about your situation in France, both of us desiring in every possible way to relieve you of unnecessary burdens, but of course to leave you with all the authority necessary to secure the best results from your forces and to supply all the support and assistance we possibly can. As the American troops in France become more and more numerous and the battle initiative on some parts of the front passes to you, the purely military part of your task will necessarily take more and more of your time, and both the President and I want to feel that the planning and executing of military undertakings has your personal consideration and that your mind is free for that as far as possible. The American people think of you as their "fighting General," and I want them to have that idea more and more brought home to them. For these reasons, it seems to me that if some plan could be devised by which you would be free from any necessity of giving attention to services of supply it would help, and one plan in that direction which suggested itself was to send General Goethals over to take charge of the services of supply, establishing a direct relationship between him and Washington and allowing you to rely upon him just as you would rely upon the supply departments of the War Department if your military operations were being conducted in America, instead of in France. Such a plan would place General Goethals rather in a coördinate than a subordinate relationship to you, but of course it would transfer all of the supply responsibilities from you to him and you could then forget about docks, railroads, storage houses, and all the other vast industrial undertakings to which up to now you have given a good deal of your time and, as you

[77] For example, see March/McCain to JJP, May 30, 1918 (cable 1426-R), in JJP Papers, Cables, Box 4, RG 200/316, National Archives. March said: "Report by cable when you move to your new Field Headquarters and take personal charge." See also Coffman, *War*, pp. 184–85. One of the rankling promotion cases involved Douglas MacArthur's promotion to brigadier general without JJP's recommendation (Coffman, *War*, p. 184). See also JJP, *Experiences*, 2:101–3.

know, we all think with superb success. I would be very glad to know what you think about this suggestion. I realize that France is very far from the United States and that our reliance upon cables makes a very difficult means of communication, so that you may prefer to have the supply system as one of your responsibilities. I would be grateful if you would think the problem over and tell me quite frankly just what you think of the subject. The President and I will consider your reply together, and you may rely upon our being guided only by confidence in your judgment and the deep desire to aid you.[78]

What did he think? Rejected! The letter confirmed a series of rumors purveyed by Pershing friends in Washington—rumors indicating that Baker came increasingly under March's malign influence and that March wanted to undercut the authority and independence of the commander-in-chief. Goethals, indeed! He was a fine canal man, surely, even proving to be a competent quartermaster general, but Goethals, a West Point teacher in Pershing's cadet days, represented the Continental army view, was of the March camp, not the AEF. If he came in a "coördinate . . . relationship" he would confuse the Allies hopelessly and hamper relations with the War Council. More than that, his higher loyalties to the War Department would work against the AEF's interests. He must not come.

A good deal of conniving probably lay behind this sudden proposition. March had raised the issue in a letter first, quickly followed by Baker's epistle, so the idea obviously had progressed pretty far. The secretary did ask for comments. Was the offer sincere, or merely a kind of post-mortem courtesy? Since Baker had ever been open in the past, better to take him at his word. While formulating a proper statement of the military absurdity of gutting the American army in France, Pershing decided he had better act swiftly to show his own concern with the SOS. Cabling Baker on July 27 that "any division of responsibility or coordinate control in any sense would be fatal," he announced his intentions to put in a new chief of the SOS, a man with his full confidence, one who would make it possible "to devote myself to military operations."[79] He had a good man in mind.

Gen. Francis Kernan had not been wholly successful in running the sprawling business enterprise that now sustained the AEF. A good administrator, he had more the staff officer's precise intellect than a commander's force. For some months Pershing had thought of shoring

[78] Baker to JJP, July 6, 1918, in JJP, *Experiences*, 2:185–86.
[79] JJP to Secwar (Confidential cable 1522-S), July 27, 1918, in Cables, GHQ, AEF to War Department, Pershing Papers, RG 200, National Archives Gift Collection.

up the crumbling organization behind the lines. He should have acted earlier when he saw the effects of too few SOS troops coming from home. Who could take over the job and do it the AEF way? What were the opinions of McAndrew, Boyd, and George Quekemeyer, whose flitting around the AEF acquainted him especially with good and bad officers? General concensus fell on Jim Harbord. Why? Trusted by Pershing, liked by Baker, he had been chief of staff, knew the SOS from its infancy, would be utterly loyal, and now had the special luster of a fighting reputation. The last point counted heavily. Too many misfits and front-line rejects had been consigned to the SOS, and morale of the whole outfit reflected failure. If Pershing sent the Marine Brigade leader, a man who now commanded the famed 2nd Division, it would perk up everybody from Marseilles to Neufchâteau!

It would be a mean trick on Harbord. He had a fighter's knack and there were too few of that kind; he loved his men, had even as a National Army brigadier fitted right into the marine tradition and added to it. When he took over the 2nd Division from Bundy's fumbling hands in July, he had fought it with distinction. In time he would command a corps, perhaps an army. But he had a wizardry with details, could handle them and delegate them and get things done. Would he take the job?[80]

Picking a man was only part of Pershing's reaction to the backfire in Washington. March's intrusions were potentially serious. If rumors were correct—Enoch Crowder pandered poisonous hints of a ruthless machine building in the War Department aimed at getting Pershing's job for March—Joffre's old worry about Limoges might become personal. To Papa Warren went a private cable and a sealed letter to the secretary of war. The letter had been written in recklessness, with a kind of spleen venting by a general tired of intrigues front and rear, a man concerned for his reputation, and a friend feeling betrayed. Warren saw Baker, raised the problem of Goethals. Baker, friendly and open, said he knew all about Pershing's views, had heard from him, had replied. The scheme, Baker thought, had started in the State Department, probably from some Paris suggestion that Pershing needed diplomatic assistance. Carefully Warren broached the possibility that March worked against Pershing, at least that he slighted some requests from France. Baker reckoned that possibly true. Then Warren thrust Pershing's sealed letter at the little secretary, with the comment: "Pershing has such confidence in you, and I also have such confidence in

[80] Harbord, *Diary*, pp. 339–40; JJP, *Experiences*, 2:179–80, 190–91.

your judgment, that instead of breaking the seals I want the letter to go directly to you intact so that you might know exactly Pershing's mind at the time he wrote." If it overstepped, Warren said, hand it back and forget it. Baker, his round glasses pushed close, leaned over his engulfing desk and read Pershing's comments on the current ways of the world. Finished, Baker tore the letter up and commented that Pershing had been entirely right. Warren left convinced that Baker's friendship flamed stronger than ever, and that March did not have undue influence.[81]

Goethals did not go. Baker, somewhat amused by Pershing's hasty guarding of his rear, accepted a general's need to run his war.[82]

"My days had always been too short."

New effusiveness had colored Fourth of July greetings. Haig announced that the BEF would celebrate America's national holiday along with their new comrades and commented on a comforting circumstance: "The soldiers of America, France, and Great Britain will stand side by side for the first time in history in the defense of the great principle of Liberty, which is the proudest inheritance and most cherished possession of their several nations. . . . With the heartfelt good wishes to you and your gallant army, believe me, Yours very truly, D. Haig, F.M." Clemenceau, fresh from watching the great Fourth of July parade in Paris, along the Avenue President Wilson, spoke glowingly: "On this holiday so wholeheartedly celebrated by all our Allies, the splendid appearance of your soldiers aroused not only our enthusiasm but our unbounded confidence as well." Foch, with simplicity, caught the point: "It is for independence that we all are fighting. With all our hearts we celebrate with you the anniversary of Indepedence Day." Belgian and Italian greetings joined the flood, even some of the Allied army commanders forwarded congratulations.[83]

Ever aware of the posture, Pershing replied gratefully to all messages. What he wrote in longhand to Haig, the field marshal published to his troops:

[81] FEW to JJP, Aug. 27, 1918 (Personal), FEW Papers, vol. 83.

[82] For the whole Goethals controversy, which sputtered in various forms for some time, see Coffman, *March*, pp. 104–9; Coffman, *War*, pp. 175–76; JJP, *Experiences*, 2:179–91. Harbord, *American Army*, pp. 345–55, gives an intensely pro-Pershing account of the episode. Peyton C. March, in *The Nation at War*, pp. 193–96, gives an oddly terse account that manages to be biased.

[83] See the messages in JJP, *Experiences*, 2:135–37.

The Independence Day greetings from the British Army in France, . . . are most deeply appreciated by all ranks of the American Expeditionary Forces.

The firm unity of purpose that on the 4th of July, this year, so strongly binds the great Allied Nations together, stands as a new declaration and a new guarantee that the sacred principles of Liberty shall not perish, but shall be extended to all peoples.

With most earnest good wishes from myself and the entire command to you and our brave British Brothers-in-Arms, I remain always, with great respect and high esteem,

Yours very sincerely,
John J. Pershing.[84]

There were ceremonial functions, too, that siphoned time from a military day. Chaumont's citizens, increasingly warm toward their American guests, gradually lavished attentions on all the men at HAEF. When Pershing moved to the stately manse, Val des Escoliers, he avoided local fuss, but on certain occasions he had to appear. On July 4, the city exulted in American Independence. Back from an impromptu meeting with the SWC that had gone well, despite some slight skirmishing with Haig about keeping American divisions with the British, Pershing joined celebrations at Chaumont's Hôtel de Ville. American and French flags were everywhere; crowds joined in listening to American and native patriotic music. As Pershing and the officers from HAEF arrived downtown, groups of people pressed greetings. Among them came a band of school children, and Pershing gave full attention to them. They had flowers for him; girls curtsied and were shy with the big American soldier who looked strong and fierce. He took the flowers, broke into a great grin, heard the speeches in the little voices, speeches of good wishes and happiness at America's birthday. The mayor of Chaumont and high civil and military officials joined in the bubbling congratulations. But it was to the children that Pershing responded—they were victims of war and would be the beneficiaries of victory. "Today," he spoke to them in French, "today constitutes a new Declaration of Independence, a solemn oath that the liberty for which France has long been fighting will be attained." Other things he said that day in the heat of good will; in fact he almost astonished himself. "I found myself almost as enthusiastic as the French speakers, though perhaps less content with my effort." On Bastille Day, July 14—an AEF holiday—the children of Chaumont's *lycée* gave Pershing a volume of French history for Warren, "which we shall long

---

[84] Special Orders of the Day, by Field Marshal Sir Douglas Haig, GHQ, July 8, 1918, copy in Haig Papers.

treasure." The general presided over prize giving at the *lycée* and mused that "Liberté, Fraternité, Egalité" were often forgotten words that shone again in anniversaries.[85]

From Paris, amid all the whelm of admiration, came Bliss's good American sense, He, too, had been deluged with flattering comments on the Americans, especially in wake of Château-Thierry and the Marne battles, and it seemed good to him, but he thought, too, that caution dictated keeping a record of all these compliments. "There may be a tendency a year or so from now," he wryly wrote, "to minimize the credit which at the moment they gave to our troops."[86] Pershing remembered every one of the comments and, especially, Bliss's admonition.

Little plagues infested HAEF: concerns with the Liberty Loans (Pershing must make statements occasionally urging purchase), with Red Cross activities so vital to army welfare, with the chaplain service (he finally snagged a major's commission in the National Army for Bishop Brent and put him in charge of chaplain affairs at GHQ), with the medical service (which came in for unjust criticism and scrutiny at a time when AEF doctors performed far better than the French and even were able to lend facilities to the British in Champagne), with prisoners of war, with visitors who flocked to Chaumont even amid campaigning, with supply problems (especially shortages aggravated now by scarce SOS personnel and by possibly purposeful opacity in the War Department). Every detail squandered time and left Pershing frustrated with the war. No harder thing could he do than tend the housekeeping of the forces fighting now in so many places. He told Enoch Crowder that he wanted fervently to "fight a division," but he could not—"and so each man to the job that has been given him!"[87]

Size had complicated all of the commander-in-chief's problems that summer. By the end of July, the AEF counted 1,169,062 officers and men, with numbers rising daily. And the AEF, so much Pershing's personal creation, hinged on policy decisions from the chief himself. Details and social obligations did almost overwhelm him, forced some

---

[85] JJP, *Experiences*, 2:135, 149–50. The speech to the children is taken from Grady Barrett, "Pershing at Close Range," typescript copy in author's possession. Mr. Barrett, of San Antonio, Tex., kindly gave a copy of this paper to the author. Barrett, an army field clerk at HAEF, was in close contact with Pershing through 1918.

[86] JJP, *Experiences*, 2:139 n.

[87] JJP to Crowder, June 28, 1918, Box 56, PP. For details of Pershing's concerns, see JJP, *Experiences*, 1:371, 2:130–33, 139–41, 192–206, 214; Essame, *Battle for Europe*, p. 96.

recognition of overcommitment. Although delegating widely to his staff, Pershing found himself enmeshed in every phase of America's effort in France. Too long he tried to do too much. Baker had been at least partly right in thinking Pershing needed to find a trusted man for the SOS. Relief from that burden would free a good deal of time.[88]

Training matters Pershing fussed with constantly; in Washington no one seemed to grasp the need for "the school of the soldier"; apparently the War Department would send over troops untutored in anything save food and sex. To the G-5 section of his headquarters staff Pershing gave much personal direction, watched carefully as relations with Allied training officers developed and deteriorated, and urged always the maintenance of American standards and methods. This function went to the heart of the forming American army, and Pershing could not really hand it to others. But he found good men to help him and fixed the attention of all staff operations officers on the urgency of battle preparation.

Diplomatic burdens he increasingly left to Bliss, whose constant attitude of cooperation won confidence. And Jack accepted with acknowledged pleasure, if some suspicion, the presence in France of Edward R. Stettinius, former assistant secretary of war, as a member of the Allied Munitions Board and negotiator for AEF ordnance supplies in Europe. They got on well enough, and Stettinius's efforts proved a valuable adjunct to Dawes's work.[89]

"My days, from the time of my arrival in France," Pershing complained, "had always been too short, but it now seemed that several days of arduous work had to be crowded into one. The sphere of our activities had become extended and many important matters required my personal attention, necessitating a great deal of travel. . . . It was necessary to spend a day or so here or there—at Paris, Chaumont, on the Marne, or in the St. Mihiel region—holding frequent conferences with Foch, Pétain, Haig and others."[90] All of these activities, vital and often highly exciting, detracted from a soldier's main interest: what about the troops? During the earlier ventures of the Doughboys along the Marne and with the British in Picardy, Pershing established an advanced headquarters at Grémévillers, a place from which he might reach any part of the fighting line speedily.[91] But as AEF opera-

[88] JJP to AGWAR, Aug. 6, 1918 (cable 1561-S), in Cables, GHQ, AEF to War Department, Pershing Papers, RG 200, National Archives Gift Collection.
[89] See Palmer, *Baker*, 2:333–34.
[90] JJP, *Experiences*, 2:214.
[91] *Ibid.*, p. 55; Bullard to JJP, May 28, 1918 (telegram), 5:00 P.M., reporting

tions spread along the Allied line, Pershing followed Mexican experience and established a kind of roving headquarters in his car; close to troops, he would stay with division or corps leaders, or in handy hotels. Some guessed he moved too much, that his constant visiting badgered field commanders and plagued people trying to find him. There may have been some truth to the argument, but an old campaigner yielded easily to the pull of the battlefield. Occasionally he would startle front-line soldiers with an appearance; more often he dropped in on division and corps commanders for briefings and to see how the troops were doing.

The Rock of the Marne

Allied reserves must be pulled into a consuming battle on bad ground, a battle so vital to France that it would ensure commitment of the precious men Foch hoarded. Where to attack? Ludendorff's best bet seemed still the Marne pocket. If he could expand it, break the Reims defensive wall, he would free rail lines into the salient and strengthen his entire posture toward Paris. Strategy remained the same —should the attack go well along the Marne, he would push it to the coming of enemy reserves, then loose Crown Prince Rupprecht against the suspicious Haig in Flanders. Two July attacks would about use up German strength, but no better chance loomed.

A spring and summer of attacking tested the stern discipline of the German army. Ludendorff had had better fiber in his divisions, corps, and armies than he reckoned; his officers, commissioned and noncom alike, had been mostly veterans, and the administration functioned well. Staff work, always efficient from Oberst Heeres Leitung (OHL) to the front lines, ensured the commander's ideas shaping events; even when the generals left the front for one of the endless conferences that so plagued the war, the well-knit entity that was the German army did whatever needed doing. But Ludendorff's stream of attacks had at last worn the edge from discipline. Replacements were not of earlier caliber, and officers were tired, many of them now less experienced; though hope of victory remained, physical limits lowered ardor.

Success through the earlier attacks came from the secrecy carefully shrouding each German drive. Secrecy depended on discipline. In the Marne bulge during July, discipline loosened a bit. Ludendorff's re-

---

on Cantigny, in HQ 1st Division, AEF, "G-3 Reports, Journals of Operations—1st Division," Folder 117-A, Box 3074, RG 120, National Archives.

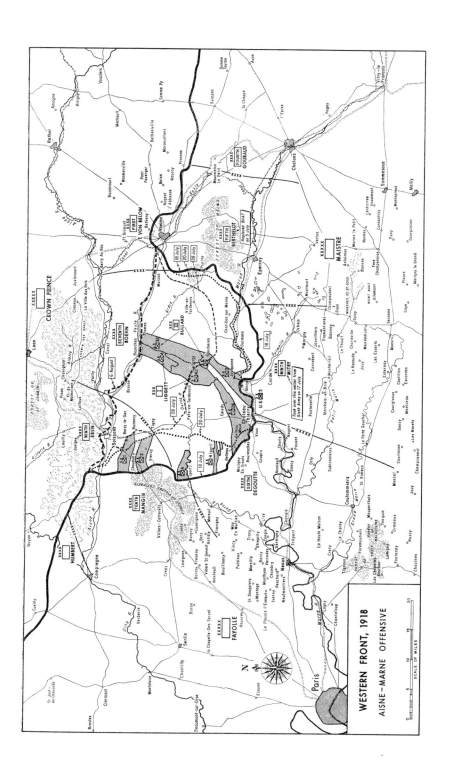

WESTERN FRONT, 1918
AISNE-MARNE OFFENSIVE

serves had thinned, and his shifts of men could be seen along the battle line. Allied intelligence officers—indeed almost anyone who looked across the lines—could guess through the last days of June and early July that the Germans' next try would come in Champagne. Prisoners confirmed the suspicion with stories of reconnaissances in the Marne area, of bridge-crossing equipment coming for use between Epernay and Château-Thierry. Through July's sweltering early days, French airmen reported vast crawling lines of trucks and wagons, poorly hidden dumps and infantry concentrations.

From the Reims sector westward around the salient, Foch disposed the French V Army aided by the British XXI Corps and the Italian II Corps, next the French IX Army, the French VI Army, aided by the forming U.S. I Corps, and finally, on the left flank beyond Soissons, Mangin's X Army. Foch built strength to twenty line divisions and fifteen reserve, and urged as many more British and American divisions forward as possible. Additional bombers and fighter planes were lent by Haig so that infantry liaison and interdiction of enemy supply lines seemed assured. Foch and Pétain schemed, this time, ahead of Ludendorff. Telling Gen. Henri Gouraud to hold the point of the salient—he made shrewd defense-in-depth plans to lure the Germans into a trap—they aimed at a heavy counterattack along the west wall of Ludendorff's exposed flank.

Pershing could take grim satisfaction that the great French plan matched exactly the one suggested to Clemenceau and Foch on June 23.

Strangely blasé about lack of security, Ludendorff scheduled "Friedensturm," a 49-division attack, for July 15, 1918. Hitting both sides of Reims, his armies would cross the Marne east of Château-Thierry and link together near Châlons. All the Reims defenders might be trapped; certainly Foch would have to drain most of his reserves far to the east—Flanders would be stripped clean!

Tipped off to the German bombardment schedule, French batteries began counterbattery and preparation fire at 11:00 P.M. on July 14; at 12:10 P.M., 2,000 German guns roared the beginning of "Friedensturm." People sat up in bed in Paris; the streets of Châlons were bright as day. East of Reims the defense in depth worked beautifully for the French; thousands of shells pounded empty trenches, and when the German infantry came over at 4:00 A.M. they occupied vacant lines suddenly churned under a bombardment of 800 Allied batteries. Here the attack stalled at the start.

West of Reims the Germans encountered different defenses. Commanders of the French V and VI Armies apparently fixed on the Marne itself as the containment point, pulled too many men close to the front, did exactly what Bruchmüller and von Hutier wanted, and paid dearly indeed. Among the unfortunates clustering the river, just east of Château-Thierry, were Dickman's men of the U.S. 3rd Division. Dickman wondered about the position and posted his artillery as best he could to cover open ground stretching alarmingly in his front and on his right flank, where French troops were supposedly to hold. Obeying orders, Dickman put some of his men right along the river with instructions to throw back the Huns. But he reinforced the river line with support battalions for counterattack, and disobeyed to the extent of keeping his main force well back. His extreme right he trusted to Ulysses Grant McAlexander and the 38th Infantry. They would have to keep the French link intact and prevent a turning movement to sweep up the whole American line.

Anxiety and near panic twitched along the river defenders from west of Château-Thierry. French officers were packed; Dickman grimly observed that if Pershing were to visit the front and see him packed, Blois would be the day's destination. Dickman's left elements held the town and connected with the French 39th and U.S. 26th Divisions on the rising ground through Belleau Wood.

Brotherly concern added to Dickman's discomfort. On his right, Charlie Muir's 28th Division, greener than grass, fresh from British training camps and without artillery, had pulled in to reinforce the French. Orders took too many of them into French units aligning the river; nobody next door really understood French—if trouble came, the 28th could be caught in a disaster.

Trouble came on schedule. On the Marne, too, French guns had anticipated German, but the attack began at 1:10 A.M., July 15, 1918, with assault teams pushing small boats into the river. General Max von Boehn's army, spruced and resupplied, swarmed across the river and grappled for beachheads, for springboards to Paris. Hard hit, six French divisions to Dickman's right fought fiercely for awhile, then pulled out, leaving four companies of the 28th Division to whatever fate lunacy provided. The four companies of Pennsylvanians, untried and surprised, fought surrounded, fought in small groups, struggled, some of them individually, against many Germans. Most were killed or captured, but a few, a heroic few, fought or sneaked their way out and joined their divisional line that held in the rear.

On Dickman's front the Germans struck McAlexander's 38th Infantry, which shared a bad bulge into the Marne with the French.

McAlexander, with cynical forethought, guessed the decamping of his allies. He understood, but told his captains that the business of the Americans was "to so impress the Germans with our fighting ability . . . that their morale would be destroyed."

With about 250 of his 3,500 men on river's edge, the rest in two lines behind, McAlexander met the Germans. Fighting raged in fanatical peaks of bravery; Germans poured incessantly into boats, onto the land; Doughboys fought them hand to hand, grenaded them, shot them down with deadly rifle accuracy, bayonetted them. The French retreated and Germans spilled across to take McAlexander in flank; his men echeloned backward and held. He beat the Germans off all day, and, when at last he pulled back to second lines, the 38th Infantry had a new name: The Rock of the Marne.

All day long the fighting on the low ground by the river, and up higher where Dickman intended his main defense, swirled in wild little melees. Pershing kept telling the Doughboys about open warfare, told them that in that kind of war they must count on "brief orders and the greatest possible use of individual initiative by all troops. . . . " They did fairly well at the initiative business that day. By late afternoon a motley gang of khaki casuals—cooks, surgeons, typists, anybody who could carry a gun—fought everywhere. By evening, although they had done well enough further east and held a considerable bridgehead with 75,000 men, the Germans had failed to cross at Château-Thierry. Bridges were held by Dickman's gunners, and the front was held by his stalwart troops. Had the flat ground of the Surmelin Valley been lost that day, Paris might well have been swamped quickly in the German overwash. But the 3rd Division and the Rock of the Marne had come to stay.

Americans all along the line—the 42nd Rainbows under Gouraud, some elements of the 26th Division—kept the proudest traditions of the United States service that day, and with their allies stalled Ludendorff's big drive. The pincers failed to close—hardly even opened—and most of the attackers were still far north of the Marne.

American deeds on July 15 added special pleasure to the congratulations that poured into Chaumont, greetings warm now with admiration and full of hope for victory. The tough fighting at Cantigny, the incessant heroism at Belleau Wood, the firm clench that the 38th Infantry and the 3rd Division put on von Boehn's main thrust showed the world an inescapable wonder—Americans fought like fiends.[92]

[92] For Château-Thierry operations sources are legion. See, for example, JJP, *Experiences*, 2:153, where he terms the fighting of the 30th and 38th Infantry

"You rushed into the fight as to a fete"

West of the Marne Salient, down below Soissons and not too far northwest of Bois de la Brigade de Marine, a vast sprawling forest land covered part of the Ourcq Valley—the Forest of Villers-Cotterêts. Buildup in that dense straggle of woods—sometimes known as the Forest of Retz—continued. Charles Mangin, angry as usual, spoiling to smash the Huns, collected anything Foch and Pétain, Haig and Pershing siphoned from lesser fronts. Pétain's nerve failed him briefly under von Boehn's Marne shock in July, but Foch stuck grimly to the offensive: Hold the front, hit them in flank. This sound plan had Pershing's stamp all over it. Mangin understood the opportunity glittering in the dark forest. If he could gather his half a million there undetected, he could hit the Germans a decisive blow. Troops kept coming.

Among the host gathering were the U.S. 1st and 4th Divisions and Hunter Liggett's U.S. I Corps. Liggett knew exactly the challenge and the chance facing him in the operations Mangin schemed. Taking over part of the front on July 4, Liggett's corps, holding the line from Château-Thierry to Belleau Wood, contained U.S. and French divisions; the general mused that "it was the first time since our Civil War that an American Army Corps had functioned in action, and the first time that an American Command had foreign troops under its control since our War of Independence." French officers respected the carefully eager staff at headquarters; cooperation posed no problems. "It was well understood," Liggett confessed, "that the success of this Corps in action would go far to remove all objections to the formation of higher units under American command and staff."[93] Confident after wresting Foch's agreement to a separate American sector,[94] Pershing had ghosted four other corps organizations, picked Maj. Gen. George Read for the II, Robert Bullard, that tried and able soldier, for the III, and the other was waiting a firm commander decision.[95]

---

regiments "brilliant"; Stallings, *AEF*, pp. 114–38, gives a colorful, sympathetic account by a former Doughboy and superb stylist; Essame, *Battle for Europe*, pp. 82–86, is a sound summary. General information can be found in Joseph T. Dickman, *The Great Crusade*, and New York Historical Commission, *The Second Division*. Special data on the 38th Infantry is found in J. W. Woodbridge, *The Giants of the Marne*. Unit histories, sadly too often ignored by historians, are bounteous sources of insight and human detail.

[93] Liggett, *Commanding an American Army*, pp. 30–31.

[94] Foch's acceptance of an American sector came during a conference at Bombon on July 10, 1918.

[95] See JJP, *Experiences*, 2:127. See also J. W. McAndrew to Commanding General, I Corps, June 10, 1918, "Utilization of Corps Headquarters and Staffs,"

Bullard, forming the III Corps, got his old 1st Division, now under Charlie Summerall, and Harbord's 2nd—the real cream of the AEF—and rushed them toward the forest at Villers-Cotterêts. The small area between Château-Thierry and Paris spawned gypsy caravans of troops, supplies, horses, camions, guns, the bulking sinews of war. Excited disorder disturbed the area; men moved back and forth, batteries careened toward unknown places, and orders wafted endlessly. Summerall got the word earlier than most, since Big Red One had been pulled into reserve in early July. Move to the French X Army zone, for attachment to the XX Corps. Troops boarded American and French trucks headed eastward. Artillery and trains marched. Changes in orders hustled men and guns on tortuous treks in the growing woodland, but by July 17 the whole division had reached assigned positions near Mortefontaine. That day attack orders arrived—Mangin would hit the German positions between the Aisne and Ourcq, push his men toward the great plain around Fère-en-Tardenois, shift northeast and try to link with other troops hitting Ludendorff's men from the Reims area on the east face of the German salient. The 1st Division would be the left element of the XX Corps, linking with the 153rd French Division and touching on the right the famed French Moroccans.

For the 2nd Division life moved in hard ways. Belleau, Vaux, these were successes come by tough sacrifice. And now came rush orders to Villers-Cotterêts. The new commander, Harbord (not yet aware of his SOS fate) pleased the tough marines mightily—his outlandish admiration for them had even amused the chief[96]—and he lent zest to every unit. When he told his men they were moving again, the news brought excitement. Aboard great old French busses on Tuesday afternoon, July 16, the men found themselves meandering to some unnamed place to do duty unguessed. Many people were on the road with them in a great ingathering of hosts. Were they going to help the 3rd Division, struggling at the Château-Thierry crossing? Quickly rumor—that immemorial telegraph of the armies—reported the rendezvous in the Forest of Retz, and that the division would be in Mangin's army, attached to the French XX Corps. Harbord, getting the word officially,

---

in AEF, GHQ, G-3, I Corps Correspondence, Folder 289, Box 3092, RG 120, National Archives.

[96] JJP, *Experiences*, 2:148. On July 12 Pershing visited the Marine Brigade and Harbord avidly described a marine who had single-handedly taken 75 Germans prisoner; Pershing smiled hugely and commented "that if he told such stories as that it was little wonder that he was popular with the Marines."

dumped headquarters gear in a truck, grabbed Preston Brown, his acerbic chief of staff, and headed for Mangin's command post.

That grim-faced, dapper soldier with the Gallic temper had decamped for some place closer to the front; instructions were vague. There would be an attack—soon. Find the XX Corps. Harbord's truck plunged into the stream of men, animals, guns, carts, infantry that struggled along the main road through the forest around Villers-Cotterêts. An hour was required to cover two or three miles—the sluggish flow almost stagnated, and Harbord despaired of finding his place. At last, long after dinnertime, he met Gen. Pierre Berdoulat, commanding the XX Corps. Courteous ever, the French general casually suggested food, and then, calmly, he said that the 2nd Division would join the attack Thursday morning! "My division," Harbord thought helplessly, "was scattered all over Champagne and entirely out of my hands."[97] He might never find it in time to lead the attack. French trucks were notoriously vagrant, their daredevil drivers always heading for some unrevealed place. Horrified, Harbord brooded that "a division of twenty-eight thousand men, the size of a European army corps, had been completely removed from the control of its responsible commander, and deflected by marching and by truck, through France to [a] destination unknown to any of the authorities responsible either for its supply, its safety, or its efficiency in the coming attack."[98] Undoubtedly, said Berdoulat, the division would be in place by jump-off time. Harbord went to look.

Finding Bullard's headquarters about midnight, Harbord also found a French staff officer who knew the ground ahead and dictated a description of the supposed attack area. It was the only intelligence briefing given.

Bullard, yielding tactical command to the French, had that essential of modern armies—a mimeograph machine. Harbord and Brown pored over maps and the brief ground description, wrote an attack order, and ran off copies for brigade commanders. One consolation: Charlie Summerall, separated from his 1st Division, shared the mimeograph machine in equal fuddlement.[99]

Through a long day American officers struggled to find their men and get them into position. Clouds lowered and the skies emptied in a kind of climatic outburst against men's follies. Still through the

[97] Harbord, *Diary*, pp. 317–18.
[98] *Ibid.*, p. 318.
[99] Stallings, *AEF*, p. 146.

drenched country came men, scattered and bedraggled, but coming to Villers-Cotterêts. With daylight on July 17, Harbord's car sloshed along a thronged avenue as he searched for his men. Finally he picked out the lead unit of the 23rd Infantry and sent an officer to direct the rest to their places in the edge of the woods. The rain, the dour darkness of the day, screened the deployment in the afternoon as units arrived. Horror stories of wandering and ignorance came with every company. Harbord commandeered a 1st Division ammunition dump to increase his men's one belt issue. As night closed its stygian grip over the forest, the men still were straggling into line. Roads were sluices, wagons slithered sideways and blocked the way, the woods rang with vulgar rage. French tanks, the Saint Chamonds, rattled along the roads, chewing up the last paving, pushing men and animals into roadside mud.

Big Red One had the dismal chore of relieving a French division during the night of July 17–18, a movement done in pitch black, dripping night. Clots of men argued, fumed, struggled in all directions, but gradually Summerall's troops reached the lines. He and his staff had been briefed by Mangin Wednesday afternoon, had snatched looks at the hard ground ahead, and knew something of the task facing the left flanking division of the corps. Their men only guessed as they slimed forward in the terrible dark. Many of them were hungry—had been for twenty-four hours—their cigarettes were wet and smoldering, their clothes sticking to them with a special paste of mud.

Southward, beyond the Moroccans, Harbord's men fought mystery, mire, and mayhem in a task he thought frankly "superhuman." But the divisional honor, national honor, was at stake, and everybody did more than possible. By 3:00 A.M. all guesses were that the 5th Marines and 9th Infantry would make it in time; by 4:00 A.M. it was almost certain they would arrive with five minutes to spare—H hour was at 4:35!

They came, all of them, hungry, infinitely weary, and learned the sudden rolling barrage would go almost instantly; they ran, then, urged forward to keep pace with the barrage.

At 4:35, Mangin's 2,000 guns fired, shells scourged German positions as 500 tanks and seven army corps surged forward.

Surprised utterly, confused in relatively light works, German survivors fought where they could, retreated, surrendered to wildly exultant enemies who charged with a forgotten élan.

Alerted by signal rockets, by the awful din of shelling, German batteries picked up resistance, machine gunners fought for pockets, and casualties mounted from the start of the drive.

First objective for the XX Corps, a road 2 kilometers ahead, came under fearful shelling and by 5:30 had been crossed by the Americans and Moroccans.

Tough for attackers, the ground became increasingly difficult—hills, ravines, plateaus, every cranny hid machine guns. Training would tell the tale here, daily infantry practice in bayonetting, bombing, rushing, flushing stubborn fighters from warrens and ditches. While the artillery ranged its stately pace of 100 meters every two minutes, Doughboys and *poilus* fought an infantryman's war—hand-to-hand, mean, decisive combats with veterans of the art. Pershing had stuck to open-warfare training—out in the open his men would know how to fight! And his men put their backs in it, their bayonets, their hides. Initiative, the Old Man preached, press on! Spotty fighting stopped parts of the attacking line through the morning, but slowly now the drive continued. German resistance increased; von Boehn did not panic, fed his reserves carefully, used his massed guns well. French tanks did yeoman duty in the early hours, but one by one were smashed.

Where was the attack going? The main thrust would cut off the salient; Mangin's men must aim for the broad plain in the middle of German ground, then swing up toward Soissons, wrest that communications center from the Boche, bag a whole army in a gigantic sack. On through the morning, lighter now, light enough for gunners to see through the dank wheatfields and chop away at advancing lines, on through the tough ground the Americans struggled. Minor tactics became vital as companies and platoons changed front, fought front and rear, aligned and charged, melted away against leaden scythes, and gained another gulch, another crag. By ten o'clock the heights above the Crise Valley were in the Yank hands, and Doughboys fought in the grim Missy-aux-Bois ravine. Southward the Moroccans and the 2nd Division kept pace with the slowing advance. Consolidation of positions took more steam out of the attack, and the Germans thought of a counterthrust.

Little went right for the Germans that day. In the morning Ludendorff held a conference at Mons with Crown Prince Rupprecht, and commanders and chiefs of staff of the armies intended for the last great Flanders offensive—"Hagen." While they talked of victory word came of defeat, of the smashed face of the Marne Salient. Ludendorff sent two divisions; more bad news; the conference ended abruptly, and Ludendorff headed east. The Germans could not launch a counterattack. Mangin, fiercely urging his weary men forward, resumed his attack in the afternoon and put the German divisions south of the Marne in jeopardy. They were ordered back across the river so rich in German blood. Von Boehn planned a withdrawal in stages, and Ludendorff cancelled all further thrusts around Reims while he halted artillery going northward for "Hagen."

Aiming for the Château-Thierry–Soissons highway, Harbord's men fought grimly throughout the hot afternoon. The whole corps front sagged a little now toward the southeast as the advance conformed to ground and enemy resistance. Heavy fighting around the village of Vauxcastille bent Harbord's right flank back, skewed his thrust. But his center units pushed on into the Vierzy ravine, and marines on the left were fighting with their left flank exposed since they had out-run the Moroccans. Orders of the afternoon to push forward Harbord delivered and moved his headquarters closer to the fighting. Late in the day, heavy resistance in Vierzy forced a concentration and a fierce attack against nests in limestone caves. Vierzy fell about 8:00 P.M., and the 2nd Division pushed almost two kilometers beyond the village. When fighting sputtered out in the night, the 2nd had advanced more than five miles, the 1st Division nearly four. The Moroccans trailed slightly, and units were well mixed.

Night positions were established, with the 2nd Division stuck ahead, flanks in the air.

Losses were frightful, especially among officers.

Mangin renewed the attack on the nineteenth against hard resistance. Von Boehn's reserves of men and guns were put in heavily—he had everything to save. Harbord's men got a late start due to slow orders from corps, but moved ahead firmly. Moving his reserves up—the 6th Marines, First Batallion, 2nd Engineers, and the 4th Machine Gun Battallion—Harbord drove toward the highway. Hard yards were bought with great valor against infantry, artillery, machine guns, and active enemy planes—including von Richthofen's *staffel*. The division took Tigny, reached the road, lost it and fell back to the Tigny–La Raperie line with guns commanding the highway.

Big Red One had trouble early. Its left contact, the French 153rd Division, lagged and held back Summerall's flank so that his advance oozed forward on the right and stretched his line. Pushing out from Missy-aux-Bois, the Doughboys ran into incredible storms of artillery and machine-gun fire that quickly swept away their last supporting tanks, withered the first lines under solid sheets of lead, and drove survivors forward in a frenzy against the machine guns. Von Boehn fought hard to hold Berzy-le-Sec and the high ground near the

Château-Thierry–Soissons road. Inevitably Summerall's left formations sagged as French support stalled. Ravine fighting and stupendous enemy fire halted the attack fairly soon on the left. The French assaulted Berzy-le-Sec and failed.

On the right going proved easier. And as the morning dragged, a gap opened between wings of the attack. The gap had to be closed, and a new attack ordered for late afternoon. Mid-day waned while troops and guns deployed for the effort. Stubborn, mean fighting raged then, and wedges of ground were taken until, at last, the Ploissy ravine fell and the gap closed. Losses were staggering.

That night, the nineteenth, Harbord secured the relief of his tired, hungry, thirsty men—minus 5,000—but Summerall's weary veterans plugged on against Berzy-le-Sec in an endless sear of battle. All through the twentieth men struggled in bad ground; on the twenty-first, with artillery help and with bald bravery, Big Red One wrenched the shattered hulk of a village from the enemy, surged across the Château-Thierry–Soissons highway, and put von Boehn's big communications center under fire. Losses came to 7,200 killed, wounded, and missing.

Von Boehn fought urgently to snake his endless columns of men and supplies and guns from the collapsing salient. Simultaneous attacks now haunted him from west, east, and south as Pétain's giant nutcracker began to smash the Marne bulge flat. Heavy resistance on the eastern flank prevented disaster for the Germans; skillful retreats saved the southern flank from annihilation. Slowly the bulge sagged like a dying observation balloon. Mopping-up operations would consume time, but the great threat to Paris faded.

American divisions joined in attacks ringing the salient, and all distinguished themselves with gallantry and dash. But it was the spearhead of Mangin's thrust, the XX Corps, that broke the bubble of Ludendorff's hopes—the U.S. 1st and 2nd Divisions and the redoubtable Moroccans put a final stop to German offensives. On July 18, 1918, the tide truly turned.

Congratulations pelted the Americans. Pershing basked in popularity outrageous and affection astounding. His men in the drive won plaudits from fighters. Charles Mangin of few words and much meanness commended them in orders, and among many nice and correct praises he said: "You rushed into the fight as to a fete. . . . I am proud to have commanded you during such days and to have fought with you for the deliverance of the world." Pretty heady words, those, from an expert.

Some, though, were even headier. On July 20 Pershing, unable to stay longer at Chaumont and study his great war map while the pins advanced, took to his car and rode forward. First to Dickman he went and heard the proud story of the Rock of the Marne; then he toiled through clogs and bog to the 28th Division, learned of some companies that got mixed with the French, were cut off and fought out, and commented that they gave "another striking illustration of the danger of having our small units serve in Allied divisions." At I Corps he found that command making "satisfactory progress," then headed for his main objective—Bullard's boys. Villers-Cotterêts still spawned men, animals, and traffic jams. Amid the maze he found Mangin, walking. They talked momentarily, and the proud French general spoke glowingly of the AEF—and Pershing's smile lit the dark tunnel of the forest. Summerall he missed, heard the 1st's exploits from the inimitable Campbell King, the chief of staff whose pouter-pigeon stuffiness irked the commander-in-chief, then talked with Bullard further on, who was "elated" at the work done by the men he had wanted to command. Then to friend Harbord, always sporting his *poilu* tin hat, and Pershing listened as the new major general burbled the boundless virtues of the 2nd Division—doubtless editing comments on the mix-ups on July 18's eve. Pershing shared his enthusiasm and burbled a bit himself. "Even though the 1st and 2nd Divisions should never fire another shot," the words were flat and toneless in that Missouri way of emphasis, "they had made themselves and their commanders immortal." It was the ultimate accolade.

Pershing left quickly. He had been summoned by Pétain, and the conference offered opportunity to strike for a separate front in the glow of Doughboy valor.[100]

---

[100] The account in the text of the Soissons battle and subsequent operations is drawn from the following: JJP, *Experiences*, 2:156–167; Frederick Palmer, *John J. Pershing, General of the Armies: A Biography*, pp. 244–49; Essame, *Battle for Europe*, pp. 86–92; Harbord, *Diary*, pp. 316–31, and *American Army*, pp. 324–38; *First Div.*, pp. 103–42; Stallings, *AEF*, pp. 141–51; "Historical Sketch of the First Division, American E.F.," AEF, GHQ, G-3 Reports, 1st Div., Folder 12, RG 120, National Archives; "Second Division Battle Northwest of Château-Thierry in June–July, 1918. Summary," by Maj. Gen. John A. Lejeune, USMC, Dec. 31, 1918, in AEF, GHQ, G-3 Reports, 2nd Div., RG 120, National Archives; "The Operations Southwest of Soissons, July 18th to 20th, 1918," by Maj. R. S. Keyser, USMC, in AEF, GHQ, G-2-A, General Correspondence of the Information Div., Folder 23.2, RG 120, National Archives; Campbell King, Chfstf, 1st Div., "Report on Operations of First Division south of Soissons, July 18–24, 1918, incl.," in 1st Div. Historical Files, 33.6, Special Reports of Operations, RG 120, National Archives. The Army War College study, approved by JJP, is *The Aisne and Montdidier-Noyon Operations, with Special Attention to the Participation of American Divisions*, and is a technically excellent military analysis, replete with splendid maps.

☆ 22 ☆

Pershing's Army

A few people knew his secret heart. Those fortunates knew him closely, watched him daily at Chaumont or recalled him of old. And they read the stories ranging stateside newspapers of this cold efficiency, his spit and polish fetish, his granite-hard manner, with toleration. A few of them—Harbord, for instance, McAndrew, Quekemeyer, Boyd, Little Collins, Georgie Patton—would snicker at some of the fulsome outrage in accounts of persistently "civilian" newsmen, would crow loudly at Newton Baker's musing that he could not understand "how any man who had such great vision as Pershing . . . thought so much about buttons."[1] Buttons were part of the constant problem of building an army. Regulars knew the need for discipline as a remedy for ennui; citizen soldiers flocked to the armies enthusiastic but unbent to regulations, and they would go "slack" in the traces of routine. Slackness led to depression, then despair. Soldiers angered about buttons, fussed about saluting, had less time to fear failure. So Pershing lectured frightened second lieutenants on the proper salutes, seared men's souls with eyes that swept everything wrong, especially dull buttons. And he kept himself an example of the standards he demanded of everyone else. Charlie Dawes, of the privileged inner circle, once searched zealously for a photograph somewhere in England reputedly showing friend John with a breast pocket unbuttoned—it would be invaluable for "defensive personal purposes."[2]

Pershing's personal appearance had a constant effect on headquarters folk; all of them did their smartest, looked their best.[3] In the field his shiny leather, his boots oddly shunned by France's herculean *boue*,

[1] Frederick Palmer, *John J. Pershing, General of the Armies: A Biography,* p. 148.

[2] Charles Dawes, *A Journal of the Great War,* 1:99.

[3] Grady Barrett, "Pershing at Close Range," pp. 3–4 (typescript in author's possession).

his immaculate uniform reflected to every Doughboy the expectations of West Point. His coming, if known ahead, caused flurries of sprucing. There were things the Old Man might tolerate—beards in the backwash of battle, perhaps—but sloven marked weakness.

Weakness Pershing deplored and fought constantly. Not because he misunderstood human nature, but simply because America's soldiers were behind in preparation and must rise above themselves to survive. Commanders could never be weak. After each engagement he would study the records of battalion, regimental, division, corps leaders for signs of indiscipline. Lapses might be remedied by a summons to Chaumont, by a talk that got down to fundamentals about men and leadership and common sense. Sufferers from those "reminder" sessions were instantly recognized for whiteness around the eyes, taut jaws, and an expression of terror. But failures that took lives were not excused. Men who did not measure up were relieved quickly and with what many thought approached unseemly zest. Yet those close to him knew the private anguish that apparent ruthlessness often brought, the wrestling with evidence, with conscience that preceded decisions that seemed too quick and hard. To Harbord, then McAndrew, trusted chiefs of staff, sometimes to old friends who listened well, Pershing often pondered aloud: "What am I going to do with him? He is not growing up to his job, but where is a better man? Do you know one?" Sometimes, watching a visitor leaving, he would wonder if his concern was correct. "What is the matter with [him]?" he would query Quekemeyer, Boyd, even Fred Palmer when he breezed in from touring newsmen around the war. Once the answer came: "He not only does not see the forest for the trees, but he is digging himself a hole under the roots of one tree." A twinkle in those blue eyes, and the quip shot back. "Why, I have considered him one of my broad-minded ones. Haven't you met any of my narrow-minded ones?"

If help could save a leader, Jack gave it. To one, hard working, devoted, but rigid, Pershing said "Read Tolstoy's *War and Peace*. It might develop your imagination."[4] Sometimes help did no good, and a saddened chief would comment, "I have known him a long time. I am very fond of him, but he has not yet gone as far as Caesar's Commentaries in studying the history of war since he forgot the history he learned at West Point." Deficiencies in old friends, especially West Pointers, irked a first captain. He fumed about relieving those types instantly, and these rages sometimes stoked the stories of intolerance.

[4] Palmer, *John J. Pershing*, p. 218.

Wise hands close by would wait for cooled ire, for an order sending the offender to easier duty. "There goes J.J.P. again in his care not to hurt the feelings of the 'lame duck' "—that comment, common among the staff, would have astounded most reporters and most Doughboys, who quaked at the thought of those cold, probing eyes. Men who worked and broke under war's pressure Pershing never condemned. "He has given all he had to give but has done noble service. But now he must have time to recover. He is very proud. Manage it if you can, so that he will not be hurt too much."[5]

Generals sometimes found themselves relieved to different challenges. Francis J. Kernan, for instance, caught in the threat of losing control of the SOS, went to Berne as American representative to a conference on war prisoners.[6] Soothed, if disappointed, Kernan remained a friend. Omar Bundy, too, suffered removal. His 2nd Division won a splendid reputation, but bits of evidence came of the general's joy in red tape. One inspector suggested the division did well in spite of Bundy, that the general gave little direction to combat and would probably "be better as a corps commander. . . . He is conscientious, loyal and full of fight. . . . " And the inspector admitted Bundy's abilities as a disciplinarian and administrator.[7] Pershing's doubts of Bundy were confirmed, as well as his points of admiration. There were valuable services that willing soldier could perform. He took command of the shadow VI Corps headquarters and trained a staff.[8] And he, too, remained a friend.

Friends were few for Pershing in France, acquaintances many, and admirers legion. His own admiration for the Doughboys expanded with every battle. He saw them close up on those quick visits of congratulation after Cantigny, Belleau, Château-Thierry, and Soissons, and he decorated new heroes with special pleasure. The Distinguished Service Cross, now authorized for bravery in action, became his talisman of courage, and he gave it solemnly, with a fighter's admiration. For the wounded, the men who gave their blood for their country, there was a special corner in Jack's heart. Resolutely he visited hospitals behind the battle line, marched through them with a tough precision that

[5] *Ibid.*, pp. 218–19.
[6] James G. Harbord, *The American Army in France, 1917–1919*, pp. 352–53.
[7] Memorandum of Maj. Gen. A. W. Brewster, I.G., July 12, 1918; *id.*, letter, July 15, 1918, in Pershing Papers, 1916–24, 1931–39, Index and Case files relating to Reclassification and Reassignment of Officers, Box 8, RG 316, National Archives; JJP, "Memorandum for the Chief of Staff" ("Confidential"), July 9, 1918, in AEF, GHQ, Office of the Chief of Staff Letterbook, RG 120, National Archives.
[8] JJP, *Experiences*, 2:239; Harbord, *American Army*, p. 422.

often infuriated unmilitary doctors; for the wounded, though, the discipline bent. Where is home? In what action were you wounded? A tough fight there; well done. Always the cheerful word, the commander's optimism, the manner that spares pity. Behind the hard face the eyes wilted, the tears held back by iron will. Charlie Dawes, who sometimes joined on those hospital calls, felt for "dear old John," whose heart was "breaking with sympathy" for those hopeful men whose respect he prized.

A commander could not melt now when his army grew into maturity and its men fought valiantly and died game. In those days after Soissons, with the hospitals filling and the new men coming, Jack hardened himself against distractions. First he must win for those men their proper place in war, and then he must send them against the German guns.

He tackled Pétain eagerly on Sunday, July 21, 1918. The meeting began well, with the French leader warm in admiration for American soldiers. On Belgium's national holiday, it would be good if Allies could form a decisive plan. Pétain and Pershing had both sent the *entente cordiale* messages of the occasion, and an atmosphere of easy charity soothed discussions. "It looked as though," Pershing thought as he judged his colleague, Pétain might "welcome the formation of an American army." Quickly the American moved to his point—"positive steps" ought to be taken toward putting an American army in its own sector. Pershing had a preference that Pétain had accepted long ago: the area east of Verdun looking toward the important rail line feeding the southern German armies down to the Swiss border. But anywhere convenient would suit. Since several divisions clustered now in the Château-Thierry area, that might be the spot. Much had to be done in preparing rear-area facilities, so decisions must come swiftly. Pétain agreed easily, seemed glad to hear that Pershing would command personally the new army when it formed. There were problems about army support troops, of course, since American shipments had run heavily to footsoldiers and machine gunners. For that reason it seemed good to put the American army under Pétain's general supervision, which would make easier logistical and staff support. Pétain accepted gracefully, nodded when Pershing reserved "entire independence regarding plans and the conduct of operations."

Together the generals rode to Foch's headquarters for his approval. Foch could be irritatingly vague. Sometimes the supreme commander's eyes drifted to some lost horizon of his own as he thought of vagrant glories, and in those moods he brushed business aside as trivial. Reminded of previous agreement at Bombon on July 10, Foch said he would think about the proposal. Disappointed but undaunted, Pershing went to Paris for conferences with Dawes and other supply people. His plans for forming his force continued. And next day, Col. Bentley Mott, the adroit American liaison officer with Foch, brought the supreme commander's agreement. The Toul sector would be American.[9]

Pershing had put part of an army staff together to do preliminary organization. Hugh Drum, growing constantly in military competence, Pershing picked as chief of staff, and since July 4 Drum had labored to build an organization and sketch outlines of an army. On July 24 Pershing issued orders creating the First Army, AEF. It would become operational on August 10. Early confusion clouded its first locale. In the brief consideration of the Château-Thierry sector, Pershing thought of putting headquarters at La Ferté-sous-Jouarre, and there Drum hastened to begin. And there came the assigned heads of staff sections, elements of available army troops, a large agglomeration of officers and men. Pershing, with pride close tethered, issued General Orders No. 1 on July 31, assuming command of his army.[10]

It was the biggest day of his war. All the preparation, the troubles behind the lines, the anguished negotiations with the Allies, the haggling, the waiting had, after all, been worthwhile. All the petty quarreling, the snipes against formation of the army faded now in the promise of achievement. As commander-in-chief of the American Expeditionary Forces, Pershing really stood above army command, might well have given it to Liggett or perhaps Bullard, to someone with line experience. But the possibility never really existed, and reasons were more personal than official. Haig and Pétain, even Foch, were fighting generals, had led units against the Germans. No matter their courtesy, some faint whiffs of doubt oozed into conversations with Pershing. And well he knew the early slurs about the "Indian fighter" who headed the Americans. That kind of thing he ignored in the rush of the overwhelming job he faced, but an old soldier listened and longed to be an equal. His men had proved their superiority in this fourth year of war —their chief could do no less. "It accorded with my own desire from the purely military point of view." Rationalizations were easy. "In the first appearance of an American army beside the Allied armies, it was clearly my place to take personal command, which I was now in posi-

[9] JJP, *Experiences*, 2:167–69.

[10] JJP and Hunter Liggett, *Report of the First Army, American Expeditionary Forces: Organization and Operations*, p. 4 (hereinafter cited as *First Army*).

tion to do. . . . "[11] And who else knew enough about the general American situation to do the daily business of army housekeeping?

That last reason was the best. Properly, of course, the commander-in-chief should not take responsibility for field success or failure, should concentrate on strategy, logistics, on getting men to the ranks. But no other American general had the perspective needed for coalition command. The point to be proved was that no one else could fight his men better. Once the army took its place and fought its ways to independence, he could step back and manage à la Haig and Pétain in the full knowledge of ability. Something had to be proved to John Pershing before he could be really comfortable behind his desk.

In a happy mood of personal participation, Pershing with Boyd and Captain de Marenches, joined Haig, Pétain, and their chiefs of staff at a conference with Foch at Bombon on July 24, 1918. An uncommon cordiality brought smiles around the table as Foch opened with a glowing recitation of the current situation. He wanted the sense of the gathering; everyone thought the initiative should be pressed by vigorous Allied attacks. Equality of numbers lent confidence to any offensives, and Foch admitted that American legions brought battle parity and gave superiority to reserves. The Allies boasted superiority now, too, in planes and tanks, even artillery, while Germany faced a mounting crisis in filling divisions. "The moment has come to abandon the general defensive," Foch proclaimed, "and to pass to the offensive." Everybody nodded agreement; Haig spoke eagerly of opportunities on his front. Foch then talked of specific objectives. Two salients now stuck into the Allied front, the huge bulge toward Amiens and the finger pointing from Saint Mihiel. Both threatened important Allied communications. These communications, once freed, would make possible vast operations against Germany in 1919. Haig readily accepted the task of pushing against the Amiens pocket; Pershing reported his preparations to move in the Saint Mihiel area. Pétain would be able, he thought, to continue pressure in the Chemin des Dames.

Carefully Pershing reported his deficiencies in artillery and recalled French promises of help. America would do its best to increase gun production; meanwhile, French artillery must be provided. Foch, true to form, waived details to lesser mortals and fixed on strategy. With the salients gone, it might be possible to launch decisive drives aimed at bagging whole segments of the German army.

No real decisions on operations were reached, but Pershing and

[11] JJP, *Experiences*, 2:168.

the others left satisfied. Coordination of programs Foch did provide, and that lent an exciting spirit of cohesion. He kept his mind firmly on the Western Front and helped others fight off siphons of their armies. Pershing had to send one infantry regiment to Russia but resisted demands for divisions in Italy.[12]

With a new army about to take the field, Pershing paid special attention to logistics. He persuaded a reluctant but ever subordinate Jim Harbord to accept command of the SOS at the end of July.[13] To prove his own concern for the SOS, Jack took Harbord on a swing through all base areas, watched happily as energy and system sprang from each visit. Harbord would do the job.

And as August—the high summer of war—arrived, Pershing basked in achievement. Baker cabled him "hearty and grateful congratulations," adding that "the whole country is thrilled with pride in our soldiers. . . . They are worthy of their country and the cause." Praise came from Japan and special recognition from the French. Lavish always in their honors to troops, the French had wanted for some time to decorate Pershing and his staff. Old American traditions frowned on foreign medals, but at last a policy change permitted inter-Allied back patting. Quickly came word that Pershing would be given the Grand Cross of the Legion of Honor by the president of France.

There must be a proper ceremony, naturally, which meant that Pershing would leave for Chaumont behind a full alert of the staff. In Paris on August 5, he looked for likely hands to take with him to the embarrassing moment. It happened that George Quekemeyer returned that evening with the U.S. minister to Sweden in tow—he had shown the distinguished guest through the British areas. Turn him over to someone else; get ready to leave for Chaumont in two hours. That took much adroit shifting, but Quekemeyer appeared in time at the railroad station and boarded the general's train. "General Pershing ordinarily travels around in an automobile," Quek mused, "but at other times by train. He has a special train all made up consisting of two sleeping cars, a diner and a baggage car so that a trip by rail can be arranged very quickly. We travelled out by train—there were about ten officers in the General's party besides a couple of clerks and some orderlies."

---

[12] *Ibid.*, pp. 171–74. For details of the meeting, see "Memorandum read at the meeting of the Commanders-in-Chief of the Allied Armies, July 24, 1918," in "Important Conferences, Memoranda, Etc. Affecting Employment of the A.E.F.," AEF, GHQ, G-3, Folder 655, Box 3110, RG 120, National Archives.

[13] See James G. Harbord, *Leaves From a War Diary*, pp. 339–40; JJP, *Experiences*, 2:179–80, 190–91.

Well rested, Pershing and a small escort went next morning to the depot and met the president's train. Poincaré, a new visitor to HAEF, must be properly shown the AEF's domain.

Raymond Poincaré had eager eyes. Quick and pleasant, he smiled his appreciation of the greeting and joined Pershing for the ride to headquarters. About 9:00 A.M. he met graciously the senior staff in the imposing offices of the AEF, then went outside to the barracks parade. An overcast sky threatened rain, but French and American troops marched in review; a spectacularly good U.S. Army band—Pershing and Boyd had cultivated it carefully—played national airs, and Pershing marched front and center. The president, short and squat, looked up into the tall Missourian's face and spoke earnestly, in "perfect English":

I am very glad to present to you to-day, before your gallant staff and your brave soldiers, the insignia of the high distinction bestowed upon you by the French Government.

It is an especial pleasure to take this opportunity of congratulating you and your splendid army for the great successes already attained and for the precious services you render to right and freedom . . . you arrived on the battlefield at the decisive hour. . . .[14]

Then the president pinned on the medal. Pershing spoke of the meaning behind the honor: "I value this decoration as a mark of recognition by France of the services of the American Army and of friendship for the American people."[15]

And then the onlookers saw what they came to see—the little Frenchman with the high-foreheaded, intelligent face muffled by a moustache and goatee, stood on tiptoe, reached up to grasp Pershing's shoulders, and there was an awkward moment when he could not reach his mark. Then Pershing bent self-consciously down and the president kissed him on both cheeks. Pershing blushed, hated the ripple of laughter that echoed in the courtyard, and hoped Poincaré shared discomfiture. But if the president heard the merriment, or felt uncomfortable, he gave no sign. Effusive and interested, he made a short tour of facilities and departed. He left behind much good feeling, and Pershing proved an especially amiable host at a luncheon for Food Administrator Herbert Hoover. Everything went well now for

---

[14] There are at least two versions of this address in print: JJP, *Experiences*, 2:213, and Harbord, *American Army*, pp. 406–7. The last phrase is included in Harbord's account but omitted from Pershing's.

[15] JJP, *Experiences*, 2:213.

the AEF; Pershing's guests could see that, in his humor, his robust good health, his high praise of American troops.[16]

While Pershing worked to get a firm grip on his new army and a firm commitment out of Foch about places and troops and aims, Haig launched his drive in the Montdidier-Albert sector. The U.S. 33rd Division was training behind Haig's lines, and one of its regiments got swept up in the attack, did splendidly, and earned a visit from the commander-in-chief. That visit coincided with one by George V to Haig's front. On August 12, the king asked Pershing and Bliss, who was also on hand, to his room. The dapper, short sovereign Pershing recalled warmly from their meetings in June, 1917. There was talk of how the war had gone, there was much praise for America's part. Americans, said the king, were needed in British lines—they were great morale boosters. He thought comradeship in battle would cement the friendship of the English-speaking peoples. Pershing thanked for the good words, but promised nothing. The king pressed a little; those divisions were needed! Then, informally, but with that special grace of his, he handed Pershing the Grand Cross of the Order of the Bath. Bliss, not forgotten, received the Order of Saint Michael and Saint George. Then the distinguished looking monarch with the trimmed moustache and goatee walked outside to decorate men of the 33rd—kind and generous in his comments as he pinned the medals on, George V made many Americans proud that day. He bothered John Pershing, who realized the pressure must come from Haig—and he was on the point of taking his men away from his British colleague![17]

Haig's gracious hospitality at lunch added to Pershing's discomfort. Well he knew the field marshal wanted to keep the American divisions, and all through the meal and afterward Pershing talked of everything but taking back his men. Finally, courage up, he talked of the forming army and the need for strength, "and said that I should be compelled to withdraw from his front at least three of the five American divisions still there in training." The Americans, Haig thought, had come for training and for service with the British and

[16] For deatils of the trip from Paris and for some details of the presentation, see George Quekemeyer to his mother, Aug. 10, 1918, Quekemeyer Papers (copy in author's possession). See also Dawes, *Journal*, 1:153, for JJP's general condition: "I never saw General Pershing looking or feeling better. He is sleeping well. He is tremendously active. He will soon strike with his field army. I know he will succeed. He is not letting anything get on his mind to absorb it from the all-important question of how to get a military victory." See also Official American Communique, Aug. 8, 1918, No. 86, in HAEF Diary.

[17] JJP, *Experiences*, 2:215–16.

lamented, strongly, that just as they were getting ready, they were to leave. Pershing, ever straightforward, reminded Haig of their agreement—the troops were always under American orders. And they would fight the common enemy on another front. A shade irked, Haig confessed disappointment at losing good men when the offensive began. But fiinally, acknowledging the agreement and understanding the reasons, Haig turned comradely. "Pershing, of course you shall have them, there can never be any difference between us." As he left BEF Headquarters, Pershing guessed how relieved Foch would be at not having to do the dirty deed.[18]

A Tuesday morning talk with Clemenceau in Paris—the Tiger, in an expansive humor, confessed he had been wrong about a separate American army and Pershing right—showed that Haig's generosity did not carry across the channel. Lloyd George still chafed for American units; a long cable to Clemenceau raised old issues of amalgamation. But the French were happy and no longer abetted the Lion.[19] Lloyd George also stirred up trouble at home. A querulous question from the War Department about why the divisions were removed required attention—and Pershing went into detail so that Baker, about to make another European visit, would know the facts before tackling the British.[20] But Haig could scarcely complain; his August 8 attack smashed the German front and brought stark realization of mortality to the enemy's high command.

Despite those old problems, Pershing still basked in achievement, in public announcement of the First Army's creation.[21] Foch accepted the idea of the Saint Mihiel region and agreed to a shift of First Army Headquarters to Neufchâteau. There were good reasons for picking that familiar town. Central to the southeastern battle zone, it served

---

[18] *Ibid.*, pp. 216–17.
[19] *Ibid.*, pp. 218–19. See also Lloyd Griscom to JJP, Aug. 22, 1918 (cable LR 2422, Secret), and JJP to Griscom, Aug. 24, 1918 (telegram), both in Box 85, PP.
[20] JJP to AGWAR for SECWAR, Aug. 15, 1918 (cable, Secret), Box 19, PP. Gen. Sir Henry Wilson, the CIGS, resented JJP's withdrawal of troops and complained to Haig (Wilson to "My General," Aug. 28, 1918, Haig Papers). Haig, replying to a note from JJP congratulating him on receiving the Medaille Militaire and thanking him for "cordial cooperation" in sending back the divisions (JJP to Haig, Aug. 20, 1918, Haig Papers), seeped some bad temper: "I was glad to be able to meet your wishes at once, and I trust that events may justify your decision to withdraw the American troops from the British battle front at the present moment, for, I make no doubt but that the arrival in this battle of a few strong & vigorous American Divisions, when the enemy's units are thoroughly worn out, would lead to the most decisive results" (Haig to JJP, Aug. 27, 1918, Haig Papers).
[21] JJP, *Experiences*, 2:214.

as a communications hub, and long American presence there disguised to some extent the sudden appearance of an army headquarters. Pershing posted the I, IV, and V Corps to duty with his new army and accepted gladly the offer of the French II Colonial Corps, which had been holding the tip of the Saint Mihiel Salient. By divisions he counted the U.S. 1st, 2nd, 3rd, 4th, 5th, 26th, 33rd, 35th, 42nd, 78th, 80th, 82nd, 89th, 90th, and 91st, with the French 2nd Dismounted Cavalry, 26th and 39th Infantry. Drum put his numerous henchmen at headquarters to the task of preparing a battle plan against the Germans in the salient. The I Corps staff had experience and could help considerably; the French staffs were war wise, but the newer American corps staffs would be planning their first operation. And the planning proved complex. French troops coming into the area as support and logistical units had to cross American communications, and the Yank divisions coming from western sectors would intrude into a zone of few roads and myriad waterways. Getting men, munitions, food, animals, forage, guns, medical supplies, hospitals, trains, dumps, billets arranged in proper places was complicated by the need to prepare the army zone with utilities, field communication facilities, airdromes, railheads, the skein of shops and depots that dotted the rear of every fighting army on the Western Front.

Among early chores loomed decisions on use of gas, tanks, huge U.S. naval guns mounted on railroad carriages; once decisions were made, finding the equipment would be a tough task made worse by traffic problems in the army zone. Drum's staff worked calmly at great charts of roads and marching schedules.

On Thursday, August 29, Pershing motored to Ligny-en-Barrois, an ancient town on the main Paris-Nancy road. Here he put his advance headquarters. Closeness to Saint Mihiel, which lay northeast about twenty miles, seemed about the only virtue this warren of narrow streets and tight houses offered—save a reputation as the final resting place of the Marshal of Luxembourg who defeated William III at Landen in 1692. But fast work by communications troops hooked the town into command points around the salient, and Pershing, as usual, felt he could control his battle better closer to the scene.

Pershing's auto, with its four-star pennant flapping, pulled into Ligny in the morning, and he soon heard that the French general who was being relieved wanted to make formal transfer of command. Usually quick words in passing sufficed in this less formal time, but Pershing readily assented—after all, this was his first assumption of a battle command in the war.

To headquarters came the French general and his chief of staff, full pantalooned in red, bloused in blue, stiff, military men with a sense of the fitness of things. The chief of staff almost staggered under two huge volumes, one the offensive plan, the other the defensive plan for the Saint Mihiel Salient. Pershing accepted the books courteously but mused on the differences in style: "My orders had been already prepared, the one for the attack comprising six pages and the one for the defense eight pages."[22] And that ceremonial moment etched clearly for Jack the gulf separating American and French methods. Trench warfare evolved a whole intricate technology and demanded a kind of mathematical rhythm; Americans relied on initiative, quickness, and attack.

"Take every advantage of cover."

No American army had ever planned an operation as colossal as the reduction of the Saint Mihiel Salient. Not even the great gathering of the Union armies against the Confederates in 1864 compared with the sprawling mass of men,, the mountainous details of movement that plagued Headquarters, First Army, in September, 1918. Once decided on the firm course of his army, Pershing issued orders swift and professional. "The Commander-in-Chief directs that the 1st Army undertake the reduction of the St. Mihiel Salient. The minimum result to be attained by this operation is the reopening of the Paris-Nancy Railroad in the vicinity of Commercy." He hoped for much larger results, for a drive into the Briey iron region, a breach of the enemy communications, perhaps a general attack into Germany.[23] Hugh Drum's corps produced, speedily, a Statement of Plan for the attack that projected twin assaults on the south and west faces to eliminate the salient in two days.[24]

Pershing approved the general scheme, including the collection nearly half a million American troops to work with 110,000 French. He had set himself the toughest task in the AEF. For the days of First Army's initiation, he would wear two hats, would divide himself

[22] *Ibid.*, p. 238.
[23] J. W. McAndrew to Hugh Drum, Aug. 16, 1918, in AEF, GHQ, G-3, Folder 1078, First Army, Letters & Instructions for St. Mihiel Operation, RG 120, National Archives.
[24] Hugh Drum, "Reduction of the St. Mihiel Salient," n.d. (ca. Aug. 20, 1918), in First Army Historical File, 32.8, Combat Plans, St. Mihiel Operation, RG 120, National Archives. Attached is the full "Plan of Engagement for Reduction of the St. Mihiel Salient. (Preliminary)."

between Chaumont and Ligny, Paris, and multiple other places, would attempt the delicate art of command and supervision. Difficult in the best of worlds, his job mired in troop and staff inexperience. Mere survival in both jobs would mean success, but he intended to do both well.

Where were his corps? Happily communications already linked him with Liggett's I Corps at Saizerais, northeast of Toul, and with Dickman's IV Corps Headquarters at Toul. Other troops were plugged into Pershing's telephones on arrival.

Communications proved something of a problem—too many people talked too much about the coming attack. Rumors had it part of nightclub banter in Paris. Officers and men clustering around the salient talked with French civilians, with men of the French II Army. Finally intelligence-wise Frenchmen tipped Pershing to the leaks. Pétain himself wrote of the exposure and suggested widely scattered reconnaissance to fool the enemy about objectives. Americans were inexpert at everything and could never keep quiet about their doings.

Much embarrassed at unmilitary manners of his men, Pershing acknowledged the errors when replying to Pétain. "I keenly regret that indiscretions may have been committed, and I consider, with you, that we must attempt to deceive the enemy upon the actual directions of the attack."[25] Privately fuming, Pershing realized that leaks were probably to be expected. "The considerable circulation of troops in the St. Mihiel area," he realized, any self-respecting agent would recognize.[26] Long American activity near Neufchâteau did not disguise the unusual traffic.

Now Omar Bundy came to mind. Take a part of the VI Corps staff, Bundy was ordered, and scout the area of Mulhouse-Belfort. Detailed studies were required of Bundy's staff, estimates of enemy defenses, sites of advance, possible depots. A special liaison officer from GHQ would coordinate activities. The officer, Col. A. L. Conger, was the only one who knew the whole venture a deception. Bundy, thoroughly professional, did a sound job of briefing staff officers assigned from seven idle divisions; together they prepared a detailed operations program for Pershing. Additional planes dotted the Vosges skies, more guns ranged on German positions, the airwaves crackled with messages.

Deliberate carelessness left copies of the operations scheme handy for prying eyes; a carbon sheet used in making duplicates disappeared from a wastebasket in Conger's hotel room.

[25] Donald Smythe, "The Ruse at Belfort," *Army* 22 (June, 1972): 35.
[26] JJP, *Experiences*, 2:239.

Clumsy the whole affair might be—the French scoffed at the American charade—but the Germans could ill afford to neglect the southern end of their front. Traffic in the Woëvre area had increased, and an attack on Saint Mihiel seemed likely to the German high command, but a few divisions did move south. So the ruse had an effect on the campaign.[27] Rumors generated by French staff officers helped distract the enemy; so did the myriad speculations germinated at Headquarters, First Army.[28]

Pershing had his own distraction. It came in the form of Marshal Foch and his alter ego, General Weygand, who came to Ligny on Friday, August 30. Just having taken command of the Western Front from Port-sur-Seille to Watronville—more than fifty miles around the salient and its shoulders—Pershing greeted his guests excitedly. Plans were far advanced for smashing the 200-square-mile triangle that jutted thirteen miles into Allied lines. Behind its 18-mile base some unfinished works of the Hindenburg Line would be the last barrier before Metz and the main German railroad. The American attack should make a 25-mile advance to the Marieulles–Mars-la-Tour–Étain line that would push the enemy ten miles behind the base of the salient.

Foch came to speak of other things. German disorder in front of the British, weakness in the Aisne area, must be exploited, he said, and the British would push hard for Cambrai and Saint Quentin, the French for Mesnil. If these drives went well, new possibilities must be considered. A number of ideas were to be presented, Foch said, gesturing grandly, and surely Pershing would need time to think about them, but he wanted first impressions. Those would be all he could give on first notice, Pershing said equably. The real chance, according to the marshal, lay not in front of the Saint Mihiel Salient, but further west in the Argonne area. He suggested drastic limitations on Pershing's attack—hit the southern face only, pinch it quickly, then switch American units to the French II Army between the Meuse and the Argonne. Another American army could form between the French II and IV Armies across the Aire River. A great Franco-American drive would aim toward Mézières for a possible link with Haig's attack on Cambrai. If successful, a huge bag of Germans and wreckage of the main enemy communications in northern France would be the least reward.

Rewards for Americans would be scant indeed, a point Pershing

[27] Smythe, "Ruse at Belfort," pp. 37–38.
[28] See JJP, *Experiences*, 2:239–40; Laurence Stallings, *AEF*, pp. 207–8.

made by suggesting the whole thing would destroy what "we have been trying so long to form—that is, an American Army."

Reasonably Foch asked for Pershing's solution. Anything would be acceptable as long as the new operations were executed. There was, Foch thought, no way to keep the Americans together—sadly. Carefully Pershing thought, then wondered about pulling the Americans from St. Mihiel and realigning them with their right on the Meuse and extending west. Foch had thought of this, he said, but the shift after action "would be very difficult."

These conversations were always awkward. Captain de Marenches, gifted interpreter that he was, Carl Boyd, whose French was better than he allowed, tried always to go beyond words, to get into minds, tried for moods and hidden meanings. But the touch of souls missed in passing, usually, and conversations were oddly flat and formal. Tough moments like the present, when so much depended on two world leaders knowing each other's hearts, put strain uncommon on translators. Foch had a strange job. His to command by suasion, to bend iron wills to him; it was a task to challenge Tallyrand, and Foch relished his role. He would have been superb save for a mystic's happy certitude. When moved by his fateful whimsy, he brooked no disagreement, for his was the way of the right. Was he in that mood now? Did his stiff insistence on the Argonne-Meuse plan spring uncoached from his mind? If so, he was unswayable.

Pershing watched his eyes in those silent moments while de Marenches changed languages. Sometimes eyes belied translators, confessed a different meaning. Foch gazed firmly at the stubborn American who seemed so blind to reason. But something disturbed Foch; he wore this role uneasily, persisted as if compelled.

His strategic idea made a good deal of sense, considered soberly. A dual advance by Haig and the French and Americans might achieve great things. And Foch had full strategic authority over the Allies; if he insisted on a concentric attack—his favorite phrase—Pershing must agree. Foch pressed his luck.

Some compulsion pulled the Allies away from an American army. Now, when it existed, Foch's petulant insistence on breaking it around French armies touched an old Missouri fury. Why, asked Pershing firmly, could not the Americans replace the French II Army between the Meuse and the Argonne Forest? Foch's blasé comment that only good could come of Americans on one side of the II Army joining up with those on the other beyond the Argonne was tactically silly—a solid front had strength. "I do not want to appear difficult," Pershing

said courteously, but "the American people and the American government expect that the American army shall act as such and shall not be
dispersed here and there along the Western Front."

All shreds of politesse vanished. Foch, livid, spoke with icy sar-
casm: "Voulez-vous aller à la battaille?" ("Do you wish to go to the
battle?") The clear insult may have been a calculated risk—there
were those who thought Foch played Pershing's prejudices artfully.
But it was a horrid moment for de Marenches, who had to put the
challenge into English.

Calmly now, politely, the answer: "Most assuredly, but as an
American Army and in no other way."

"That means it will take a month," Foch sniffed. There was no
time.

"If you will assign me a sector I will take it at once," Pershing said
firmly, and added that if the marshal considered the situation carefully he would agree with the American view.

Where would the sector be? Foch wondered, and Pershing said,
quickly, "Wherever you say."

Artillery, auxiliary troops, were needed by the Americans, Foch
argued, and Pershing reminded him that the French had insisted on
bringing infantry and machine gunners. Foch himself had promised
to make up deficiencies—and now Pershing demanded the promises
be kept.

Uncomfortably Foch blustered. "It is now August 30th, and the
attack must begin on September 15th; it is a question of time." He
would listen to any proposition, but the attack must start on schedule.

They argued the same ground for a time, Foch continuing to
press for American units in the French II Army, Pershing looking for
ways to consolidate. Both men got madder as they talked. De Marenches and Boyd, knowing their man, waited for the boiling point. At
one last demand Pershing lost his temper.

"Marshal Foch, you have no authority as Allied Commander-in-
Chief to call upon me to yield up my command of the American Army
and have it scattered among the Allied forces where it will not be an
American army at all."

Eyebrows up in surprise, Foch fumed "I must insist upon the
arrangement," and rose brusquely from the table. Pershing, too, stood,
and answered coldly:

"Marshal Foch, you may insist all you please, but I decline absolutely to agree to your plan. While our army will fight wherever you
may decide, it will not fight except as an independent American

army." Too long had critics at home wondered where the army was; President Wilson's message to the embassies in Washington left no doubt about the AEF sticking together.

Foch rather lamely professed himself disposed to help form the American army, but he felt sure that Pershing, on reflection, would agree no other plan would work. Then, pale and exhausted, he swept up his maps and papers and walked to the door, turned, handed Pershing the written proposal, and asked for comments. Pershing agreed to reply quickly and formally.

As Foch left, Pershing thought of the meeting. Something had bothered the marshal all through the argument. Pershing got the impression that Foch approved the American army idea, but that someone pushed him to split it after the Saint Mihiel venture. Nothing would justify such a course. The meeting had been tough, angry, showed the touchiness of alliances. An American army fighting on its own front would do more to win the war than any other Allied weapon. Pershing would preserve it.

Next day a long, courteous rejection of Foch's plan was drafted, polished by Pershing, and sent. And, realizing that communications might well collapse with the French, Pershing sought out Pétain on his headquarters train at Nettancourt.

Together the two generals—they were now almost friends—discussed Foch's plan of limiting the Saint Mihiel action and shifting American units westward. A smaller Saint Mihiel attack would free several French and American divisions for Foch's planned Meuse-Argonne offensive, but Pershing insisted that dual attacks on the salient's faces were essential. He would use seven divisions in line, two in reserve. A smiling Pétain uncovered a map of the salient marked with his own attack ideas—he had the same number of divisions listed! Cordiality warmed the talk now, and Pétain sympathized with Pershing's predicament. Foch, he said, had no right to interfere in tactical arrangements by an army commander—his to order the strategy, theirs to carry it out according to circumstances. Pershing nodded emphatically.

As to Metz, Pétain thought the direction important to breaking down German resistance, but that no attack could succeed in that area until the Meuse-Argonne sector had been taken. Later, certainly, he would support a drive there.

Adroitly Pétain assessed his guest and the thinking of Foch as well and suggested turning over the front from the Moselle to the Argonne; he would leave General Hirschauer's French II Army in place under Pershing for such logistical and staff help as needed. In time an American Second Army could extend westward toward the Argonne, a Third up toward Reims. As long as Pétain understood American units would fight under their own commanders, the plan looked great. But Foch must be cajoled into acceptance.

Pétain doubtless had few worries as Pershing left—the Meuse-Argonne area loomed fearsome with woods, ravines, watercourses, crags and gulches, all honeycombed with machine guns. If the fanatical Americans wanted to dig through that maze, fine. Pershing had not been fooled. He knew the challenge ahead, if Foch approved. "In my opinion . . . none of the Allied troops had the morale or the aggressive spirit to overcome the difficulties to be met in that sector."[29]

At Bombon on September 2, Pershing, Pétain, and Foch came to quick understanding. Foch, having digested Pershing's long explanation of his intransigence, seemed resigned if not happy; he heard the results of the Nettancourt conference with obvious relief. Did Pershing want to cancel the Saint Mihiel operation? Not unless the marshal thought it necessary. Despite difficulties, especially shortages of transportation, Pershing felt he could smash the salient and still move his main force to the Meuse-Argonne sector. Circulation behind the front would be horrendous, but he expected to be able to extract his Saint Mihiel troops, join them with unused American divisions, and attack again on September 25. If Saint Mihiel were dropped, he could attack earlier. And when he went, he promised "all the vigor and enthusiasm" he could muster, every man and gun in battle.

Impressed with Pershing's pugnacity, Foch thanked him for a "splendid expression of good will." If Pershing could hit the salient on September 10, there might be time for the whole complicated venture. At last Foch gave approval to both operations, and Pershing left in vast relief at a decision.[30]

Even with Pétain's energetic aid, "our commitments now represented a gigantic task, a task involving the execution of the major operation against the St. Mihiel salient and the transfer of certain

[29] For the two conferences, see JJP, *Experiences*, 2:243–54; Carl Boyd, "Notes on Conversation Between General Pershing and Marshal Foch on August 30, 1918 at Ligny-en-Barrois," in AEF, GHQ, G-3, Folder 986-A, RG 120, National Archives; [Boyd?] "Notes on Conversation Between General Pershing and General Pétain, August 31, 1918. On General Pétain's Train at Nettancourt," *ibid.*, Folder 986-B. See also T. Bentley Mott, *Twenty Years as Military Attaché*, pp. 242–43.

[30] See JJP, *Experiences*, 2:254–55; [Boyd?] "Notes on Conference Between General Pershing, Marshal Foch, and General Pétain at Bombon, September 2, 1918," in AEF, GHQ, G-3, Folder 656, Important Conferences—Foch-Pétain-Pershing, RG 120, National Archives.

troops employed in that battle, together with many others, to a new front, and the initiation of the second battle, all in the brief space of two weeks." Drum's staff got a sudden influx of men from HAEF— they were going to need all the help they could get. But the Old Man offered no options. The double attack was on; plans must be made immediately.[31]

Artillery still lagged from the French armies; transportation, barely adequate to sustain the Saint Mihiel offensive as originally planned, would be critical: moving 600,000 men and 2,700 guns into the Meuse-Argonne line would baffle Solomon, but to extract more than half of them from a battle, shift them sixty miles, and hurl them against the enemy would boggle Jules Verne's mind. The job would be done.

There were odd delays—Lord Reading called in Paris to ask for more Americans with the British; Gen. Armando Díaz, Italian commander, asked for twenty-five divisions on his front; and Pershing, amused, confessed his own need for men. But nothing really distracted the new battle commander. Off to Ligny at every chance, Pershing kept close check on needed supplies, especially tanks and planes. Air cover would be vital in a sector heavily guarded by German aircraft. Bombing operations against the big rail and supply center at Conflans had damaged German rail yards and bridges and showed the havoc determined flyers could wreak. Those raids had alerted the Germans fully to coming trouble, but apparently no reinforcements were heading into the salient.

On his rides into Ligny, Pershing crossed the old Marne battle-fields and thought, suddenly, of the mortals in his hands—how many would die in the next days? Saddened, he worried about hospital facilities and was reassured by Gen. Merritte Ireland that 100,000 beds were ready. That seemed, somehow, a tragic boast.[32]

Guns rumbled nightly toward the German ditches. Khaki-clad men came marching gaily in thronging lines that sometimes were slowed by traffic and seen by daylight. Trains came, filled with shells, ammunition of all kinds, grenades, mortars, gas cylinders, food, medicine, arms, replacements for everything likely to be used up in battle, even men. Slowly but in a comforting kind of system the American First Army grew into a mighty host.

Much of the preparation for battle Pershing consigned to Hugh Drum. Delegation of authority and responsibility marked a wise com-

[31] JJP, *Experiences*, 2:254–55.
[32] *Ibid.*, pp. 255–58.

mander, and the present problems of divided attention made Drum an essential extension of command. But an all-seeing eye swept activities in the Ligny zone. Visits to gathering divisions showed the state of morale, equipment, training. Studies of recent AEF battles modified tactical ideas. At the daily staff conferences Drum had with his deputies—à la McAndrew—memos from the army commander were reviewed. Daily comments came in short paragraphs of advice, of complaints at some deficiency spotted on a visit or on the road, of orders for movements or changes in routine. The smallest things seemed to catch the commander-in-chief's notice. "I think you should seize the first opportunity to emphasize the necessity of our men taking every advantage of cover," he wrote on August 15, and developed his point: "That is, they should, where the ground at all permits of it, advance by rushes. I can readily see that advancing by rushes in ground covered with crops might be the cause of considerable straggling, but under other circumstances, instead of advancing in the open in groups or in solid line, as pointed out by a captured German officer, our men should be cautioned against bunching, and also warned to get over the ground rapidly and fire from the prone position when they can do so effectively."[33]

His comments were reinforced by a staff note: "Please have the Operations Section make a tactical study of the question of attack. It seems to me that perhaps we are losing too many men by enemy machine guns. I think . . . this might be met by tanks or possibly by artillery."[34] Treatment of war prisoners, handling of self-inflicted wounds, efficiency of military police in such congested areas as Commercy and Toul, road discipline of infantry, care of billets, all these details caught Pershing's attention. Lax standards brought sharp words to division commanders. Proper training aids for company commanders were stressed in battle preparations, and special emphasis went to handy maps of the Saint Mihiel zone. One hundred thousand were prepared and up-dated.[35]

In the regiments, too, little details fixed his attention. Bangalore

[33] JJP to Gen. H. B. Fiske, Aug. 15, 1918, in AEF, GHQ, Office of the CIC, Correspondence, File 15125–27, RG 120, National Archives. Drum circulated the observations of German prisoners on American tactics to corps commanders in "Memo . . . French Interrogation of . . . prisoners," Aug. 7, 1918, in First Army Historical File, RG 120, National Archives.

[34] JJP, Memorandum for the Chief of Staff, Aug. 7, 1918, in AEF, GHQ, Office of the Chfstf., Letterbook, RG 120, National Archives.

[35] "The Taking of the St. Mihiel Salient; Immensity of the Operation," Current History 9 (Nov., 1918): 235.

torpedoes—the big ones that ripped up enemy wire—were issued to pioneer companies; heavy wire cutters went to selected riflemen. White tape strips were cut to fix the march axis on the morning of attack; bigger strips issued to mark front lines for observation planes when the infantry got into German positions. Gas masks were checked. Ammunition supplies were replenished, but some battery commanders fussed over special powder and shell shortages.[36]

Lines of callers flocked to army headquarters in Ligny, officers reporting conditions and worries, the French chief of aviation to put air units under Pershing and Billy Mitchell, division commanders to review last-minute changes in plan because of the sudden restriction of attack. Artillery officers got Pershing's special attention, since guns had been short throughout August. By the beginning of September, statistics comforted the commander-in-chief: 3,010 guns of all kinds, over half of them manned by Yank gunners; 40,000 tons of ammunition in dumps, ready; 5,000 miles of field-telephone wire, some laid, some ready to reel out in enemy territory and connect 6,000 telephones to all parts of First Army.[37]

Pershing became increasingly interested in air cover. If German light bombers dominated the battlefield, casualties would be excessive. He had, much earlier, ordered Mitchell to build an umbrella of planes above the battlefield, and that zealous colonel—always eager, sometimes reckless—worked closely with British, French, and Italian officers to create a combined air force of almost 1,500 planes, an incredible armada for the Western Front.[38]

Infantry took position behind the old French front—with luck the Germans would not be certain of the attack date. Drum reported the attack order ready for distribution: Main thrust aimed at the southern face of the salient, to be delivered by Liggett's I Corps on the extreme right, from Pont-à-Mousson to Limey, and by Dickman's IV Corps from Limey to Xivray; secondary thrust by Cameron's V Corps directly east toward Saint Remy and across the base of the salient to meet Summerall's 1st Division, IV Corps, somewhere near middleground at Hattonchâtel. Eight American divisions would be in the first rush. One French division with five and a fraction American divisions would constitute the reserve. Around the tip of the

[36] Charles D. Rhodes, "Diary of the World War," Sept. 5, 11, 1918, USMA Library.

[37] "The Taking of the St. Mihiel Salient," pp. 235–36.

[38] Brig. Gen. William Mitchell, "The Air Service at St. Mihiel," *World's Work* 38 (Aug., 1919): 364, 370.

salient the French II Colonial troops held the line and would advance as the enemy cleared out of Saint Mihiel, abandoned frowning Montsec, and fell into the Yank trap in the rear.

General Pétain arrived at Ligny on September 9 for reassurance and gaped, amazed, at the crisp system functioning everywhere at headquarters, at the high morale, the confidence of Americans. Reduction of scope from twenty-five divisions in the advance had been handled easily; the divisions not now required were en route to staging areas in the Meuse-Argonne. Although Pershing had hoped to attack on the tenth, tardy French heavy artillery forced a postponement to the twelfth—and for that day everything looked ready to the Frenchman's veteran eye.

Enthusiastic and eager, wanting to see everything, to talk to all the men at hand, Newton Baker arrived at Ligny on Tuesday, the tenth. Pershing had known he was coming, hoped he would make it in time for the First Army's baptism. The secretary had a politico's grasp of loyalties and wondered about the divisions about to go forward— what were they, where did they come from, what states were represented. He heard a wondrously American roll call: 1st (Summerall), 2nd (Lejeune), and 5th (McMahon) Regular Divisions; two veteran National Guard Divisions, New England's 26th (Edwards) and the 42nd Rainbow (Menoher); three National Army divisions, 82nd (Burnham), 89th (Wright), and 90th (Allen), all filled with a year's draftees. Recently, Baker noted happily, all had been redesignated the United States Army, and the subtle niceties of status faded in comradeship. Not everything wore an American label—in the center was the fine II Colonial Corps with France's superb black troops. The planes and guns, too, were French. But everything ran according to a new system, a method peculiarly American.

Constantly Pershing preached the wisdom of pilfering good things from Allied methods and blending them into the U.S. Army's style— and that style could be glimpsed around the sudden fascinating Saint Mihiel Salient. Pressed, Pershing could have explained the style as a mixture of his own devotion to detail and the iron routine inculcated at the Fort Leavenworth Staff College. Most of the higher staff officers—and they numbered few enough—were graduates of Leavenworth, and they showed common passion for precision planning, clear orders, simple movements, care for troops. Hugh Drum ranked perhaps as the brainiest of the chiefs of staff, smarter even than McAndrew, but the genius of operations was Fox Conner at HAEF. In the

Operations Section he had pulled together a skilled team of brilliant technicians, including George Marshall, a freshly minted bird colonel come far from the terrible moment of confrontation with Pershing at Sibert's headquarters. Conner and Marshall, with others in operations at HAEF and First Army, mulled various action plans through August, tried different drafts, and soon Marshall's schemes took prominence in the final attack order. His, too, the eyes that roved constantly over the army as it inched into line—everywhere Marshall's tall figure might be seen as he asked about positions, ammunition, maps, tiny details of preparation. Pershing pushed all commanders to get close to things, and Marshall believed. He regretted the attack's restriction, thought possibilities for a smashing victory great. But his plans reflected orders.[39]

Leaving HAEF to McAndrew's competency, Pershing moved into the Ligny command post on September 5. Immediately the service and combat commanders clustered for final review of operations. What of a barrage? Should there be one, or should the Doughboys jump off unannounced? Pershing listened to various views. Liggett and one or two others opposed a bombardment, "arguing that the advantages of a complete surprise would outweigh any amount of shell fire." Others argued the moral virtue of preparation, the good effect on their troops before attacking, the damage certainly done German reserve concentrations, batteries, and wire entanglements. A good deal depended on whether tanks would be available in quantity. They had been promised by the British and French, but so far only French light tanks had arrived. It seemed likely that Haig, entangled in his own offensive, would need his heavy tanks.

Without heavy tanks limited artillery preparation became almost essential. Although many American gunners had not yet fired an angry shot, training levels were high and morale excellent. The army's chief of artillery guessed that even inexperienced shooting would take effect; he recommended a four-hour shelling before the attack. Careful aerial reconnaissance located every enemy battery in the salient, and the 600 German guns would take a pasting in four hours. Some at the conference urged the cosmetic need for preparatory fire, and Hugh Drum finally conceded that a four-hour pounding of the German lines was a reasonable compromise with secrecy and would "meet public

[39] Forrest Pogue, *George C. Marshall: Education of a General, 1880–1939*, pp. 171–74; Charles Rhodes, "Diary of the World War," Sept. 5–11, 1918; George C. Marshall, *Memoirs of My Services in the World War, 1917–1918*, ch. 10.

opinion."[40] In four hours no fresh reserves could reach the enemy front line.

Conferences with intelligence people indicated that General von Fuchs, commanding Group C in Gen. Max von Gallwitz's Composite Group, appeared to be pulling men out of the salient. A few weeks earlier some indecision had reigned, and Fuchs had seemed on the point of a disruptive attack. But now, with the British pushing forward after their great victory on August 8—the "Black Day of the German Army," Ludendorff thought—much starch wilted in those usually good enemy divisions. Fuchs's units were under strength and had been holding quiet lines long and complacently; he apparently felt discretion led back to the "Michel" line in the dreaded Hindenburg defense system. If, indeed, the Germans were pulling out, the Yank attack might catch him on the road, defenses down, and wreck his whole retreat; at least, withdrawal would derange his artillery and soften resistance at such places as Montsec, Longmont, and in the myriad runs and "rupts" that watered the valleys of the Meuse Heights. Any assistance would be welcomed. Pershing considered the whole salient "practically a great field fortress."[41]

Billy Mitchell came with spectacular news—he had assembled "the greatest concentration of air forces" in the history of the war and, with "barrage" flights that would deny the salient to enemy planes, he could guarantee control of the air for three days. That would be enough![42]

On Tuesday afternoon, September 10, Pershing held his final conference with corps commanders and chiefs of staff. Initiative, always give the infantryman his head, this the commander-in-chief preached; let the men do heroic things, take and hold ground, fight—fight—fight. H hour was 5:00 A.M. on the twelfth. Pershing had done everything an army commander could do—the battle now rested with his men.

Weather turned poor. All through the eleventh a great stirring of men disturbed the front as Doughboys moved closer to the jump-off line. Down in the 82nd Division hugging the shoulder of the line near Pont-à-Mousson, Charlie Rhodes, Pershing's suffering plebe of yore, made final adjustments to the guns of the 157th Artillery Brigade. Fussing about "all the endless, little details, a thousand and one things,

[40] See endorsement by Hugh Drum on Maj. Gen. E. F. McGlachlin, Jr., Chief of Artillery, First Army, to Drum, Sept. 10, 1918, in AEF, GHQ, First Army Reports, G-3, First Army, File 122.04, Miscellaneous Correspondence re-Preparation of Plan for the St. Mihiel Operation, RG 120, National Archives; Hunter Liggett, A.E.F. Ten Years Ago in France, pp. 145–46.

[41] JJP, Experiences, 2:263.

[42] Mitchell, "Air Service at St. Mihiel," p. 369.

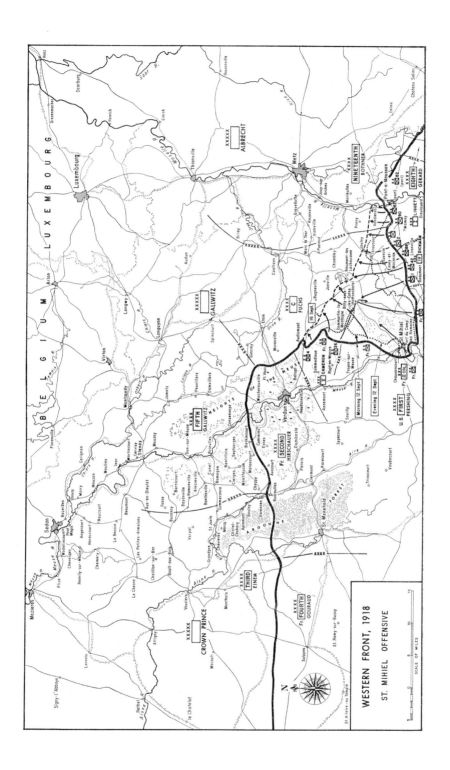

WESTERN FRONT, 1918

ST. MIHIEL OFFENSIVE

apt to be forgotten by a 'green' artillery brigade,"[43] he moved in a kind of eerie calm. And he watched such omens as the weather. Rain and sunshine alternated, splotching the heights and the Woëvre Plain beyond in a kind of climatic prelude. Up further toward those distant hills Rhodes must push his guns when the attack got going, must load with special shells to sweep I Corps targets.

Nervous fire plagued the night; German registration shelling spattered rear areas, stuttering guns along the lines told the tension of waiting. Rain drenched men going forward, drenched gunners and brought much swearing at the elements.

One o'clock in the morning, September 12, 1918. Promptly the terrible collection of American guns thundered on the southern face of the salient. As the guns continued, a weird flickering light etched the battlefield. Dampness strangely muffled the noise, and it came back to gunners in a dull echo—on it went through the night.

Pershing sent Secretary Baker to a relatively safe observation point overlooking the field, then took some of his staff to Fort Gironville, on a high hill south of Apremont and Montsec.

Five o'clock. Promptly Doughboys clambered out of their trenches, wire parties ahead. They hunched against the bullets and the chill wind, watched the little tanks ahead—267 of them—and marched into an inferno of star shells, explosions, and light resistance. The bombardment, mixed with gas and smoke, drove the retreating Germans underground, and Doughboys grenaded many of them from dugouts.

On his hill Pershing could see his battle shaping according to plan. A wheeling turn northeast hinged on the 82nd Division, was pushed by the 90th Dvision, by the 5th and 2nd Divisions of the I Corps; the IV Corps's 89th, 42nd, and 1st Divisions drove on toward Vigneulles and Hattonchâtel and the linking with the 26th Division. The French pinned a few Germans in the tip of the salient. And at 8:00 A.M. the secondary strike at the west face by the 26th Division began. A diversion, this attack drove into bad ground and tough resistance, and the fighting grew fierce, bloody, and personal.

A good many greenhorns learned war that day; even the untried divisions did nobly. Steadily the attack rolled ahead on the southern face. Confused and surprised, the Germans blew up dumps, fired villages as they scrambled to escape. Casualties on both sides seemed light.

From his high lookout Pershing now could see little save the roll-

[43] Rhodes, "Diary of the World War," Sept. 11, 1918.

ing barrage—that told him how fast the line moved and he was pleased. The churning smoke, the advancing lines of dim figures touched a fierce pride in him that morning—that was the United States Army out there, his own men, going to war at last on their own and doing great and terrible deeds. For one locked moment he felt the touch of great captains, and then the mood passed to concern for gallant soldiers. Down from Gironville and back in Ligny, Pershing began getting reports at 9:00 A.M. Along the entire 25-mile battle line "everything was going well, with losses light."[44]

An exultant war secretary joined Pershing at headquarters. Flushed with excitement, Baker bubbled at the successes. This first great American effort, so long building, erased all frustrations, ended doubts.

French observers were astounded at American dash and innovation. Wire entanglements, so long the bane of the Western Front, Americans crossed on chicken-wire bridges reeled out ahead as they advanced; their wire parties were marvelously athletic, their open-warfare methods sure and brutal.[45]

By noon early objectives were taken and the attack rolled on. In the afternoon IV Corps gambled on a cavalry raid that failed against machine guns, but that proved the sole setback. Pershing noted, though, as the afternoon lingered, the hard fighting on the west face, the fierce resistance against Clarence Edwards's New Englanders of the 26th Division. Reports of streaming escapees jamming roads out of the salient excited Pershing. Grabbing a field telephone, he called Dickman and Cameron, urged their IV and V Corps forward faster. Cameron got a special order: push at least one of Edwards's regiments straight for Vigneulles—the trap must close behind at least some Germans![46] Fighting flickered into night as the enemy pressed his withdrawal. Edwards threw most of his 51st Brigade forward, and it struggled to the outskirts of battered Vigneulles shortly after 2:00 A.M. Taking defensive positions in all directions, the isolated men closed the main road junction in the salient and hung on. Near dawn on the thirteenth, troops of the 1st Division marched to the Yank roadblock, and the gigantic sack had closed on thousands of hapless Germans.

Back at the point of the bulge, the French moved ahead, mopping up; Saint Mihiel fell. Later that Friday, the thirteenth, Pétain came to

[44] JJP, *Experiences*, 2:267.

[45] See *ibid.*, pp. 267–78; General Buat to Commanders, Army Groups Center, East, and the 1st U.S. Army, Sept. 18, 1918, in AEF, GHQ, G-3, First Army Correspondence, Folder 234, RG 120, National Archives.

[46] JJP, *Experiences*, 2:269.

Ligny all smiles and congratulations and suggested a trip into captured territory. Pershing took his guest out on the battlefield, finally into Saint Mihiel itself. Frenzied citizens, waving French flags long in hiding, thronged the streets; four years they had been virtually prisoners, and deliverance was almost unbearable. At the Hôtel de Ville the assistant mayor—where was His Honor?—complained that the Germans took all men between sixteen and forty-five with them. But they were later found abandoned by captors and returned. Pétain, ever ready for drama, spoke to the people and confessed that although the splendid black troops that freed them were French, they served with a powerful American army. It was altogether a good occasion in which both generals reaped rewards. As they left town they met Baker coming, and Pershing wished they had found him earlier. But there had been pleasures enough for Jack's birthday—he was fifty-eight years old, and a victor in war.

Operations continued for the next few days, local advances expanded the front slightly, several counterattacks were repulsed, and a defensive zone stabilized along a line from Haudiomont on the northwest through Fresnes en Woëvre–Doncourt–Jaulny–Vandieres. The Saint Mihiel Salient was no more. Threats to the Allied southern flank vanished. Trophies were many—freed Frenchmen, villages, more than 16,000 prisoners, and 450 enemy guns. Nothing on the Western Front came cheaply: the attacks cost more than 7,000 Doughboys.[47]

Considering the formidable terrain and old defensive system, the losses were light. And Pershing looked longingly at the unfinished work ahead in the Hindenburg Line. Continued attacks would succeed, he knew, and the damage inflicted on Germany might be fatal. But the shift to the Meuse-Argonne had already started.

Sadly the new assignment prevented real celebrating, but messages deluged headquarters in Ligny. Wilson cabled:

Accept my warmest congratulations on the brilliant achievements of the Army under your command. The boys have done what we expected of them and done it in a way we most admire. We are deeply proud of them and of their Chief. Please convey to all concerned my grateful and affectionate thanks.

Foch waxed effusive about precocious students.

[47] Casualty figures are various. JJP in *Experiences*, 2:270, gives the 7,000 figure, which is widely copied. In "Notes on Operations—C: Reduction of the St. Mihiel Salient," prepared by Brig. Gen. Fox Conner (n.d., but apparently a wartime broadside), the estimate is "about 11,000" (in AEF, GHQ, G-3, Folder 1085, Notes on Reduction of the St. Mihiel Salient, RG 120, National Archives).

The American First Army, under your command . . . has won a magnificent victory by a maneuver as skillfully prepared as it was valiantly executed. I extend to you as well as to the officers and to the troops under your command my warmest congratulations.

Haig sent his accolade:

All ranks of the British Armies in France welcome with unbounded admiration and pleasure the victory which has attended the initial offensive of the great American Army under your personal command. I beg you to accept and to convey to all ranks my best congratulations and those of all ranks of the British under my command.[48]

No more sniping now from Haig about laggard Americans, no more doubts about Yankee courage. Pershing's Army had earned its independence.

"If we strike hard enough we may end this war this fall."

Old battlefields have odd jetsam—bits of wreckage, human and material—and they attract endless curiosity. Into the waste of Saint Mihiel's seared land wanderers trekked to see how bad it had been. Some such interest was obviously masochistic, some maudlin, and some simply honest fascination for war. Pershing understood the gawkers who roamed the field, shared the roads with them, but worried lest some of the civilians step on unexploded shells or suffer other accidents.

That concern kept Clemenceau out of the ruined area. "Mr. President, we cannot take the chance of losing a Prime Minister."[49] Huffing displeasure, the Tiger visited safer places. But President Poincaré and his wife came that same Sunday, September 15, joined Jack for lunch, and beamed their pleasure at American victory. This part of France had been the Poincarés' home; they wanted to see their house. Near Sampigny, they said, the house had long been within German gun range. After lunch Pershing served as escort, and they found the ruins of home. "A beautiful though modest house" had been flattened by shelling. The Poincarés stood briefly thinking of easier days, then they shrugged, turned away with one remark—"C'est la guerre." The three sightseers strolled a bit and were joined by two Yank artillerymen who, taking Pershing's identification of his guests as an introduction, walked up easily and shook hands. Poincaré, who knew Amer-

48 Quotes are from JJP, *Experiences*, 2:273–74.
49 *Ibid.*, p. 274.

icans, seemed charmed by the cordial greetings. Later, at dinner with the Tiger, Pershing confessed that Poincaré had bullied his way up into hot country around Thiaucourt, and the prime minister fumed.[50] Foch and Weygand toured with Pershing on Friday, the twentieth, and the marshal "spoke with enthusiasm regarding the battle."

Pershing did his best to see everybody in the postattack days. Without warning he descended on division command posts day or night, talked brusquely about conditions of men, guns, animals, supplies, looked hard for signs of command failure. And he cast wide a search for new commanders. Battle consumed men fiercely: they fell in action, some cracked under strain, others simply faded in fatigue. In the hectic rounds he perked up always at good words about his friends. Gen. William Burnham of the 82nd boasted the fine fire support his men got from the 157th Field Artillery Brigade. Old plebe Charlie Rhodes headed that outfit; reports were all good about his efficient command, his skill in shooting. Where is he, the Old Man wondered? On Monday, when he visited the 82nd, Pershing sent for his long-suffering friend. Rhodes, caught out on the lines inspecting observation posts, got the summons and responded in West Point style. "I 'beat it' with all speed forthwith, to MARBACHE, and had 'JOHN' . . . 'look me over.'" Jack swept the little brigadier with those professional eyes—they had not warmed any—and noticed that conditions modified West Point polish. Soaked, his khaki raincoat dripping where he walked, Rhodes touched his tin hat, smiling, stood unblushing in shoes gooey with mud. He looked like a fighting soldier; Pershing chatted briefly with Rhodes and a few others, waved "adios," and vanished. Later that day Rhodes learned Pershing had talked of making him a major general. First Captain Pershing climbed notches in Rhodes's esteem.[51]

Those divisions of Saint Mihiel were America's veterans. They ought to spearhead the Meuse-Argonne drive, but logistics barred them from early participation. New ones, mostly untried, some even without trench experience, would be Pershing's instruments farther west.

Intricacies of logistics hounded the Operations officers of First Army and AEF. By best estimates, the new attack would require nine divisions in line, with four in corps reserves (one of them French cavalry), three in army reserve. Which imposed considerable pressure on the staff—but efficiency prevailed among those careful young men under Conner and Drum. Conner handed the biggest chore of plan-

[50] *Ibid.*, pp. 274–75.
[51] Rhodes, "Diary of the World War," Sept. 16, 1918. See also JJP, *Experiences*, 2:279.

ning to George Marshall. If Marshall had had time to count, he would have been mildly surprised to find he must plan the movement of 600,000 U.S. soldiers into the attack sector and the removal of 220,000 French troops. Schedules of daily marches, bivouac areas, regulations for supply traffic, concentration of munitions, medical stores, railroad facilities, all the needs of war, must be plotted to bring everything to the attack zone over three main roads and insufficient trackage.

Marshall's plan hinged utterly on Harbord's SOS. If the ports, depots, all the intermediate and forward regulations stations—especially the one at Saint Dizier—did their jobs, the plan had an outside chance to work. Harbord was screaming at Pershing's skeletonizing his stations for forward troops. If men were stripped from the SOS, how could supplies move? Pershing knew Harbord would manage; it was confidence Dawes understood best. "John is going to strike his maximum blow. He is taking his chances on his supply. He believes a reserve is meant to be used in emergency."[52]

In the midst of concentration statistics totaled differently every day, but by September 21 experts could predict certain levels of equipment and of need. American and French gunners would man 3,980 guns of all sizes—two-thirds of the gunners would be Yanks—and ammunition piled to the staggering total of 40,000 tons for a beginning barrage; after that 12 to 14 carloads of artillery shells must come to the army daily, enough cars to provide at least 3,000 tons every twenty-four hours, since estimates were that divisional and corps batteries would use 350,000 rounds each day. Ordnance repair and issue depots numbered 12; ammunition dumps 24; gasoline and oil depots 9, although these might not be enough in a modern, mechanized war where machines consumed petroleum like men ate "corned Willy." Uniforms, puttees, belts, underclothes, all the garments of battle poured into 9 quartermaster depots, which issued new, and cleaned old, clothes and equipment. Technical supply points mounted as the infinite tooling of slaughter expanded—the engineers filled 12 depots; gas and flame equipment, 6. Signal, medical, motor, and tank supplies filtered into the battle zone in floods. Hospital trains rolled to convenient sidings; evacuation stations appeared behind the battle front, and 34 intermediate hospitals opened for business.[53]

Transport consisted largely of French trucks aimed by reckless drivers who had just a few days ago hurtled *poilus* to war and were

[52] Dawes, *Journal*, 1:175.
[53] See JJP, *Experiences*, 2:285 n; Stallings, *AEF*, pp. 226–27, leans heavily on JJP's account, as does Palmer, *John J. Pershing*, pp. 302–3.

wearied to daze on the road. Some American commanders would have refused to feed these strange and melancholy stalwarts of the highways, but George Marshall smashed prejudice with orders.[54]

Marshall's plans were good, considered all the tangibles of time, space, exposure, fatigue, bulk, rail speeds, road conditions. And Marshall justly reaped high regard for his shrewd guessing on what the First Army could do—but the plans broke down almost from the start. Men did unscheduled things, wandered from the roads to steal a nap, find a latrine, rest and eat, flirt with a pretty girl, cuss at buddies, the weather, Fritz, officers, and the whole situation. Long wear racked more than 90,000 horses that pulled guns, wagons, ambulances, searchlights, and caissons through the waterlogged country by the Meuse— thousands collapsed or died in the traces, and behind them traffic jams exploded to astounding size. In the constant drizzle, men, wheels, hooves, squashed roads to mire, and engineer troops toiled endlessly with rocks, gravel, mud, and logs to rebuild after every column. When, at last, columns compressed into mass, engineers worked between men, wheels, and any small gap in the jam.

Pershing expected trouble in the concentration. Saint Mihiel's experience revealed weaknesses in military police training—Yank MPs were inexpert at traffic control and were rushed through quick courses in arm waving and nervelessness. Staff officers hoped for tidy approaches to assigned spots in the line, but delays, confusion, the constant mixing of units forced assignment by arrival. French officers of the veteran II Army, left with alleged control over movements in their zone, were appalled by the shambles that passed for Yank traffic management.[55] French General Hirschauer, II Army, complimented Pershing on the personal discipline and concealment of infantry in the U.S. First Army, but threw up his hands at the highway chaos—"road discipline not so good," he said.

Actually road discipline was terrible, and without the constant plague of staff officers haunting the lines, urging division and brigade commanders to find their men and push them forward, chaos would probably have escalated into disaster. Marshall roamed the roads daily to see how far awry his plans had gone; the commanding general, disdaining rain, mud, and the growing chill of September, stormed division headquarters with scathing instructions on organization. All kinds of training defects were revealed in the Saint Mihiel operations;

[54] Pogue, *Marshall*, p. 177.
[55] JJP, *Experiences*, 2:279.

new ones erupted each night on the roads. Two weeks were not enough —unscrambling this military mess would take a month!

Somehow, in ways peculiar to American initiative, the divisions struggled ahead in the dripping dark. A kind of amiable anger touched the lines as men knew each other's misery and made allowances. Officers showed happy flexibility in bending orders to circumstances. By D day minus one, line divisions were almost on hand. The night of September 11–12 stuck in the minds of all who struggled to the front. Out of the trenches came the French, who had been holding in feigned unconcern for two weeks; into their places went scared and eager Doughboys, most of them unbroken to hostile fire, most wondering what the world would be like with dawn, wondering whether they would know another night. The enemy showed no signs of alarm.

In briefings with his corps commanders, in frequent talks with division leaders, General Pershing emphasized the hard future for them all. Foch's orders aimed the American army at a breach of the Hindenburg Line from Dun-sur-Meuse to Grandpré, a farther push to a line from Stenay to Le Chesne; when they got that far, the Yanks would flank the German Aisne River positions, force a general withdrawal toward Mézières. Together with the French IV Army, driving on their left, the Americans could wreck German hopes for an orderly retreat to the Fatherland. Once their main lateral rail line broke behind their front, German supplies and troops must evacuate France through a bottleneck between the Ardennes and Holland. The prize seemed worth a high price.

What price the Meuse-Argonne? Even rookie officers read the omens of their maps. On the right of the attacking force the Meuse angled northwest, and just across it, lofty and menacing, the Meuse Heights guarded the Woëvre Plain. Among those heights were promontories that gave splendid observation of the whole American line to enemy artillery on the Consenvoye Heights, especially on the fearsome Borne de Cornouiller—soon famed as "Corned Willy Hill." On the American left flank, just west of the Aire River, loomed the Argonne Forest, running well over ten miles long and far wider than a man could see. What lurked in that dense wilderness was anybody's guess. Dead in front of the Yank center lay the wintering country of Champagne, not so winning now as in spring, but rocky, wooded land, enriched by the water of the Meuse and the Aire. Between those rivers loomed high ground that rose in ridges to the distant feather of Barricourt Woods. Bulking from the high ground were hilly bastions that frowned over the battlefield—Montfaucon, Cunel, Romagne Heights, each lofty and wooded and bristling with guns. Patches of woods rode the ridges and broke up ground for infantry. Pershing's Army faced a terrible natural fortress of rocks, forests, small streams and valleys, hills and tiny towns with names lost to France.

Devilish German engineers had for four years improved on nature. In front of the Americans ran a battle line marked by rusty festoons of wire, much of it properly staked and crisscrossed, the impassable barrier of Loos, Lens, Ypres, Chemin des Dames. Pillboxes dotted the front positions and almost five kilometers behind them ran the Giselher Stellung, first of three trenchlines—named after Wagnerian witches —in the Hindenburg system. Centered on Montfaucon, this line of works, machine-gun nests, and forward mortar positions covered the front; another six kilometers back loomed the great rocky ridges of Romagne Heights and the Kriemhilde Stellung—strongest enemy position. Beyond that still, perhaps eight kilometers, lurked the last-stand trenches of the Freya Stellung, hugging Buzancy's hills.

Pershing had said it earlier: no other Allied troops "had the morale or the aggressive spirit to overcome the difficulties to be met in that sector." True, and no other Allied general would have dared order his men to attack that fearsome place. Pétain thought the Americans would do well to take Montfaucon before winter halted fighting, but Pershing's battle orders set the Kriemhilde Stellung as the first day's objective.[56]

Stripping out a skeleton group, Pershing moved his Advanced Command Post to Souilly on September 21;[57] he moved his headquarters train to a handy siding, and set up First Army's working office in the town hall. On the way to his new official residence, Pershing visited Verdun—the town would soon come under his command, a great act of confidence on Pétain's part—and he looked at the bombproofs and scars of long siege battling. In the Officer's Club with the French commander and some American staff officers, Pershing stopped and looked hard at a sign writ large on a wall: "On ne passe pas." Those words of Pétain's, spoken two years before in a crisis time for Verdun, moved

56 *Ibid.*, p. 254; "Special Operations Report, 1st Army . . .," pt. C. The Argonne-Meuse Operation (pt. 2 of pt. C, Plans for the Attack), AEF, GHQ, G-3, First Army Report, File 110.01, RG 120, National Archives. The attack preparations are well covered in Pogue, *Marshall*, pp. 175–80; Palmer, *John J. Pershing*, pp. 298–305; JJP, *Experiences*, 2:279–88; Stallings, *AEF*, pp. 225–27; JJP and Liggett, *First Army*, pp. 46–48. See, especially, Frederick Palmer, *Our Greatest Battle (The Meuse-Argonne)*, pp. 1–74; Marshall, *Memoirs*, pp. 148–59.

57 Memorandum, Chief of Staff's Office, First Army, Sept. 17, 1918, "The Advance P.C.," Chief of Staff, HQ, First Army, RG 120, National Archives.

Pershing greatly. "It would be difficult to describe my feelings," he said, and mused on the responsibility of holding a place so sacred to France.[58] At midnight, September 22, he assumed command of the Meuse-Argonne sector.[59]

By now he had formed habits of command that subordinates knew well; they expected nervous visits before action. They knew these peripatetic wanderings were as much release as review; the Old Man had to be out with the troops, close to the war. Once fixed in Souilly, Pershing began a last round of inspections and conferences with corps and division commanders "to give a word of encouragement here and there. . . . "[60] He never minced words before battle. The expectations were greater, he thought, than possibilities. Although he hoped that gallantry would go well against experience, that the initial advance would be better than Pétain's gloomy prediction, he prophesied hard fighting, no easy spots anywhere. What had been done at Saint Mihiel would be repeated.

At 5:30 A.M., September 26, the First Army would attack; artillery preparation would start at 2:30, after a long period of harassing and interdiction. When his boys went, they would surge along a 25-mile line and aim to push salients on either side of Montfaucon, flank that formidable barrier, breach the Giselher Stellung, and drive through the Kriemhilde Stellung on the Cunel and Romagne massifs. Surprise was the key; if the concentration had gone undetected, if the attack hit the enemy in the complacent certainty of his veteran strength, then a ten-mile penetration could happen. Montfaucon must fall on the first day, Côte Dame Marie (in the third line) on the second, or things would get extremely sticky.

To questions Pershing replied that he felt good about the "vigor and . . . aggressive spirit" of the Doughboys in this final test of army maturity. They had every chance to accomplish an impossible task— but if firm German fighters stopped the drive, there were plans handy for a series of small, mincing operations designed to grind the Germans up the hills and down the Meuse Valley to Sedan—that was the hard and costly way. If it came down to a siege battle, morale and initiative would decide victory.

[58] JJP, *Experiences*, 2:287.
[59] *Ibid.*, p. 289; Order, signed by General Hirschauer, Sept. 21, 1918 (Personal and Secret): "Beginning Sept. 22nd at midnight, General Pershing will assume command of all Allied forces stationed in the American area . . ." (in AEF, GHQ, G-3, Folder 983, RG 120, National Archives).
[60] JJP, *Experiences*, 2:294.

Pershing toured the front that last night in nervous eagerness. German guns dropped shells on the Clermont-Varennes road, but the big khaki car with its four stars splashed forward. Suddenly a group of Doughboys arose from cover by the roadside and stood rigid in salute. It was the highest tribute of soldiers. One of those unknown fans was tanker George Patton.[61]

On his left, in the Argonne, Pershing had put Liggett's I Corps, in the center Cameron's V, and Bullard's III on the right extending to the Meuse. At 11:30 P.M., September 25, scattered American batteries began a general searching of German positions; it was apparently random harassment, but some enemy observers had come to a healthy appreciation of Yank gunners. They had a nasty habit "of scattering fire systematically over the whole battlefield."[62] Veteran troops were not much bothered by this kind of shelling; they simply settled deeper in their comfortable bunkers—turned almost into home through four years of garrison work—and slept well. The Americans obviously supported the long, thunderous French bombardment on the IV Army front. At 2:30 Thursday morning, every American battery opened fire in a flickering staccato drumming of the front lines, the support areas, the second German positions. Confused about intents, the Germans waited for developments.[63] At 5:30 the shelling stopped, and the infantry came up from the trenches and raced for the German wire. On the right, Bullard's men struggled down into the slough of Forges Brook, tangled in the wire, came up and out and smashed on to wheel right and block the Meuse banks. Farther along the line, other divisions crossed wire barriers that seemed impassable to Germans—the Yanks' feet were big, their boots spanned cords of barbs, their chicken-wire bridges reeled out for followers—and pushed out into deceptively easy ground. Canny old German infantrymen came out of their dugouts, fixed their machine guns, and began to chop away at these reckless boys who charged so gleefully. A ragged line advanced on the left, and in the center two divisions raced to bypass Montfaucon, but they were hit from three sides by galling machine guns and artillery. On the left, where part of Liggett's line was in the Argonne, some men partly in the open, the drive also gained costly ground. But the salients did not girdle Montfaucon that day; the spire in the town

[61] Martin Blumenson, *The Patton Papers, 1885–1940*, p. 609.

[62] Lt. Col. Hermann von Giehrl (German Army), "The American Expeditionary Forces in Europe, 1917–1918," *U.S. Infantry Journal* 20 (Feb. 1922): 143.

[63] Von Giehrl, "American Expeditionary Forces" (pt. 2), *U.S. Infantry Journal* 20 (March, 1922): 298.

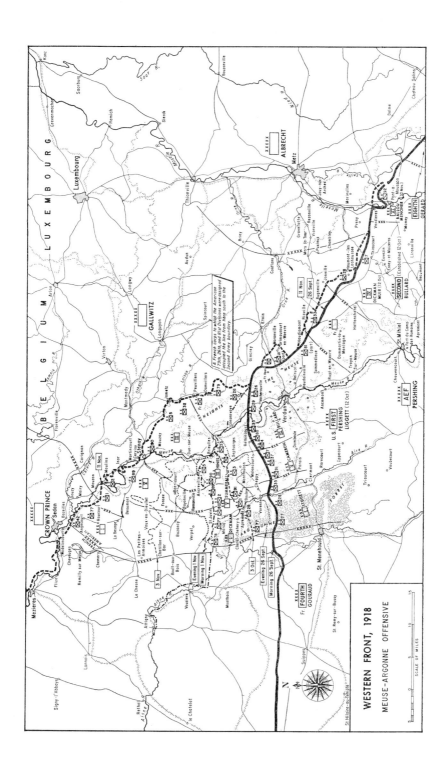

WESTERN FRONT, 1918

MEUSE-ARGONNE OFFENSIVE

mocked men who struggled against leaden buffeting and hostile ground.

Tanks would have helped, but they were too few and too small. The ones that did advance were pieces of iron poetry to the Doughboys clustering about their bulk. Most of them were battered into scrap by dark. By nightfall, Bullard had driven into the enemy's second position after fierce fighting in tough, marshy ground and in scattered woods. Cameron's troops had a harder day—some of them did dig their ways into Malancourt but were stopped in open ground beyond, and they could not put a clamp on Montfaucon. On the left Liggett's men did heroic things that first day—Vauquois, Cheppy, Very, Varennes, where inches were miles in blood, were taken or partly taken—but on the extreme left the enemy clung to spurs in the Argonne with nests of guns and hit attackers in flank. From across the Meuse all day, German guns on the heights scourged American infantrymen with flanking fire, crossed with guns in the Argonne and on Montfaucon, so that many divisions took punishment from three sides. But some parts of the line advanced eight and nine kilometers.

Pershing knew the problem. German reserves were coming up; the first line had been lightly held; the big test would come on the morrow. Montfaucon must be taken to clear the center of the battlefield, and something would have to be done about the guns east of the Meuse as well as the batteries screened in the Argonne Forest.

At dawn of the twenty-seventh, Cameron's men tried again for Montfaucon. They started with a few surviving tanks. Montfaucon fell about noon, the town a wreck, but with the crown prince of Germany's old observation post and telescope intact. On other parts of the line grudging advances were hacked from furious and stubborn defenders. The field remained bad: enfiladed, raked by fire from the front as well as from distant battery positions where the enemy put his bigger guns in, Americans fought hand to hand increasingly in a classic siege battle, an infantryman's war. Each attacking division lost about 5,000 men that first day.[64] By the end of September Pershing could report an inching advance that averaged about four miles. With the chance to take Montfaucon the first day gone, the battle shifted character. Had that central bastion fallen that first day, along with dreaded Le Chêne Tondu—a rocky finger jutting from the Argonne and pointing eastward at killing open ground—the Kriemhilde Stellung would have been in

[64] Stallings, AEF, p. 248.

dire jeopardy. But they had held long enough for reserves to arrive and settle the battle to butchery.

Casualties continued high, especially among company and field officers, and organization wavered when command lapsed. Untried troops, though, had withstood a holocaust of fire with fine bravery; individual acts of heroism defied counting. Pershing roamed his battlefield, taking pulse of command, organization, morale. Morale remained superb, humor buoyed the hurt, and resolution stiffened the generals. Corps commanders did herculean labors of management and kept their battles going. Some division commanders showed the confusion of inexperience, some the baseness of mettle. Those good troops, especially the National Guardsmen, who had fought without real training, needed relief; the lines needed unscrambling; a general refitting seemed necessary. Pershing decided on September 29 to stabilize his line where it held, go on the defensive briefly, and gird for another drive.[65]

In the lull visitors poured into army headquarters. They were the bane of victory.

On Sundays Clemenceau took to the battlefield—and for his September 29 tour, he selected the American front. Excited at Pershing's success in wresting Montfaucon from the enemy, the Tiger burst upon Souilly with a demand to visit the crown prince's old vantage point. Although his new cordialty pleased Pershing, who wanted to maintain good relations, Clemenceau's insistence was simply bothersome. Dangerous ground lay ahead, Pershing cautioned, especially Montfaucon —the Mount of the Falcon drew incessant fire. Traffic clotted everywhere, going would be difficult. Off Clemenceau went in his limousine, clearly expecting to follow the splendid system of the Voie Sacrée that fed Verdun in its harsh travail. But the Sacred Way seemed now a squalid swamp of goo, stuck camions, cursing Americans, wallowing guns, foundered horses. Some kind of relief operation scrambled along the road. If Clemenceau inquired, he learned that Big Red One was going in to replace the Missouri and Kansas guardsmen of Peter Traub's not-so-green-anymore 35th Division. Eighteen thousand survivors tramped the road back, weary, chalky white with fatigue, and wiser. Summerall's men, already wise to the ways of Fritz, inched

---

[65] "Special Operations Report, First Army, American Expeditionary Forces," pt. C, The Argonne-Meuse Operation, pt. 4, "The 1st Operation," citing FO 32, Sept. 29, 1918, AEF, GHQ, First Army Reports, G-3, First Army, File 110.01, RG 120, National Archives.

forward with the endless banter of dread. But the "road discipline" appalled Clemenceau, accustomed, he thought, to French *système*. His parting remarks were friendly, his impression nearly fatal.

Unknown to Jack at the moment, the prime minister would quickly write Foch of his horrid discoveries, claim his higher responsibility to French soldiers, and demand the removal of the incompetent commander-in-chief of the American Expeditionary Forces.

Pershing also had removals in mind. Reports from various outfits showed human attrition; small-unit commanders generally did well, but some regimental and brigade leaders lacked force and discipline, had failed to inspire, or simply wilted under fire. Doubts were heard of a few division commanders. All of Pershing's men knew his philosophy of command—"a man will stand or fall by his machine." If a unit failed, the man failed. For some the ruthlessness Pershing practiced could scarcely be grasped, but as the list of removals grew, a dawning understanding permeated the army—nobody had tenure of command. Secretary Baker knew fully Pershing's fetish for efficiency and during the early days of the Meuse-Argonne agreed with suggestions about high officer removals. There were sticky cases. John E. McMahon of the 5th Division showed awkwardness that might cause relief. George Cameron, heading the V Corps, looked close to exhaustion. The stickiest case, though, would be Clarence Edwards, who led the New Englanders in the 26th Division. These prickly National Guardsmen had their breed's suspicion of regulars, but old Clarence's saucy wit and dash they liked. He babied them some, commented often on the dirty jobs they got, and made hilariously snide remarks about high officers in other places—and those things earned affection among fellow sufferers. But those things had no place in an army. Pershing had bawled Edwards out several times in stiff letters about slurs against superiors in the hearing of his men, cautioned him about pessimistic claptrap that could only dull his division's honed fighting edge. But Edwards went his way, promising in one memorable note that Jack could "count upon me to play with particularity the role of Caesar's wife."[66]

Edwards pushed his men, but not hard enough. If he failed to "run his machine" now that the 26th would go into battle in the Meuse

[66] C. R. Edwards to Harbord, Mar. 31, 1918, "In the Matter of the Investigation of Major General Clarence R. Edwards, N.A. (Personal File of Gen. J. J. Pershing), May 7, 1919," Reclassification and Reassignment of General Officers, Pershing Papers, RG 200, National Archives Gift Collection.

area, he would be relieved—and that would raise a loud ruckus in New England and in some regular circles at home. But just as friends knew no quarter in efficiency's name, neither did misfits. With the higher ranking men, Pershing often did his best to assure them some duty at home that would preserve their status—training camp command, something of that sort. There were a few whose status he had long thought inflated; their shrinkage gave him no pangs.

Lesser ranks usually got a quick brush, a physical, and a one-way ticket to Blois, then home. Those whose incapacity stemmed only from ignorance, Pershing tried to save by training. Corps and division commanders received careful instruction in the care and preservation of good men. Recent fighting chipped a good deal of rhetoric from open-warfare training. And while some French and British critics, gloating over high casualties in Saint Mihiel and in the first days at the Meuse-Argonne, were wrong about erroneous instructions, there were important changes necessary in Doughboy tactics. Pershing's battlefield tours showed him some of the defects in maneuver; his staff officers, who ranged everywhere in battle, reported others. Worst blunders came in attacks on machine guns. Although iron-voiced Hanson Ely might wonder about using the 37mm cannon against machine guns— he thought they were too accurate for shooting at invisible targets, their shells too tight in damage[67]—the small cannons must be used where possible; so, too, the invaluable Stokes mortars which went forward with the attack. More flanking and less full-on rushing at German nests would save lives—small-unit commanders must drive that difficult lesson home to their reckless men. Taking cover branded no man a coward!

Discipline ranked high on the list of problems following the first hard battles. "Squad and platoon commanders," Pershing noted, "too often do not hold their personnel up to that high standard of sportsmanlike cooperation that appeals to our fine young American soldiers. There is no question of their personal bravery, but there is not always present a well directed sporting instinct that holds men together and indicates to each his obligation to do his part in the team, always striving to aid in the success of his squad, platoon or company." All officers from division commanders down must reinforce West Point discipline. Lack of it produced unsoldierly straggling and pointless

[67] Col. S. R. Gleaves to Fox Conner, Sept. 21, 1918 (Secret), in AEF, GHQ, G-3, Folders 1069 & 1071, Comments on the St. Mihiel Operation, RG 120, National Archives.

meandering. Sometimes poor discipline and poor spirit led to funking before the enemy.

That conduct Pershing would not tolerate. "When men run away in front of the enemy, officers should take summary action to stop it, even to the point of shooting men down who are caught in such disgraceful conduct. No orders need be published on the subject, but it should be made known to younger officers that they must do whatever is required to prevent it. The immediate trial by court-martial of cases not handled on the spot, imposing the death penalty where proved, will go far toward ending this sort of thing." President Wilson might shrink from widespread death sentences, but quailing in battle transcended executive squeamishness.

A good deal of the army's looseness sprang from uncertainty in younger officers. Many of them lacked self-confidence, "too often consider themselves much in the same class as the men whom they are leading." They are often right, Pershing thought, in matters of intelligence and attainment, but "they must understand that they are the designated leaders, clothed with official responsibility, and they must be inspired to assume that attitude of mind and action, otherwise there is hesitation and delay instead of decision, aggressiveness and leadership." That same confidence must be given to noncoms as well.

In the fighting ahead, initiative could make the difference between winning and losing. Everyone must fight, fight, fight.[68]

Endless attention to detail, the constant visits to forward headquarters, the constant damnable drizzling rain that turned air to a kind of muddy paste, wore Jack down. He lost weight, his high Mexican tan faded to a ghostly gray, his eyes sank into dark holes, sometimes he even slumped at his desk. The crisis of his army hit him the hardest.[69] Staff members saw the strain, sympathized, but marveled at the intense concentration JJP achieved. The battle and his army were the boundaries of his world. Outside distractions he handled, but not willingly—the map on the headquarters wall consumed him; he marked the slightest change in the front, could tell anyone where every division was every day. His devotion achieved a domination of command; the army seemed an extension of his personality. Other American generals had concentration, devotion, grasped details of armies and

---

[68] JJP to Maj. Gen. William M. Wright, Oct. 24, 1918, in 89th Div. Records, File 330.1, Efficiency of Organizations, RG 120, National Archives. This is a typical letter of instruction to division commanders. Pershing sent many.

[69] See Palmer, *John J. Pershing*, p. 321.

actions, but none before were so much the fulcrum of force. Pershing's will was the army's armor; his nerve, the army's spur.[70]

Some visitors brought welcome ease by siphoning tension. Charlie Dawes was best at that—his earthy humor, warmth, and affection gave Jack a chance to think aloud. One morning Jack worked over his map for Dawes's benefit, pointed out plans, and guessed things would go well. A quick turn to his friend who shared so much, a shrug, a smile, and a fond memory to fit the moment: "When Frankie and I were in the Philippines she would ask, 'Jack, how do things stand?' I would say, 'Very well at present.' Then she would reply, 'Look out! Something is going to happen.'" A raised, amused eyebrow, "And," Charlie, "something always did happen!"[71]

Something was going wrong right enough. Baker, on a swing to London, fell foul of Lloyd George in one of his postprandial pets, and heard a pent suspicion. After all the ships Britain provided for American troops, precious few of those troops were serving with Haig's beleaguered legions. Divisions trained by British officers were jerked away by Pershing to do duty with the French. Yanks, said the prime minister, had been of "no service to the British." Stung to response, Baker, with icy courtesy, pointed out that Pershing commanded his army as fully as Haig did the BEF, and could move his divisions when and where he pleased. As for service to England, Americans fighting at Belleau, Château-Thierry, Saint Mihiel, now in the Argonne, attracted numerous German divisions, hence relieved pressure elsewhere. More than that, the American II Corps had been slugging along with Haig's men in the mean fighting around Saint Quentin. What really bothered Lloyd George, Baker guessed in his letter to Pershing recounting the meeting, was creeping Franco-American closeness. Anglo-American understanding seemed vital to the prime minister; he counted on it in the postwar world. And, diffidently, the secretary suggested Pershing might leave the II Corps with Haig for a time.[72]

Pershing needed George Read's two divisions, the 27th and 30th, but he had no hope of pulling them into the Meuse-Argonne cauldron. In late September they were committed to desperate fighting in the

[70] See Dawes, *Journal*, 1:187–88.

[71] *Ibid.*, p. 188. In Dawes's text JJP refers to Frankie as "my wife." I have personalized the conversation, since he would hardly have been formal with Dawes.

[72] Baker to JJP, Oct. 2, 1918, in JJP, *Experiences*, 2:315–18.

Cambrai–Saint Quentin canal tunnel complex. On September 29 they gallantly stormed the Saint Quentin tunnel at Bellicourt and pushed to a clear break of the Hindenburg Line in that sector.[73] No help to the British?

But everybody wanted some of Pershing's divisions. Foch asked for two as aids to the French IV Army, struggling to pass Blanc Mont. Although loath to spare any more troops, Pershing sent John Lejeune's 2nd Division and Billy Smith's Texans of the 36th Division. They stormed Blanc Mont and were hard at fighting when Pershing pushed his own army forward once again.

Three of his green divisions, the 37th, 79th, and 35th, bloodied now and well thinned, Pershing pulled out of line and replaced with Summerall's men who tangled on the road with Clemenceau in the September slush, with the 32nd under William ("Bunker") Haan, and the 3rd under Beaumont Beauregard Buck. Pershing's front line had pushed out more than four miles, flanks sagging a little, and the ground ahead remained the same sodden, merciless, rocky menace crammed with guns and increasingly irked Germans. One Doughboy, after a tough day's work getting at machine guns, summed up the inferno that was the Meuse-Argonne's three lines of Wagnerian stellungs—"What bitches they were. Every goddam German there who didn't have a machine gun had a cannon."[74]

Cannons bothered all American commanders. Concealed gun positions in the Argonne had to be taken; so did the great booming terrors on Corned Willy Hill. Flank attacks were likely to be hit from behind by guns on the Romagne Heights, from Cunel and from countless other wicked eyries for Boche gunners. A general assault again, along the whole front, depressing as it loomed, offered the best chance to get through the Kriemhilde works and into the last Hindenburg positions. That was the next order of business.

Replacements were a problem. Shipping, ever scant, had choked back the flow of men for fighting units. Pershing had asked for 50,000 replacements during July, August, and September, and they were still absent. This forced the skeletonizing of some line divisions—a practice Jack had intended to avoid through the depot division scheme. At the rate of shipping now, Pershing guessed that not even the 80-division plan could be realized by 1919. But he had an eye to the present. Strip the SOS, clean out the depots, use everything handy—

[73] JJP, *Experiences*, 2:304; Stallings, *AEF*, ch. 15, pp. 257–66.
[74] Stallings, *AEF*, p. 225.

this just might be the drive to end drives. He wanted to push it off on October 1, but changes, road repairs, resupply snarls held up everything. Finally the orders were issued: Attack on October 4.

Fortune had shifted since the glittering chance on September 26. The kind of surprise he planned then—total air domination, a swamping thrust by waves, backed by reserves to leap-frog forward, murderous artillery support—had been original, a scheme tuned to American morale and resources. It had failed, just barely, because of disorganization and inadequate transport, and now the battle would be a thing of shards and bombs and bayonets, of inches grubbed by bones, of odd and fiery heroism, of grim and bulldog defense. The only way now was to go through the leaden hails of the Meuse Heights, grind through Argonne's labyrinths.[75]

Reports from other fronts stimulated everyone in the Souilly town hall—Haig's men drove on through the Hindenburg Line, and the French in the Aisne country and around the old 1917 battlefields were pushing forward well. The French IV Army on the American left had kept pace with Pershing's men. Reports of casualties in the three active corps seemed average, although the word "heavy" appeared too frequently.

In the midst of this expanding Allied success, Foch sent a curious message on October 1, by Weygand in person. Resistance seemed so heavy in front of the Americans, Weygand said, that Foch thought of inserting another French army between Pershing and the French IV; this intruding force would take over some of Pershing's divisions. No, came the flat rejection that rang in Pershing's town hall room. That smacked of the old August plan and was even more wrong now than then. The American army would go on with its assignment. Pershing guessed that Clemenceau had some malign hand in the new suggestion. And he guessed, too, that the last had not been heard of the scheme.[76] Dawes had told him that gleeful Paris rumors flew about the mess behind American corps and that criticism mounted of poor supply management. That gossip might spawn another Goethals incident, and Pershing acted to protect himself. About to leave for home, Baker stayed temporarily at 73, rue de Varenne, and Pershing asked Harbord to get up to Paris and tell the secretary some home truths about the Allies.[77] And in a final letter before Baker departed France on October

[75] For a professional appreciation of Pershing's September attack plan, see H. Essame, *The Battle for Europe, 1918*, pp. 167–68.

[76] JJP, *Experiences*, 2:306–7.

[77] Dawes, *Journal*, 1:179, 181, 182, 189–90.

5,[78] Pershing reiterated his irritations with lax handling of requisitions by the General staff—a clear shifting of blame homeward.[79]

No blame tainted Baker's generous heart. His visit at the fruition of so many hopes touched him with the grandeur of America's effort in the war. His admiration for the soldiers, the officers, the toilers in the ports and stations and hospitals carried back to the States and shaped a fresh wind in the War Department.

Pershing made his regular round of corps headquarters calls on October 3. Objectives he hardly needed to discuss. They stuck up in front of all eyes—Romagne Heights and its near outcrop, Côte Dame Marie, Cunel and its heights, the hostile bulk of the Argonne on the left. Tactically the problem came clearer now. The First Army attack would finally resemble a fan opened to its right half; the army's line finally would slant along the Meuse, which meant that divisions on the left would have farther to go in reaching the river than those on the right. Corps commanders all nodded at warnings of hard fighting, but they were eager to get going. Pershing put it to them firmly: "The thing to do is to drive forward with all possible force."[80]

Jump-off time on the fourth—5:30 A.M. Bombardment could hardly be distinguished midst the general racket of the field. An almost continual drumming dinned ears daily now; heaves of dirt broke across the open, cracked limbs in the *bois* and scattered rocks and arms and legs and broken guns in the strange cordite clouds of war. Misting gases fogged the front as the infantry scrambled out of shelters and into the struggle for height. On the right, Bullard's men, aimed at Cunel and its inviting lofts, made some progress, fought their way into Bois de Fays. In the center Cameron's men struggled out of Cierges, heading northwest for Gesnes and possibly a flanking hold on Romagne Heights. On the left, Liggett's 1st Division slammed into scythes of fire near Exermont, and the 28th, scrambling along the valley of the Aire, did well. Some units attacked the tough stronghold, Chéhéry, and after hand-to-hand encounters with numberless machine gunners, forced their way into the ruins. Farther left, part of the 28th stalled in the Bois de Taille l'Abbe and had to change front to a north-south axis along the Aire, the main line facing west.

In the gloomy Argonne proper, the 77th inched up to Charlevaux Creek, stopped, fell back, and left a mixed body of troops surrounded

---

[78] See Harbord, *Diary*, pp. 366–67.
[79] JJP, *Experiences*, 2:312.
[80] Quote, altered to the present tense, is from *ibid.*, p. 321.

behind German lines. This "lost battalion" was under Maj. Charles Whittlesey, a thin, bespectacled lawyer in civilian life who hated war but had dutifully studied it at Plattsburg. Left with his men in a bad place, he kept them there and lived to take a good many survivors out. He and his men were stuck in the dank Argonne from October 2 to 7; they ran out of cigarettes, food, water, most of their ammunition, had many killed and wounded, were down to their last carrier pigeon —a noble bird that gave up an eye and a leg taking the final message out. Every man in that never-really-lost-only-surrounded battalion deserved the Medal of Honor, and the Yankee lawyer got it.

Heroism ran so common in those early October days that medals became almost cheap. But one thing Pershing noticed in the resumption of fighting on the fifth; American initiative did pay dividends. New tactics were devised on the spot to grenade gun emplacements, to work into ravines and flank machine-gun nests. In the fighting around Apremont and Le Chêne Tondu, which, praise all, fell on the fifth, Yanks rushed woods and learned how to help each other leap-frog through villages. But all the while they took withering fire from Corned Willy Hill, from those spewing crags in the Argonne; still the terrible, three-sided chopping cut them down.

Resistance picked up bitterly as the Germans pumped new divisions in against the First Army. By October 1, seven German divisions joined the eleven in line; and during the first week of the month, the number swelled to twenty-seven, with seventeen in reserve.[81] Using skillfully their narrow-gauge rail network behind the lines, the enemy brought artillery forward in swamping amounts until the whole battle front seemed a thing of caroming rock, dirt, and shrapnel. Enemy infantry, veteran, tough, had the support of highly trained and fatalistic machine gunners who held their positions beyond common. Smart tacticians, German infantry officers directed small, telling counterattacks on favorable ground, regained heights and crags, and made Yanks pay twice, three times, sometimes more often, for the same blood-claimed land. Those first October days were bleached horrors of shelling that searched the front, roamed back into billet areas, scourged all ruins for stray observation points. Sleep came fitfully, snatched midst alarms and always in the suspicion of a sudden gas attack that could catch men unmasked. Rations were lost somewhere behind the lines; men ate what they carried, drank the water in canteens, and

[81] JJP and Liggett, *First Army*, pp. 54, 58. JJP estimated there were eleven German divisions between the Argonne and the Meuse, fifteen between the Meuse and the Moselle.

raced for clear streams when fire permitted. Daylight plagued the clumps of men clinging to woods and bluffs, grenading and bayoneting, holding what they had, yielding here and there, tired into a kind of stupor that sometimes craved death. And still the orders were onward; fight through the Romagne barrier; pierce the Kriemhilde Stellung.

At least no one could say the officers had no idea of the front—staffers from corps and army were everywhere, encouraging, occasionally commanding, but aware. Officers sometimes had strange fancies, though; they were fond of saying that German morale sagged, that the troops opposite were feeble second liners. Low morale? Spandaus, .77s, 220s sizzled, sang, and killed everywhere as the old 5.9s crumped into foxholes, clanged into kitchens and command posts, ferreted the meek and flailed the strong.

Big French guns, many worked by fine Yank artillerists, pounded the field, too, and flung mountains of steel at opposite numbers in that strange counterbattery war that seemed, sometimes, apart from the killing in the lines.[82]

Tough as he was, Fritz backed up under the young bravery of the Doughboys. They had scant style and battle ken; they were raw and eager and knew too little of the odds they faced; they went into the whizzing maelstrom in angry crouches; they died in rows and bunches, sometimes in graceful sprawls of slumber; but on they went into the Romagne claws, on the approaches to Cunel, until they came to the thinnest touches with mortality. Others of them off on the left, unseen save by odd flashes, unheard in the reigning din of dying, fought a squirrel hunter's war in the Argonne, sniping, stalking, stopped by sudden leaden tongues that hissed and cracked in hate. And by October 8 some of them were pushing across the Meuse, told to get at the tormentors on Corned Willy Hill. They moved up the heights, the *bornes*, and the impossible crags, bled, and retired; some died, some stuck to the bases of the hills, but the guns boomed still against their buddies anguished in the snares of Kriemhilde Stellung. This was not war; it had no pomp, just awful circumstance and the baffling grandeur of sacrifice. When, after constant days of attack Pershing called a halt on October 11, fearful lists of casualties—100,000 some said[83]—made melancholy way to headquarters, and the front line ran north of Consenvoye, west across the Meuse, wobbled around Cunel

---

[82] Charles Rhodes's "Diary of the World War," for Oct., 1918, gives an excellent account of an American artillery battery's life and hard work.
[83] Edward M. Coffman, *The War to End all Wars*, p. 332.

and Romagne Heights, and broke out of the Argonne at Sommerance. Pershing's army had footholds all along the Kriemhilde Stellung. The enemy fought fiercely as the Yank threat increased. More German divisions came to stall Pershing's terrible grinding machine.

Various shiftings and reliefs of divisions consumed three days. Pershing expanded his battlefield, added the French XVII Corps on the right, under Corned Willy Hill, until at last his men held a front of more than thirty miles. Out came the battle-weary 1st Division, replaced by the 42nd in V Corps; John McMahon's 5th Division took up the 80th's line in III Corps.

Big changes swept the top command. Pressures and politics, long neglected, at last engulfed the commander-in-chief. He decided to step back from active battle leadership and assume the role of an army group commander, the equal, at length, of Haig and Pétain. He would give First Army to thoroughly trusted Hunter Liggett and the new Second Army to Robert L. Bullard—whose neuritis had not slowed him a whit as a corps commander. The Second Army had been forming in Pershing's mind and on paper since the Saint Mihiel period, days when Pershing realized he would soon have more divisions than one man could handle. And he had tested himself, had seen his army gear into a full-panoplied Western Front battle, overcome all kinds of defects, and fight better than the enemy. He had not done all he would have liked, had not seen his good plan for the September 26 attack succeed, but he had watched green troops learn with lightning speed the skills of fine infantry, had prodded and scolded a staff organization equal to the greatest mass movement of the war, and had managed a battle with increasing confidence. Now he could talk to his Allied colleagues as a battle-proved equal.

Promotion of Liggett and Bullard to lieutenant generals and army commanders vacated two corps; a third opened when George Cameron confessed himself frazzled and asked to return to his old 4th Division. Who were the fighters that deserved promotion? Pershing always had a list handy of the trusted ones. Charles Summerall handled the good 1st Division brilliantly, was an aggressive, tireless battlefield leader with administrative skill—he got the V Corps. John L. Hines, known from the Villa days, who had done well with the 4th Division, moved up to Bullard's old III Corps. Joseph Dickman, whose handling of IV Corps showed great dexterity, shifted to Liggett's crack I Corps, and Charles Muir, of the proud Pennsylvanians' 28th Division, moved into IV Corps. Those were solid, battle-trained generals who knew how to run efficient machines. The army's organization could stand the next test of the Meuse-Argonne.[84]

Pershing gave orders for a last attack before stepping up to his General Headquarters—the sweeping push scheduled first for October 15, then redated for the fourteenth to join the French IV's attack. That last battle had all kinds of disappointments. The first disappointment appeared almost fatal. It came on October 12 with a visit of Maxime Weygand, messenger of madness. Be it said for him that he bore this duty squeamishly—but he had a message for General Pershing from the marshal commanding the Allied armies. Picking up Captain de Marenches in First Army Headquarters at Souilly and leaving an aide to talk with Colonel de Chambrun, Weygand went upstairs to beard Pershing in his den. Weygand's aide, excited and talkative, showed Lafayette's descendant a copy of the message Weygand carried. It was an order from Foch: General Pershing was relieved from command of the First Army and placed in command of the sector from Pont-à-Mousson to the Selle—a nice, quiet area unhampered by traffic problems or enemy activity. General Hirschauer would assume command of the U.S. First Army. De Chambrun, astounded, said the order could not be obeyed, "it was a great mistake in policy." And he wondered what horrors Weygand suffered in the room above. Weygand stayed briefly, came downstairs, and asked if de Chambrun had seen the order? Yes. Huffily, Weygand said "it is all off!" He then sent an opéra-bouffe cryptogram to Foch: "General Pershing received the fifteen carloads of ballast but cannot receive the remainder of goods until his transportation facilities are improved. I am coming home."

Warily de Chambrun climbed the stairs, found his general sitting patiently at his desk. Did the colonel know what had happened? Yes. What did de Chambrun think? "It would never do," he blurted, "it would be a fatal blunder and would forever obliterate the part America had taken in the war." Nodding sharply, Pershing asked de Chambrun to get Pétain on the telephone and ask him to come to Souilly right away. Pétain's headquarters at Nettancourt had been warned—the general could not take the phone. Finally, after several requests, the message changed. General Pétain would not come to the phone. De Chambrun delivered Pershing's request. Pétain had seen Weygand going through Nettancourt but had not yet seen him return, hence he

[84] JJP, *Experiences*, 2:336.

could not go to Pershing. De Chambrun faced a crisis in loyalties. Somehow he must preserve amity between his two countries.

To Pershing he explained Pétain's regret at entertaining important guests; he would come next morning. And later in the day, excused by Pershing from further duty, de Chambrun went to Nettancourt. Pétain greeted him in anguish and said that "he loved General Pershing and admired him greatly but that it was impossible under the circumstances for him to come to his headquarters." Weygand had told him of the order, said it would be executed "at all costs," and had stopped on his way back to say that Pershing "refused to accept the order and that Foch would have to go to Clemenceau for drastic action." Next morning Pétain called at Souilly.[85]

Foch would have to explain himself. Pershing, having heard rumors of Clemenceau's conniving, guessed that the prime minister had put the marshal on the spot. But Pershing rejected the spot Foch contrived for him. In company with the ubiquitous Carl Boyd, Pershing climbed into his car and headed for Bombon. It was Sunday, October 13, and the date had every chance of being bad for the Allies. At Bombon the Americans were ushered into the drawing room of Foch's headquarters. Weygand the ever present watched Pershing especially—he had noted the day before how weary the tall man seemed, the sallow skin and slackening jawline. Today Pershing seemed different, his blue eyes snapped, he carried himself erect, walked forcefully. Pershing wondered just how the marshal would save the Alliance.

Always a student of Pershing's moods, Foch tried an oblique tack— that likely would throw the direct American from the point. "What do you think President Wilson expects to do under present conditions?"

That vague question could have referred to Wilson's attitude toward rumored German peace feelers or his reaction to Clemenceau's latest gambit in command. Pershing parried with the truth. "I have received no communication whatsoever from President Wilson."

"I hope," Foch said grandly, "he will not presume to speak for the Allies. I am afraid the President will allow himself to become involved . . ." There was pause while he phrased the idea. "Involved in *long conversations*."

"Newspapers at home," Pershing said flatly, "find everyone resolved to push the war to a definite conclusion."

[85] Preston Brown, "Memorandum of a Conversation with Colonel de Chambrum at Army War College, 2:30 P.M., January 18, 1920," Box 35, PP.

Waving his hands, Foch fumed at politicians' chicanery with another thrust at Wilson: "I have no confidence in the Germans. A *long conversation* would give them an opportunity to withdraw and reform their armies." Clearly the French worried about American influence at the peace table; that had not been behind Clemenceau's poisonous maneuver.

Carefully Pershing said, behind his thin smile: "The talk around the White House is that Mr. Wilson will not become involved in long conversations."

"Good!" Foch turned to the big map on his wall. "And now, how are matters progressing on the American front?"

Quietly, firmly, Pershing talked of the hard fighting, the tough resistance. That sparked irritation.

"On all other parts of the front, the advances are very marked. The Americans are not progressing as rapidly."

Foch, master of the reptilian thrust, almost goaded Pershing to anger. But he explained patiently, "Our fighting facilitates the advance of the other armies. We are drawing enemy divisions away from the other fronts."

Foch wanted to see better performances from the Americans. Quickly came the icy response: "No army in our place would have advanced farther than the Americans." Pershing choked back comments on the terrible ground so generously handed his army by the French command.

Foch crushed the defense with a churlish line: "Every general is disposed to say the fighting on his front is the hardest." Waving at the map, he said, snidely: "I myself only consider results."

Results Pershing boasted: His men had engaged and eroded twenty-six German divisions. Foch disputed the figures, asked if Pershing wanted to see his list, and got a flat "No" for reply.

Finally the marshal said, less belligerently, "I want to see the Americans come up to the level of the other Armies in the direction of Mézières."

"I will continue my attacks until the Germans give way." Then Jack added with venomous courtesy, "Provided, of course, that this is Marshal Foch's desire."

"By all means," Foch said, and then changed his tone to podium cadence as he gave a lecture in elementary tactics to an old first captain of the Long Gray Line. The American practice of doing things without detailed written orders bothered Foch. Written orders were standard American policy, Pershing explained.

"Yes?" Foch shrugged maliciously.

Pershing added that he got copies of attack orders, written reports from the battlefield; those told him of the desperate German resistance. "The Germans," he added, "could hold up any troops Marshal Foch has at his command."

"Ah," again the chilly shrug, "I judge only by results."

That broke through the iron will. "Nothing any French general could say," Pershing snapped, "will put more goodwill, energy, or coordination into our operations. I have done all in my power, as have the officers under me."

Punctiliously Foch rang changes again on proper plans and professional execution in battle—"If an attack is well planned and executed, it succeeds with small losses. If not, the losses are heavy and there is no advance."

That old doctrine, denied on most French fields, Pershing rejected. "True only to a certain extent. Much depends upon what your enemy does." Now he took the offensive: "Why bring all this up? I am speaking of conditions that actually exist on my front. *No other troops could overcome them!* I would like to call your particular attention to the terrain."

Foch knew the ground; Pershing chose it, Foch allowed him to attack there. Then they both argued old feuds about splitting the American army here and there; Pershing reiterated his demands for a solid American army and Foch at last realized that the flashing blue eyes showed no weakness at all.

"Oh, well, it is a matter of no consequence now," he sighed. "The only thing that matters is results."

Weygand, who watched the two contestants in fascination, knew just the moment, always, to rescue his chief. "Here is General Pershing's plan for the formation of two armies."

Happily Foch said, "Ah, yes," without looking at the plans. "I am inclined to grant your request." Then a caustic order: "However, you are not to construe this as a plan for you to withdraw to Chaumont."

"As usual," Pershing said in controlled rage, "my headquarters train will remain in the woods at Souilly. I will visit Army, Corps, Division, and Brigade as often as possible."

"Very good," said Foch, standing at last, "General Pétain is agreeable to your plan."

Pétain's name triggered a final Pershing demand: Now that he commanded an army group, he said, he expected to be on footing equal with Pétain and Haig. Foch, knowing he was negating his whole argument, grudgingly agreed. And the meeting ended in careful courtesy.[86]

Returning to the tidied battlefield, straightened remarkably well, Pershing plunged into his last offensive as a field commander. To his new corps leaders Pershing put the attack problem clearly enough: "It was again practically a problem of forcing our way through a defile. The defenses of the Bois de Romagne and of the Bois de Bantheville may be compared to those of the Bois de Montfaucon, Bois de Cheppy, and Montfaucon; the defenses of Cunel Heights to those of the Bois de Forges; and those of Champigneulles, Bois des Loges and Bois de Bourgogne to the Argonne Forest." And still the Germans held splendid positions for defense; screened in woods that largely nullified American big guns, the increasingly worried Boche waited with thirty-two divisions and eight in reserve.[87]

Problems of coordination, unexpected and irritating, forced a double jump-off time—a straight thrust at Côte Dame Marie by center elements of the V Corps to start at 5:30 on the fourteenth, followed by the general assault three hours later. A two-stage jump-off confused artillery preparation, but quick shifts in assignments solved battery problems. On schedule the two attacks started, ran into fanatical fire, struggled for slithering yards in a cold, misty wind. There seemed that day a kind of eerie hostility in nature that aided enemy machine gunners, hid some from view, and wrapped the attackers in a special isolation. Quickly staff officers noticed a strange lapse in army efficiency. Plans called for a double penetration around Bois de Romagne, a cut through the defile in front of Cunel, a link up behind the Kriemhilde Stellung near Les Grands Carres, and a push toward Barricourt Woods and Buzancy. But one of the new divisions, McMahon's 5th, floundered under poor leadership, broke up and stalled.

[86] This episode is variously reported. JJP in *Experiences*, 2:335, mentions only that he visited Foch and talked of his new organization. Harbord, in *American Army*, p. 450, mentions Foch's postwar recollection of a letter from Clemenceau demanding Pershing's removal, and that he (Foch) turned the Tiger's anger since he "could not acquiesce in the radical solution contemplated by Monsieur Clemenceau." Frederick Palmer, in *JJP*, pp. 327–28, accepts Foch's version. Stallings, in *AEF*, pp. 325–28, reprints Carl Boyd's minutes of the meeting, slanting them to the view that Foch did not intend Pershing's removal. The conversation between Preston Brown and Colonel de Chambrun, cited earlier, is not mentioned in these sources. It changes the whole view of the Bombon conference. Foch must have worried for some time about Pershing's handling of their meeting. Would he tell Baker, the president, the AEF? But Missouri tact spared everyone embarrassment. See also Foch, *Mémoires*, 2:244–54.

[87] JJP and Liggett, *First Army*, pp. 64, 67.

Some units struggled ahead of the main body, fought their way into the dismal Bois des Rappes, and flanked Cunel. One battalion, sent on a quirky reconnaissance, filtered into the Kriemhilde positions; one company under Acting Capt. Samuel A. Woodfill meandered into the Kriemhilde Stellung unawares. Caught in a machine-gun crossfire, Woodfill set out to kill the gunners. An Old Army sergeant who wore brass uncomfortably, Woodfill had an expert rifleman's badge and that day proved the virtue of long shooting. At ranges often of more than 200 yards, he killed the crews of five machine guns—twenty-five men —captured three ammunition carriers, and extracted his command. This was the kind of fighting the Old Man expected of the U.S. regular soldier.[88] Woodfill was one of the fighters.

McMahon was not. Unsure of his position, of the general situation, a man tuned too much to rumors, he recalled his men from the Bois des Rappes. It took six days to get back in those bloodied woods. Corps commander John Hines, hard and driving and intolerant of timidity, ordered McMahon on October 15 to reorganize his division under close scrutiny. Pershing, who appeared at III Corps headquarters just after Hines blasted McMahon out into his troops, heard the whole story—and McMahon was through. Growling Hanson Ely got the 5th Division.[89]

Clarence Edwards, too, was through. Pershing had almost made up his mind about the New Englanders' darling in early October, had discussed removing Edwards with Baker, and watched the progress of the 26th with care. In the quiet Saint Mihiel area the division had no problems, but it lacked the kind of polish Pershing liked. He had orders for Edwards' removal drawn and approved by Washington, then waited. On the twentieth the order went to Edwards along with a saccharine letter from Chief of Staff McAndrew allowing that Pershing was inaugurating a policy of rotating line generals home to train recruits in the rigors of modern war. Edwards could be one of the first of that dubious crew with a particular blessing: "It is understood here that in compliance with General Pershing's specified request, you will retain your present rank and will be assigned to duty . . . ap-

[88] Stallings, *AEF*, pp. 29, 335–38.

[89] See "Index and Case Files Relating to Reclassification and Reassignment of Officers," Pershing Papers, 1916–24, 1931–39, in Box 8, RG 316, National Archives; Hugh Drum to G. C. Marshall, Sept. 27, 1919, in Pershing Papers, Correspondence re the First Army Report, 1919–1920, RG 200, National Archives Gift Collection. Stallings, in *AEF*, pp. 338–39, laments McMahon's removal without more evidence than Ely's sudden appearance to take over the command. He missed the Pershing Papers.

propriate to such rank. . . . He wishes you a safe and pleasant return home and every good that the future can bring to you."[90]

Somehow there seemed no consolation in Pershing's personal solicitude. Eruptions of horror swept the 26th's troops, morale reportedly sagged, but the new commander, Brig. Gen. Frank Bamford, found them hardy fighting men.[91]

Pershing had shown considerable irritation on October 15; his final attack stalled with only one notable objective taken—Côte Dame Marie. Through the fifteenth and sixteenth, Doughboys slugged their way to no real gain, save a penetration of Bois de Romagne's western reaches by Douglas MacArthur's 84th Brigade in the 42nd Division.

On the sixteenth the attack ended, and the First Army licked wounds and refitted.

That day Pershing received his most important message from Foch:

Allied G.H.Q., Oct. 16, 1918.

MARSHAL FOCH,
    Commander-in-Chief of the Allied Armies.

To GENERAL PERSHING,
    Commander-in-Chief of the American Expeditionary Forces in France.

My dear General:

I have the honor of confirming to you the conclusions of our interview of October 13th by informing you that in future I will send instructions of a tactical order directly to you without passing through the intermediary of the Commander-in-Chief of the Armies of the North and North-East, as I proceed toward Marshal Haig. . . .

Very sincerely yours,
F. FOCH [92]

As an army group commander Pershing intended to keep close to operations. At Liggett's request, he sent a mission order to the First Army on October 16 that permitted no relaxation of the Meuse-Argonne struggle. The army would drive on into and through the Kriemhilde and Freya Stellungs, crack enemy communications, and strike for Mézières. The general Allied situation improved daily. British and Belgian armies were driving through Flanders toward

[90] J. W. McAndrew to C. R. Edwards, Oct. 20, 1918, "In the Matter of the Investigation of Major General Clarence R. Edwards, N.A. (Personal File of Gen. J. J. Pershing), May 7, 1919," Reclassification and Reassignment of General Officers, Pershing Papers, RG 200, National Archives Gift Collection.

[91] Stallings, AEF, p. 305. See also JJP, Experiences, 2:353 and n.

[92] AEF, GHQ, G-3, Folder 656, Important Conferences, Memoranda, Etc., Affecting Employment of the A.E.F. (Foch-Pétain-Pershing), RG 120, National Archives.

Brussels—Pershing helped them with two divisions—other British forces were driving, too, toward Mézières; French armies, now free of the Aisne tentacles, pushed the center of the sagging German pocket. Foch's intended bag looked likely to close on rich prizes. Pershing ordered Liggett to launch a general attack on October 28— take Buzancy, Barricourt Woods, push to the Meuse. Foch, in flashing rhetoric, had ordered *tout le monde à la bataille*, and the Americans were a considerable part of the world of war.

Pershing had been right in arguing that the Meuse-Argonne thrusts by his men were putting unbearable pressure on the Germans. "It was . . . the advance of the Americans west of the Meuse which necessitated the withdrawal of the Aisne front,"[93] one German officer said, as more and more divisions were pulled in to hold the Freya Stellung.

Liggett unleashed a thoroughly remodeled army on November 1, 1918—the French IV Army's preparations lagged and delayed the assault. From positions along the Kriemhilde's remaining pockets, Doughboys plowed through the stuttering resonance of Romagne's guns, swept up past Grandpré, and toiled painfully on the slopes of Corned Willy Hill. Everywhere resistance hit that old killing standard as small, bitter, personal combats flamed across the battlefield. Slowly the Yank attack drove on. Those guns on Corned Willy Hill still killed many in flank. Hanson Ely's 5th Division regulars, helped by others, stormed the hill on November 7, and the whole line surged forward toward the Meuse. From Barricourt's ridge Doughboys at last looked down on a great valley stretching to the distant spires of Sedan. The objective was in sight of the survivors, but almost 120,000 of their buddies were dead, wounded, or gassed.[94]

By the first of November, political battles outstripped military ones in interest. As trouble bubbled in the Fatherland, morale eroded behind Germany's tottering legions. They retreated everywhere, but were not yet finished, and some Allied leaders like Haig worried lest they rekindle somehow the old spirits of Flanders. But Ludendorff cracked in the long crisis after his grisly failures in the summer; in a vision of despair he resigned on October 27, after Hindenburg, a tough old trooper who took his medicine, told the German government that peace negotiations must start. Steadily through October the German position eroded, home and front. The kaiser decamped and

[93] Von Giehrl, "American Expeditionary Forces" (pt. 2), p. 301.

[94] JJP and Liggett, *First Army*, p. 90. Pershing wrote this report for the period Aug. 10, 1918 to Oct. 15, 1918; Liggett wrote it from Oct. 16, 1918 to Apr. 20, 1919. See also Marshall, *Memoirs*, pp. 173–92.

Prince Max von Baden finally inherited the shambles of government and pushed hard to get terms according to Wilson's Fourteen Points. While diplomats studied each other's notes for nuances, the Americans drove on through Buzancy, hit the Meuse on a broad front, and were threatening Stenay and Beaumont.

Most of Pershing's days were spent on his headquarters train near Souilly or out in the field with various units. But in the pulsing days of October he ran increasingly to Paris. On the twenty-second a meeting there with Clemenceau caught that redoubtable rogue in high good humor. Ambassador Sharp and Tasker Bliss chattered gleefully about armistice prospects. Armistice or not, Pershing told them he would press his drive, extend it to the Second Army front for that thrust he had so long intended toward Metz and the Briey iron region. Bullard had organized his army speedily, and it would do good work in that open land where Metz lay unprotected.[95]

A visit to Foch at Senlis on the twenty-third produced warm greetings, high praise of American toughness, and some speculation on peace. There would have to be a conference of Allied generals. At Bertincourt with Haig, who was in high fettle at news of his gallant legions rushing forward with that recollected dash, Pershing talked seriously of possibilities. Less belligerent than Foch, Haig thought the Germans would accept armistice but not humiliation.[96]

Germany had had humiliation aplenty by late October. Austria buckled after the woeful disaster at Vittorio Veneto and sued for separate peace by the end of the month. Rumania collapsed and Germany's remaining outworks crumbled. She stood alone, stricken, bleeding, wracked with unrest. And still diplomats pondered periods and commas while men died across France.

Influenza stalked the armies and the world that chill winter, and Pershing himself, as he journeyed to Senlis on Friday, the twenty-fifth, felt worrisome symptoms. But the conference's importance beggared disease. All the army commanders-in-chief were present, plus several staff officers, including Pershing's faithfuls, Boyd and de Marenches. Pershing had hoped for instructions from Washington about terms, about things he ought to say, but talks with Bliss and Sharp, with Fox Conner, James McAndrew, and the army's judge advocate were his only priming.[97]

This meeting lacked the pressure of other Allied conferences.

---

[95] Robert L. Bullard, *Personalities and Reminiscences of the War*, pp. 282–90.
[96] JJP, *Experiences*, 2:355.
[97] *Ibid.*, p. 359.

Pershing felt no qualms this time, heard no frothing desires to steal his army. High merriment touched everyone and business seemed a little hard to confront. Foch at last achieved order. Germany negotiates, he said, through the Americans along the Fourteen Point line. He had assembled them, he told his colleagues, to sound their armistice views; he thought the terms should prevent Germany's resumption of war. After he had Wilson's Fourteen Points read aloud, he asked for ideas. Pétain, phlegmatic, said peace terms were politicians' business, and he agreed that any armistice should break German war powers. Pershing questioned the authority of the delegates—had the governments asked Foch to call them together? Yes, the Allied and Associated governments wanted the commanders-in-chief's views. Foch thought they should draft a statement of conditions acceptable to all.

Haig echoed the liberal sentiments that Pershing recently had heard. The German army still could resist; the Allies, Haig said, were thoroughly tired; the American army—here came a phrase to hurt—was not organized, "had suffered a great deal on account of its ignorance of modern warfare," and needed time to get in shape. If the Allied armies could fight vigorously, they should stick for hard terms. But in their reaches of attrition, easy terms were advisable. He sounded as though he thought the Allies needed the armistice as much as the Germans.

Pershing, next queried, passed to Pétain, since, as he said, "the French and British had been in the war longer than the Americans. . . ." Pétain thought the Germans expected harsh conditions and still negotiated. He wanted only to fix military boundaries on the Germans, to prevent them from resuming the war—he urged guarantees of territorial advantages to the Allies in case they had to finish the enemy. Political conditions such as occupation of Alsace-Lorraine meant little "from the military point of view"—surely heresy from France's hero of Verdun! Cars and locomotives captured by the Germans—some of them—ought to be returned.

Pershing listened in mounting dismay. His colleagues all seemed too ready to quit. He had just recently told his army that "there can be no conclusion to this war until Germany is brought to her knees"; it was a sentiment he felt deeply. Over the last weeks, as possibilities grew for an end to the horrors, his conviction hardened that Germany, if granted an armistice, would rebuild her power, try it all again. These ideas he voiced at the meeting, adding that he believed in hard lines. He agreed that terms should give every favorable edge to the Allies, thought, really, there should be no leniency shown to those

who had ruined so much of Europe. Haig's ideas of Allied fatigue
Pershing countered with the thought that victorious armies are seldom
fresh but that constant attack builds its own momentum. The American
army, he pointed out acidly, had done pretty well since July 18, was
growing in numbers and competence, and would be able to take on
heavier burdens should hostilities resume. He outlined a seven-point
program that included evacuation of occupied territories; repatriation of captives; withdrawal of German forces east of the Rhine;
surrender of U-boats, perhaps to a neutral power pending a peace
settlement; unrestricted transportation of U.S. forces from the States;
and return of railroad stock to France and Belgium.

Foch liked the American's views, praised the American army in
a pointed rebuff of Haig. Discussion focused finally on Pétain's scheme.
Foch, as usual, had everybody write out his ideas and collected them
the next day. In substance they all agreed with Pétain's middle-ground
position and with repatriation. Foch pushed Pershing's U-boat suggestion. Pétain wanted a withdrawal schedule for German troops
that would prevent their extracting heavy guns or equipment; he
wanted, also, occupation of Rhine bridgeheads by Allied forces and
the return of rolling stock—which apparently fascinated him.[98]

Back in Paris, Pershing cabled the ideas to Washington. His flu
symptoms worse, he finally went to bed. But not before he made a
considerable blunder. Wilson, through Baker, cabled a critical assessment of the severity of terms proposed at Senlis, but added an invitation to submit ideas on peace terms. The president would be glad,
Baker said, "to have you feel entirely free to bring to his attention any
consideration he may have overlooked which in your judgment ought
to be weighed before settling finally on his views."[99]

Ill and wearied, Pershing had dictated a long statement of his
ideas—they sounded like he was abandoning armistice for unconditional surrender—and submitted it to the Supreme War Council. A
copy went to Col. E. M. House, apparently for his submission to the
council—that would have been the proper channel. But Pershing had
sent it directly to the council, and it raised a storm of eyebrow wig-
gling and behind-hand whispering. How could Pershing have usurped
so much political authority? Stiff little House took it personally but

[98] *Ibid.*, p. 351; "Notes on Conference Held at Senlis, October 25, 1918";
"Meeting of the Commanders-in-Chief to discuss the terms of the Armistice"
(apparently an edited copy of the proceedings, possibly for public consumption),
both in Box 16, PP.

[99] Baker to JJP, Oct. 27, 1918, in Baker Papers, Correspondence 1916–21, Box
8, 1918 W-2 (Wilson), item stamped 167, Library of Congress.

refused to brave Pershing's flu bug to get the facts. Baker, when he learned that Pershing apparently had ignored Wilson's ideas about armistice terms, sat down and drafted the only letter of reprimand he ever aimed at Pershing. But on November 7, having heard from House that the whole thing had been a misunderstanding, Wilson quashed the letter. Pershing explained that his recital of unconditional terms had been merely military advice; no intent to intrude on political ground should be inferred. Pershing had blundered, but not seriously enough to cloud success.[100]

There were other blunders. In the last days of the race for the Meuse, looking down on the Sedan plain, Pershing saw the First Army close to a moment of history. Apparently, he wanted his army to take Sedan. There were boundary problems. The French IV Army aimed almost straight at that historic place, the place where Germany humbled France in 1870, but with a little fudging the Americans might win the race. Sedan would be a prize for France, certainly, but if the AEF could get there first a lot of doubts would be dissipated. Haig's insult at Senlis—for which the field marshal made handsome apologies in a personal letter to Pershing[101]—left scars that Sedan could

---

[100] JJP, *Experiences*, 2:363–69, gives his version of the complex maneuvers during the period October 25–November 3, and indicates no knowledge of the serious difficulties surrounding him. He recognized some misunderstanding, especially by the flu-shy House, but had no sense of overstepping authority. For his correspondence in this period, see JJP to the SWC, Oct. 30, 1918; JJP to House, Oct. 30, 1918; JJP to AGWAR, Oct. 25, 1918; House to JJP, Oct. 30, 1918 (all in Box 16, PP). See also Bullitt Lowry, "Pershing and the Armistice," *Journal of American History* 55 (Sept., 1968): 281–91.

[101] Haig, learning that his words about the American army hurt Pershing deeply, wrote a graceful apology on Oct. 27: "I have just heard that some of the remarks which I made at the Conference at Senlis. . . in French, were misinterpreted so as to give an idea of failure to the work of the American Army since it came to France. I write at once to correct this most incorrect impression of what I said. I yield to no one in my admiration for the grand fighting qualities of the American soldier nor for the manner in which you & your staff have overcome the greatest difficulties during the war. So such an idea has never entered my mind. At the conference. . . I was anxious to direct attention to the actual state of all the Allied Armies in France. . . . Foremost amongst [our] difficulties is that of creating enough American armies to make up for the rapidly dwindling numbers of the French and British. . . . Possibly the double translation of my thoughts . . . is responsible for the impression produced . . . but I trust that this letter puts matters in their true light. . . ." Pershing accepted the apology handsomely on the twenty-ninth, saying that "I am more than satisfied with the official correction that you have made" (Haig changed the minutes of his remarks) and added that the cordiality between British and Americans gratified him (both letters in Haig Papers). See also Haig Diary, Oct. 28, 1918, where Col. Robert Bacon is credited with reporting JJP's hurt feelings to Haig. "The Americans have been so criticised by the French that they are very touchy," Haig mused on hearing Bacon's report.

erase. Pershing sent Fox Conner to arrange Sedan's fate. What followed, had Foch heard it, would have amused him mightily—would have confirmed his faith in rereading written orders.

Conner went to Souilly late in the afternoon of November 5, found neither Liggett nor Drum handy, but saw George Marshall and dictated on the spot a memorandum for Marshall to issue to the I and V Corps, both of which might have a shot at the city. Drum arrived shortly after Conner left, heard the story from Marshall, and joined him in telephoning orders to corps headquarters.

1. General Pershing desires that the honor of entering Sedan fall to the First American Army. He has every confidence that the troops of the 1st Corps, assisted on their right by the 5th Corps, will enable him to realize his desire.

2. In transmitting the foregoing message, your attention is invited to the favorable opportunity now existing for pressing our advance throughout the night. Boundaries will not be considered binding.

Dickman of I Corps understood the message—French-American boundaries would not be binding. Summerall of V Corps apparently thought the message meant corps boundaries would be broken. At any rate, during the night of November 6, elements of the 1st Division of Summerall's corps stumbled over men of the U.S. 42nd Division, men they had not expected to meet. One of those men looked like a German officer in his greatcoat and rakish cap—and Gen. Douglas MacArthur had to talk his way out of arrest. During the day a mixed group of Americans struggled toward the city through French IV Army territory but reached only the environs.

As news of the snarl spread, tempers exploded. The commander of the French IV Army wrote an elaborate indictment of American indiscipline and preached morals on battlefield safety. Yank generals fumed at each other, friendships cracked, and the tangle finally unravelled—to leave dark suspicions and "secret" recollections which hinted that Pershing deliberately wrote a vague order to steal Sedan from the French. He shared the irk of some of his generals, but thought he had made arrangements with the French IV Army to slide a little out of the Americans' way and that confusion explained the mixup. He did think, though, that whoever had ordered the 1st Division's movement ought to be disciplined—in other, harder times. But not when victory ticked closer on the clock.[102]

[102] The Sedan episode became a cause célèbre in some circles and whetted tempers for years. It also became something of a historiographical problem in view of the bulking testimony from interested participants. For a survey of the events

About to enter formal negotiations with German representatives on November 9, Foch sent instructions for another general advance by all his armies. "Make decisive," he urged, "the results obtained."[103] The U.S. Second Army went forward on November 9—there was good progress toward the Briey iron area, but the fighting flared hot and fearsome. Still the Second Army earned much credit in three hard days. American divisions with the Belgians, too, earned credit and the U.S. Army took prominence from the channel to Metz's outskirts.

Word came to Pershing at Chaumont at 6:00 A.M. on November 11, 1918, that German delegates had signed armistice terms earlier that morning in a railroad car at Compiègne. Hostilities would cease. Phones connected him with First and Second Army Headquarters; he talked quickly about orders. At 11:00 A.M., November 11, the shooting stopped. Pershing thought the armistice too lenient, thought firmly that unconditional surrender was the only cure for German revival.[104] So the bickering began.

---

and the evidence, see JJP, *Experiences*, 2:381, where he dismisses the tangle as the result of a "misconception in the V Corps of the exact intent of the orders . . .;" Harbord, *American Army*, pp. 455–60, in which Harbord attempts a dispassionate unravelling of the events; Pogue, *Marshall*, pp. 186–88, reviews Marshall's role; Donald Smythe, "A.E.F. Snafu at Sedan," *Prologue: The Journal of the National Archives*, Fall, 1973, pp. 135–49, offers a general survey of the historiography. See also "Special Operations Report, First Army," Part IV of Section C, Meuse-Argonne, the Second Operation, AEF, GHQ, G-3 First Army, File 110.01, RG 120, National Archives; First Army Historical File 33.6, Special Reports of Operations; Sedan Incident, RG 120, National Archives; Coffman, *War*, pp. 348–53, offers a succinct account of the Sedan imbroglio. George Marshall in his *Memoirs*, pp. 189–90, discusses his meeting with Conner and asserts that Conner initiated the controversial order without reference to JJP.

103 JJP, *Experiences*, 2:382.
104 Dawes, *Journal*, 1:195–96.

☆ 23 ☆

Old Echoes, New Trumpets

DISAPPEARING armies have their own echoes. These blend with the happiness of sudden peace, blend, too, with the sadness of fading comradeship and crisis into the lasting history of men who raged and died in generations somehow larger than life. Silence on the Western Front came in great relief and in stunned enthusiasm. Men walked trench-lines in strange ease. Along those old hostile lines celebrating seemed somehow subdued, tempered by release. Behind the lines the wildness came. Crowds thronged Parisian boulevards in surges of excitement; London, long staid in austerity, erupted into mobs remindful of Mafeking night in Victoria's days. As the news raced wires to the world, America awoke slowly to a finished crusade—a finish that caught the nation in mid-strides of preparation.

Armistice had crowned a night's close vigil at Pershing's Chaumont headquarters.[1] Margaret Wilson, the president's daughter currently attached to the YWCA, joined the headquarters family for dinner on November 10, and talk had buzzed on pending negotiations with the Germans. "It will be an easy date for the future generations to remember," George Quekemeyer thought, "for it was the eleventh month, the eleventh day and the eleventh hour."[2] Orders went to America's armies, and struggles along the Marne and the Moselle stopped. Pershing prepared to visit Paris on November 12, 1918.

A Touch of History

"Le jour de gloire est arrivé," the "Marseillaise" proclaimed, and Paris proved the promise. Where could a man of triumph go? Pershing tried hiding, with moderate success. Orders from Foch about pursuit of retreating Germans were discussed with McAndrew—and with

[1] JJP, *Experiences*, 2:388.
[2] George Quekemeyer to his mother, Nov. 12, 1918, Quekemeyer Papers.

Harbord who had come from Tours in search of directions and excitement, found both, and barely contained seriousness enough for business.[3] Waving all but faithful Quek and Boyd back to their revels, Jack rode toward Senlis and a rendezvous with Ferdinand Foch. They met there for the first time in peace. The marshal, now the Victor Supreme, shook hands and seemed to bounce in ebullience. Everything about the war was wonderful—especially the Americans and their tall, straight general. The marshal raved awhile and Pershing listened in benign amusement.

Of the Americans what could an honest man say? They were magnificent, they fought like tigers, they were invincible, their commanders intrepid and stalwart. Their commander-in-chief? A man of "cordial cooperation," he was, "straightforward," even guileless. Foch in some excess boasted of knowing always where Jack stood because he had said what he thought "frankly and clearly and then lived up to it." Warmed to enthusiasm himself, Pershing spoke of Foch's brilliant leadership, his consideration for American desires, his indomitable will to victory. And then the speeches stopped in a sudden rush of awareness—it all was over. The terrible challenges, the arguments, the ceaseless, grinding warring that consumed days and hearts and lives for what had seemed eternity, were now done. Two comrades who remembered looked silently at each other. Words carried none of the realities of strife—they suddenly embraced and "gave each other the time-honored French 'accolade.'"[4]

Unashamed the warriors wept. And then they pulled themselves together for a ceremony—this was the time of ceremonies, of praising, and of gratitude.

In the yard behind Foch's quarters stood a small guard of honor, headed by a grizzled sergeant of the line. Trumpeters opened with a flourish. A long, fond look at Foch, then sincere, admiring words in French that ran much more melodiously than eighteen months before, and, with a hand tucked inside the marshal's tunic, Pershing pinned on the red, white, and blue ribbon of the Distinguished Service Medal. It was the first of its kind given to a foreign officer, and it came at Jack's personal suggestion to President Wilson.[5] Quekemeyer handed one of Foch's aides a copy of the remarks and then Foch began talking.

[3] See James Harbord, *Leaves From a War Diary*, pp. 392–98.

[4] JJP, *Experiences*, 2:393.

[5] *Ibid.*, p. 394; Baker to Wilson, Oct. 15, 1918, Correspondence 1916–21, Box 8, W-s (Wilson), item stamped 146 (also 1154), Baker Papers, Library of Congress.

An honor he cherished, he said, had just come, cherished especially since it marked the closeness between France and America and would remind him ever of how "brilliantly" Doughboys fought beside *poilus*. Emotion filled his eyes again, his voice faltered, and at last he stopped. Jack took his hand and they stood together while trumpets flourished once again and the troops marched away.

Foch proved a voluble host at lunch and fascinated everyone with his recollections of negotiating armistice with the Germans. Quek, as he heard of high councils, thought "it was one of the most interesting things" he had ever experienced.

After lunch the Americans drove back to Paris—only to find it a wildering bedlam. "It looked as though the whole population had gone entirely out of their minds," Jack thought, as he saw the crush on every street and boulevard, heard the singing and cheering, watched the dancing and celebrating.[6] As Jack's auto struggled through the Place de la Concorde, people recognized "Général Pairshing, Général Pairshing"; celebrants clambered all over the running boards, hood, roof, and refused all pleas to leave; some climbed in with le Général! A group of happy Doughboys, spotting their chieftain's plight, formed a wedge and led him through the maze—the crossing of the Place took two hours!

"Ridiculous things" happening on all sides amused Jack, but business caught his mind. Dawes, good old Charlie always thinking ahead, suggested a general order reversing the supply machine—and it had been issued on the eleventh.[7] A War Department cable on the twelfth suggesting the same thing proved Dawes's prescience. That energetic bundle talked now of new problems in supplying food to Belgium, to riot-torn Germany, to Austria, and of things more serious. "The day of the civilian is approaching," Dawes brooded, and guessed that the intricacies of dismantling the AEF offered boundless chances for unpopularity. Battle heroes spoil quickly in peacetime, and that good friend worried lest Jack's repute fade in the wrangles of demobilization. As for himself, Dawes wanted to go home—"I wish selfishly I could stop my military work at this juncture. Personally there is nothing to gain by success and much to lose by mistake."[8] Command continued past war's end, and Jack thought hard about his own responsibilities. Those good men who came from America, who fought, bled, died, and sur-

---

[6] Quekemeyer to his mother, Nov. 12, 1918, Quekemeyer Papers; JJP, *Experiences*, 2:395.

[7] Charles Dawes, *A Journal of the Great War*, 1:209.

[8] *Ibid.*, pp. 205, 222.

vived, wrote the history of the AEF—the finest army surely ever fielded by the United States. Those men came to discharge a duty, did it, and would now be eager to go home. Their care and future rested in their commander's hands. Nothing must tarnish the record of the AEF.

In a nearly emotional order, he told his men how he admired them and called for further service.

G.H.Q.
American Expeditionary Forces,

France, *Nov. 12, 1918.*

General Orders
No. 203

The enemy has capitulated. It is fitting that I address myself in thanks directly to the officers and soldiers of the American Expeditionary Forces who by their heroic efforts have made possible this glorious result. Our armies, hurriedly raised and hastily trained, met a veteran enemy, and by courage, discipline and skill always defeated him. Without complaint you have endured incessant toil, privation and danger. You have seen many of your comrades make the supreme sacrifice that freedom may live. I thank you for the patience and courage with which you have endured. I congratulate you upon the splendid fruits of victory which your heroism and the blood of our gallant dead are now presenting to our nation. Your deeds will live forever on the most glorious pages of American history.

Those things you have done. There remains now a harder task which will test your soldierly qualities to the utmost. Succeed in this and little note will be taken and few praises will be sung; fail, and the light of your glorious achievements of the past will sadly be dimmed. But you will not fail. Every natural tendency may urge towards relaxation in discipline, in conduct, in appearance, in everything that marks the soldier. Yet you will remember that each officer and each soldier is the representative in Europe of his people and that his brilliant deeds of yesterday permit no action of today to pass unnoticed by friend or foe. You will meet this test as gallantly as you have met the tests of the battlefield. Sustained by your high ideals and inspired by the heroic part you have played, you will carry back to our people the proud consciousness of a new Americanism born of sacrifice. Whether you stand on hostile territory or on the friendly soil of France, you will so bear yourself in discipline, appearance and respect for all civil rights that you will confirm for all time the pride and love which every American feels for your uniform and for you.

JOHN J. PERSHING,
General, Commander in chief.[9]

In a long afternoon conference on November 12, Pershing talked with Dawes, McAndrew, Harbord, and General Merrone of the Italian Army, and he set the first patterns of inter-Allied collaboration in

---

9 *USWW*, 16:533–34.

peace. Whatever measures must be taken for disengagement and for German occupation would follow careful, measured lines. America's position would not be compromised on the threshold of a new era.[10]

No seriousness could survive, though, Parisian ecstasy. Charlie Dawes never lost perspective—his swath of pleasure ran wide in Paris, and his repute for *joie de vivre* ranked with the finest. Jack had too long fussed with the AEF; this was the time for fun. Charlie had tickets for the Folies Bergères. The show was *Zig Zag* and, although he had seen it the night before with Harbord, Charlie pressed his old friend to share his box. A good show, Harbord said, agreed himself to go again, and promised a certain cleanliness and patriotism on stage. Jack accepted without much persuasion—pretty girls were always a priority. Besides, Carl Boyd thought enough of the performance to bring his lovely wife. And the show did boast Allied prowess—scenes depicting French and British triumphs, Australian bravery, Scottish pluck brought raucous cheering. Pershing had behind the box partition, peeped at the stage in awkward anonymity, and joined in Yank yelling for the tableaux praising Saint Mihiel and the Meuse-Argonne.

Word of Pershing's presence somehow raced through the theater, and the crowd, less boisterous than the night before, tired from roistering, held back until the last curtain—and then they simply stayed and looked toward the general's box! Hurrying out by the stage entrance, Pershing's party made for his car. At the stage door a crowd waited and cheered thunderously when the general appeared. Amiable now, happily tired, the merrymakers let the auto leave without hindrance.[11]

Camaraderie still caught the old Allies. Pershing had several medals yet to bestow. On Wednesday, the thirteenth, he called on Marshal Joffre, the hero shelved but not forgotten, and at the Ecole de Guerre gave the decoration with simple words of praise. "It gave me the greatest pleasure to make this presentation."[12]

One above all others Pershing yearned to give—this to Henri Philippe Pétain. In the finalities of fighting Jack remembered the growing closeness of the French commander, his firm aid in troubles with Foch and Haig, his deference to American hopes. Now a "good friend," Pétain almost more than Joffre deserved America's recognition. After the Joffre presentation Pershing, Harbord, Boyd, and Quek piled into the khaki auto with its four stars and motored to Provins, where

[10] Dawes, *Journal*, 1:210–11.
[11] *Ibid.*, p. 206; Harbord, *Diary*, pp. 397–98.
[12] JJP, *Experiences*, 2:396.

Pétain waited. At lunch the taciturn hero of the armies of France presided over a large table of aides, generals, and dignitaries and after dessert led everyone out to the front courtyard. There a twenty-man guard of honor stood rigidly in waiting; Pétain marched to their front, and Jack faced him. Words of thanks came easily to the Missourian as he pinned the Distinguished Service Medal on the light tunic. When Pétain beamed, Jack basked. "It was especially gratifying for me to decorate Pétain, as my relations with him were always closer than with any of the other Allied officers and we had become fast friends." Pétain spoke eloquently of the AEF—the surest way to Jack's heart—and obviously enjoyed the recognition.

One more honor must be paid.[13] Troubles, bickers, and quibbling dogged Anglo-American relations, but Douglas Haig kept firm the façade of cooperation. His own dogged courage had held the BEF together, made it finally a sure weapon of victory, and no full compliments could be paid without him. To Cambrai on November 14 Pershing went in his special train, still served by the faithful Boyd and Quek and accompanied this time by Charlie Dawes and faithful Robert Bacon, liaison with Haig. Dawes's reputation among the British made him an asset at Cambrai; his quick, quirky curiosity charmed the staid English, and Haig seemed especially fascinated by the strange Yankee so casual, so shrewd. Breakfast with Haig's staff started the day, and then a short auto trip to Ewey landed the visitors in a dense fog. Worried about Dawes's foul cigars, Jack threatened personal damage if a trickle of smoke marred the meeting. The car stopped, and out of the swirling grayness came the trim, moustached face of Douglas Haig, commanding British Armies in France. His aide, General Lawrence, joined Dawes, and the four soldiers stalked into the murk.

Suddenly trees yielded on a large open space with the American flag atop a small pole. Pershing peered hard into the fog, saw dimly a British square guarding the Stars and Stripes, a square made by a brigade from the 51st Highland Division. "Present Arms." To the flag Pershing marched with Haig. Dawes and Quek attended Pershing; Lawrence and General Horne, commanding the British I Army, attended Haig. A chilly breeze flapped the flag as pipers swung past the generals in an echo of Scottish airs. Pershing turned to Haig, spoke briefly, pinned on the Distinguished Service Medal. Haig spoke, too, and briefly, as a galaxy of generals gathered. Five minutes had passed. Smartly to the flag came a Highlander, who moved it carefully a hun-

[13] *Ibid.*; Pétain to JJP, Nov. 9, 1918, and JJP to Pétain, Nov. 11, 1918, Box 160, PP.

dred yards to left center of the square. "Pass in Review." Pipes skirled, and first came the Black Watch. Thinning fog gave a good view of these splendid troops who marched with veteran ease and precision. Pipers switched to the Black Watch air. On came the men. "Eyes left," the order rang and heads turned to look as the men passed by. Next came the Argyll and Sutherlands. Then the tune changed to the "Campbells Are Coming," and, quickly, they came. In that gray but shining morning, the Highlanders moved off at last to fading notes and history.

Back Pershing and friends went to Cambrai once again to board the special train. "Moving-picture operators of the Signal Corps" covered the Haig presentation, buzzed around Pershing as he settled in his new office car on the train, and photographed everything in sight. They were bothersome, but they were tolerated in relaxation.[14] A slow trip back to Paris—the roadbed, just relaid after fighting, provided uncertain comforts—gave opportunity to think of others to be honored. March, after all his struggles as chief of staff, surely deserved the Distinguished Service Medal,[15] and Pershing cabled a recommendation.

That slow, rocking trip to Paris gave time, too, to talk further with Dawes about the housekeeping details of demobilization. It seemed almost sinful to impose on Charlie, but needs transcended people. He must stay in Europe and advise on the dwindle of materiel. With Edward Stettinius representing Baker and Harbord representing the SOS, Pershing thought that Dawes, aided by them and by the AEF's finance officer, could fashion a system to disperse equipment and excess American supplies honestly and with some profit. Those men, under Harbord's chairmanship, would constitute an Advisory Settlement Board of the AEF, which could sell surplus goods to Allied governments. Anything that could be dispensed fairly must go— returning vast tonnages of lumber, pipe, railroad iron, and specialized machinery to the States for scrap looked woefully wasteful. What did Charlie think? He agreed with the need but seemed lukewarm about staying in France. Loyalty, though, and affection for Jack prevailed—he accepted the necessity to "complete my work and remain as long as duty requires." Jack had, certainly, not demanded Charlie's acquiescence, but his mere request was enough. Those good Missouri blue eyes looking straight at Charlie, the honest question, and the obvious need all touched a sympathetic heart. "The General has now become one of the first figures in the his-

14 JJP, *Experiences*, 2:397; Dawes, *Journal*, 1:211–13.
15 Edward M. Coffman, *March*, p. 170.

tory of our nation," Charlie mused, and noted comfortably that "to me he is always the faithful and affectionate friend and congenial associate of twenty-four years' standing. His head is not turned in the least."[16]

Enough rankling continued to dim conceit. In the midst of euphoria some old tinges of inter-Allied competition intruded to tarnish slightly the shine of victory. Pershing's growing concern fastened on getting as many of his men home as might be spared from France. Despite some cherished fears of Foch's and Haig's that the Germans might not go through to a final peace settlement, Jack thought the enemy nearly finished. He doubted that unrest in the Fatherland and the war weariness of veteran German troops would permit resumption of conflict. And the heavy burdens of supply in Europe, the senseless pouring of men and treasure into a quiet war zone, must be stopped. From Baker came ample evidence that mobilization efforts would stop, the machinery would be reversed, and the fond American dream of getting the "boys" home quickly would be realized. But pressure from Allied leaders hampered Pershing's plans to return his men home.[17]

Confusion hampered Allied plans. Foch and Pétain worried about demobilized *poilus* and problems they might present to France's economy and politics; they worried, too, about policing the devastated areas. These double worries prompted some indiscretion. To Pershing on November 23 Foch sent an impassioned letter that rang oddly like a statement of obligation:

The reconstitution of the soil and the means of habitation of the devastated regions will necessitate considerable labor and effort. It will be impossible for France to furnish, within the time limit set for restoring the country to the economical condition which is indispensable to it, this labor and effort after she has been reduced to her own resources.

French troops in rest areas Foch generously offered as aides to civilians. Surely the American army, also in its rest areas, would continue

to give . . . the aid which you have so generously given . . . during the war. I am . . . convinced that your troops will put all their soul into repairing, as far as they are able to do so before leaving France, what has necessarily been destroyed during the course of the operations.

---

[16] Dawes, *Journal*, 1:218.

[17] Baker to JJP, Dec. 1, 1918 (cable 2374-R), in AEF, GHQ, G-3, Folder 653, RG 120, National Archives; JJP to AGWAR, Dec. 18, 1918 (cable 1972-S), in Pershing Papers, Cables, Box 4, RG 200/316, National Archives; James G. Harbord, *Personalities and Personal Relationships in the American Expeditionary Forces*, p. 15.

As laborers Doughboys would do "precious service" for a crippled Ally.[18]

Infuriated, Pershing sent an icy acknowledgement of Foch's letter with the comment that its questions touched on "the policy of my Government" and so he had sent it to Washington. In his covering cable to Baker, Jack offered sober reasons against Foch's request. Delays in withdrawal would occur; the time until departure could be used far better for training; more to the point, "the temper of the soldier, if not that of their relatives at home, precludes any idea of the general employment of the American soldier as a laborer in rebuilding France." The issue had serious potential, he warned, since there seemed a growing sentiment among the Allies "that American Armies or a part of them should largely perform such police or garrison duty as may possibly arise." A clear policy statement by the United States would settle the matter, and Pershing hoped it would come swiftly. Clearly the commander-in-chief thought any attempt to reduce his good men to ditch fillers ranked as a supreme, incredible insult. Other nuances Pershing felt as well, nuances of exclusion in occupation positions in Germany, of a subtle downgrading of American presence in Europe. None of these possibilities could be tolerated.

Baker read his general's banked outrage aright and replied on December 1. No published announcement seemed wise, he said, but a policy had been adopted for private expression to Allied officers—and it ran much to Pershing's pleasure.

The policy of the United States is to bring about immediate return to the United States of our soldiers in France as rapidly as transportation facilities are available or can be supplied. . . . no soldier of the United States can be retained in France to be used as [a] laborer or in reconstruction work, and the most that can be done in that regard is to offer to our soldiers such opportunities as are consistent with the necessary military situation to work voluntarily upon such reconstruction enterprises. . . . The gift of service, however, is from them as individuals to France. No part of their duties to their own Government as soldiers would justify our Government in requiring them to perform such labor. . . .[19]

Fiercely defensive of his soldiers' honor, Pershing reported Baker's views to Foch in conciliatory sympathy but without concession. French troops would have to rebuild their own country. At the same time he

18 Foch to JJP, Nov. 23, 1918, in AEF, GHQ, G-3, Folder 653, RG 120, National Archives.
19 JJP to Foch, Nov. 28, 1918; JJP to AGWAR, Nov. 28, 1918 (cable 1933-S); Baker to JJP, Dec. 1, 1918 (cable 2374-R, Confidential), (all in AEF, GHQ, G-3, Folder 653, RG 120, National Archives).

pressed the marshal to release American divisions. How many combat-ready units were really needed? Foch, in a harried meeting at Strasbourg on December 8, guessed that the thirty divisions discussed in the November 12 talks ought to be kept handy. Pershing urged twenty-five, though he thought a reduction by half would not jeopardize peace chances. Concentrating around Le Mans, he said, were some 80,000 men of the SOS waiting for shipment home. Before the SOS could be cut further, some combat forces must go. Reluctantly Foch agreed to let five divisions move toward Le Mans, but refused others until "J" day, the day the preliminary peace treaty would be signed. Pershing accepted, promised to keep the marshal informed of American base port arrangements and troop movements. Privately he determined to keep pushing Foch on force reduction—suddenly the marshal coveted the AEF and his eagerness needed curbing.[20]

How face the easing pressure? Alarms so long the elixir of each day, crises always pulsing adrenalin, excitement and anguish for the fighters in Romagne, in Cunel's clutches, hacking upward on Corned Willy Hill, all ebbed now in the ennui of an old war. Time could be wasted. Conviviality rekindled with Micheline Resco at her studio, with Charlie Dawes, and with the myriad guests ever flocking to that gay man's company. In stray moments with so old a friend, frustrations could be aired and sometimes eased. And cherished cohort that he was, Charlie could assess the waves of sentiment washing over Pershing and his army from the world. Nostalgia suddenly swept pique aside, and the American press for the moment lavished adulation on everyone with the tinest part of the "great crusade." Pershing more than others claimed popular clamor—he ranked now with the greatest captains, an American Napoleon, a man who had commanded more men and done more fighting than U. S. Grant. That kind of talk seemed overdrawn to Jack, whose admiration for Grant grew with his own experiences in high responsibility. That kind of wild boasting, too, had backfiring possibilities. As streams of official and lesser visitors bubbled around Paris, streamed to Chaumont, and claimed any spare moments of the commander-in-chief's time, rumors wafted with them to bother a professional soldier now remote from Senator Warren's political coils. Pershing for president! Headlines, if not bold ones, did suggest that chance, backed by reams of newsprint wasted in speculation about his politics, his predilections, his preferences. Clippings

[20] [Carl Boyd?] "Notes on Conversation Between General Pershing and Marshal Foch at Strassbourg, December 8, 1918," Box 16, PP.

came in bales from well-wishers at home—would the general let his name go formally to the people?

Adulation and honors were fine, coveted in fact, but a Republican general serving a Democratic administration must keep strictly neutral in political realms. Wilson and Baker had been steadfast and remarkably wise in support. Their good will and appreciation had been quickly confirmed at war's end when Tasker Bliss journeyed in mid-November to Chaumont to do a happy duty for the president. As he watched doughty Bliss of the Old Army pin on the Distinguished Service Medal, Pershing's pride broke bounds. He spoke a soldier's thanks truthfully, "I know of no honor that could come to an American greater than the honor which has come to me to-day . . . from the President and the American people whom I serve. I can simply say that I thank them. . . . "[21] And in the full feeling of affection for his country, John Pershing had grown beyond the last twinges of ambition. When he basked in the fullest triumph of a soldier, what other careers could matter? Calls to high office could not flatter, could only tarnish a world reputation. If the presidency charmed—and it did—the charm should be ignored.

But rumors indicated canonization for Pershing. Newsmen, fond always of the random guess as a stimulant to confession, persistently suggested Pershing as presidential material. Papa Warren, still clipping items about his son-in-law, dutifully bundled the sheaves of guesses and shipped them to Chaumont. Embarrassed at personal attention, acutely aware of the poor timing—President Wilson was about to arrive at Versailles—Jack growled his displeasure to an amused Dawes. Should he deny the rumors in strong terms? Shrewd Dawes urged a glacial unconcern—"not worthy of notice," Jack, Charlie said, "at least for the present."[22] Those rumors were natural—a point Senator Warren made—and must be accepted stoically. If Jack's fancy turned—well, the opportunity might linger.

Some interesting family suasion clouded the presidential issue. Carefully, without telling Jack, Warren had been testing the political climate for a Pershing breeze. He had not planted the stories, but when they began he took a cryptically noncommittal stand to the press. Questions he fended as "premature," "speculation," the kind of thing likely to "embarrass" a soldier in his job. To questions about Jack's politics, Warren was apparently candid:

21 Remarks of JJP in accepting the Distinguished Service Medal, Chaumont, Nov. 16, 1918, Box 342, PP.
22 Dawes, *Journal*, 1:223.

I have never asked him; . . . I do not know; . . . Pershing is a soldier, does not want office and will refuse to consider it; . . . being educated at West Point, and having been in the Army serving in the field in this and foreign countries ever since, and never having visited his home station, where he might vote, more than two or three times since his graduation, it is easy to imagine that he has never had an opportunity to vote, and hence may never have voted. He came from a Democratic State, although that particular part of it might have been, and probably was, Republican. His father was a standard Union man throughout the Civil War; his only brother is a Republican; he married an ardent Republican; and hence they may guess as to his politics, but must not consider him a candidate.

Ingenuously reporting his bland actions to Jack, Warren admitted the vagaries of political reaction: "Of course I know what the result of all this will be, that the more [Pershing] or his friends, say 'No,' the more people will rise out of the cane-brakes and yell . . . 'You must.'" Both parties, Warren boasted, asked confidential reports on Jack's position, with the Democrats wistfully willing to boom him if he simply had not "declared" himself Republican.[23]

Bales of clippings recalled early events in Pershing's life—many hilariously fictional—and suggested the crown of responsibility in France conferred uncommon wisdom. Outrageous praise brought a grin to the thin mouth, creased the laugh lines around the blue eyes, and touched that old current of glory deeper sunk now in maturity. He would have grasped for the brass ring a few years ago, he knew it, and would have played some cagey game of noncandidacy, but now the return of the men, the care for those not going home, the guarding of an army's repute seemed duty fitting for history. Generals, some of them, made bad presidents. He asked Warren for a canny politico's views. Warren's answers blended affection with surrogate ambition. "There is no answer you can make at this time and no declaration that will stop this flow. If you keep still and let it run, it will run no faster and perhaps . . . slower than if you made continued declarations." A lofty declaration of devotion to "great tasks of reconstruction" would sit well. But Warren leaned and showed it—"way down underneath I must tell you that it looks very much as if *you are in for it*. . . . Best prepare for the White House!"[24] Election time in 1920 could be exciting for the whole Warren-Pershing clan.

Nothing now was more important than getting the Doughboys home in reasonable time and condition. The country owed those good

[23] FEW to T. Blake Kennedy, Dec. 4, 1918; *id.* to JJP, Dec. [date illegible], 1918 (both in FEW Papers, vol. 85).

[24] FEW to JJP, Dec. [date illegible,] 1918, FEW Papers, vol. 85.

soldiers careful care until they were demobilized. Special orders went to Hugh Young and his heroic VD men to redouble efforts at prophylaxis—and the job would be especially touchy with fighting ended and time abundant. But there would be no relaxing health regulations.[25]

A series of stories scurried the army about the Old Man's penchant for prophylaxis. One such story reported outrage on the part of Bordeaux's city fathers when they heard Pershing had put the red-light district off limits to the AEF. This would ruin the city's economy! Others, more rueful than funny, reported soldiers' bouts with gonorrhea and general orders, with syphilis and segregation. But together the stories showed attention—the men had enough respect for the regulations to joke.

Joking ran thin in the hospitals. Pershing kept up his visits to the wounded, urged better care on every doctor, fussed about food and comforts for men who were heroes, each and every one.

Heroes put a heavy burden on their commander as he trekked the fields of their shining glory. Showers of decorations, lavish dinners in praise of all, glittering poesies of congratulation, all seemed somehow limp and shabby against the sacrifice of so many whose future lay now in the ground of France. Whispers from home of problems and speculations in France dishonored the living and shamed the dead. Rumbles from the dissatisfied irked all American leaders in France—they seared John Pershing. As far as he could tell, all officers who survived the harsh testing he demanded, who survived the fighting in France, were honorable men whose devotion to America transcended pettiness. Silence proved hard to keep, but friend Dawes again urged no answer from Chaumont. If rumors and carping turned on the members of the AEF, then their general would speak.

Critics were careful about aim. Mostly they struck away from GHQ, slammed lesser folk in the supply system or speculated on wastage as an accepted fact on the Western Front. Somehow the commander-in-chief, AEF, escaped blame—so far—for heavy battle

---

[25] Hugh Young, A *Surgeon's Autobiography*, pp. 387–90; GO no. 32, GHQ, AEF, Feb. 15, 1919, in *USWW*, 16:656–57, included these strictures: "The recent adoption of more liberal leave privileges for the men of these forces renders it timely to emphasize the necessity of redoubling our efforts to advise continence and discourage illicit sexual intercourse on the part of all ranks. . . . In case of venereal disease where it appears that prophylaxis has not been taken as required there will be a trial on a separate charge of failing to obey the requirements of G.O. No. 6, these headquarters, as well as on the charge of contracting a venereal disease."

losses in the Meuse-Argonne, for suspected cheating in purchasing and construction.

> *Yes, makin' mock o'uniforms that guard you*
> *while you sleep*
> *Is cheaper than them uniforms, an' they're*
> *starvation cheap . . .* —Kipling

Woodrow Wilson came to the Peace Conference on December 14. For ten days he basked in sea air aboard the *George Washington* and during the crossing, now tranquil and serene, pondered the future of his world. Suspicious already of the shifting motives of Allied colleagues, aware of nuances and possible side agreements, Wilson came with the naïveté of a scholar and the confidence of honesty. Europe, save for its leaders, waited for his coming in messianic excitement. His Fourteen Points had brought Germany to the peace table, and, if most knew none of the points or the principles under them, people knew instinctively that this tall, graying professor came with good intent. In Paris on the Saturday of his arrival, Wilson wallowed in the tumult of exultation—crowds thronged the avenues, held children aloft to see the savior of the world, and waved American flags as they had done that June day in 1917 when John Pershing brought America's first mite to the war.

Clearly the generals would have little to do with the peace deliberations. Delegates—Bliss stood in for Baker—would discuss German needs and punishments, consult on martial matters only with selected officers, and leave the old heroes to the new shelves. Pershing came to Paris to meet the commander-in-chief. The old coldness in a military presence tinged the meeting, but the president's happiness bridged the moment. Worn, tired, but smiling, he promised hard work to achieve the kind of peace to last. If any rankling remained of Pershing's stand on the armistice negotiations, it failed to show, and Pershing asked the president's consent to a Chaumont review. Jack had, before Wilson's departure from the States, urged that the president include a battlefield review of veterans in the Meuse-Argonne country. Not only would such an occasion please the troops, but "I believe that [it] would afford the President the best opportunity he will probably have to emphasize to Europe, in an address to his own troops as their Commander-in-Chief, the purposes he had in mind in sending this

Army to France." That good idea failed of a place on the presidential agenda, although a visit to Chaumont won approval.[26] Pershing thought Wilson missed his best moment—a battlefield address had immortalized the Union's cause. Many veterans felt snubbed. But the general had nothing save admiration—and concern—for the president. "He has been a good President to us, backed the army well, but he has his hands full now."[27]

No clashes came over rumored presidential possibilities. Wilson, like Pershing, ignored the speculation—although he heard, surely, of the triumphs marking Pershing's progression through Luxembourg on his pilgrimage into Germany at Treves. Wild gratitude marked the visits, and when, with Albert of the Belgians, Pershing entered Brussels, the scenes almost beggared Parisian eruptions. London wanted him at a great parade; Paris planned one final spasm of victorious congratulation. But the president's presence damped martial panoply—at least for the Americans.

Serious, idealistic, ascetic, Wilson had the hauteur of rectitude. His righteousness irked lesser folk like Clemenceau and Lloyd George and forged a closer bond of selfishness between them. Through the parlors of Paris, London, and Rome, Wilson's aloof chill repelled enthusiasm, and when the Peace Conference at last got to business at Versailles, he had a completely distorted view of world realities. Remoteness begat distortion, and he moved in a closing vision of his own.

Restless and uncertain about peace terms, half wondering if the war would somehow erupt again, Pershing turned his eyes to the AEF. Demobilization continued as the organization of dispersal took hold. Gathering Boyd and Quekemeyer close, Pershing resumed his flits around the countryside—now to inspect units before they left for the States. Each division rated an inspection before embarkation, and these became famed as ordeals beyond the call of duty. Troubles came in the Old Man's inflexible discipline, in the harsh training rules he maintained, all the physical conditioning that continued in peacetime. Regulations seemed tougher than ever; MPs fixed everyone with cold looks for transgressors, and the army hunched under traces too hard for necessity. Grumbling echoed louder; jokes in the *Stars and Stripes* became more pointed than funny, and drill returned to its place of damnation. But Pershing would not omit the visits—his men had fought and offered themselves as sacrifice; he would see them as they

26 JJP to AGWAR, Nov. 29, 1918 (cable 1941-S), Pershing Papers, Cables, Box 4, RG 200/316, National Archives.
27 Frederick Palmer, *John J. Pershing, General of the Armies*, p. 344.

returned from their crusade. Staffers worked feverishly to arrange parades of whole divisions, and stories soon erected Pershing's reviews into marathons of waiting, in cold, sleet, rain or snow, for the Old Man ever late. His reviews were woefully thorough; through bottomless mud he slogged across France, eyed sodden men and logy uniforms, rain-streaked guns and bayonets, talked with bravery's beribboned, and made speeches of thanks to anguished multitudes. Good weather or bad made no difference in his way of reviewing—the standards of West Point stood.[28]

Not much given to exhortation, the Old Man waxed uncommonly eloquent in some of these last talks to his men. Boasting came easier in the wake of victory, and sometimes he reminded the veterans of what they had done. To the 77th's officers, for instance, he told his own appreciation for valor, added that the whole AEF had "done a very valuable service to humanity and to civilization, more important perhaps than is realized by those who have represented America in France." Any fair appraisal of the war's history would show that "it is not too much to say . . . that America won the war, or at least that if it had not been for America the war would have been lost." Lifted eyebrows at such hyperbole brought quick elaboration. "No man here should stand for minimization of America's effort in the war. History later will bear out America's proud part."

No division escaped Pershing's concern for venereal disease—he would send home a clean army. Every division heard a homiletic on the subject in which the words varied, the sentiments never: "It is a proud thing to go back to our mothers, and our wives, and our sisters and sweethearts . . . [and] be able to say that [we] belonged to an organization of two million men absolutely free from venereal disease and it will be the proudest thing in my life if it can be done."[29]

As the army dwindled so did the griping, but discipline remained tight. In the chill of that first peace winter, most Doughboys still abroad would vote for Jack Pershing as villain of the year.

[28] See, for example, "Remarks . . . to the Officers of the 77th Division, . . . Sable, France, February 24, 1919," and "Remarks . . . at Inspection and Review of the 92nd Division, Le Mans, January 29, 1919," Box 100, PP. There are countless recollections extant by men who heard Pershing's divisional departure speeches. For example, see William B. Ruggles to the author, Dec. 16, 1973, describing Pershing's fear of public speaking and the fear of men who suffered his parting scrutiny (letter in author's possession). See also Frank Freidel, *Over There*, pp. 366–69.

[29] Speech to Officers of 77th Division, Sable, France, Feb. 24, 1919, Box 100, PP.

While Pershing tended his army, President Wilson's vision of peace was clouded by the knavery of his colleagues. When, at last, he took his lovely wife to Chaumont for Christmas festivities, he was haunted by a crumbling dream. Idealism and lasting peace Wilson still clutched, while the other powers of the war plotted retribution and revenge. Had Pershing's first guess in October, 1918, been right, that snap judgment about unconditional surrender? The president still pinned the future on the League of Nations—that hallowed hall of reason where right would make power and candor brand deceit. Like Candide, Wilson believed in the best of all possible worlds—winsome and woebegone, he still championed man.

Out from Paris came the presidential train, puffing importantly through whistle stops and little towns. Woodrow Wilson approached his army with a weary man's resolve; his wife, Edith, whose eyes missed no pomp, suffered in the drafty car through the night of December 24. A broken heating system, sheets that were icily damp, brought fond recall of Paris's plush Hôtel de Mûrat, where celebrities were properly pampered. She firmly expected pneumonia to come from the night ride. Up in Lorraine the weather turned sulky, and by the time the train reached Chaumont about nine on Christmas morning snow flurried in the gray light.

General Pershing and a motley entourage waited on the platform, and when the Wilsons emerged they were swept into Pershing's smiling introductions—the mayor of Chaumont, the French commanding general of the district, their staffs, their friends, and others. As quickly as French protocol permitted, the multitudes bundled into cars for a ride to the Hôtel de Ville.

Again a race through the elements into the Town Hall, where the mayor, the préfect, the general all made welcoming speeches in excited French; the president, dignified but cold, replied with his innate formality. Edith Wilson noted with some anxiety that plans called for a full day of sightseeing—bad enough on good days, wretched this Christmas. A twenty-mile ride over questionable roads brought the presidential party to Langres, the great AEF training center, a place, said Pershing, of military higher education. Squalid and forlorn the wooden barracks, the squat schools looked in the drizzle; mud resisted perambulation, but Pershing relentlessly launched everyone on a long duckboard to a reviewing stand. At least that flag-draped enclosure offered chairs.

Proudly, before elements of two divisions—some 12,000 men altogether—Pershing, in brief remarks, introduced the commander-in-chief of the army and navy. Wilson, who looked good in his long fur coat, spoke thinly to the wind and most men missed his words. Then bands played, the troops passed in review—not much hampered by the mud but obviously blue with cold. They were impressive, their lines moving true, their steps in cadence, their eyes shifted to the reviewers, their long khaki columns sodden, mud-spattered, yet somehow glowing like their bayonets as they showed their chieftain his battle strength.

Dampened but pleased, the visitors—the crowd had grown considerably to include General Liggett and his staff—motored to 26th Division Headquarters at Montigny-le-Roi for Christmas dinner. Good food, spirits, charming companions brought special sparkle to Pershing's blue eyes; his dimpled smile won even Edith Wilson. But an afternoon of billet watching in wet Lorraine frosted everyone's temper. Still the cheerful acceptance of discomfort by all the troops warmed Wilson's heart—the "boys" were all they were touted.

By four o'clock, chilled thoroughly but firmly bouyant, the presidential party reached Chaumont and took refuge in the Val des Escoliers, where a great roaring fire and hot tea restored resilience. Resilience everyone needed, for an iron schedule took them into a receiving line at 4:30 P.M. Pershing invited all of Chaumont—town and sash—to meet the president and his lady. Quekemeyer and Boyd presented the visitors and kept the line moving. At last, by six o'clock, the visitors boarded their wet, cold train—Pershing watched the cars rumble across the points toward Paris. Despite the realities of the Great War, Wilson still resisted martial circumstance—clearly ill at ease with generals, he thawed partially with the "boys." Soldiers somehow soiled the symmetry of society. He had reluctantly listened to details of the occupation. Pershing had described an advanced headquarters for the AEF at Treves and briefed the president on the American zone of occupation running through Luxemburg, then on astride the Moselle to Rhine bridgeheads at Coblenz and Neuwied, thence on to a neutral zone beginning just beyond Montabaur. Suspicions, nothing more, Pershing had voiced of French and British intent to reduce American importance in Germany—and these suspicions Wilson seemed to doubt. All would come right with the final peace settlement. Switching to the topic of troop returns, Pershing had met a happier reception. Shipping remained the problem—Allied enthusiasm cooled with peace, and badgering continued for space. Repatriation of war prisoners complicated the schedule. Brest, Saint Nazaire, and Bordeaux were the homing ports, with Le Mans a great staging center for processing. All this seemed fine to the president.[30] Pershing had pushed Foch for troop reduction; thirty U.S. divisions were unnecessary and might halt the steady flow of men toward home. Wilson seemed confident war would not resume—troop reduction ought to be increased. All details Pershing would work out with Baker.

Aware that the burden remained where it had always been, glad enough to have some understanding of his curious chief, Pershing took one last look at the train. His blood quenched by principle, Wilson lost his sense of people—it was sad for him, possibly tragic for the world. Although haunted by the thought, Pershing raced for the highlight of Christmas—the headquarters party. He had invited the close staff to conjure again the "family" that built the AEF in early times. George Patton came; he was out of the hospital, almost recovered from a tanker's wound in the Meuse-Argonne. Carl Boyd's charming wife and little daughter brightened the festivities. Capt. Frank Pershing, James's son, joined the group, much to Jack's pleasure. Food and drink came in quantities, especially plum pudding. Georgie loved plum pudding, kept eating it until, at last, "the general ordered the waiter to give me no more there by saving my life."[31]

A great, stately tree, beautifully decorated, presided over gift giving after dinner. Patton, embarrassed because he had been the only giver last year, brought no presents, but received lavishly; Pershing gave him a handsome scarf. Pershing gave the whole staff something personal and received in kind, and the family feeling increased when the orderlies, chauffeurs, and servants were summoned and Pershing personally passed out gifts. Spirits flowed and rose apace, there was dancing and happiness, even some dice shaking, and a cold day closed in human warmth.[32]

It had been a long war. A long grind at headquarters had worn the staff, but Pershing felt the drain himself. Pressure continued but in a different way, and the time seemed right to pull the close group of friends out of Chaumont's chill for a vacation in warmer climes. Word of vacation stunned the younger men, but they dove into plans and

---

[30] JJP, FR, p. 57; Baker to JJP, Nov. 23, 1918 (cable 2245-R), in Cables—War Department to AEF, RG 200, National Archives Gift Collection.

[31] Martin Blumenson, The Patton Papers, 1885–1940, p. 666.

[32] Sources for the Wilson visit and festivities of Dec. 25 include ibid., pp. 666–67; John Dos Passos, Mr. Wilson's War, pp. 450–51; Edith Bolling Wilson, My Memoir, pp. 188–90, and especially Quekemeyer to his mother, Jan. 1, 1919, Quekemeyer Papers, in which he describes the day in splendid detail.

arrangements with an old zeal. The trip would start the evening of the twenty-sixth with a night run to Paris.

So Christmas night passed in bloated anticipation for most at GHQ. In the reflecting hours of that night, Pershing could count the things done with satisfaction. His own conviction of the AEF's decisive role in the war grew with daily observation; so did his admiration for his men. They wanted to go home, hated the cold foreign winter; they resented the hard drilling and regulations imposed, but they took it all with the Doughboy's sardonic humor. A lot of them had died in hard fighting, but the casualty lists were minor compared with those of other belligerents. Vast construction projects were still underway, since peace had caught the AEF forming, but machinery already worked toward selling the sites, the raw materials, the spare equipment to France. Within six months, if shipping were found, most of the troops would be home and America's crusade gallantly ended. For a brief moment the chief might rest, might think of personal pleasures.

Paris looked gayer to vacationers. While his staff buzzed round the city searching for civilian clothes and sports equipment for a Riviera sojourn, Jack conferred again with Charlie Dawes. Charlie approved the vacation utterly, observed with his old cynicism that the president's pending triumph in England relieved Jack of necessity to be handy, and promised to keep close to Herbert Hoover's food needs and the business of liquidation.

At eight in the evening of December 27, Pershing's party boarded his special train and headed south for Monte Carlo. Everyone talked of ways to relax, speculated on golf, swimming, other diversions. But relaxing had to be postponed. Somehow word raced ahead of the train that Pershing was coming. In every town of any size crowds thronged depot platforms, calling for a view of America's general. A wave, a beam, sufficed usually, but in Marseilles everyone had to detrain and join French officials in a champagne toast to victory, to France, America, Britain, everything else. By the time the train reached Monaco, Pershing knew the excited weariness of a conqueror returning to Rome. His staff loved every minute of the adulation, and Jack enjoyed their pleasure while he played his proper role.

Monte Carlo's attractions were many and varied, not the least of them lovely ladies who captivated the staff—especially "Peter" Bowditch, Quek, and another aide, Capt. John G. Hughes. The gaming halls were off limits to uniformed officers, but the young men plotted mufti raids, which were kept from the Old Man's ken. Pershing and Boyd became objects of sympathy. Quek felt almost guilty in his escapades. "The poor General on account of the way tongues would wag if he did go around a little has to cut out . . . parties and stay at home. . . . Boyd being a respectable married man stays at home too."[33] But the dashing Quek and the darkly handsome Hughes overcame consciences sufficiently to scout the good bars and entertainment sites—and reported with gusto.

Jack enjoyed himself, although relaxing came harder than in those days when Frankie shared in fun. Daily stints on the high golf course in Monte Carlo worked up fine appetites eased by a special cook who worked wonders in the kitchen of Pershing's borrowed apartment. After lunch Pershing usually took Quek to a gymnasium for exercise followed by a Turkish bath and massage. Back to the apartment for dinner with the whole party, and then Jack and Boyd faced bachelor evenings.

Change seemed helpful, although Jack guessed the concern of friends for his health unnecessary. True, the strain had lasted long and been hard, but he thrived on activity. If, as Dawes, Harbord, Boyd, even faithful Quek, said, he looked drawn and weary, the wear was "more apparent than real." He slept well, always, and boasted that he banished worry before retiring.[34] That proved invaluable; it kept problems in perspective. And the Monte Carlo carefree days did refresh the staff—hence were worthwhile. Pershing would have especially enjoyed relaxing in Paris.

"There is always Paris"

Ogden Mills renewed the invitation to use 73, rue de Varenne—even after the Millses returned to Paris. It would be hard to leave that lovely place. In the months of war, during those rush visits from Chaumont, the Mills house stood a reminder of graces worth defending, and it became far more than a house. Many good memories ghosted its hallways, memories of urgent meetings, of crises, of convivial dinners, of visitors, of excitement, depression, fear and triumph—even of love.[35]

Jack often found life in Paris and Chaumont lonely, but his quick eye for the ladies kept him interested and interesting. He and Charlie never ignored the need for female diversion. A few ladies came to mean much to Pershing. He had problems with distaff alliances—too

[33] Quekemeyer to his mother, Jan. 1, 1919, Quekemeyer Papers.
[34] JJP to Dawes, Nov. 29, 1918, Box 59, PP.
[35] Mills to JJP, Feb. 10, 1919, Box 85, PP.

many eyes searched him too often for easy privacy. Dorothy Canfield Fisher's visits to Chaumont were simple joys of friendship that pleased the entire celebrity-conscious staff.[36] Daisy Harriman, whose political concerns for Jack were real and whose help at home in fighting rumors was vital, came with open happiness to see how the general's projects prospered. But she touched the strong romance in Jack that witched so many hearts. Once he took her in early 1919 to a review in Nancy, and the mixture of man, place, and nature brought special appreciation. "It is a moonlight night and this beautiful city is a dream."[37]

Daisy's friendship Jack valued too much to jeopardize. From her he won companionship and steady understanding. From other lady visitors to Chaumont and to Paris he won solace and fleeting ease to loneliness. In the hectic weeks of peace making he suffered the surges of fame. Everyone wanted his picture, autographed of course; everyone claimed a mite of his time for good causes. In those happy days of basking, he sat for an American sculptor in Paris, favored photographers as often as possible, and trekked more frequently than ever to Micheline Resco's studio. Her nimble, lovely hands etched his firm chin, his eyes punctuated by laugh lines, his distant look of war. The picture was a thing of love, one that showed Jack's inner self. The hours of posing were times of renewal, moments of quiet turbulence in a growing affection.

Young, serious, enormously talented, Micheline lived quietly with her mother in an apartment on the rue des Renaudes. From first meeting in 1917 Jack felt Micheline's fascination; months of association proved her love. Carefully he cultivated their relationship—never obtrusively lest both be hurt by prying. He shared her affection but worried about the spring-winter spread of years—she was scarcely twenty-one, he fifty-eight. Formidably guileless, Micheline cared only for him, feared convention only as it might hurt his reputation. And with the war ended and his fame soaring, she hung further in the background. That devoted withdrawal charmed and bothered Jack. He knew her growing seriousness, her open intent to marry him. And he wanted marriage.[38] But there were complications.

[36] See correspondence between JJP and Dorothy Canfield Fisher throughout 1917–1918, Box 74, PP.

[37] From Mrs. J. Borden Harriman, *From Pinafores to Politics*, entry for Mar. 22, 1919, cited in Richard O'Connor, *BJP*, p. 341.

[38] For a summary of the Resco-Pershing relationship, see Henry Wales, "Pershing and the Lovely Parisienne," *Chicago Sunday Tribune Graphic Magazine*, Nov. 30, 1952, p. 7, reprinting an article from *Samedi Soir* entitled "During 30 Years a Frenchwoman Played 'Back Street' for Pershing." Indications of Pershing's

There was, for instance, Nita Patton. The ardor between them had chilled in distance, but Georgie still coveted an alliance, Nita's parents wrote fond recollections, and Nita played a waiting game. She had not been able to come to France during the war, but peace changed circumstances. She wrote of visiting England; obviously she wanted to see if embers could be fanned.[39] Pershing wondered, too, and suffered the irk of an ambivalent swain. His ambivalence was increased by further fickleness on his part.

Easily he had slipped into closeness with a charming lady who visited Chaumont late in 1917 with a plea to aid a troubled Doughboy. Pershing gallantly helped the soldier and charmed the lady. Elizabeth Hoyt's visit to France ended soon, but he asked her to return and see him.[40] She did, in the winter of 1918, and renewed friendship in Paris.

Busy with multifarious maneuvers of unbuilding, Jack took time to show Elizabeth the glitter and grace of the Paris he knew. Always complete in female company, Jack proved masterful, gentle, and winning. Elizabeth proved witty, coquettish, and impressed. Happy in quick affection, Jack pushed their relationship and found a warm, immensely understanding heart to share when he could. Elizabeth's easy accommodation to his business seemed somehow more comfortable than Micheline's utter devotion. "Merry Christmas," Elizabeth wrote Jack, and added a hope: "some day when you get settled in your new advanced HQ perhaps I may be allowed to call on you again or if not that there is always Paris. I do not bother you as I should like to when you are here because by now I hope that you know we are good enough friends to know that I am here when you want to or have time to play—and that when I am silent it is only because I do not want to add to your bothers. . . . "[41]

Paris in that gay winter seemed suddenly too small for comfort. Official entertainments in the capital took too much time for personal things, but Jack managed to neglect neither. He did worry about

desire to marry Micheline came from Maj. Gen. Thomas North, USA (Ret.) in an interview with the author, Washington, D.C., February, 1974, as well as from the *Tribune* article.

[39] Blumenson, *Patton*, pp. 702, 707.

[40] JJP to Elizabeth Hoyt, Dec. 29, 1917, Box 98, PP.

[41] See JJP to Hoyt, Nov. 27, 1918, in which he said: "Although I had a chat with you last night, may I still write you a note to show my appreciation for your invitation . . . I telegraphed you today." Hoyt to JJP, Dec. 8, 1918: "I found . . . a copy of your Thanksgiving address. I give thanks over again on reading it—thanks largely that my country has had a real man at the head of its victorious army." The "Merry Christmas" quotation is from Hoyt to JJP, Dec. 22, 1918. All these letters are in Box 98, PP.

neglecting one or the other of his ladies, and the schedule must have kept the staff socially nimble. There were no complaints; the young men approved the general's tastes, and Charlie Dawes always appreciated lovely ladies.

Tragedy stalked Parisian gaiety early in the new year. Carl Boyd, peerless aide and warm friend, caught a cold which grew worse and settled into pneumonia, and a distracted wife called for help. Pershing sped to Paris on February 12, conferred with doctors attending Boyd, and heard a grim prognosis. A specialist had been summoned, would arrive on the thirteenth, but probably could do little. Mrs. Boyd, the dear friend and charming hostess of so many convivial evenings, visited Carl, found him delirious. Pershing took her and her little daughter Ann home and stayed with them for dinner. Expectations were that Carl would survive another thirty-six hours, but at midnight a phone call announced him dead. A quenched, grief-stricken group went back to the hospital for sad details.

Pershing arranged burial in the cemetery at Surennes, in the French soil Carl so loved. A solemn guard of mourners attended, and Pershing, Dawes, and Quekemeyer shared Mrs. Boyd's desolation. Death came so easily now; graves dotted French soil in a kind of grim scything. Boyd's death brought an anguished reminder of the Presidio and the dwindle of affection.[42]

But nothing—neither death nor romance—distracted Jack from the AEF.

Die Wacht am Rhine

Behind the retreating Germans, Allied armies had pushed on into the Fatherland. Crises, political, economic, and social, riddled that country, but Americans noted the unsullied lands of the enemy. Pershing, concerned lest the slightest tarnish touch the shield of his army, soon put an advanced headquarters at Treves, and on the way to that ancient town he, too, noted the unmarked countryside and seethed. How humbled could the German army be in the full knowledge that war's scars fell only on France and Belgium? Still, no outrages must be done to the losers. American armies were famed for restraint; this army would be more famous than its predecessors.[43]

[42] See Memorandum concerning Boyd's death, Box 33, PP; Dawes, *Journal*, 1:236.

[43] In GO no. 218, HAEF, Nov. 28, 1918, Pershing set the rules of occupation conduct: "You have come not as despoilers or oppressors, but simply as the instruments of a strong, free government whose purposes towards the people of Germany are beneficent. During our occupation the civil population is under the

Discipline stood the main problem. Pershing's solution—hard training—rankled the rank and file. Grumblings continued and General Dickman, commanding the Third Army in its occupation role, combatted them as he could. Orders from GHQ offered little relief. Redlight districts were *verboten,* recreation scant, and rapid maneuvers constant. Weather in that north country hardly enhanced outdoor work. As he went forward through the old battle belt, Pershing's eye fell on special hardships of his troops. Many of his men had huddled in the funk holes of the Meuse-Argonne for weeks after the armistice—something about Foch wanting them handy for renewed strife. "Still in the lousy, stinking dug-outs to get influenza and pneumonia," Pershing fumed. "I thought I had settled that with Foch. They must be moved. . . ."[44] Concern was appreciated, but would have been cheered if relief had combined with liberal leaves. For some reason the Old Man hated good times and took it out on the men.

But if Foch and the Doughboys battled Pershing, the people who followed the AEF back to broken homes wrapped Americans in warmth and admiration. Affection shown to his men touched Jack always with that old kinship of humanity. Once, on the battlefield near Beaumont, Pershing encountered a group of French civilians carrying flowers to American graves. An old man told him that the people of the neighborhood would always care for those lost resting places. The simple declaration, the children's bouquets, the serried white wooden crosses broke through military reserve. Tears rolling down his face, Pershing said, "It is very hard for us to say 'Good-bye' for the last time to our dear comrades. . . . But since they cannot go home with us, there is no land save their own in which we would rather have them rest—no people with whom we can more surely leave their ashes to tender care and lasting memory than the dear people of France. I thank you in the name of their bereaved and in the name of our whole people who are mourning them to-day and whose hearts are here."[45]

Front-line troops were pulled back to better training grounds, and divisions freshly arrived before the war ended were shipped up slowly

---

special safeguard of the faith and honor of the American Army. . . . It is not believed that any acts of pillage or violence will be committed by members of the American Forces, but, should any persons prove themselves unworthy of this confidence, their acts will be considered not only as crimes against the sufferers, but as dishonoring the American Army. . . . Such transgressions . . . will be punished with the severest penalties known to our military law." (*USWW,* 16: 549–50.)

[44] Palmer, *John J. Pershing,* p. 349.
[45] Dawes, *Journal,* 1:251.

to relieve veterans of Dickman's Third Army. A healthy leaven of battle-hardened units would remain to shape the new divisions to AEF mold, but rotation of fighting men toward Le Mans began. Aside from normal friction with French and British commanders about roles and precedence in Germany, the occupation went smoothly. No serious incidents disturbed the peace, and the Stars and Stripes flew tranquilly over Coblenz's famed fortress, Ehrenbreitstein. Demobilized German soldiers showed normal curiosity toward fellow professionals; German civilians were too friendly in some cases, and Jack issued orders against fraternization.[46]

Discipline held firm but morale sagged. Muttered resentment filtered across the Atlantic, and Pershing suddenly enjoyed Secretary Baker's friendly concern. "I get reports," Baker cabled in February 1919,

that our soldiers in Europe are many of them living under conditions of very great hardship, and that there is no group which has as its special problem relieving as far as possible the depressing conditions surrounding them. Earnest and sympathetic men tell me that the effect of this is a great depression of morale, and a feeling on the part of many soldiers of bitterness toward the A.E.F. and the War Department for permitting these conditions to go unremedied. . . . Among the accounts given me are many which deal with discomforts growing out of strict adherence to minor regulations, in spite of conditions which would seem to justify abatement of them.

Baker suggested a mixed committee of officers and civilians look into living conditions and recommend changes.[47]

This uncommon interference from the war secretary caught Jack by surprise. Regulations were necessary, adherence essential to prevent an unused army dribbling into rabble. Baker knew that; pressures from home must be growing. There had been indications of trouble from Baker and from Senator Warren earlier. Rumblings from disaffected New England areas where Clarence Edwards and Leonard Wood made political hay from Pershing's derelictions came in several letters. Warren, who cautioned Jack to watch his rear, thought the troubles would pass. Baker, who felt most of the thrusts personally, talked with Warren about slurs against the AEF. He showed a letter written to Pershing that summed the complaints and offered wry philosophy on victories dimmed by scrutiny. Congressional concern seemed likely to generate an investigation of the conduct of the war—shades of Lincoln's troubles with the Radicals! Baker could take care of the War Department; he

---

[46] GO no. 218, Nov. 28, 1918, in *USWW*, 16:549–50.
[47] Baker to JJP, Feb. 3, 1919, in Frederick Palmer, *Newton D. Baker: America at War*, 2:405.

felt special responsibility to defend the AEF. Pershing's distance, his military posture, precluded public rebuttal of rumors. Perhaps he could send a couple of officers, armed with AEF statistics, to deny accusations of heavy casualties, reckless leadership, wasteful administration. Angered at any slurs on the AEF, Pershing agreed he could make no general refutation but wrote Baker, "I do not fear the investigations—on the contrary."[48]

The secretary's concern for the army Pershing understood. He had, fortunately, already modified the drill regulations and urged commanders to a full athletic program for recreation and physical conditioning.[49] In January he had begun an extensive tour of installations and units, turned out men and officers for scrutiny, searched the buildings with that old Mindanao eye.[50] A letter to Baker, written two days before the secretary's cable, reported on the embarkation sites and SOS facilities. "It is my endeavor," he wrote, "to send the army home with high morale, clean physically and clean morally."[51]

Privately he knew his information scant. So much had happened so fast that the usual runs to troop units for inspection and conversation had lapsed. Much as he wanted to, he had not been with the Occupation forces enough to know the real state of the army. There had been complaints. Rumors ran the Third Army about the chief. Had he "lost interest in them?" Bad weather, bad rules, bad morale fostered anger toward the top—and Pershing, who still awed the lowest ranks, began to draw ire.[52]

[48] JJP to Baker, Feb. 23, 1919, Box 19, PP; Baker to JJP, Jan. 22, 1919 (cable 2521-R—Confidential and Personal), in Cables, War Department to AEF, Pershing Papers, RG 220, National Archives Gift Collection; FEW to JJP, Jan. 21, 1919, in FEW Papers, vol. 85, in which Warren recounts a visit with Baker on Jan. 20 during which the secretary read a letter he had just written JJP. "This was after he first asked me if I was forwarding you what the New England papers were saying and what Edwards' friends were doing, and he remarked that General Wood likewise was scrapping. . . . The Secretary said he believed the matter would blow over pretty soon, and, if not, he might ask an investigation by either House or Senate Committees, or both. . . . He expressed himself as feeling it was his duty as well as his pleasure to protect you in your absence and inability to respond to accusations against your Army, etc. He said that he really believed it was in fact an attack upon him and the War Department." See Baker to JJP, Jan. 20, 1919 (Personal and Confidential), Box 19, PP, which is obviously the letter Warren heard in Baker's office.

[49] GO no. 241, Dec. 29, 1918, which prescribed a full competitive program of athletics in the AEF leading to AEF championships. The order is in USWW, 16:589–91.

[50] "List of Places Visited and Inspected by the C-in-C on Tour of Inspection from January 21st to March 18, 1919," Box 100, PP.

[51] JJP to Baker, Feb. 1, 1919 (Personal), Box 19, PP.

[52] See O'Connor, BJP, p. 340, citing Charles MacArthur, A Bug's Eye View

He had to get forward. Advanced headquarters at Treves soon ceased to be advanced enough. On to Coblenz Pershing moved for a look at the American bridgehead in enemy country. Dickman's army welcomed him happily—the Old Man had not forgotten them after all! In that city Pershing found relaxed gaiety among the officers at army headquarters and a special camaraderie with news correspondents assigned to the farthest point of Yank domination.

Pershing resumed his ritual of inspections, set a tough standard, and fixed hard eyes on everyone. Granite faced, he stalked parade lines with few words and scarce smiles. Clearly the men needed a model and a focus of frustration—the Old Man offered both. In the camps around Coblenz, Montabaur, Regensdorf, Neuwied, men huddled in winter's discomforts. Raymond Fosdick, head of the War Department commission on training camps, had reported "the situation . . . here is . . . little short of desperate. . . . The feeling of bitterness among the troops is growing."[53] Policing of tents, huts, barracks had been maintained, but some units were lax in weak traces—their officers must sharpen discipline or be replaced. Morale appeared fair— judged by grumbling, that age old thermometer of armies. American ingenuity helped morale. Men in rags sewed, patched, cleaned their clothes and gear, washed mud from vehicles and wagons, spruced leather and horses, and vied with each other for prizes in poverty. Quick visits to wretched billets often surprised smiles from huddling denizens; questioned about living conditions, the men usually answered "fine." How is the food? "Fine," came the stalwart deceit. But a soldier knew the signs of wear, and Pershing suggested increased athletic programs, liberalized leave policies, and began "one of the most interesting school and college systems ever inaugurated." With the help of the Army Educational Commission, supported by the YMCA,

---

of the War (Oak Park, Ill., 1919). For the question about interest, see A. S. Kuegle to [?] Birnie, Feb. 10, 1919, AEF, GHQ, G-3 Reports, Third Army, Folder 276, Box 3091, RG 120, National Archives. For intelligence problems, see Klaus Schwabe, *Deutsche Revolution und Wilson-Frieden: Die Amerikanische und deutsche Friedensstrategie zwischen Ideologie und Machtpolitik 1918/19*, and Fritz T. Epstein, "Zwischen Compiègne und Versailles: Geheime Amerikanische Militärdiplomatie in der Periode Waffenstillstandes 1918/19: Die Rolle des Obersten Arthur L. Conger," *Vierteljahrshefte für Zeitgeschichte* 3 (Oct., 1955), 412–45.

[53] For troop dispositions, see Hunter Liggett, *Commanding an American Army*, pp. 126–27; "Notes on Conversation Between General Pershing and Marshal Foch at Strassbourg, Dec. 8, 1918," Box 16, PP; James Harbord, *The American Army in France*, pp. 559–60. For Fosdick's comments, see D. Clayton James, *The Years of MacArthur*, 1:251.

secondary and high schools were opened for Doughboys; a correspondence college offered courses ranging from citizenship and personal development to farm management, mathematics, history, and elementary engineering; the AEF University at Beaune stood at the top of the educational structure and by spring 1919 boasted six thousand soldier students. By special arrangement, limited numbers of American troops could enroll in British and French universities. With the closing of AEF schools at Langres, officers wanting advanced work could take advantage of the general educational program along with their men. This special instructional system reached a fraction of the AEF, but that fraction might benefit the country.[54]

Satisfied that life for the men improved, Pershing cabled Baker on February 23, 1919, that "generally speaking, conditions are good," and added that "[I] shall continue efforts without cessation to further improve the living conditions of our splendid troops." Complaints of poor management were groundless.[55] All pressures would ease when large numbers of men could go home. Baker and March convinced Congress, for the moment, to accept success as virtue.[56]

Baker's concern for Pershing's personal morale brought special joy in April. The secretary of war decided, at last, to make another visit to the army before it all left France. Once decided, he broached a happy possibility to Senator Warren: Could Warren Pershing go with him to France? For most of the war, most of the months of his father's soaring fame, Warren had lived with Aunt May Pershing in Lincoln, Nebraska. Too much away from his son, Pershing kept close tabs on him through May and Papa Warren, read with joy of Warren's manning a little "recruiting station," crowned by a small American flag. May had done her best with Warren, so had the rest of the family, but Pershing feared too much female influence. Senator Warren guessed a doting daddy would gleefully receive a ten-year-old boy who basked in the light of his father. He had not been forgotten; letters kept going to him; Madame Foch had sent him a miniature uniform of a marshal of France; newsmen noted him occasionally. But Pershing knew the ache of prolonged absence, hoped it had not been

[54] See Anson Phelps Stokes, American University Union in Europe, to "Dear Sir," Apr. 11, 1919, enclosing press release entitled "American Soldiers at School" (copy in author's possession).

[55] JJP to Baker, Feb. 23, 1919 (cable), Box 19, PP; Palmer, *Baker*, 2:405–6. For a general assessment of AEF morale in the winter and spring of 1919, see Brig. Gen. M. B. Stewart, "The A.E.F. Follows Through," *U.S. Infantry Journal* 16 (Oct., 1919): 259–66 (especially p. 263 for persistent optimism of the troops).

[56] Palmer, *Baker*, 2:408.

too long. Papa Warren's news brought the happiest prospects since May, 1917.

Baker corresponded with May Pershing and Mary Elizabeth (Bessie) Butler, won their consent, and won the agreement of one to go along. The trip would be kept a secret from Pershing—but no secrets concerning the secretary or the Pershings kept well. Photographers caught the party en route to New York, and accounts of the gesture hit newspapers and movie news programs.[57]

Warren came with Baker in early April and arrived in a splendid khaki uniform provided by the War Department, replete with sergeant's stripes and scattered decorations. Reunions after long parting are awkward, but dad did his best to knit stretched threads of love. Proud of Warren's development, impressed with his behavior, his growth, Pershing tried to avoid excessive parental doting. What would the staff think? Most were happy in the general's happiness; Charlie Dawes thought Warren's coming would vastly lighten Jack's last months in Europe.[58]

A budding sergeant should learn his trade from an old hand—so Warren found himself handed to the care of Sgt. Frank Lanckton. Fresh from lengthy hospital treatments for a bad leg, Lanckton took his job seriously. He and the boy got along. Warren, not accustomed to hard discipline, quickly adjusted to military rules. Serious offenses brought stern threats to take away the stripes! Lanckton's hard "Sergeant Pershing, go to your quarters" pronounced the harshest sentence —and brought instant obedience. And during dad's inspection trips, the two sergeants went along. They kept each other company when the general did business or went to official functions.

Official functions hindered fatherly affection, but Jack took Warren wherever he could. Especially exciting was a visit to the Third Army, made in May. All the men fussed over Warren; he watched, fascinated, as dad inspected long lines of big men. Generals entertained him, and dad was always handy. That was the best part of the trip.

For Jack, too, that was the best of the trip. They stayed in grand places for a boy. In Neuwied, where Gen. John L. Hines had his III Corps Headquarters, they were guests in a great, soaring castle belonging to the prince of Wied. At the end of an exciting day, Warren climbed into a huge bed under "a German feather-tick three times as big as he." Lanckton said his "Lights Out," and the boy slept. Later,

[57] FEW to JJP, Mar. 22, Apr. 16, 1919, FEW Papers, vol. 86.
[58] Dawes, *Journal,* 1:245.

during a large party in his honor, Father Pershing disappeared. A scout found him sitting quietly by his sleeping son's bedside. He offered a simple confession: "I like to be with my boy. I have seen so little of him in the last few years that it seems as if we hardly know each other. I want to see all of him I can. I wouldn't feel right if I let the evening pass without spending part of it with my son, even if he is asleep."[59]

Time spent in the hectic entertainments of these inspection trips wearied most of the staff; they marveled at Pershing's iron energy. He kept up with the strongest, threw himself into dancing and merry-making, encouraged his men in relaxation, and won their hearts utterly. Quek, after months of association, told his mother that Pershing "is really a dear and I like him more and more every day. He is so considerate, human and natural and yet so very efficient and such a strong character that one just has to admire him."[60]

His efficiency showed. By the end of May over 300,000 men had sailed for home; thousands more were in the final stages of departing. Shipping increased, and Pershing pushed facilities at Brest to accommodate increased numbers for the delousing, physical examinations, and refitting needed before departure. Foch seemed increasingly willing to reduce reserves but clung fervently to the five divisions in the Army of Occupation. Until the peace treaty was signed, the marshal of the Allied Armies would not wholly relax. Until then the Americans at Coblenz, the French at Mayence, and the British at Cologne would keep close watch on the Rhine.

A Last Great Round of Glory

Shrinking armies, fading challenges gave hope of early return to the States for everyone at GHQ. President Wilson and Secretary Baker broached the topic of returning home to Pershing several times. There ought to be a grand review of American troops, selected ones, in honor of the AEF and its commander—the kind of thing New York did well, perhaps even Washington on an apolitical day. Pershing hesitated; a triumphal parade at home would be a crowning moment for a soldier. But there were reasons to stay in Europe—good reasons. "It would certainly be a memorable occasion for me if I could be present at a review of a number of available divisions," Pershing had

[59] Quoted in O'Connor, *BJP*, p. 342.
[60] Quekemeyer to his mother, May 4, 1919; see also *id.* to *id.*, Mar. 28, 1919 (both in Quekemeyer Papers).

written Baker in February, 1919, but he confessed a preference for a quieter return and a concern to see more of his army embarked for home. "It will be necessary of course to wait until we see how rapidly troops can be sent home, and then determine according to circumstances when my own return would be considered opportune."[61] Baker renewed inquiries when he saw Pershing in April and met continued reluctance. Pershing had talked with the president; decisions were pending—but problems in getting the AEF out delayed the CIC. A congressional committee, with Julius Kahn in charge, came to check on U.S. operations. Hearings at Chaumont in April, 1919, gave Jack, George Marshall, and corps commanders a chance to boast and to explain matters of tactics and casualties.

Going home posed problems—official and personal. Uncertainty of rank stood an official problem; if he went too soon, he, like his officers ahead of him, would drop back to his regular rank. Two stars no longer seemed adequate after so much power and so much success. Congress had been wrestling with a bill to create two full generals, a bill pushed by March, to include Pershing and the chief of staff. Senator Warren reported scant interest among his colleagues, especially since the war secretary seemed lukewarm. Delay might permit realignments on the Hill—at least Papa Warren would have maneuvering time.[62] Poor tactics on Baker's part obstructed the bill. He suggested the chief of staff as the general of precedence over the entire army; Pershing would come next in the *Army Register*. Warren said that March was not "well thought of and seems to have stalled everything so far."[63] But the bill waited action and hopes were alive.

Personal considerations were hard to express—they sounded, out loud, oddly selfish, archly ambitious. What would Jack go home to do? Who was home to care? Micheline, in Paris, kept a steadfast heart for him, and with her he felt something of an old contentment. Elizabeth Hoyt's discreet welcome also warmed Paris. Warren had stayed with Jack when Baker returned home. And most of Jack's good friends were now in Europe. Charlie Dawes would soon go back to family and business, but his friendship would last over time and distance. The Millses, the Harjes, and Marshal Pétain ranked now among a small coterie of dear people; so did the Astors in England, who wanted Jack to attend the christening of their son John Jacob as soon as he could. Popularity had to be admitted; in Europe the

61 JJP to Baker, Feb. 1, 1919, Box 19, PP.
62 FEW to JJP, Mar. 22, 1919, FEW Papers, vol. 86.
63 FEW to JJP, May 31, 1919, FEW Papers, vol. 86.

name John Pershing called up visions of victory, of help in dire times—
he was a hero matching the greatest of the war. How would it be
at home? Would Americans hail a returned general, deck him in ticker
tape and medals, cocoon him in words and forget? Probably—for
Americans shied quickly from heroes. Why did it matter?

It mattered because his ego had grown in France to match his
achievements; it mattered, perhaps mainly, because America would be
lonely. So there were reasons to stay with his dwindling legions. He
knew he must finally go home, but not until the future looked clearer.
Meanwhile he would enjoy his job.

Enjoying caught him a whirl of public functions. Friends claimed
him for parties, receptions, formal and informal soirees. Public appearances often led to private invitations.

One creation of the AEF led to an impressive, even embarrassing,
public benediction done by Pershing. Allied leaders, vying with each
other in ways to keep men usefully occupied, devised the Inter-Allied
Games to involve as many deft competitors as possible in athletic
combat. So huge were these games in concept that a new stadium
must be built to encompass all the simultaneous events. The YMCA,
aided by AEF engineers and pioneers, built Pershing Stadium in
Paris for the games. The general, on June 22, smiling his pleasure but
still oddly shy, dedicated the stadium. He spoke brief words of welcome, especially to old battle comrades, then evoked the spirit of
competition:

Conscious of the service which athletes have rendered, and aware of the
influence that athletic training had in making possible the victory, it would
seem fitting that the conclusion of our labors . . . in a common cause should
be celebrated by a great tournament. . . . On this opening day of the gathering of Allied representatives, it is appropriate to mention that this is the
second anniversary of the arrival of the first contingent of American combatant troops in France. . . . Through this tournament we Americans hope
to return in some slight measure the generous and gracious spirit that has
been accorded us from the beginning. . . . This tournament would not be
possible except for the liberal support of France in donating the ground for
this stadium, and for aid in its construction. . . . It will soon be my agreeable
duty to transfer this amphitheatre to the French Government in the name
of the Y. M. C. A. of America . . . with the hope that it may become not
only a permanent testimonial of our esteem, but also an enduring monument
of the sportsmanlike spirit that has inspired and sustained France throughout
the war.[64]

Done with that, Jack took a group of cronies, including Dawes,

[64] JJP, speech dedicating the stadium for the inter-allied games, Box 106, PP.

to Le Mans to open the Inter-Allied target shoot. Teams from about fifteen nations enrolled. Here was a contest for an old sharpshooter! Making a few welcoming remarks to the contestants, Pershing met all the officers, shook their hands, and begged permission to open the "trap-shoot." Up flew the first clay pigeon, bang went Pershing's shotgun, on flew the pigeon unmarked. A rusty shooter must try again—ready consent was given midst much mirth. "Pull!" Again the pigeon flew, again Pershing fired, and the bird exploded in mid-air. Half a success felt better than total failure.[65] Once the shooting began, Pershing rushed into a full round of inspections and entertainments. Everything, including a dance with Red Cross ladies, had to be crowded into a day, since the general's party was scheduled for an English visit on June 24.

A telegram announcing their arrival went to Lloyd Griscom, serving as Pershing's liaison with the British. The consternation it caused Pershing heard with amusement when he met Griscom at Dover on the morning of the twenty-fourth. Pershing explained he was making an "informal" visit to receive a Doctorate in Civil Law from Oxford University—an honor long proffered and coveted. Griscom appreciated the reason, had himself stood as proxy for Pershing in May when Earl Haig, now Lord Rector of Saint Andrews University, gave Pershing an honorary degree, but insisted that courtesy calls on the prime minister and secretary for war were essential. Griscom had, in fact, made the appointments!

"Griscom, I can't do that."

"But, General, I'm afraid the English may be offended if you don't. They'll only take a minute or two."

"No. Sorry. I can't do it."

"Well, I'll have to make some sort of excuse so that they will understand."

Actually, Pershing confessed "sheepishly," "the truth is, I've promised to go that day to the christening of Charlie Dawes's godchild."

Griscom's jaw dropped, but he struggled manfully to save the situation.

"Well, where do you have to go? How far is it from London?"

A tiny town in Kent, Mount Ephraim, Pershing said, and explained that the irrepressible Charlie had found relatives in England—at least he claimed the Kent Dawes clan—had written introducing himself, and suddenly became the godfather of a baby bearing his name!

---

[65] Quekemeyer to his mother, June 23, 1919, Quekemeyer Papers.

Fulsomely he insisted on full godfatherly duties and had pressed Pershing into the role of co-godfather. Griscom must have looked astounded for Pershing added, lamely:

"I promised Charley I'd do this."

There were all kinds of reasons unnecessary to add—not the least of which was love for Charlie—but also there was perception of Charlie's awkward position. Pershing had inherited "children" in the Philippines, had, in fact, "adopted" a French boy and girl whose father had been lost in the first onrush of war and whose mother clung desperately to a destitute family shred.[66] A gentleman could find himself impelled to unsought responsibilities. Jack would not desert a friend in the pursuit of gallantry. Griscom would simply have to understand. Griscom tried.

There were possible alternatives; his diplomat's guile, challenged, assessed distances against time.

"Well, General, the only way out is to explain that you committed yourself weeks ago to a private engagement of the greatest importance, but that you'll be able to reach Downing Street at five and the War Office a half-hour later."

"All right. That'll be fine," Pershing agreed, and took the party to London for the night.[67]

Next morning Griscom found, to his horror, that Charlie, who invited him to "a bang up time at the christening," had broadcast invitations all over the War Office and that almost everyone was going!

Dawes's energetic artlessness charmed some happy response in his British friends. At about eleven in the morning on the twenty-fifth, London watched as a cavalcade of fourteen army automobiles, crammed with beribboned officers, threaded through the streets, out through astounded little towns, and at last cluttered the Kentish village of Mount Ephraim. Normally sleepy, assured behind its bricks and thatch, Mount Ephraim suddenly bulged with fame. Denizens had tried to brace for the day; across the narrow street hung a great banner: "Welcome General Pershing."

On the porch of the manor house, the resident Dawes greeted everyone and presented his lady; in the "great hall" stood the relatives of all ages and sources. Horror of horrors, there looked to be at least

[66] See JJP to various authorities (Stars and Stripes, the Red Cross, the Women's Auxiliary of the American Legion), dating from July 25, 1918, to Oct. 24, 1930, in Box 43, PP. For the conversation with Griscom, see Lloyd C. Griscom, Diplomatically Speaking, pp. 454–55.
[67] Quekemeyer to his mother, June 23, 1919, Quekemeyer Papers.

a hundred to meet! Dawes loved them instantly and they him, and he pitched in to find the prettiest "cousins." "How are you, Cousin Mary, Cousin Imogene, Cousin Betsy," he said as he bestowed kisses. So large a contingent of renown confused the reception only briefly, then everyone settled to the business of christening and entertainment. To music provided by the band of the 8th Hussars—Pershing's presence produced unexpected frills—the party clambered back into cars and rode to the Norman church at nearby Hernhill village. Villagers crowded the aisles for glimpses of the visitors; the red-robed rector stood with the baby, and Charlie, Pershing, and pretty eighteen-year-old Betty Dawes stood as sponsors and godparents, and then took a pew in front of the rector.

When the ceremony ended, everyone went back to the Dawes home for lunch and found added guests were invited to share a moment of glory. Betty Dawes liked the big American general and chatted long with him. After lunch local schoolchildren came to present an "address" to General Pershing, who listened in rapt attention. His host asked Charlie to join the children, who then sang "Auld Lang Syne," the custom when a family member returned from long absence. "The General and I," said Charlie, "were much impressed and found ourselves choked up a little several times."

Quick good-byes, waves, then Pershing, Griscom, and Quekemeyer dashed to London, skidded to a stop in front of 10 Downing Street at fifteen seconds to five, and the general was, for once, on time.[68]

Hasty calls on proper officials led to a trip to Paris. On June 23 German delegates had at last agreed to peace terms, drawn tortuously and acrimoniously and not exactly along Woodrow Wilson's line. There would be a big signing ceremony at the Palace of Versailles on June 28; Pershing wanted his friends and leading generals present. There were, it seemed, innumerable problems about getting military people into the signing session. Generals, soldiers, had had their day—now was the day of frock-coated deceivers. In London Pershing heard first rumblings of scarce seats for the great occasion. Furious that many who had made the ceremony possible would be excluded, he wired Harbord—again AEF chief of staff since McAndrew had gone home in May—an angry question about tickets.[69] Harbord quickly caught the sentiments—"there did not seem to be much desire to have that historic ceremony attended by mere soldiers." But Pershing, in "plain

---

[68] For the Dawes visit, see Dawes, *Journal*, 1:254–57; Griscom, *Diplomatically Speaking*, pp. 454–55.

[69] Harbord, *American Army*, p. 558; Dawes, *Journal*, 1:250.

vigorous words" got grudging concession "so late that it practically prohibited the attendance of those at any distance from Paris, accompanied by the injunction to return the tickets at once if unable to use them."

By Pershing's insistence, a goodly number of khaki uniforms sprinkled the audience in the Galerie des Glaces du Château—the same room where the German Empire was announced to the world in 1871—that solemn Saturday afternoon, June 28, 1919. Maj. Gen. Henry Allen, shortly to command the American forces in Germany, Brig. Gen. Fox Conner, trusted chief of operations, aides John Hughes and Quek, and later Major General Summerall and Mason Patrick of the air service joined Pershing's party. A hasty scan of the room told too much by absence. Where were Foch, Joffre, Pétain? Sir Henry Wilson, CIGS, represented Britain's martial might. No soldiers came from Italy or Belgium to remind the vultures of harder times.[70] Not that the room was empty—over five hundred people crowded to watch the signing process as it began at 3:10. For thirty-five minutes pens scratched and dark-coated men hovered around the table, as officials provided needs and herded crowds. Protocol had returned to the world with high public ceremony. Wilson sat straight through the proceedings, his face drawn, his body worn with fatigue, his eyes haunted by bartered possibilities. But he signed, harping still on the battered League of Nations. He would leave Paris that afternoon for home and a looming war with Congress.

As the American officers left the Galerie, Pershing asked Harbord to join him for a run to the Gare Saint Lazare and a farewell to the president. He was aboard the train when Pershing and Harbord arrived but came out on the platform for a moment's talk. Shaking hands with him, Pershing noted the harried hope still in Wilson's eye. With peace accepted, Foch could no longer require five divisions— the AEF could go home.

Could John Pershing go home?

Foch did agree to siphon away the last divisions. Pershing on June 30 pushed for a final departure schedule, announced he would leave some American troops under Henry Allen, but wanted the main forces gone. Two divisions could quit the Rhine watch at once; Harbord's gallant 2nd Division could leave on July 15; then the 3rd; and at last Pershing's Pets, the Old Guard of the AEF could leave on August 15.

With Baker and the president, Pershing had discussed the re-

<hr>

[70] Harbord, *American Army*, pp. 558–59.

maining contingent needed; Wilson thought no troops should stay in Europe, but finally agreed to a brigade-sized unit under Maj. Gen. Henry Allen, to show the flag and support American interests in the occupation. Pershing had not minimized the importance of the "American Forces in Germany" and picked Allen for his tough repute.[71]

Whoever stayed behind would have a highly visible role, would probably enjoy high popularity and much fun—and Pershing wanted the job. But he knew he must go home.[72] About the only official duties left to him were ceremonial. July coming would be filled with pageantry, including victory parades—perhaps the last any of the AEF would know, unless people remembered still at home. And remembering grew harder with the passage of time. With the rest of the troops getting back, the country likely would pull the men into civilian routine and hope nothing military disturbed them again—especially not generals who led them all toward death. So Jack looked forward to a last round of glitter and pomp, the last good echoes of cheers.

First came the Fourth of July, now almost a French national holiday. Celebrations began on July 3, with a reception given by the *Municipalité de Paris* for the American army and navy. Pershing and staff went to the Hôtel de Ville at five. Receiving a great plaque in testimony of Paris's affection, Pershing spoke, and listened to many other speeches, met hundreds, and heard his country lavishly appreciated. Dubbed the guest of honor for an evening gala, Pershing, taking Quek firmly in tow, went to the Pre-Catalan in the Bois de

[71] See JJP, "Memorandum Regarding the Retention of American Troops in Army of Occupation," Paris, May 18, 1919, Box 16, PP; T. H. Bliss to Wilson, June 25, 1919, in *ibid.*, in which Bliss writes: "General Pershing informs me that you said to him (as you had already said to me) that under an agreement that you and Mr. Lloyd George had made with Mr. Clemenceau you would retain here, at the most, one American regiment. General Pershing desires to add to this regiment the necessary hospital and sanitary service and such other auxiliary services as are necessary to make the regiment independent of French resources. . . . General Pershing also thinks that a general officer should be left in command of this organization. He thinks that nothing but the presence of an American general officer will prevent the regiment from being handled in about the same way that our single regiment in Italy was handled, and also our single regiment at Archangel—that is to say, in a way which caused a feeling of bitterness and resentment among our officers and men. I concur in General Pershing's views. . . ." Wilson noted: "Approved." See also Heath Twichell, Jr., *Allen: The Biography of an Army Officer*, pp. 215–52.

[72] Brig. Gen. Frederick W. Sladen to his wife (Lil), Aug. 3, 1919, in Sladen Family Papers, Box 16, U.S. Military History Research Collection, Carlisle Barracks, Pa. Reference supplied through the kindness of Dr. Richard Sommers of the MHRC.

Boulogne, where Foch and Pétain also shared the limelight. This dinner, given by French Minister of Marine Georges Leygues, honored military folk, and the uniforms of eighty high ranking officers glistened in the lamplight. Here was a moment to recall Fort McKinley, a moment when war ebbed and happiness flowed, when a kind of lambent cheer made comrades into friends. Pershing spoke in French, to Pétain's anguish and Harbord's happy understanding.[73]

Friday, July 4, continued the hectic activities of the AEF headquarters party. At 9:00 A.M. Jack attended a review of American troops with President Poincaré, Marshal Foch, and American ambassador Hugh Wallace. As the last of the good marching troops passed, Pershing and party headed again for Picpus cemetery and Lafayette's tomb for a wreath laying. To the Hôtel du Palais d'Orsay he went with Harbord, Quek, and Little Collins, who had once more joined the official family. More than four hundred people milled in a great hall, ate lunch, and listened to lengthy declamations of abiding affection.

Later the general went to Pershing Stadium for a look at the Inter-Allied games. Amid all kinds of activities, Pershing looked with special eye on a selected regiment of American troops as they competed for drilling honors. Surely with thoughts of West Point's Corps and of the Lincoln cadets, he watched men picked for their soldierly qualities and trained in a "Provisional Regiment" as America's contingent for the victory parades in Paris and London. They were as good, almost, as those Nebraska boys had been so many years ago. Quek, a West Pointer who had not seen the university unit, thought his comrades in khaki "simply superb."[74]

Evening passed at the opera with a performance of *Faust*. Pershing sat with Marshals Foch and Joffre, their ladies, and Generals Bliss and Harbord, and enjoyed the show—and the pageantry. There was a dance after the opera that lasted until 2:00 A.M.—then the headquarters group collapsed at 73, rue de Varenne. They all slept late Saturday morning. Which was as well, since Pershing had to go to the stadium again for presentation of prizes in the games. America's representatives did well and he was proud.[75]

All of this activity might be considered preliminary, though, a prelude to the great spasm of Bastille Day—the first peaceful one in five years. But the Fourth of July orgy was a fitting climax to America's

[73] Harbord, *American Army*, p. 562; Dawes, *Journal*, 1:261.
[74] Quekemeyer to his mother, July 5, 1919, Quekemeyer Papers.
[75] *Ibid.*; Harbord, *American Army*, p. 562.

role in the war. In the ten days until July 14, Pershing ordered the closing of headquarters at Chaumont. He would give up Val des Escoliers, move back to the Mills house, reopen the office on the rue Constantine, and begin the final withdrawal of the AEF.

Closing Chaumont brought heartaches. Everyone in the small town mourned the Americans' departure. How bid such good friends goodbye? Whatever ceremony seemed appropriate would have to be fitted among departing boxes and troops. Pershing took time to call on Mayor Lévy-Alphandéry and to give his fellow citizen a Distinguished Service Medal in thanks for so much good will. Rounds of farewells to city fathers and daughters brought floods of tears, heartfelt desolation, and, finally, departure for Paris on July 12. The train rolled back through the Lorraine hills, and Pershing looked on the old land, washed again in blood. It was, forever, part of America. He had brought America to her triumphs here; he was leaving so many of his men. A mournful rhythm echoed from the wheels.

Bastille Day roared toward the explosive climax of a great parade through the Arc de Triomphe. The city throbbed all day with building excitement—a great rising wave of exuberance that bubbled and rustled in the crowds thronging the boulevards. Banners dappled every tree and light, people carried rosettes remindful of the Revolution and the sacrifices to preserve it. All the allies, save poor Russia, would be represented in the huge march. This was the occasion Pershing had been expecting, the one for which he had picked the Provisional Regiment; those men gathered, with so many Allied buddies, far out in Neuilly on the avenue de la Grande Armée. Formation began early in the morning, amid people who had been sleeping on the curbs to hold places for the view. Viewing would be difficult, but the sight unforgettable—Dawes knew that, and had declined a place in the column in order to see Jack's greatest moment[76]—and the wait was a small price. At 10:00 A.M. trumpets sounded from massed bands, and the march began—countries placed alphabetically, America came first. Pershing, sitting his horse as befitted a trooper of the cavalry, headed the American column, behind Foch and Joffre. Next came Jack's standard bearer, then Harbord, followed by the aides abreast on three white horses ahead of fifteen American generals. Finally came the crack Provisional Regiment, its exquisite precision an honor to every unit in the AEF. All American flags were bunched this time, carried by the center battalion, and they flashed a bank of color as the men

[76] Dawes, *Journal*, 1:262.

filed through France's sacred arch. Those stalwart Americans began the crowd's wild applauding, the cheering that buffeted the column as it snaked its seven-mile course. Along those avenues the people thundered their thanks, and the cheering rose dramatically as the overcoated *poilus* came with rifles and fixed bayonets. They passed, at last, a place where the *Mutilés* took the review—the maimed, dauntless men who had held back the Boche, watched as their comrades turned to salute them on the march. Pershing, moved beyond expression, saluted, too, and Harbord caught the spirit in recollection: "The world has never seen anything quite like it before, for it was France and the French in their own capital, enshrined in the memories of a thousand years of Old France." And then the last man passed and the drums stopped, the trumpets hushed—victory was remembered.

Happy recollections with Joffre and Foch, with doughty Pétain who headed France's men, then a quick farewell, for a tight schedule beckoned. That night Pershing, with Harbord and a few other generals, plus Quek (a new colonel) and Major Hughes headed for Boulogne and a trip to London.

By the time Pershing reached British soil, Griscom had abounding good news. Winston Churchill, Griscom's nominal boss in the War Office, had determined that Pershing would lead the Victory Parade, despite Foch's self-invitation. "Pershing shall lead," Churchill thundered to Griscom, but admitted that a Victory Parade must include all the Allies. The Provisional Regiment—known in Britain as "Pershing's Own"—would have honored place ahead.

Ensconced at the Carlton Hotel, Pershing discovered a hectic week of ceremonials scheduled. He must bestow some Distinguished Service Medals on British civilians in the War Office and on some officers after the Prince of Wales' review of the Provisional Regiment. Dinners and functions were legion, offered by ambassadors, friends, the king, the Commons; the eager Prince of Wales was going to take Pershing to a boxing match![77]

There were special honors pending, honors more important than were usually given to foreigners. Field Marshal Haig invited Pershing and his personally selected attendants to a special dinner at the Carlton. Pershing, understanding Haig's old shyness, realized the tribute implied and took a few of his military intimates. Haig invited

---

[77] Paraphrase of Harbord, *American Army*, pp. 564–65. For Griscom's role, see his *Diplomatically Speaking*, p. 456.

a stellar lists of generals, including Canada's Arthur Currie, Australia's John Monash, British army commanders, and staff officers.[78]

These friends respected each other and showed it through a convivial dinner and especially after the two speeches of the evening—Haig's and Pershing's. They spared no pains in praising each other and each other's armies. From that dinner came lasting affection.

At 12:25 P.M. on July 18, Pershing presented himself at the Guildhall to be greeted by an honor guard of Grenadiers, was met on the porch by a committee, and inspected his guard. Conducted then to the dais in the Guildhall by frock-coated hosts, he met the lord mayor and two sheriffs. The town clerk then read the Order of the Court—General Pershing was presented the Honorary Freedom of the City. The chamberlain offered him a hand of fellowship, presented a copy of the Court Resolution, asked him to accept the Sword of Honor. Pershing, ramrod straight, solemn, made a short acceptance statement and met various officials. Throughout the proceedings the Royal Artillery band played a special program—"Hands Across the Sea," "America," "Omaha," "Missouri," "Stars and Stripes." As the ceremony ended, the band played "God Save the King." The lord mayor then hosted a luncheon at the Mansion House.

After lunch Pershing had barely time to get ready for dinner at the House of Commons. Churchill presided over more than eighty guests, a glittering array of military and civil dignitaries refulgent in decorations. In grand form, Churchill entertained with witty remarks and a special toast to Pershing. Clearly he thought the Anglo-American alliance must stand fast in the future. As Pershing glanced around the table he saw Harbord and many British generals, but missed Haig. Sir Henry Wilson smiled from a distance; Cavan, Plumer, Rawlinson, others were warm in welcome, as were the Geddes brothers and Viscounts Haldane and Milner. Exhausted but excited, Pershing sought sleep to fortify against the parade on the morrow.[79]

Churchill's plans for the parade almost miscarried. Pershing and the American army did take precedence—by alphabet, obviously—in that line that rivaled the Paris march. For seven miles the route ran from Albert Gate, over the Thames, then across Westminster Bridge to the Unknown Soldier's monument, on through Whitehall, the Ad-

[78] Harbord, *American Army*, pp. 565–67. The dinner was given on July 16, 1919. See George C. Marshall, *Memoirs of My Services in The World War, 1917–1918*, pp. 214–15.
[79] This account is taken from Harbord, *American Army*, pp. 567–68. See also Marshall, *Memoirs*, p. 218.

miralty Arch, up the Mall past the king and queen waiting at Queen Victoria's Memorial, on to Hyde Park Corner. Griscom hoped all arrangements were in order—though he fussed about the horses.

Starting time was 10:00 A.M. Long before the hour, Quek and Griscom went to Rotten Row to check the mounts. Griscom hoped for a "fine old steady charger" for the general and gaped in dismay at the small, nervous animal presented. Snorting, cavorting, the horse seemed unused to noise. Quek swung on for a trial ride; the horse almost threw a colonel of the U.S. Cavalry! Furious, he tested others, found a large one that looked "placid" for his general. Pershing arrived, noted Quek's problems, but accepted the horse, swung on, and started. Behind him rode Harbord with Maj. Gen. John Headlam, Pershing's liaison from Haig, followed by other American generals. Next came the band and then the Provisional Regiment, brought especially for the march.

Griscom, mounted on a touchy animal himself, best described the Americans' ride:

We managed to get in formation and danced out of Hyde Park Gate across Knightsbridge and down Sloane Street. A drizzling rain had made the pavement like glass. The music and the jangling of our swords seemed to madden the horses. One moment I would be up in the air and the next down. It was impossible to keep a proper interval. . . . Just as we turned safely left under the broad Admiralty Arch, the band burst forth anew, the sound reverberated in a terrific roar, and every horse was immediately again on its hind legs. Marshall's mount reared and tumbled over backwards, but he himself slid from beneath with amazing agility. . . .[80]

Pershing's horse, restless and balky, fought hard but submitted at last to tough cavalry handling.

Precise and marvelously disciplined compared to the horsemen, the Provisional Regiment set a splendid standard for all the Allied forces. Pershing and Harbord dismounted after passing the reviewing stand and entered the Royal Pavilion. There they could see the rest of the troops in endless ranks surging along the Mall and the crowds that clustered in wild density to cheer. Haig—that day an earl—looked superb at the head of Britain's legions. And when the last man passed, Pershing and Harbord along with many Allied officers joined the king and queen for lunch at Buckingham Palace.

Britain had more honors for Pershing. He was weary but happy, aware, too, that all the pomp had political circumstance. It was vital

---

[80] Griscom, *Diplomatically Speaking*, p. 457. See Marshall's laconic account in his *Memoirs*, pp. 219–20.

to America's interests that ceremonial duties be done with aplomb—victory had catapulted the country into world prominence, and her representatives must maintain the position. Vital, too, was the realization that much of the adulation, many of the honors were for his country, not him. He must do his duty with grace and serve his nation.

At Cambridge University on July 23, he received an honorary LL.D., along with several British leaders and General Currie. Impressive, solemn, traditional, the proceedings called up old visions of Britain's history and her power. Pershing the American was properly pleased.[81]

Quickly across the channel in a British destroyer, Pershing was back in his Paris office in time for lunch with Charlie on July 24. Dawes was going home—his Liquidation Commission had done a masterful job, had arranged to dispose of surpluses to France for $400,000,000. Happy in his honors—he had the French Legion of Honor, the croix de guerre, Belgium's Order of Leopold, was a Companion of the Bath, and from Jack had the Distinguished Service Medal—Dawes at last felt able to quit. He had been loyal and diligent, had done more than perhaps anyone else to consolidate Allied supply efforts, and had arranged liquidation details shrewdly. His business sense, his boisterous manners, his disdain for red tape had angered and finally captivated his colleagues; his appointment had been one of Jack's finest. Jack would miss him sorely—with no other man could he be completely himself, to no other could he tell his frustrations, confess his ambitions. Suddenly Europe seemed lonely—despite Micheline and other ladies. After lunch and some talk of business, the two cronies talked about the near future. Charlie left the restaurant warm in Pershing's friendship. "Dear old John," he thought, "nothing changes him from what he has always been. His feet are always on the ground."[82]

They would have one last meeting, a long one, before Charlie sailed on the *Leviathan* August 30. They talked again of the future. Pershing assessed his own position coldly, guessed at scant chances for higher things, doubted they could mean as much as heading the AEF. "Several times during our long visit," Charlie noted, "we both were greatly affected, but it was when we spoke of the sorrows in our life, not of anything material that there may be left in it for either of us."

[81] Griscom, *Diplomatically Speaking*, pp. 457–59; Harbord, *American Army*, pp. 569–71.
[82] Dawes, *Journal*, 1:270.

What remained to do? The AEF had shrunk virtually to nothing; Jack commanded ghost legions, marched to old echoes. He would fight for the right of those legions to the Sam Browne belt. For obscure reasons March and even Baker opposed the belt and forced returning AEF men to discard it—they looked bare to Jack. It had been a mark of rank and responsibility; it made a man look snappy. Surely the secretary would allow it worn in the final review promised for Pershing's homecoming? The issue seemed worth a battle, anyway.[83]

Old friends and helpers, Americans and Allies, remained to be thanked. That should be done in the form of returned hospitality. He would give a farewell party, a great assembly of many who had entertained and consoled, helped and persuaded, wished well, fought and forgiven. More than a thousand invitations were sent to an "At Home" at the Crillon on Tuesday, July 29. The gaiety seemed obscured by the future, but everyone enjoyed himself, and the glitter outshone almost every other gathering in brass and gowns and prominence—generals, their ladies, officers, and civilian leaders of all Allied nations graced the hall. Micheline was invited, as were other special friends.[84]

Then there was time for one final act before he could leave in August or early September. He would make a last inspection tour, a sentimental journey to towns and stations and battlefields and to the troops still watching the Rhine.

At Coblenz the troops were in fine shape, Allen doing a splendid job. Clearly the commander-in-chief could do nothing there. He could, at least, see the places forever famed in American military history. Taking his aides to Pont-à-Mousson near Saint Mihiel, he put them in cars and began a fearsome tour of the salient—fearsome because he saw everything, studied the actions closely from maps, talked of the lessons that should have been learned. For the young officers he gave personal lessons in tactics and logistics. Conflans and Verdun were stops, followed by a plunge into the sprawling Meuse-Argonne country. Two tough days hiking and checking map references followed, days of talks on tactics and questions to the young men. These two days were "in the field," with lunches carried and rest ignored. Jack called off sightseeing about eight at night, and no one had trouble

---

[83] For background on the belt issue, see JJP to AGWAR, May 23, 29, 1918 (cables), in Open Cables Sent; JJP to Baker, July 11, 1919 (Personal), Box 19, PP; Palmer, *Baker*, 2:410–11.

[84] See "General Pershing's 'At Home,' July 29, 1919—4 to 7, List of People to Whom Invitations Were Sent," Box 253, PP.

sleeping. From the Meuse-Argonne he took his troops to Champagne, showed them the damaged cathedral in Reims, then the Marne sites at Château-Thierry, Belleau Wood, the Soisson woods where the 1st and 2nd Divisions attacked. Next he led on to the British line in the Somme, to Arras, Vimy Ridge, the tank battlefield at Cambrai, up to the Lys area, Messines ridge, and on to the Ypres Salient. Wherever Americans had fought, Pershing lectured with authority on their deeds. Warren, tucked along with Sergeant Lanckton, did as much of the touring as he could, and enjoyed especially the end when he and his dad had lunch with the king and queen of Belgium.

It was August 10, and their majesties entertained the American general, his son, and Colonel Quekemeyer at a private luncheon in their country home near Dinant. Pershing sat at the head of the table, the queen on his right, the king, his left. King Albert and the queen were soon coming to America and Pershing made arrangements to see them.

Following the royal interlude, Pershing picked up Fox Conner and George Marshall, saw Waterloo again (without Frankie), and made a swing to Antwerp, an American base port. It had been a tough, wearing trip, but it refreshed Jack's memory on the intrepid bravery of his fine soldiers. His lessons had been well learned and his battle-field lectures had taught his young staff. Quek said "I wouldn't have missed this trip for anything in the world. It was most instructive and so very interesting."[85]

For Pershing there remained one last trip—one protocol demanded. He had not yet visited Italy and had to pay a courtesy call on those southern allies. His official train sped southward, and he toured vigorously. King Victor Emmanuel entertained happily, as did Gen. Armando Díaz and old friend General Cariglia. Carefully Pershing decorated numerous Italian officers, inspected their battle fronts in admiration, and managed to cram in several operas. He was glad he made the excursion.[86] At every station Italian and American flags were in evidence, people were excited, and when Pershing stopped to sight-see, he was the leading attraction.

There were no more reasons to stay. Micheline confessed willing-ness to visit the United States. Most of Jack's friends were home now,

---

[85] Quekemeyer to his mother, Aug. 11, 1919, Quekemeyer Papers. George Marshall kept a diary of the trip, Aug. 1–12, 1919. See his *Memoirs*, pp. 226–29.

[86] See Grady Barrett, "Pershing at Close Range," pp. 12–13 (typescript in author's possession); JJP to AGWAR Aug. 17–20, 1919, Box 106, PP; Marshall, *Memoirs*, pp. 230–39.

or back to business in Europe. On September 1, 1919, he and Warren would board the *Leviathan* for the United States.

His era appeared to be passing. People in Paris bustled in old courses of affairs; the boulevards hummed now with commerce, not war. Near the Invalides the AEF's offices were being closed, records packed, furniture scattered, men leaving. No crowds clustered to salvage mementoes, no mourners stood vigil in good-bye. There were many who cared, many who were close to that fading army and remembered what it had done for France. Many, too, wanted to bid Pershing farewell, had, in fact, done so in the functions that so filled the last months. But the mood was different in Paris, in France, in all of Europe—the Great War was over and men change with the times.

He wanted his closest associates to go home with him—and some were summoned for the trip. Lloyd Griscom, far traveled now from America's legation in Tokyo, received the call and accepted gladly. George Marshall, a close staff family member, would go; so would good George Quekemeyer, loyal and diligent and secretly thrilled by Pershing's words in a recent efficiency report. But Harbord had gone to Armenia on a special mission, Dawes had gone home, Boyd was dead, so many were dead and staying in France.

On Sunday, August 31, 1919, Pershing, with Quek, made a pilgrimage of parting to the Surennes Cemetery. There, bareheaded, they stood in tribute and fond remembrance of Carl Boyd. Back at the rue de Varenne Pershing finished some writing, said good-bye to the housekeeper and the servants who had done so much so willingly. Train time was 6:35 and Pershing determined to be early, since "I had been told that there would be a number of people down to see me off." At 6:15 he reached the Invalides and perked up quickly. A guard of honor lined his way to the tracks. Once ensconced in his car, he returned to see who had come—and the list brought mild surprise: General Allen; Gen. William Connor; Ambassador Wallace with many from the embassy; good old Bliss, smiling but sad; the Tiger of France himself, blustery and sentimental now; Tardieu, the faithful; Jusserand, so long America's votary; and a flock of personal friends. He was not to slip unnoticed from Paris. When the train left, he was smiling as he and Warren waved.

At 8:40 A.M., Monday, the train chuffed to a stop on the docks at Brest. Pershing stepped into the midst of a French guard of honor and was greeted warmly by Marshal Foch, who had come down the night before to say good-bye. The guard lined the quai where a tug waited to take Pershing and other passengers out to the *Leviathan*. A band, smartly accoutered, stood at attention as the two generals walked toward the dock. As they passed the band struck up "The Star Spangled Banner," and people cheered. Vive Pershing! Vive Foch! There was a moment of poignant recollection. Then Pershing and party boarded the tug, went to the *Leviathan*, and were welcomed by the captain and officers. Staterooms assigned, Pershing soon hosted Foch in his sitting room and they talked "intimately" for a while. They went, finally, to the lounge to greet the GHQ contingent and ship's officers. Foch, saying that he wanted to share Jack's last moments in France, made a fine, stalwart speech: "On arriving you said, 'Lafayette, nous voilà.' Allow the French soldier of today to answer 'Thanks be to you,' and in a few words to recall the great work that you have done for the rights and the liberty of the world." Remembering America's unprepared state in April, 1917, Foch recounted quickly the hasty mobilization of men and material, described the raw troops put into Pershing's hands, troops needing

discipline, military spirit, training and tactical knowledge, as well as . . . offensive spirit. . . . By your method, your work, your spirit of organization, your tenacity, you fully realized these results and when the moment came to enter the fight, . . . remarkable resolution animated the American army and their chief. . . . Thus you have shown yourself, in the largest sense of the word, an organizer, a soldier, a chief, and still more a great servant of your country. You have crowned the generous efforts and the noble intention of America with . . . the victory of your armies. Of this achievement you can be proud. And in leaving France you leave your dead in our hands. On our soil we will care for them religiously, jealously, as the witness of the powerful aid you brought to us. . . . By their sacrifice, you carry henceforth an immortal glory in the folds of your Star Spangled Banner.

Deeply touched, both by the speech and by Foch's presence, Pershing answered, in English:

My Dear Marshal: You have done me signal honor in paying this final visit, as I am about to sail for my own country. In leaving France it is fitting that you should be the last to whom I say farewell because of our intimate service together in days of anxiety and in days of victory. These will ever live in my memory as of yesterday. The American Army, in fulfillment of the will of our people, came to France because we stood for the same principles of right and because the common ideals of our two countries called for mutual action. Upon this foundation close comradeship and cooperation rapidly moulded our fresh and aggressive young manhood into an army, which under you, as the Allied leader, was to turn the tide of war. To have fought beside the glorious army of France and to have been of your people during more than two years, has given our relations an affectionate touch that makes our parting one of sadness. But in these deep sentiments there is an abiding confidence between our people that insures to the world our constant friendship and our common purpose in behalf of humanity. In leaving with France our dead we are consoled to feel that their graves will be tenderly cared for. . . . In saying farewell to you, my dear Marshal, I say farewell to France—to her gallant Poilus, to her patriotic men and to her noble women, and leave with full confidence in France's glorious future.

Then the two old soldiers clasped hands, nearly wept. Pershing walked Foch to the gangway, they shook hands again, embraced briefly, then the marshal walked down to the tug. Pershing watched, saluted when the marshal turned back; the salute was returned. At 3:00 P.M. the *Leviathan* blew for clearance, her whistle was echoed by all other ships in the harbor, her engines throbbed, and she made way. As she headed out, Pershing noted, lump in his throat, that Foch was aboard a small cutter that kept pace with the *Leviathan*; bands aboard flocking French destroyers played distant songs of war, and as the ship cleared the harbor, up on the captain's bridge Pershing saluted Foch and France.[87]

Some things about the trip home reminded Jack of the *Baltic*— the feeling of camaraderie, the closeness of the military family, the casual troops aboard. There were, too, happy contrasts—Warren was aboard, no submarine threat darkened pleasure, and lights burned gaily at night. Pershing had wired ahead the names of his party so that provision could be made for their inclusion in any celebration planned. But he had heard nothing of such plans and was worried. Would there be a reception? Baker had often spoken of a proper welcome home; the president, too seemed amenable. Had anything gone wrong? Had he pushed too hard about the Sam Brownes? He had asked that the men on board with him be allowed to wear the belt in any official functions—had that been too much to ask? Or had trouble intruded about the question of rank? Papa Warren reported stalled proceedings still on the bill to create full generals—and Jack had hoped that he would be confirmed in permanent possession of four stars before he got home. It looked now as though the rank might not come; there were complications over naming permanent lieutenant generals that irked Pershing. He thought good fighters like Liggett, Bullard, and Harbord deserved recognition. Rank in the AEF had always been a nagging bother, especially during the last year. Some

[87] For the farewell proceedings, see Griscom, *Diplomatically Speaking*, p. 459, where details are erroneously recalled; see, too, the *Leviathan's* newspaper, *Transport Ace*, Tuesday, Sept. 2, 1919, for copies of the speeches and details of embarkation; JJP, Diary, Aug. 31, Sept. 1, 1919, Boxes 4–5, PP.

finicky parsimony choked off promotions abroad and led to bitter complaints about stateside officers who got stars for attending parties! Baker had tried to rectify the matter, had pushed March to permit promotion in the Army of Occupation, but had achieved only limited success.[88] Temporary ranks were allowed, to revert on return home. It was under that temporary authority that Pershing had upped Quekemeyer and many others. They would all lapse the minute they touched American soil and it seemed, somehow, a shabby reward. Probably March's petty concern for punctilio, and especially for his own aggrandizement, caused the trouble, but Baker should not have agreed. Renewed talks with Baker might yet win a reversal of policy. Pershing was the only man to fight for the AEF—he would not shirk the honor.

Things like rank seemed small in the good will suddenly washing over the *Leviathan.* Cascades of telegrams came from everywhere welcoming Pershing back, wishing him well, saying all kinds of nice things. But by contrast the official silence from Washington seemed ominous.

One good result Pershing realized quickly at sea—he rested, truly rested, for the first time since April, 1917. It was a new and awkward feeling to have time to rest, to choose between idle occupations. But the awkwardness faded quickly; he might get used to being lazy.

Unfortunately, the sea disturbed leisure by turning ugly, and the second day out the *Leviathan* rolled and pitched in heavy troughs. She was big, an old German passenger ship, still crazed with camouflage, and her size steadied her slightly. But Pershing stayed close to his room and listened to the engines labor against the elements. He tried working on his final report, but writing and seasickness seemed a bad combination. And he worried in those queasy hours about the Washington silence. Warren, unaware of dad's worries, rushed around the ship in glee and dashed in often to report discoveries.

Thursday morning, the fifth, Pershing was shocked awake by Warren landing on his bed, waving a message from the wireless room —it was something important, Warren said, read it! Pershing read slowly and with rising excitement—Congress had voted him the rank of General of the Armies. He missed the full import for a time, basked simply in being a permanent general. The officers wanted to congratulate him, and he dressed for the occasion. On deck after lunch, at the

[88] See March to JJP, Jan. 27, 1919 (cable 2557-R-Confidential), in Cables— War Department to AEF, Pershing Papers, RG 200, National Archives Gift Collection.

request of the commander of the Provisional, or Composite, Regiment, he stood and shook hands with a long line of officers who filed proudly by. There was a formal picture-taking ceremony, and many men took candid shots of their own. The more he heard, the more he appreciated the new rank—it was unusual. Some speculated that only George Washington had held it before. That seemed doubtful—Grant, surely, had held that rank, perhaps Sherman, as head of the army? But it was nice, a great gesture by Baker and the president, and it changed the temper of the trip, even of the sea! He worked that afternoon on a speech he would "probably have to make before Congress."[89]

More bright news came Saturday; McAndrew wired that he and Collins would be in charge of New York City's reception, and it would be a humdinger! Work on the speech and the report flew easily—the preliminary report was finished by Saturday night. Next day clouds of congratulations flooded the radio room along with invitations to speak, to appear, to dedicate all kinds of things. A senator offered his house during Pershing's Washington sojourn. The ship would dock at 9:00 A.M. on Sunday, September 8, but by 7:00 A.M. a new world dawned.

Shrieking whistles and sirens from a motley flotilla of boats, ships, and destroyers clustering out of New York harbor awakened everyone on board. Quek urged haste—the United States waited! Dressed, Pershing took Warren to the bridge and looked in amazement at the mass of boats and ships and people. Forests of arms waved, great, deep foghorns hooted, and a guard of honor made by tugs escorted the *Leviathan* toward Hoboken. At eight Pershing pointed to a destroyer maneuvering alongside—on the bridge were Baker and General March, McAndrew, Senator Wadsworth, and a flock of former AEF staff officers. The mayor of New York waved from another tug; yet another carried the families of the official party, including May and Bessie and brother Jim. Pershing gaped at the wholehearted, hysterical warmth of his welcome. "I was frankly overwhelmed by its size and enthusiasm." When the ship docked, floods of newsmen and photographers crowded aboard, "some hundred" pictures were taken, and then the famed frost of the Iron Commander opened the way ashore.

Protocol demanded a handclasp with the secretary of war, who came representing the president. Baker, jaunty in a new-cut suit with vest and a broad-brimmed fedora, grinned hugely behind his rimless glasses. Pershing, his smile fetching an elusive dimple, shook hands and listened to Baker's little speech. He came, he said, with a dual

---

[89] See O'Connor, *BJP*, p. 343, for Warren's arrival with the message; JJP, Diary, Sept. 2, 3, 4, 5, 1919, Boxes 4–5, PP.

purpose—to greet Pershing as a friend and as a representative of President Wilson. Wilson sent a message, and a freshly signed commission. The president, embattled for the League, had gone on a "swing around the circle" to win support, else he would have been in Hoboken. His message had uncommon warmth:

My dear General Pershing, I am distressed that I cannot greet you in person. It would give me the greatest pleasure to grasp your hand and say to you what is in my heart and in the hearts of all true Americans as we hail your return to the home land you have served so gallantly. Notwithstanding my physical absence, may I not, as your commander-in-chief and as spokesman of our fellow countrymen, bid you an affectionate and enthusiastic welcome,—a welcome warmed with the ardour of genuine affection and deep admiration? You have served your country with fine devotion and admirable efficiency in a war forever memorable as the world's triumphant protest against injustice and as its vindication of liberty, the liberty of people and nations. We are proud of you and of the men you commanded. . . . It is delightful to see you home and well and fit for the fatigue you must endure before we are done with our welcome.[90]

And the president had told Baker he envied him the privilege of greeting Pershing. As Baker thrust the commission in his hand, Pershing's pride was full—how Frankie would have beamed. How May and Bessie and Jim beamed, how everyone seemed so happy—it was gratitude beyond wishing, more than a triumph, an engulfing of love. Home looked different but was not strange.

[90] Wilson to Baker, Sept. 3, 1919, Correspondence 1916–21, Box 11, 1919 Wilson, item stamped 229, Baker Papers, Library of Congress. See also JJP, Diary, Sept. 8, 1919, Boxes 4–5, PP, for details of going ashore.

☆ 24 ☆

"The True Soldier"

RUMORS about the new rank had substance. Research into the labyrinths of legislation showed that Congress, seeking every possible
way to skirt the intricacies of promotions en masse, revived a title to
solve a dilemma. Senator Warren had rightly guessed that March's
name tied to the full-general bill scuttled its chances in the House. An
old vendetta waged by at least one angry member snarled consideration of the joint bill of promotion. Even Wilson's recommendation and
Baker's cordial testimony in favor of both Pershing and the chief of
staff failed to move Congress.[1]

Congress sought safety in precedent, and a precedent offered from
1799. In that year Congress created for George Washington the rank
of General of the Armies, although he had probably been given the
rank earlier by the Continental Congress. General Grant received the
title of General of the Army in 1866, and it was construed as being the
same as full general by the comptroller general. Carefully Congress

---

[1] For Wilson's recommendation, see Peyton C. March, *The Nation at War*, pp.
349–50. For Baker's firm endorsement of both men, see Baker to Senator Wadsworth, July 26, 1919, FEW Papers, vol. 86. Of Pershing, Baker said, in part: "General Pershing led the Armies of America in the greatest war in the history of the
world, and led them to a victory of which the world had begun to despair, and the
fruits of which are of incalculable value to mankind. He led them with leadership
in keeping with the highest traditions of American genius." Much public interest
in Pershing's welfare spurred Congressional action. Sentiment in the army ran
strongly for Pershing. See, for example, an editorial, "General Pershing and His
Rank," in *U.S. Infantry Journal* 16 (Sept., 1919): 248. See also, "Miller" to "Dear
General," Office of the Judge Advocate General, Aug. 1, 1919, in Western Historical MSS Collection, University of Missouri, Columbia, containing this comment:
"Apparently the Pershing-March bill will not pass this month. . . . I dont suppose
that General Pershing will return until it does pass, as my understanding is that he
will revert to a Major General upon his arrival in the U.S., unless the legislation
is meanwhile enacted." See the adulatory comments concerning Pershing in *Congressional Record*, 66th Cong., 1 sess., 58, pt. 5:4463–68.

wrote a bill (HR 7594) to revive the rank of General of the Armies for General Pershing alone to hold during his lifetime. The rank would cease to exist upon Pershing's death. Public Law 45, 1919, passed easily, and Wilson had appointed Pershing as expected. So he and Washington shared a rare and lofty perch.[2]

Riding the crest of new adulation occupied Pershing's immediate future—he would enjoy receptions, reviews, parades in New York and Washington, could go virtually anywhere on as many speaking engagements as he wanted. But after the tumult what would he do? March still held the top soldier's job as chief of staff, and, although Jack had pushed his Distinguished Service Medal, March still resented the independence of the AEF and the ruthless strength of its commander. Was the army big enough for both? Pershing had tried to ease relations by friendly letters, which March reciprocated, but strain continued. With Pershing the ranking general and March the chief of staff, clashes seemed inevitable.

Pershing reckoned that Baker would have trouble finding work for the General of the Armies.

He reckoned, too, that the immediate future would take care of brooding time for everybody. Arrival day had flitted in a rush of presentations for his party and himself: freedom of New York, guests of the city at the Waldorf-Astoria; the same waves of visitors as on the remote day at the Crillon in 1917; a late afternoon session with forty newsmen; a stag dinner at the Ritz, guests of Redman Wanamaker, chairman of the mayor's entertainment committee; then a coeducational evening at the Hippodrome with embarrassing notice from the crowds. Happy exhaustion claimed his whole party, and they clutched sleep eagerly against the new day.

Old friends claimed part of the day, especially Charlie Magoon, now ex-governor, and William Jennings Bryan, of Lincoln days. Pershing visited a riding academy to see a gift horse; he looked so like a warhorse Jack decided to ride him in the big parade on September 10. Fifty thousand school children greeted the general in Central Park, and he was "deeply touched" by their happy enthusiasm; they were open and happy, and the little girls brought tender memories. Later, after many callers, he went to have tea with the Warrens at the Plaza Hotel. An Elks Club dinner thronged with no less than five thousand

---

[2] See "Legislative History of the Rank of General of the Armies," in Pershing File, Truman Library, Independence, Mo.; *Statutes at Large of the United States of America*, 41, pt. 1:283, for "An Act Relating to the creation of the office of General of the Armies of the United States."

howling Elks led to a mobbed evening at the Gayety Theater. But Jack was looking ahead to the big parade.

Not just the Provisional Regiment would go this time; the entire 1st Division, Pershing's Own, would stream its full length and complexity along New York's streets, and Pershing was happy it would give people "an opportunity to see just what a complete American division is like and how many various units it contains besides the actual fighting men." New York had prepared for this parade with lavish care. A full-sized replica of the Arc de Triomphe stood athwart Fifth Avenue; through that memorial Pershing would lead his Composite Guard and Big Red One—and they were ready, all of them, tough men now, battle tested and proud that they were the first of the AEF, which meant they were the first of the best.

Like so many he had been in, this parade began at 10:00 A.M.; it formed far out on 110th Street, began its cadenced progress toward downtown through dense crowds who cheered and waved and listened. Veteran parader that he was, Pershing walked his mount gracefully at the head of the column, followed by his standard bearers, staff, officers, and his fine, fine men. A halt at 57th Street for a change of horses gave Pershing a chance to speak to Cardinal Mercier at the cathedral, then on to Washington Square through denser hordes of onlookers. When he reached that objective, he climbed into a car, sped to the Waldorf, and watched the troops pass for another hour. He was as pleased as any sightseer, beamed as the men marched, pointed to special things, and felt that keen kinship with the AEF.[3] He thought the whole show "most successful."

Through careful liaison between General McAndrew and the Wanamaker committee, Pershing avoided a good many functions, but he still had no real time to himself. His family he saw in snatches. He did insist on giving a small reception for the families of his official party, and he enjoyed a Pershing Welcome concert in Central Park conducted by Walter Damrosch, whose work with the AEF bands Pershing remembered gratefully. "The concert was a splendid one." An official dinner at the Waldorf packed in hundreds, and he stood shaking hands for endless stretches. On the eleventh, the parade still fresh in mind, he did a duty of affection—out to Oyster Bay he went with Quek to call on Mrs. Theodore Roosevelt. The colonel's death after the war had saddened all his loyal admirers, and Pershing, ever since, had wanted

[3] JJP, Diary, Sept. 9, 10, 1919, Boxes 4–5, PP. Frank Vandiver, *Illustrious Americans: John J. Pershing*, p. 113.

to pay personal respects to his widow. Mrs. Roosevelt showed the old, charming, Roosevelt hospitality, showed her visitors "the Colonel's grave," and sent them away relieved. A "Pershing Club" in New York where AEF officers had enjoyed themselves on the way from France, claimed a short moment of Jack's time when he got back from Oyster Bay, then he checked with George Marshall on the state of correspondence. Two thousand telegrams, Marshall reported, most of them invitations, cluttered the hotel suite, plus several hundred letters—they rained steadily on an overworked mail desk!

People knotted the halls, delegations from everywhere, all seeking speeches from the man of the moment. He tried to be pleasant, to shake as many hands as possible, to smile and be appreciative, but adulation had its difficult side. Gauche though it would sound publicly, Pershing wearied of sycophancy and looked toward return of official duties, especially toward his address to a Joint Session of Congress, scheduled for September 18. There he could talk of gallant men, sound old trumpets of remembrance. He purloined moments to work on his speech.

A special 1st Division train took Pershing and multitudes of his men to Washington. There was a stop at Philadelphia while the honored passenger rode a motorcade to Independence Hall, and a spontaneous flood of well wishers darkened the streets. Pleased at the honesty of affection, Pershing accepted a Liberty Bell medal crusted with diamonds, said a few words, and spoke his thanks for the whole AEF to a crowd outside; a side visit to the Union League Club demanded more words, but at last the trip continued toward Washington. Wilmington would not be ignored; Pershing spoke to a crowd in the station. In Washington, Baker and March met the train—a replay of New York's reception—and Vice President Thomas R. Marshall said welcome in Wilson's name. A suite at the Shoreham decked with flowers and telegrams awaited; once located, Pershing, Quek, Hughes, and Jack's nephew, Jim, had dinner with the Marshalls.

Official and personal calls and callers filled the next days, especially on the thirteenth, Jack's fifty-ninth birthday. Baker, during an official visit by Jack that day, agreed to let Pershing continue his headquarters in Washington while records and reports of the AEF were processed. A call on the chief of staff went well. Then he saw his offices in the Land Office Building on 7th and E Streets, divided up the cubicles, and prepared to get back to work. The Warrens gave a birthday dinner for him in the evening.

From the wilderness of invitations came confusion; how many should a soldier accept? Baker "intimated that he thought it advisable for me to accept some of the invitations I have received from cities throughout the South and Middle West. . . . " Pershing wanted a vacation, worried, too, lest his motives in traveling around making speeches would be misunderstood. Still, these invitations did give chances to encourage "real appreciation of what the A.E.F. has done. . . . "[4] Much perturbed about whether or not too much exposure might hurt rather than help both the AEF and his own personal cause—he had not forgotten the coming political conventions[5]—Pershing considered carefully and finally decided against a speaking "swing" for the present.[6] Instead, he begged and instantly received a renewed invitation to visit old friend Governor Forbes, of fond Philippine memories, in Cape Cod. Before the vacation he would parade and would address Congress.

He liked the parade in Washington better than the one in New York. The Composite Regiment and the 1st Division were tighter and more professional; everyone's horse behaved. It started in the afternoon of September 17; he arranged good seats for many personal friends, including Mrs. Carl Boyd.[7] His new horse, Jeff, rode well as the parade wended along Pennsylvania Avenue to 15th Street, then right, on through the Victory Arch, left past the reviewing stand in front of the White House where Vice President Marshall received the salute. A few blocks past, then Pershing and his officers joined the reviewers and watched in glee as the men showed the prowess of training.

He was to have a day reserved for few mortals, a day when all the assembled members of the Congress of the United States would listen to him talk of the AEF and of what America had done in the Great War. There were to be friends in the gallery, newsmen in the corridors, lights and movies and microphones as a conqueror, American style, reported to the representatives of his countrymen. It was Thursday, September 18, 1919; Pershing rose uncommonly excited, nervously worked on his speech—already rewritten often—greeted brother Jim Pershing who came from New York for the occasion, ate an early lunch with close associates, then went to the House entrance of the Capitol. Met by Senator Wadsworth, Julius Kahn, whom he had seen in France, Champ Clark, Missouri Senator Spence, Fiorello LaGuardia of New York, and others, who served as an escort, Pershing found himself ushered to an anteroom, and on the stroke of two he went into the

[4] JJP, Diary, Sept. 10–14, 1919, Boxes 4–5, PP.
[5] See JJP to Charles G. Dawes, Sept. 12, 1919, Box 59, PP.
[6] See statement to the press in JJP, Diary, Sept. 16, 1919, Boxes 4–5, PP.
[7] See JJP, Diary, Sept. 17, Boxes 4–5, PP, referring to seats for Mrs. Boyd and her daughter, Anne.

House. Galleries were banked full of people, the circling seats filled with members of both houses. For an old Missouri farm boy this was the truly tall cotton. Charlie would have agreed that it sure "beat Hell!" Impressed, Pershing looked around the imposing room, the waiting crowd, and deep down inside felt "that I have [n]ever received a greater honor." The president pro-tem of the Senate made some complimentary opening remarks, Gillette of the House followed with "delightful" words, and then Champ Clark, the famed ex-Speaker, strode forward and read a Joint Resolution "Tendering the thanks of the American people and the Congress of the United States to General John J. Pershing, and to the officers and men of the American Expeditionary Forces." Not surprised—he had heard there would be a resolution—Pershing was suddenly struck by the personal citation, followed by the general inclusion of the AEF—it was all for him, the resolution, the Joint Session, the people, honored him as well as his men. Despite everyone hanging on his words, he could speak easily of the men who had done the deeds that brought him here, of the country they all loved. He did not speak long, his flat voice rose rarely in emphasis, but his praise and love for the "boys" needed no artificial periods. The general talked like a general and a concerned fellow American, a man who loved his country and his army. His account was of stewardship, of trust discharged, of opportunity appreciated. He thanked the American people for their steadfastness and the Allies for their aid. His words were in Grant's and Lee's tradition—they would have understood.[8]

His moment passed and so some of the hectic fame; he could, at last, get to the AEF's business. Housekeeping details were settled with Quek, George Marshall, and Mrs. Warren helping him find a rented home in Chevy Chase, and with full staffs and furniture at work in headquarters. Baker proved amenable about HQAEF still issuing orders concerning its own tiny contingent—on everything save courts martial. Hasty orders issued from the chief of staff transferring officers and demoting generals Pershing discussed with Baker; the orders were modified to allow Pershing's office to work unimpaired. March had simply been too quick in his duty.[9]

[8] See *ibid.*, Sept. 28, 1919; the text of the Joint Resolution can be found in FEW Papers, vol. 86, as well as in *U.S. Statutes at Large*, 41, pt. 1:291. The text of JJP's address to Congress can be found in *Congressional Record*, 66th Cong., 1 sess., p. 5562.

[9] Baker to JJP, Sept. 17, 1919, AEF, GHQ, Office of the CIC, Correspondence, File 21968, RG 120, National Archives. See also Chief of Staff, AEF (Fox Conner) to JJP, Sept. 13, 1919, *ibid.*; JJP, Diary, Sept. 15, 1919, Boxes 4–5, PP.

About supper time on September 20, Pershing, in mufti, slipped out of the Shoreham's servants' entrance, took a Ford taxi to the station, and caught the Federal Express for Boston. His companions were fewer than usual; Quek had headed for Mississippi and a long-delayed visit with his mother—Pershing felt close to the families of all his official family—and George Marshall asked for a few days' delay in Washington with his wife.[10] Two aides and two sergeants completed the party. Governor Forbes brought two cars and whisked his guests to New Bedford, put them aboard his yacht, *Mangosteen,* and sailed to Naushon Island, near Woods Hole. Pershing had decided on a month's rest and the island looked like a marvelous place to begin—isolated, beautiful, with beaches, inlets, docks, boats, obviously lots of fishing, bracing air. And Forbes was his old kind self.

Days passed in delicious idleness, in long morning sleeps, lazy lunches, fishing excursions, hikes, and playing. Guests—young and not so young, boys, girls, men and lovely ladies—ebbed and flowed through the governor's hospitality. Handsome and well-knit, in fine shape still, Pershing attracted women always; he did on the island. He threw himself heartily into "Highseas," a kind of horseback "tag" game in which "pirates" try to capture "cruisers." Jack, a "pirate," spent most of his time captured by distaff "cruisers," "since all these seemed to single me out for capture."[11] Evenings were filled with "all sorts of foolish games."

There were moments of conscience, when Jack would try to attack the bales of correspondence that filtered to him through his office, but the efforts were halfhearted. He played polo, hiked with girls, danced, fished—and rested. On October 6 he packed his gear, and with Forbes went to the mainland; together they climbed into a handsome Cadillac—a gift to Jack from the manufacturer. George Marshall (who had joined the party a few days earlier) and Pershing took Forbes as far as Middleboro, then drove to a night's stop at a Berkshires hotel. Pershing hated leaving Naushon Island; the governor's house, his easy hospitality, reminded so much of the Philippines. On the seventh Jack's route led through the Mohawk Valley to Utica, for a rendezvous with Fox Conner. Fighting off reporters, Pershing's party took a train for Brandreth and the Conner lake camp.

At this rustic place of many cabins, Pershing began another bout of resting. Rusty in his shooting, he rapidly improved and began to bag deer in impressive style. Conner's sister-in-law, Paulina Brandreth,

[10] JJP, Diary, Sept. 19, 1919, Boxes 4–5, PP.
[11] *Ibid.*, Sept. 21–27, 1919.

not according to Virginia Conner

fortyish, self-possessed, became a frequent companion on the hunting treks, as was her fetching friend Elsie Robinson. At the lake Pershing and Marshall worked on the AEF final report and on correspondence, but kept at least half of every day for fun. Marshall and Fox Conner finally focused Pershing's attention on army reorganization problems mentioned by Baker before vacation began.[12]

Vacation ended on the twenty-fifth—Quek never saw the general look better—with Pershing going to New York for a visit with Jim and his family, with the Martin Egans, and to join a soiree on Long Island for his friend, the queen of Belgium. Back in the Washington office on October 27, Pershing plunged into reorganization matters. March and Baker had planned a small, highly professional army run by the chief of staff and regulars. Pershing, caught uncomfortably in the middle of a struggle between a parsimonious Congress and a determined Baker, could not support a 500,000-man regular army as proposed by March. The Baker-March bill, as it was called, whipped up much debate and anger. Congress had co-opted John McAuley Palmer, who had helped draft the Baker-March proposal, to write a congressional version. Testimony was piling up on both sides of the issue; Pershing was asked by Senator James Wadsworth of New York, Chairman of Papa Warren's old Military Affairs Committee, and by Representative Julius Kahn's opposite committee in the House, to give his views. Consulting twenty key officers throughout the top army structure, Pershing prepared his views, always with Marshall and Conner at hand.

The testimony began on October 31 in an atmosphere unlike any Pershing had known for years. Deferential, the Joint Committee members were nonetheless technically Pershing's superiors—at least partly —and he felt some unease in their presence. Most of them he knew, at least through Papa Warren, and they were friendly. But Washington was not Chaumont, the House Office Building hardly GHQ. For three days he gave his ideas; he was against the 500,000-man concept, found it too expensive, essentially unnecessary, and likely to be unpopular with the people. No more than 300,000 men were needed, they to instruct the National Guard and reserves. Essentially Pershing confirmed congressional prejudice and so made a good witness—but he was not as effective as he might have been.

Caught sometimes in uncertainty, apparently waiting for opinions to show, he backed and filled and was not always the crisp man of decision whose legend awed the committees. But they were impressed,

[12] George Quekemeyer to his mother, Oct. 24, 1919, Quekemeyer Papers.

even with his controversial support of universal military training, his support for a flexible single promotion list (March advocated a complicated multi-list system based on branches of service which would create a crazy-quilt of inequality). Pershing explained his views to Baker as well as to Congress and thought he scored with both. He did. He scored, especially, with his steadfast views on democratic forces, on an army of the people, serving the nation. Eleven months' compulsory training he thought sound not only from the military view, but also from the view of citizenship. Things in the country bothered him—the rising Bolshevism touted daily in the press, the rampant crime in cities, the strange decay in morality that seemed to be softening the national backbone. Spoken like a true soldier, and tuned to the rising Red Scare, Pershing's views were unoriginal—but vigorously defended.

He had another avenue of attack on a large army: cost. His business friends, men like Cameron Forbes, Charlie Dawes, and Martin Egan of J. P. Morgan's interests, conveyed the growing mood of the banker class. He, too, held conservative financial views, thought that sound money came from balanced budgets, had practiced that kind of fiscal responsibility in the AEF. A smaller army, geared to rapid expansion through a pool of trained men, would do the best job for America. A large standing army had not helped Germany—but then, most men in Congress were not experts on Schlieffen's and Moltke's expansible-army ideas. Economy would be the loudest voice in the army debate.[13]

But Pershing's voice rang the last knell of doom on the Baker-March reorganization. Pershing and Palmer pushed their own conception of a modern weapon for national defense, and Baker accepted gracefully the end of an idea. The two remained cordial friends, and Baker kept a concerned eye on Pershing's job. What did he want to do in his role as General of the Armies?[14] First he wanted to finish his AEF report. He had been working on it, with able assistants, for months. Records of the AEF were combed, statistics checked, maps redrawn, SOS charts digested and cross-checked, the whole General Organization Project outlined in reusable detail. The report, though a

[13] For an admirable summary of the controversy and for Pershing's views, see Forrest C. Pogue, *George C. Marshall: Education of a General, 1880–1939*, pp. 206–10. See also March, *Nation at War*, pp. 330–43; U.S., Senate, Military Affairs Committee, *Reorganization of the Army. Hearings Before the Committee on Military Affairs, United States Senate, 66th Congress, 2 Session, on S. 3792 To Reorganize and Increase the Efficiency of the United States Army, and for other Purposes*, pp. 1571–1704.

[14] JJP, Diary, Nov. 22, 1919, Boxes 4–5, PP.

product of many contributors, Pershing wrote himself in that spare, unaffected prose that seemed to hide so much of the author. It was, after all, the record, and that was the place for facts. "In the record" was a soldier's citation—what the AEF had done, what he had done as its commander-in-chief, needed no more elaboration than straight history. Daily stints on the report continued through October and November.

People kept calling, asking Pershing's blessing or approval for all kinds of projects—songs, books, monuments, personal advancement—most of which he avoided as deftly or as bluntly as possible. He played, too, attending parties, dinners, receptions—the Belgian royal family stayed some time, and the Prince of Wales made a state visit that took more of Pershing's attention than expected. Elsie Robinson, she of Brandreth Lake, accepted his invitation to lunch; he saw Elizabeth Hoyt in New York.[15] Several times he slipped from staff supervision to lunch with "a friend." Evenings were often occupied with plays or parties—at which Pershing proved indefatigable. He watched a "better" Navy team beat Army 6–0 on November 29 in one of the "cleanest" games he ever saw.

At last he sent a draft of the report to Baker, who liked it and cleared it to the Government Printing Office.[16]

Now he would take up Baker's next assignment—a great swing around army installations, a national trip of inspection. It would be useful, indeed, to his knowledge of the home forces; it would help in his reorganization ideas, but it would also be a grand tour of triumph —if invitations were any guide to popularity. He picked a staff carefully, including Marshall, Quek, Pete Bowditch, Fox Conner as chief of staff, Generals Moseley and Nolan of HAEF, four field clerks, a railroad representative, and five orderlies. He arranged to split up inspection duties so that each station could be covered speedily.

Beginning in mid-afternoon of December 4, the trip covered, literally, the entire country. Stopping sometimes only minutes, sometimes several days—depending on the size of the installation, the size of the town, the local arrangements—Pershing's expedition sped first south into Georgia and Alabama, then up through Tennessee into Ohio, thence to Chicago. Here an inspection of Leonard Wood's Headquarters of the Central Department included a huge parade and two large receptions in the evening, during which Wood and Pershing spoke, as

15 *Ibid.*, Nov. 7, 20, 1919.
16 The report was published under date of 1920 as *Final Report of Gen. John J. Pershing, Commander-in-Chief, American Expeditionary Forces.*

did Charlie Dawes, who recalled thrillingly the days in France, and people cheered.

Clearly one drawback above others marred this kind of trip—Pershing shook hands all day! He reckoned he had shaken over 50,000 hands by Chicago; before the trip ended, if his own good right survived, he might well have shaken a million hands! But people liked it; they seemed to like the smile they got with the handshake, and making friends ranked high in his job.

Most of the time the trip ran smoothly; a private Pullman carried Pershing, the staff, and their gear easily; it was shunted to sidings for longer waits, picked up by scheduled trains, and moved to the next objective. Sometimes Pershing's penchant for getting out, especially at places where he was supposed to wave demurely from the car, slowed the scheduled trains more than the companies appreciated. But there were so many diverting distractions; the American Legion folks always clustered, usually with children bearing gifts or flags or posters, and if little girls came, Pershing was lost. He always devoted himself to their little speeches, paid special courtesy to them all. People saw the glistening tears as he talked to the children and loved him for it.[17]

For Jack the happiest days were in Laclede, Missouri, and Lincoln. Laclede, scheduled out of Chicago and Saint Louis, was to be a day's visit, but the train rumbled in late in the morning. As the Pullman "New York" slowed, Pershing walked along the corridor looking at the familiar faces crowding the platform. Scenes from the past, people not forgotten, clouded his eyes. By now Warren and May, up from Lincoln where they had gone for the school year, and Frank Pershing had joined the trip. They went with Jack into the crush of humanity.

Reporters marveled at his recall—here the staff could not prompt him, for they were strangers. Pershing pushed into the crowd, trying to herd Warren with him, and grabbed hands, embraced friends— a band played, raucously, "When Johnny Comes Marching Home"— and he virtually vanished amid admirers. "Toad Welch," he yelled, pressed through people to a surprised woman, threw his arms around her, kissed her on the mouth, "and gave her a hug," said an awed *Kansas City Star* man, "such as younger men would envy." "Whom did you marry and where do you live?" he asked. She was, she said, Mrs. Bosworth and lived in Kansas City; he was pleased, she thrilled.

[17] See Quekemeyer to his mother, Feb. 9, 1920, Quekemeyer Papers. See also JJP, Diary, for the months of Dec. 1919, Jan. and Feb. 1920, Boxes 4–5, PP, for details of the trip.

An elderly Negro crawled under the car and stood straight in front of Jack: "Hello, Al," the general said to Allen Warfield, a bus driver for a local hotel. Beaming, trying to get Warren to share a picture, Pershing found him crouched behind him. "Come on up here, Warren, I want your picture by my side here in my home town. It is a picture I'm going to prize." A roiling mob eddied out to the Pershing home, and as Jack climbed the steps people called for a speech. A raised hand, quick silence, then a moment's thought, and he said, "I'm mighty glad to be welcomed home by you, my friends."[18]

He was getting weary from the constant rolling wheels, the endless swaying of the train, the faces, the hands, the inspections running into one long blur. He sent the staff home for Christmas and, when the train reached Lincoln, felt he, too, was home. To the house where May and Warren lived he went, met Bessie there, too, and relaxed. Christmas morning with Warren touched old memories; as the boy laughed and ripped into presents, the father watched with a saddened smile. Home had heartaches never eased.[19]

Lincoln had lots of good memories, and the days filled with nostalgia. Jack called on the chancellor of the university—the way to the office seemed vastly different now—who, with the faculty, presented a resolution of thanks from the old school; receptions, handshakings, dances, all showed that life in Nebraska had lost none of its zest.

On January 3, 1920, the tour resumed. Pershing and the staff, refreshed, anticipated the old routine—Rock Island Arsenal, Illinois, came first, then Iowa, back through Nebraska, Kansas, to a major stop at Fort Leavenworth. Devoted utterly to the value of staff training, Pershing spoke to the faculty and students, many of them AEF veterans, on the contributions made by people at HAEF who had Leavenworth schooling. They had made the war work; their training, their ideas, formed a common bond of language and systems that would succeed in any American staff organization at any time. What was learned at Leavenworth would knit the army into its fullest strength.[20] Entertainments at Leavenworth were warm and nostalgic; Hugh Drum, now a major, gave a dinner, and his humble station reminded everyone of rank's mortality.

Fort Riley touched old cavalry chords in the hearts of both Pershing and Quek, and the post seemed, somehow, modern even in the age of

---

[18] Editors of the *Army Times*, *The Yanks Are Coming*, pp. 151–53; JJP, Diary, Dec. 23, 1919, Boxes 4–5, PP.

[19] JJP, Diary, Dec. 25, 1919, Boxes 4–5, PP.

[20] *Ibid.*, Jan. 9, 1920.

the machine gun. Finally out on the West Coast, Pershing caught the fresh breezes of the Pacific and made a three-day rest stop in Seattle. Then down to California the travelers went, east to Phoenix and Tucson, Arizona, where Jack received an honorary LL.D. degree from the state university.

At El Paso proceedings at Fort Bliss brought floods of recollection, and Texas hospitality again impressed Pershing. At one of the functions, an informal supper, he noted: "There were a number of ladies present and I enjoyed the occasion very much indeed."[21]

In San Antonio, Gen. Joseph Dickman, commanding the Southern Department, greeted his mentor; Harbord, commanding Fort Sam Houston, beamed a welcome, and many retired army friends gave a special greeting. Inspections, receptions, speeches, handshakings, air shows, and greetings from Chinese refugees saved from Mexico in 1917 (a few had greeted him in Leavenworth) telescoped time until departure for Houston on February 4. Texas Governor William Hobby, Mayor A. E. Amerman, and Comdr. Lindsey Blayney of the American Legion met the train at Houston, and rushed the general into a schedule. Harry Pollard, a former Pershing chauffeur in France, drove the official Locomobile.

Inspection of Ellington Field led to a Rotary luncheon at the Rice Hotel and a reception where more hands were shaken. In the afternoon the hosts whisked Pershing out Main Street to Rice Institute "where I met Dr. E. O. Lovett, president . . . a Princeton man and warm personal friend of President Wilson's." A few remarks, a tree planted, a gaze at the "new institution . . . located in a beautiful section on the outskirts of the city," left scant time for a reception at the Municipal Auditorium. Handshakes again, this time even with Civil War veterans, then a round of receptions and a Shriner's Ball finished a hectic day.[22]

Always impressed by their chieftain, the staff now held him in awed affection. He never flagged. On a trip to break younger hearts, he hurtled through each day with warmth and human kindness as well as a soldier's keen eye for detail. His inspections, larded though they were with socializing, remained models of precision. Although he never talked of presidential ambitions, the staff cherished them for him. Hundreds of thousands of people had shaken hands with him; towns were named for him—babies, schools; on this trip he filled more column inches of newsprint than almost anyone else; the exposure had

[21] *Ibid.*, Feb. 1, 1920.
[22] *Ibid.*, Feb. 5, 1919. See photographs of JJP's visit to Rice Institute in the Rice University Archives, Houston, Tex.

been good everywhere. "General Pershing is receiving a most cordial reception everywhere we go and more and more people are talking about him for President," Quek reported to his mother in January, 1920. "I wonder what the outcome of it all will be?" So did Pershing.

A final swing took the inspectors up through Oklahoma, Arkansas, Tennessee again, down to New Orleans for Mardi Gras. Celebrations in New Orleans were fabulous, but Pershing's round of duties took him to Jackson Barracks, to Tulane University, and to Sophie Newcomb College for young ladies—where he mixed happily and shook hands warmly with pretty southern belles. Antoine's restaurant also impressed him. The great Rex parade seemed happily unmilitary and the evening balls gay and abandoned. Pershing enjoyed them and turned his staff loose in New Orleans for such entertainment as they wanted.

A run up through the Carolinas into Virginia—where the general spoke to a Joint Session of the Assembly in Richmond—brought Pershing's party to Boston on February 25. This was Yankee Division country, and Clarence Edwards himself greeted Pershing at Headquarters of the Northeastern Department. Governor Calvin Coolidge shared honors of greeting the general and brought several committeemen, including Cameron Forbes. The New England swing, including more speeches, handshakings, and weeks proclaimed in his honor, ended for Pershing early on the morning of March 1, 1920. The General of the Armies knew more about the army than anyone else. George Marshall and Malin Craig, who joined in January, shared most of that knowledge. Pershing confirmed his convictions for universal military training and formed close estimates of the potential leadership of regular and emergency forces.

What would he do with the knowledge? The trip had, in a sense, been an adroit maneuver by Baker to keep Pershing and March apart. The chief of staff would hold office until July, 1920. Would Jack follow March? The chief of staff's job would crown Pershing's career. Some argued that his new rank put him above the chief of staff, made that office minor. But Pershing wanted it, "was keen to have it." There he could put his own views of a democratic army in practice—at least some of them. A lot depended on the rest of the year. If a presidential boom for him burgeoned during the summer, his plans might alter permanently. If he did not seek the presidency, would the new president want him as chief of staff?

Lofty symbols tend toward ennui. Pershing began to wonder again about the army. He had done just about everything, and if the chief of staff's spot could not be certain, what about leaving the service? If he did that he would have a variety of opportunities. Dawes, ever quick with usually sound advice, cautioned against hasty wreckage of a reputation. Much in terms of an earlier session in Lincoln when Jack pondered quitting the field for the law, Dawes bade him wait. Political winds shifted whimsically; no one could tell what the parties would do, but a groundswell of Pershing sentiment Dawes could not see. Another Lincoln friend, Mark Woods of the Cadet Corps, now a wealthy man and full of hope for his old chieftain, urged the general's candidacy. Pershing held aloof but did not say no, so Woods schemed to get the great name on the Nebraska primary ballot. As things worked out there would be three names—Pershing's, Leonard Wood's, and Senator Hiram Johnson's. News of these activities stirred that restless ambition; conqueror of one profession, why not try another?

That the White House bug had bitten Pershing, George Marshall knew and deplored. He had tried to fend petitioners for Pershing's approval and irked his boss. Pershing came back from the great trip infected with public enthusiasm—so many thousands had shaken his hand, spoken warmly, and would surely back their friendliness with votes! But the route ahead lay filled with rubble. Papa Warren cautioned propriety in America's leading figure. It would hardly do for Pershing, a creature of a Democratic administration, to repay glory with ingratitude. The objective must be sought indirectly. Deny so often as to rouse suspicion. These tactics were doubtless the political way, but they ran against Pershing's grain. If a man wanted something he said so and went out for it. Coyness was all right in some people; it ill fitted a man.

On April 14, 1920, at a Washington meeting of the Nebraska Society, he heard himself suggested as a possible candidate. It was unexpected and blatant, and if there were ever a chance to squelch political rumors, the moment had come. Eagerly the audience listened, were depressed as Pershing started: "Speaking of the great office with which you have been kind enough to connect my name, it seems fitting that I should say to you, my friends, that my whole life has been devoted to the service of our country. . . . " He paused, and people could write the soldier's conclusion, but he went on. "And while in no sense seeking it, I feel that no patriotic American could decline to serve in that high position if called upon to do so by the people." Screams of delight, cheering, seemed echoes of the future.[23]

Meetings continued, speeches multiplied; veterans organizations

[23] JJP, Diary, Apr. 14, 1920, Boxes 4–5, PP.

and benevolent societies called for Pershing; patriotic groups eagerly sought a man who spoke so forcefully on Americanism. Universities of prestige, Harvard, Yale, Columbia, and others, offered honorary degrees. Each such public moment brought fresh tumult and touting— and they were altogether far more exciting than humdrum work on the army reorganization bill or the report of the U.S. First Army, which Hugh Drum wrote with Pershing's advice. The streams of visitors to GHQ, official and private, emphasized the essentially ceremonial duties of the General of the Armies. Even the Board for Appointment of Officers, which would finally produce a slate for rationalizing advancement, seemed dull and red-tapey by comparison to the "affairs" calling an active man.[24]

In a kind of personal doldrum Pershing struck at his circumstances. After talking with Baker—who understood him far better than anyone guessed—Pershing wrote the secretary a letter, released for publication, a letter which showed more frustration than foresight, more pique than prudence. His duties were too light, Pershing said; obviously he could be spared, and "under the circumstances, I feel that, after the completion of the work contemplated by the Army Reorganization Act, I could relinquish military duty without detriment to the service and thus be free to engage in something more active. Therefore, unless a situation should develop to justify my remaining, I shall plan to take the step indicated within the next few months." He was, as ever, at the country's call in any emergency. Pershing noted, in odd surprise, that newsmen "were attempting to put some political significance to this letter." It had political significance, but Pershing could not bring himself to admit the pull of the hustings—it would be too public a thing for a private man.

Baker, who assessed shrewdly Pershing's ambivalence about politics, replied cordially that he was sure the president would agree to a course, when expressed, but made no fuss about the letter and let it float on Pershing's dreams. A good friend, he took no offense at the implied blackmail for a better job, nor did he resent the amateur's hedging of bets. Pershing deserved free run of his ambitions; whatever he did, he did well.[25]

What he was doing was hoping—hoping, somehow, that the Repub-

[24] *Ibid.*, Apr.–July, 1920, for myriad meetings and speeches and adulatory convocations.

[25] The letter is in *ibid.*, June 7, 1920. In an interview with Senator Warren in January, 1919, Baker had said, philosophically, that Pershing "had as good a right as anybody else to run for President. . . ." FEW to JJP, Jan. 21, 1919, FEW Papers, vol. 85.

lican convention in Chicago during the second week of June would look toward Washington. Nebraska's primary had been scant comfort —in the three-way race there, Pershing had lost out to Hiram Johnson —but he had achieved something by knocking Leonard Wood's richly supported candidacy onto a siding. That consolation had important personal impact: if Wood secured the nomination he would likely win —the Republicans were licking their chops over the moribund administration of a stricken Woodrow Wilson who left affairs of state to his wife—and if Wood won, John J. Pershing must resign from the army. Others might deny it; Pershing knew he would have to go, so he would accept anyone else as the standard-bearer.[26] Public announcement of near resignation might tip the balance.

Wood and Governor Frank Lowden of Illinois fame fought through the convention's early ballots—and Lowden's candidacy had put Dawes on the spot. He liked the governor, thought him an admirable man, and supported him wholly. But Lowden committed a kind of Republican apostasy in supporting Wilson's peace treaty, and Wood was outgaining him in the tallies. Still, Lowden picked up support from many of the favorite-son men and had a chance to win if the balloting continued. There was a recess, and after behind-the-scenes maneuvering, handsome Senator Warren G. Harding got the nod. Pershing, who had pensively stayed at his house, "Highwood" on Rittenhouse Street, hoping for a call to service, heard the news in sadness and some relief —his course had been cleared, he would stay in the army along with Leonard Wood. To Charlie in Chicago, Jack sent a crony's message: "Could anything be better? The victory is ours. I die content."[27] Pershing had some Democratic nibbles—a Pershing–Al Smith ticket was mentioned but gained no strength.[28]

He was neither dead nor content. But Baker kept him busy. In addition to the promotion board, which would require a detailed report of its deliberations, Pershing made a springtime quasi-diplomatic trip to Panama, where he inspected military installations and tried to repair a crumbling American image. Happily he took Warren along, helped him with navigation, tried to teach him rudimentary mathematics, read to him, fished and played as much as possible—they almost got reacquainted. On the way home Pershing stopped at Saint Thomas and Puerto Rico, and there he and Warren shared the excitement of a

---

[26] Bascom N. Timmons, *Portrait of an American: Charles G. Dawes*, pp. 192–93.

[27] *Ibid.*, p. 193.

[28] Pogue, *Marshall*, p. 215.

grounded ship. Afloat again fairly quickly, the excitement lasted for Warren, to dad's amusement.[29]

Washington in the last somber months of Wilson's era drifted in uncertainties and unfinished business. Baker, whom Pershing regarded as the best war secretary he had ever known, would soon be gone. The good things he had accomplished might not survive him. March, too, would be gone, and the evil he had tried to do might not survive him, either.

The National Defense Act of 1920, allegedly an amendment to the defense charter of 1916, went into effect on June 4 and created a new and different army. With John Palmer's views written in, the bill suited Pershing: 297,800 officers and men in the regular forces sounded just right. Especially did Pershing like the configuration of a small regular force designed to cooperate with and train National Guard and reserve divisions. Although March disapproved, he issued the orders necessary to replace geographical commands with nine corps areas, each with an organic regular division, a shadow reserve, and two National Guard divisions. Auxiliary units would be state provided. The areas and divisions would be grouped into three armies. Old provisions from the 1916 act allowed federalizing the guard when necessary. Despite March's fears, the General Staff would be stronger, although its personnel less. A War Council would give overall consideration to military policies—a gesture toward congressional fears of a German-type General Staff.

Suspicions and public opposition to universal training forced a sad compromise, one that Palmer and Pershing recognized as dubious but essential to reorganization—universal military training, even cut to four months, had to be dropped in favor of volunteers. This left the army training centers in doubtful circumstances. If trained citizen units were not maintained, the success of the new system seemed dim. But at least there was an organization.[30]

Baker's time faded in a flurry of parties and farewells to which Pershing went with growing sadness. Who would replace him?

Much depended on Harding's grasp of men. Speculations wafted Washington's salons as usual in a change of regime. Would Pershing be war secretary? The senator seemed amiable and determined to regard ability, but he had solid obligations that he would not dishonor. And the War portfolio lacked the importance of recent years. The vital problems of America were now economic, social; the country,

[29] JJP, Diary, Apr. 25–May 20, 1920, Boxes 4–5, PP.
[30] For the new law and its implications, see Pogue, *Marshall*, pp. 213–14.

wracked by unrest and protest, tried to return to "normalcy" and to forget the waste of war. Harding picked Bostonian John W. Weeks, graduate of the Naval Academy, former Massachusetts congressman and U.S. senator, now a successful broker, for the War job. The choice looked good. Rotund, bald, his size caricatured by a handle-bar moustache, Weeks's shrewd eyes belied his comic bulk. He would do nothing hasty, but would surely support the Pershing-Palmer military view.

Those last Democratic weeks Pershing passed in heavy social rounds; farewells were depressing this time, since so many of the men leaving had had so much to do with the AEF's success. But in those saddened days there were good moments, too, especially at frequent hops and dances. Pershing loved dancing, always found comely and willing partners, could usually be counted on to stay late if the band was good. He enjoyed good health and vigor, nursed his hair by frequent treatments at the Frances Fox Institute, and kept his weight steady. Several ladies caught his special notice—Ramona Lefevre (he met her on the Panama trip), Elizabeth Hoyt, and others whom he tantalizingly identified as "friends."[31]

Home life ran smoothly, though a rent rise forced him to more modest quarters on Connecticut Avenue.[32] Warren, in May's good care, did well in school and grew apace; James, with his family in Rosslyn, New York, did as well as usual. From a personal standpoint, Jack was as ready for a new administration as he was likely to get, as ready for any assignment. Baker had kindly never mentioned the resignation, nor had anyone else, seriously, so his career lay open to orders.

Harding he knew from casual acquaintance; their association had been cordial during the campaign, and he anticipated no trouble from the president. The secretary of war came unknown.

Pershing participated in the inaugural activities and took occasion to greet a shockingly enfeebled Woodrow Wilson, who was helped to the Capitol where he signed some last minute legislation with a shaking, untypical scrawl. Then the new team took the reins. Pershing knew the vice president, Calvin Coolidge, from earlier ceremonies in Boston. Secretary Weeks saw Jack early and talked favorably of the new legislation, listened to his ideas, backed by the War Department and the General Staff, of a mobile field headquarters for an active army. So much did he like the idea that he announced in April a

31 JJP, Diary, Apr. 1920–Mar., 1921, Boxes 4–5, PP.
32 The address was 2029 Connecticut Avenue (see *ibid.*, Feb. 24, 1921).

special assignment for the General of the Armies; he would supervise a special staff considering contingency war plans.

A version of something Fox Conner had once proposed, Weeks's scheme brought military outcry—the way he described the idea, Pershing's duties would overlap the chief of staff's and cause horrendous confusion. When Pershing told Harbord of the plan, that loyal soldier expostulated at the legal and personal snarls inevitable in the arrangement. Apparently surprised over the complaints, Pershing studied the idea more carefully. Finally he protested to the secretary that the scheme was unworkable. Harding apparently became embroiled in the argument and soon realized the coadjutor status could produce chaos. Weeks, no dummy, realized too the snarls inherent in dual command.[33] On May 13, 1921, he announced that Pershing would wear two hats—as commanding general of a battle staff and also as chief of staff. So the job had come at last. The last pinnacle in Pershing's view, the chance he coveted was his. There were intricacies in the new scheme almost beyond even Fox Conner's solution, but time and determination would unravel the puzzle. What Weeks proposed and Pershing sanctioned created two sets of offices for the General of the Armies, who would be responsible for the organization and training of the army and also for fighting it in war. Harbord got orders to come to Washington as executive assistant to Pershing. There would be an attempt to run the army on a businesslike basis.

Some could see traces of the old commanding general scheme in all this, a return to the anomalies of Nelson Miles's position during the Spanish-American War, a serious undercutting of the General Staff as conceived by Elihu Root and advanced by Newton Baker. But Weeks and Pershing understood each other, could work together— and Harbord could work with both of them. People could make any system go—usually.[34]

Harbord set the proper tone for change. "I think," he said with typical candor, "that there should be something done at once to mark the fact that a new power has taken over—some visible sign—and I suggest the restoration of the shoulder belt associated with all our victories. . . ." He resented the delay in changing chiefs of staff, thought it left too much to March, and wanted Pershing to get going. Pershing had his own plans. A thorough reorganization of the office seemed in order, a kind of sweeping of the chaff, but he did not want to appear

[33] See Pogue, *Marshall*, pp. 217–18.
[34] See Edward M. Coffman, *March*, pp. 227–28; Pogue, *Marshall*, pp. 218–19; Vandiver, *Illustrious Americans: John J. Pershing*, p. 223.

ruthless beyond necessity. Many of March's deeds were sound, many of his friends powerful, and the administration could ill afford an intra-army civil war. Suffice it for the moment that on July 1, 1921, the AEF's time had come!

Chaumont seemed re-created in the State, War, and Navy Building. Pershing set up the old five staff divisions and put trusted aides in chief positions. Quickly he learned that running the office of the chief of staff lacked the urgency of Chaumont. There was not nearly enough to do; routine dragged its course, mired in the sludge of regulations and army precedent. With the reorganization going almost as well as Pershing had hoped, challenge lapsed for the General of the Armies. And he reacted as old friends expected—he delegated. Close by were Harbord and Marshall. Most papers normally routed to the chief of staff went to Harbord, who shuffled through them with an eager eye to change, to clearing the fustiness of an office he thought the army distrusted.[35]

Marshall, equally close to "the chief," found himself increasingly deluged with draft letters, reports, memoranda. Knowing the keen intelligence of Marshall, his thoroughly professional view, Pershing seldom acted without the younger man's opinion. Marshall could be counted on for the discretion that Harbord surmounted. Pershing himself found his routine hardly disturbed. Ceremonial duties still took much time, not all of it happy. On July 10, in Hoboken, he stood mute and sad while the bodies of 7,160 American soldiers were unloaded on their home soil. There were religious services, then Senator Lodge spoke; finally Pershing, moved as always by the bravery of those "boys," spoke briefly, feelingly.[36]

There were more visits to the secretary's office than before, more discussions of vexing budget matters, more concern for political nuances. But this kind of high-level manipulation fascinated an old conniver. Preparation of actual estimates Pershing left to others; he would present the results and defend the army appropriations. And that likely would be his main function—defending the army.

Despite the general approval of the new reorganization, Congress sulked in an economy mood. Fiscal responsibility seemed to fix more firmly on the army, though, than on other branches of the government. Pershing urged retention of the numbers agreed, but congressional leaders hacked away in the surety that the country would

---

[35] Coffman, *March*, p. 229; James G. Harbord to JJP, May 24, 1921, Box 58, PP.

[36] JJP, Diary, July 10, 1921, Boxes 4–5, PP.

not need more than 150,000 men. Harding and Weeks opposed the cut, Pershing vehemently argued for at least the minimum written in the law, but reduction had to be achieved by October. Pershing sought Warren's help, thought a Republican Congress ought to follow a party administration, but encountered that peculiar rigidity Congress shows when piously guarding the purse strings. As both sides dug in, Pershing realized that the role of General of the Armies, on the outside gazing in, had been far easier, happier. He now had the hot seat to himself.

True, he had growing friendship with his bosses. Harding he liked, the feeling was cordially reciprocated; they saw each other fairly often, officially and socially—Pershing gave the president a bottle of 112-year-old Scotch, which Harding announced would be kept for Pershing's visits to the White House.[37] And Weeks came to full trust and confidence. But Congress kept pushing, and clearly the fight would be uphill.

Beyond working toward the creation of an effective war-plans office, Pershing wanted to coordinate interservice activities and used his chairmanship of the Joint Army-Navy Board to foster good relations.[38] He had a four-step plan that, with luck, might result in a much improved defense position. First, various changes in procedure and field regulations must be instituted to raise the army's morale. Two years of uncertainty eroded pride and turned many good men toward civilian jobs. A corollary to higher morale would be the second objective: increased efficiency. There was, as he could tell during his countrywide inspection, considerable duplication and wastage in units everywhere—a lot of it encouraged by archaic practices defended without reason. Increased efficiency would enhance the next objective: economy. Economy, demonstrated, would ease congressional relations —and that stood the main hope of his tenure.[39]

These objectives would be hard to achieve without shifting people in and out of the office. Rumors reached Pershing of army dissatisfaction with general staff officers too long absent from troops, hence out of touch with reality. Poor officers were in key spots, with the militia getting the worst for trainers. Wasteful procedures in the staff departments, Pershing knew damaged morale.

An old hand at running military activities, Pershing realized that

[37] *Ibid.*, July 16, 1921.
[38] *Ibid.*, July 14, 1921.
[39] See James G. Harbord, "Confidential Memorandum for General Pershing," June 26, 1921, Box 88, PP.

economy could easily be enhanced by coherent centralization, by combining activities, perhaps even consolidating stations—horror of horrors! Reduction of staff and closer supervision of travel would cut the outgo of money.

To his new cohorts Pershing emphasized an obvious point about congressional relations. Too often people from the chief of staff's office had wandered before key committees, offered maundering, imprecise, fumbling testimony, were unable to answer questions, and seemed at best incapable. Long-standing furor over deceitful army practices had damaged the repute of military men; inconsiderate treatment of congressional requests at the War Department made matters worse. A little pampering might work wonders.

In dealing with the army itself, common courtesy toward field commanders would be enforced; where local preferences were reasonable in personnel and practice, they should be allowed. If all these things were done, the chief of staff's office might begin to regain lost prestige. At least people would know who to talk to for information and assistance. Harbord got the task of supervising administration, and he went at it with gusto.[40]

Pershing realized his regime entered at a time of rapid military change, not in America alone, but the world over. George Patton had long predicted the perfection of the tank and he was right. New machines, more maneuverable, speedier, better armed, were being built. How many could the army afford? Billy Mitchell shouted raucously the utter superiority of the airplane. March had underwritten aerial bombing experiments; and in July, 1921, Pershing, with other army and navy observers and congressional onlookers, watched Mitchell's planes sink the "unsinkable" *Ostfriesland,* late of the German fleet. All watchers were stunned; many realized both armies and navies were unsafe. The Joint Army-Navy Board took note of this shocking blow but reported, with that sanctimonious certitude Harbord so hated, that "the battleship is still the backbone of the fleet and the bulwark of the nation's sea defense."[41] What would Patton have said about the future of his tanks?

Pershing, not really an innovator, had used Mitchell's ideas effectively in France, had seen the uses of combined operations, but could not surmount the ossification of his colleagues; nor could he, honestly, recommend large expenditures for planes when infantry and artillery

40 *Ibid.*
41 Richard O'Connor, *BJP,* p. 357.

units were barely operational. But he did believe in military aviation and should have pushed harder for its cause.[42]

What were the real defense needs of the country? Pershing knew the answer before taking office. A well-regulated militia system, tied in with the guard and the regular army. That had been the heart of his arguments for the National Defense Act of 1920; that remained his message at every public and private opportunity to speak professionally. Using the force of his reputation, the power of his office, Pershing spoke widely on the abilities of the army to protect the country when closely tied to a citizen force. The tie was the key, and it would last only so long as equipment and manpower were well supported by the country. His constant reminders of the professional competence of the officer corps, of the importance of well-schooled officers, of the leadership provided by citizen officers who properly taught the basic staff and line procedures, pleased the army. Those speeches, faithfully recorded in the *Army and Navy Journal*, gradually rebuilt self-confidence in officers and men—and those speeches were likely Jack's most important contribution to saving the army in the early 1920s.[43]

Public documents could deal useful blows for defense. Pershing had learned the value of well-aimed reports back in Moro Province days; he used his reports as chief of staff, as well as his reports to congressional committees, to buttress his public utterances. In developing his points, he wrote articles for such magazines as offered space. He worried at inroads of disloyalty, of softness that threatened decay in democracy. Defense, democracy, and decay—these were often his themes. In the *Saturday Evening Post*, March 10, 1923, he wrote under the chief of staff's rubric that America had entered the World War in a state of dismal unpreparedness and reminded the country how lucky it was that the Allies held off the Germans and gave a year's grace to draft, train, and begin supplying millions of Doughboys.

All we can say is that through the years we, the people, and those who make our laws, have gone from bad to worse, learning little, doing less, still prejudiced, lulled into inaction by an unwarranted sense of security and by false ideas of economy, instead of using plain, practical common sense and making reasonable provision in time of peace for the maintenance of a moderate policy of national defense. . . . A group of pacifists, who, by carrying

[42] See JJP's testimony before the Senate Military Affairs Committee, *Reorganization of the Army Hearings*, pp. 1573, 1608–11, 1668, 1682–1702.

[43] For examples, see *Army and Navy Journal* 60 (Dec. 30, 1922): 419, in which a column is devoted to an appreciation of Pershing's speaking tours; *ibid.* 61 (Oct. 27, 1923): 194; *ibid.* 62 (Sept. 6, 1924): 1305.

placards and applying epithets, think they can end wars, proclaim in favor of our complete disarmament as a beginning to world peace, entirely ignoring the experience of the World War and the palpable fact that we should be in a class by ourselves and probably become at once the object of aggression by wiser nations. It is one of the inconsistencies of this group to be among the first to demand protection at home and intervention abroad.[44]

In his three-year administration of the army, Pershing came to know all too clearly the anguish of near success. The organization, the structure, the program, the schools, all existed to build a solid military foundation. If the army could be kept at a decent minimum, supported in its basic needs and experimentation, it need not grow large to be effective. But Congress dawdled. His words, comforting to the army, merely vexed a languid nation—why weren't those old AEF people quieter? Their time had passed.

Pershing cast aside some of his worries in September, 1921, and accepted happily the president's commission to go abroad and lay the Congressional Medal of Honor on the grave of the French Unknown Soldier. It would be a sentimental journey, a chance to see those old fields of glory, to see old comrades—perhaps a friend in Paris. Before he sailed on September 14, he tangled toughly with Samuel Gompers. At the Chevy Chase Club on Tuesday evening, September 6, the short, rotund president of the American Federation of Labor shared the Lafayette–Marne Day program with Pershing. Gompers, never bashful, spoke of labor's unstinting contribution to the war, of labor's ceaseless efforts in the war, of labor's winning of the war. The more he talked, the madder Pershing got, and when his turn came, he pitched in hard against praisers of the rear. Not one to detract from anyone's help for the cause, Pershing would not permit the slightest derogation of the AEF's "boys." "While I did not directly attack Mr. Gompers or his speech, in my address which followed I let it be distinctly understood that no particular organization or group of people could claim any especial credit for winning the war; that it was the American people as a whole who had brought about the result."[45]

Newsmen rushed to telephones, stories were quickly filed, and Pershing's "attack" on labor made headlines. He was not sorry—guessed that such friends as Charlie Dawes and President Harding would be secretly tickled that someone had faced the giant of labor in patriotic fray. It was probably just as well he was going abroad!

[44] JJP, "A Discussion of National Defense," *Saturday Evening Post*, March 10, 1923, pp. 3–4; see also Eds. of *Army Times, Yanks Are Coming*, pp. 155–57.
[45] JJP, Diary, Sept. 6, 1921, Boxes 4–5, PP.

He was gone until late October, and the trip had triumphs unexpected. A Medal of Honor was placed at the Arc de Triomphe; he visited battlefields and old acquaintances near the ghostly quiet front, looked at the cemeteries, stayed in Paris, and frequently dined "with friends"—one of them surely being Micheline Resco. He went to England, saw Earl and Lady Haig, the high government officials and, in an especially impressive ceremony, placed a Medal of Honor on the Unknown Soldier's tomb in Westminister Abbey. It was a rare privilege and he did it well.

There was time to recall, on the way home, that in Europe his army was held in high regard.

Routine galled on return. More and more details went to the staff, and Pershing took up again the inspection role. The army still ebbed in public esteem, in congressional largesse, but nothing daunted the message Pershing preached steadily—preparedness was the price of liberty. Preparedness must be based on a soundly schooled officer corps, trained in such places as Leavenworth's Command and General Staff School or the Army War College, places where professionalism mixed with learning to produce democracy's skilled soldiers.

In San Francisco in August, 1923, he called on Mrs. Harding at the Palace Hotel in concern at the president's condition. The president died on August 2, and Calvin Coolidge became president. Would he want Pershing to remain as chief of staff? How did he feel about the army? There had been changes in the department. Harbord, wooed by industry, decided to leave the army. Pershing coaxed John L. Hines, of AEF fame, to assume the role of deputy chief of staff, and the machinery seemed to work well. Perhaps, after all, the time had come to leave. If the president said nothing, what should a soldier do? Finally, in an anguished breach of protocol, Pershing called on the president. They shook hands, and Coolidge waited. Embarrassed, Pershing stumbled through his question—did the president want him to stay? Silence, then Coolidge cleared his throat, and said in that clipped New England voice: "General, I'm surprised you should ask that question." And that was the end of the interview. Pershing still had no clear answer! A friend interceded and got a direct response: "Of course."[46]

Coolidge did not dislike the army and did like Pershing. But he was no spendthrift. Appropriations languished and problems multiplied. The chief of staff continued his propaganda efforts, and he tried optimism as a brake on sagging morale. In a General Order of January

[46] Eds. of *Army Times, Yanks Are Coming,* pp. 158–59.

1923, he told his colleagues that things were better, that the worst was over. Conditions were improving, he said, reciting better living facilities, pay, a closer knit officer corps, and increasing interest on the public's part. Every army man hoped the general was right.[47]

That year Pershing got an additional assignment dear to his heart. After much fumbling with policies toward foreign cemeteries, Congress created the American Battle Monuments Commission to supervise proper interment and memorials for the Doughboys—and others. Pershing gladly accepted the chairmanship and began to spend increasing amounts of time in France. In the fall of 1923, for instance, he made a six-month tour of the burial sites and worked on architectural plans for monuments and small chapels. During those months George Marshall held the chief of staff's office together. Hines, less belligerent than Harbord, did splendid work, but Marshall knew the chief's mind, and everyone in the office accepted his decisions. While the general was gone, Marshall put the finishing touches on the chief of staff's report for 1923. It was a firm reaffirmation of defense needs, but extremely modest in requesting small additions to regulars, guard, and reserves— there should be 13,000 officers and 150,000 men. After explaining the cooperation needed between components, Marshall's document, over Pershing's name, said:

> We have made progress in the organization of the framework for a great citizen Army to maintain the honor and prestige of America in the event of a national emergency, but the total number of individuals under military supervision has decreased by 15,000 during the past three years. . . . I sincerely hope that it is the will of the American people that we should carry out a conservative and balanced program for the national defense in preparation for whatever emergency we may be destined to encounter.[48]

Marshall knew army structure and potential thoroughly—so did Pershing.

But Pershing's concerns were increasingly personal. During his sixty-third birthday celebration in Washington, before the French trip, he had basked in affection and remembrance, but he kidded friends and himself with the thought that in "just about one more year . . . I will become a wheedling, ossified, doddering, mendicant knocking at the doors of my friends here and there for a few kind words and crumbs. . . ."[49]

With any kind of luck the General of the Armies would not retire.

[47] See *Army and Navy Journal* 60 (Mar. 3, 1923): 1, 645.
[48] *Ibid.*, 61 (Dec. 8, 1923): 342.
[49] JJP to Harbord, Apr. 28, 1923, Box 88, PP.

There had been a good deal of speculation in the army about Pershing's fate on September 13, 1924. Would the government permit his services to end? Pershing wanted to stay in harness, but there were increasingly petty problems in the office. He found himself getting testy when he should have been generous. A silly argument with Douglas MacArthur about failing to call on the chief of staff during a Washington visit hardly was worthy of a soldier.[50] But the prolonged vacations did help, and simply being retired had scant attractions.

Secretary Weeks thought he should remain in a developmental role for the army, perhaps build up the guard and reserve units he had so strongly pushed. Weeks suggested that to both military committees of Congress, and there was considerable discussion.

Pershing felt embarrassed at the thought of a law exempting him from normal regulations, but he confessed to Weeks that "if such a provision should be made of course it will be very gratifying, and I shall be glad to continue on duty as long as my services are of value to the government."[51]

Months flew faster as September, 1924, approached. Congress hung fire on the continuation issue, and Pershing hesitated to press too hard. Enough cudgels were raised in his defense without calling all chargers to the fray—a man must be seemly in his going. Pershing at last announced, "As the clock strikes noon, Saturday, I retire; that's all there is to it." Newspapers cried that there was much more to it, that an ungrateful country was wasting a great talent, that he would be cut off on half pay, that it was all somehow shabby.[52]

It was a sad day, one to be borne, one to say things to old and new comrades that would tell the heart of a soldier, one to receive battalions of well-wishers and tokens of affection; it was one to think of the AEF, of the "boys," of Warren, and of Frankie and the girls—and of the fact that the General of the Armies remained always on duty.

Soldier Diplomat

That solemn march of farewell on John Pershing's birthday marked the end of an era. He was gone from stage center. For two-score years

---

[50] See JJP to MacArthur, Jan. 30, 1922, and MacArthur to JJP, Feb. 2, 1922, Box 120, PP.

[51] JJP to Weeks, Dec. 13, 1923, Box 207, PP; *Army and Navy Journal* 61 (Dec. 8, 1923): 342; *ibid.* (May 17, 1924): 912.

[52] See, for example, "Gratitude or Ingratitude Toward General Pershing," *Literary Digest*, Sept. 27, 1924, p. 15.

he had soldiered; his career shaped the army and sustained his nation. As he shook those friendly hands, looked in faces familiar from all parts of the service, he could remember the roll and its changes: his gray-clad cadet cronies; the men of the 6th Cavalry in dust-blown New Mexico; Indians who fought toughly to the end; black troopers of the 10th Cavalry who taught so much human wisdom; the expeditionary force that marched around Lanao; the Moros and their warrior code; short, brave *Nippon denji* and his hulking, ill-led foe; Villa, the arid alkali fastness of Chihuahua, Charles Boyd of Carrizal; Big Red One, the Tommies ever steadfast, the *poilus* philosophical in dying, Fritz who charged so often so well and who retreated at Saint Mihiel and the Meuse-Argonne; and always the blue and the khaki, the long, long lines of Americans who fought valorously, hated war, and slept in battlefields around the world—his soldiers they had seemed to everyone in France, for the army was his own. For forty-two years he served the colors, and in those years his world and his army became complex, sophisticated organisms,[53] increasingly machine managed. In the war the army's size put it beyond camaraderie and made it an impersonal force. But Pershing never conceded inhumanity to his men and kept the AEF an entity. The new army, small and dwindling, again had the closeness of penury, but Pershing had planned for expansion in crisis to a size perhaps larger than ever. If he abhorred impersonal systems, he knew how to make them workable. So he left behind a legacy of humanity, honor, and military integrity that seemed, somehow, in the 1920s altogether archaic and unnecessary.

In a way he was lucky, and he knew it. A nation tired of heroics might easily have forgotten its greatest hero—but America respected Pershing. True, Heywood Broun's comment during the war that "nobody will ever call him 'Papa' Pershing" showed a certain lack of warmth in respect. He was not loved, but few hard fighters are. Respect better suited a soldier. Respect gave some weight to martial views he held, and he would keep trying to protect his country.

He was tired and a little depressed at the thought of shelfsitting, but there were things to occupy him, once he got back to work. Work on a book about the World War had sputtered along through the years since 1920. That project grew more or less logically from his *Final Report* and the *Report of the First Army*.[54] Most of the documents he needed were hoarded in the AEF offices, and Pershing had used many

[53] According to the census of 1920, the population of the United States was 105,710,620 (*Abstract of the Fourteenth Census of the United States, 1920*, p. 18).
[54] JJP and Liggett, *First Army* (August 10, 1918 to October 15, 1918).

in working on early drafts. He had some of the staff do special studies for him but stubbornly put the narrative together in his own spare prose. Careful, determined that the AEF would have its innings in his pages, he struggled with various versions and was far from finished. Actually he had not quite decided whether to write a full book of memoirs or limit himself to the war years, but the war years took precedence in the initial writing. Even that important labor would not occupy his full energies, and for the moment an officer might unwind. He missed Warren, at school in Switzerland, and decided to visit him.

That kind of trip would renew those good European ties, revive low spirits, and maybe something would happen along. Over on the *Leviathan*—she sailed on October 4—he recalled an earlier trip, and in Europe the old style of lionizing worked its charm. Much time with Warren cheered a father's heart. Warren had gone to Europe alone in September, had been a little saddened, but began to do manly things. The boy seemed not quite as interested in the great war days as he might have been, but the war, after all, had gone to history. Warren grew splendidly, was tall, good looking, had much of Frankie's charm and outgoing personality. Altogether Pershing liked him as a man and loved him as a son. They traveled across Europe together. It was a good vacation—and something did turn up.

When the S.S. *Paris* reached New York in November, Quek stood waiting at the dock. President Coolidge had asked Pershing's diplomatic aid in Latin America. Relations there had seesawed endlessly, and domestic quarrels among South American nations usually spilled partly on North American relations. Particularly vexing had been the running feud between Peru and Chile over the disputed Tacna-Arica strip of high and low country lying between those nations. Coolidge had become involved in arbitration, a process begun by Charles Hughes as secretary of state, and found the situation thornier than diplomatic politeness could explain. Troubles lingered from an old war between Chile and her enemies, Peru and Bolivia; Chile won, with victory, domination of the nitrate-rich strip of mountain and coastline. By the Treaty of Ancon, 1883, a plebiscite had been promised within ten years to determine the lasting fate of the province. The vote had not been held, the territory lingered a thorn to peace—the sticking point was the "form" of the plebiscite. And with the naïveté of power, Coolidge schemed somehow to make a settlement. So much ill will, though, clotted even formal relations, and he looked for a graceful way to enter negotiations.

Peru offered a chance. There would be a great celebration of the one-hundredth anniversary of the great battle of South American liberation—Ayacucho, where Antonio de Sucre defeated the Spanish army on December 9, 1824—a celebration forever memorable to the world. All nations, especially those in the hemisphere, were urged to send delegates. In honor of so great a moment, the United States would send her greatest soldier! If he would go. Coolidge asked and Pershing accepted the assignment. The president hoped for usable contacts and for insights into the Tacna-Arica imbroglio.

There were all kinds of chances for disappointment in the job—the task seemed clearly symbolic and wearisome, the kind of diplomatic posturing that Pershing hated. But he would do what the president asked.

Quek had made his usual efficient arrangements—and Pershing was grateful that he had been continued as an aide. The navy provided a battleship, the *Utah*, for the official mission of eight people. Pershing was the chief; Admiral Dayton and lesser ranks went along to attend to some ceremonial duties. The trip as Quek outlined it would tax a mule. The Ayacucho festivities, beginning on December 9, would run for several days, then the party would undertake an incredible tour of South America. And with rare lapses, the plan succeeded. The *Utah* dropped anchor in Callao harbor on the sixth; Pershing and henchmen were taken to Lima for rounds of official entertaining—which included not only speechmaking but also dancing. Glittering diplomatic missions arrived from all South America, and Pershing met each of them —his grace and obvious interest in South America quickly won friends. He knew the opportunity and the duty—he could and would learn all possible about conditions in the southern hemisphere, do as much to mend fences as he could, and report in detail to the president.

Experience had taught the value of study for any assignment, and as the *Utah* had steamed southward Pershing pursued a crash course in South American history and customs. All of which showed off well in the formal and informal gatherings in Lima.

Sucre's victory properly celebrated and the new statue of the hero unveiled, ceremonies next centered on other Latin American luminaries—Bolívar, San Martín, and George Washington. General Pershing, immaculate in his khaki uniform, his brass glittering, eyes somber, reverently laid wreaths on the tombs of Bolívar, San Martín, and Sucre, and on December 14, 1924, proudly participated in homage to Washington. The minister of foreign affairs laid a wreath on the statue, spoke feelingly of Washington's impact on the world; the mayor of Lima spoke, as did representatives of Venezuela and Colombia. Then

Pershing stood bareheaded in the cool, clear air. He had a manuscript in his hand, but he barely glanced at it as his Missouri voice warmed to the respect shown his countryman. Unabashedly in English he said:

We Americans of the North sincerely appreciate the honor extended by the Government of Peru to the memory of Washington on this one hundred and twenty-fifth anniversary of his death. . . . These surroundings are resonant with recollections of those immortal heroes of South American independence; San Martín, Sucre and Bolívar, and it is fitting, at this time, that we should pause at the foot of this shrine to pay homage, because wherever men are gathered together in the name of liberty, there engraved on each and every heart will be found the name of Washington. . . .

This was not a canned evaluation, but one that saw Washington in Pershing's terms.

Washington's masterly conduct of the campaigns that led to Yorktown made of him a great military figure, yet the deep conviction of his continued obligations to his countrymen was never altered by the excess of their acclaim, nor tinged by the vanity of martial glory. . . . I would rather go down into history like those great patriots of the two Americas, Washington, Bolivar, San Martín and Sucre, with the love and admiration of succeeding generations of free men, than to sit on the throne and wear the jewelled crown of the greatest monarch that ever ruled over an oppressed people. This national celebration in Peru of the final victory for American independence . . . shows full well that the spirit of democracy runs high. . . . But mere words do not carry us far enough, and the very sacred duty of positive action devolves upon us to whom these men have given freedom. It is for us wisely and unselfishly to apply their glorious example to our every day problems. Not only do the principles handed down to us demand liberty and justice for the humblest citizen within the boundaries of our respective countries, but they point the way to still closer relations among our several republics themselves. . . .[55]

He made a hit.

From Lima the mission began a great trek, first up the high railway into the Andes toward Bolivia, then by horseback, boat, and sometimes automobile over wretched roads through Chile, Argentina, Uruguay, Brazil, countries where the military authorities and highest officials paid constant honor. Pershing basked in renown, even in the remotest villages of the highest mountains—Inca Indian chieftains came to small towns to greet the great American general. Christmas in Arequipa, Peru, offered unique touches between past and present. In the great cities—Santiago, Buenos Aires, Montevideo, Rio de Janeiro, where old custom blended with new graces to make societies charming and warm

[55] "Remarks of General John J. Pershing at the Statue of Washington, Lima, December 14, 1924," Box 331, PP.

—Pershing and his party were heroes. United States diplomats and nationals and other "gringo" colonies entertained the visitors when they could snatch them from officialdom. When, on February 6, 1925, Pershing put his coterie aboard the *Utah*—which had followed around South America—for a run to Trinidad and Venezuela, the trip had become an incredible triumph of good will.

Veteran traveler and observer, Pershing cherished no illusions about understanding the complexities of South American relations; he did have a fair knowledge of economic and transportation problems, a feel for the people, and an appreciation of the potential seen everywhere on the western coast and southern end of the continent.

Trinidad, raised on February 17, offered a touch of British hospitality and reminded Pershing of so many drawingroom sessions in England. Three days later the *Utah* sailed for La Guaira, the harbor for Caracas, where Pershing presided over honors at another Washington statue. A visit to the Venezuelan military academy reminded him of the odd currents of foreign martial influences seen in South America. French teachers instructed the Peruvians, but goose-stepping troops in several countries showed the sinister revival of German militarism. The United States ought to encourage acceptance of training missions in as many Latin American nations as possible.[56]

On Sunday, March 1, the *Utah* anchored at Guantanamo for a day's inspection of the great U.S. naval base. Monday the American ambassador met Pershing and his party at Santiago, and it was a reunion of old Missouri cronies—Enoch Crowder grabbed Jack's hand and embraced him warmly. There were, he announced, big things planned for the general. Luncheons, dinners, dances to Jack's taste, a presidential reception. All sounded fine, but Pershing had a touch of tropical trouble. Even a rest in Havana's sumptuous Sevilla-Biltmore Hotel failed to restore him fully. By Tuesday he reported "on the sick list," and an American doctor who specialized in tropical medicine came for an examination. Pershing had amoebic dysentery, not a bad case, but not likely to get better without care. Always eager to do a doctor's bidding, Jack followed orders; that doctor, Jack reported, "managed to straighten me out in about a week, and I think entirely eradicated the bug from my system."[57]

In a week Pershing returned to duty, spoke at the unveiling of the *Maine* monument, paid respects to the president of Cuba, and gladly

[56] JJP to John W. Weeks, on board the U.S.S. *Utah* at sea, Dec. 23, 1924, Box 207, PP.

[57] JJP to George Marshall, May 29, 1925, Box 124, PP.

boarded the *Utah* for return to the States. He reached New York on March 13, 1925, which incidentally was Friday.[58]

When he arrived back in Washington on March 16, Jack found a large crowd waiting at the station—they greeted him as they used to, as a returning conqueror. Diplomats had some fun, after all. A reception in the president's room at the station involved more hand shaking —he wondered if he'd shaken more hands than anybody—and a return to office routine. He had noticed that retirement had not reduced the daily stream of visitors or the number of consultations with John Hines. For all practical purposes he functioned as the *éminence gris* of the War Department and now added the laurels of elder statesman. Retirement simply varied activities. Mail continued its avalanche in the office, and invitations came in quantities to occupy him constantly.[59]

In two days he, in company with the rest of his mission, paid a formal call on the president and made a short assessment of South America. A round of entertainments by and for Peruvian diplomats consumed a few days. Still, Jack had time to enjoy the company of the new vice president of the United States—a man whose inaugural address had caught the country by surprise and the U.S. Senate in disbelief. Charlie Dawes, in a precedent-shattering speech upon taking the oath of office, had castigated senators for antique and unbusinesslike rules. Happily he reported his transgressions to Jack, who understood him. Charlie's technique remained constant—in France he had pitched into fusty Allied colleagues on the supply board with outrageous language, fogged the room with vile cigar smoke, and been altogether gauche. Usually he made someone angry early, and from anger came remorse and then agreement. He boasted of his method; he used it before the "Graham Committee" in 1921. Picky they were about big affairs and they wasted his time. "Is it not true," one of the inquisitors had asked mincingly, "that excessive prices were paid for some articles?" Dawes fumed: "When Congress declared war, did it expect us to beat Germany at twenty per cent discount?" Raising his decibles he stormed, "Sure, we paid high prices. Men were standing at the front to be shot at. We had to get them food and ammunition. We didn't stop to dicker. Why, man alive! We had a war to win! It was a man's job!" After a question about high mule prices, Charlie had yelled

[58] Two logs of the trip offer excellent detail. For Pershing's own account, see his log, attached to JJP to George Marshall, May 29, 1925, Box 124, PP. For a fuller account, kept by another member of the mission, see Maj. Edward W. Sturdevant, USMC, "Log of Special Mission to Peru," Box 331, PP.

[59] JJP, Diary, Sept., 1924–Mar., 1925, Boxes 4–5, PP.

"Helen Maria," and become famous as the prime cusser of the haute monde.[60]

When he stood before the Senate while Jack was off in South America, Dawes had preached a sermon of change—it was effrontery, it was egotism, it was improper, and it was Charlie Dawes. Senators, strangers to his complex mix of warmth and bombast, thought him absurd, but the public read his remarks with glee. A Boston paper reported that "Dawes has no one but the people with him."[61]

Jack guessed some hidden purpose in Charlie's indelicacy and, when they lunched together on March 20, listened eagerly to accounts of the row. Charlie proved pretty cagy. He spoke of his days on the rostrum with pleasure; presiding with fairness had become a fetish. But explanations for his outburst he avoided, let Jack guess at his motives. And Jack did—knowing Charlie, he thought he saw method behind folly. "My own private opinion is that he has set up a straw man to knock down principally for the purpose of getting himself talked about," Pershing wrote George Marshall, now on China station,

and to have an excuse to travel around the country carrying his fight into various states where senators are to be reelected. He seems not to discriminate between Republican and Democratic senators and as the Republicans' chances for retaining control of the Senate are very slim, Dawes is getting himself into quite a little bit of hot water with the party. . . . However, it is amusing to stand on the side lines and see these people play politics.[62]

Watching Charlie's gyrations and those of his colleagues amused Jack and may have caused a twinge or two of envy. But he went on with the hectic ceremonials and increasing business. The American Battle Monuments Commission obviously would be a time taker, but Jack fully approved of its purposes and wanted to give it his best attention. Old friends demanded moments of his days, too, and he could never really turn people away—a happy weakness he shared with Charlie.[63]

Nor was Pershing good at avoiding presidential duties—it was a manner born at West Point and trained through the years. When Coolidge asked him, during a meeting at the White House on Monday, March 23, if he would head a commission to "conduct the Tacna-Arica" plebiscite, he said, simply, "yes, sir." The president's request was a

[60] Timmons, *Dawes*, p. 195.
[61] *Ibid.*, p. 245.
[62] JJP to Marshall, May 29, 1925, Box 124, PP.
[63] JJP, Diary, Mar., 1925, Boxes 4–5, PP; Timmons, *Dawes*, pp. 256–57.

soldier's command. "The President asked me to go." [64] It was "very important duty," to be sure, but he had spent months in the area, knew the problems inherent in winning cooperation between two nearly primordial enemies, and realized chances for success were slim. "I am not particularly keen about this job," Pershing recorded, "but there seemed to be no way out of it, so after some hesitation I finally accepted it." [65] At least he would not have to leave instantly—there would be time for a visit to Lincoln and the family. But in a way lonesomeness engulfed him—Quek departed for the Staff School at Fort Leavenworth. [66]

Army schools were dear to Pershing's heart. He had watched them grow—Infantry at Fort Benning, Artillery at Fort Sill, the old Remount Station at Fort Riley turning more and more toward mechanized work. But it was at places like Leavenworth and the Army War College that the future staff leaders would be trained. Those schools and West Point —its curriculum at last back to four years, thanks to some Pershing pushing—were the custodians of the martial future of the nation. Progression through the successive schools would fit any man of sense with the highest tools of his profession. Once, congratulating graduates of the War College, Jack boasted of the system. The United States, he said, at last had a coordinated military educational program, "probably the most effective in the world," which fitted officers for the broadest missions of national defense; they would be leaders and managers, coordinators and analysts, soldiers, statesmen, businessmen. For the army a new scope and reliance offered challenge and opportunity. Men like Quek would outdo their predecessors. It was good to have helped create the school system; it would have been thrilling to be a student again. [67]

Good times pass too soon and the future rushes in. Summer had flown, most of it, in visits and rest and some research into the background of the Tacna-Arica morass. Pershing's days were filled with cramming on protocol and in hearing the views of the State Department, a bureaucracy fascinated ever with the punctilio of peace. Clearly, Coolidge and Secretary of State Frank Kellogg virtually expected miracles from Pershing—perhaps his high repute with the world could prevail over local jealousies. Well, it seemed dubious.

[64] Frederick Palmer, *John J. Pershing, General of the Armies: A Biography,* p. 357.
[65] JJP to Marshall, May 29, 1925, Box 124, PP.
[66] JJP, Diary, Mar. 24, 1925, Boxes 4–5, PP.
[67] JJP, "Address at Army War College Graduation Exercises," Box 343, PP.

Hopeless Task

No one could guess how long the mission would take, but optimism always felt better than pessimism. Pershing picked his aides carefully, had to take some from State, and discovered that he would be given a cruiser by the navy—the U.S.S. *Rochester*—for transportation. For advisors he would have William J. Dennis, Dr. Harold Dodds, and Col. Edward A. Kreger of the Judge Advocate's Department. Dodds, as a Latin American expert in the State Department, had some experience in southern-hemisphere elections and could inject a tinge of reality into a group of enthusiasts. Kreger's legal knowledge ought to keep the Tacna-Arica Plebiscitary Commission within bounds of the International Arbitration under which it would function. Happily for Pershing, Quekemeyer received orders to go along as the general's aide, and two old friends—Sergeants Lanckton and Steve B. Ceto—would attend to personal and housekeeping details. There would be secretaries, including old friend Ralph Curtin, and presumably the navy would keep the *Rochester* handy for any sudden emergencies. Two correspondents were assigned to the mission.

Everybody boarded for departure on July 17, 1925. By then goodbyes had been said, skeptics had clucked again about Pershing letting himself in for so strange a task, and nothing but going was left. A special escort for Ambassador Pershing had been provided by the U.S. Marine Corps, the detachment commanded by Capt. John W. Thomason, soldier, artist, writer, veteran of the 2nd Division's hardest days in Belleau Wood. He had served under Harbord and would care for his general's special friend.

And Thomason became a friend. During the good sailing days to Key West and beyond toward the Panama Canal, Pershing much enjoyed touring the ship, once the battleship *New York*, and in the evening would have a few cronies into his sumptuous mahogany-panelled admiral's quarters for talk or poker. Talk ran mainly to the war, for most of the men with him had done a stint in the AEF. Thomason had the most distinction—he wore ribbons of the croix de guerre, Navy Cross, and other decorations, and he combined soldiering with wit, humor, and wry wisdom. Of the war Pershing spoke freely and nostalgically. Thomason found a kindred soul. "He loved stories of men under arms," Thomason said, "troops were his whole life."[68] Recollections sometimes brought the cold blue to the general's eyes, especially recollections of the armistice. That last offensive he had planned would

[68] Laurence Stallings, *AEF*, p. 373.

have ended military problems for a long time. Thomason argued that the Germans still were able to fight at the end and would have; Pershing conceded that, but said flatly that when "we came down the Linden as an army with banners," all fighting would have stopped. Might there have been sniping and street fighting in Berlin? "We would have flushed them out and hanged them to the lamp posts of the Linden to let the Germans know who won the war. The Germans are being told the people let the armies down." Ideas of *revanche* could thrive on those fairytales—the AEF was not permitted to finish the job. The more he thought about it, the madder the general got; once he banged the table, sat forward and snapped, "They never knew they were beaten in Berlin. It will all have to be done all over again." [69]

Men of the mission who did not know Pershing, some of them, came with trepidation. Famed as the cold "Black Jack," he loomed a fearsome taskmaster. Harold Dodds had that anticipation when he joined the party en route. Pershing liked the scholarly young man with the quiet certitude and gathered him instantly into the official family. He picked associates, always, that he trusted and could like—Dodds had been a wild card that proved a winner. He liked poker, could joke with the best, and enjoyed war stories.

In those "headquarters" sessions no one talked about the mission. Pershing cherished few illusions—it would be touchy.

From Key West the sea smoothed under gentle skies; easily the *Rochester* glided through the Panama Canal, turned south to run along the coast of Ecuador, and at last crossed the equator—where the rites of Neptunus Rex were gleefully celebrated by all "shellbacks" aboard. Landlubbers were suitably shriven in delightfully pagan ways; Pershing enjoyed the view—he had been through it all on the *Utah!* [70] The good-natured, if sometimes rowdy, hazing showed fine ship morale.

Down beyond the Galapagos Islands, past the western shoulder of South America, the *Rochester* steamed, her brass bright, her crew proud of having the General of the Armies and Admiral Latimer, commanding the special fleet for South American maneuvers, aboard. The Pacific rolled in long reaches close to the west-trending Humboldt Current and turned deep blue as the ship approached the Peru-Chile Trench. Shortly after 9:00 A.M. on Sunday, August 2—a fine, bright, windy day—the *Rochester* dropped anchor in Arica harbor. Proper

[69] *Ibid.*, p. 374.
[70] For the orgy of making shellbacks and Pershing's pleasure at watching the proceedings, see John W. Thomason, Jr., "Crossing the Line with Pershing," *Scribner's Magazine*, Aug., 1926, pp. 115–24.

salutes to the port and the Chilean cruiser *O'Higgins,* riding anchor in the roadstead, were given; out from the dock came Agustín Edwards, Chile's delegate to the Plebiscitary Commission. Suave, urbane, a diplomat with long experience as ambassador in London and as president of the League of Nations, Edwards seemed almost too smooth. Charming, cordial he certainly was, eager to introduce the general to Arica and to his countrymen.

Arica, decked for high celebration, spread before the ship's company. Flags snapped from every building in a gala bombardment of color. They all seemed to be Chilean, but a close sweep with glasses spied two Stars and Stripes over two buildings, the ones readied for Pershing's company, and other national standards mixed over the city —all but Peru's. That one was glaring in its absence. Bothered by this singular blot on amity, Pershing put Edwards a question: How could there not be any Peruvian flags flying? Edwards had no real answer but suggested there were not enough Peruvians in Arica to make that banner necessary. Curious.[71]

Hearty optimism oozed in the atmosphere. Edwards blithely assured Pershing that the plebiscite would be quickly accomplished— the Tacna-Arica population, about 80 percent Chilean, fervently wanted to remain under Chile. This kind of blatant suasion rankled an old Missouri distrust; Pershing wanted to see the Peruvians. They were not in sight.

Going ashore in the admiral's barge, Pershing and most of his colleagues were welcomed by a variegated panoply of officialdom and smart formations of Chilean soldiers and sailors. A band began a raucous sound and Pershing finally deciphered the tune. "The band murdered the Star Spangled Banner horribly," he realized, and snapped to a salute as, mercilessly, the cacophony continued. Finally, discouraged, he dropped his hand and a Chilean general waved frantically to stop the music. Speeches of welcome made and answered, Pershing led his company toward the two houses assigned. Crowds lined the streets, waved, and the "vivas" brought smiles to gringo faces.

[71] See JJP, Journal of Tacna-Arica, August 9, 1925, Box 334, PP. References in this section are from Pershing's journal, unless otherwise noted. For the reception in Arica, see also "Joint Report to the Arbitrator, Tacna-Arica Arbitration, By General John J. Pershing, First President, and Maj. Gen. William Lassiter, Second President, of the Plebiscitary Commission, Tacna-Arica Arbitration," p. 38, in Early History of the Plebiscitary Commission—Arrival of the Commission at Arica, Records Relating to International Arbitrations, RG 76, National Archives. The entire proceedings are covered in detail by the Minutes of the Commission meetings, in *ibid.*

First Pershing paid a call on Commissioner Edwards at his residence, and Edwards then escorted Jack to the North American quarters. All the way enthusiastic people waved and cheered—but they were Chileans. Pershing, eyes roving the crowd closely, noted "the atmosphere . . . entirely Chilean."

Quarters were comfortable. Someone had gone to considerable trouble to repaper and paint the buildings, to alert the servants to new tenants—they stood aligned and nervously curious as these strange Norte Americanos packed in baggage, papers, and themselves.

After lunch Pershing inspected the Quartel, a new concrete structure built for troops but as yet unused—here the commission would hold its sessions. A large office, Pershing noted, had been reserved for him. Commissioner Edwards, with a host's enthusiasm, showed the general around and basked in Pershing's guileful hyperbole—these halls, said the veteran of so many Allied conferences, compared with Versailles. He did not specify in what respect.

Edwards entertained most of the Pershing mission at dinner. At the table Pershing sized up Edwards' advisors and henchmen, noted that a Washington lawyer named Van Dike had been retained by the Chilean mission. Edwards, sliding smoothly from host to advocate, "talked about fairness and how they [Chile] would easily win the plebiscite." Always attentive—it was an attractive trait—Pershing listened to Edwards with genuine interest but took Van Dike aside after dinner to chat about general conditions. They shared sadness at the Peru-Chile dispute "over a piece of territory which intrinsically is hardly worth the price of the plebiscite." Sentiment, they agreed, counted more than reality in this controversy. And that disturbed the chairman of the Plebiscitary Commission mightily, for sentiment yields nothing to reason.

On the third, a proper Monday, the Peruvians arrived on the transport *Ucayali*,[72] which dropped anchor at midmorning. She carried Commissioner Freyre y Santander and cohorts, including Dr. Alberto Salomón, former prime minister, who had wisdom crusted in a cynic's wit and viewed the plebiscite as a charade to sanction Chilean brigandage. He spoke of the years of occupation, of Chilean ruthlessness in colonizing, and doubted any chance of fairness.

Determined that fairness and honesty were the main ingredients his mission offered, Pershing listened in dismay. Salomón seemed reasonable, though his comments biased. But he could cite an incident al-

[72] "Joint Report," p. 38. Pershing misspelled the ship's name in his Journal of Tacna-Arica, Aug. 3, 1925, as "Ucalayi."

ready, one he thought likely to be typical. When a Peruvian member of the Boundary Commission (which was meeting simultaneously with the plebiscite) came ashore, he was roughly knocked from the dock by a snickering Chilean enthusiast—and no official action followed.[73]

Hangers-on bothered Pershing. Each delegation, save his own, collected "experts" on everything, especially did they collect stray American women with specialties and bodies they tried to exploit.[74]

The chairman could take scant heart from the first formal session of the commission on August 5, 1925. He opened with praise of arbitration as a solution to international problems, congratulated Peru and Chile for adopting it, and recalled the horrors of war. He pronounced the prime duty of the commission to be that of assuring fairness in voting for all parties in the disputed territory and reminded his colleagues that they had full powers to insure honesty and freedom of choice to all citizens. Reassuring them that "the Government of the United States has no ambition other than to aid in the attainment of these aims, no policy that does not conform to these . . . aspirations," Pershing concluded with confidence in the triumph of justice. Edwards and Freyre y Santander each gave "moderate" statements, but Pershing sensed the undercurrents of hostility. Edwards had said to him during dinner the night before that "we shall differ on every point. If they say a thing is white we shall say it is black and vice versa," and the cautious sniping at the opening seemed to confirm the prophecy. The first fight occurred over the suggested rules of procedure. On the sixth the Chileans proposed to limit the commission's action by labeling it a court of law subject to judicial circumscription. Colonel Kreger quickly objected, and trouble hung leaden over the conference.

Dodds, drawing on his experience with other Latin American balloting, and on his discussion with the various staffs, told Pershing that nothing could be done until a "plebiscitary atmosphere was achieved." In an atmosphere of open hostility, fairness would be a joke. There were specific obstacles: (1) too many Chilean governmental officials functioning in Tacna-Arica with opportunities to sway opinion; (2) too many Chilean troops, "carbineers," police, and secret-service men in the province; (3) too few Peruvian voters left on hand for a fair test

---

[73] Harold W. Dodds to the author, Sept. 29, 1970.

[74] A Sarah Wambaugh, who had written "a book of large size giving the history of recent European plebiscites" [*A Monograph on Plebiscites with a Collection of Official Documents*], Pershing thought a problem, along with Mrs. Jackie Deitrick, whose reported attack on her person by Chileans almost caused an incident (JJP, Journal of Tacna-Arica, Aug. 3, Nov. 22, 1925).

of strength. Before any plebiscite could occur, Chile would have to take steps to lighten its yoke on the area.

Obviously this seemed altogether silly to the Chileans; if there were few Peruvians, fine, a vote should be taken quickly. For several days the commissioners wrangled over procedural matters. Pershing sent for a group of Spanish-speaking Americans from Panama to go into the various districts as fact-finders. Freyre y Santander and his colleagues claimed fearsome oppression by Chile, harassment of Peruvians still in Tacna-Arica, a virtual reign of terror to drive out the diehards. Those charges required investigation. And as the days passed, specific charges accumulated. A group of zealots calling themselves Sons of Tacna-Arica bullied, threatened, even attacked Peruvians in remote places. If these charges seemed at first outlandish, treatment of the American and Peruvian missions lent confirmation. In a short time the Americans noticed they were shadowed, trailed, presumably by Chilean secret agents—it all seemed melodramatic to the Anglo-Saxon mind. But it was real enough.

So many petty cases of bellicosity occurred and so much bickering disturbed the commission meetings that Pershing, by September, began to doubt the chances of success. "I am not a defeatist," he noted in his journal, "but this old difference has existed so long and so much bitterness has been engendered that all sense of fairness is entirely lacking in reality. They both see things through a cloud of intense hatred and both views are very much prejudiced."[75]

Delay is the surest defense—and Chileans were deft in polite confusion. They misunderstood requests; Edwards required conferences with his government; both sides used the regular sessions—which Pershing finally ran daily in a kind of attempt at exhaustion—for public damnation of each other. Votes were rarely possible, even on the simplest procedural matters. Chile demanded that Pershing and the commission set dates for the plebiscite; Pershing stuck toughly to the need for proper "atmosphere." Complaints leaked to Washington; Secretary Kellogg, unable to understand the poisonous air in Arica, kept urging speed on Pershing. The general dug in; he would not be coerced—Foch would have been amused! Dodds became a grateful admirer of Pershing's. "I was much heartened by the manner in which Pershing withstood high pressures from Washington to yield. . . ."[76]

[75] "Address of General Pershing at First Meeting of Plebiscitary Commission, at Conference Hall, Arica, August 5, 1925," JJP, Journal of Tacna-Arica; JJP, Journal of Tacna-Arica, Aug. 5, 1925; Dodds to author, Sept. 29, 1970.
[76] Dodds to the author, Sept. 29, 1970.

There would be no plebiscite until it could be run in an honorable way.

Incidents increased and began to sound like Belgian atrocity stories. From up north came a tale of three carbineers tying up a Peruvian and raping his wife in front of his eyes. That produced fierce local reaction, and a mob killed the leading culprit—but Chileans turned the incident to good effect by saying it was planned by Peruvians, and the dead villain became a folk hero!

Pershing insisted from the start that all commission proceedings be confidential, but Edwards began to leak important discussions to the press. Pershing called him to task, received the usual bland disclaimers, and fumed when Edwards produced a lengthy indictment of the commission's practices, allegations of Pershing's bias, and denial of any Chilean perfidy. Edwards also gave his letter to the press in violation of the rules. His intemperate and absurd charges and his indiscretion thoroughly angered Pershing, who wrote a vitriolic answer, which he put on the commission's record. But he would not hurry.

Outside influences worked on Edwards. Pershing noted the arrival on the scene of a leftist former president of Chile, Arturo Alessandri, who seized on every convolution of the negotiations to suggest Yankee intrigues. And the Peruvian government postured as fiercely as the Chilean. All incidents and pressures Pershing dutifully reported to the State Department but grew certain that nobody read his dispatches. "It is a pity," he mused, "that this whole thing cannot be suspended until somebody goes to Washington and puts the State Department on the right track." He much desired to go home for Christmas, wanted to see Warren, but slowly abandoned hope. So did Quek and the others of the mission, all of whom were losing patience.[77]

Realizing that delay put heavy weapons in Chilean hands and allowed men like Alessandri to claim manipulation, Pershing sought a way to bludgeon compliance with prerequisites for a plebiscite.

He worked carefully. Long experience had taught the value of consultation and he knew his staff competent, wise in local prejudices, and willing to advise. He walked along the beach daily with different staff members—out in the open, surveillance would be difficult. These walks were intelligence sessions for him; questions were always incisive, direct, and he wanted the whole truth in reply. And he wanted all shades of opinion. William Dennis had been a legal advisor to Charles Hughes during the early stages of the award; he opposed

[77] JJP, Journal of Tacna-Arica, Dec. 2, 1925; Quekemeyer to his mother, Nov. 8, 1925, Quekemeyer Papers; Quekemeyer, Tacna-Arica Diary, Nov. 7, 1925, Quekemeyer Papers.

Pershing's delaying until a "plebiscitary atmosphere" could be created. Dodds agreed fully with the general, as did Kreger and Quek.

From these consultations Pershing developed two possible lines of action. One he deplored, for it smacked of blackmail, but it might be necessary: threaten a resolution citing outrages committed and declaring that unless "the situation is changed without delay . . . the plebiscite is a failure and that the blame rests directly on Chilean shoulders." The other had simplicity and a directness not likely to appeal to either side, grounded as they were in sentiment and unwillingness to negotiate directly: a diplomatic settlement of the boundary without a vote. Anything done would have future implications. Pershing worried about precedents. By November he confessed to many at home his conviction that the plebiscite "is absolutely impossible." But he felt he must carry on until events convinced the State Department—the secretary would probably not take his word, would want an unimpeachable stance for United States withdrawal. That legal bent Pershing considered disastrous. "If we pursue this legal idea . . . much farther it is going to lead to a calamity. I mean that we shall arrive at an impasse between ourselves and the Chileans that will make a future settlement by negotiation well nigh impossible. It will produce unfriendly relations between the two governments for years to come and will also . . . weaken our influence in South America."

Finally the Chileans withdrew from the meetings, using blackmail themselves; Edwards, egged on probably by Alessandri, attacked Pershing's honesty, accused him of provoking both sides. Pershing had feared for some time that the Chileans would boycott the meetings and use their outside position as a club to force a quick plebiscite. But Edwards's charges infuriated him. "I get to a point here in this matter where my usual control and equanimity are about to disappear. These people have not the slightest sense of honor nor a remote consideration for truthfulness. It is mighty up hill business to carry on with such people." To Harbord he wrote with uncommon despair that "it looks just about as near a hopeless task as could well [be] imagin[ed]—the bitterness, antagonism, animosity that exists between these two people is almost beyond comprehension—it is almost as if they were at war at this moment. . . . "[78]

Staff members worried about him. His kindness to them never flagged, but he seemed less and less robust. His appetite dwindled, and he slept fitfully. Quek, who worked diligently at running a smooth

[78] JJP to Harbord, Sept. 13, 1925, Box 88, PP. See also JJP, Journal of Tacna-Arica, Nov. 16, 24, 25, 1925.

office and at maintaining equanimity at mealtimes, noted that the special canapés he fixed each afternoon no longer attracted Pershing. Queried, Pershing confessed they were giving him nightmares—he told of one that dissolved Quek in laughter: the top of his head was off and he was trying to screw it back on but couldn't get it straight! A dream analyst might have done wonders with that revelation.[79]

Pershing disliked being irritable and realized that frustration would induce error. He came, slowly, to realize that pressures would force him to concede dates for voting, even though Chile had not complied with prerequisites. He delayed still, worried about the position of the mission. The *Rochester* had been recalled, would be replaced by the *Denver*; he longed to go back with his flagship. The *Denver*, much smaller, would be dwarfed by the *O'Higgins*, and that status decline would not go unnoticed by protocol lovers in Chile.

Animosity clogged the air; he grew worried about the safety of his charges in their yellow house near the waterfront. He worked out a system of distress signals with navy officers and tested them one Sunday. Lanckton and Ceto pulled up the signal flags, fired their small gun, and waited. In about twenty minutes a launch came with an officer who asked, "Say, did you fellows call for a launch?" The sergeants erupted, but Pershing stopped them. If there had been real trouble, he said, the navy "would have been right on the job."[80]

Part of the problem was lack of diversion—there was simply not enough entertainment in Arica. The *Rochester* showed movies, the staff gathered for cocktails, dinner, for good, low-stake poker games—at which the Old Man excelled with his cold, implacable eye—but time hung heavy as the air. Visitors were few and were clutched in desperation when they came.

Christmas passed, the New Year crept in, and still the meetings dragged. As he finally moved toward setting dates, Pershing encountered fresh outrages that forced another delay. Kellogg fumed. There was a respite when former Secretary of War and Mrs. Weeks sailed into Arica. He had been ill, was better, and listened to Pershing's problems with a sensitive, comprehending ear. Kellogg had told him, he said, that the situation in Arica "was impossible," and that the United States "had made a very grave mistake to mix up with this problem." Pershing echoed that heartily, but guessed "if anybody is to be left in the lurch when the time comes that it will be those of us who

[79] Quekemeyer, Tacna-Arica Diary, Nov. 5, 1925.
[80] Robert Ginsburgh, "Pershing as His Orderlies Know Him," *American Legion Monthly* 5 (Dec., 1928): 61.

are down here trying to pull the chestnuts out of the fire for the State Department." He confessed to Weeks that he would not have taken the assignment had he known more about it when offered.

Weeks suggested he go to Washington and explain things; it was impossible at the moment, Pershing thought. Weeks would send a cable himself explaining how badly the situation had coagulated. Pershing accepted the offer gladly—Washington would listen to Weeks.

Gradually Pershing's health deteriorated. Lanckton and Ceto noticed he ate and slept less and less. Kellogg, who had feared Pershing might leave too soon, heard of his illness. Rumor had it that a tooth bothered him. The secretary of the navy offered to send a dentist, but Pershing declined. His trouble would require "expert surgical dentistry"; if it got worse he would have to go home. By mid-January navy doctors were worried seriously; his blood pressure shot up, possibly caused by the inflamed tooth, and his general physical condition sank alarmingly. Against his own good judgment, he finally boarded ship late in January, 1926, for the United States.

There were chortles from his enemies—foreign and domestic—as he had dreaded. Pershing had failed, had developed a "diplomatic" illness, and was slinking home. But the staff knew better. He had been ill for some time; they hoped he had not stuck to his post too long. Quek went with him. And Harold Dodds, waiting for Pershing's old friend Maj. Gen. Bill Lassiter to take over, regretted the going of a man he loved "second only to . . . my father."[81]

Pershing suffered physical torment and mental anguish. He knew he had done all that could have been done, that he had been in "the most exasperating situation . . . any man or set of men representing what we represent could ever be placed in . . . without hope of successful termination. . . . " But he had been in that kind of spot often enough, and had never failed. No matter the rationalizing done by his admirers, if he had not failed this time, he had certainly not succeeded. It was not a good feeling. There were two consolations: he had stuck to his job until his health broke, and he left things as tidy as possible for Lassiter. And it was good to be home—even in the hospital.[82]

[81] Dodds to the author, Sept. 29, 1970. See, for previous quotations, JJP, Journal of Tacna-Arica, Nov. 29, Dec. 2, 1925. The worries of the staff are well covered in a memorandum by Harry W. Frantz, formerly United Press Correspondent, who accompanied Pershing's mission. The memorandum, dated Aug. 2, 1960, is attached to Dodds to the author, Feb. 5, 1971.

[82] JJP to Elmer J. Burkett, Feb. 26, 1926, Box 37, PP. See also JJP, Journal of Tacna-Arica, Jan. 7, 1926.

A Memory for Fighters

He recovered, returned to his office, and picked up his large correspondence, but he had been badly scared. Heart trouble, that old bugaboo George Deshon had pooh-poohed years before, finally hit hard. Some of Jack's health problems in Tacna-Arica were probably small heart attacks, and an old fighter would have to slow down. That looked to be easy enough. There really was little serious business to occupy an old soldier. There were flurries of interest from the world. Some hints of possible success had come during the election excitement in 1924; Pershing steered a careful course of encouraging denial of concern.[83] But now, in wake of diplomatic disaster and health collapse, who would want him for much of anything?

As soon as recovery permitted, he began a regime of annual pilgrimages to Europe for looks at the developing monuments and graveyards. On these excursions he often stayed with Micheline Resco in her rue des Renaudes flat. There he found the only kind of solitude a lonely man desires. And there, too, he often worked long, long hours on his evolving manuscript. In the twenties the book took its own form. It would be an account of his role as commander-in-chief of the AEF. Finical with his own prose—he once consoled Harbord about one of his books with the wry thought that "neither of us is from Harvard and of course we are unable to give the Harvard touch to anything we do"[84]—he wrote and rewrote passages, checked his memory against AEF documents, and asked former staff associates to read his drafts for style and fact. George Marshall proved his most honest critic. Marshall noted the enormous damage done to reputations in memoirs and reminiscences. That strange compulsion of ego led droves of World War I figures to historical suicide. Once armed with pen and foolscap, generals of judgment became contenders against their comrades for glory. Few, Marshall thought, emerged unsullied. Pershing's achievements were so important that they ought not be dimmed by criticism—and memoirs usually evoked varieties of condemnation. That would be especially true if Pershing lapsed to criticism himself—and, as Marshall read the unfolding account of the AEF, he realized that his old chieftain had at last vented the spleen pent from so many months of frustration in France. With his sparse Missouri language, ever precise, pointed, icy, Pershing chopped away at Foch, Haig, Pétain in the early days, Clemenceau, and Lloyd George; he twitted Bliss, mused at

[83] JJP to Jacob M. Dickinson, Apr. 29, 1924, Box 64, PP.
[84] Cited in O'Connor, *BJP*, p. 376.

House, virtually damned Peyton March and his War Department, but praised Wilson and friend Newton Baker. Marshall should not have been surprised. Pershing simply wrote the truth as he felt it—he could do nothing else. But truth is slippery and meets eyes differently. Marshall knew a different truth about the AEF and realized that March would have his version, as would all others swept into Pershing's prism. Each really would read only what Pershing said about him and would praise or condemn accordingly.

Better far, urged Marshall, to write as Pershing acted in France—impersonally and with "marvelous restraint."[85] The manuscript as Marshall read it in 1930 "presents you in a different light, because of the frequency of criticism of the War Department and the Allies." Pershing diluted some of his vitriol, but much of his resentment seeped still across the pages. Various people helped him with his work. Beyond Micheline and Marshall were Maj. Dwight Eisenhower, who also worked on the Battle Monuments Commission's superior guide book, *American Armies and Battlefields in Europe*; 1st Lt. Thomas North, faithful friend from Chaumont's War Room; and others who served closely as aides and assistants, including Quek, Collins, and long-time secretary at last turned aide, George Adamson. All contributed critical eyes and sometimes rewrote sections within their competence. But the book remained Pershing's. Marshall feared at one time that there was too little color in the manuscript for popularity. Pershing grumbled about such a thing as too much color but added dashes here and there.[86]

Uncommonly personal, Pershing's book read straightforwardly, unemotionally, and on quick perusal might seem dull. It was anything but dull, given close reading. During a decade Pershing wrote different sections and fitted them together finally into two volumes entitled *My Experiences in the World War*. Three benchmarks set the tone of his writing—his dedication: "To the Unknown Soldier"; his foreword's last sentence: "No commander was ever privileged to lead a finer force; no commander ever derived greater inspiration from the performance of his troops"; his portrait as frontispiece to the second volume: by Micheline Resco. The book told the saga of the AEF according to the lights of the Iron Commander. His portrait of his men was true and affectionate altogether; Micheline's portrait of him, the same. And

---

[85] Quoted in Forrest Pogue, "General Marshall and the Pershing Papers," *Quarterly Journal of the Library of Congress* 21 (Jan., 1964): 10.

[86] Author's interview with Maj. Gen. Thomas North, USA (Ret.), Washington, D.C., Apr., 1974.

when this peculiarly good book was published by the Frederick A. Stokes Company of New York in 1931, it attracted a gradually growing audience.

Pershing, like all authors, hoped for instant immortality through his words, but his words were cast to the public in a bad year for buying books. Depression notwithstanding—Bernard Baruch helped Jack with personal finances—Pershing's book found syndication in many newspapers, its two blue volumes increasingly graced coffee tables, and reviews rained in on Washington. Most comments were glowing, a few neutral, fewer caustic. Hostile appraisals were expected from special pleaders, friends of March, of Clarence Edwards, of Leonard Wood, and others cast from the Pershing circle. Some adumbrations from Europe showed misunderstanding or fatuous acceptance. Military men wrote Pershing from everywhere in compliment or supplement; Harbord admired, as he would. Perhaps the most serious misappraisal came from an unlikely source, Capt. B. H. Liddell Hart of England. An old admirer, as much so as an Englishman might be, Liddell Hart, famed military critic and historian, had written a highly touted book in 1928 titled *Reputations—Ten Years After*, in which Pershing had fared fairly well. Upon reading Pershing's book, Liddell Hart lost some respect for the AEF's commander because "he revealed strange limitations of outlook and of knowledge in a man cast by fate for so big a role. More significantly still, he showed such an ingrained suspicion of other people's motives and recited with such obvious pride his own unconciliatory rejoinders that one could not help seeing that he must have been a very difficult team-mate."[87] This assessment showed the Englishman touchy about Pershing's candid recitation of troubles with Haig and Lloyd George and of English attempts to undercut and run around HAEF. Pershing's "limitations of outlook" were simply recognition of noncooperation.

Unexpectedly from his own viewpoint, Pershing won the Pulitzer Prize for history in 1932. The honor struck some critics as a sop to hero worship, but, if the book did not rank as great literature, it did deserve admiration as a splendid historical source. At least Pershing's book had considerable power of attraction. In 1932 Peyton March published *The Nation at War*, neither, he said, as rebuttal nor justification, but for the record. In fact March's book did abrade on Pershing's often: March found his own work usually responsible for Pershing's successes and attributed the commander-in-chief's criticisms to prejudice.

[87] B. H. Liddell Hart, "Pershing and His Critics," *Current History* 37 (Nov., 1932): 136.

Harbord, whose 1925 edition of *Leaves from a War Diary* offered a splendid primary account of his AEF career, refurbished that sparse diary in a full history of *The American Army in France* and put it into print in 1936—as a counterbattery action against March. So the war's leaders battled each other as Marshall had feared. But Pershing's almost glacial volumes endured controversy well and stood as his special monument to the AEF.

Increasingly the American Battle Monuments Commission consumed his days. He worked closely with the officers who served as secretaries; they found him helpful, always eager that cemeteries and monuments were tastefully, carefully done in ways to last. And he ran the commission as he ran everything else—by finding good men, backing them to the hilt, and looking over their shoulders.

And he pushed them with vigor. A concept gradually formed for the American Battle Monuments Commission that Pershing thought would maximize exposure and minimize expense: A cemetery near major cities would hold the hospital dead; major battlefields would have large cemeteries to which bodies from that battle and nearby fields would be consigned. Pershing insisted on this plan to give fallen soldiers a place on or near the fields they won.

Closely connected with graves preparation was the work of locating, designing, and constructing monuments. Pershing urged the commission to wide appreciation of American battle sites, including areas served by the navy. For the army it seemed to him that three kinds of service deserved recognition: minor action by Americans in training or Allied support sectors; major fighting by American units assigned to Allied armies; and decisive American battles. There would be small monuments at Blanc Mont Ridge in the French zone, near the Saint Quentin Canal Tunnel, and at Cantigny, between Ypres and Kemmel Hill in the British zone; small memorials, too, would commemorate the SOS at Tours and the Americans in Italy at Rome; there would be tablets at GHQ in Chaumont and at First Army Headquarters in Souilly. Three large monuments would mark the Second Marne at Château-Thierry, the Saint Mihiel offensive at Montec, and the Meuse-Argonne battle at Montfaucon.[88]

No field would be missed, no grave neglected; American families would be able to find their lost ones and to follow the advance of every American unit by the finest battlefield guide ever published.

[88] See Brig. Gen. Henry J. Reilly, "Pershing's Job Today: What the Wartime Leader Does," *World Today*, 1929, pp. 452, 454–55. Also in *World's Work* 57 (Nov., 1928): 31–36.

Endless details demanded Pershing's attention: selection of architects for the chapels to grace each cemetery, selection of materials, preparation of grounds, procurement of labor, preparation of budgets, defense of the program before Congress. The commission relied on Pershing for most of these activities; he was retired, after all. But these were sacred duties. Pershing picked architects with great care, accompanied them frequently to the battlefields, always had ideas on what they should design, and never hesitated to criticize plainly the things he disliked.[89] Sometimes this resulted in artistic heartburnings and military disgust—but the work progressed. All bodies left in France were collected for interment in the centralized cemeteries by 1922, a year before the commission received its congressional charter. Work had centered on cemetery construction and beautification. Pershing wanted visiting mothers to have places to sit amid well-kept rows of crosses; often, when he was on the grounds, he would escort Gold Star mothers through cemeteries with such pride as a bereaved commander knew.

A high moment came in the summer of 1937 when the great, soaring pillar crowned by Liberty's statue was dedicated at Montfaucon, France. In October the monument at Château-Thierry was dedicated by Jack, Charlie Dawes, and Jim Harbord together; it stood the proudest, gayest occasion, surely, of a long retirement.[90] Pershing spent much of 1937 in Europe, although his health troubled him a good bit. He went as official military representative of the United States to the coronation of King George VI. Papers picked up one facet of his trip that irked him a great deal—a special uniform he designed himself at a rumored astounding cost. He went because the president asked him to, not because of any attraction for royalty. "I suppose," he quipped to Martin Egan in April, 1937, "the representatives of democracy will be at the tail end of the procession."[91] But he looked impressive, anyway, in his blues and cockade, when he joined the glittering procession as cohort to knee-breeched U.S. Ambassador James W. Gerard. His presence caused much pleasure in England. Haig and Foch were gone, and Pershing came one of the last of the great World War leaders—a link with Britain's heritage that counted.

He always enjoyed England and France; they were places of his glory. Visits there eased some of the loneliness at home. Papa Warren

89 Author's interview with Maj. Gen. Thomas North, USA (Ret.), Apr., 1974.
90 See various letters of the American Battle Monuments Commission throughout 1937 in Box 27, PP.
91 JJP to Egan, Apr. 14, 1937, Box 69, PP.

was gone—he died on November 24, 1929, while still a member of the Senate. Son Warren pursued the active life of youth. Jack's own health seemed fragile. During his London visit in 1937, he suffered another slight heart seizure; arthritis increasingly irked, and he began to forego appearances in public. It seemed expected of a seventy-seven year old, but it bothered a normally active John Pershing. Friends noticed that he showed age now, his face lined heavily and his ramrod figure shrinking. That sort of thing bothered him, too; people should not see him as a ruin!

News of the world indicated ruin of another kind. Hitler's rise followed a hard treaty but no defeat, and the course of German resurgence cast a pall on the world. Armaments were changing rapidly. Although Pershing shared the general army glee that Billy Mitchell had been quenched if not squelched,[92] the reckless airman's prophecies were all too true. A German Luftwaffe was building. George Patton's fascination with tanks proved prophetic as well; the cavalry had gone into shining armor. Pershing's appreciation of new weapons alerted him to Germany's threat. In response to a request from President Franklin Roosevelt, Pershing prepared an estimate of Germany's military strength in September, 1935. Impressed himself at his findings, Jack reported that "there is no doubt that Germany is planning a strong army." He misjudged Teutonic speed when he guessed that "it will take some time." Still, within ten years he thought Hitler could handle "any eventuality."[93] It seemed, sadly, that Jack's own dread prediction of having to do "it all again" might be accurate. Indeed, as Germany menaced fearsomely in 1936, French sources were already wishing they had listened to him.[94]

Winters worked hardships on old joints, and in the hateful months he normally went to Tucson, where he lived in a hotel and took as much sun as possible. The winter of 1937–38 found him ensconced in that city noted for warm climate and warm people. A welcome guest much lionized locally, he became a kind of adopted Arizonan and enjoyed races and other sports events. That winter he seemed well enough, but in the spring severe chest pains signaled far more than rheumatism. Doctors rushed him to the Desert Sanitarium and called army specialists. Dr. Roland Davidson put him on oxygen; Dr. Shelly

[92] See JJP to John L. Hines, Nov. 22, 1925 (cable), in Tacna-Arica envelope, PP; JJP, Journal of Tacna-Arica, Nov. 22, 1925.

[93] JJP report to the president on the size and status of the German army, Sept. 6, 1935, Box 177, PP.

[94] See W. Morton Fullerton, "If They Had Listened to General Pershing," *Le Figaro*, March 30, 1936.

Marietta of San Antonio came, along with Dr. Verne Mason and the University of California's heart expert, Dr. William Kerr.

Bulletins signaled a long retreat: February 24, acute damage to heart muscles, coma; on the twenty-sixth, brief rally, coma, irregular pulse. The doctors called the family. May was already there; Warren, now a tall, handsome towhead like his father, arrived and gave May someone to fuss over. A faithful orderly, Sgt. C. C. Shaeffer, tried to spread optimism by announcing that "we refuse to believe it is the end." The doctors offered scant hope.

February 27 brought renal failure, uremic poisoning "of considerable magnitude." Headquarters of the Army was asked to send a funeral train to Tucson; two black-draped Pullmans (they would have sparked memories of a bygone train at Garrison, across from West Point) and an engine came from the Southern Pacific Railroad. Sergeant Shaeffer, wallowing in grief, called Washington for the general's best uniform.

February 28 found Pershing restless with fever; no renal improvement. The end could be expected at any moment.

Dr. Marietta hated to give up on an old fighter. He tried psychotherapy. Early in the morning, in those ebbing hours of darkness, he took Sergeant Shaeffer into Pershing's room. Red-eyed and heartsick, the sergeant bent over the bed and asked, "General, do you know who this is?"

Dr. Marietta, the nurses, all watched in despair, but the eyes opened, almost clear blue, and the General of the Armies snapped, "I don't know what you call yourself now, but you used to be Sgt. Schaeffer [sic]!" Everybody dissolved; the general was fighting back.[95] From that moment Pershing pushed recovery: by March 3 he was sitting up in bed; by the sixth his bed was wheeled into the sun and his kidneys were back to work; and by the 8th the bulletin read, "Kidney out put ample, heart regular."[96]

As symbol of his ultimate triumph, Pershing, slightly aided by George Adamson and Warren, boarded his "funeral train" and rode it happily to New York. At the station under the Waldorf, Pershing climbed into an elevator and sped to his suite on the twenty-fifth floor. Reason for the quick trip to New York: Warren's marriage, in late

[95] Eds. of *Army Times, Yanks Are Coming*, pp. 168–70. For an earlier account of JJP's illness, see an Associated Press story, "The Man Who Bosses Pershing Keeps Sad Vigil at Bedside," dated February 25, 1938.

[96] For the bulletins see Benjamin S. Abeshouse, M.D., *A Medical History of General John J. Pershing* (Eaton Laboratories, Norwich, N.Y., 1971), n.p., section entitled "Black Drapes at Tucson."

April, 1938, to Muriel Bache Richards, a lovely girl whom the general adored.

Warren pleased him mightily. He had, at last, accepted the idea that his son was a man. Their relations were not always clear—separation caused simple strangeness. Warren, raised by Aunt May and Grandpa Warren, found his father usually a tough "old gent" to know. They had become real friends in the last few years, and it warmed the marrow of Pershing's rheumatic bones. Warren, too, enjoyed knowing that "Black Jack," unlikely as it seemed, could be a man of affection and wit.[97]

Marriages and funerals took up a lot of time, with funerals running ahead. Most of Pershing's friends were gone or going. Correspondence in the late thirties became a clot of condolences to widows and, sometimes, widowers. There were bright spots. He watched the "Pershing men" in the army with pride. Especially did he watch George Marshall's continued rise to recognition. There had been a halt during Douglas MacArthur's tour as chief of staff. MacArthur, despite his spirited defense of Pershing's pension against a mean congressional streak, lost little love for the man who had pestered him in the past. There had been an unfortunate public episode—not a private one— connecting Pershing to Louise Cromwell Brooks, MacArthur's first wife. Pershing knew and liked her immensely, and she him, but romance really flamed between Louise and George Quekemeyer. Quek's tragic death in 1926 ended it. Stories of a Louise-Jack liaison lingered in the capital. One rumor had it that Pershing sent MacArthur to the Philippines in a kind of banishment as soon as he married Louise. Pershing resented the whole outcry, as did MacArthur.[98] Pershing kept pushing Marshall, though, and noted happily his promotion to a star and his rapid elevation afterwards. Malin Craig's career had soared and ebbed with time; the list ran long of distinctions for the Pershing clan. Marshall remained the brightest hope. Quek surely would have shared that limelight.

"You Are Magnificent"

Pershing realized as things worsened in Europe that Marshall might be the answer to American's unrecognized military problems. Although Pershing had worked to prepare a system for building an American

[97] Author's interviews with F. Warren Pershing, New York, N.Y., 1963, 1969, 1970.

[98] D. Clayton James, *The Years of MacArthur*, 1:291–92, 319–20, 672.

army in another emergency, the country languished in the same kind of unpreparedness he had faced in 1917. Years of preaching on every podium, preaching of the need to be ready, had fallen on closed ears. No country is ever as unready as a democracy convinced of its own virtue. Nothing could bother the United States. Even Charles Lindbergh, who ranked the greatest American hero of the twentieth century—not excluding John Pershing—talked openly of trouble in Europe being kept there; America ought to think of itself first. But Hitler marched on Poland in September, 1939, and the world was again at war.

By every military and economic consideration he could assess, Pershing had guessed against war so soon. So had Charlie Dawes. But, as Jack confessed to Charlie on September 6, 1939, their "conclusions would have applied had we been considering normal human beings, but as it turns out it is clear that the leader of the German Government today does not belong to that class. In my opinion he is really a mad man. . . . It is a tragic thought for all of us who fought in the last World War. . . ."[99]

Age's infirmities increased. Pershing had made a last swing to his European fields in the spring of 1939 and still tried to attend the annual gatherings of the *Baltic* Society—that convivial group who met to commemorate the voyage of so long ago—but finally moved into a suite in Washington's Walter Reed Hospital. From his fourth floor eyrie, he looked out on a warring world. He read the news avidly and basked in the realization that his patronage of Marshall probably made George chief of staff in 1939—no better man could manage the expansion of the army. Marshall tried to keep his old chieftain informed, would brief him frequently. But it was hard to escape a sense of exclusion.

A "sitzkrieg" following Germany's initial thrust into Poland made scant sense to a fighter, but Pershing realized that Germany simply worked to assess the lessons of early campaigns and would strike France when ready. Roosevelt, keenly aware of Allied deficiencies, eager to win American friendship to Britain and France, aware, too, that America would probably have to enter the war to keep it away, invited Pershing to the White House in May, 1940. It was an official visit, replete with black limousine. France had been invaded; Pershing was a symbol of a firm alliance. He put aside his cane on the porch, straightened the gray Homburg, pulled himself to attention, fixed the cameras with cold eyes, and had his picture taken—a hateful business.

[99] JJP to Dawes, Sept. 6, 1939, Box 60, PP.

Then he went inside to talk to the president. One newsman said in awe: "Here we go again."[100]

A group of preparedness-minded citizens, men like Will Clayton of Texas, agreed with Roosevelt that the United States must aid the Allies. Britain, perhaps compelled to stand alone, would need all shipping support possible, something Pershing understood. But isolationism swept the nation; people watched in horror as Europe crumbled and wanted no part in the wreckage. There must be a gesture, some offer of help, not just to encourage the flagging Allies but also to tip the sentiments of Americans. Who had sufficient prestige to command an audience and compel compliance? John Pershing. Would he make a nationwide radio broadcast urging the offer of fifty World War I destroyers to Britain in exchange for Atlantic bases? His doctors advised against it, but the president asked him.

In the evening of August 4, 1940, his Missouri voice, still with that flat crack Foch had heard so long ago, went across the land.

Fellow citizens: I am speaking tonight because I consider it my duty. It is my duty to tell you that in my opinion we face problems of the utmost seriousness, and all the things we hold most dear are gravely threatened. . . . More than half the world is ruled by men who despise the American idea and have sworn to destroy it. They know that while one great people remains independent and free because it is strong and is brave, they can never crush finally the people they have conquered. . . . The appeasors of eight nations are dead or in jail or discredited and ruined. . . . It is not hysterical to insist that democracy and liberty are threatened. . . . We must be ready to meet force with a stronger force. . . .

Then he spoke of the destroyers, of Britain's need for help on the sea, and he urged the next few weeks as critical. This was no time to shrink from duty; America had to face its peril openly and do everything it could to be ready for defense. It was a new kind of war Americans would have to meet—one fought everywhere, including home. The general closed with a call to recognize the new revolution against democracy: "We can see it developing right before our very eyes. It must be faced with daring and with devotion. We must lift up our hearts. We must reaffirm our noble traditions and make ourselves so strong that the traditions we live by shall not perish from the earth."[101]

Britain got her destroyers. In December, 1941, Japan, Pershing's loved old haunt, attacked Pearl Harbor. Pen went to paper and the General of the Armies wrote his Commander in Chief:

100 *Time*, Nov. 15, 1943, p. 60.
101 Vandiver, *Illustrious Americans: John J. Pershing*, pp. 227–29.

December 10, 1941

Dear Mr. President:

All Americans today are united in one ambition—to take whatever share they can in the defense of their country.

As one among these millions, I hasten to offer my services, in any way in which my experience and my strength, to the last ounce, will be of help in the fight.

With supreme confidence that, under your calm and determined leadership, we will retain our balance, despite foul blows, I am

Faithfully yours,
John J. Pershing.

Touched and impressed, pleased, too, at a letter valuable in the press, Roosevelt replied:

Dear General:

You are magnificent. You always have been—and you always will be. I am deeply grateful to you for your letter of Dec. 10.

Under a wise law, you have never been placed on the retired list. You are very much on the active list, and your services will be of great value.

Always sincerely,
Franklin D. Roosevelt.[102]

Pershing, though, knew he would not be a partner in the war. In fact he seemed a ceremonial mannequin bowed to on needful occasions. Time passed in Walter Reed without much save old friends to fill the days. Letters from the Harbords and the Daweses continued; George Marshall came when he could, to talk of the war. But what, really, did an eighty-one-year-old have to contribute? He watched with pride as the Pattons and the Marshalls did well. He had given Georgie his blessing in a touching Walter Reed farewell.

Marshall and MacArthur, who was, after all, a kind of Pershing man, both looked out for Warren. The young Pershing enlisted in the army, asked especially that his father do him no favors, and worked up through Officer's Candidate School; Marshall handed him his commission in 1942, and MacArthur asked the general to send Warren to him as an aide.[103] It was a fine gesture from a good soldier. Warren made it on his own. So did other Pershing relatives; he never tried to interfere in personnel arrangements.

Save once. In 1943 the Joint Allied Staff decided to trade Marshall and Eisenhower and have Marshall lead the invasion of France. Mar-

102 "Pershing Offers Aid to the Last Ounce," United Press dispatch printed in *New York Times*, Dec. 10, 1941. See Box 177, PP, for letters to and from FDR.
103 Douglas MacArthur to JJP, Feb. 15, 1942, Box 120, PP.

shall coveted the job, FDR virtually promised it to him; even old friend Henry Stimson, secretary of war, agreed. But Pershing, approached by Malin Craig as spokesman for a group of worried officers, agreed that Marshall alone could run a multi-theater war. He wrote Roosevelt that he had been so greatly disturbed by reports of Marshall's possible departure that he wanted to "express my fervent hope that these reports are unfounded. . . . We need our most accomplished officer as Chief of Staff. . . . that officer is General Marshall. . . . I know of no one at all comparable to replace him as Chief of Staff."

Roosevelt replied that Pershing was both right and wrong; Marshall was the most valuable man as chief of staff, but the operations he was likely to conduct might be the most important of the war. And FDR ended on a flattering note. "I want George to be the Pershing of the second World War—and he cannot be if we keep him here. I know you will understand."[104] But Marshall stayed chief of staff.

Strange that Pershing should have so changed his views as to think the most important job was chief of staff, that he would think field command in Europe secondary. Peyton March must have smiled.

Finally the war dwindled toward an Allied—especially an American—victory. On September 13, 1944, Pershing's eighty-fourth birthday, Eisenhower sent a thoughtful teletype: "The A.E.F. of 1944 sends birthday felicitations and best wishes to the great American soldier who led their fathers to victory twenty-six years ago over the same battlefields we are traversing today. . . . Please permit me personally to wish you many happy returns of the day and to express to you my sincere and respectful admiration and regard. Your example has been an inspiration to me in many moments of trial." It was handsome amends for not taking proper leave of the General of the Armies before going to England. Ike, too, commented that first looks indicated the American battle monuments and cemeteries were in good shape— once a Pershing man, always one![105]

Pershing wanted desperately to go to Europe to salute Ike's men on their victory but was too weak. He admired these new Doughboys as the old, had written survivors of the class of '86—he still kept his duties as class president—in glowing terms of American bravery in the war. He would have liked to acknowledge it personally.[106]

During the war various visitors called; there was an embarrassing

[104] Quoted in O'Connor, *BJP*, pp. 384–85.
[105] Dwight D. Eisenhower to JJP, Sept. 13, 1944 (cable), copy in Box 37, Eisenhower Papers, Johns Hopkins University Library, Baltimore, Md.
[106] Eds. of *Army Times, Yanks Are Coming*, p. 172.

moment for the staff when General De Gaulle came in 1944, and Pershing asked about Marshal Pétain! Callers were increasingly unhappy at Pershing's appearance; he did get crotchety. May Pershing moved to a nearby room in the hospital, read to him frequently, as did shifts of nurses. And at the real end of the war, in the Age of the Atomic Bomb, Harry S. Truman, new president, sent his former chieftain a marvelous birthday message:

September 13, 1945

Dear General Pershing:
    This should be one of the happiest of your many birthdays as you remember that this time we went all the way through to Berlin, as you counseled in 1918. I hail a great soldier who happily exemplified also the vision of the statesman.
    With every good wish.
Very sincerely yours,
Harry S. Truman.[107]

There were little annoyances of being shuffled off what little stage remained—the administration got involved in a laughable business of moving the Office of the General of the Armies from the Old State, War and Navy Building to the new Pentagon—and lots of veterans roared anger from around the nation. That brought the frosty smile.

A warm smile came in 1946 when Congress passed an act "Authorizing the President of the United States to award a special medal to General of the Armies of the United States John J. Pershing." The act said, flatteringly, that the medal would recognize "peerless leadership, heroic achievements, and great military victories . . . gallant and unselfish devotion to the service of his country in his contribution to the preparation for, and the prosecution of, World War II," and would be presented by the president in the name of the people.[108] A good deal of administrative slippage followed passage of the act—it seemed to lack urgency. But Congressman Henry D. Larcade, Jr., of Louisiana had a deep interest in this medal—he kept pushing. And at last, on October 17, 1947, Maj. Gen. Harry Vaughn, Truman's military aide, presented the specially designed medal. It was in Walter Reed, but on one of the good days. And the medal seemed, somehow, to say a lot of things the American people had not said, seemed to reach back to rub away neglect and denial, and to thank a soldier for his life.

    [107] Harry S. Truman to JJP, Sept. 13, 1945, Pershing Papers, Truman Library, Independence, Mo.
    [108] Private Law 831, 79th Cong., 2 sess., ch. 828, copy in Pershing Papers, Truman Library.

Winter passed in its chilling time and spring came again to Washington. The cherry trees, people said, looked beautiful as ever, and the boulevards were bustling with lovely young things. Good days dwindled in a long retreat, but there were lucid times when the eyes cleared and May was there, often Warren and his boys, others, old Charlie Dawes, who kept on doing good, Barney Baruch, solid friend of later years, generals—Marshall, the victors of the war, but not Georgie, who was dead. Visitors came who remembered and who admired duty done with honor.

It was 3:50 A.M. the morning of July 15, 1948. A nurse, suddenly worried, called Dr. Marietta—that good friend—who bent over a stethoscope on the shrunken chest, listened, and arose. The General of the Armies was dead. Harry Truman told the world that "in peace, no less than in war, he retained the dignity and modest bearing characteristic of the true soldier."

He had asked to be buried in Arlington Cemetery. After a great state funeral he was interred beneath an enlisted man's headstone in that section of Arlington reserved for the AEF—he was out on a knoll in front of his men. They had been waiting for their commander-in-chief.

Bibliography

Interviews and Oral History Memoirs

Aguinaldo, Emilio. Interview. Manila, P.I., Aug. 14, 1962.

Baruch, Bernard. Interview. New York, N.Y., Oct. 17, 1961.

Castle, Benjamin. Memoir. Oral History Collection, Columbia University, New York, N.Y.

Collins, Brig. Gen. James L. Interview. Carlisle Barracks, Pa., Apr., 1974.

Foulois, Maj. Gen. Benjamin. Interviews with author and Maj. Perry Craddock. Andrews Air Force Base, Md., Mar. 8, 9, 1960.

————. Memoir. Oral History Collection, Columbia University, New York, N.Y.

Frey, John P. Memoir. Oral History Collection, Columbia University, New York, N.Y.

Gilhouser, Col. Henry. Interview. Manila, P.I., Aug. 15, 1962.

Hoover, Herbert. Interview. New York, N.Y., Oct. 17, 1961.

Marshall, Brig. Gen. S. L. A. Interview. Colorado Springs, Colo., Oct. 5–6, 1972.

North, Maj. Gen. Thomas. Interviews. Washington, D.C., Feb., Apr., 1974.

Pershing, F. Warren. Interviews. New York, N.Y., various times, 1960–1970.

Rickenbacker, Capt. Eddie. Interview. Houston, Tex., 1961.

Simpson, Gen. William Hood, and Mrs. Simpson. Interviews with author and his wife, San Antonio, Tex., various times, 1960–1969, 1974.

Spalding, Brig. Gen. Isaac. Interview with Lt. Col. Thomas Stone. Jan. 6, 1971.

Steeves, Mrs. Myron. Interview. Houston, Tex., 1963 (Mrs. Steeves lived as a child in quarters near the Pershings at the San Francisco Presidio).

Newspapers

Army and Navy Journal, 1885–1924, and scattered later issues.

Cheyenne (Wyo.) *Leader*, May 10, 1912.

Chicago Sunday Tribune Graphic Magazine, Nov. 30, 1952.

El Paso (Tex.) *Herald*, Sept. 8, 1915.

Houston Chronicle, April 25, 1967.

Houston Tribune, Oct. 13, 1966.

Kirksville Normal School Index, 1880–1881.

Laclede (Mo.) *Review*, Sept. 13, 1960.

Lincoln (Neb.) *Evening Journal*, Feb. 6, 1938.
Linneus (Mo.) *Bulletin*, Oct. 27, 1881.
The Times (London), 1917–1948.
Manila Times, 1906–1914.
New York Herald, 1906.
New York Sun, June 11, 1912.
New York Times, 1897–1948.
New York Evening World, May 27, 1912.
New York World, June 7, 1913.
Omaha (Nebr.) *World*, May 4, 1937.
Philadelphia North American, June 11, 1912.
San Francisco Bulletin, Jan. 13, 1914.
San Francisco Chronicle, 1914–1915.
San Francisco Examiner, Jan. 14, 1914.
San Francisco News Letter, Jan. 24, 1914.
Silver City (N.M.) *Enterprise*, 1886.
Stars and Stripes, 1917–1919.
Sombrero (University of Nebraska), 1895.
Sulu News, 1911.
Transport Ace (S.S. *Leviathan*), Sept. 2, 1919.
The Hesperian (University of Nebraska), 1891–1895.
Washington (D.C.) *Evening Star*, 1896–1898.
Washington (D.C.) *Herald*, March 11, 1910, June 11, 1912.
Washington (D.C.) *Post*, June 7, 1913.
Washington (D.C.) *Sunday Star*, Apr. 19, 1942.

Unpublished Sources

American Expeditionary Forces War Diary, 1917–1919, kept at headquarters daily. Typescript volumes in Records of the AEF, Record Group 120, National Archives, Washington, D.C.

Baker, Newton D. Papers. Library of Congress, Washington, D.C. An important collection for any work on America's part in World War I.

Baldwin, T. A. "Report of Operations Tenth Cavalry, Since July 1, 1898." 3849 ACP 1886, Record Group 94, National Archives, Washington, D.C.

Barrett, Grady. "Pershing at Close Range" (typescript in author's possession). Mr. Barrett, of San Antonio, Tex., was an army field clerk at HAEF.

Bateman, Mrs. Cephas C. "True Indian Stories and Ft. Assinniboine, Montana." Manuscript owned by Mrs. Diane Davidson, Fair Oaks, Calif. (copy in author's possession).

Benson, Sir Rex. "Diary of the World War." Manuscript in possession of the heirs of Sir Rex Benson, London, England.

Bliss, Tasker H. "Report of General T. H. Bliss on the Supreme War Council" to Secretary Newton D. Baker, Washington, D.C., Feb. 6, 1920. Typescript in AEF, GHQ, G-3, Folder 1338-C, Record Group 120, National Archives, Washington, D.C.

[Boyd, Carl ?] "Notes on Conference Between General Pershing, Marshal Foch, and General Pétain at Bombon, September 2, 1918." AEF, GHQ, G-3, Folder 656, Record Group 120, National Archives, Washington, D.C.

[Boyd, Carl ?] "Notes on Conversation Between General Pershing and General Pétain, August 31, 1918. On General Pétain's Train at Nettancourt." AEF, GHQ, G-3, Folder 986-A, Record Group 120, National Archives, Washington, D.C.

Boyd, Carl. "Notes on Conversation Between General Pershing and Marshal Foch on August 30, 1918 at Ligny-en-Barrois." AEF, GHQ, G-3, Folder 986-A, Record Group 120, National Archives, Washington, D.C.

Brown, William Carey. Papers. U.S. Army Military History Research Collection, Carlisle Barracks, Pa.

Chynoweth, Bradford G. Papers. U.S. Army Military History Research Collection, Carlisle Barracks, Pa.

Clemenceau, Georges. Collection. French Military Archives, Vincennes, France. An extensive collection of papers dealing with Clemenceau's direction of, and interest in, military affairs.

Collins, James Lawton. "Report of Bagsak Campaign." Copy furnished by Brig. Gen. J. L. Collins, Washington, D.C.

de Francisco, Joseph E. "Amalgamation: A Critical Issue in British-American Command Relations, 1917–1918." Master's thesis, Rice University, 1973.

Dewees, A. Draper. "Fifth Corps Headquarters; A Record of Experiences with the American Expeditionary Forces during the World War in France." A. Draper Dewees Papers, U.S. Army Military History Research Collection, Carlisle Barracks, Pa.

Dodds, Harold. Letters to the author, 1970–72.

Drum, Hugh. "Diary of General Hugh Drum, USA: 17 May 1917–15 May 1918." In possession of Hugh Drum Johnson, Closter, N.J. (copy furnished by Prof. Alan R. Millet, Ohio State University).

Duncan, George B. "Reminiscences of the World War." Typescript in University of Kentucky Library, Lexington (copy furnished through the courtesy of Prof. Edward Coffman, University of Wisconsin).

Eisenhower, Dwight D. Papers. The Johns Hopkins University Library, Baltimore, Md.

Eltinge, LeRoy. "Plan for Keeping Lists of Officers for Staff Duty and Higher Command." Attached to JJP to Chief of Staff, HAEF, Oct. 2, 1917, Office of CIC Correspondence, File 3358, Record Group 120, National Archives, Washington, D.C.

Finley, John P. "A Synopsis of the Progressive Development of the Moro Province." Typescript in Finley Papers, U.S. Army Military History Research Collection, Carlisle Barracks, Pa.

Fitzhamon, E. G. "The Only True & Accurate Story of the Dreadful Fire at S. F. Presidio, Where Mrs. Pershing and Three Children Perished" (written Aug. 27, 1915). Archives of the Presidio, San Francisco, Calif.

Funston, Frederick. "Annual Report for the Southern Department, 1916." AGO Records, Record Group 94, National Archives, Washington, D.C.

Goodin, Katherine K. "The Early Life of General John Joseph Pershing." Master's thesis, Northeast Missouri State Teacher's College, 1954.

Great Britain. War Cabinet Minutes (Cab. 23). Public Record Office, London.

————. War Office papers relating to the AEF (WO 106/468). Public Record Office, London.

Haig, Douglas. Papers. National Library of Scotland, Edinburgh. An extensive collection covering all phases of Haig's military and personal life. There is a detailed "Diary" (in multiple volumes) included which illuminates every day of the British army's service in France, 1914–1918. The papers of Haig constitute one of the essential sources for the history of the Great War. The author is indebted to the present Earl Haig and to Prof. Hugh Trevor-Roper, Oxford University, for permission to use the Haig Papers.

Hines, Gen. John L. Memoir. Typescript in John L. Hines Papers, U.S. Army Military History Research Collection, Carlisle Barracks, Pa.

Hixson, John A. "The United States Army General Staff Corps, 1910–1917: Its Relationship to the Field Forces." Master's thesis, Rice University, 1971.

"Important Conferences, Memoranda, Etc., Affecting Employment of the AEF." GHQ, G-3, Folder 655, Record Group 120, National Archives, Washington, D.C.

"Important Letters and Memoranda on Employment of the AEF." GHQ, G-3, Folder 675, Record Group 120, National Archives, Washington, D.C.

Lee, Fitzhugh. Papers. University of Arizona Library, Tucson. These papers contain copies of daily situation reports from Pershing's Mexican expedition, sent to General Funston. Colonel Lee was Funston's aide.

Lindt, Mrs. John H. Recollections of Presidio of San Francisco Fire (copy in author's possession).

Lloyd George, David. Papers. Beaverbrook Library, London. An important collection, with much material on British-American relations.

MacArthur, Douglas. Statement concerning General Pershing, Aug. 22, 1960 (copy in author's possession).

Meiklejohn, George D. Papers. Nebraska State Historical Society, Lincoln.

"Memorandum of Conference Between General Alvaro Obregón, Secretary of War of the Republic of Mexico, Major General Hugh L. Scott, Chief of Staff, U.S.A., and Major General Frederick Funston, U.S.A. . . ." (May 2, 1916). Lee Papers, University of Arizona, Tucson.

Palmer, John McA. "Report of Official Journey—August 18–21, 1917." Typescript in AEF, GHQ, G-3, Folder 1108-A, Record Group 120, National Archives, Washington, D.C.

Pershing, (Helen) Frances Warren. "New Pocket Diary for 1907." Box 2, Pershing Papers, Library of Congress, Washington, D.C.

Pershing, John Joseph. Papers. Library of Congress, Washington, D.C. This large aggregation of personal letters, memoranda, diaries, memorabilia, official correspondence, and Christmas cards fills over one hundred file boxes. It is carefully catalogued (save for some recently added material) and access is made easier by an index. This collection is vital to any Pershing study and to any serious study of World War I. Especially important is Pershing's Diary, 1917–1925 (Boxes 4–5), which formed the basis for much of his book *My Experiences in the World War* and chronicles his postwar life. Pershing paraphrased his wartime diary entries as chapter introductions in *My Experiences in the World War*.

Although the original is often fuller, sometimes different, the author has generally followed the printed version. This was done to enable others to check material more easily. In instances where differences are substantial, both versions are given.

Recent additions (in 1975–1976) to the papers vastly enhance their value as a source for Pershing's personal life. Perhaps the most useful material in the whole collection is contained in the two unpublished volumes of Pershing's "Memoirs" (the draft of 1937 is the best), which recount his prewar career in vivid prose.

Also of value is Pershing's Journal of Tacna-Arica in Box 334, which offers special insight into frustration.

———. Appointment, Commission, and Promotion (ACP) File, AGO, filed under 3849 ACP 86, Record Group 94, National Archives, Washington, D.C. This file contains invaluable official material on Pershing's military career.

———. "Report of the Punitive Expedition to June 30, 1916," and "Report of the Punitive Expedition, July 1916–February 1917." AGO Records, Record Group 94, National Archives, Washington, D.C.

———. Papers. Gift Collection, Record Groups 200, 220, National Archives, Washington, D.C.

———. Papers, 1916–1924, 1931–1939. Record Group 316, National Archives, Washington, D.C.

———. File. Harry S. Truman Library, Independence, Mo.

———. Student record card of, First District Normal School. Manuscript in Northeast Missouri State College Archives, Kirksville.

———. Papers. Pershing Home, Laclede, Mo.

———. File. Nebraska Historical Society, Lincoln.

———. Papers. In possession of Mrs. Marlene Muffie MacNeal, Houston, Tex. A small collection of family papers from a collateral Pershing line.

———. Papers. Rice University Archives, Houston, Tex. A small group of miscellaneous Pershing letters.

[———, and Maj. Gen. William Lassiter.] "Joint Report to the Arbitrator, Tacna-Arica Arbitration. . . ." Records Relating to International Arbitrations, Record Group 76, National Archives, Washington, D.C.

Quai d'Orsay, Records of. Etats-Unis, Armée Américaine. A series of volumes dealing with U.S. troops in France during World War I. Highly important for French views. Copies of these papers are in the French military archives at Vincennes.

———. Opérations Stratégiques, Dossier Général. Copies in French military archives, Vincennes.

Quekemeyer, George. Papers. Yazoo City, Miss. An important collection of letters and official documents concerning the career of one of John J. Pershing's most trusted aides. The author is indebted to Mrs. Andrew B. Clark, Yazoo City, for permission to use this collection.

Rhodes, Charles D. "Diary (10 June 1885–25 April 1886.)" Typescript in U.S. Military Academy Library, West Point, N.Y.

———. "Diary Notes of the Pine Ridge or Brulé Sioux Indian Campaign of 1890–91." Typescript in U.S. Military Academy Library, West Point, N.Y.

———. "Diary of the Spanish War, June 7–14, 1898." Typescript in U.S. Military Academy Library, West Point, N.Y.

———. "Diary of the World War." Typescript in U.S. Military Academy Library, West Point, N.Y.

Scott, Hugh L. Papers. Library of Congress, Washington, D.C. An extensive collection dealing with the full career of General Scott in the American West and during the border crisis. There are many letters to and from John J. Pershing in this collection.

Sladen, Frederick W. Family Papers. U.S. Army Military History Research Collection, Carlisle Barracks, Pa. This collection contains letters from Brigadier General Sladen to his wife during 1919. The author is indebted to Dr. Richard Sommers of the Research Collection for this reference.

Straight, Willard. Papers. Collection of Regional History and University Archives, John M. Olin Library, Cornell University, Ithaca, N.Y. There are some fine letters from Straight to his wife from France, 1918, contained in these papers.

University of Nebraska Archives, Lincoln. Record Group 1/1/1.

Warren, Frances. "Diary, 1903–1904." Box 2, Pershing Papers, Library of Congress, Washington, D.C.

Warren, Francis Emory. Papers. Western History Research Collection, University of Wyoming, Laramie. A large body of letters, ledgers, business archives, and personal papers that touch on all facets of Warren's active life and careers. These papers are essential for any Pershing, Warren, or Wyoming historical study. Microfilm copies of many letter press volumes are in the author's possession.

Washington, D.C. National Archives. Record Groups 76, 77, 94, 98, 107, 108, 120, 200, 220, 316, 393, and 395. For complete information, see citations of specific letters, reports, and documents listed by author and title.

Wilson, Woodrow. Papers. Library of Congress, Washington, D.C. An extensive collection dealing with all phases of Wilson's career. The wartime papers were consulted for this study. There is an additional source of Wilson material contained in the editorial offices of the Woodrow Wilson *Papers* at Princeton University, Princeton, N.J. Prof. Arthur Link, editor of this admirable documentary collection, is invariably helpful to all students of any facet of Wilson's life. He was generous in his searchings for Pershing material.

Winnia, Lt. Col. Charles. Papers. Fondren Library, Rice University, Houston. These papers contain a map issued to Punitive Expedition officers by the War College Division of the General Staff. The collection preserves a lively exchange of letters between Winnia, who enlisted for the Spanish-American War and remained in the regular army, and his family. The papers were presented to Rice University by Colonel Winnia's daughter, Mrs. Diane Davidson, of Fair Oaks, Calif.

Published Sources

A Brief History of the Sixth Armored Cavalry Regiment from Its Establishment to the Current Day, 1861–1968. N.p., n.d.

Abell, Tyler, ed. *Drew Pearson Diaries, 1949–1959.* New York, 1974.

Abeshouse, Benjamin S., M.D. *A Medical History of General John J. Pershing.* Norwich, N.Y., 1971.

"Adair of Carrizal." *United States Cavalry Journal* 27 (Nov., 1916).

Adam, G. Mercer. *The Canadian North-West: Its History and Troubles.* Toronto, 1885.

Adams, Henry. *The Education of Henry Adams: An Autobiography.* Boston and New York, 1918.

Alger, Russell A. *The Spanish-American War.* New York and London, 1901.

Almada, Francisco R. *La Revolución en el Estado de Chihuahua.* 2 vols. Chihuahua, Mexico, 1964.

Ambrose, Stephen E. *Duty, Honor, Country: A History of West Point.* Baltimore, 1966.

American Battle Monuments Commission. *American Armies and Battlefields in Europe: A History Guide and Reference Book.* Washington, D.C., 1944.

Andrews, Avery D. *My Friend and Classmate, John J. Pershing.* Harrisburg, Pa., 1939.

"Annual Report of the Bureau of Insular Affairs." In *Annual Report of the Secretary of War,* vol. 10. House Doc. No. 2, 59th Cong., 1st sess. Washington, D.C., 1905.

Applin, R. V. K. "Tactics of the Machine Gun." *United States Infantry Journal* 14 (Apr., 1918).

The Army Almanac: A Book of Facts Concerning the United States Army. Harrisburg, Pa., 1959.

Association of the United States Army. *Infantry in Battle.* Washington, D.C., 1939.

Atherton, Lewis E. "The Merchant Sutler in the Pre–Civil War Period." *Southwestern Social Science Quarterly* 19 (1938–39).

"The Attack on Our Cavalry at Parral." *United States Cavalry Journal* 27 (Oct., 1916).

Atterbury, W. W. "The Army and Its Future." *United States Infantry Journal* 16 (Sept., 1919).

Augur, Col. J. A. "The Cavalry in Southern Luzon." *United States Cavalry Journal* 13 (Apr., 1903).

Ayres, Leonard P. *The War With Germany: A Statistical Summary.* Washington, D.C., 1919.

Bacon, Robert, and James B. Scott, eds. *The Military and Colonial Policy of the United States: Addresses and Reports by Elihu Root.* Cambridge, Mass., 1916.

Baker, Ray Stannard. *Woodrow Wilson: Life and Letters.* Reprint, 8 vols. New York, 1968.

Behymer, F. A. "General Pershing's Human Qualities Recalled by St. Louis Dentist." *Missouri Legionnaire* (July, 1948).

Beisner, Robert L. "Gloom, Gloom, Gloom, and Scarce One Ray of Light: Ruminations of E. L. Godkin and Charles Eliot Norton." *American Heritage* 18 (Aug., 1967).

———. *Twelve Against Empire: The Anti-Imperialists, 1898–1900.* New York, 1968.

Bennitt, Rudolf, and Werner O. Nagel. *A Survey of the Resident Game & Furbearers of Missouri.* University of Missouri Studies, no. 12. Columbia, Mo., 1937.

Bethel, Elizabeth. "The Military Information Division: Origin of the Intelligence Division." *Military Affairs* 11 (Spring, 1947).

Bliss, Tasker H. "The Strategy of the Allies." *Current History* 29 (Nov., 1928).

Blumenson, Martin. *The Patton Papers, 1885–1940.* Boston, 1972.

Bray, Willis J. "General John Joseph Pershing." *Nemoscope* (Summer–Fall, 1948).

Briscoe, Edward. "Pershing's Chinese Refugees in Texas." *Southwestern Historical Quarterly* 62 (Apr., 1959).

Brooke, Lord. *An Eye-Witness in Manchuria.* London, 1905.

Brophy, Leo P. "Origins of the Chemical Corps." *Military Affairs* 20 (Winter, 1956).

Broun, Heywood. *The A.E.F.: With General Pershing and the American Forces.* New York, 1918.

Broun, W. C. "Incidents in Aguinaldo's Capture." *United States Infantry Journal* 26 (June, 1925).

Brownell, Atherton. "Turning Savages Into Citizens." *Outlook,* Dec. 24, 1910.

Buhn, Mina Clark. "Early Days Along the Niobrara." *Nebraska History Magazine* 14 (1933).

Bullard, Robert Lee. *Personalities and Reminiscences of the War.* Garden City, N.Y., 1925.

Byron, George Gordon, Lord. *Childe Harold's Pilgrimage.* London, 1816.

Campbell, Clark S. *The '03 Springfield.* Beverly Hills, Calif., 1957.

Campobello, Nellie. *Apuntes Sobre la Vida Militar de Francisco Villa.* Mexico City, 1940.

Carter, W. H. *From Yorktown to Santiago with the Sixth U.S. Cavalry.* Baltimore, 1900.

——. *The Life of Lieutenant General Chaffee.* Chicago, 1917.

Cashin, H. V., and others. *Under Fire with the Tenth U.S. Cavalry.* Reprint. New York, 1969.

Castle, Benjamin F. "Possibilities of the Air Service." *United States Infantry Journal* 16 (Oct., 1919).

"The Cavalry Fight at Columbus." *United States Cavalry Journal* 27 (Nov., 1916).

"The Cavalry Fight at Ojos Azules." *United States Cavalry Journal* 27 (Jan. 1917).

"Cavalry Lessons of the Great War from German Sources." *United States Cavalry Journal* 30 (Oct., 1921).

Chamberlain, Weston P. "Hints for Line Officers Regarding the Diseases Liable to be Met With in Mexico and the General Methods of Combating Them." *Journal of the Military Service Institution of the United States* 54 (May–June, 1914).

Citizen's Military Training Camp [Maj. Earl L. Parmenter, USA, Director]. *The Peep Sight of Fort Sam Houston, 1923.* Dixon, Ill., 1923.

Clark, William F. *Over There with O'Ryan's Roughnecks.* Seattle, Wash., 1966.

Claudy, C. H. "Fighting With Axe and Saw." *Scientific American,* Sept. 22, 1917.

Clendenen, Clarence C. *Blood on the Border: The United States Army and the Mexican Irregulars.* New York, 1969.

————. "The Punitive Expedition of 1916: A Re-Evaluation." *Arizona and the West* 3 (Winter, 1961).

————. *The United States and Pancho Villa: A Study in Unconventional Diplomacy.* Ithaca, N.Y., 1961.

Coffman, Edward M. "Army Life on the Frontier, 1865–1898." *Military Affairs* 20 (Winter, 1956).

————. "The Battle Against Red Tape: Business Methods of the War Department General Staff, 1917–1918." *Military Affairs* 26 (Spring, 1962).

————. *The Hilt of the Sword: The Career of Peyton C. March.* Madison, Wisc., 1966.

————. *The War to End All Wars: The American Military Experience in World War I.* New York, 1968.

Collier's War Correspondents. *The Russo-Japanese War: A Descriptive Review of the Great Conflict in the Far East.* New York, 1905.

"The Conquest of Bubonic Plague in the Philippines." *National Geographic Magazine* 14 (May, 1903).

Connolly, C. P. "Senator Warren of Wyoming." *Collier's,* Aug. 31, 1912.

Coox, Alvin D. "General Narcisse Chauvineau: False Apostle of Prewar French Military Doctrine." *Military Affairs* 37 (Feb., 1973).

Cotton, Robert C. "A Study of the St. Mihiel Offensive." *United States Infantry Journal* 17 (July, 1920).

Craig, George C. "The American Victories Before Manila." *Journal of the Military Service Institution of the United States* 26 (Jan., 1900).

Cram, George F. *Cram's Unrivaled Family Atlas of the World.* Chicago, 1885.

Cramer, Stuart W., Jr., "The Punitive Expedition from Boquillas." *United States Cavalry Journal* 27 (Nov., 1916).

Dallam, Samuel F. "The Punitive Expedition of 1916." *United States Cavalry Journal* 36 (July, 1927).

Daly, H. W. "The Geronimo Campaign." *United States Cavalry Journal* 19 (July, 1908).

Daniel, Hawthorne. "They Have Come for the Sake of France." *World's Work* 35 (Dec., 1917).

Davis, Richard Harding. *The Cuban and Porto Rican Campaigns.* New York, 1898.

Dawes, Charles G. *A Journal of the Great War.* 2 vols. Boston and New York, 1921.

de Barneville, Maurice F., "The Remount Service in the A.E.F." *United States Cavalry Journal* 30 (Apr., 1921).

de Chambrun, [Jacques], and [Charles] de Marenches. *The American Army in the European Conflict.* New York, 1919.

de Los Reyes, Isabelo. "Biographical Sketch of Emilio Aguinaldo." *United States Cavalry Journal* 12 (Jan., 1903).

Dewar, George A. B., assisted by J. H. Boraston. *Sir Douglas Haig's Command, December 19, 1915 to November 11, 1918.* 2 vols. London, 1922.

DeWeerd, Harvey A. *President Wilson Fights His War: World War I and the American Intervention.* New York, 1968.

De Witt, John L. "Supply Functions of the General Staff." *United States Infantry Journal* 16 (May, 1920).

Dick, Everett N. "Problems of the Frontier Prairie City as Portrayed by Lincoln, Nebraska, 1880–1890." *Nebraska History* 28 (June, 1947).

Dickman, Joseph T. *The Great Crusade.* New York, 1927.

"Dictionary of the A.E.F." *United States Infantry Journal* 20 (Apr., 1922).

Dierks, Jack C. *A Leap to Arms: The Cuban Campaign of 1898.* Philadelphia, 1970.

Dos Passos, John. *Mr. Wilson's War.* Garden City, N.Y., 1962.

Downey, Fairfax. *Indian Fighting Army.* Reprint. Fort Collins, Colo., 1971.

Duffy, Herbert S. *William Howard Taft.* New York, 1930.

Dusenberry, Verne. *The Montana Cree: A Study in Religious Persistence.* Stockholm, 1962.

———. "The Rocky Boy Indians." *Montana Magazine of History* 4 (Winter, 1954).

Eastman, Elaine Goodale. "The Ghost Dance War and Wounded Knee Massacre of 1890–91." *Nebraska History* 26 (1945).

Editors of the *Army Times*. *The Yanks Are Coming: The Story of General John J. Pershing.* New York, 1960.

Edmonds, James E. *A Short History of World War I.* London, 1951.

Edwards, Clarence R., "Governing the Philippine Islands." *National Geographic Magazine* 15 (July, 1904).

———. "The Work of the Bureau of Insular Affairs." *National Geographic Magazine* 15 (June, 1904).

Elliott, Charles P. "The Geronimo Campaign of 1885–6." *United States Cavalry Journal* 21 (Sept., 1910).

Elser, Frank B. "General Pershing's Mexican Campaign." *Century Magazine,* Feb., 1920.

Epperson, Ivan H. "Missourians Abroad. No. 1. Major General John J. Pershing." *Missouri Historical Review* 11 (1916–1917).

Epstein, Fritz T. "Zwischen Compiègne und Versailles: Geheime Amerikanische Militärdiplomatie in der Periode Waffenstillstandes 1918/19: Die Rolle des Obersten Arthur L. Conger." *Vierteljahrshefte für Zeitgeschichte* 3 (Oct., 1955).

Essame, H. *The Battle for Europe, 1918.* New York, 1972.

Estep, Raymond. "John F. Stevens and the Far Eastern Railways, 1917–1923." *Explorers Journal* 48 (Mar., 1970).

"Europe's War Welcome." *Literary Digest,* Apr. 14, 1917.

Evans, Ellwood W. "Cavalry Equipment in Mexico." *United States Cavalry Journal* 27 (Nov., 1916).

Fergusson, James. *The Curragh Incident.* London, 1964.

Feyler, F. "The Defeat of the German Army." *United States Infantry Journal* 16 (May, 1920).

"The Field Artillery of the United States Army." *Scientific American,* Aug. 5, 1916.

"Field Notes from Mexico and the Border." *United States Cavalry Journal* 28 (Nov., 1916).

Finney, Robert T. "Early Air Corps Training and Tactics." *Military Affairs* 20 (Fall, 1956).

Fiske, H. B. "General Pershing and His Headquarters in France." *Military Review* 20 (Sept., 1940).

Fleming, Thomas J. "Pershing's Island War." *American Heritage* 19 (Aug., 1968).

————. *West Point: The Men and Times of the United States Military Academy.* New York, 1969.

Foch, Ferdinand. *Mémoires.* 2 vols. Paris, 1931.

"Foch's Ten Commandments." *United States Infantry Journal* 16 (Apr., 1920).

Follmer, Harry R. *Footprints on the Sands of Time.* 9 vols. in 12. N.p., 1950?–1953.

Forbes, W. Cameron. *The Philippine Islands.* 2 vols. Boston and New York, 1928.

Foulois, Benjamin. *From the Wright Brothers to the Astronauts.* New York, 1968.

Frazer, Robert W. *Forts of the West.* Norman, Okla., 1965.

Freidel, Frank. *Over There: The Story of America's First Great Oversea Crusade.* Boston, 1964.

————. *The Splendid Little War.* Boston, 1958.

Frothingham, Thomas G. *The American Reinforcement in the World War.* Garden City, N.Y., 1927.

Fullerton, W. Morton. "If They Had Listened to General Pershing." *Le Figaro,* Mar. 30, 1936.

"Funston and Pershing, the Generals in Charge of the Chase After Villa." *Current Opinion* 60 (May, 1916).

Gannett, Henry. "The Philippine Islands and Their People." *National Geographic Magazine* 15 (Mar., 1904).

Gates, Paul W. "The Railroads of Missouri, 1850–1870." *Missouri Historical Review* 27 (1931–1932).

"General Information Concerning Members of the American Expeditionary Forces." *United States Infantry Journal* 14 (June, 1918).

"General Pershing and His Rank." Editorial in *United States Infantry Journal* 16 (Sept., 1919).

"General Pershing During Operations." *United States Infantry Journal* 16 (June, 1920).

"General Pershing's Address to the Graduates of General Staff College— Class of 1920." *United States Infantry Journal* 17 (Aug., 1920).

"General Pershing's Official Story." *Current History* 9 (Jan., 1919).

"General Pershing's Opinion of Infantry." *United States Infantry Journal* 11 (July–Aug., 1914).

"General Pershing's Tribute to General McAndrew." *United States Infantry Journal* 20 (June, 1922).

"German Trench Defense Methods." *Current History* 9 (Oct., 1918).

Gilheuser [sic], Henry. "Mindanao: Its Early American Military Government." *Military History Review* (Philippines) 4 (Dec., 1956).

Gill, Charles C. "Overseas Transportation of United States Troops." *Current History* 9 (Nov., 1918).

Ginsburgh, Robert. "Pershing as His Orderlies Know Him." *American Legion Monthly* 5 (Oct., Nov., Dec., 1928).

Glass, E. L. N., comp. and ed. *The History of the Tenth Cavalry, 1866–1921*. Reprint, with Introduction by J. M. Carroll. Fort Collins, Colo., 1972.

Gleaves, Albert. *A History of the Transport Service: Adventures and Experiences of United States Transports and Cruisers in the World War*. New York, 1921.

Goodale, Roy, ed. "A Civilian at Old Fort Bayard, 1881–1883." *New Mexico Historical Review* 25 (Oct., 1950).

"Gratitude or Ingratitude Toward General Pershing." *Literary Digest*, Sept. 27, 1924.

Green, Constance McL. *Washington: Capital City, 1879–1950*. Princeton, N.J., 1963.

Greer, Allen S. "A General Staff Corps for Our Army." *United States Infantry Journal* 14 (Nov., 1917).

Greer, Thomas H. "Air Arm Doctrinal Roots, 1917–1918." *Military Affairs* 20 (Winter, 1956).

Gregg, Andrew K. *New Mexico: A Pictorial History*. Albuquerque, 1968.

Griscom, Lloyd C. *Diplomatically Speaking*. New York, 1940.

Grunder, Ganel A., and William E. Livezey. *The Philippines and the United States*. Norman, Okla., 1951.

Guzmán, Martín Luis. *Memoirs of Pancho Villa*. Translated by Virginia H. Taylor. Austin, Tex., 1965.

Hagedorn, Hermann. *Leonard Wood: A Biography*. 2 vols. New York, 1931.

Hagood, Johnson. *The Services of Supply: A Memoir of the Great War*. Boston and New York, 1927.

Haig, Dorothy, ed., *Douglas Haig: His Letters and Diaries*. Vol. 1, *Before the Great War, 1861–1914* (First vol. of two projected vols. Proof copy, to have been published in Edinburgh, 1934, but never issued). Douglas Haig Papers, National Library of Scotland, Edinburgh.

"Haig on the Need of Preparedness." *United States Infantry Journal* 16 (Sept. 1919).

Halle, Louis J. "1898: The United States in the Pacific." *Military Affairs* 20 (Summer, 1956).

Hanly, Thomas. "The Brain of the Army." *Van Norden Magazine* 4 (Jan., 1909).

Harbord, James G., *The American Army in France, 1917–1919*. Boston, 1936.

———. *The American Expeditionary Forces: Its Organization and Accomplishments*. Evanston, Ill., 1929.

———. *Leaves from a War Diary*. New York, 1925.

———. *Personalities and Personal Relationships in the American Expeditionary Forces*. U.S. Army War College, Washington, D.C., 1933.

———. *Serving With Pershing*. Address delivered before the University Club of Port Chester, Port Chester, New York, May 26, 1944.

———. "Universal Military Training." *United States Infantry Journal* 28 (Jan., 1921).

Harriman, Mrs. J. Borden. *From Pinafores to Politics.* New York, 1923.

Hart, Basil H. Liddell. "Pershing." *Atlantic Monthly,* Aug., 1927.

———. "Pershing and His Critics." *Current History* 37 (Nov., 1932).

———. *Reputations Ten Years After.* Boston, 1928.

Hays, Robert E., Jr. "Military Aviation in Texas, 1917–1919." *Texas Military History* 3 (Spring, 1963).

Hein, O. L. *Memories of Long Ago.* New York, 1925.

Heitman, Francis B. *Historical Register and Dictionary of the United States Army.* Reprint. Champaign, Ill., 1965.

Helmick, Eli A., "Leadership." *United States Infantry Journal* 25 (Nov., 1924).

———. "Psychology of Command." *United States Infantry Journal* 16 (Mar. 1920).

Hicken, Victor. *The American Fighting Man.* New York, 1969.

Hines, Walker, *War History of American Railroads.* New Haven, Conn., 1928.

History of Linn County, Missouri. Kansas City, Mo., 1882.

Hobart, E. F. *Teacher's Register Arranged for Recording Attendance, Deportment and Scholarship for the Use of Public and Private Schools.* St. Louis, Mo., 1873.

Horgan, Paul, *Great River: The Rio Grande in North American History.* 2 vols. New York and Toronto, 1954.

Horne, Alistair. *The Price of Glory: Verdun, 1916.* New York, 1964.

Howard, Joseph Kinsey. *Strange Empire: A Narrative of the Northwest.* New York, 1952.

Howells, William Dean. *Letters of An Altrurian Traveller (1893–94).* Reprint. Gainesville, Fla., 1961.

Howland, Lt. H. S. "Field Service in Mindanao." *United States Infantry Journal* 2 (Oct., 1905).

Huidekoper, Frederick L. "The Armies of Europe." *World's Work* 28 (Sept., 1914).

———. "How to Read the War News." *World's Work* 28 (Oct., 1914).

———. "The Lessons of Our Past Wars: I. A Nation Never Ready to Fight." *World's Work* 29 (Feb., 1915).

———. "The Truth Concerning the United States Army." *United States Infantry Journal* 7 (May, 1911).

Hunn, Bobby. "Groom, Graze, and Growl." *Texas Historian* 33 (Nov., 1972).

Hunt, Frazier. *The Untold Story of Douglas MacArthur.* New York, 1954.

Hurley, Victor. *Jungle Patrol: The Story of the Philippine Constabulary.* New York, 1938.

———. *Swish of the Kris: The Story of the Moros.* New York, 1933.

Hyman, Harold M., *Soldiers and Spruce: Origins of the Loyal Legion of Loggers and Lumberman.* Los Angeles, Calif., 1963.

Illustrated Historical Atlas of Linn County, Missouri. N.p., 1876.

"Information as to Uniform and Equipment for Officers in France." *United States Infantry Journal* 14 (Feb., 1919).

"Invading Mexico to Avert Intervention." *Literary Digest,* Mar. 25, 1916.

James, D. Clayton. *The Years of MacArthur*. 2 vols. Boston, 1970–.

James, Edward L. "The Battle for Argonne Forest." *Current History* 9 (Oct., 1918).

Jessup, Philip C., *Elihu Root*. 2 vols. New York, 1938.

Johnson, Alvin. *Pioneer's Progress: An Autobiography*. New York, 1952.

Johnson, Melvin M., Jr., and Charles T. Haven. *Automatic Arms: Their History, Development and Use*. New York, 1941.

Johnson, Thomas M. *Without Censor: New Light on Our Greatest World War Battles*. Indianapolis, Ind., 1928.

Johnson, William Walter. *Heroic Mexico: The Violent Emergence of a Modern Nation*. New York, 1968.

Johnston, E. S. "Evolution of Infantry Tactics, 1914–1918." *Review of Military Literature*, Dec., 1934.

Johnston, R. M. "Staff and Command." *United States Infantry Journal* 16 (Aug., 1919).

King, James T. "Forgotten Pageant: The Indian Wars in Western Nebraska." *Nebraska History* 46 (Sept., 1965).

———. *War Eagle: A Life of General Eugene A. Carr*. Lincoln, Nebr., 1963.

Laffargue, André. *The Attack in Trench Warfare: Impressions and Reflections of a Company Commander*. Washington, D.C., 1916.

Landor, Arnold Henry Savage. *Everywhere: The Memoirs of an Explorer*. 2 vols. New York, 1924.

———. *The Guns of the East*. New York, 1904.

Lasch, Christopher. "The Anti-Imperialists, the Philippines, and the Inequality of Man." *Journal of Southern History* 24 (Aug., 1958).

Lattin, Paul L. "Pursuit of Villa" [Letter in reply to an article]. *Montana* 19 (Winter, 1969).

Leckie, William H. *The Buffalo Soldiers: A Narrative of the Negro Cavalry in the West*. Norman, Okla., 1967.

Leech, Margaret. *In the Days of McKinley*. New York, 1959.

Leland, Waldo G., and Newton P. Mereness. *Introduction to the American Official Sources for the Economic and Social History of the World War*. New Haven, Conn., 1926.

Leupp, Francis E. "President Taft's Own View: An Authorized Interview." *Outlook*, Dec. 2, 1911.

Liggett, Hunter. *A.E.F. Ten Years Ago in France*. New York, 1928.

———. *Commanding an American Army: Recollections of the World War*. Boston and New York, 1925.

Link, Arthur. *Wilson: The Struggle for Neutrality, 1914–1915*. Princeton, N.J., 1960.

———. *Woodrow Wilson and the Progressive Era, 1910–1917*. New York, 1954.

Lister, Florence C., and Robert H. Lister. *Chihuahua: Storehouse of Storms*. Albuquerque, N.M., 1966.

Lowry, Bullitt. "Pershing and the Armistice." *Journal of American History* 55 (Sept., 1968).

MacAdam, George. "The Life of General Pershing." *World's Work* 37 (Nov., 1918) through 39 (Dec., 1919).

Malone, Dumas, ed. *Dictionary of American Biography*, 20 vols. New York, 1934.

March, Peyton C. *The Nation at War*. Garden City, N.Y., 1932.

Marcosson, Isaac F. *S.O.S.: America's Miracle in France*. New York, 1919.

Marshall, George C. *Memoirs of My Services in the World War, 1917–1918*. Foreword and notes by Brig. Gen. James L. Collins, Jr. Boston, 1976.

Marvin, George. "Invasion or Intervention." *World's Work* 32 (May, 1916).

———. "Scott, U.S.A." *World's Work* 29 (Feb., 1915).

Mason, Gregory. "The Dough-Boy and the Truck: Some Lessons of our Mexican Expedition." *Outlook*, May 31, 1916.

Mason, Herbert Molloy, Jr. *The Great Pursuit*. New York, 1970.

Mattison, Ray H. "The Army Post on the Northern Plains." *Nebraska History* 35 (Mar., 1954).

Maurice, Frederick. "General Pershing and the A.E.F." *Foreign Affairs* 19 (July, 1931).

McArthur, C. N. "Rock of the Marne." *United States Infantry Journal* 17 (Sept., 1920).

McClellan, Edwin N. *The United States Marine Corps in the World War*. Washington, D.C., 1920.

"Messages from Mexico." *World's Work* 32 (Aug., 1916).

Miles, Nelson A. *Personal Recollections*. Chicago and New York, 1897.

———. *Serving the Republic*. New York, 1911.

Miles, Perry L. *Fallen Leaves: Memories of an Old Soldier*. Berkeley, Calif., 1961.

Miley, John D. *In Cuba With Shafter*. New York, 1899.

Mills, A. L. "The Military Geography of Mexico." *United States Cavalry Journal* 10 (Dec., 1897).

Missouri State Normal School, First District. *Annual Catalogues of the Officers, Alumni and Students of the State Normal School, First District, Kirksville, Missouri*. Kirksville, Mo., 1891–92, 1897–98, 1904.

———. *Fifteenth Annual Catalogue of the Missouri State Normal School, First Normal District, for the School Year 1881–82*. Hannibal, Mo., 1882.

Mitchell, William. "The Air Service at St. Mihiel." *World's Work* 38 (Aug., 1919).

———. "The Air Service at the Argonne-Meuse." *World's Work* 38 (Sept., 1919).

Mooney, James. *The Ghost Dance Religion and the Sioux Outbreak of 1890*. 14th Annual Report of the Bureau of American Ethnology, 1892–93, pt. 2. Washington, D.C., 1896.

Moore, Robert W. "The Glory of Their Deeds." *National Geographic Magazine* 65 (Jan., 1934).

Moorman, Frank. "Code and Cipher in France." *United States Infantry Journal* 16 (June, 1920).

Morison, Elting E., ed. *The Letters of Theodore Roosevelt*. 8 vols. Cambridge, Mass., 1951–54.

Morey, Lewis S., "The Cavalry Fight at Carrizal." *United States Cavalry Journal* 27 (Jan., 1917).

Morton, Louis. "Military and Naval Preparations for the Defense of the

Philippines During the War Scare of 1907." *Military Affairs* 13 (Summer, 1949).

Mott, T. Bentley. *Twenty Years as Military Attaché.* New York, 1937.

Munro, J. N. "The Philippine Native Scouts." *United States Infantry Journal* 2 (July, 1905).

Myers, Lee, "Military Establishments in Southwestern New Mexico: Stepping Stones to Settlement." *New Mexico Historical Review* 43 (Jan., 1968).

"The Naval ABC." *World's Work* 28 (Oct., 1914).

Nelson, William H., and Frank E. Vandiver. *Fields of Glory: An Illustrated Narrative of American Land Warfare.* New York, 1960.

New York Historical Commission. *The Second Division.* New York, 1937.

Nichols, Vernon R. "Our Battle of the Argonne." *United States Infantry Journal* 16 (Sept., 1919).

Norvell, S. T. "Las Guasimas." *United States Cavalry Journal* 12 (Dec., 1899).

"Notes from Here and There in Mexico." *United States Infantry Journal* 13 (Feb., 1917).

"Notes on Campaigning in Mexico." *United States Cavalry Journal* 27 (July, 1916).

Nouailhat, Yves-Henri. *Les Américains à Nantes et Saint-Nazaire, 1917–1919.* Paris, 1972.

O'Connor, Richard. *Black Jack Pershing.* Garden City, N.Y., 1961.

Official Catalogue of the Exhibits on the Midway Plaisance, World's Columbian Exposition, Department M—Ethnology. Chicago, 1893.

Official Programme of the National Peace Celebrations, 19th July, 1919. London, 1919.

Official Register of the Officers and Cadets of the U.S. Military Academy, West Point, N.Y. Vols. *1882, 1883, 1884, 1885,* Washington, D.C., 1882–1885.

"Old Soldier." *Time,* Nov. 15, 1943.

Order of Battle of the United States Land Forces in the World War, American Expeditionary Forces, General Headquarters, Armies, Army Corps, Services of Supply, and Separate Forces. Washington, D.C., 1937.

"Our Progress in the Mexican 'War.'" *American Review of Reviews* 43 (May, 1911).

"Outline Histories of Infantry Regiments." *United States Infantry Journal* 19 (Dec., 1921).

Page, Arthur W. "The Truth About Our 110 Days' Fighting." *World's Work* 37 (Apr., 1919).

Page, Victor W., "Substituting Gasoline for Horseflesh; Work of Motor Trucks With the Army in Mexico." *Scientific American,* Aug. 5, 1916.

Palmer, Frederick. *John J. Pershing, General of the Armies: A Biography.* Harrisburg, Pa., 1948.

———. *Newton D. Baker: America at War.* 2 vols. New York, 1931.

———. *Our Greatest Battle (The Meuse-Argonne).* New York, 1919.

———. *With Kuroki in Manchuria.* New York, 1904.

Parker, James. "Some Random Notes on the Fighting in the Philippines."

Journal of the Military Service Institution of the United States 27 (Nov., 1900).

Patton, George S., Jr., "Cavalry Work of the Punitive Expedition." *United States Cavalry Journal* 27 (Jan., 1917).

——. "Comments on Cavalry Tanks." *United States Cavalry Journal* 30 (July, 1921).

——. "What the World War Did for Cavalry." *United States Cavalry Journal* 31 (Apr., 1922).

Pédroncini, Guy. *Le haut commandement francais de mai 1917 à novembre 1918.* Paris, 1972.

Pegler, Westbrook. "When Pershing Bawled Out Raw, Gum Chewing Recruits." *Omaha World,* May 4, 1937.

Penrose, Charles. *James G. Harbord (1866–1947), Lieutenant General: USA, Chairman of the Board: RCA.* New York, 1956.

Perry, G. A. "W.W.I Battlefields, Then and Now." *Texas Magazine* (from *Houston Chronicle*), Nov. 10, 1968.

"Pershing, A Great Soldier of the Republic." *Literary Digest,* Sept. 27, 1919.

Pershing, Edgar. *The Pershing Family in America.* Philadelphia, 1924.

Pershing, John J. "Address Delivered Before the National Civic Federation, Armistice Day, 1922." *Bulletin of the Women's Department, National Civic Federation* 8 (Nov., 1922).

——. *Annual Report of Brigadier General John J. Pershing, United States Army, Commanding the Department of Mindanao, June 30, 1912.* Zamboanga, P.I., 1912.

——. *The Annual Report of the Governor of the Moro Province, for the Fiscal Year Ended June 30, 1913.* Zamboanga, P.I., 1913.

——. "The Campaign of Santiago." In *Under Fire with the Tenth U.S. Cavalry,* by H. V. Cashin and others. New York, 1969.

——. "A Discussion of National Defense." *Saturday Evening Post,* Mar. 10, 1923.

——. "A Message to the Cavalry from General Pershing." *United States Cavalry Journal* 39 (Apr., 1920).

——. *Final Report of General John J. Pershing, Commander-in-Chief, American Expeditionary Forces.* Washington, D.C., 1920.

——. *My Experiences in the World War.* 2 vols. New York, 1931.

——. "Our National War Memorials in Europe." *National Geographic Magazine* 65 (Jan., 1934).

——. "Report of the Department of Mindanao." (June 30, 1910). In *War Department Annual Reports, 1910.* 4 vols. Washington, D.C., 1910.

——. "Report of the Department of Mindanao" (June 30, 1911). In *War Department Annual Reports, 1911.* 4 vols. Washington, D.C., 1912.

——, and Hunter Liggett. *Report of the First Army, American Expeditionary Forces: Organization and Operations.* Fort Leavenworth, Kans., 1923.

"Pershing's 'Jinx' Birthday, and Something about His Boyhood." *Literary Digest,* Sept. 7, 1918.

Pickering, Col. Abner. "The Battle of Agua Prieta." *United States Infantry Journal* 12 (Jan., 1916).

Pitt, Barrie. *1918: The Last Act*. New York, 1963.
Platt, Rutherford H. "There Was a Captain by the Name of Pershing." *World's Work* 47 (Dec., 1923).
Poe, Sophie A. *Buckboard Days*. Caldwell, Idaho, 1936.
Pogue, Forrest. "General Marshall and the Pershing Papers," *Quarterly Journal of the Library of Congress* 21 (Jan., 1964).
———. *George C. Marshall: Education of a General, 1880–1939*. New York, 1963.
Pool, William C. "Military Aviation in Texas, 1913–1917." *Texas Military History* 2 (Feb., 1962).
Pratt, Walter M. *"Tin Soldiers": The Organized Militia and What It Really Is*. Boston, 1912.
Pringle, Henry F. *The Life and Times of William Howard Taft*. 2 vols. New York and Toronto, 1934.
———. *Theodore Roosevelt: A Biography*. New York, 1931.
Program of the Military Tournament and Athletic Meet, Department of Luzon, Philippine Division, Manila, P.I., 1908. Manila, P.I., 1908.
Quirino, José A. "Datu Ali—Lord of the Rio Grande." *Philippine Armed Forces Journal* 7 (May, 1954).
———. "Moro Outlaws." *Philippine Armed Forces Journal* 7 (June, 1954).
Rand, Oscar. "Army Week in Georgia." *United States Infantry Journal* 17 (July, 1920).
Reddick, L. D. "The Negro Policy of the United States Army, 1775–1945." *Journal of Negro History* 34 (Jan., 1949).
Reilly, Brig. Gen. Henry J. "Pershing's Job Today: What the Wartime Leader Does." *World Today* 53 (1929). Also in *World's Work* 57 (Nov., 1928).
Remington, Frederick. "A Scout with the Buffalo Soldiers." *Century Illustrated Monthly Magazine* 37 (Apr., 1889).
Report of the Committee on Awards of the World's Columbian Exposition: Special Reports upon Special Subjects or Groups. 2 vols. Washington, D.C., 1901.
Requin, E. "The Strategy of the French Command." *Current History* 29 (Nov., 1928).
"The Retreat of Our Ten Thousand." *Literary Digest*, Feb. 3, 1917.
Rhodes, Charles D. "The Utilization of Native Troops in our Foreign Possessions." *Journal of the Military Service Institution of the United States* 30 (Jan., 1902).
Rippy, J. Fred. "Some Precedents of the Pershing Expedition into Mexico." *Southwestern Historical Quarterly* 24 (Apr., 1921).
Rockenbach, S. D. "Some Experiences and Impressions of a 2nd Lieutenant of Cavalry in the Santiago Campaign." *United States Cavalry Journal* 40 (Mar.–Apr., 1931).
Rodwell, J. M., trans. *The Koran: Translated from the Arabic*. Reprint. New York, 1913.
Russell, Bertrand. "Autobiography, 1914–1918." *Harper's Magazine*, Jan., 1968.
Russo-Japanese War Fully Illustrated. 3 vols. Tokyo [?], 1904–1905.
Sargent, Herbert H. *The Campaign of Santiago de Cuba* 3 vols. Chicago, 1907.

Scammell, J. M. "A.E.F., S.O.S., and U.S.A." *United States Infantry Journal* 20 (Mar., 1922).

Schwabe, Klaus. *Deutsche Revolution und Wilson-Frieden: Die Amerikanische und deutsche Friedensstrategie zwischen Ideologie und Machtpolitik 1918/19.* Dusseldorf, 1971.

Scott, Hugh L. *Some Memories of a Soldier.* New York, 1928.

Scott, James B. *Robert Bacon: Life and Letters,* New York, 1923.

"The Secret of the 'Baby' Tank." *Scientific American,* Nov. 30, 1918.

Selden, Charles A. "The Chief of the General Staff." *World's Work* 36 (May, 1918).

"Senator Warren and the Infantry." *United States Infantry Journal* 16 (June, 1920).

Seymour, Charles. *The Intimate Papers of Colonel House.* 4 vols. Boston and New York, 1926–1928.

Shannon, James A. "With the Apache Scouts in Mexico." *United States Cavalry Journal* 27 (Apr., 1917).

Sharpe, Henry G. *The Quartermaster Corps in the Year 1917 in the World War.* New York, 1921.

Sherman, Richard G. "Charles G. Dawes, A Nebraska Businessman, 1887–1894: The Making of an Entrepreneur." *Nebraska History* 46 (Sept., 1965).

Sherrill, Stephen H. "The Experiences of the First American Troop of Cavalry to Get into Action in the World War." *United States Cavalry Journal* 32 (Apr., 1923).

Shunk, William A. "The Military Geography of Mexico." *United States Cavalry Journal* 6 (June, 1893).

Slote, Bernice, ed. *The Kingdom of Art: Willa Cather's First Principles and Critical Statements, 1893–1896.* Lincoln, Nebr., 1966.

Smith, Capt. C. C. "The Mindanao Moro." *United States Cavalry Journal* 17 (Oct., 1906).

Smith, C. H., "Motor Mobilizing." *Out West Magazine* 45 (Mar., 1917).

Smythe, Donald, "A.E.F. Snafu at Sedan." *Prologue: The Journal of the National Archives,* Fall, 1973.

———. "The Battle of the Books—Pershing versus March." *Army* 22 (Sept., 1972).

———. "The Early Years of John J. Pershing, 1860–1882." *Missouri Historical Review* 58 (Oct., 1963).

———. *Guerrilla Warrior: The Early Life of John J. Pershing.* New York, 1973.

———. "John J. Pershing at Fort Assinniboine." *Montana, The Magazine of Western History* 18 (Jan., 1968).

———. "John J. Pershing at the University of Nebraska, 1891–1895." *Nebraska History* 43 (Sept., 1962).

———. "John J. Pershing: Frontier Cavalryman." *New Mexico Historical Review,* 38 (July, 1963).

———. "John J. Pershing in the Spanish-American War." *Military Affairs* 30 (Spring, 1966).

———. "Never Have I Witnessed a Sight So Marvelous." *Montana, The Magazine of Western History* 13 (Apr., 1963).

————. "Patton and Pershing: The Men Behind George C. Scott's Oscar." *Family, The Magazine of Army/Navy/Air Force Times*, Jan. 30, 1974.

————. "Pershing and Counterinsurgency." *Military Review* 46 (Sept., 1966).

————. "Pershing and the Disarmament of the Moros." *Pacific Historical Review* 31 (Aug., 1962).

————. "Pershing and General J. Franklin Bell, 1917–1918." *Mid-America: An Historical Review* 54 (Jan., 1972).

————. "Pershing at West Point, 1897–1898." *New York History* 48 (Jan., 1967).

————. "Pershing Biographer Takes Issue with Carrizal Affair Motives." *Montana, The Magazine of Western History* 19 (Spring, 1969).

————. "Pershing's Great Personal Tragedy." *Missouri Historical Review* 60 (Apr., 1966).

————. "The Ruse at Belfort." *Army* 22 (June, 1972).

————. "When General Pershing Missed the Chance to Make a Million, Solve Unemployment, Become President, Save the World, and Do Everything Else That Needed Doing." *Army* 20 (Nov., 1970).

Society of the First Division. *History of the First Division During the World War, 1917–1919*. Philadelphia, 1922.

Solbert, O. N., and George Bertrand. "Tactics and Duties of Small Units in Trench Fighting." *United States Infantry Journal* 14 (Jan., 1918).

"Soldiering with Pershing in the Philippines." *Literary Digest*, Nov. 17, 1928.

Spears, E. L. *Prelude to Victory*. London, 1939.

Stallings, Laurence. *The Doughboys: The Story of the AEF, 1917–1918*. New York, 1963.

Stallman, R. W., and E. R. Hagemann, eds. *The War Dispatches of Stephen Crane*. New York, 1964.

Stanley, F. (pseud.), *Fort Stanton*. Pampa, Tex., 1964.

Stanley, George F. G. *The Birth of Western Canada: A History of the Riel Rebellions*. Toronto, 1960.

Stewart, Brig. Gen. M. B. "The A.E.F. Follows Through," *United States Infantry Journal* 16 (Oct., 1919).

————. "The Army of the United States." *United States Infantry Journal* 20 (Apr., 1922).

Stockbridge, Frank P. "If the War Had Lasted Until Spring." *World's Work* 37 (Mar., 1919).

Stockle, G. E. "Military Instruction in Colleges." *United States Cavalry Journal* 12 (Mar., 1899).

Swift, Eben, Jr. "Experiences in Mexico." *United States Cavalry Journal* 27 (Nov., 1916).

"The Taking of the St. Mihiel Salient: Immensity of the Operation." *Current History* 9 (Nov., 1918).

Taft, William Howard. "Ten Years in the Philippines." *National Geographic Magazine* 19 (Feb., 1908).

Taylor, A. J. P. "Politics in the First World War." *Proceedings of the British Academy* 45 (1959).

Taylor, John R. M. "An Estimate of the Situation." *United States Infantry Journal* 17 (Aug., 1920).

Taylor, William. "The Debate Over Changing Cavalry Tactics and Weapons, 1900–1914." *Military Affairs* 28 (Winter, 1964–65).

Thomason, John W., Jr. "Crossing the Line with Pershing." *Scribner's Magazine*, Aug., 1926.

———. "When the Storm Broke on the World." *New York Times Illustrated Magazine*, July 29, 1934.

Timmons, Bascom N. *Portrait of an American: Charles G. Dawes.* New York, 1953.

Tolman, Newton F. *The Search for General Miles.* New York, 1968.

Tompkins, Frank. *Chasing Villa: The Story Behind the Story of Pershing's Expedition into Mexico.* Harrisburg, Pa., 1934.

Toulmin, H. A., Jr. *With Pershing in Mexico.* Harrisburg, Pa., 1935.

Trask, David F. *The United States in the Supreme War Council: American War Aims and Inter-Allied Strategy, 1917–1918.* Middletown, Conn., 1961.

Traub, Capt. Peter E. "The First Act of the Last Sioux Campaign." *United States Cavalry Journal* 15 (Apr., 1905).

Troxel, Capt. C. C. "The Tenth Cavalry in Mexico." *United States Cavalry Journal* 28 (Oct., 1917).

Turner, Martha Anne. " 'With All My Love—John': A World War I Letter from John W. Thomason, Jr." *Texas Military History* 7 (Summer, 1968).

[Twain, Mark.] *The Family Mark Twain.* New York and London, 1935.

Twichell, Heath, Jr. *Allen: The Biography of an Army Officer, 1859–1930.* New Brunswick, N.J., 1974.

Ueland, Alexander. "John J. Pershing, Crusader and Mason." *The New Age* 68 (Dec., 1960).

U.S. *Statutes at Large of the United States of America.* Vol. 41, pt. 1.

U.S. Army. *Army Register.* Washington, D.C., annually, 1906–1948.

———. *Centennial for a Soldier.* Army Information Series, PAM 355-200-10. Washington, D.C., 1960.

U.S. Army, General Staff, Historical Branch. *A Study in Battle Formation.* Washington, D.C., 1920.

———. *A Study in Troop Frontage.* Washington, D.C., 1920.

———. *Organization of the Services of Supply, American Expeditionary Forces.* Washington, D.C., 1921.

U.S. Army, Historical Division. *United States Army in the World War, 1917–1919.* 17 vols. Washington, D.C., 1948.

U.S. Army War College. *Statement of a Proper Military Policy for the United States.* Washington, D.C., 1916.

———. *The Aisne and Montdidier-Noyon Operations, with Special Attention to the Participation of American Divisions.* Washington, D.C., 1922.

U.S. Army War College, Historical Section. *Order of Battle of the United States Land Forces in the World War—Divisions.* Washington, D.C., 1931.

———. *The Genesis of the American First Army.* Washington, D.C., 1938.

U.S. Bureau of the Census. *Abstract of the Fourteenth Census of the United States, 1920.* Washington, D.C., 1923.

U.S. Coast and Geodetic Survey. *Special Publication No. 3, Atlas of the Philippine Islands.* Washington, D.C., 1900.

U.S. Congress. *Congressional Record*. 1903–1948.

U.S. Department of State. *Papers Relating to the Foreign Relations of the United States* [1917]. Washington, D.C., 1926.

U.S. Militia Bureau. *Report on Mobilization of the Organized Militia and National Guard of the United States, 1916*. Washington, D.C., 1916.

U.S. Philippine Commission. *Report to the President*. Senate Doc. No. 138, 56th Cong., 1st Sess. (Serial Set No. 3885). 4 vols. Washington, D.C., 1900.

U.S. Senate, Military Affairs Committee. *Reorganization of the Army. Hearings Before the Committee on Military Affairs, United States Senate, 66th Congress, 2 Session, on S. 3792 To Reorganize and Increase the Efficiency of the United States Army, and for other Purposes*. Washington, D.C., 1920.

U.S. Senate, *Reports*. Vol. 4, Doc. No. 821, 54th Congress, 1st Sess. (Serial Set No. 3365). Washington, D.C., 1896.

U.S. War Department. *Annual Reports of the War Department for the Fiscal Year Ended June 30, 1901*. Washington, D.C., 1901.

————. *Annual Reports of the War Department for the Fiscal Year Ended June 30, 1916*. 3 vols. Washington, D.C., 1916.

————. *Extracts from General Orders and Bulletins, War Department, 1917, with List of Paragraphs of Army Regulations and Other Regulations and Manuals of the War Department That Have Been Changed Since Latest Edition of the Publication*. Washington, D.C., 1918.

————. *Index to Monthly Extracts, General Orders, and Bulletins, War Department, January 1 to December 31, 1918 and List of Paragraphs of Army Regulations and Other Regulations and Manuals of the War Department That Have Been Changed Since January 1, 1913*. (Dec., 1918.) Washington, 1919.

U.S. War Department, Adjutant General's Office. *Military Notes on the Philippines*. Washington, D.C., 1898.

————. *Tables of Organization, United States Army, 1917*. Washington, D.C., 1917.

University of Nebraska. *Announcements*. Lincoln, Nebr., 1892.

————. *Catalogue (Law College)*. Lincoln, Nebr., 1893.

————. *History of the Military Department, University of Nebraska, 1876–1941*. Lincoln, Nebr., 1942.

Utley, Robert M. *The Last Days of the Sioux Nation*. New Haven and London, 1963.

Van Horn, R. O. "Notes on Field Service in the District of Cotabato, Mindanao, P.I." *United States Infantry Journal* 2 (Jan., 1906).

Vandiver, Frank E., "Commander-in-Chief–Commander Relationships: Wilson and Pershing." *Rice University Studies* 57 (Winter, 1971).

————. "Haig, Nivelle, and Third Ypres." *Rice University Studies* 57 (Winter, 1971).

————. *Illustrious Americans: John J. Pershing*. Morristown, N.J., 1967.

————. "John J. Pershing and the Anatomy of Leadership." *The Harmon Memorial Lectures in Military History, Number Five*. United States Air Force Academy, Colo., 1963.

Violette, E. M. *History of the First District State Normal School, Kirksville, Missouri.* Kirksville, Mo., 1905.

von Giehrl, Hermann. "Battle of the Meuse-Argonne." *United States Infantry Journal* 19 (Aug., Sept., Oct., Nov., 1921).

―――. "The American Expeditionary Forces in Europe, 1917–1918." *United States Infantry Journal* 20 (Feb., 1922).

von Kuhl, H. J., "The Strategy of the Central Powers." *Current History* 29 (Nov., 1928).

―――, and General von Bergman. *Movements and Supply of the German First Army During August and September 1914.* Fort Leavenworth, Kans., 1929.

Waldron, W. H. "The Tactical Employment of Motor Transportation." *United States Infantry Journal* 13 (Apr., 1917).

Wales, Henry. "Pershing and the Lovely Parisienne." *Chicago Sunday Tribune Graphic Magazine*, Nov. 30, 1951.

Wambaugh, Sarah. *A Monograph on Plebiscites with a Collection of Official Documents.* New York, 1920.

"War Chiefs of the Army." *World's Work* 30 (Oct., 1915).

War of the Rebellion: A Compilation of the Official Records of the Union and Confederate Armies. 70 vols. in 128 and index. Washington, D.C., 1880–1901.

Warner, Ezra J. *Generals in Blue: Lives of the Union Commanders.* Baton Rouge, La., 1964.

Watson, James W. "Scouting in Arizona, 1890." *United States Cavalry Journal* 10 (June, 1897).

Weissheimer, J. W. "Field Ovens in Mexico." *United States Infantry Journal* 13 (Feb., 1917).

Wharfield, H. B. "The Affair at Carrizal." *Montana, The Magazine of Western History* 18 (Oct., 1968).

Wheeler, Harold F. "The Romance of General Pershing." *Ladies Home Journal*, July, 1919.

"Who's Who in General Pershing's Army; Names of Chief Officers and Titles of All Units in the First Five Army Corps." *Current History* 9 (Oct., 1918).

Wiener, Frederick B. "Five Is Higher Than Six When Fact and Legend Clash." *Army* 21 (Jan., 1971).

―――. "How Many Stars for Pershing?" *Army* 20 (Dec., 1970).

Williams, S. M. "The Cavalry Fight at Ojos Azules." *United States Cavalry Journal* 27 (Jan., 1917).

Wilson, Edith Bolling. *My Memoir.* Garden City, N.Y., 1938.

Williams, Walter, ed. *The State of Missouri: An Autobiography.* Columbia, Mo., 1904.

Wise, J. C. "Organization and Initial Training of a Company." *United States Infantry Journal* 14 (Sept., 1917).

"With the Army in Texas." *Outlook*, Apr. 1, 1911.

Wolff, Leon. "Black Jack's Mexican Goose Chase." *American Heritage* 13 (June, 1962).

―――. *Little Brown Brother: America's Forgotten Bid for Empire Which Cost 250,000 Lives.* Reprint. New York, 1970.

Wood, Walter Shea. "The 130th Infantry, Illinois National Guard: A Military History, 1778–1919." *Journal of the Illinois State Historical Society* 30 (July, 1937).

Woodbridge, J. W. *The Giants of the Marne.* Salt Lake City, Utah, 1923.

Woolley, Paul G. "Rinderpest." *Philippine Journal of Science* 1 (July, 1906).

Worcester, Dean C. "The Non-Christian Peoples of the Philippine Islands." *National Geographic Magazine* 24 (Nov., 1913).

Young, Hugh H. *A Surgeon's Autobiography.* New York, 1940.

Young, Karl. "A Fight That Could Have Meant War." *American West* 3 (Spring, 1966).

Younghusband, Maj. G. J. *The Philippines and Round About.* London, 1899.

Index

Abainville, France: 760
Abbeville, France: 745, 891
ABC Powers: 583
Acosta, Julio: 641
Adair, Henry R.: 653
Adair County, Missouri: 16
Adam, Emil: 89
Adams, Charles Francis, Jr.: 221
Adams, Henry: 130
Adams, Robert: 560
Adamson, George: 700, 1085, 1090
Adta of Paiogoay (*datto*): 279–80
AEF University (Beaune, France): 1014
Aero Squadron, 1st: with Punitive Expedition, 605, 613, 622–24, 630
Africa: 236, 452, 455
Aguadores River (Cuba): 195, 198, 201, 202
Aguinaldo, Emilio: as Insurrecto leader, 225, 242, 244, 250, 253, 257, 259, 424, 495
Agus River (Mindanao): 315
Agusan River (Mindanao): 509, 512
Ahern, George: 297
Ahmai-Benanning (of Gata): 312
Ahmai Ben Kurang (*datto* of Oato): 302
Ahmai-Manibilang (*datto*): Pershing meets with, 265–69, 298–300, 315; mentioned, 465, 475, 489
Ahmai-Tampugao (*datto*): 379, 475
Ahumada, Mexico: 650–51, 653
Aire River (France): 936, 968
airplanes. *See* aviation
Aisne River (France): 1917 battle on, 681; Nivelle's drive on, 743; German forces at, 852, 889, 936; AEF troops on, 862; in Meuse-Argonne drive, 955. *See also* Marne sector, second battle of

Ainsworth, Fred C.: and promotion of Pershing, 374, 385; and Pershing's orders for Japan, 390, 391 n; and Philippine policies, 498 n, 543
Alabama (ship): 71
Alabama: 218–19, 319, 1047
Albany (U.S. cruiser): 515
Albert (king of Belgium): 1000, 1031
Albuquerque, New Mexico: 50, 51, 85
Alessandri, Arturo: 1080, 1081
Alexandria, Egypt: 238
Alger, Russell A.: appointed secretary of war, 162–63; and Spanish-American War, 179, 183, 186, 209; and promotion of Pershing, 213, 402; blamed for detention camp conditions, 215; and problems of military government, 219; removed from office, 221–22
Allaire, Bill: 760, 764
Allen, Henry T.: with Punitive Expedition, 630, 654; with AEF, 944, 1022; with occupation troops, 1022, 1023, 1030, 1032
Allen, John C.: 102
Allenby, Edmund: 711
Allied Munitions Board: 909
Allies (World War I): AEF preparedness compared to, 603, 688–89, 690; failing war efforts of, 645, 671, 676, 704, 707, 713, 725–26, 752, 757, 810–11, 819, 826; commission of, to United States, 681, 726; on amalgamation of AEF troops, 682, 693, 695–96, 741–42, 786, 842; use of U.S. arms by, 692; comparison of staffs of, 700; rivalry among, over use of AEF troops, 711, 721, 734, 740, 741–42, 743, 755–56, 786–90, 829 and n, 830, 834–36, 847–48, 874–75, 879–80, 891–94, 965–66; Armies of the North of, 735,

Chemin des Dames region, 888–90; in Marne drives, 890, 899–900, 910, 912, 914, 919–20, 921; effects of second Marne battle on planning of, 919–21; on Montdidier-Albert sector loss, 946; resigns, 979

Luftwaffe, German: 1089

Luger pistol: 809

Lunéville, France: 862

Luxembourg, grand duchy of: 933, 1000

Luzon, Department of (Philippines): Insurrectos in, 242, 244; reaction in, to Fort McKinley command charge, 423; Baguio as summer HQ of, 437; Pershing as temporary commander of, 437; troop maneuvers in, 486; R. Potts as commander of, 501; visitors from, in Zamboanga, 511; mentioned, 572. *See also* Fort McKinley; Manila

Lys sector (Western Front): 882, 883, 1031. *See also* Cantigny, France

Macajambo (peoples of Mindanao): 258

McAlexander, Ulysses Grant: 760, 913–14

McAndrew, James: in establishment of AEF schools, 771; on AEF staff, 894, 905, 923, 924, 944, 945, 977, 980, 987; brilliance of, 944; in victory celebrations, 989, 1036, 1040; returns home, 1021; mentioned, 942

MacArthur, Arthur: in Philippines, 256, 262, 270; Pershing visits, in California, 324; observes Russo-Japanese War, 354–55, 358, 364, 366–67, 373; Pershing and, in Tokyo, 382

MacArthur, Mrs. Arthur: 355, 357, 382

MacArthur, Douglas: Pershing's first meeting with, 324; on death of General Funston, 672 and n; and selection of head of AEF, 682; promotion of, 903 n; at Sedan, 984; Pershing quarrel with, 1065, 1091; Warren Pershing as aide to, 1094

McCabe, W. P.: 653

McCarthy, Daniel H.: 180, 729

McCarthy Light Guards (of Little Rock): 121

McClellan, George Brinton: 329

McCook, Alexander McD.: 80, 133

McCormick, Cyrus: 130

McCormick, Vance: 832

McCoy, Frank: 202, 738

McClernand, E. J.: 185–86, 202

machine guns: in Spanish-American War, 370; in Russo-Japanese War, 370–71, 434; in Philippines, 422, 486, 487, 557; in troop training at El Paso, 591; used by Punitive Expedition, 608, 611, 642, 656, 670–71; selected for AEF, 692, 700; at Belleau Wood, 603, 808, 887, 895, 897; Allied demands for troops trained in use of, 874–75, 883, 891–93, 938; at Château-Thierry, 899; in second Marne battle, 920; difficulty of attack on, in Meuse-Argonne, 963, 966, 969. *See also* Gatling guns; Vickers-Maxim guns

Maciricampo (*datto* of Marahui): 271–72

Maciu, Lake Lanao area, Mindanao: first expedition to, 282–87; second expedition to, 288–97, 305, 306; sultan of, in battle, 292, 293–95; Lake Lanao expedition at, 311, 312; death of *cambugatan* of, 314

McKim, Rev. Dr. Randolph H.: 347, 350

McKinley, William: election of, 153–54, 158; political appointments of, 162–67; description of, 166; inauguration of, 166–67; and Spanish-American War, 174, 177–80, 183, 209, 232; and Pershing promotion, 213; at Camp Wikoff, 215; and problems of military government, 219; and removal of Alger from office, 221–22, 225–26; Philippine policies of, 243–44, 250–51, 253, 256, 426; assassination of, 264

McKinley, Mrs. William (Ida): 173, 221

McKinney, C. F.: 561, 563, 564

Maclay, Sir Joseph: 843–44

McLeod Trail (Montana): 148

McMahon, John E.: commands 5th Division with AEF, 944, 962, 971; loses command, 962, 976–77, 977 n.

McNair, Captain: on first Maciu expedition, 283, 284, 285, 286; on second Maciu expedition, 288, 290–94; on Marahui expedition, 304–08; mentioned, 311

Macready, Sir Nevil: 706

Madalum, Lake Lanao area, Mindanao: 316

Madaya, Lake Lanao area, Mindanao: Pershing and sultan of, 265, 268, 269; Pershing at, 272–73, 299, 315; mentioned 490

Madera, Mexico: 616